MATERIALS FOR THE STUDY OF ĀRYADEVA, DHARMAPĀLA AND CANDRAKĪRTI

MATERIALS FOR THE STUDY OF ĀRYADEVA, DHARMAPĀLA AND CANDRAKĪRTI

The Catuḥśataka of Āryadeva, Chapters XII and XIII with the Commentaries of Dharmapāla and Candrakīrti: Introduction, Translation, Notes, Sanskrit, Tibetan And Chinese Texts, Indexes

TOM J.F. TILLEMANS

Volume I
INTRODUCTION & TRANSLATION
Volume II
TEXTS & INDEXES
(Bound in one volume)

MOTILAL BANARSIDASS PUBLISHERS
PRIVATE LIMITED • DELHI

First Indian Editon : Delhi, 2008
After arrangements with "Arbeitskreis für Tibetische und Buddhistiche Studien, Universität Wien"

ISBN: 978-81-208-3112-4

MOTILAL BANARSIDASS
41 U.A. Bungalow Road, Jawahar Nagar, Delhi 110 007
8 Mahalaxmi Chamber, 22 Bhulabhai Desai Road, Mumbai 400 026
203 Royapettah High Road, Mylapore, Chennai 600 004
236, 9th Main III Block, Jayanagar, Bangalore 560 011
Sanas Plaza, 1302 Baji Rao Road, Pune 411 002
8 Camac Street, Kolkata 700 017
Ashok Rajpath, Patna 800 004
Chowk, Varanasi 221 001

The cover photo by Nicholas Halpin of *Eyes Wide Open Photography* (www.eyeswideopen.ca), Gabriola Island, B.C., Canada

PRINTED IN INDIA
By Jainendra Prakash Jain at Shri Jainendra Press,
A-45 Naraina, Phase-I, New Delhi 110 028
and Published by Narendra Prakash Jain for
Motilal Banarsidass Publishers Private Limited,
Bungalow Road, Delhi 110 007

For Shelley, Leah and Sylviane

PREFACE TO THE INDIAN EDITION

Since 1990, when the present work was first published, various translations and studies on Madhyamaka and Yogācāra have appeared, sufficiently numerous that it would be impossible to incorporate them; nor is it possible to incorporate here the generally minor corrections suggested by reviewers such as J.W. de Jong or Akira Saito.* Accordingly this edition is a simple reproduction of the 1990 work. Naturally, my own interpretations of Madhyamaka themes have undergone evolution in the fifteen year interval from the initial publication. For the question of the tetralemma and that of the problem of scriptural authority, I can refer the reader to respectively the preface and part one ("Scripturally Based Argumentation") of my *Scripture, Logic, Language* (Boston: Wisdom 1999) ; on the Madhyamaka stance concerning perception and the given, see the article "Metaphysics for Mādhyamikas" in G. Dreyfus and S.McClintock (eds.), *The Svātantrika-Prāsaṅgika Distinction* (Wisdom, 2003). Note too that we finally have a good translation and study of the Chinese text of a significant portion of Dharmapāla's commentary, the chapter in which is found his debate with Bhāviveka/Bhāvaviveka. This translation, by the late Paul Hoornaert in *Studies and Essays, Behavioral Sciences and Philosophy*, Faculty of Letters, Kanazawa University 24 (2004), enables us to form a much clearer idea of what Dharmapāla's position actually was. One can only hope that work on Dharmapāla of this quality will somehow continue.

Tom J.F. Tillemans
Lausanne, Switzerland
April 2006

*Two mistakes should however, be corrected here. First of all, on P. 172, line 2, the translation should be emended to read "certain flowery trees, known as Aśoka [trees], are such that when... ." Secondly, the claim on P. 12 that there is no trace of Dharmapāla's poetry is wrong, although it is not certain that the poetry we do have is by the same Dharmapāla as the author of the commentary on Āryadeva.

PREFACE

The following work takes as it nucleus a series of seminars given by Prof. J. May during which, over a number of summer semesters, we read the Sanskrit texts of Āryadeva's *Catuḥśataka* (CS) and Candrakīrti's *Catuḥśatakavṛtti* (CSV). Subsequently, in Japan, while working mainly on Dharmakīrti with Prof. S. Katsura, I began to read the Chinese commentary of Dharmapāla, and was impressed with the importance and philosophical interest of the latter text, not only for understanding Āryadeva in a different manner, but also for its connections with the Epistemological school founded by Dignāga.

Below the reader will find translations of two chapters from Āryadeva, Candrakīrti and Dharmapāla, chapters which are diverse in style and content, CS XII and its commentaries being largely rhetorical — a polemic against the infidels — while the subsequent chapter on perception and its commentaries are full of dense philosophical argumentation. My approach has been, in effect, to show a representative sample of Candrakīrti and Dharmapāla's interpretations of Āryadeva. Nonetheless, two chapters are hardly exhaustive: we should mention that the eighth chapter of Dharmapāla's commentary, which is of considerable philosophical and historical interest, remains to be translated.

The translations are preceded by a three chapter introduction. The first seeks to present the usual introductory matters, such as material on previous research, lives, dates and works of the authors, as well as a few methodological points. The subsequent two chapters are loosely based on topics in the commentaries to CS XII and XIII respectively, but instead of summarizing the details of Āryadeva and his commentators' numerous arguments, I have preferred to treat of the dominant themes in CS XII and XIII by placing them in a larger context of Yogācāra and Madhyamaka philosophies. Nonetheless, the structure of the arguments themselves should be comprehensible from the subheadings which I have added to the translations and from the presentation of rGyal tshab Dar ma rin chen's topical outlines (*sa bcad*) which I have appended to the introduction (i.e. Appendices III and IV).

A few brief words are in order on the transcriptions of Tibetan and Chinese words and on some other conventions which I have adopted. Tibetan transcription is in the system recommended by the American Library Association and the "Verein Deutscher Bibliothekare", that is, with the *n* + superdot (ṅ), *n* + tilde (ñ), *z* + *accent aigu* (ź) and *s* + *accent aigu* (ś) instead of the *ng, ny, zh, sh* which one would use in the system of T. Wylie. (See e.g. Steinkellner and Tauscher 1983 p. ix or Mimaki 1976 p. 185 for the details.) Chinese is transcribed in *Pinyin*, with the first tone (flat) being indicated by macrons (i.e. ā, ē, ī, etc.), second tone (rising) by an *accent aigu* (i.e. á, é, í, etc.), the third tone (falling-rising) by a superscribed "*v*" (i.e. ǎ, ě, ǐ, ǒ, ǔ) and fourth tone (falling) by means of an *accent grave* (i.e. à, è, ì, etc.). I have repunctuated the *Taishō*'s Chinese text by placing a small circle (i.e. °) *beside* the character which I take as ending the Chinese sentence. The *Taishō*'s own rather misleading punctuation, consisting in points *after* the characters, can safely be ignored. Footnotes are used in the introductory chapters, while endnotes figure in the translations. The former are indicated simply by superscribed numbers, whereas the latter are indicated in the text by numbers in parentheses, the actual endnotes themselves being found in the section "Notes to the Translations". In cross-references and in the indexes "footnote" is abbreviated by "fn." and "endnote" by "en." Finally, it may be remarked that many Sanskrit words, such as "dharma", "karma" and "nirvāṇa", have been left unitalicized: this is because they are now bona fide English words. Nonetheless, in many cases, such as "skandha", "śraddhā", "dharmakāya", etc., where the reader might very well have difficulties, I have still followed a more conservative approach, i.e. putting the term in italics and providing a translation. For a partial list of these surprising new English words included in *Webster's Third New International Dictionary* see Jackson (1982).

Numerous are those who have in one way or another assisted me in accomplishing this work: amongst them let me single out a few names for special mention. First and foremost is Jacques May, who was the director of my thesis and who has shown me great personal kindness and careful guidance over the years that I have been in Switzerland. My gratitude also goes to the other members of the jury, i.e. J.F. Billeter, J. Bronkhorst and D.S. Ruegg, as well as to Shōryū Katsura, and (last but not least) to Ernst Steinkellner, for his encouragement and willingness to publish this work. Karen Lang, who has made and is making important contributions on the *Catuḥśataka*, has kindly provided Prof. May and me with copies of her publications. Her work has been of constant use to me, and has been consulted at every stage in working on the CS and CSV. As in the case of Richard Hayes' recent book on Dignāga, which is also a valuable contribution, my occasional disagreements should not at all be misinterpreted: they are, hopefully, constructive disagreements and are intended as such.

Tony Duff, of *Help! Computer Consulting* in Boulder, Colorado, has the incalculable merit of satisfactorily solving the problem of printing Sanskrit, Tibetan and *Pinyin* diacritical marks. Georges Dreyfus, with whom I've had a running dialogue on common philosophical concerns for approximately ten years, has had an important influence on the development of my ideas: no doubt many of our discussions have in one way or another found their course into the positions which I've adopted in this book. Finally, my sincere thanks to my parents, and especially to my wife, Shelley, whose support, comments and patience were indispensable to my being able to accomplish this work.

Financial support was gratefully received from the Japanese Ministry of Education (1983-85), the Social Sciences and Humanities Research Council of Canada (1984-85) and the *Fonds national suisse de la recherche scientifique* (1985 until the present). The University of Lausanne partially subsidized the costs of publication.

Tom J.F. Tillemans
March, 1990.

ANALYTICAL TABLE OF CONTENTS

VOLUME I

PREFACE vii

ABBREVIATIONS xv

BIBLIOGRAPHY xvii

I. INTRODUCTORY REMARKS 1

A. Past research on the *Catuḥśataka* and its commentaries; the scope of our project. 1

B. Lives and works of Āryadeva, Dharmapāla and Candrakīrti 5

C. Some methodological remarks 14

1. The question of an Indo-Tibetan approach 14
2. Can we legitimately speak of Dignāga, Dharmapāla and Dharmakīrti as belonging to one unified school? 18

II. THE PROBLEM OF SCRIPTURAL AUTHORITY 23

A. The Epistemological school's position 24

B. Āryadeva, Dharmapāla and Candrakīrti 29

C. Some final remarks on appeals to authority 32

III. CANDRAKĪRTI AND DHARMAPĀLA ON PERCEPTION 37

A. Candrakīrti on perception and the status of the given 41

B. Dharmapāla on perception 54

IV. A SUMMARY OF OUR ARGUMENTS IN CHAPTERS II AND III 67

A. The problem of scriptural authority 67

B. Candrakīrti on perception and the status of the given 67

C. Dharmapāla on perception 68

APPENDIX I: TEXTS AND TRANSLATIONS FROM PSV AND PST; A NOTE ON DHARMAKĪRTI'S AND DIGNĀGA'S *APOHA* 69

APPENDIX II: REMARKS ON THE *CATUṢKOṬI* 72

APPENDIX III: RGYAL TSHAB RJE'S TOPICAL OUTLINES TO CATUḤŚATAKAVṚTTI XII 77

APPENDIX IV: RGYAL TSHAB RJE'S TOPICAL OUTLINES TO CATUḤŚATAKAVṚTTI XIII 81

ENGLISH TRANSLATIONS 85

DHARMAPĀLA'S COMMENTARY TO THE CATUḤŚATAKA,
Chapter IV: Refutation of Heretical Views (*jiàn* 見 = *dṛṣṭi*) 87
A. The qualities of the auditors of the teaching 87
B. The Outsiders' and Buddhist notions of liberation compared 88
C. The problem of the authority of the Outsiders' and Buddhists' treatises and scriptures 90
1. The Outsider's objection 90
2. The Buddhist reply appealing to voidness 91
3. Voidness 92
4. The Outsiders are untrustworthy 93
5. Arguments against the Vaiśeṣikas 94
6. Arguments against the Sāṃkhyas 96
7. Conclusions and rhetorical exhortations 97
D. The fear of nirvāṇa 99
E. Moral and philosophical faults compared 102
F. Selflessness (*nairātmya*) 102
1. Debates 102
2. Consequences of inappropriately teaching selflessness 104
3. Selflessness was not taught for the sake of argumentation 106
G. Arguments against the Brahmins and Jains 108
1. Refutation of the Vedas 109
2. Jains and Brahmins compared 109
3. Refutation of asceticism and high birth as means to liberation 110
H. Résumé of the Buddhadharma 112
I. Conclusions 113

CATUḤŚATAKAVṚTTI XII: REFUTATION OF HERETICAL VIEWS (*dṛṣṭi*) 115
A. The qualities of the auditors of the teaching 115
B. The Outsiders' and Buddhists' notions of liberation compared 117
1. Citations and some grammatical remarks 117
2. The Outsiders do not know the method for liberation 119
C. The problem of the authority of the Outsiders' and Buddhists' treatises and scriptures 120
1. Citations 120
2. The untrustworthiness of the Outsiders 121
D. Fear of voidness and nirvāṇa 122

E. Moral and philosophical faults compared 124
F. Selflessness (*nairātmya*) 125
1. Consequences of teaching selflessness 125
2. Explaining what selflessness is 126
3. Selflessness was not taught for the sake of argumentation 128
G. Arguments against the Brahmins and Jains 130
1. Jains and Brahmins compared 131
2. Refutation of asceticism and high birth as means to liberation 132
H. Résumé of the Buddhadharma 132
I. Conclusions 133

DHARMAPĀLA'S COMMENTARY TO THE CATUḤŚATAKA, Chapter V: Refutation of the sense organs and their objects (*gēn jìng* 根境 *=indriyārtha*) 135
PART I: SENSE OBJECTS 135
A. Against Sāṃkhya. Refuting sense objects because one never sees the whole 135
B. All sense objects are to be similarly refuted 136
C. One cannot see the whole object by merely seeing its visual form 137
1. Discussion as to whether the visual form itself is indeed perceptible 137
2. The whole form cannot be seen 138
D. Against Buddhist Vaibhāṣikas and other realists. Part-whole arguments used against various positions on the reality of atoms 139
1. *Sādhyasama* 139
2. Atoms and *akṣara* are analogous 140
E. Examination of the Abhidharma's notion of the domain of visual form (*rūpāyatana*): the relationship between shape and colour 141
1. Shape is not different from colour 141
2. Shape is not the same as colour 143
3. Shape, colour and atoms 143
F. Critique of Vaiśeṣika positions 144
1. Refuting the Vaiśeṣika views on colours and their causes: substances are not the cause for colour 145
2. Refuting the Vaiśeṣika views on colours and their causes: colourness is not the cause for colour 145
3. The Vaiśeṣika view that the eye and the body apprehend earth, water and fire 147
4. Substances like earth, etc. are in fact imperceptible 148

5. General refutation of the Outsiders and the other Buddhist vehicles 149
PART II: SENSE ORGANS 150
A. Refuting other Buddhist schools' positions on the reality of the sense organs 150
1. All sense organs are alike in being derivatives from the elements. Why then do only the eyes see? 150
2. The view that the sense organs' characters are the same but their functions differ 150
3. Could the eyes and other organs have different characters because they exist separately from the elements? 151
4. The view that it is the combination of karma and the elements which produces the different effects, such as vision, hearing, etc. 152
5. Does one karma cause different effects? 152
6. Could the powers of karma alone produce the different effects? 153
7. Conclusion: Karma is responsible for the sense organs, but is unanalysable and inconceivable 154
B. Refutation of the Sāṃkhyas' view that form, etc. are apprehended by the sense organs and the inner mind 155
C. Refuting prāpyakāritvavāda — contact between the object and the sense organ 156
D. Refuting aprāpyakāritvavāda — no contact between the object and the sense organ 157
E. Refutation of the Sāṃkhyas' position that the eye and its object are fundamentally identical 159
F. Refutation of the Aulūkyas (Vaiśesikas) 160
1. Refuting the Vaiśeṣikas' four conditions for vision 161
2. Buddhist Hīnayāna views also refuted by the same arguments 161
3. Conclusions 162
G. Critique of sounds and words 162
1. Critique of sound's universal characters 163
2. Refuting prāpyakāritvavāda and aprāpyakāritvavāda with regard to sound 165
3. Sounds cannot be cognized in their totality 165
4. Temporal arguments against the reality of sounds 166
H. Critique of some Sāṃkhyas' views on the mind (*manas*) 167
I. Discussion of "notions" (*saṃjñā*) 168
J. The unreality of consciousness 169
1. Debates about illusions 170

2. Dharmapāla's position 171
K. Replying to the charge that the Madhyamaka is simply counterintuitive 171
L. Similes for dharmas' mode of existence 172

CATUḤŚATAKAVṚTTI XIII: REFUTATION OF THE SENSE ORGANS AND THEIR OBJECTS (*indriyārtha*) 175
PART I: SENSE OBJECTS 175
A. Refuting sense objects because one never sees the whole 175
1. Debate with the logicians on *pratyakṣa* 176
2. Candrakīrti's view: it is the object which is *pratyakṣa*, rather than the mind 178
3. Conclusions 179
B. All sense objects are to be similarly refuted 179
C. One cannot see the whole object by merely seeing its visual form 180
D. Part-whole arguments applied to visual form and atoms 180
1. *Sādhyasama* 181
2. Atoms and *akṣara* are analogous 181
E. Examination of the Abhidharma's notion of *rūpāyatana*: the relationship between shape and colour 182
F. Critique of form and its causes, i.e. the elements 183
1. The view that form and its causes are not different 183
2. The view that form and its causes are different 184
G. Refuting perceptibility (*draṣṭavyatva*) 184
PART II: SENSE ORGANS 185
A. Refuting other Buddhist schools' positions on the reality of the sense organs 185
1. All sense organs are alike in being derivatives from the elements. Why then do only the eyes see? 185
2. Karma is responsible for the sense organs, but is unanalysable and inconceivable 186
B. The view that the eyes, etc. must exist because we observe their effects, viz. the sense consciousnesses 187
C. Refuting prāpyakāritvavāda — contact between the object and the sense organ 188
D. Refuting aprāpyakāritvavāda — no contact between the object and the organ 189
E. Sight is not the nature (*svabhāva*) of the eye 190
F. Refuting the Buddhist's three conditions for vision 190
G. Critique of sounds and words 191

H. Critique of the mind (*manas*) 192
I. Discussion of "notions" (*saṃjñā*) 193
J. The unreality of consciousness 194
K. Replying to the charge that the Madhyamaka is simply counterintuitive 196
L. Similes for dharmas' mode of existence 197
1. Explanations 197
2. Citations 198

NOTES TO THE TRANSLATIONS 201
A. Notes to Dharmapāla's commentary, chapter IV 203
B. Notes to Catuḥśatakavṛtti XII 234
C. Notes to Dharmapāla's commentary, chapter V 246
D. Notes to Catuḥśatakavṛtti XIII 271

VOLUME II

PREFACE TO THE TEXTS AND INDEXES iii

TABLE OF CONTENTS v

ABBREVIATIONS AND SIGLA vi

SANSKRIT AND TIBETAN TEXTS OF CATUḤŚATAKAVṚTTI XII 1

SANSKRIT AND TIBETAN TEXTS OF CATUḤŚATAKAVṚTTI XIII 59

CHINESE OF DHARMAPĀLA'S COMMENTARY 129
Chapter IV 131
Chapter V 138

INDEXES 147
Sanskrit terms 149
Tibetan terms 160
Chinese terms 165
Proper names 180

Candrakīrti. *Catuḥśatakavṛtti* or *Catuḥśatakaṭīkā*. Skt. fragments edited in Haraprasād Shāstrī (1914); skt. and tib. ed. by V. Bhattacharya (1931); Chapt. IX transl. in May (1980), (1981a), (1981b), (1982), (1984); Japanese transl. of Chapt. IX in S. Yamaguchi (1964); Japanese transl. of Chapt. XI in I. Ogawa (1977); unpublished transl. of Chapt. XIV in Lang (1976). Chapters XII and XIII edited and translated in the present work. Bibliographical details concerning the Tibetan translations: P. vol. 96, 5266 ya 33b4-273b6; D. ya 30b6-239a7; C. ya 29a6-236a7; N. ya 34b2-264a6.

Candrakīrti. *Madhyamakāvatāra*. P. 5261 and 5262. Ed. Louis de la Vallée Poussin (i.e. "LVP") (1907a-1912). Transl. LVP (1907b, 1910, 1911) up to Chapt. IV, 165; the rest (viz. VI, 166-226) is transl. in Tauscher (1981).

Candrakīrti. *Pañcaskandhaprakaraṇa*. P. 5267. Ed. Lindtner (1979).

Candrakīrti. *Prasannapadā Madhyamakavṛtti*. Sanskrit ed. in LVP (1903-13).

Candrakīrti. *Śūnyatāsaptativṛtti*. P. 5268.

Candrakīrti(?). *Triśaraṇasaptati*. P. 5366 and 5478. See Sorensen (1986).

Candrakīrti. *Yuktiṣaṣṭikāvṛtti*. P. 5265.

Candramati. *Daśapadārthaśāstra*. See Ui (1917).

Carnap R. (1967). *The Logical Structure of the World* and *Pseudoproblems in Philosophy*. Berkeley and Los Angeles: University of California Press. An English translation by R.A. George of the second edition of Carnap's *Der Logische Aufbau der Welt*, 1961.

Chandra, Lokesh (1971). *Tibetan-Sanskrit Dictionary*. New Delhi, 1971. Reprinted Kyoto: Rinsen Books, 1976.

Chandra, Lokesh (1984). "Vaipulya sūtras and the tantras". In Ligeti (1984): 99-115.

Chimpa, Lama and A. Chattopadhyaya (1970). See Tāranātha.

Chu fei-huang (= Zhū fèihuáng)(1967). *Fǎ xiāng dà cí diǎn* 法相大辭典. 2 Volumes, Taipei, 1967.

Clark R. and L. Jamspal (1979). "The Dialectic which refutes errors establishing logical reasons", *The Tibet Journal* 4: 29-50.

Co ne bstan 'gyur. Micofiches. Stony Brook, New York: The Institute of the Advanced Study of World Religions.

Cousins L., A. Kunst and K.R. Norman (eds.)(1974). *Buddhist Studies in Honour of I.B.* Horner. Dordrecht: D. Reidel.

Dà zhì dù lùn 大智度論 attributed to Nāgārjuna. T. 1509. See Lamotte, *Traité*.

Dag yig gsar bsgrigs. See Blo mthun bsam gtan et al. (1979).

Dantinne J. (1983). *La Splendeur de l'Inébranlable (Akṣobhyavyūha)*. Tome I, Les Auditeurs. Publications de l'Institut Orientaliste de Louvain 29. Louvain-la-Neuve: E. Peeters.

Daśabhūmikasūtra. Ed. J. Rahder. Louvain: J.-B. Istas, 1926.

Dayal H. (1931). *The Bodhisattva Doctrine in Buddhist Sanskrit Literature*. London: Routledge and Kegan Paul. Reprinted Delhi: Motilal Banarsidass, 1970.

dBu ma'i spyi don. See Se ra rje btsun Chos kyi rgyal mtshan, *dBu ma'i spyi don*.

dBus pa blo gsal Byaṅ chub ye śes (14th C.). *Grub pa'i mtha' rnam par bśad pa'i mdzod.* Partially ed. and transl. in Mimaki (1982).

De Jong J.W. (1949). *Çinq chapitres de la Prasannapadā.* Paris: Geuthner.

De Jong J.W. (1971). Review of E. Lamotte, *Traité de la Grande Vertu de Sagesse de Nāgārjuna*, III. *Asia Major* 17: 105-112.

De Jong J.W. (1972). "The problem of the absolute in the Madhyamaka school", JIP 2: 1-6.

De Jong J.W. (1978). "Textcritical notes on the *Prasannapadā*", *Indo-Iranian Journal* 20: 25-59; 217-252.

De Jong J.W. (1986). Review of J. Hopkins' *Meditation on Emptiness*. JIABS 9,1: 124-128.

Demiéville P. (1987). *Le Concile de Lhasa.* Une controverse sur le quiétisme entre bouddhistes de l'Inde et de la Chine au VIIIe siècle de l'ère chrétienne. College de France, Institut des Hautes Etudes Chinoises, Paris. 1st edition published 1952.

dGe 'dun chos 'phel. See A mdo dGe 'dun chos 'phel.

dGe 'dun grub pa (1391-1474). *Tshad ma rnam 'grel legs par bśad pa. Collected Works of the First Dalai Lama, dGe 'dun grub pa,* Vol. 5. Gangtok, 1981.

dGe 'dun grub pa. *Tshad ma rigs rgyan = Tshad ma'i bstan bcos chen po rigs pa'i rgyan.* Mundgod, Karnataka: Drepung Loseling Press, 1984.

Dharmakīrti. *Nyāyabindu: with Dharmottara's Nyāyabinduṭīkā and Durveka Miśra's Dharmottarapradīpa.* Ed. by D. Malvania, Patna: Kashi Prasad Jayaswal Research Institute, 1955, second edition 1971.

Dharmakīrti. *Pramāṇavārttika.* Ed. by Y. Miyasaka. *Pramāṇavārttika-kārikā (Sanskrit and Tibetan).* Naritasan Shinshoji: Acta Indologica 2 1972, pp. 1-206. Ed. R. Sāṅkṛtyāyana in appendices to JBORS 24 (1938), parts I-II. Japanese transl. of PV III in Tosaki (1979), (1985). (PV I = *Svārthanumāna*; PV II = *Pramāṇasiddhi*; PV III = *Pratyakṣa*; PV IV = *Parārthānumāna*.)

Dharmakīrti. *Pramāṇavārttikasvavṛtti.* Ed. R. Gnoli. *The Pramāṇavārttikaṃ of Dharmakīrti.* Serie Orientale Roma 23, Rome, 1960.

Dharmakīrti. *Pramāṇaviniścaya.* P. 5710. Chapt. I ed. and transl. by Vetter (1966); Chapt. II ed. in Steinkellner (1973), transl. Steinkellner (1979).

Dharmapāla. *Chéng wéi shí lùn* 成唯識論 . T. 1585. See Xuán zàng, *Chéng wẹi shí lùn.*

Dharmapāla. *Chéng wéi shí bǎo shēng lùn* 成唯識寶生論 . T. 1591. Transl. Yì jìng.

Dharmapāla. *Guān suǒ yuán lùn shì* 觀所縁論釋 . T. 1625. Transl. Yì jìng.

Dharmapāla. *Guǎng bǎi lùn shì lùn* 廣百論釋論 . T. 1571. Transl. Xuán zàng.

Dharmapāla(?). *Theg pa chen po'i chos brgya gsal ba'i sgo bstan bcos.* P. 5564. See Vasubandhu T. 1614.

Dharmapāla. *Yi ge'i mdo'i 'grel pa.* P. 5570.

Dharmottara. *Nyāyabinduṭīkā.* See Dharmakīrti, *Nyāyabindu.*

Dīgha = *Dīgha Nikāya*. Ed. T.W. Rhys Davids and J.E. Carpenter in 3 volumes. London: Pali Text Society, 1889-1910. Reprint 1947-1949.

Dignāga. *Ālambanaparīkṣā*. Ed. and transl. with *vṛtti* in S. Yamaguchi and H. Meyer (1929) and in F. Tola and C. Dragonetti (1982).

Dignāga. *Ālambanaparīkṣāvṛtti*. See Dignāga's *Ālambanaparīkṣā*.

Dignāga. *Nyāyamukha*. T. 1628. Ed. and Japanese translation in S. Katsura, *Inmyō Shōrimonron Kenkyū*. Hiroshima Daigaku Bungakubu Kiyō 37 (1977) 106-127, 38 (1978) 110-130, 39 (1979) 63-83, 41 (1981) 62-83, 42 (1982) 82-100, 44 (1984) 43-75, 46 (1987) 46-65. Transl. G. Tucci, Heidelberg: Materialen zur Kunde des Buddhismus. 1930.

Dignāga. *Pramāṇasamuccaya*. P. 5700. Chapter I transl. and ed. by Hattori (1968a). Chapter V edited by Hattori (1982) and partially translated in Hayes (1988).

Dignāga. *Pramāṇasamuccayavṛtti*. P. 5701 (i.e. PSVa) transl. Vasudhararakṣita and Seṅ rgyal; P. 5702 (i.e. PSVb) transl. Kanakavarman and Dad pa śes rab.

Dignāga?. **Upādāyaprajñaptiprakaraṇa*. *Qǔ yīn jiǎ shè lùn* 取因假設論 . T. 1622 Transl. Yì jìng. Partial English translation in Kitagawa (1973).

dKon mchog 'jigs med dbaṅ po (1728-1791). *Grub mtha' rnam bźag rin chen phreṅ ba*. Ed. by K. Mimaki (1977).

Durveka Miśra. *Dharmottarapradīpa*. See Dharmakīrti, *Nyāyabindu*.

Dutt N. (1934). "The Birthplace of Āryadeva", *Indian Historical Quarterly* 10; 137-142.

Dutt N. (1930). *Aspects of Mahāyāna Buddhism and its relation to Hīnayāna*. London: Luzac.

Eckel M. (1985). "Bhāvaviveka's critique of Yogācāra philosophy in chapter XXV of the *Prajñāpradīpa*". In Lindtner (ed.) (1985b): 25-75.

Eckel M. (1987). *Jñānagarbha's Commentary on the Distinction Between the Two Truths*. An Eighth Century Handbook of Madhyamaka Philosophy. Albany N.Y.: State University of New York Press.

Edgerton F. (1953). *Buddhist Hybrid Sanskrit Grammar and Dictionary*. Volume I: Grammar. Volume II: Dictionary. New Haven, 1953. Reprinted Delhi: Motilal Banarsidass, 1977.

Endō N. (1932). *Daijō kōhyakuron shakuron*. In *Kokuyaku Issaikyō*, *Chūgan-bu* 3. Tokyo: Daitōshuppansha.

Fǎ xiāng dà cí diǎn. See Chu Fei-huang (1967).

Foucher A. (1949). *Le Compendium des topiques d'Annambhaṭṭa*. Eléments de systématique et de logique indiennes. Paris: A. Maisonneuve.

Franco E. (1984). "On the interpretation of *Pramāṇasamuccaya(vṛtti)* I, 3d", JIP 12: 389-400.

Franco E. (1989). "Was the Buddha a buddha?", JIP 17: 81-99.

Frauwallner E. (1953,1956). *Geschichte der Indischen Philosophie*. 2 volumes. Salzburg: Otto Müller Verlag.

Frauwallner E. (1958). "Die Erkenntnislehre des Klassischen Sāṃkhya-systems", WZKSO 2: 84-139.

Frauwallner E. (1959). "Dignāga, sein Werk und seine Entwicklung", WZKSO 3: 83-164.

Frauwallner E. (1961). "Landmarks in the history of Indian logic", WZKSO 5: 125-148.

Frauwallner E. (1961b). "*Mīmāṃsāsūtram* 1.1.6-23", WZKSO 5: 113-124.

Gaṇḍavyūhasūtra. Ed. P.L. Vaidya, Buddhist Sanskrit Texts n° 5, Darbhanga, 1960.

Garbe R. (1894). *Die Sāṃkhya Philosophie: Eine Darstellung des Indische Rationalismus.* Leipzig: Hessel. Reprinted 1917.

Gauḍapāda. *Sāṃkhyakārikābhāṣya.* See Īśvarakṛṣṇa.

Gautama. *Nyāyasūtra.* Ed. with the *bhāṣya* of Vātsyāyana by P. Shāstrī and H. Shukla. Kashi Sanskrit Series 43. Varanasi: Chowkhamba Sanskrit Series Office, 1970. See Vidyābhuṣana (1913).

Gillon B. and R. Hayes (1982). "The role of the particle *eva* in (logical) quantification in Sanskrit", WZKS 26: 195-203.

Gokhale V. (1930). *Akṣara-Çatakam, the Hundred Letters.* Heidelberg: Materialen zur Kunde Buddhismus 14.

gŹan dga' gŹan phan chos kyi snaṅ ba (1871-1927). *bsTan bcos bźi brgya pa źes bya ba'i tshig le'ur byas pa'i mchan 'grel.* Vol. 5 in *gŹuṅ chen bcu gsum gyi mchan 'grel,* Commentaries expanding the texts of the chief Indic Buddhist *śāstras* in their Tibetan translations. Reproduced from a set of the 'Bri guṅ prints from the library of Ñi ma lcaṅ ra rin po che. Published by the Ven. D.G. Khocchen Tulku, Nyingmapa Lamas' College, Clement Town, Dehra Dun U.P., and printed at the Jayyed Press, Delhi, 1978.

Haack S. (1974). *Deviant Logic. Some philosophical issues.* Cambridge: Cambridge University Press.

Hahn M. (1982). *Nāgārjuna's Ratnāvalī, Vol. 1 the basic texts (Sanskrit, Tibetan, Chinese).* Indica et Tibetica 1, Bonn.

Hall B.C. (1986). "The meaning of *vijñapti* in Vasubandhu's concept of mind", JIABS 9, 1: 7-23.

Haraprasād Shāstrī (1911). "Notes on the newly-found manuscript of Chatuḥśatika by Āryadeva", *Journal of the Asiatic Society of Bengal* 7: 431-436.

Haraprasād Shāstrī (1914). "Catuḥśatika of Ārya Deva", *Memoirs of the Asiatic Society of Bengal,* Vol. III, 8, Calcutta: 449-514.

Haribhadra. *Abhisamayālaṃkārālokā Prajñāpāramitāvyākhyā.* Ed. U. Wogihara, Tokyo 1932, reprinted 1973. See Moriyama (1984).

Hattori M. (1968a). *Dignāga on Perception: being the Pratyakṣapariccheda of Dignāga's Pramāṇasamuccaya.* Harvard Oriental Series 47. Cambridge, Mass.: Harvard University Press.

Hattori M. (1968b). "Two types of non-qualificative perception", WZKSO 12-13, Festschrift für E. Frauwallner: 161-169.

Hattori M. (1982). *The Pramāṇasamuccayavṛtti of Dignāga with Jinendrabuddhi's Commentary, Chapter Five: Anyāpoha-parīkṣā.* Tibetan Text with Sanskrit Fragments. Memoirs of the Faculty of Letters, 21, Kyoto University.

Hattori M. (1988). "Realism and the philosophy of consciousness-only", *The Eastern Buddhist* XXI, No. 1: 23-60. English translation by W. Powell of a chapter in M. Hattori and S. Ueyama. *Ninshiki to chōetsu: Yuishiki*, 1970.

Hayashima O. (1976). "Hō-zuihō-gyō (dharma-anudharma-pratipatti) — sono gogi to igi", *Nanto Bukkyō* 36: 1-24.

Hayes R. (1984). "The question of doctrinalism in the Buddhist epistemologists", *Journal of the American Academy of Religion* 52: 645-670.

Hayes R. (1988). *Dignāga on the Interpretation of Signs.* Studies of Classical India 9. Dordrecht: Kluwer.

Herzberger R. (1986). *Bhartṛhari and the Buddhists*: an essay in the development of fifth and sixth century Indian thought. Studies of Classical India 8. Dordrecht: D. Reidel (= Kluwer).

Hirabayashi J. and S. Iida (1977). "Another look at the Mādhyamika vs. Yogācāra controversy concerning existence and non-existence", in L. Lancaster and L.O. Gómez (eds.) *Prajñāpāramitā and Related Systems*: Studies in honor of Edward Conze. Berkeley: Berkeley Buddhist Studies 1, pp. 341-360.

Hirakawa A. (1973, 1977, 1978). *Index to the Abhidharmakośabhāṣya (P. Pradhān edition).* Part One, Sanskrit-Tibetan-Chinese, 1973; Part Two, Chinese-Sanskrit, 1977; Part Three, Tibetan-Sanskrit, 1978. Tokyo: Daizō shuppan Kabushikigaisha. References abbreviated as "H." are to Part Two.

Hōbōgirin, Dictionnaire encyclopédique du bouddhisme d'après les sources chinoises et japonaises. Tokyo: Maison franco-japonaise. Paris: Librairie d'Amérique et d'Orient, 1929- .

Hobson-Jobson. See Yule, H. and A.C. Burnell.

Honda M. (1974). "Ārya Deva's critique against Sāṃkhya", IBK 23,1: 491-486.

Honjō Y. (1984). *A Table of Āgama-citations in the Abhidharmakośa and the Abhidharmakośabhāṣya*, Part I. Kyoto: Koseisha.

Hopkins J. (1975). *The Precious Garland and The Song of the Four Mindfulnesses.* Wisdom of Tibet Series 2. London: George Allen and Unwin.

Hopkins J. (1977). *Tantra in Tibet*, The Great Exposition of Secret Mantra by Tsong-ka-pa. Wisdom of Tibet Series 3. London: George Allen and Unwin.

Hopkins J. (1983). *Meditation on Emptiness.* London: Wisdom Publications.

Hopkins J. (1989). "A Tibetan delineation of different views of emptiness in the Indian Middle Way school", *The Tibet Journal* XIV, 1: 10-43.

Huì lì 慧立 . *Dà táng cí ēn sì sān zàng fă shī zhuàn* 大唐慈恩寺三藏法師傳 . T. 2053. Transl. S. Beal. *The Life of Hiuen-Tsiang.* London 1888, reprint. 1911, 1914.

Hulin M. (1978). *Sāṃkhya Literature.* In J. Gonda (ed.), *A History of Indian Literature*, Vol. 6, fascicule 3. Wiesbaden: O. Harrasowitz.

Ichigō M. (1985). *Madhyamakālaṃkāra of Śāntarakṣita with his own commentary or Vṛtti and with the subcommentary or Pañjikā of Kamalaśīla.* Kyoto: Buneido.

Iida S. (1973). "The nature of *saṃvṛti* and the relationship of *paramārtha* to it in Svātantrika-Mādhyamika", in M. Sprung (ed.), *Two Truths in Buddhism and Vedānta*. Dordrecht: D. Reidel, pp. 64-77.

Iida S. (1980). *Reason and Emptiness*: a study in logic and mysticism. Tokyo: Hokuseido Press.

Iida S. and E. Conze (1968). "'Maitreya's questions' in the *Prajñāpāramitā*", in *Mélanges d'Indianisme à la mémoire de Louis Renou*. Publications de l'Institut de Civilisation Indienne, Fascicule 28. Paris.

Inami M. and T. Tillemans (1986). "Another look at the framework of the *Pramāṇasiddhi* chapter of *Pramāṇavārttika*", WZKS 30: 123-142.

Inde Classique. See L. Renou and J. Filliozat (1947 & 1953).

Īśvarakṛṣṇa. *Sāṃkhyakārikā*. Transl. and edited with Gauḍapāda's *Bhāṣya* by T.G. Mainkar. Poona: Oriental Book Agency, revised edition, 1972.

Īśvarakṛṣṇa. **Suvarṇasaptati, Jīn qī shí lùn* 金七十論. T. 2137. Chinese version of *Sāṃkhyakārikās* with *bhāṣya*. Transl. Takakusu (1904). Iwata T. (1981). "Bemerkung zur *sahopalambhaniyama*-Schlussfolgerung Dharmakīrtis und seiner Kommentatoren", IBK 30, 1: 493-486.

Iwata T. (1984a). "One interpretation of the *saṃvedana*-inference of Dharmakīrti", IBK 33, 1: 397-394.

Iwata T. (1984b). "Dōji ninshiki ni tsuite", *Tōyō no Shisō to shūkyō*, June, 1984: 1-25.

Jackson R. (1982). "Terms of Sanskrit and Pāli origin acceptable as English words", JIABS 5-2: 141-142.

'Jam dbyaṅs bźad pa'i rdo rje Ṅag dbaṅ brtson 'grus (1648-1722). *Tshig gsal stoṅ thun gyi tshad ma'i rnam bśad zab rgyas kun gsal tshad ma'i 'od brgya 'bar ba skal bzaṅ sñiṅ gi mun sel*. Included in Vol 11 pp. 483-619 of *The Collected Works of 'Jam dbyaṅs bźad pa'i rdo rje*. Published by Ṅag dbaṅ dge legs bde mo, Delhi, 1973.

'Jam mgon 'Ju mi pham rgya mtsho. See Mi pham rgya mtsho.

'Jam mgon koṅ sprul Blo gros mtha' yas (1813-1899). *Śes bya kun khyab = Theg pa'i sgo kun las btus pa gsuṅ rab rin po che'i mdzod bslab pa gsum legs par ston pa'i bstan bcos śes bya kun khyab*. 3 Volumes. Beijing: Mi rigs dpe skrun khaṅ (Minzu chubanshe), 1982.

Jinendrabuddhi. *Pramāṇasamuccayaṭīkā (Viśālāmalavatī)*. P. 5766. Chapter V ed. Hattori (1972).

Jīn qī shí lùn. See Īśvarakṛṣṇa.

Jñānagarbha. *Satyadvayavibhaṅgakārikā*. D. 3881. *sDe dge bstan 'gyur (dbu ma)* vol. 12. See Eckel (1987).

Jñānagarbha. *Satyadvayavibhaṅgavṛtti*. D. 3882. *sDe dge bstan 'bgyur (dbu ma)* vol. 12. See Eckel (1987).

Kaḥ thog mkhan po Ṅag dbaṅ dpal bzaṅ (1879-1941). *dBu ma bźi brgya pa'i rnam par bśad pa rgya mtsho'i zeg ma*. Reproduced from a print from the Kaḥ thog blocks. Published by Ven. Pad ma Nor bu Rin po che, rÑiṅ ma pa Monastery, Bylakuppe and printed at M.M. Offset Press, Delhi, 1984.

Kajiyama Y. (1963, 1964). "Bhāvaviveka's *Prajñāpradīpaḥ*", WZKSO 7: 37-62; WZKSO 8: 100-130.

Kajiyama Y. (1965). "Controversy between the *sākāra-* and *nirākāra-vādins* of the Yogācāra school — some materials", IBK 14, 1: 429-418.

Kajiyama Y. (1966). *An Introduction to Buddhist Philosophy,* an annotated translation of the *Tarkabhāṣā* of Mokṣākaragupta. Memoirs of the Faculty of Letters of Kyoto University 10, Kyoto.

Kajiyama Y. (1968). "Bhāvaviveka, Sthiramati and Dharmapāla", WZKSO 12-13, Festschrift für E. Frauwallner: 193-203.

Kajiyama Y. (1971). "The atomic theory of Vasubandhu, the author of the *Abhidharmakośa*", IBK 19, 2: 1001-1006.

Kajiyama Y. (1973). "Three kinds of affirmation and two kinds of negation in Buddhist philosophy", WZKS 17: 161-175.

Kajiyama Y. (1977). "Realism of the Sarvāstivāda school", in L.S. Kawamura and K. Scott (eds.), *Buddhist Thought and Asian Civilization.* Essays in honour of Herbert V. Guenther on his sixtieth birthday. Berkeley: Dharma Publishing.

Kajiyama Y. (1978). "Later Mādhyamikas on epistemology and meditation", in M. Kiyota (ed.), *Mahāyāna Buddhist Meditation: Theory and practice.* Honolulu: University of Hawai Press. pp. 114-143.

The above-mentioned publications of Y. Kajiyama are now reprinted in *Y. Kajiyama, Studies in Buddhist Philosophy.* Selected papers. Ed. by K. Mimaki et al. Kyoto: Rinsen Book Co., 1989.

Kamalaśīla. *Madhyamakālaṃkārapañjikā.* P. 5286. Ed. Ichigō (1985).

Kamalaśīla. *Madhyamakāloka.* P. 5287.

Kamalaśīla. *Sarvadharmaniḥsvabhāvasiddhi.* P. 5289.

Kamalaśīla. *Tattvasaṃgrahapañjikā.* See Śāntarakṣita, *Tattvasaṃgraha.*

Kambala. *Ālokamālā.* Ed. and transl. by C. Lindtner in Lindtner (ed.) (1985b): 108-220.

Kaṇāda. *Vaiśeṣikasūtra.* Ed. M. Jambuvijayaji (1961). *Vaiśeṣikasūtra of Kaṇāda, with the commentary of Candrānanda.* Gaekwad's Oriental Series 36. See transl. by Sinha (1911).

Karṇakagomin. *Pramāṇavārttikasvavṛttiṭīkā.* Ed. R. Sāṅkṛtyāyana. Reprinted Kyoto: Rinsen Books, 1982.

Kāśyapaparivarta. Ed. A. von Staël-Holstein. *The Kāśyapaparivarta, a Mahāyānasūtra of the Ratnakūṭa class edited in the original Sanskrit, in Tibetan and in Chinese.* Reprinted Tokyo, 1977.

Katsura S. (1982). See Dignāga, *Nyāyamukha.*

Katsura S. (1984). "Dharmakīrti's theory of truth", JIP 12: 215-235.

Katsura S. (1986a). *Indo Ronrigaku ni okeru Henjū Gainen no Seisei to Hatten — Carakasaṃhitā kara Dharmakīrti made.* Hiroshima Daigaku Bungakubu Kiyō 45, special supplement 1, Hiroshima.

Katsura S. (1986b). "On the origin and development of the concept of *vyāpti* in Indian logic", *Tetsugaku* 38, Hiroshima University: 1-16.

Katsura S. (1986c). "On *Trairūpya* formulae", in *Buddhism and Its Relation to Other Religions*: Essays in honour of Dr. Shozen Kumoi on his seventieth birthday, Kyoto, pp. 161-172.

Kelsang T. and S. Onoda (1985). *Textbooks of Se-ra Monastery for the Primary Course of Studies.* Kyoto: Biblia Tibetica 1.

Kitagawa H. (1973). *Indo Koten Ronrigaku no Kenkyū: Jinna no taikei.* Revised edition. Tokyo: Suzuki Gakujutsu Zaidan.

Kobayashi M. (1986). "Kamalaśīla no ri-itsuta-ronshō — 'chūganmyō' shiyaku I (The 'neither one nor many' argument for *śūnyatā*, an annotated Japanese translation of the *Madhyamakāloka* of Kamalaśīla (I))", *Tōhoku Indogaku Shūkyō Gakkai Ronshū* 13: 90-72.

Kobayashi M. (1987). "Mujishōshō-ronshō to shoe-fujō no mondai — Kamalaśīla no 'chūganmyō' o chūshin to shite (The Mādhyamika argument for *niḥsvabhāvatā* and the fallacy of *āśrayāsiddha* — Kamalaśīla's view in his *Madhyamakāloka*)", *Bunka* 50: 41-60.

Kokuyaku Issaikyō, Chūgan-bu. 3 vols. [i.e. "Canonical texts translated into the national language, Madhyamaka section"]. Tokyo: Daitō shuppansha, 1930-1932. See also *L'Inde Classique* II, § 2165 and *Hōbōgirin* IV, Supplement, pp. ii, ix for more information on the *Kokuyaku Issaikyō*, which is a collection of Japanese translations of various Chinese texts.

Kripke S. (1981). "Wittgenstein on rules and private language", pp. 238-312 in I. Block (ed.), *Perspectives on the Philosophy of Wittgenstein.* Oxford: Basil Blackwell.

Kuī jī 窺基. *Chéng wéi shí lùn shù jì* 成唯識論述記 . T. 1830.

Kuī jī. *Chéng wéi shí lùn zhǎng zhōng shū yào* 成唯識論掌中樞要 . T. 1831.

Kuī jī. *Wéi shí èr shí lùn shù jì* 唯識二十論述記 . T. 1834.

Kumārila Bhaṭṭa. *Ślokavārttika, with the Commentary Nyāyaratnākara of Śrī Pārthasārathi Miśra.* Ed. D. Shāstrī. Varanasi: Tara Publications, 1978.

La Vallée Poussin L. de. (1903-1913). *Mūlamadhyamakakārikās (Mādhyamikasūtras) de Nāgārjuna*, avec la *Prasannapadā* commentaire de Candrakīrti. St. Petersburg: Bibliotheca Buddhica IV. Reprinted Osnabrück: Biblio Verlag, 1970.

La Vallée Poussin L. de. (1907a-1912). *Madhyamakāvatāra par Candrakīrti*, traduction tibétaine. St. Petersburg: Bibliotheca Buddhica IX, reprinted Osnabrück, 1970.

La Vallée Poussin L. de (1907b, 1910, 1911). "*Madhyamakāvatāra*, Introduction au Traité du Milieu de l'Ācārya Candrakīrti, avec le commentaire de l'auteur, traduit d'après la version tibétaine", *le Muséon*, Louvain, VIII, 1907, pp. 249-317; XI, 1910, pp. 271-358; XII, 1911, pp. 235-328.

La Vallée Poussin L. de. (1913). *Théorie des douzes causes.* Université de Gand, Recueil de travaux publiés par la Faculté de Philosophie et Lettres. London: Luzac and co.

La Vallée Poussin L. de. (1928-1929). *Vijñaptimātratāsiddhi, La siddhi de Hiuan-Tsang,* traduit et annotée par Louis de la Vallée Poussin. Buddhica, Documents et travaux pour l'étude du bouddhisme publiés sous la direction de Jean Przyluski, Tome I (1928), Tome II (1929). Paris: Librairie Orientaliste Paul Geuthner.

La Vallée Poussin L. de. (1923-1931). *L'Abhidharmakośa de Vasubandhu:* traduction et annotations. Paris: Geuthner; Louvain: J.-B. Istas, 1923-1931 6 volumes. New edition prepared by E. Lamotte, MCB vol. XVI, 6 volumes. Brussels: Institut Belge des Hautes Etudes Chinoises, 1971.

La Vallée Poussin L. de. (1932). "Le *nirvāṇa* d'après Āryadeva", MCB I: 127-135.

La Vallée Poussin L. de. (1933a). "Le petit traité de Vasubandhu-Nāgārjuna sur les trois natures", MCB 2: 147-161.

La Vallée Poussin L. de. (1933b). "Réflexions sur le Madhyamaka", MCB 2: 1-59.

Lakatos I. (1978). "History of science and its rational reconstructions", pp. 102-138 in J. Worral and G. Currie (eds.), *Imre Lakatos, The Methodology of Scientific Research Programmes.* Philosophical Papers Vol. 1, Cambridge: Cambridge University Press, 1978.

Lalitavistara. Ed. P.L. Vaidya. Buddhist Sanskrit Texts 1, Darbhanga, 1958.

Lamotte E. (1935). *Saṃdhinirmocanasūtra, L'Explication des mystères:* texte tibétain édité et traduit par Etienne Lamotte. Recueil de travaux publiés par les membres des Conférences d'Histoire et de Philologies 2e Série, 34e Fascicule. Université de Louvain, 1935.

Lamotte E. (1936). "Le Traité de l'acte de Vasubandhu, *Karmasiddhiprakaraṇa*", MCB 4: 151-288.

Lamotte E. (1949, 70, 76, 80). *Le Traité de la Grande Vertu de Sagesse de Nāgārjuna (Mahāprajñāpāramitāśāstra).* Tome I and II, Bibliothèque du Muséon vols. 18 and 19 (1949), reprinted 1966 and 1967. Tome III, IV, V printed in Publications de l'Institut Orientaliste, Louvain, 2, 12, 24, in 1970, 1976, 1980 respectively.

Lamotte E. (1962). *L'Enseignement de Vimalakīrti (Vimalakīrtinirdeśa).* Traduit et annoté par Etienne Lamotte. Bibiothèque du Muséon, vol. 51. Institut Orientaliste, Louvain.

Lamotte E. (1965). *La Concentration de la Marche Héroïque (Śūraṃgamasamādhisūtra).* MCB Vol. XIII, Brussels.

Lamotte E. (1973). *La Somme du grand véhicule d'Asaṅga (Mahāyānasaṃgraha).* Tome I: versions tibétaine et chinoise (Hiuan-Tsang). Tome II: traduction et commentaire. Publications de l'Institut Orientaliste de Louvain 8. Louvain, 1973.

Lamotte E. (1974). "Passions and impregnations of the passions in Buddhism", in L. Cousins et al. (eds.) (1974), pp. 91-104.

Lang K. (1976). *"Showing the realization of the refutation of holding extreme views": Chapter XIV of Candrakīrti's Bodhisattvayogācāracatuḥśatakaṭīkā.* Critical edition, English translation, study. Unpublished M.A. Thesis, University of Washington, Seattle. 270 p.

Lang K. (1983). *Āryadeva on the Bodhisattva's Cultivation of Merit and Knowledge.* Ph.D Thesis for University of Washington, available from University Microfilms International, Ann Arbor, Michigan.

Lang K. (1986). *Āryadeva's Catuḥśataka.* On the bodhisattva's cultivation of merit and knowledge. Indiske Studier VII. Copenhagen: Akademisk Forlag.

lCaṅ skya rol pa'i rdo rje (1717-1786). *lCaṅ skya grub mtha' = Grub pa'i mtha' rnam par bźag pa gsal bar bśad pa thub bstan lhun po'i mdzes rgyan.* Sarnath: PES Press, 1970.

Lévi S. (1925). *Vijñaptimātratāsiddhi,* Deux traités de Vasubandhu, *Viṃśatikā* (la Vingtaine) accompagnée d'une explication en prose et *Triṃśikā* (la Trentaine) avec le commentaire de Sthiramati. Paris: Honoré Champion.

Lévi S. (1929). "Autour d'Aśvaghoṣa", *Journal Asiatique* Oct-Dec.: 255-285.

Lévi S. (1932). *Matériaux pour l'étude du système vijñaptimātra.* Paris: Honoré Champion.

Ligeti L. (ed.) (1984). *Tibetan and Buddhist Studies Commemorating the 200th Anniversary of the Birth of Alexander Csoma de Körös.* Budapest: Akadémiai kiadó.

Lindtner C. (1979). "Candrakīrti's *Pañcaskandhaprakaraṇa,* I. Tibetan Text", *Acta Orientalia* 40: 87-145.

Lindtner C. (1980). "A propos Dharmakīrti — two new works and a new date", *Acta Orientalia* 41: 27-37.

Lindtner C. (1981). "Atiśa's introduction to the two truths, and its sources", JIP 9: 161-214.

Lindtner C. (1982a). "Adversaria Buddhica", WZKS 26: 167-194.

Lindtner C. (1982b). *Nāgārjuniana:* Studies in the writings and philosophy of Nāgārjuna. Indiske Studier IV. Copenhagen: Akademisk Forlag.

Lindtner C. (1984). "Bhavya's controversy with Yogācāra in the appendix to *Prajñāpradīpa*, chapt. XXV", in L. Ligeti (ed.) (1984): 77-98.

Lindtner C. (1985a). "A treatise on Buddhist idealism, Kambala's *Ālokamālā*", Ed. and transl. in Lindtner (1985b): 108-220.

Lindtner C. (ed.) (1985b). *Miscellanea Buddhica.* Indiske Studier V. Copenhagen: Akademisk Forlag.

Lindtner C. (1986). "Bhavya's critique of Yogācāra in the *Madhyamakaratnapradīpa*", in B. Matilal and R. Evans (eds) (1986): 239-264.

Lipman K. (1980). "*Nītārtha, neyārtha,* and *tathāgatagarbha* in Tibet", JIP 8: 87-95.

Liu Ming-Wood (1982). "The three-nature doctine and its interpretation in Hua-Yen Buddhism", *T'oung Pao* 68, 4-5: 181-220.

Lokesh Chandra. See Chandra, Lokesh (1984).

Lopez D.S. (1987). *A Study of Svātantrika.* Ithaca, New York: Snow Lion Publications.

Mahāvyutpatti. Ed. R. Sakaki. 2 volumes. Kyoto, 1916-1925. Reprinted Tokyo, 1965.

Mainkar T.G. (1972). See Īśvarakṛṣṇa.

Maitreya. *Abhisamayālaṃkāraprajñāpāramitopadeśaśāstra*. Ed. T. Stcherbatsky and E. Obermiller. Bibliotheca Buddhica 23. Reprinted Osnabrück: Biblio Verlag, 1970.

Maitreya. *Biàn zhōng biān lùn sòng* 辯中邊論頌 . Transl. of *Madhyāntavibhāga* by Xuán zàng, T. 1601.

Maitreya. *Madhyāntavibhāga*. Ed. by G. Nagao, *Madhyāntavibhāgabhāṣya*. Tokyo: Suzuki Research Foundation, 1964. Ed. R. Pandeya, *Madhyāntavibhāga-śāstra, containing the kārikās of Maitreya, [the] Bhāṣya of Vasubandhu and [the] Ṭīkā by Sthiramati*. Delhi: Motilal Banarsidass, 1971. *Madhyāntavibhāga*, *bhāṣya* and *ṭīkā* transl. in Stcherbatsky (1936). See also Maitreya, T. 1601 and Vasubandhu, T. 1600.

Majjhima = *Majjhima Nikāya*. Ed. by V. Trenkner and R. Chalmers in three volumes. London: Pali Text Society, 1948-1951.

Manorathanandin. *Pramāṇavārttikavṛtti*. Ed. by R. Sāṅkṛtyāyana with the notes of Vibhūticandra in the appendices to JBORS 24 (1938) part III. Also ed. by D. Shāstrī, Varanasi: Bauddha Bharati 3, 1968.

Matilal B.K. (1970). "Reference and existence in Nyāya and Buddhist logic", JIP 1: 83-110.

Matilal B.K. (1971). *Epistemology, Logic and Grammar in Indian Philosophical Analysis*. The Hague: Mouton.

Matilal B.K. (1974). "A critique of Buddhist idealism", in L. Cousins et al. (eds.) (1974), pp. 139-169.

Matilal B.K. (1977). *Nyāya-Vaiśeṣika*. In J. Gonda (ed.), *A History of Indian Literature*, Vol. 6, fascicule 2. Wiesbaden: O. Harrasowitz.

Matilal B.K. (1986). *Perception*. An essay on classical Indian theories of knowledge. Oxford: Clarendon Press.

Matilal B.K. and R.D. Evans (eds.) (1986). *Buddhist Logic and Epistemology:* Studies in the Buddhist analysis of inference and language. Studies of Classical India 7. Dordrecht: D. Reidel.

Matsumoto S. (1981). "*Svabhāvapratibandha*", IBK 30: 498-494.

May J. (1959). *Candrakīrti Prasannapadā Madhyamakavṛtti*. Paris: Adrien-Maissonneuve.

May J. (1971). "La Philosophie bouddhique idéaliste", EA 25: 263-323.

May J. (1979). "*Chūgan*". *Hōbōgirin* V, Paris-Tokyo: 470-493.

May J. (1980). "Āryadeva et Candrakīrti sur la permanence (I)", in *Indianisme et Bouddhisme, Mélanges offerts à Mgr Etienne Lamotte*. Louvain: Publications de l'Institut orientaliste de Louvain.

May J. (1981a). "Āryadeva et Candrakīrti sur la permanence (II)", *Bulletin de l'Ecole française d'Extrême-Orient*. Tome 69 à la mémoire de Paul Demiéville: 75-96.

May J. (1981b). "Āryadeva et Candrakīrti sur la permanence (III)", EA XXXV, 2, Hommage à Constantin Regamey: 47-76.

May J. (1982). "Āryadeva et Candrakīrti sur la permanence (IV)", *Etudes de Lettres*, University of Lausanne, 3: 45-76.

May J. (1984). "Āryadeva et Candrakīrti sur la permanence (V)", *Acta Indologica*, Studies of Mysticism in honor of the 1150th Anniversary of Kōbō Daishi's Nirvāṇam. Narita: Naritasan Shinshoji. pp. 115-144.

May J. and K. Mimaki (1979). "*Chūdō*", *Hōbōgirin* V, Paris-Tokyo: 456-470.

Mi pham rgya mtsho = 'Jam mgon 'Ju mi pham rgya mtsho (1846-1912). *gŹan stoṅ seṅ ge'i ṅa ro. Collected Writings of 'Jam-mgon 'Ju mi-pham-rgya-mtsho*, published by Sonam Topgay Kazi, Gangtok, 1976.

Mikogami E. (1979). "Some remarks on the concept of *arthakriyā*", JIP 7: 79-94.

Mimaki K. (1976). *La Réfutation bouddhique de la permanence des choses (sthirasiddhidūṣaṇa) et la preuve de la momentanéité des choses (kṣaṇabhaṅgasiddhi)*. Paris: Publications de l'institut de civilisation indienne, fascicule 41.

Mimaki K. (1977). *Le Grub mtha' rnam bźag rin chen phreṅ ba de dKon mchog 'jigs med dbaṅ po (1728-1791)*. Text tibétain édité, avec une introduction. Kyoto: Zinbun Kagaku Kenkyusyo.

Mimaki K. (1980). *Le chapitre du Blo gsal grub mtha' sur les Sautrāntika.* Un essai de traduction. Kyoto: Zinbun Kagaku Kenkyusyo, University of Kyoto, Research Institute for Humanistic Studies, pp. 143-173.

Mimaki K. (1982). *Blo gsal grub mtha'.* Kyoto: Zinbun Kagaku Kenkyusyo.

Mimaki K. (1983). "The *Blo gsal grub mtha'*, and the Mādhyamika classification in Tibetan *grub mtha'* literature", pp. 161-167 in E. Steinkellner and H. Tauscher (eds.) (1983).

Mimaki K. (1987). Entries for "Āryadeva", "Candrakīrti" and "Śīlabhadra", pp. 431a-432a, 58b-59a and 320b-321b respectively in Mircea Eliade et al. (eds.), *The Encyclopedia of Religion*. New York: Macmillan Publishing.

Mitsukawa T. (1976). "Shihyakuron no Gohō-shaku to Gesshō-shaku ni tsuite," IBK XXIV, 2: 50-55.

Miyasaka Y. (1972). See Dharmakīrti, *Pramāṇavārttika*.

Mokṣākaragupta. *Tarkabhāṣā*. See Kajiyama (1966) for transl. Skt. ed. R. Iyengar, Mysore, 1952.

Monier-Williams, M. (1899). *A Sanskrit-English Dictionary*. 1976 reprint. Oxford: Clarendon Press.

Mookerjee S. (1935). *The Buddhist Philosophy of Universal Flux.* University of Calcutta, 1935. Reprinted Delhi: Motilal Banarsidass, 1980.

Moriyama S. (1984). "The Yogācāra-mādhyamika refutaion of the position of the Satyākāra and Alīkākāravādins of the the Yogācāra school. Part 1: a translation of portions of Haribhadra's *Abhisamayālaṃkārālokā Prajñāpāramitāvyākhyā*", Kyoto: Bukkyō Daigaku Daigakuin Kenkyū Kiyō 12: 1-58.

Nāgārjuna. **Bodhisaṃbhāra. Pú tí zī liáng lùn* 菩提資糧論 . Chinese transl. by Dharmagupta, T. 166O. Transl. Lindtner (1982).

Nāgārjuna. *Mūlamadhyamakakārikās*. Sanskrit ed. by LVP with Candrakīrti's *Prasannapadā*, 1903-1913, reprinted (1970); ed. J.W. de Jong, Adyar: The Adyar Library and Research Center, 1977.

Nāgārjuna. *Ratnāvalī*. Ed. Hahn (1982). Transl. and ed. Tucci (1934, 1936), transl. Hopkins (1975).

Nāgārjuna. *Śūnyatāsaptati*. Ed. and transl. in Lindtner (1982b).

Nāgārjuna. *Yuktiṣaṣṭikā*. Ed. and transl. in Lindtner (1982b).

Nagao G. (1954). *An Interpretation of the Term "saṃvṛti" (Convention) in Buddhism*. Silver Jubilee Volume of the Zinbun Kagaku Kenkyusyo, Kyoto University, Kyoto, 1954.

Nagao G. (1978). "'What remains' in *śūnyatā*: a Yogācāra interpretation of emptiness", in M. Kiyota (ed.), *Mahāyāna Buddhist Meditation*: Theory and Practice. Honolulu: University of Hawai Press, pp. 66-82.

Nagao G. (1979). "From Mādhyamika to Yogācāra, an analysis of MMK, XXIV.18 and MV [= MAV], I.1-2", JIABS 2-1: 29-43.

Nagatomi M. (1959). "The framework of the *Pramāṇavārttika*, book one", *Journal of the American Oriental Society* 79: 262-266.

Nagatomi M. (1967-68). "*Arthakriyā*", *Adyar Library Bulletin* 31-32: 52-72.

Nagatomi M. (1980). "*Mānasa-pratyakṣa*: a conundrum in the Buddhist *pramāṇa* system", pp. 243-260 in M. Nagatomi et al. (eds.), *Sanskrit and Indian Studies*, essays in honour of Daniel H.H. Ingalls. Dordrecht: D. Reidel.

Nakamura H. (1983). *Bukkyō-go dai jiten*. Reprinted Tokyo: Tōkyo shoseki.

Obermiller E. (1932). "The Doctrine of *Prajñāpāramitā*, as exposed in the *Abhisamayālaṃkāra* of Maitreya", *Acta Orientalia* 11: 1-133, 334-354.

Ogawa I. (1977). "Jikanron ni taisuru Daijōbukkyōteki Shiten — Gesshō zō 'Shihyakuron Shaku' Daijūisshō 'Hajibon' no Kaidoku. Kyoto: Otani Daigaku Kenkyū Nenpō 29, pp. 1-56.

Pañcaviṃśatisāhasrikā Prajñāpāramitā. Ed. N. Dutt, Calcutta Oriental Series 38, London, 1934.

Pāṇini. *Aṣṭādhyāyī*. See Renou (1966) for text and transl.

Patañjali. *Vyākaraṇa-Mahābhāṣya*. Ed. F. Kielhorn. Second edition. Poona, 1892.

Peri N. (1911). "A propos de la date de Vasubandhu", *Bulletin de l'Ecole française d'Extrême-Orient* 11: 339-390.

Potter K. (1977). *The Encyclopedia of Indian Philosophies,* Vol. II Nyāya-Vaiśeṣika. Delhi: Motilal Banarsidass.

Prajñākaragupta. *Pramāṇavārttikabhāṣya*. Ed. R. Sāṅkṛtyāyana, Patna: Tibetan Sanskrit Works 1, 1953.

Prajñākaramati. *Bodhicaryāvatārapañjikā*. Ed. P.L. Vaidya, *Śāntideva, Bodhicaryāvatāra, with the commentary Pañjikā of Prajñākaramati*. Buddhist Sanskrit Texts, Darbhanga, 1960.

Praśastapāda. *Praśastapādabhāṣya (= Padārthadharmasaṃgraha), with the commentary Nyāyakandalī of Śrīdhara.* Ed. by V.P. Dvivedin. 1st ed. Banaras 1895; 2nd ed. Delhi 1984. Transl. G. Jha, Varanasi, Chaukhambha Orientalia, reprint. 1982.

Price H.H. (1950). *Perception.* London: Methuen. Second edition.

Python P. (1973). *Vinaya-viniścaya-upāli-paripṛcchā,* Enquête d'Upāli pour une exégèse de la discipline. Traduit du sanscrit, du tibétain et du chinois, avec introduction, édition critique des fragments sanscrits et de la version tibétaine, notes et glossaires. Paris: Adrien-Maisonneuve.

Randle H.N. (1926). *Fragments from Diṅnāga.* Royal Asiatic Society Prize Publication Fund, Vol. 9. London.

Red mda' ba' gŹon nu blo gros (1349-1412). *dBu ma bźi brgya pa'i 'grel pa.* Sarnath: Sakya Student's Union, 1974.

Renou L. (1966). *La Grammaire de Pāṇini,* traduite du sanskrit avec des extraits des commentaires indigènes. 2 volumes. Paris.

Renou L. (1975). *Grammaire sanscrite.* 2nd edition. Paris: A. Maisonneuve.

Renou L. and J. Filliozat (1947 & 1953). *L'Inde Classique,* manuel des études indiennes. Tome I, Paris, Payot. Tome II, Paris, Imprimerie Nationale, Ecole française d'Extrême-Orient, Hanoi.

rGyal tshab rje = rGyal tshab Dar ma rin chen (1364-1432). *bŹi brgya pa'i rnam bśad legs bśad sñiṅ po.* Sarnath: PES Press, 1971.

rGyal tshab rje. *rNam 'grel thar lam gsal byed = Tshad ma rnam 'grel gyi tshig le'ur byas pa'i rnam bśad phyin ci ma log par gsal bar byed pa.* 2 volumes. Sarnath: PES Press, 1974.

rJe btsun pa'i don bdun cu. See Se ra rje btsun Chos kyi rgyal mtshan, *Don bdun cu.*

rJe btsun pa'i grub mtha'. See Se ra rje btsun Chos kyi rgyal mtshan, *Grub mtha'.*

Robinson R. (1967). *Early Mādhyamika in India and China.* University of Wisconsin Press. Reprinted in 1976 by Motilal Banarsidass, Delhi.

Rorty R. (1980). *Philosophy and the Mirror of Nature.* Princeton: Princeton University Press.

Ruegg D.S. (1969). *La Théorie du tathāgatagarbha et du gotra.* Publications de l'Ecole française d'Extrême-Orient. Paris: A. Maisonneuve.

Ruegg D.S. (1973). *Le Traité du tathāgatagarbha de Bu ston rin chen grub.* Publications de l'Ecole française d'Extrême-Orient, Vol. LXXXVIII. Paris: A. Maisonneuve.

Ruegg D.S. (1977). "The uses of the four positions of the *catuṣkoṭi* and the problem of the description of reality in Mahāyāna Buddhism", JIP 5: 1-71.

Ruegg D.S. (1981). *The Literature of the Madhyamaka School of Philosophy in India.* In *A History of Indian Literature* ed. by J. Gonda, Vol. VII, fasc. 1. Wiesbaden: O. Harrassowitz.

Ruegg D.S. (1982). "Towards a chronology of the Madhyamaka school", in L. Hercus et al. (eds.), *Indological and Buddhist Studies*: Volume in honour of Professor J.W. de Jong on his sixtieth birthday. Canberra: Faculty of Asian Studies, pp. 505-530.

Ruegg D.S. (1983). "On the thesis and assertion in the Madhyamaka / dBu ma", in E. Steinkellner and H. Tauscher (1983), pp. 205-241.

Ruegg D.S. (1985). "Purport, implicature and presupposition: Sanskrit *abhiprāya* and Tibetan *dgoṅs pa / dgoṅs gźi* as hermeneutical concepts", JIP 13: 309-325.

Ruegg D.S. (1986). "Does the Mādhyamika have a thesis and philosophical position?", in B.K. Matilal and R.D. Evans (1986), pp. 229-237.

Ruegg D.S. (1988). "An Indian source for the Tibetan hermeneutical term *dgoṅs gźi* 'intentional ground'", JIP 16: 1-4.

Śālistambasūtra. Skt. ed. LVP (1913).

Samādhirājasūtra. Ed. P.L. Vaidya. Buddhist Sanskrit Texts 2, Darbhanga, 1961.

Saṃdhinirmocanasūta. Ed. and transl. E. Lamotte (1935).

Saṃyutta = *Saṃyutta Nikāya.* Ed. by L. Feer and C.A.F. Rhys Davids in six volumes. London: Pali Text Society, 1884-1904.

Śaṅkarasvāmin. *Nyāyapraveśa.* Ed. and transl. in M. Tachikawa (1971), "A sixth-century manual of Indian logic", JIP 1: 111-129.

Śāntarakṣita. *Madhyamakālaṃkāra.* P. 5284. Transl. and ed. by M. Ichigō (1985).

Śāntarakṣita. *Madhyamakālaṃkāravṛtti.* P. 5285. Ed. Ichigō (1985).

Śāntarakṣita. *Tattvasaṃgraha.* Ed. with Kamalaśīla's *Pañjikā* by D. Shāstri. 2 volumes. Varanasi: Bauddha Bharati 1. Transl. by Ganganatha Jha in *The Tattvasaṅgraha of Śāntarakṣita with the Commentary of Kamalaśīla.* Baroda: Gaekwad's Oriental Series, 1937, 1939.

Sasaki E. (1978). "The Chapter V of the *Catuḥśatakaśāstra* or the Four Hundred Treatise by Āryadeva. *Ikenobōtanki Daigaku Kiyō* 8: 49-98.

Schayer S. (1931). *Feuer und Brennstoff.* Ein Kapitel aus dem Mādhyamikaśāstra des Nāgārjuna mit der Vṛtti des Candrakīrti. *Rocznik Orjentalistyczny* 7: 26-52.

Schmithausen L. (1969). *Der Nirvāṇa-Abschnitt in der Viniścayasaṃgrahaṇī der Yogācārabhūmiḥ.* Wien: Verlag Österreichischen Akademie der Wissenschaften.

Schmithausen L. (1970). "Zur Lehre von der vorstellungsfreien Wahrnehmung bei Praśastapāda", WZKS 14: 125-129.

Schmithausen L. (1987). *Ālayavijñāna*, On the Origin and the Early Development of a Central Concept of Yogācāra Philosophy. 2 parts. Studia Philologica Buddhica Monograph Series IVa and IVb. Tokyo: The International Institute for Buddhist Studies.

sDe dge Tibetan Tripiṭaka, bsTan 'gyur. dBu ma Vol. 1-17, 1977-79. Sems tsam Vol. 1-16, 1979-81. Tshad ma Vol. 1- , 1981- . Tokyo: Faculty of Letters of Tokyo University.

Se ra rje btsun Chos kyi rgyal mtshan (1469-1546). *dBu ma'i spyi don = bsTan bcos dbu ma la 'jug pa'i rnam bśad dgoṅs pa rab bsal gyi dka' gnad gsal bar byed pa'i spyi don legs bśad skal bzaṅ mgul rgyan.* Blockprint, textbook (*yig cha*) of Se ra byes monastery, Bylakuppe, Mysore District, Karnataka, India, 197?.

Se ra rje btsun Chos kyi rgyal mtshan. *Don bdun cu = bsTan bcos mṅon par rtogs pa'i rgyan gyi brjod bya dṅos po brgyad don bdun cu ṅes par 'byed pa'i thabs dam pa.*

Ed. by S. Onoda, *Rje btsun pa'i don bdun cu, An Introduction to the Abhisamayālaṃkāra.* Nagoya University: Studia Asiatica no. 6, 1983.

Se ra rje btsun Chos kyi rgyal mtshan. *Grub mtha' = rJe btsun 'jam dpal dbyaṅs chos kyi rgyal mtshan gyis mdzad pa'i grub mtha'i rnam gźag.* Facsimile edition in T. Kelsang and S. Onoda (1985), pp. 90-97.

Se ra rje btsun Chos kyi rgyal mtshan. *rNam 'grel spyi don = rGyas pa'i bstan bcos tshad ma rnam 'grel gyi don 'grel rgyal tshab dgoṅs pa rab gsal źes bya ba le'u daṅ po'i dka' ba'i gnad la dogs pa gcod pa.* Blockprint, textbook of Se ra byes, 197?

Se ra rje btsun Chos kyi rgyal mtshan. *sKabs daṅ po'i spyi don = bsTan bcos mṅon par rtogs pa'i rgyan 'grel pa daṅ bcas pa'i rnam bśad rnam pa gñis kyi dka' ba'i gnad gsal bar byed pa legs bśad skal bzaṅ klu dbaṅ kyi rol mtsho źes bya ba las skabs daṅ po'i spyi don.* Blockprint, textbook of Se ra byes, 197?.

Shāstrī P.S. (1955). "Nāgārjuna and Āryadeva", *Indian Historical Quarterly* 31: 193-202.

Shimaji D. (1932). *Historique du système vijñaptimātra.* Transl. from the Japanese by P. Demiéville. Chapter III in Lévi (1932).

Sinha N. (1911). *The Vaiśeṣikasūtras of Kaṇāda with the Commentary of Śaṅkara Miśra and Extracts from the Gloss of Jayanārāyaṇa.* The Sacred books of the Hindus, Vol 6. 1st edition, Allahabad: The Pāṇini Office, 1911. Reprinted New York: AMS editions, 1974.

sKabs daṅ po'i spyi don. See Se ra rje btsun Chos kyi rgyal mtshan, *sKabs daṅ po'i spyi don.*

Sorensen P. (1986). *Candrakīrti's Triśaraṇasaptati:* The septuagint on the three refuges. Wiener Studien zur Tibetologie und Buddhismuskunde Heft 16. Wien: Arbeitskreis für Tibetische und Buddhistische Studien Universität Wien.

Śrīdhara. *Nyāyakandalī.* See Praśastapāda.

Stcherbatsky T. (1923). *The Central Conception of Buddhism and The Meaning of the Word "Dharma".* London, 1923. Reprinted Delhi: Motilal Banarsidass, 1970.

Stcherbatsky T. (1926). *La Théorie de la connaissance et la logique chez les bouddhistes tardifs.* Transl. I de Manziarly, P. Masson-Oursel. Annales du Musée Guimet, Bibliothèque d'études, tome 36. Paris: P. Geuthner.

Stcherbatsky T. (1927). *The Conception of Buddhist nirvāṇa.* Leningrad: Publishing Office of the Academy of Sciences of the USSR. Reprinted by Mouton and co.: The Hague, 1965.

Stcherbatsky T. (1930, 1932). *Buddhist Logic.* 2 volumes. Leningrad: Bibliotheca Buddhica. Reprinted The Hague: Mouton and co., 1958.

Stcherbatsky T. (1936). *Madhyānta-vibhaṅga,* Discourse on discrimination between middle and extremes ascribed to Bodhisattva Maitreya and commented by Vasubandhu and Sthiramati: translated from the Sanscrit by Th. Stcherbatsky. Bibliotheca Buddhica XXX. Reprinted Osnabrück: Biblio Verlag, 1970.

Steinkellner E. (1971). "Wirklichkeit und Begriff bei Dharmakīrti", WZKS 15: 179-211.

Steinkellner E. (1973). *Dharmakīrti's Pramāṇaviniścayaḥ, Zweites Kapitel: svārthānumānam.* Teil I. Wien: Österreichische Akademie der Wissenschaften.

Steinkellner E. (1973a). "On the interpretation of the *svabhāvahetuḥ*", WZKS 18: 117-129.

Steinkellner E. (1979). *Dharmakīrti's Pramāṇaviniścayaḥ, Zweites Kapitel: svārthānumānam.* Teil II. Wien: Österreichische Akademie der Wissenschaften.

Steinkellner E. (1982). "The spiritual place of the epistemological tradition in Buddhism", *Nanto Bukkyō* 49: 1-15.

Steinkellner E. (1983). "*Tshad ma'i skyes bu*: meaning and historical significance of the term", in E. Steinkellner and H. Tauscher (eds.) (1983): 275-284.

Steinkellner E. (1984). "*Svabhāvapratibandha* again", *Acta Indologica*, Studies of Mysticism in honor of the 1150th Anniversary of Kōbō Daishi's Nirvāṇam. Narita: Naritasan Shinshoji. pp. 457-476.

Steinkellner E. and H. Tauscher (eds.) (1983). *Contributions on Tibetan and Buddhist Religion and Philosophy.* Wiener Studien zur Tibetologie und Buddhismuskunde Heft 11. Wien: Arbeitskreis für Tibetische und Buddhistische Studien Universität Wien.

Steinkellner E. and H. Krasser (1989). *Dharmottaras Exkurs zur Definition gültiger Erkenntnis im Pramāṇaviniścaya.* Wien: Österreichische Akademie der Wissenschaften.

Sthiramati. *Dà chéng zhōng guān shì lùn* 大乘中觀釋論. T. 1567.

Sthiramati. *Madhyāntavibhāgaṭīkā.* See Maitreya, *Madhyāntavibhāga.* Ed. R. Pandeya. Transl. Stcherbatsky (1936).

Sthiramati. *Triṃśikābhāṣya.* Skt. ed. S. Lévi (1925); transl. Lévi (1932).

Taishō = Taishō Shinshū Daizōkyō, The Tripiṭaka in Chinese. Ed. by J. Takakusu and K. Watanabe. 100 volumes. Tokyo, 1925-1935.

Tāranātha (1575-?). *rGya gar chos 'byuṅ.* Text ed. in A. Schiefner, *Tāranāthae de Doctrinae Buddhicae in India Propagatione.* St. Petersburg, 1868, reprint. Tokyo, 1963. Transl. Schiefner, *Tāranātha's Geschichte des Buddhismus in Indien.* St. Petersburg, 1869, reprint. Tokyo, 1963. Transl. by Lama Chimpa and A. Chattopadhyaya and edited by D. Chattopadhyaya, *Tāranātha's History of Buddhism in India.* Simla H.P., India: Indian Institute of Advanced Study, 1970.

Takakusu J. (1896). *A Record of the Buddhist Religion as Practised in India and the Malay Archipelago (A.D. 671-695) by I-tsing.* London 1896. Reprinted Delhi: Motilal Banarsidass, 1966.

Takakusu J. (1904). "La *Sāṃkhyakārikā* étudiée à la lumière de sa version chinoise I", *Bulletin de l'Ecole française d'Extrême-Orient* 4: 1-65. Id. II: 978-1064.

Takakusu J. (1947). *The Essentials of Buddhist Philosophy.* 1st edition University of Hawai. Reprinted Delhi: Motilal Banarsidass, 1975.

Tauscher H. (1981). *Candrakīrti — Madhyamakāvatāraḥ und Madhyamakāvatārabhāṣyam (Kapitel VI, Vers 166-226).* Wien: Wiener Studien zur Tibetologie und Buddhismuskunde.

The Tibetan Tripiṭaka, Peking Edition. Tokyo-Kyoto: Tibetan Tripiṭaka Research Institute, 1957.

Thomas F.W. and H. Ui (1918). "The Hand Treatise, a Work of Āryadeva", *Journal of the Royal Asiatic Society*: 267-310.

Thurman R. (1984). *Tsong kha pa's Speech of Gold in the Essence of True Eloquence.* Princeton: Princeton University Press.

Tillemans T. (1982). "The 'neither one nor many' argument for *śūnyatā*, and its Tibetan interpretations: background information and source materials", *Etudes de Lettres*, University of Lausanne, 3, July-September: 103-128.

Tillemans T. (1983). "The 'neither one nor many' argument for *śūnyatā* and its Tibetan Interpretations," in E. Steinkellner et H. Tauscher (ed.), (1983): 305-320.

Tillemans T. (1984a). "On a recent work on Tibetan Buddhist epistemology", EA XXXVIII, 1: 59-66.

Tillemans T. (1984b). "Sur le *parārthānumāna* en logique bouddhique", EA XXXVIII, 2: 73-99.

Tillemans T. (1984c). "Two Tibetan texts on the 'neither one nor many' argument for *śūnyatā*", JIP 12: 357-388.

Tillemans T. (1986a). "Dharmakīrti, Āryadeva and Dharmapāla on scriptural authority," *Tetsugaku* 38, Hiroshima: 31-47.

Tillemans T. (1986b). "*Pramāṇavārttika* IV (1)", WZKS 30: 143-162.

Tillemans T. (1987). "*Pramāṇavārttika* IV (2)", WZKS 31: 141-161.

Tillemans T. (1988a). "On *bdag, gźan* and related notions of Tibetan grammar", in H. Uebach and J.L. Panglung (eds.), *Tibetan Studies*: Proceedings of the fourth seminar of the International Association for Tibetan Studies. Studia Tibetica, Band II. Kommission für Zentralasiatische Studien, Bayerische Akademie der Wissenschaften, Munich. Pp. 491-502.

Tillemans T. (1988b). "Some reflections on R.S.Y. Chi's *Buddhist Formal Logic*", JIABS 11, 1: 155-171.

Tillemans T. (1989a). "Formal and semantic aspects of Tibetan Buddhist debate logic", JIP 17: 265-297.

Tillemans T. (1989b). "Indian and Tibetan Mādhyamikas on *mānasapratyakṣa*", *The Tibet Journal* XIV, 1: 70-85.

Tillemans T. (1990). "On *sapakṣa*", in press for JIP 17.

Tillemans T. and Derek D. Herforth (1989). *Agents and Actions in Classical Tibetan.* The indigenous grammarians on *bdag* and *gźan* and *bya byed las gsum*. Wien: Wiener Studien zur Tibetologie und Buddhismuskunde.

Tola F. and C. Dragonetti (1982). "Dignāga's *Ālambanaparīkṣāvṛtti*", JIP 10: 105-134.

Tosaki H. (1979, 1985). *Bukkyō Ninshikiron no Kenkyū.* (Jōkan = 1979; Gekan = 1985). Transl. of PV III. Tokyo: Daitōshuppansha.

Tsoṅ kha pa = Tsoṅ kha pa Blo bzaṅ grags pa (1357-1419). *Collected Works (gSuṅ 'bum) = Khams gsum chos kyi rgyal po Tsoṅ kha pa chen po'i gsuṅ 'bum.* Delhi:

dGe ldan gsuṅ rab mi ñams rgyun phel series 79-105, published by Ṅag dbaṅ dge legs bde mo, 1975-79.

Tsoṅ kha pa. *Draṅ ṅes legs bśad sñiṅ po.* Sarnath: PES Press, 1973 (References are to this edition.) *Collected Works*, Vol. **pha**. Transl. Thurman (1984).

Tsoṅ kha pa. *dGoṅs pa rab gsal = bsTan bcos chen po dbu ma la 'jug pa'i rnam bśad dgoṅs pa rab gsal.* Sarnath: PES Press, 1973. *Collected Works*, Vol. **ma**.

Tsoṅ kha pa. *Legs bśad gser phreṅ = Śes rab kyi pha rol tu phyin pa'i man ṅag gi bstan bcos mṅon par rtogs pa'i rgyan 'grel pa daṅ bcas pa'i rgya cher bśad pa'i legs bśad gser phreṅ. Collected Works*, Vol. **tsa**.

Tsoṅ kha pa. *rTsa ba'i śes rab kyi dka' gnas chen po brgyad kyi bśad pa.* Sarnath: PES Press, 1970. *Collected Works*, Volume **ba**.

Tsoṅ kha pa. *rTsa śe ṭīk chen = dBu ma rtsa ba'i tshig le'ur byas pa śes rab ces bya ba'i rnam bśad rigs pa'i rgya mtsho.* Sarnath: PES Press, 1973. *Collected Works*, Vol. **ba**.

Tsoṅ kha pa. *sDe bdun la 'jug pa'i sgo don gñer yid kyi mun sel.* Sarnath: PES Press, 1972.

Tsoṅ kha pa. *sṄags rim chen mo = rGyal ba khyab bdag rdo rje 'chaṅ chen po'i lam gyi rim pa gsaṅ ba kun gyi gnad rnam par phye ba. Collected Works*, Vol. **ga**.

Tsoṅ kha pa. *Tshad ma'i brjed byaṅ chen mo = rGyal tshab chos rjes rje'i druṅ du gsan pa'i tshad ma'i brjed byaṅ chen mo. Collected Works* Vol. **pha**.

Tucci G. (1925). *La versione cinese del Catuḥśataka di Āryadeva, confrontata col testo sanscrito e la traduzione tibetana.* Rome, Rivista degli studi orientali X: 521-567.

Tucci G. (1926). "Un Traité d'Āryadeva sur le 'nirvāṇa' des hérétiques", *T'oung Pao* 24: 16-31.

Tucci G. (1929). *Pre-Diṅnāga Buddhist Texts on Logic from Chinese Sources.* Baroda: Gaekwad's Oriental Series. Reprinted by the Chinese Materials Center, San Francisco, 1976.

Tucci G. (1934, 1936). "The *Ratnāvalī* of Nāgārjuna", *Journal of the Royal Asiatic Society of Great Britain and Ireland*, 1934: 307-325. Id. 1936: 237-252 and 423-435.

Tucci G. (1980). *Tibetan Painted Scrolls*, Vol. 1. Reprinted Kyoto: Rinsen Books.

Ui H. (1917). *The Vaiśeṣika Philosophy according to the Daśapadārtha-śāstra:* Chinese text with introduction, translation and notes by H. Ui. 1st edition London, Royal Asiatic Society, 1917. Reprinted Varanasi: Chowkhamba Sanskrit Series Office, 1962.

Vātsyāyana. *Nyāyasūtrabhāṣya.* See Gautama, *Nyāyasūtra.*

Vaidya P.L. (1923). *Etudes sur Āryadeva et son Catuḥśataka.* Paris: Paul Geuthner.

Vajracchedikā. Transl. by Max Muller. Sacred Books of the East °49. London: Oxford University Press, 1927.

van Bijlert V.A. (1989). *Epistemology and Spiritual Authority.* The development of epistemology and logic in the old Nyāya and the Buddhist school of epistemology with an annotated translation of Dharmakīrti's *Pramāṇavārttika* II (*Pramāṇasiddhi*) vv. 1-7. Wiener Studien zur Tibetologie und Buddhismuskunde Heft 20. Wien: Arbeitskreis für Tibetische und Buddhistische Studien Universität Wien.

Van den Broeck J. (1977). *La Saveur de l'immortel (A-p'i-t'an Kan Lu Wei Lun)*. La version chinoise de l'Amṛtarasa de Ghoṣaka (T.1553), traduite et annotée par José Van den Broeck. Publications de l'Institut orientaliste de Louvain, vol 15. Louvain-la-Neuve.

van der Kuijp L.W.J. (1978). "Phya-pa Chos-kyi seng-ge's impact on Tibetan epistemological theory", JIP 5: 355-369.

van der Kuijp L.W.J. (1979). "Introductory Notes to the *Pramāṇavārttika* based on Tibetan sources", *The Tibet Journal* IV, 2: 2-28.

van der Kuijp L.W.J. (1983). *Contributions to the Development of Tibetan Epistemology.* From the eleventh to the thirteenth century. Wiesbaden: Franz Steiner Verlag.

van der Kuijp L.W.J. (1985a). "Notes on the transmission of Nāgārjuna's *Ratnāvalī* in Tibet", *The Tibet Journal* X, 2: 3-19.

van der Kuijp L.W.J. (1985b). "Studies in the life and thought of mKhas-grub-rje I: mKhas-grub-rje's epistemological oeuvre and his philological remarks on Dignāga's *Pramāṇasamuccaya* I", pp. 75-106 in *Berliner Indologische Studien* Band I, Reinbek: Verlag für Orientalistische Fachpublikationen.

van der Kuijp L.W.J. (1987). "An early Tibetan view of the soteriology of Buddhist epistemology: the case of 'Bri-gung 'jig-rten mgon-po", JIP 15: 57-70.

Vasubandhu. *Abhidharmakośakārikā* and *Abhidharmakośabhāṣya*. Skt. ed. P. Pradhān. *Abhidharma-Koshabhāṣya of Vasubandhu.* Patna: K.P. Jayaswal Research Institute, 1967. Transl. LVP (1923-1931) 6 volumes. See Chinese T. 1560 and 1558.

Vasubandhu. *Ā pí dá mó jū shè lùn* 阿毘達磨俱舍論 . Chinese of AK-bhāṣya, transl. Xuán zàng, T. 1558.

Vasubandhu. *Ā pí dá mó jū shè lùn běn sòng* 阿毘達磨俱舍論本頌 . Chinese of AK-kārikās, transl. Xuán zàng, T. 1560.

Vasubandhu. *Biàn zhōng biān lùn* 辯中邊論 . Xuán zàng's transl. of *Madhyānta-vibhāgabhāṣya* , T. 1600.

Vasubandhu (?). *Dà chéng bǎi fǎ míng mén lùn* 大乘百法明門論 . T. 1614. = Dharmapāla P. 5564.

Vasubandhu. *Karmasiddhiprakaraṇa.* See Lamotte (1936) for texts and transl.

Vasubandhu. *Madhyāntavibhāgabhāṣya.* See Maitreya, *Madhyāntavibhāga.* Transl. Stcherbatsky (1936). See also Chinese in T. 1600.

Vasubandhu. *Triṃśikā.* Skt. ed. S. Lévi (1925); transl. Lévi (1932).

Vasubandhu. *Trisvabhāvanirdeśa.* Skt. and Tib. edited and translated in LVP (1932-33).

Vasubandhu. *Viṃśatikā.* Skt. of *kārikās* and *vṛtti* edited in S. Lévi (1925). Transl. Lévi (1932).

Vasubandhu. *Vimśatikāvṛtti.* See *Viṃśatikā.*

Vetter T. (1964). *Erkenntnisprobleme bei Dharmakīrti.* Wien: Österreichische Akademie der Wissenschaften.

Vetter T. (1966). *Dharmakīrti's Pramāṇaviniścayaḥ, I. Kapitel: Pratyakṣam.* Wien: Österreichische Akademie der Wissenschaften.

Vetter T. (1984). *Der Buddha und seine Lehre in Dharmakīrtis Pramāṇavārttika.* Der Abschnitt über den Buddha und die vier edlen Wahrheiten im Pramāṇasiddhi-Kapitel. Wien: Wiener Studien zur Tibetologie und Buddhismuskunde.

Vibhūticandra. See Manorathanandin.

Vidyābhūṣaṇa S.C. (1913). *The Nyāyasūtras of Gotama.* The Sacred Books of the Hindus. Allahabad: The Pāṇini Office, 1913. Reprinted by AMS editions, New York, 1974.

Vidyābhūṣaṇa S.C. (1971). *A History of Indian Logic.* Delhi: Motilal Banarsidass. Reedition of *A History of the Mediaeval School of Indian Logic.* Calcutta, 1909.

Vogel C. (1970). *The Teaching of the Six Heretics according to the Pravrajyāvastu of the Tibetan Mūlasarvāstivāda Vinaya:* edited and rendered into English by Claus Vogel. Abhandlungen für die Kunde des Morgenlandes 39, 4. Wiesbanden: F. Steiner Verlag.

Vostrikov A. (1970). *Tibetan Historical Literature.* Transl. H.C. Gupta, Calcutta.

Wayman A. (1979). "Yogācāra and the Buddhist logicians", JIABS 2: 65-78.

Wezler A. (1986). "A note on *Mahābhāṣya* II 366.26: *guṇasaṃdrāvo dravyam.* Studies on Mallavādin's *Dvādaśāranayacakra* II", in *Buddhism and its Relation to Other Religions*: Essays in honour of Dr. Shozen Kumoi on his seventieth Birthday. Kyoto, pp. 1-33.

Williams P.W. (1979). "Tsoṅ kha pa on *kun-rdzob bden-pa*", pp. 325-335 in M. Aris and Aung San Suu Kyi (eds.), *Tibetan Studies in Honour of Hugh Richardson.* Warminster, England: Aris and Phillips Ltd.

Xīn biān zàng wén zì diǎn. See Blo mthun bsam gtan et al. (1979).

Xuán zàng 玄奘 = Hiuen tsiang; Hsüan tsang. *Chéng wéi shí lùn* 成唯識論 . T. 1585. See LVP, Siddhi.

Xuán zàng. *Dà táng xī yù jì* 大唐西域記 . T. 2087. Transl. S. Beal, *Si-yu-ki. Buddhist Records of the Western World from the Chinese of Hiuen Tsiang.* London, 1884. Reprinted Delhi, 1969.

Yamaguchi S. (1941). *Bukkyō ni okeru Mu to U to no Tairon.* Kyoto, 1941, Reprinted Tokyo, 1964.

Yamaguchi S. (1947). *Gesshō-zō Chūronshaku I.* Tokyo: Kōbundō.

Yamaguchi S.(1964). "Gesshō-zō Shihyakuron-chūshaku Hajō-hon no kaidoku." *Suzuki Gakujutsu Zaidan Kenkyū Nenpō,* Annual of Oriental and Religious Studies, 1, Tokyo: 13-35. Reprinted in *Yamaguchi Susumu Bukkyōgaku Bunshū,* Tokyo: Shunjūsha.

Yamaguchi S. (1974,1979). *Index to the Prasannapadā Madhyamakavṛtti.* Part One: Sanskrit-Tibetan, 1974. Part Two: Tibetan-Sanskrit, 1979. Kyoto: Heirakuji-shoten.

Yamaguchi S. and H. Meyer (1929). "Dignāga, Examen de l'objet de la connaissance (*Ālambanaparīkṣā*), textes tibétain et chinois et traduction des stances et du commentaire, éclaircissements et notes d'après le commentaire tibétain de Vinītadeva", *Journal Asiatique* January-March: 1-65.

Yaśomitra. *Sphuṭārthā Abhidharmakośavyākhyā*. Ed. D. Shāstrī, Varanasi: Bauddha Bharati, 5-6, 1981.

Yì jìng 義淨 = I-tsing; I-ching. *Nán hái jì guī nèi fǎ zhuàn* 南海奇歸内法傳. T. 2125. Transl. Takakusu (1896).

Yoṅs 'dzin bsdus grwa (*blo rigs, rtags rigs*). See Yoṅs 'dzin phur bu lcog Byams pa tshul khrims rgya mtsho.

Yoṅs 'dzin phur bu lcog Byams pa tshul khrims rgya mtsho (1825-1901). *Yoṅs 'dzin blo rigs = Tshad ma'i gźuṅ don 'byed pa'i bsdus grwa'i rnam bźag rigs lam 'phrul gyi lde mig ces bya ba las rigs lam che ba yul yul can daṅ blo rigs gi rnam par bśad pa*. In T. Kelsang and S. Onoda (1985).

Yoṅs 'dzin phur bu lcog. *Yoṅs 'dzin rtags rigs = Tshad ma'i gźuṅ don 'byed pa'i bsdus grwa'i rnam par bśad pa rigs lam 'phrul gyi lde'u mig las rigs lam che ba rtags rigs kyi skor*. Included in T. Kelsang and S. Onoda (1985). See also the critical edition by S. Onoda, *The Yoṅs 'dzin rtags rigs* — A manual for Tibetan logic. Nagoya: Studia Asiatica 5, 1981.

Yoṅs 'dzin phur bu lcog. *Yoṅs 'dzin bsdus grwa = Tshad ma'i gźuṅ don 'byed pa'i bsdus grwa'i rnam bźag rigs lam 'phrul gyi lde'u mig* (3 books: *chuṅ*, *'briṅ*, *che ba*). Included in T. Kelsang and S. Onoda (1985).

Yuktidīpikā. Ed. R.C. Pandeya (1967). *Yuktidīpikā*: An ancient commentary on the *Sāṃkhya-Kārikā* of Īśvarakṛṣṇa. Delhi: Motilal Banarsidass.

Yule H. and A.C. Burnell (1903 / 1968). *Hobson-Jobson*. A Glossary of colloquial Anglo-Indian words and phrases [...]. New edition edited by William Crooke. London: J. Murray, 1903. Reprinted by Munshiram Momoharlal, Delhi, 1968.

I. INTRODUCTORY REMARKS

A. Past research on the Catuḥśataka and its commentaries; the scope of our project.

The *Catuḥśataka* (CS), the major work in sixteen chapters of the Madhyamaka author, Āryadeva, has remained less accessible and less well understood by contemporary scholars than the major work of the founder of the Madhyamaka school, Nāgārjuna. The situation is partly explained by the fact that, apart from a few fragments in Candrakīrti's *Prasannapadā*, the CS is only conserved in Sanskrit in the incomplete eleventh century manuscript discovered by Haraprasād Shāstrī (HPS)[1], but another no doubt non-negligible factor is the difficult argumentation to be found in Āryadeva, argumentation which is frequently directed against fairly obscure non-Buddhist opponents and which demands recourse to commentarial exegeses if we are to have any hope to follow its sinuous development. There is thus an obvious necessity to translate and edit the commentaries to CS.

Recent work on the *Catuḥśataka*, such as that of K. Lang and J. May, has almost exclusively interpreted the CS in the light of Candrakīrti's commentary, the *Catuḥśatakavṛtti* (CSV), alternatively known as the *Catuḥśatakaṭīkā*, the only exception being Giuseppe Tucci's (1925) Italian translation of the Chinese version of CS in which he incorporated a few excerpts from Dharmapāla's commentary. Now, contemporary Western and Japanese scholars are not alone in viewing CS via Candrakīrti, i.e. from the perspective of the so-called Mādhyamika-Prāsaṅgika school. Traditional Tibetan scholars, apart from their few isolated references to Dharmapāla's general position which they might have, in part, gleaned from accounts of the famous Dharmapāla-Bhāvaviveka debate[2], generally take Candrakīrti's perspective too. A cautionary result

---

[1] Haraprasād Shāstrī (1914) p. 449: "The following fragments of Āryadeva's Catuḥśatikā [sic] with their commentary by Candra Kīrti are published from 23 old palm leaves written on in Newari character[s] of the 11th century." About one third of CS and the commentary by Candrakīrti is conserved in Sanskrit. Haraprasād Shāstrī (1911) is a preliminary study of the manuscript which he discovered

[2] Some remarks on the Tibetan perception of Dharmapāla. rGyal tshab rje (chapter I, p. 4), after paraphrasing a few lines of Candrakīrti, makes the following accurate comment which is not found in Candrakīrti: *sñiṅ po'i don yaṅ kun brtags raṅ gi mtshan ñid kyis grub pa 'gog pa rnam par rig pa tsam gyi* tshul du 'grel par*

which emerges from our integral translation of both Dharmapāla and Candrakīrti's commentaries to the twelfth and thirteenth chapters of CS is that, paradoxically, Āryadeva's thought is even less well understood than we, or the Tibetans, might feel it is. Dharmapāla's commentary, which approaches the text from the standpoint of the Idealist school, or Vijñānavāda, and which very often explains Āryadeva's verses as directed against very specific non-Buddhist schools, provides an interpretation of the CS which is coherent and thorough, but one which nonetheless radically differs from that of Candrakīrti, who was frequently more inclined to take Āryadeva as simply giving more general Madhyamaka-style arguments directed against no school in particular.

Now, the first major task which lies before us in researching the thought of Āryadeva and his commentators is the problem of a readable text. As the Sanskrit of CS and CSV is incomplete, we need to have recourse to the Tibetan and Chinese: fortunately, the CS was translated in its entirety into Tibetan by Sūkṣmajana and Pa tshab Ñi ma grags and into Chinese — the second half only — by Xuán zàng 玄奘. In the case of Dharmapāla's commentary, i.e. the so-called "Commentary on the Extensive Hundred Treatise" (*guǎng bǎi lùn shì lùn* 廣百論釋論), which is in fact on the last eight chapters of CS, we have only the Chinese of Xuán zàng: nothing remains in Sanskrit and the work was never translated into Tibetan.

---

mdzad do /. "He [i.e. Dharmapāla] explained the essential point from the point of view of Vijñaptimātra, refuting that thoroughly imagined phenomena (*kun brtags* = *parikalpita*) were established by their own natures." * rGyal reads *gyis*. On the Bhāvaviveka-Dharmapāla debate see Chapter III, section B. Note that other Tibetans, such as gSer mdog paṇ chen Śākya mchog ldan (1428-1507) and 'Jam mgon koṅ sprul Blo gros mtha' yas (1813-1899), were also, at least to some degree, familiar with Dharmapāla's thought. They included him in the "other-voidness" (*gźan stoṅ*) lineage with Nāgārjuna, Asaṅga and Vasubandhu and characterized him as explaining Madhyamaka from the Vijñaptimātra point of view. Curiously enough, following this depiction, Dharmapāla ends up in the same camp as Tāranātha and the Jo naṅ pas. See van der Kuijp (1983), p. 42 and n. 146 for references. As van der Kuijp n. 146 points out, Dharmapāla was sometimes represented as having written a commentary on Nāgārjuna's MMK. See Ruegg (1973) pp. 2-4, n. 2-3 on pp. 3-4 for the Jo naṅ pa doctrine and p. 7, n. 1 for the question of its (obscure) Indian antecedents. One oddity in placing Dharmapāla (and many other Vijñānavādins) in the camp of the gŹan stoṅ pas is that he seems to assign real and ultimate existence to *paratantrasvabhāva* ("dependent natures") (see fn. 116, 119, 126), whereas gŹan stoṅ pas usually take *paratantra* and *parikalpitasvabhāva* ("thoroughly imagined natures") as being only conventionally existent. See below pp. 45-50 for the three natures (*trisvabhāva*). See 'Jam mgon koṅ sprul's *Śes bya kun khyab* Vol. 3 p. 38: *kun brtags gźan dbaṅ kun rdzob don dam ni / yoṅs grub raṅ rig ye śes gźan stoṅ lugs /*. "The Other-voidness tradition is that thoroughly imagined phenomena (*kun brtags* = *parikalpita*), dependent phenomena (*gzan dbaṅ* = *paratantra*) are conventional; the ultimate is what is thoroughly established (*yoṅs grub* = *pariniṣpanna*), viz. the wisdom consisting in self-awareness (*raṅ rig* = *svasaṃvedana*)." See also ibid. p. 39 for the interpretation of the Jo naṅ pa, Dol po pa Śes rab rgyal mtshan (1292-1361), on the question of the three natures — *paratantra* is just conventional. See Ruegg (1977) n. 126 on an Indian Vijñānavādin source — i.e. the *Mahāyānasūtrālaṃkārabhāṣya* — which held that *paratantra* was not ultimately real.

Finally, note that Candrakīrti in CSV I, P. 34a7 refers to the commentary on the *Catuḥśataka* by the "contemporary poet, Bhadanta Dharmapāla" (*da lta'i sñan dṅags mkhan bstun pa chos skyoṅ*); Tāranātha's *rGya gar chos 'byuṅ*, probably following Candrakīrti's lead, praises Dharmapāla's poetic skills at greater length; see ed. Schiefner (1868) pp. 123-124, transl. Schiefner (1869) p. 160.

In 1923 Vaidya presented the available Sanskrit of the *kārikās* and attempted the dubious project of "reconstructing" the Sanskrit of the others from the Tibetan; on this basis he attempted a French translation. Bhattacharya (1931) presented the available Sanskrit of the *kārikās* to the last eight chapters of CS along with that of CSV to these chapters and sought to reconstruct the missing Sanskrit in CS and CSV from the Tibetan version. (The latter work was not translated into Chinese.)

While Bhattacharya's work no doubt represented a significant advance, it was marred by two principal flaws: (a) his reconstructions, like virtually all reconstructions into Sanskrit of long passages from Tibetan, are untrustworthy. (b) Bhattacharya's Tibetan text was based only on the edition of sNar thaṅ, which indeed he frequently misread.

In short, the enterprise of reconstructing CS and CSV's Sanskrit from the Tibetan is probably only of value when it is a question of a few words here and there which are missing in Shāstrī's manuscript; to understand the large passages which are missing in Sanskrit, it is certainly of use to find equivalences and to imagine possible structures in Sanskrit, but basically we must read the text as a Tibetan text. Another factor which serves to complicate the picture is that Haraprasād Shāstrī's manuscript of CS and especially of CSV, even disregarding the extensive lacunae, is not the same text as what we find in Tibetan. Not only does the Tibetan text contain numerous sūtra quotations left out in HPS's manuscript, but, what is more, in the parts where it does seem to correspond approximately to HPS, it often has words or phrases which do not figure in the latter text at all: there seems little doubt that the Sanskrit original which Pa tshab Ñi ma grags (1055/1054 -?)[3] used was significantly different from the version we have in HPS. Bhattacharya, when faced with this problem, took what seems to me the least satisfactory solution: he systematically amended HPS's text, adding words here and there and unnecessarily changing the Sanskrit so that (with the exception of missing sūtra quotations) it would correspond to the Tibetan. My proposal will be to translate on the basis of HPS's text without trying to blur its difference from the text which Pa tshab Ñi ma grags must have used. As a guiding rule I have adopted a "maxim of minimum change", only modifying HPS's text when it seemed clearly erroneous, corrupt, badly edited or badly punctuated: if HPS is comprehensible as it stands, I have not attempted to change it simply in order to make it conform to the Tibetan.

Lang (Thesis) and (1986), besides presenting HPS's Sanskrit of the *kārikās* and a readable translation, also edited the Tibetan of CS, comparing the Peking, sDe dge, Co ne and sNar thaṅ editions of the *kārikās*, thus yielding a satisfactory Tibetan text of CS. In her doctoral thesis, she summarized Candrakīrti's commentary, but did not edit it nor translate it; her 1986 translation and edition is only of the *kārikās* in CS.[4] It is worthwhile remarking that in fact there are two Tibetan versions of the *kārikās* of

---

[3] The date is that of Vostrikov (1970) p. 149 and Tucci (1980) p. 99. For some arguments against this date, see van der Kuijp (1985) p. 4, who situates him somewhat later.

[4] In addition she has prepared a summary of CS and CSV which will appear in the *Encyclopedia of Indian Philosophies*, vol. on Mahāyāna Buddhism, ed. K. Potter, Motilal Banarsidass.

CS, one being only the *kārikās* and the other incorporating the *kārikās* into CSV: the two often differ significantly in their readings. Lang (1986), dealing only with CS, compared the editions of the former text; I give priority, whenever reasonably possible, to the latter, as the present study is concerned primarily with CS as seen via its commentaries. The variants from the simple *kārikā*-texts in the four editions of the canon are given in the notes.

As for work on the CSV, J. May in a series of articles, viz. (1980), (1981a), (1981b), (1982) and (1984), translated the ninth chapter of CSV into French, also editing the Tibetan whenever the Sanskrit was unavailable. Japanese translations of CSV IX and XI were respectively published by S. Yamaguchi 山口 益 (1964) and by I. Ogawa 小川 一乗 (1977). K. Lang, in her unpublished (1976) M.A. thesis, edited and translated the fourteenth chapter. We should also mention an edition of the fifth chapter by E. Sasaki 佐々木 恵精 (1978).

The Chinese version of CS and the commentary of Dharmapāla occupy two entries in the Taishō, viz. T. 1570 and 1571 respectively, but the text in T. 1570 simply consists of the *kārikās* extracted from Dharmapāla's commentary and exhibits no differences from the *kārikās* in the latter. Dharmapāla's commentary has as yet received little attention, much less than it merits. N. Endō 遠藤 二平 (1932) published a literal Japanese translation in the *Kokuyaku Issaikyō*, a translation which I have systematically consulted, but which in its literalness is of limited utility in shedding light on the meaning of the Chinese terms. (The Japanese translator's understanding of the syntax is also in many cases misleading.[5]) The Japanese translator does, however, provide a number of corrections or choices of variants for the Taishō text which I have taken into account and which are often helpful.[6] Apart from some excerpts in Tucci (1925) and Louis de la Vallée Poussin's (1932) translation of CS k. 220-221 along with Dharmapāla's commentary, nothing has been translated into European languages.

One final point needs to be mentioned in this connection. Just as the Sanskrit original which Pa tshab Ñi ma grags had in front of him probably differed significantly from the Sanskrit in HPS, so it seems that the Sanskrit text on which Xuán zàng based his Chinese translation may very well have been quite different too. At any rate, be it due to differences in the Sanskrit original or due to Xuán zàng's way of translation, the result is that the Chinese of CS does exhibit important divergences and has to be treated separately from the Sanskrit and Tibetan. To avoid confusion between different texts and different commentarial perspectives, I have, therefore, given priority to Dharmapāla's interpretation in translating the Chinese of CS and have generally

---

[5] I generally do not indicate my numerous divergences from the Japanese translator's interpretations.

[6] In his foreword (Kyik. p. 145) the Japanese translator mentions six commentaries on CS listed in catalogues; unfortunately only one *juàn* of one of the commentaries seems to be extant. Amongst the names of the commentators we find the Korean, Yuán cè 圓測 (Wŏn ch'uk), of the Xī míng 西明 temple in Chang An who belonged (temporarily) to Xuán zàng's school and wrote an important commentary on the *Saṃdhinirmocanasūtra* which is conserved in the *Zokuzōkyō* Vol. 34 and was translated into Tibetan. See Hirabayashi and Iida (1977), and their n. 22 for references to S. Inaba's restitution of some missing parts of the commentary plus references to G. Nagao's review of Inaba.

adopted Candrakīrti's perspective in translating the Tibetan and HPS' Sanskrit of Āryadeva's text.

B. Lives and Works of Āryadeva, Dharmapāla and Candrakīrti

According to the commentator Candrakīrti's account[7], Āryadeva seems to have been born on the island of *Siṃhala* as a prince and to have subsequently become a monk in South India under the great Madhyamaka master, Nāgārjuna. Other perhaps less credible biographies maintain that he was a South Indian Brahmin who studied with Nāgārjuna, particularly skilled in defeating non-Buddhist opponents, indeed so much so that he finished his life murdered by a vengeful student of one of these teachers.[8]

The question as to whether *Siṃhaladvīpa* is to be identified with Ceylon is subject to some controversy[9]; if, however, we accept this identification, as seems reasonable, then it may very well be that Āryadeva is the Deva referred to in Sinhalese chronicles.[10] From this some scholars, such as Lamotte, have concluded that Āryadeva was associated with the Ceylonese kings Vohārikatissa and Saṃghatissa and lived in the second half of the third century during the time of the Mahāyāna heresy, or Vetullavāda, in Śrī Laṅka.[11] K. Lang, however, takes somewhat different dates for Vohārikatissa's reign from those of Lamotte and stresses that Nāgārjuna, and possibly Āryadeva, were associated with one of the Śātavāhana kings, a dynasty which ended in the middle of the third century; hence she places Āryadeva's literary activity between 225 and 250 A.D.[12] At any rate, while his being a student of Nāgārjuna and co-founder of the Madhyamaka is beyond doubt and his preoccupation with refuting non-Buddhist

---

[7] CSV, Peking p. 34b. On the life and works of Āryadeva, see the Introduction to Lang (1986), (Thesis) chapter II; Ruegg (1981) p. 50 et seq.; Robinson (1967) pp. 27-28; Lamotte, *Traité* III, pp. 1371-1374, n. 2; V. Bhattacharya (1931) Preface and Introduction; May *Hōbōgirin*, s.v. *Chūgan* p. 479.

[8] Based on the *Dī pó pú sà zhuàn* 提婆菩薩傳 (T. 2048); see Robinson (1967) pp. 27-28; Lang (1986) p. 7.

[9] Dutt (1934) p. 660 took Siṃhapura as being in North India; P.S. Shāstrī (1955) maintained that Āryadeva's birthplace was in Andhra, from where he subsequently went to Ceylon. See Ruegg (1981), p. 50, n. 136.

[10] Namely *Mahāvaṃsa* (xxxvi, 29) and *Dīpavaṃsa* (xxii, 41, 50). See *Traité* III, p. 1373.

[11] On the Vetullavādins, or Vetullaka, see Bareau (1955) Chapter XXXIV; see also Lokesh Chandra (1984) pp. 105-113 on Vetullavāda in Śrī Laṅka.

[12] See Lang (1986) p. 8; Lamotte, *Traité* III p. 1373. Lamotte also relies on Xuán zàng's *Xī yóu jì* for references to Xuán zàng's detection of traces of Āryadeva's journeys in North India. Cf. Ruegg (1982) pp. 506-507 on Nāgārjuna's possible affiliation with different Śātavāhana monarchs. Ruegg opts for c. 150-200 as dates for Nāgārjuna. On the Śātavāhana kings see *L'Inde Classique* § 449.

doctrines is amply attested to by all sources and certainly by his own major work, the *Catuḥśataka*, the problem of his dates is probably no more or less clear than that of his teacher, Nāgārjuna, with many contemporary scholars following Kumārajīva's chronology and situating Nāgārjuna in the latter half of the third century A.D., others placing him in the first or second centuries.

Generally nowadays one differentiates between two Āryadevas, viz. the Mādhyamika disciple of Nāgārjuna (Āryadeva I) and a Tantric author also known as Āryadeva (Āryadeva II). One also differentiates the Mādhyamika Nāgārjuna from a Tantrika of the same namesake, viz. Nāgārjunapāda, and indeed the names and careers of the key figures in the Tantric lineages mirror those of their Mādhyamika counterparts: Āryadeva II seems to have been a disciple of the Tantric master, Nāgārjunapāda, who founded the important commentarial lineage of the *Guhyasamājatantra*, the so-called Ārya tradition. Major Tantric works attributable to this Āryadeva include the *Cittaviśuddhiprakaraṇa* on Nāgārjunapāda's *Pañcakrama* on *Guhyasamāja*. There is, however, little doubt that these Tantric writers lived much later than their Mādhyamika counterparts. Indeed, if we hypothesize that Āryadeva II was also the author of the *Madhyamakabhramaghāta*, attributed to "Āryadeva" in the Tibetan canon (see below), then he must have lived well after the sixth century, for he cites the *Madhyamakahṛdayakārikā* and *Tarkajvāla* of Bhāvaviveka (500-570) in his *Madhyamakabhramaghāta*.[13]

Besides the *Catuḥśataka* — the only work of Āryadeva I which remains partially conserved in Sanskrit —, numerous other philosophical works are attributed to "Āryadeva" in the Tibetan and Chinese canon. Let us begin with the works according to the Chinese canon. Here we can presume authorship by Āryadeva I as the Chinese canon, unlike the Tibetan, does not confuse Āryadeva I with the Tantrika of the same name:

1. *Guǎng bǎi lùn* 廣百論 (i.e. the last half of the *Catuḥśataka*) T. 1570 and 1571. T. 1570 is only the *kārikās*, whereas T. 1571 is with Dharmapāla's commentary.
2. *Bǎi lùn* 百論 (**Śata(ka)śāstra*), T. 1569. Only the first half is conserved and is integrated with the commentary by Vasu .[14]

---

[13] See Mimaki (1987), "Āryadeva", pp. 431a-432a and Ruegg (1981) pp. 105-106.

[14] Transl. Tucci (1929). As for the question as to which half of the *Bǎi lùn* was in fact translated, the *Preface to the Bǎi lùn* by Sēng zhào 僧肇 T. 1569 makes it clear that Kumārajīva did not think the last ten chapters were worth translating for his countrymen. See Robinson (1967) p. 211. On Vasu and the *Bǎi lùn*, see e.g. Peri (1911) pp. 361-368; the attribution of this work to Deva = Āryadeva has been questioned by De Jong (1971).

3. *Băi zì lùn* 百字論 (**Akṣaraśataka*) T. 1572 with a commentary which may be by Āryadeva himself.[15]
4. *Dī pó pú sà shì léng jiā jīng zhōng wài dào xiăo chéng sì zōng lùn* 提婆菩薩釋楞伽經中外道小乘四宗論 T.1639.[16]
5. *Dī pó pú sà shì léng jiā jīng zhōng wài dào xiăo chéng niè pán lùn* 提婆菩薩釋楞伽經中外道小乘涅槃論 T. 1640.[17]

In the Tibetan canon we find the following works, of which only the first and second are attributable to Āryadeva I:

a. *Catuḥśataka*. P. 5246 (*kārikā*s only) and P. 5266 (*kārikā*s with Candrakīrti's commentary).
b. *Akṣaraśataka* P. 5234. In fact, the Tibetan canon attributes this work and its commentary to Nāgārjuna. However, not just the Chinese but also the Tibetan Dunhuang translation of this text attribute it to Āryadeva.
c. *Hastavālaprakaraṇa* P. 5244 and 5248 (*kārikā*s only), P. 5245 and P. 5249 with the commentary, the *Hastavālaprakaraṇavṛtti* or *Hastavālavṛtti* respectively. The work is also in the Chinese canon, but is attributed there to Dignāga.[18]
d. *Skhalitapramathanayuktihetusiddhi* P. 5247 (Āryadeva II?)[19]
e. *Madhyamakabhramaghāta* P. 5250 (Āryadeva II?).
f. *Jñānasārasamuccaya* P. 5251 (Āryadeva II?). The text gives a fourfold presentation of Buddhist doctrine typical of doxographical (*siddhānta*) texts, a genre which considerably post-dates Āryadeva I.[20]

---

[15] See May *Chūgan* p. 479; Lang (Thesis) pp. 82-85. Transl. Gokhale (1930). The Tibetan canon attributes this text and its commentary to Nāgārjuna, but as Lang p. 82 and Gokhale p. 2 point out, the Tibetan Dunhuang translation made by Chos 'grub on the basis of the Chinese refers to Āryadeva and suggests that someone else (unnamed) wrote the commentary.

[16] A work on a version of the *catuṣkoṭi* dealing with identity and difference.

[17] Transl. Tucci (1926). It should be mentioned that there are some scholars who are inclined to identify Āryadeva with Qīng mù 青目 (= *Piṅgala) as the author of commentaries (T.1564 and 1568) on the *Zhōng lùn* 中論 (i.e. MMK) and the *Shí èr mén lùn* 十二門論. See e.g. Lamotte *Traité* III p. 1373; cf. Robinson (1967) p. 29; Peri (1911) pp. 365 n. 4 and May *Hōbōgirin* s.v. *Chūgan* p. 481 for further references.

[18] T. 1620, 1621. Cf. Hattori (1968a), p. 7 n. 41, who also attributes this text to Dignāga. Transl. F.W. Thomas and H. Ui (1918); Tibetan text in Frauwallner (1959).

[19] Transl. R. Clark and L. Jamspal (1979). The attribution of this text and the **Madhyamakabhramaghāta* to Āryadeva I is questioned. See Lang (Thesis) p. 85. See also Lang (1986) p. 15 who mentions that the former work is cited in the *Ratnapradīpa*; Lindtner (1982a) p. 173, n. 21 points out that the *Madhyamakabhramaghāta* is identical with a part of the *Tarkajvāla* of Bhāvaviveka.

[20] Edited and transl. along with the commentary by Bodhibhadra in Mimaki (1976).

Turning now to Dharmapāla and Candrakīrti, the information gleaned from Xuán zàng's *Xī yóu jì* 西域記 leads most scholars to fix Dharmapāla's dates at 530-561 A.D.[21] We find other information to the effect that he was born in Kāñcī in South India as the eldest son of a high official; subsequently, fearing that he was to be forced to marry a daughter of the king, he fled to a monastery and later became a famous Vijñānavādin teacher in the monastic university of Nālandā in the North. In 559 A.D. at the age of twenty-nine he retired from Nālandā to meditate in Bodh Gaya, where he remained until his death in 561 A.D.

In spite of his short life, he had a considerable influence on the development of Indian and Chinese Mahāyāna Buddhist thought, in part due to his celebrated debate with the Mādhyamika, Bhāvaviveka, but also because of his influence on Xuán zàng, who wrote his famous *Chéng wéi shí lùn* (**Vijñaptimātratāsiddhi*) as a compilation of various Indian Vijñānavāda masters' thought. The latter relied especially heavily on Dharmapāla's commentary to the *Triṃśikā* of Vasubandhu,[22] very possibly because Dharmapāla was himself the teacher of Xuán zàng's guru, Śīlabhadra.

Crucial to understanding Dharmapāla's thought is his connection with the Epistemological school. Indeed he may have been a grand-pupil of Dignāga[23], or at least he had very close ties with this branch of Vijñānavāda, as is evidenced by his commentary on Dignāga's *Ālambanaparīkṣā* and by the fact that he wrote a (now lost) commentary on the *Nyāyamukha*. Moreover, his philosophical standpoint in his commentary on the *Catuḥśataka*, and especially his discussions there on particulars (*svalakṣaṇa*), universals (*sāmānyalakṣaṇa*) and the philosophy of language, bear witness to a marked affinity with the Epistemologists. In the *Chéng wéi shí lùn* we also see that, like Dignāga's branch of the Vijñānavāda, he accepted and placed great importance on the existence of a "self-awareness" (*svasaṃvitti*; *svasaṃvedana*) not distinct from the mind which divides itself into objective and subjective parts (*fēn* 分 = *bhāga*). These

---

[21] See Frauwallner (1961) pp. 132-134, who summarizes the reasoning of H. Ui. See also Kajiyama (1968), Peri (1911) pp. 383-384 and N. Aiyaswami Shāstrī (1942) p. xx et seq. on the life and dates of Dharmapāla. In fact, at the risk of making a heretical statement, I doubt that these dates are quite as sure as they are often made out to be. The whole argument rests on calculations from the fact that Xuán zàng met Dharmapāla's pupil Śīlabhadra who was supposedly 106 years old at the time, a "ripe old age" which inevitably suggests exaggeration. Note that Śīlabhadra, at age 106, then supposedly taught Vijñānavāda to Xuán zàng for a few years. On Śīlabhadra's life see Mimaki (1987), "Śīlabhadra", pp. 320b-321b.

[22] Contrary to what is often thought, the *Chéng wéi shí lùn* (**Vijñaptimātratāsiddhi*) is not an Indian text. In the Chinese canon we find the work attributed to "the bodhisattva Dharmapāla and others", but in fact the work must be regarded as essentially an indigenous Chinese work, a kind of digest of Indian Vijñānavāda based on paraphrases and résumés of the works of writers such as Dharmapāla, Nanda, etc., but compiled and written by Xuán zàng himself. Cf. D. Shimaji in S. Lévi (1932) p. 16: "Les commentaires décisifs [de la *Triṃśikā*] furent ceux de 'dix grands maîtres en śāstra', comprenant chacun dix chapitres, soit en tout cent chapitres. Hiuan-tsang [= Xuán zàng] les rapporta de l'Inde et en fit une traduction éclectique en dix chapitres, prenant pour base l'interprétation de Dharmapāla et y combinant celles des neuf autres maîtres: c'est le *Tch'eng wei che louen*."

[23] See Hattori (1968a) p. 2.

latter two "parts" consist respectively in the "image" or "aspect of the object" (*viṣayākāra*; *arthākāra*) and the "aspect of [the awareness] itself (*svākāra*), or in other equivalent terms the objective aspect (*grāhyākāra*) and the subjective aspect (*grāhakākāra*)[24] . As is well known, postulating a *svasaṃvitti* "part" of the mind is a key element in the Epistemologists' proof of idealism in that it eliminates the need for external objects to explain cognition: mind simply knows its own objective and subjective aspects, i.e. mind just knows itself. We will return to the question of *ākāra* in more detail in Chapter III, but for our purposes now in showing Dharmapāla's affiliation with the Epistemologists, it should be stressed that he also seems to have embraced Dignāga's account of *pramāṇaphala* ("the result of the means of valid cognition"), which Dignāga had taken as *svasaṃvitti*.[25]

---

[24] See e.g. the explanations in Hattori (1988) p. 51 et seq. and May (1971) p. 306. See fn. 131 for Dharmakīrti's and Dignāga's Idealism. See also Kuī jī's characterization of Dharmapāla's position, fn. 127.

[25] See *Chéng wéi shí lùn* T. 1585 ii 10b et seq.; *Siddhi* pp. 132-135. In Dignāga's Idealist system there are in fact three divisions or "parts" to consciousness: the apprehended object (*grāhya*), the apprehending perception (*grāhaka*) and the self-awareness (*svasaṃvitti*; *saṃvitti*) of the perception. The first is the *prameya* ("what is validly cognized"), the second the *pramāṇa* ("the means of valid cognition") and the third is the *pramāṇaphala* ("the result of the means of valid cognition"). See PS I k. 10: *yadābhāsaṃ prameyaṃ tat pramāṇaphalate punaḥ / grāhakākārasaṃvittī trayaṃ nātaḥ pṛthakkṛtam //*. Transl. Hattori (1968a) p. 29: "Whatever the form in which it [viz. a cognition] appears, that [form] is [recognized as] the object of cognition (*prameya*). The means of cognition (*pramāṇa*) and [the cognition which is] its result (*phala*) are respectively the form of the subject [in the cognition] and the cognition cognizing itself. Therefore, these three [factors of cognition] are not separate from one another." See also Hattori's note 67 and PV III k. 354. As Hattori pointed out, PS I k. 10 is quoted in *Chéng wéi shí lùn* ii 10b 13-16; *Siddhi* p. 131.

Now it might perhaps be objected that Dharmapāla's position — if we are to believe Xuáng zàng and Kuī jī — is *not* in fact completely the same as that of Dignāga. The *Chéng wéi shí lùn* passage referred to above describes a position where a fourth "part" (*fēn* 分 = *bhāga*) is postulated for consciousness: besides *svasaṃvittibhāga* ("self-awareness"), there is also, according to this view, *svasaṃvittisvasaṃvittibhāga*, the "self-awareness of self-awareness", i.e. an additional part. Moreover, LVP (*Siddhi* p. 133) cites Kuī jī's commentary on the *Viṃśatikā*, viz. the *Wéi shí èr shí lùn shù jì* 唯識二十論述記 T. 1834, specifying that *Dharmapāla* not only accepted *svasaṃvitti* (= *zì zhèng* 自證) but also *svasaṃvittisvasaṃvitti* (*zhèng zì zhèng* 證自證). (LVP was no doubt thinking of T. 1834 *xià* 999a24-28.) This, however, is probably of less importance than it may at first sight seem, for the fourth part is in fact included in the third, both being classified as *pramāṇaphala*. (See *Siddhi* p. 134 and Kuī jī T. 1834 *xià* 998c 27 - 999a 4). Indeed, evidence that this "divergence" from Dignāga was not of great consequence comes from Kuī jī's own repeated statements in the *Wéi shí èr shí lùn shù jì* that Dharmapāla held *three* parts of consciousness, i.e. the perception (*jiàn* 見), the characters (*xiāng* 相) of the object and the self-awareness (*zì zhèng* 自證). See e.g. T. 1834 *shàng* 982c 12-16 and *xià* 1007b 18-19. See fn. 127 for text and translation. In short Dharmapāla does not seem to be significantly different from Dignāga in his interpretation of *svasaṃvitti*, nor in the doctrine of *pramāṇa*, *prameya* and *pramāṇaphala*.

Note also that Kuī jī (op cit.) stresses the important point that Dharmapāla accepted that all three parts were "dependent phenomena" (*paratantra*), a position which Kuī jī contrasts with that of Sthiramati who held that the first two were "thoroughly imagined" (*parikalpita*). Here then is another similarity with Dignāga that is worth noting: both were *sākāravādins*. Cf. Kajiyama (1965) pp. 423-421 who gives a brief account of Dharmapāla's *sākāravāda* (i.e. the position usually ascribed to Dignāga and Dharmakīrti that consciousness

Finally, if we are to follow Tāranātha, he was in fact a guru of Dharmakīrti, a claim which, from a doctrinal point of view, is not at all implausible, but which is, alas, chronologically problematic.[26]

---

has real aspects) and the differences between Dharmapāla and Sthiramati's positions, the latter being a *nirākāravādin.* (See our Chapter III, A for the general issues at stake.) He quotes, with some apparent skepticism, Frauwallner's opinion (in *Die Philosophie des Buddhismus*) that Dharmapāla's theory is based on Asaṅga. As Kajiyama (p. 421) points out, this latter view would contradict usual characterizations (e.g. in Bodhibhadra) of Asaṅga as being a *nirākāravādin.*

Indigenous Tibetan writers too provide arguments for affiliating Dharmapāla with Dignāga and Dharmakīrti on the question of acceptance of *svasaṃvitti*. Vasubandhu and Asaṅga are generally classified by Tibetan doxographical literature as *luṅ gi rjes su 'braṅ pa'i sems tsam pa*, "Vijñānavādins who follow scripture", while Dignāga and Dharmakīrti are *rigs pa'i rjes su 'braṅ pa'i sems tsam pa*, "Vijñānavādins who follow reasoning". See e.g. *Grub mtha' rin chen phreṅ ba* p. 91 ed. Mimaki (1977) or *lCaṅ skya grub mtha'* p. 158: *sa sde sogs kyi rjes 'braṅs luṅ gtso bor smra ba luṅ gi rjes 'braṅs daṅ / tshad ma'i bstan bcos sde bdun mdo daṅ bcas pa nas bśad pa ltar gyi rigs pa'i rjes 'braṅs gñis su yod pa ni grags che la /*. As *lCaṅ skya grub mtha'* p. 193 points out, *svasaṃvitti* occupied a major place in the position of the Vijñānavādins who follow reasoning, but it is not clear to what degree the other branch of Vijñānavāda accepted it at all: *...rigs pa'i rjes 'braṅ gi sems tsam pas mṅon sum la dbaṅ yid raṅ rig rnal 'byor mṅon sum bźi 'dod do / luṅ gi rjes 'braṅ gi sems tsam pas gźan gsum 'dod kyaṅ raṅ rig 'dod mi 'dod ni gsal bar ma bśad la rje btsun dam pa 'jam dbyaṅs bźad pa'i rdo rjes sa sde'i rjes 'braṅ gi sems tsam pas raṅ rig mi 'dod de / sa sde lṅa nas ma bśad pa'i phyir źes gsuṅs so.* "...The Vijñānavādins who follow reasoning accept that perception has four [sorts], i.e. physical sense [perception], mental [perception], self-awareness and yogic perception. The Vijñānavādins who follow scripture accept the other three, but do not clearly explain whether or not they accept self-awareness. So 'Jam dbyaṅs bźad pa'i rdo rje [Ṅag dbaṅ btson 'grus (1648-1722)] said that the Vijñānavādins who follow the "Collections of the *bhūmis*" [, i.e. the *Yogācārabhūmiśāstra,* etc. of Asaṅga,] do not accept self-awareness, because it is not asserted in the five 'Collections of the *bhūmis*'." Given the clear importance that Dharmapāla placed on *svasaṃvitti* it seems more reasonable to place him in the camp of Dignāga on this point, rather than in Asaṅga's.

[26] If we take Dharmakīrti as having lived in the seventh century — Frauwallner (1961) pp. 136-139 opts for c. 600-660 A.D. — he would not have met Dharmapāla. In brief the usual argument is as follows: if we accepted the hypothesis of a meeting between the two, we would have to situate Dharmakīrti in the sixth century, with a few years of his old age perhaps occurring in the seventh century. In that case, Xuán zàng's silence on Dharmakīrti becomes difficult to explain, as the Chinese pilgrim, who was an aficionado of epistemology and Vijñānavāda and left India in 644 A.D., would certainly have mentioned Dharmakīrti if he had known of him. Yì jìng, who left India around 685 A.D., does mention Dharmakīrti, a fact which leads Frauwallner to conclude that the beginning of Dharmakīrti's fame must be between these dates. The problem remains open. Cf. the arguments of Lindtner (1980) to place Dharmakīrti c. 530-600, and the discussion in Ruegg (1982)'s postscript. On Dharmakīrti's life according to Tāranātha's *rGya gar chos 'byuṅ*, See ed. Schiefner (1868) pp. 134-142; transl. Lama Chimpa and A. Chattopadhyaya (1970) pp. 228-240; Schiefner (1869), pp. 175-185. See Tosaki (1979) pp. 3-24 on Dharmakīrti's life; ibid p. 4 for a résumé of Tāranātha's account; ibid pp. 20-21 for an evaluation of the hypothesis that Dharmapāla was the teacher of Dharmakīrti.

As Ruegg (1981) n. 148 points out, Tāranātha also relates that Dharmadāsa, who was supposedly a direct pupil of Asaṅga and Vasubandhu and a teacher of Ārya Vimuktisena, was also a teacher of Dharmapāla. See *rGya gar chos 'byuṅ*, transl. Schiefner (1869) p. 124; Lama Chimpa and A. Chattopadhyaya (1970) pp. 188-189 as well as pp. 212-214 for Tāranātha's account of Dharmapāla's life. That this Dharmadāsa (Chos

None of Dharmapāla's works survives in Sanskrit, nor were they translated into Tibetan.[27] In the biography of Xuán zàng by Huì lì 慧立 we find mention of four works:

a) *Shēng míng zá lùn* 聲明雜論 in twenty-five thousand *ślokas*;
b) a commentary on the *Guǎng bǎi lùn* (= *Catuḥśataka*);
c) a commentary on *Vijñaptimātratā*, i.e. *Wéi shí lùn* 唯識論 ;
d) a commentary on logic, i.e. *Yīn míng* 因明 . (*Yīn míng lùn* = *Nyāyamukha*)

The titles of a), c) and d) were given rather improbable Sanskrit reconstructions by Beal and later N. Aiyaswami Shāstrī[28], viz. **Śabdavidyāsaṃyuktaśāstra,*

---

kyi 'baṅs) was a teacher of Dharmapāla is also mentioned in Sum pa mkhan po Ye śes dpal 'byor's *dPag bsam ljon bzaṅ*, (ed. Das) pp. 99 and 102. This Vijñānavādin teacher is mentioned in CSV P. 35a4-5 as giving examples for the first eight chapters of CS: *'dir rab tu byed pa brgyad kyi tshig le'ur byas pa dag re re la* ***slob dpon chos kyi 'baṅs*** *kyis sbyar ba'i dpe rnams 'don pa de dag daṅ lhan cig rnam par bśad par bya'o /.* It is tempting to speculate that some of the aspects of Dharmapāla's philosophical stances which seem to resemble Asaṅga's might have been communicated to him by this Dharmadāsa. Cf. e.g. Dharmapāla's and Asaṅga's views that it is only *manas* and *manovijñāna* (and not sense consciousnesses) which are responsible for *parikalpita*, or "thoroughly imagined natures". See *Siddhi* p. 518 et seq. which quotes Asaṅga's *Mahāyānasaṃgraha* in this context; cf. Dharmapāla's commentary to CS XIII k. 322.

A confusion to be avoided is that between the Dharmapāla who was the teacher of Śīlabhadra, died in Bodh Gaya, etc. etc. and a Vijñānavādin Dharmapāla of Suvarṇadvīpa, who was a guru of Atiśa Dīpaṃkaraśrījñāna c. 1000. (Tāranātha p. 214 transl. Chimpa and Chattopadhyaya has this confusion.) N. Aiyaswami Shāstrī (1942) p. xix also warns against confusion with the Dharmapāla of the Theravāda school, who was, according to the *Viśuddhimaggaṭīkā* colophon, a native of Badarititha, not far from Ceylon. According to Shāstrī, this is "near Negapatam, a small seaport town in South India." Hence, Shāstrī reasons that our Dharmapāla, who fled Kāñcī to go North and who had no connection with Badarititha, is clearly different from the Theravādin.

[27] The Tibetan *bsTan 'gyur* does, however, mention two works by a "Dharmapāla":

1) *Theg pa chen po'i chos brgya gsal ba'i sgo bstan bcos* P. 5564. This work, which was translated from the Chinese, *Dà chéng bǎi fǎ míng mén lùn* 大乘百法明門論 T. 1614, is according to the Tibetans by Dharmapāla, but is by Vasubandhu according to the Chinese. The work gives a list of various Abhidharmic entities, e.g. the consciousnesses, *citta-caittas*, etc. In fact the colophon in Tibetan says merely that the work is "generally thought by Tibetans to be by Dharmapāla". *rgya'i dpe las slob dpon dbyig gñen gyis mdzad par snaṅ / deṅ saṅ bod rnams dpal ldan chos skyoṅ gis mdzad ces grags so /.* "In the Chinese text it appears that it was composed by Vasubandhu, but nowadays Tibetans generally think that it was composed by the exalted Dharmapāla."

2) *Yi ge'i mdo'i 'grel pa*, i.e. *Varṇasūtravṛtti* P. 5770. A short commentary in eight folios on Candragomin's *Varṇasūtra*; if we situate Candragomin as fl. 650, this makes it impossible that our Dharmapāla is the author.

[28] See fn. 30 and transl. Beal p. 139; cf. also N. Aiyaswami Shāstri (1942) p. xx. The restitutions are those of Aiyaswami Shāstrī; clearly *Vijñaptimātratāsiddhi* is preferable instead of his *Vidyāmātrasiddhi*. Kuī jī's phonetic commentary on the Sanskrit term in his *Chéng wéi shí lùn zhǎng zhōng shū yào* 成唯識論

**Vidyāmātrasiddhi* and the **Nyāyadvāratarkaśāstra* (= the *Nyāyamukha* of Dignāga) respectively.

The first work was also spoken about by Kuī jī 窺基 as being a profound work on grammar in 25,000 *ślokas*, especially prized in the "Western regions"; he gave the title as *Zá bǎo shēng míng lùn* 雜寶聲明論.[29] Now, Yì jìng had spoken of a work by Dharmapāla in 14,000 *ślokas* on "Bì ná", which was in turn in 3,000 *ślokas*.[30] Takakusu had transcribed the characters 蓽拏 as "Pei na" and speculated that the text might be a work on the *Vedas*[31], but this is unlikely and it is probably in fact a *Vyākaraṇa* treatise — Brough (1973) argues that, inspite of the phonetic dissimilarity, "bì ná" is "*Prakīrṇaka*", i.e. a section of Bhartṛhari's *Vākyapadīya*. If that is so, then the grammatico-philosophical work of Dharmapāla mentioned in Yì jìng is a commentary on the *Vākyapadīya*, and the question naturally arises as to whether it is identical with a) above. What seems possible is that Kuī jī (whose account is similar to that of Huì lì) was talking about the same commentary as Yì jìng but exaggerated its length.[32]

At any rate, neither a) nor d) are extant, and in fact it is probably wise to keep a dose of skepticism about *Vyākaraṇa* works attributed to Dharmapāla. There is, to our knowledge, no trace of such works. Nor is there, for that matter, any trace of Dharmapāla's supposed "poetry", although both Candrakīrti and especially Tāranātha (see fn. 2) insisted on his being a notable poet (*sñan dṅags mkhan*) — it is, again, not clear how we should take these affirmations. What does remain in the *Taishō* are the following works:

掌中樞要 T. 1831 *shàng běn* 608c23-27, makes it clear that this is what it must be.

[29] *Chéng wéi shí lùn zhǎng zhōng shū yào*, T. 1831 *shàng běn* 623a29-b2: 然護法 菩薩造二万五十頌名雜寶聲明論西方矣以爲聲明究竟之極論。. See Peri (1911) p. 377 n. 4. Note that Kuī jī, Yì jìng and Huì lì speak of "the bodhisattva Dharmapāla", thus suggesting that it is not a different Dharmapāla who produced the work on *Vyākaraṇa*. Finally, it is worthwhile to remark that "*śloka*" in this context does not necessarily mean that the work is in verse, but can refer to groups of thirty-two syllables. See Brough (1973) p. 259, n. 40.

[30] T. 2125 iv 229b5-6: 次有蓽拏頌有三千釋有十四千頌乃伐㰚可利所造釋則護法論師所製。Cf. *Life of Xuán zàng* T. 2053 iv 241c22-24: 造聲明雜論二万五千頌 又釋廣百論唯識論及因明數十部並盛宣行。

[31] Takakusu (1898) p. 180 and endnote.

[32] Brough (1973) p. 260: "... 'Pei-na' is the *Prakīrṇaka*. Rangaswamy Iyengar and Subramania Iyer have already made this proposal, and the latter suggested that the Chinese name might represent a Prakrit *paīṇṇa*. Unfortunately (unless Takakusu had a different reading before him), the modern transcription should not be *pei-na*, but *pi-na* 蓽拏 [= *bì ná* in *pinyin*], Mid. ch. *pit-ṇa*. It is hard to reconcile this with *paīṇṇa*. At the same time, it is equally hard to reject the identification. One can only suggest that I-ching misheard the Prakrit name, and that his transcription reflects a distortion, **piṇṇa*. ... This is not a very satisfying solution; but no better alternative has yet suggested itself." As Brough shows, Yì jìng's account of grammatical works contains some inaccuracies but is far from being a work of pure inventive fiction.

1. *Guǎng bǎi lùn shì lùn* 廣百論釋論 T. 1571.
2. *Chéng wéi shí lùn* 成唯識論 T. 1585.[33]
3. *Chéng wéi shí bǎo shēng lùn* 成唯識寶生論 T. 1591. A commentary on Vasubandhu's *Viṃśatikā* translated by Yì jìng. The commentary on the *Triṃśikā* on which Xuán zàng relied is not extant.
4. *Guān suǒ yuán lùn shì* 觀所緣論釋 T. 1625. A commentary on Dignāga's *Ālambanaparīkṣā* translated by Yì jìng.[34] The text comments on the *Ālambanaparīkṣā* only up to the seventh verse and then abruptly stops.

As for Candrakīrti, we have almost no reliable information concerning his life, the only material being the largely fabulous biographies of Candrakīrti by the Tibetan historians, Bu ston Rin chen grub, Tāranātha and Sum pa mkhan po Ye śes dpal 'byor. In addition to recording legend, these writers tend to confuse the philosopher Candrakīrti with another Tantric Candrakīrti who wrote the *Guhyasamājatantra* commentary known as the *Pradīpoddyotana* (P. 2650). Indeed it may even be that there was a third writer of this name who wrote the **Madhyamakaprajñāvatāra* (P. 5264) and collaborated with 'Gos khug pa lhas btsas to translate it into Tibetan, thus enabling us to date this "Candrakīrti" in the eleventh century — it is, however, unclear whether the Candrakīrti of the *Pradīpoddyotana* is to be identified with this author or with the philosophical writer who commented on Nāgārjuna and Āryadeva. At any rate, these confusions between two or possibly three figures led Tibetans to claim a lifespan of three to four hundred years for "Candrakīrti".[35]

Taking a more sober perspective, the dates for the Madhyamaka philosopher and commentator, Candrakīrti, are generally held to be from approximately 600 A.D. to 650, although some would wish to place him in the sixth century. (Lindtner [1979] p. 91 opts for 530-600.) As is well known by now, he and Buddhapālita were responsible for a method of Madhyamaka philosophy based on the use of *reductio ad absurdum*, or "consequences" (*prasaṅga*), and hence he is considered as one of the principal figures in the Prāsaṅgika school of Madhyamaka thought.[36] Contrary to Mādhyamikas such as Bhāvaviveka or Śāntarakṣita, who borrowed heavily from the Epistemologists, Candrakīrti's standpoint is often quite opposed to Buddhist

---

[33] See fn. 22 for the question as to who wrote this work. Transl. Louis de la Vallée Poussin (1928-1929), i.e. *Siddhi*.

[34] Translated into Sanskrit and English by N. Aiyaswami Shāstrī (1942).

[35] See Mimaki (1987) "Candrakīrti" pp. 58b-59a, Ruegg (1981) pp. 71, 81 and 105, Lindtner (1979) pp. 87-91.

[36] On Candrakīrti's approach, see Ruegg (1981) pp. 76-80; May (1959) pp. 15-16; Tillemans (1982) pp. 105-112 for Tsoṅ kha pa's view on Prāsaṅgikas. Note that the term itself is convenient Sanskritizing of a Tibetan term, *thal 'gyur pa*. It may very well be Pa tshab Ñi ma grags who first came up with the distinction into *thal 'gyur pa* and *raṅ rgyud pa* (*svātantrika*). See Mimaki (1983) pp. 163-164.

epistemology, and in fact shows a marked preference for certain aspects of Nyāya-Vaiśeṣika logic and analyses of conventional truth.[37]

His main works (viz. 1-5 below), with the exception of the *Madhyamakāvatāra*, consist in commentaries on works of Nāgārjuna and Āryadeva:

1. *Prasannapadā Mūlamadhyamakavṛtti.*[38]
2. *Yuktiṣaṣṭikāvṛtti* P. 5265. Conserved only in Tibetan.[39]
3. *Śūnyatāsaptativṛtti* P. 5268. Conserved in Tibetan.[40]
4. *Madhyamakāvatāra* and *Bhāṣya*. Conserved in Tibetan.[41]
5. *Catuḥśatakavṛtti* or *Ṭīkā*.
6. *Pañcaskandhaprakaraṇa* P. 5267. Conserved in Tibetan.[42]
7. *Triśaraṇasaptati* P. 5366 / 5478. Conserved in Tibetan.[43]

In terms of relative chronology little can be said except that it was probably in the *Madhyamakāvatāra* that Candrakīrti initially formulated his thought on Madhyamaka — we see that this work is cited in *Prasannapadā* and in the *Catuhśatakavṛtti.*

C. Some methodological remarks

1. The question of an Indo-Tibetan approach

First of all, the rather thorny question might arise as to the use and value of indigenous Tibetan materials in interpreting the *Catuḥśataka* and *Catuḥśatakavṛtti.*[44]

---

[37] See fn. 89. In logic, for example, he deliberately uses the Nyāya five-membered reasoning instead of the two-membered (or sometimes three-membered) Buddhist *parārthānumāna*. He also accepts the four Nyāya *pramāṇas*, viz. perception (*pratyakṣa*), inference (*anumāna*), comparison (*upamāna*) and testimony (*śabda*).

[38] Sanskrit in Pr. edited by Louis de la Vallée Poussin. Transl. by several scholars; see May (1959) p. 10 for the details.

[39] An edition and French translation is in preparation by C. Scherrer-Schaub

[40] Translation in preparation by F. Erb.

[41] Text ed. by LVP (1907-12). Transl. of chapters I-V and VI k. 1-165 in LVP (1907), (1910), (1911). Transl. of VI k. 166-226 in Tauscher (1981).

[42] Tibetan edited in Lindtner (1979).

[43] Edited and translated by P. Sorensen (1986). The authorship here is questionable. It may be the work of the Tantric author of the same name. See Ruegg (1981) p. 105 n. 334.

[44] Cf. the following sampling of opinions pro and contra: Hattori (1968a) p. 15: "There is a commentary on PS(V) by the great Tibetan scholar Darma Rinchen. However, I have not utilized it since I thought that the examination of it might serve to clarify only the Tibetan interpretation of Dignāga's thought." (My

There are Tibetan commentaries on CS and CSV[45]; what is more, there is a wealth of Tibetan literature on the philosophies of Candrakīrti, Āryadeva and Nāgārjuna, not to mention the corpus of writings on epistemological problems, the doxographical literature, much of which, depending upon one's methodology, could be potentially relevant. Without any pretensions of exhausting the issue, I would make the following observations on the suitability of an Indo-Tibetan approach.

1) I take it as obviously true that Tibetan commentaries or Tibetan oral traditions cannot *replace* a thorough study of the Indian texts in the context of the Indian, rather than Tibetan, philosophical discussions and that this study must rely primarily upon the Sanskrit originals of the texts when the Sanskrit is available.[46]

2) Tibetan word-commentaries (*tshig 'grel*) on Indian texts are useful in understanding as to what would be the most natural way for an educated Tibetan to read the Tibetan translation. Some drawbacks of relying on such commentaries: a) The Tibetan translation which the indigenous Tibetan commentators rely upon often differs substantially from the Sanskrit. The reasons for these divergences are complex and have to be evaluated case by case, but it has to be granted that not too infrequently the

---

comment: It is not clear whether Hattori is thinking of just the situation with regard to PS or whether he would generalize. It is true that the indigenous literature on PS is very meager and of a much lower quality than that on PV. No doubt the difficulty of PS and the abysmally bad Tibetan translations played a role.)

Ruegg (1981) p. viii: "In Tibet for example there has existed for over a millennium a tradition of study of a very considerable portion of Indian literature, including even works that are not specifically Buddhist; and with a view to both translation and exegesis Tibetan scholars developed remarkable philological and interpretative methods that could well justify us in regarding them as Indologists avant la lettre."

R. Hayes (1988) p. 8: "But while it may be a mistake when discussing Buddhist philosophy to rely too heavily on Brahmanical works to the exclusion of Buddhist works, it is no less a mistake to rely too heavily upon Buddhist works, and especially on works of the later Tibetan tradition, as guides to understanding Indian Buddhist thought."

K. Mimaki (1982) p. 3: "On entend souvent la critique suivante à propos de l'étude des *grub mtha'* [i.e. Tibetan doxographical literature]: dans l'étude des *grub mtha'*, s'agit-il du bouddhisme indien ou du bouddhisme tibétain? Cette question revient à dire que ce n'est ni le bouddhisme indien, parce que ce sont des tibétains qui écrivent les *grub mtha'*, ni le bouddhisme tibétain parce que ce sont des écoles indiennes qui y sont décrites. Il est facile de répondre à cette critique, en disant, comme pour sortir d'un dilemme, que les *grub mtha'* constituent justement le bouddhisme tibétain, parce que ce sont des tibétains qui les écrivent: c'est aussi le bouddhisme indien, parce que c'est la philosophie bouddhique indienne qui y est exposée."

45 There are four Tibetan commentaries available on CS and CSV, generally of uneven quality. The longest is that of the Sa skya pa, Red mda' ba gŹon nu blo gros (1392-1481), i.e. *dBu ma bźi brgya pa'i 'grel pa*; also of interest is the *bŹi brgya pa'i rnam bśad legs bśad sñiṅ po* of rGyal tshab Dar ma rin chen (1364-1432). Kaḥ thog mkhan po Ṅag dbaṅ dpal bzaṅ (1879-1941) wrote the *dBu ma bźi brgya pa'i rnam par bśad pa rgya mtsho'i zeg ma*, which is largely a remake of rGyal tshab, apart from a few additional remarks. The nineteenth century rÑiṅ ma pa writer, gŹan dga' gŹan phan chos kyi snaṅ ba, wrote an interlinear commentary on the *kārikās* entitled, *bsTan bcos bźi brgya pa źes bya ba'i tshig le'ur byas pa'i mchan 'grel*. I thank J. Dantinne for kindly making a microfilm of the latter commentary available to me; thanks also to G. Dreyfus and Z. Horváth for help in obtaining Red mda' ba's commentary.

46 Cf. the remarks of De Jong (1986), p. 128.

translators, who were of course of varying competence, did not fully understand their texts. b) What is equally problematic is that even when the Tibetan does not really differ from the Sanskrit, it often has to be read in an artificial and unnatural manner, one which eludes the word-commentaries. c) The Tibetan word-commentaries on many occasions adopt an interpretation which is not philosophically inaccurate in the light of the Sanskrit and the Indian commentaries, but which so transforms and adds to the original that the Indian author's own wording and syntax is no longer clear — there are, then, obvious perils in adopting these interpretations for translational purposes.[47] Now, as mentioned in the previous paragraph, priority should normally go to the Sanskrit originals and commentaries. If, however, the Sanskrit original is lost and there are no Indian commentaries (as is the case for much of CSV), then indigenous Tibetan word-commentaries can come to the rescue.

3) The *forte* of the indigenous Tibetan writers is their philosophical interpretations and their philological discussions of certain issues, rather than their word-by-word commentaries. In another context (viz. Tsoṅ kha pa's explanations of Śāntarakṣita's argumentation in the *Madhyamakālaṃkāra*) I argued that the distinction between internal and external history in the history of science made by the Hungarian historian and philosopher of science, Imre Lakatos, is also relevant for our field of study. To prevent this digression from becoming unduly long, let me simply cite these remarks:

> "I think it is fair to say that Tsoṅ kha pa was less concerned with what Śāntarakṣita and others said, than with rationally reconstructing the logical situations they faced. We follow Imre Lakatos and make a distinction between internal and external history, the former being primarily logical deductions of what could have been said, given the key ideas of the philosopher in question, the latter being what was actually said, what actually took place. In this light, there is no doubt that Tsoṅ kha pa, the great debater, was a specialist at internal history; as such his stretching of terminology, his imposition of concepts which have no obvious textual justification, should not be judged by the severe criterion of the external historian. Bearing this distinction in mind, we deprive neither Tsoṅ kha pa, nor for that matter, ourselves, of the possibility of using fertile but foreign concepts."[48]

---

[47] Take the case of a very useful Tibetan word-commentary on PV: dGe 'dun grub pa's *Tshad ma rnam 'grel legs par bśad pa*. Often the typical dGe lugs pa method of paraphrasing into "sequence and reason" (or *thal phyir* to use Stcherbatsky's phrase) makes so many changes in PV's word-order and so many additions that the original syntax is unfindable. Nonetheless, it should be stressed that dGe 'dun grub *does* usually manage to capture Dharmakīrti's thought quite accurately and insightfully. For a discussion of *thal phyir* logic, see Tillemans (1989a).

[48] Tillemans (1983) p. 312. See Lakatos' *History of Science and its Rational Reconstructions* pp. 102-105, 118-121 in the edition of his papers by J. Worral and G. Currie (1978). (Cf. M. Broido [1988] n. 12 who suggests that my approach works somewhat better for writers like Tsoṅ kha pa than for others like Pad ma dkar po, in that Tsoṅ kha pa "perhaps had a more highly developed sense of the way the systems he interpreted might be expected to evolve.")

Obviously, the dominant current in our field is towards external history, and this is probably as it should be. However, I would also make a plea for sufficient flexibility to account for what I am terming "internal history." What is to be avoided is a certain type of stultifying narrowness in the name of "history" or "philology". To take an example: we typically find investigations as to whether or not a certain term occurs in a particular philosopher's writing; if it does not, but occurs later in a commentary, the natural tendency is to say that it reveals the commentator's thought, an "historical development", rather than that of the philosopher in question. This reasoning is not at all probative. But more significantly, the question is what we mean when we speak of a certain philosopher's "thought", viz. his subjective states (henceforth "thought$_1$"), or his philosophy taken as a set of propositions forming a system (henceforth "thought$_2$") — in the latter sense it is highly possible to attribute to him things which he never wrote, nor perhaps even thought$_1$ of. Indeed, there may be an enormous discrepancy between, for example, the tortuous and roundabout psychological processes which constitute the thought$_1$ of a logician such as Kurt Gödel or Bertrand Russell and, on the other hand, their thought$_2$, viz. Gödel's Proof, Gödel's work on the foundations of mathematics, or Russellian logic. We will probably study Gödel's proof in a form in which he never conceived of it (e.g. that of Barkley Rosser or perhaps in a *Scientific American* type of presentation such as that of E. Nagel), but that in no way prevents us from attributing this form of the proof to Gödel in that it represents a *rational reconstruction* (to use Lakatos' term). To take another example: the creative, philosophical interpretation of Wittgenstein in Saul Kripke's 1981 work on Wittgenstein's argumentation on rules and the private language. It is probably of secondary importance to Kripke's arguments about "Wittgenstein" whether or not the actual man subjectively had in mind the very same connections between rules and private language that Kripke finds in reading the *Philosophical Investigations*. In short, to resume this approach to history and hermeneutics, internal history is a study of the history of thought$_2$, thought taken in its impersonal, non-psychologistic sense, much like Frege's *Gedanke* and Popper's "third world".

For the Tibetan hermeneuticians' own interpretations of "thought / intention" (*dgoṅs pa = abhiprāya*) and "intentional foundation" (*dgoṅs gźi*), see Broido (1984) and Ruegg (1985), (1988); see also Thurman (1984), Lipman (1980) on aspects of Tibetan hermeneutics. Buddhist hermeneuticians themselves, however, seem to be generally speculating on the thoughts$_1$ of authors, or perhaps it might be more accurate to say that the distinction which we are making is unknown to them, and as such the Buddhists' own hermeneutics is probably significantly different from what we are advocating here.

A few examples of some important Tibetan developments which we maintain arguably represent Indian philosophers' thought$_2$:

a) the notion of a *tshad ma'i skyes bu* ("person of authority"). See Steinkellner (1983), van der Kuijp (1985b), (1987), M. Inami and T. Tillemans (1986) pp. 127-128.

b) In Madhyamaka: Tsoṅ kha pa's important elaboration and development of the term *kun rdzob tsam* in M. av. VI: 28; see Williams (1979). The identification of the object to be refuted (*dgag bya*) in Madhyamaka argumentation; see Tillemans (1982).

c) the interpretation of PS III's definition of the thesis as making a difference between real and nominal subjects (*raṅ rten chos can* vs. *chos can 'ba' źig pa*); the use of this and the *don spyi* ("object-universal") in Tibetan analyses of *āśrayāsiddha*. Tillemans (1984c), see n. 42; Kobayashi (1987); see also Kobayashi (1986) on Kamalaśīla's analysis which was an important source for Tsoṅ kha pa.

d) Tibetan doxographers' classifications of Mādhyamikas and Yogācāras. See Mimaki (1982), (1983).

e) Se ra rje btsun Chos kyi rgyal mtshan, in his *rNam 'grel spyi don* ff. 56a-58b, gives a good example of the internal historian's approach to the problem of *niścitagrahaṇa* and the fact that *niścaya / niścita* are missing in PS's version of the *trairūpya*.

2. Can we legitimately speak of Dignāga, Dharmapāla and Dharmakīrti as belonging to one unified school?

A second methodological point. Is it meaningful to speak of an Epistemological school to which Dignāga, Dharmakīrti and Dharmapāla belonged? Can we reasonably use Dharmakīrti's thought to interpret Dignāga or Dharmapāla, as I obviously do? There is a current tendency to make a radical distinction between Dignāga and Dharmakīrti, a position strongly argued for by Richard Hayes (1988) and Radhika Herzberger (1986). Here is Hayes' position:

> "Both Frauwallner and R. Herzberger have helped to advance our understanding of the Buddhist epistemologists to the point where we can no longer speak of them as being anything like a uniform school of thought with a single agenda."[49]

As I am primarily concerned here with the problem of scriptural authority in the Epistemological School and in Āryadeva and his commentators, I will concentrate my attention on Hayes' views on this matter; an extensive treatment of Herzberger's views, which concern Dignāga's logic, would take us too far afield.

Hayes, in his admirable work on Dignāga's philosophy of language, argues that Dignāga's position represented a type of skepticism which was completely distorted by Dharmakīrti and later commentators. On this he becomes quite polemical:

---

[49] Hayes (1988) p. 310. For an earlier article on the problem of doctrinalism and the authority of scripture in the Buddhist epistemologists, see Hayes (1984). One observation that must be made: Hayes in (1984) seeks to make a difference between Dignāga and Dharmakīrti which turns on Dignāga's definition of the thesis in PS III k. 2, and hence, on the refutation of theses by scripture. Unfortunately this definition is misrepresented, with the result that Hayes' discussion on pp. 656-657 is marred. The Sanskrit of the PS III passage in question is found in PVBh 545,7 and 549,6 and reads: *svarūpeṇaiva nirdeśyaḥ svayam iṣṭo 'nirākṛtaḥ / pratyakṣārthānumānāptaprasiddhena svadharmiṇi*. The definition, inter alia, includes *four* ways in which a sound thesis is not refuted: 1) by objects of *pratyakṣa* (perception); 2) by *anumāna*; 3) by authorities (*āpta*); 4) by commonly acknowledged (*prasiddha*) linguistic conventions. See PV IV k. 109-130 on refutation by *prasiddha*. In Hayes' translation (p. 656) there are only three ways: "the person advancing the argument himself believes it and it is not overthrown by anything that is known through sensation, inference or the testimony of a competent witness." The result is that he leaves out *prasiddha* and then he takes the example of the moon being called *śaśin* ("that which has a rabbit") as a proposition whose truth should be established by "competent witnesses". Thus *acandraḥ śaśī* is claimed to be an example of a proposition refuted by *āptavacana*. (See p. his 657 and n. 12.) This is wrong. The latter proposition is an example of a thesis refuted by *prasiddha*, as we see by the discussion in PV, and also in Dignāga's PSV ad PS III and NM. We therefore must reject Hayes' conclusion (p. 657): "And so it turns out that these 'competent witnesses' to whom Diṅnāga refers are simply the linguistic community at large from whom we learn the proper usage of words, phrases and constructions."

"It could be said, taking R. Herzberger's observations a step further, that Dharmakīrti not only washed away Diṅnāga's philosophical accomplishments but also washed away much of the accomplishment of the Buddha as well. It is ironic that in his very attempt to secure the truth of the traditional teachings of Buddhism, to establish the authority of the Buddha himself as a teacher, and to defend established Buddhist doctrine as much as possible from the sharp-minded critical attacks of some non-Buddhist thinkers, Dharmakīrti managed to violate the essentially open-minded and critical spirit of many of his predecessors, putting in its place a dogmatic edifice that eventually very nearly imprisoned a number of the later Indian and Tibetan Buddhist traditions."[50]

Strong stuff, but is it really plausible? I think the evidence for a charge like this would have to be much stronger than what Hayes is giving. Below we will take up the question of Āryadeva and the Epistemologists' views on scriptural authority, but for the moment suffice it to say that Hayes' main point is that Dignāga and Dharmakīrti differed on their views of the use of scripture or verbal testimony. The basic difference which emerges from Hayes is that Dharmakīrti maintained that with regard to imperceptible, supra-sensible states of affairs one can formulate valid inferences based on scripture and testimony, providing these scriptures meet certain criteria for trustworthiness. Dignāga, however, according to Hayes' comment on PS II, k. 5, maintained that

"a passage of scripture can be regarded as authoritative only insofar as what it says is true. So, rather than saying that something is true on the authority of scripture, we can only say that something in scripture has authority only if it is already known to be true."[51]

This would indeed be different from Dharmakīrti, and for that matter from Āryadeva, Candrakīrti and Dharmapāla, (whose views I maintain are similar to Dignāga and Dharmakīrti). It seems to me, however, that the Sanskrit passage of Dignāga on which Hayes may very well have based his remarks does not support this interpretation. The Sanskrit of PS II, k. 5ab reads:

---

[50] Ibid. p. 310.

[51] Ibid. p. 239. Compare also Hayes' (p. 253) explanation of why Dignāga did not accept verbal testimony (*śābda*) as a means of knowledge (*pramāṇa*) for supra-sensible matters:

"First, some things mentioned in scripture, such as heaven and primordial matter (*prakṛti*), are utterly unknowable; belief in them is not knowledge at all, but only unjustified belief. Of these things it is inappropriate to speak of a means of acquiring knowledge (*pramāṇa*). Second, some things mentioned in scripture are knowable, but our knowledge of them turns out to be justifiable by ordinary sense experience or inferences that rest in the final analysis on sense experiences."

āptavākyāvisaṃvādasāmānyād anumānatā[52]

Hayes translates (the italics are my doing):

> "The statements of credible persons are inference *insofar* as they have the common character of not being false."[53]

My translation:

> *Because* authoritative words are similar in not belying, they are [classified as] inference.[54]

The problem is that one cannot translate the ablative *°sāmānyād* as "insofar". It is giving a reason for authoritative speech being classified as inference; it is not saying that such speech is inference *provided, or to the degree that*, it is not *visaṃvāda* ("false"; "belying"), a sense which would have been better expressed by a *yāvat ... tāvat* construction. Note also that PS and PSV, in Tibetan translation, are unambiguous about taking the ablative (*...mtshuṅs pa'i phyir*) as "because" or "therefore" (as Hayes

---

52 Skt. in Randle (1926) p. 17; PVSV ed. Gnoli p. 108,1.

53 Hayes (1988) p. 238.

54 Cf. Tillemans (1986a), p. 32. Note that in the discussion which follows I understand *āptavacana* / *yid ches pa'i tshig* as the words of an authoritative person, although for brevity I speak of "authoritative words". The interpretation fits the Sanskrit *āpta* (cf. M. Monier-Williams, *Sanskrit-English Dictionary* p. 136: "a fit person; a credible or authoritative person") better than the Tibetan *yid ches pa*, which clearly puts the accent on trustworthiness. Cf. Monier-Williams ibid. s.v. *āptavacana*. The translation of *visaṃvādin* / *visaṃvāda* by "belie" is that of Eli Franco. For *avisaṃvādin*, I occasionally use a neologism, "non-belying", instead of the longer "... does not belie". Cf. *The Concise Oxford Dictionary* s.v. belie: "Give false notion of; fail to fulfil (promise etc.); fail to justify (hope etc.); fail to corroborate." Note that this translation, which has the distinct advantage of capturing the etymological sense, could be understood as also expressing the positive quality of *reliability*. Dharmottara's gloss on *avisaṃvādakatva* in his *Pramāṇaviniścayaṭīkā* brings out the sense of "not failing to fulfil a promise" or "reliability": *ji ltar 'jig rten na khas blaṅs pa'i don daṅ phrad par byed pa mi slu ba yin pa de bźin du śes pa yaṅ bstan pa'i don daṅ phrad par byed pas mi slu bar blta bar bya'o // de'i don ni 'di yin te / dṅos po 'dzin par byed pas ni yaṅ dag pa'i śes pa ñid ma yin gyi 'on kyaṅ dṅos po thob par byed pa ñid yin no //*. Text and translation in Steinkellner and Krasser (1989) p. 26 and 75: "Ebenso, wie in Alltag einer, der eine (von ihm) versprochene Sache erreichen lässt, ein Verlässlicher (*saṃvādakaḥ*) ist, ist auch eine Erkenntnis, sofern sie die (von ihr) gezeigte Sache erreichen lässt, als verlässlich (*saṃvādakam*) anzusehen. Der Sinn dieser (Formulierung im PVin) ist folgender: Nicht dadurch, dass das Ding erfasst wird, hat [eine Erkenntnis] den Charakter einer richtigen Erkenntnis, sondern das zum Erreichen des Dinges Führen [ist dieser Charakter einer richtigen Erkenntnis]." This dimension of "reliability" or even "infallibility" in *avisaṃvādakatva* would be insisted upon by certain Tibetan philosophers, who would argue that it is possible to have a simply correct cognition which is nonetheless not *avisaṃvādin*: this is the case of *yid dpyod* ("true presumption"), which is not *avisaṃvādin*; it just happens to be correct, but cannot elicit sufficient certainty to dispel erroneous opinions. See fn. 86.

himself implicitly recognized in translating the PSV passage by "because..."). PSV(a) 29b7:

> *yid ches pa'i tshig gzuṅ nas kyaṅ mi slu bar mtshuṅs pa'i phyir de yaṅ rjes su dpag pa ñid du brjod do* /. My translation: "When one apprehends authoritative words, they are similar in not belying, and therefore, they too are said to be inference."

If we translate PS without surreptitiously changing the ablative into a *yāvat ... tāvat* construction, much of the textual basis for Hayes' commentary on k. 5 may go by the board and with it Dignāga's supposed skepticism about scriptural authority. However, there is one other point on which Hayes places store: the fact that, according to PSV, some scriptures speak of "heaven" or *prakṛti* / *pradhāna* (the "Primordial Nature" in Sāṃkhya philosophy) and other such imperceptible and unknowable things.[55]

> "...[S]tatements the truth of which cannot be ascertained through sensation or reasoning are statements the truth of which cannot be ascertained at all. In *Pramāṇasamuccaya* 2:5ab and his own commentary on it, for example, Diṅnāga cites the Sāṃkhya doctrine that all mental and physical phenomena are transformations of a primordial substance (*pradhāna*) as a doctrine the truth of which is unknowable. Presumably his reason for declaring primordial substance unknowable is that such a substance is in principle impossible to experience in its primordial form, but one can never in Diṅnāga's view infer the general form of anything if one has not previously experienced a particular instance of it. Thus in general Diṅnāga's view of those religious, moral and metaphysical doctrines that can neither be established nor repudiated by direct experience or reasoning would most likely be that it is a mistake to say that *knowledge* of them can be acquired only through scriptures."[56]

It should be fairly obvious that this view would lead to skepticism about scriptural authority, but once again, I would understand Dignāga somewhat differently.

First of all, Hayes lumps Dignāga's talk about "heaven" and *prakṛti* together as giving examples of unknowable entities on which Dignāga remains agnostic. I doubt that they do belong together: Dignāga accepted the heavens as things which were unknowable by sense perception or ordinary inference but which could be known by scripture; *prakṛti*, on the other hand, is an example of something which does not exist, and where the scriptures describing it are bogus.

Let me try to give an alternative explanation of PSV ad k. 5ab. (Texts and translations of the key passages of PSV and PST are to be found in Appendix I.)

---

55 See Appendix I pp. 71, 72, 73 for the "heavens".

56 Hayes (1988) p. 180. Cf. Kitagawa (1973) p. 93 who takes k. 5 as showing Dignāga's "pragmatism" (*jitsuyō shugi*).

1) The general underlying principle in Dignāga is that the object of inferences is not a real particular, or *svalakṣaṇa*, but that, nonetheless, via these mentally created objects we do gain knowledge about *svalakṣaṇa*.

2) In the immediately preceding passage to k. 5, Dignāga had made a distinction between two types of inference, depending upon whether the object is empirical or non-empirical, arguing that in the former case we can apply names to what is empirical, but in the latter case we only have a concept (*rnam par rtog pa = vikalpa*) and do not cognize the *svalakṣaṇa* object.[57]

3) An opponent then tries to find an absurdity, saying that in that case authoritative statements about imperceptible objects would just express the conceptually invented object and not the real particular at all: hence there would be no difference between authoritative and unauthoritative statements.

4) Dignāga then replies that authoritative statements about heaven and the like do not express *just* the conceptually invented object: they are similar to normal inference because they too are non-belying with regard to the real particular. For, although the heavens and so forth are beyond our sense range, authoritative people have directly seen them and hence were able to apply the words "heaven", etc. Dignāga then says, "This position refutes inferences with regard to natures such as *pradhāna* and so forth." In other words, the word "*pradhāna*" has never been applied by an authoritative person to a real particular.

5) His conclusion from all this is to restate his general view, now safe from attack: "therefore, the object of inference is not a *svalakṣaṇa*."

It should be clear that this interpretation of Dignāga differs from that of Hayes and does not support the view that Dignāga was essentially agnostic on scripturally-known matters. At least on the question of scriptural authority I see no reason to make a split between Dignāga, on the one hand, and Dharmakīrti, the perverter of Dignāga's thought, on the other, but then, in general, I confess that I am very reluctant to accept R. Herzberger's account of the supposed "differences" in their philosophy of language and *apoha* too. But *that* is something which (apart from a few remarks in Appendix I) will basically have to be put on hold for the present. At any rate, there seems to me little reason to question *across the board* the whole legitimacy of speaking of the Buddhist Epistemologists as being a unified school thought; and if that is so, then circumspectly using Dharmakīrti's, Dignāga's and Dharmapāla's works to explain each others' thought must be unobjectionable.

---

57 PSV(a) P 29b5-6: *sgra yaṅ yul thun moṅ ma yin pa daṅ 'brel pa'i yod pa ma yin pas rnam pa gñis ka rjes su dpag par brtag par bya ste / mthoṅ ba'i don ma mthoṅ ba'i don no // de la mthoṅ ba'i don la miṅ bstan pa'o* / ma mthoṅ ba'i don la ni rnam par rtog pa tsam 'ba' źig ste / don gyi bye brag rtogs par byed pa ni ma yin no* /* I follow PSV(b) and PST here. PSV(a) reads: *de la mthoṅ ba'i don mi gsal bar byed pa'o.*

II. THE PROBLEM OF SCRIPTURAL AUTHORITY

Having thus attempted to define a stance on these methodological preliminaries, let me now turn to what I maintain became the predominant Buddhist interpretation in the problem of appeals to authority, namely, an approach which we find in Āryadeva's *Catuḥśataka* XII and its commentators and which, according to some insightful remarks of Tsoṅ kha pa, is precisely the same thought developed in the Epistemological school of Dignāga and Dharmakīrti. The approach is of some philosophical interest in that it seeks to resolve the inevitable tension between scripture[58] and reason in a way which permits certain "propositions of faith", but nonetheless retains a rationalistic orientation and extreme parsimony with regard to acceptable means of knowledge. At the end of this chapter we shall attempt a brief analysis as to how far it succeeds, but first the details.[59]

---

[58] In what follows the difference between *āgama* ("scriptures") and *śāstra* ("treatises") is of no consequence. Also, as Dharmakīrti argues in PV IV k. 93-107 (Sāṅkṛtyāyana's heading: *āgamasvavacanayos tulyabalatā*), there is no essential difference in the force or trustworthiness of one's own words and those of scripture. The same evaluative procedures apply to both.

[59] The general problem of the soteriology of the Epistemological school is treated in numerous publications, notably Steinkellner (1982), and Vetter (1964), (1984). Particularly important is the opening verse of PS and PV II's comment on this verse. See Nagatomi (1959), Hattori (1968a) p. 23 et seq. and 74 et seq., Inami and Tillemans (1986), Franco (1989) pp. 82-84. Worthwhile pursuing in this connection is Franco's suggestion (p. 84 and n. 8) that the key term in this verse, viz. *pramāṇabhūta*, finds parallels in the *Mahābhāṣya*, where Pāṇini is so called. On Dharmakīrti's and the early Naiyāyika's view of scriptural authority, cf. the recently published book of V.A. van Bijlert (1989), pp. 16-19, 30-34, 80-82 and 122-125.

An earlier version of this chapter appeared in an article in *Tetsugaku*, the *Journal of Hiroshima University's Philosophical Society*. See Tillemans (1986a): "Dharmakīrti, Āryadeva and Dharmapāla on Scriptural Authority". In that article as well as in the present chapter, I, like most writers on these subjects, deliberately treat the problem of authority from a theoretical and philosophical point of view. I am, however, aware that the problem is not *just* theoretical, but has important sociological and political dimensions as well. Indeed, as may even be implicit in both Candrakīrti's commentary on CS XII, k. 294 (see §64) and Dharmapāla's commentary to CS XII, k. 280, one of the motivations for trying to prove that a teacher was trustworthy on matters beyond the range of the senses was to defuse opponents' criticisms about the impropriety of his behaviour or the questionable behaviour of certain monks. The dark side of it all is that the Buddhist's theoretical argumentation about *atyantaparokṣa* was probably fairly frequently misused to rationalize power-politics and

A. The Epistemological school's position

As discussed in the previous chapter, the key elements in the Epistemologists' position are to be found in *kārikā* 5 of the *Svārthānumāna* chapter in Dignāga's *Pramāṇasamuccaya* and *Pramāṇasamuccayavṛtti*. They were subsequently given a sophisticated development by Dharmakīrti in the *Svārthānumāna* and *Parārthānumāna* chapters of *Pramāṇavārttika* (i.e. PV I and PV IV respectively).

Pramāṇasamuccaya II (*Svārthānumāna*) k. 5a:
"Because authoritative words (*āptavāda*) are similar in not belying, they are [classified as] inference."[60]

Pramāṇasamuccayaṭīkā to PS II k. 5a:
"Authoritative words which concern completely imperceptible things (*śin tu lkog tu gyur pa'i yul can = atyantaparokṣaviṣayin*) are similar in being non-belying to the other authoritative words which concern states of affairs seen by direct perception and inference. Therefore, they are [classified as] inferences. Such is the meaning of [Dignāga's] statement."[61]

Pramāṇavārttika I (*Svārthānumāna*) k. 215, 216, 217:
"A [treatise's[62]] being non-belying [means that] there is no invalidation of its two [kinds of] propositions concerning empirical and unempirical things by direct perception or by the two sorts of inference [viz. inference which functions by the force of reality (*vastubalapravṛtta*) and inference which is based on scripture (*āgamāśrita*)[63]]." **(k.215)**[64]

---

corruption by saying that such-and-such things are too subtle for us to understand or criticize. Certainly amongst Tibetans the Tantric precept that the one should transform all "apparent" faults of the master into virtues because his purposes are too subtle for us to perceive was and still is being widely abused.

[60] See the previous chapter p. 22 for Sanskrit text and Appendix I, §*a* and §*b* for PSV.

[61] PST P. 104a5-6: *yid ches pa'i tshig śin tu lkog tu gyur pa'i yul can ni cig śos mṅon sum daṅ rjes su dpag pas mthoṅ ba'i don gyi yul can gyi yid ches pa'i tshig daṅ mi bslu bar mtshuṅs pa ñid kyi phyir rjes su dpag pa ñid do źes pa ṅag gi don no* /.

[62] Cf. PVSV-ṭīkā: 392,15: *asya śāstrasyāvisaṃvādaḥ*.

[63] PVSV-ṭīkā: 392,14-15: ...*anumānena ca dvividhena vastubalapravṛttenāgamāśritena ca* ... Cf. also PVV ad k. 215.

[64] *pratyakṣenānumānena dvividhenāpy abādhanam / dṛṣṭādṛṣṭārthayor asyāvisaṃvādas tadarthayoḥ* //. Van Bijlert (1989) p. 123 seems to have gotten this wrong, which adversely affects the clarity of his exposé. He translates: "The trustworthiness of this [useful sentence] about visible and invisible things which are [i.e. can

"As authoritative words are similar in not belying, the understanding of their imperceptible (*parokṣa*) object is also termed an inference, for [otherwise] there would be no way [to know such objects[65]]." **(k.216)**[66]

"Or, they do not belie with regard to the principal point [viz. the four noble truths[67]], for the nature of what is to be rejected and what is to be realized as well as the method is acknowledged. Therefore [the understanding arising from the Buddha's words can properly] be an inference in the case of the other things [too, i.e. completely imperceptible (*atyantaparokṣa*) objects[68]]." **(k.217)**[69]

Now, first of all, the usual types of inferences which we associate with Dignāga and Dharmakīrti, such as those of sound's impermanence and the like, are said to be *vastubalapravṛttānumāna* in that they derive their truth from the fact that the reason, being a product (*kṛtakatva*), is in reality, or objectively, related with the property, impermanence, and qualifies the subject sound. However, an important point which needs to be clear is that in spite of the numerous passages in which these authors talk about one state of affairs proving another, or, in the case of Dharmakīrti, about essential connections (*svabhāvapratibandha*) between the terms in an inference, it is not so that every inference functions by the force of reality (*vastubalapravṛtta*).[70] *Vastubalapravṛtta* is certainly an unbending requirement for the normal or "straightforward" type

be] objects of the [two *pramāṇas*, perception and inference], consists in the fact that [the information contained in such a sentence] is neither contradicted by perception nor by twofold inference." In fact, *tadarthayoḥ* and *dṛṣṭādṛṣṭārthayor* are not to be connected with *avisaṃvāda*, but rather with *abādhanam*, as we see in PVV and very clearly in PV Tib: *mthoṅ daṅ ma mthoṅ dṅos po yi // don de dag la mṅon sum daṅ // rjes su dpag rnam gñis kyis kyaṅ // gnod med 'di yi mi slu ba'o //*. See n. 75 for dGe 'dun grub pa's *Tshad ma rnam 'grel legs par bśad pa*, which shows the Tibetan's understanding of the syntax of k. 215.

65 Vibhūticandra comments on PVV's (p. 365) phrase *agatyānumānatoktā: ato 'nyathā parokṣe pravṛttyasaṃbhavāt.*

66 *āptavādāvisaṃvādasāmānyād anumānatā / buddher agatyābhihitā parokṣe 'py* asya gocare //.* *PVV reads *niṣiddhapy.* But cf. Tib. *lkog gyur na'aṅ* = *parokṣe 'py.*

67 Cf. PVSV 109,15-16: *heyopādeyatadupāyānāṃ tadupadiṣṭānām avaiparītyam avisaṃvādaḥ / yathā caturṇām āryasatyānāṃ vakṣyamāṇanītyā* /...* * PVSV-ṭīkā reads *vakṣyamāṇayā nītyā.*

68 Cf. PVV ad k. 217: *paratrātyantaparokṣe 'py arthe bhagavadvacanād utpannaṃ jñānam anumānaṃ yuktam iti vā pakṣāntaram /.*

69 *heyopādeyatattvasya sopāyasya prasiddhitaḥ / pradhānārthāvisaṃvādād anumānaṃ paratra vā //.*

70 Cf. for example PV IV k. 15: *arthād arthagateḥ* , etc. See Tillemans (1987). For Dharmakīrti's development of the notion of *svabhāvapratibandha* ("essential connections"), see Katsura (1986a) pp. 96-107 and the English summaries in (1986a) pp. 121-122 and (1986b) pp. 13-14; classic sources on *svabhāvapratibandha* are to be found in passages such as PVSV ad PV I, k. 14; see Steinkellner (1971) , (1984) and Matsumoto (1981).

of inferences with which we are familiar, but, as we see in PV I k. 215, there are also inferences based on scripture, that is to say, a scriptural passage rather than a state of affairs is given as the reason. The question then easily arises as to (a) which sorts of scriptural passages can be used in such inferences, and (b) how the admittance of scriptural proofs can be harmonized with the general tenor of Dignāga and Dharmakīrti's thought, which is, no doubt, oriented towards *vastubalapravṛttānumāna*.

Let us begin with (b). The Epistemological school solves this problem by introducing three sorts of objects: perceptible (*pratyakṣa*), imperceptible (*parokṣa*) and completely imperceptible (*atyantaparokṣa*).[71] The first sort consists of those things such as form (*rūpa*), vases, etc. which are accessible to direct perception, the second being things (such as impermanence, selflessness [*nairātmya*], etc.) which can be proven through the usual *vastubala* kind of inference. The third kind, however, are objects such as the different heavens (*svarga*) or the details of the operation of the law of karma, all of which are, of course, inaccessible to direct perception, but also cannot be proven by citing some or another state of affairs as a reason: in short, we might say that they are beyond the limits of *ordinary* rationality. A slight complication which should perhaps be cleared up at this point is that Dharmakīrti often uses *parokṣa*, a term which also has an extremely important place in PS II and PV III (*Pratyakṣa*), in the sense of *atyantaparokṣa*.[72] However we see in the commentaries that what is at stake in PV I k. 216 — as well as in PS II k. 5 — is indeed *atyantaparokṣa*, and moreover, it is abundantly clear from certain passages elsewhere (in PV IV) that Dharmakīrti himself did explicitly accept this threefold division of objects.[73]

---

[71] In my (1986a) article I chose different translations, i.e. "evident", "obscure" and "extremely obscure", arguing on p. 44, n. 12 that literalness was impossible because "it is anomalous in English to make a difference between 'imperceptible', and 'extremely imperceptible': there are no degrees of imperceptibility. (Cf. the problem of translating the Tibetan term *cuṅ zad lkog gyur* by 'a little bit imperceptible'!)" This time I choose to bite the bullet, essentially because the discussion of *pratyakṣa* in the next chapter demands that I stay literal.

[72] E.g. PV I k. 216.

[73] In k. 216, its *Svavṛtti* and subsequently, Dharmakīrti does not himself use the term *atyantaparokṣa*, but his commentators Manorathanandin and Karṇakagomin do. (Cf. PVV and PVSV-ṭīkā ad k. 216) However, it is clear from passages such as PV IV k. 51 (*tṛtīyasthānasaṃkrāntau nyāyyaḥ śāstraparigrahaḥ*) that Dharmakīrti does accept the threefold classification. *Tṛtīyasthāna* refers to *atyantaparokṣa*. Cf. also k. 50 where Dharmakīrti speaks of the first two sorts of objects: *tathā viśuddhe viṣayadvaye śāstraparigraham / cikīrṣoḥ sa hi kālaḥ syāt tadā śāstreṇa bādhanam //*. PVV ad k. 50: *śāstropadarśite viṣayadvaye pratyakṣaparokṣe rūpanairātmyādau tadā pramāṇapravṛttyā viśuddhe nirṇīte sati paścād atyantaparokṣe svargādau śāstreṇa śāstrāśrayeṇānumānaṃ cikīrṣoḥ sataḥ sa hi kālo 'bhyupagamasya* yadi śāstrabādho na bhavet /*. "Suppose that the two [types of] objects taught in a treatise -viz. perceptible and imperceptible [objects], such as form and selflessness, etc.- are ascertained by *pramāṇas* as faultless. Then subsequently, when one wishes to make an inference concerning completely imperceptible [objects] such as heaven, etc. by means of a treatise, i.e. by recourse to a treatise, then if the treatise is not invalidated, this would indeed be the occasion to accept it." *Sāṅkṛtyāyana: *abhyupagamya*. Cf.PVBh 505,4: *sa hi kālaḥ syād abhyupagamasya*. Finally note that in the usual Dharmakīrtian interpretation of PS II k. 5a and PSV by Jinendrabuddhi, we find the term *śin tu lkog gyur* =

So what Dharmakīrti and Dignāga do is to limit the scope of scripturally based inferences to cases where the object is *atyantaparokṣa*, and hence beyond the range of ordinary ratiocination. By means of this strict delimitation, the theory that ordinary inference must be objectively grounded can be preserved, for this will be a requirement of logical reasoning which applies to the first two kinds of objects, viz. *pratyakṣa* and *parokṣa*. The Epistemologist can also at the same time distance himself from the non-Buddhist schools' use of scripture: in effect the error which a Mīmāṃsaka or Sāṃkhya makes in citing scriptural passages as a means of proof (*sādhana*) is that they apply scriptural arguments to propositions, such as sound's impermanence, etc., which can and should be decided by *vastubalapravṛttānumāna*, and which are not at all outside the bounds of ordinary ratiocination.[74]

As for question (a), viz. the kinds of scriptural passages which can be used, Dharmakīrti (and Dignāga, if we read him via Jinendrabuddhi's commentary) introduces what Tibetan scholastics would come to call "the threefold analysis" (*dpyad pa gsum*) for testing as to whether particular scriptures (*luṅ* = *āgama*) are sound bases for inference.[75] Specifically, as PV I k. 215 makes clear, such a scripture must be unrefuted

---

atyantaparokṣa.

[74] Cf. e.g. PV IV k. 2 and our commentary in Tillemans (1986b).

[75] Cf. e.g. rGyal tshab rje's commentary (*rNam 'grel thar lam gsal byed*) to k. 215, Vol. I pp. 177-8, where the three criteria in k. 215 are presented as a formal reasoning (*sbyor ba* = *prayoga*): *śin tu lkog gyur ston pa'i bcom ldan 'das kyi gsuṅ chos can / raṅ gi bstan bya la mi slu ba yin te / dpyad pa gsum gyis dag pa'i luṅ yin pa'i phyir /*. ("Take as the topic the speech of the Illustrious One which describes completely imperceptible [objects]; it does not belie with regard to the [states of affairs] described, because it is a scripture which is [judged] immaculate through the three [kinds of] analyses."). Cf. dGe 'dun grub pa, *Tshad ma rnam 'grel legs par bśad pa* p. 58 on k. 215: *luṅ de btsan bya'i don la ji ltar mi slu że na / khyad par gsum ldan gyi luṅ 'di chos can / bstan bya'i don la mi slu ba yin te / dpyad gsum gyis dag pa'i luṅ yin pa'i phyir te / mthoṅ ba mṅon gyur daṅ lkog gyur la mṅon sum daṅ rjes dpag daṅ / ma mthoṅ ba śin tu lkog gyur gyi dṅos po'i don de dag la yid ches rjes dpag gis kyaṅ gnod pa med pa'i luṅ yin pa'i phyir /*. These are more or less standard versions of what in *rTags rigs* literature is categorized as a "reason based on authority" (*yid ches kyi rtags*). Interestingly enough, this literature then goes on to treat such reasons along the same lines of other types of valid reasons, classifying them in terms of effect (*kārya*), essential property (*svabhāva*) and non-perception (*anupalabdhi*). Cf. *Yoṅs 'dzin rtags rigs*, ed. Onoda p. 46. On the Tibetan interpretations see also Ruegg (1969) p. 229 n. 2 and van der Kuijp (1979) pp. 4-5.

Note that here it is not actually the words of a suitably tested scripture which prove or refute anything but rather the fact that the words pass the three tests: the reason used is *dpyad gsum gyis dag pa'i luṅ*, and it is this reason which can be said to have the necessary connection with the property to be proved. There does, however, seem to be a position which took the *prayoga* differently, citing an actual scriptural passage as the reason. Tibetan texts speak of an Indian Buddhist debate on the question as to whether the scripture itself can refute or invalidate (*gnod byed*) opposite propositions or can only create an "impediment" (*gegs byed*) to them — the debate between *luṅ gnod byed du 'dod pa'i lugs* and *luṅ gegs byed du 'dod pa'i lugs*. The former position was apparently held by some followers of Dignāga who maintained that the scripture itself could both refute and prove. See dGe 'dun grub pa's *Tshad ma rigs pa'i rgyan*, pp. 268-269: *slob dpon phyogs glaṅ gis / luṅ rnam dag raṅ lugs la brjod bya sgrub pa'i rtags yaṅ dag tu mi bżed kyaṅ / re żig gżan ṅor* brjod bya sgrub pa'i rtags yaṅ dag yin pa'i rnam gżag mdzad pa la 'khrul nas / slob dpon gyi slob ma kha cig na re*

by direct perception and by *vastubalapravṛttānumāna*, and cannot come into contradiction with other propositions whose truth is scripturally inferred. Put in this way it might seem that what is being said is simply that the scripture cannot be refuted by *any pramāṇa* or that it cannot come into conflict with any of the other three kinds of objects. However, the point at stake, as we find it elaborated in PV I k. 216, the *Svavṛtti* and Karṇakagomin's *Ṭīkā*, is more subtle and is essentially an argument by analogy: the scripture's assertions concerning perceptible (*pratyakṣa*) and imperceptible (*parokṣa*) objects do not belie, and so, *similarly*, its assertions about completely imperceptible (*atyantaparokṣa*) objects, if not internally inconsistent, should also be trustworthy. The same type of analogical argument is given an alternative formulation in the next *kārikā* when Dharmakīrti says that because the (Buddhist) scriptures do not belie concerning the principal points, viz. the four noble truths, they should also be authoritative on completely imperceptible matters. The four noble truths are accessible to proof by *vastubalapravṛttānumāna* — as we see in the second chapter of PV — and thus, as these propositions in the Buddhist scriptures are trustworthy, so the others should be too.

In short, scriptural argumentation — when applied to *atyantaparokṣa* objects, which is its only proper domain — is an inference: there is no need to postulate an additional *pramāṇa* such as the *śābda* ("testimony"), etc. of certain Hindu schools. It is,

---

*/ luṅ rnam dag de raṅ gi brjod bya sgrub pa'i rtags yaṅ dag daṅ log phyogs la gnod byed yin te / gźal bya'i gnas daṅ po gñis la dpyad pa dag nas / sbyin sogs dkar po'i chos ni tshe 'phos nas bde ba ster ba daṅ sdug bsṅal ster*** *ba la 'jug ldog bya dgos la / 'jug ldog byed pa de'i gźi tshad mas grub dgos śiṅ / luṅ las gźan pa'i sgrub byed yaṅ dag med pa'i phyir / gal te luṅ gnod byed min na gegs byed du yaṅ mi 'gyur te / gegs byas pa'i gźi tshad mas ma grub pa'i phyir ro // źes zer ro //* *Text has *dor.* **Text: *stor.* "Although the Master, Dignāga, did not hold that immaculate scriptures, in our own tradition, are valid reasons for establishing their content, still a disciple of the Master once went astray on the position that [scriptural passages] are valid reasons for establishing their content to the opponent and argued as follows: 'An immaculate [passage of] scripture is a valid reason for establishing its content and does invalidate the opposite [of what it says]. This is so because after the analyses of the first and second sort of *prameya*, one then must affirm and negate [the respective propositions] that giving, etc. will bring happiness or will bring suffering in subsequent lives — the basis for these affirmations and negations must be established by means of a *pramāṇa*, and [yet] apart from scripture there is no other valid *sādhana*. If scripture were not something which invalidates then it would not create an impediment either, for the basis for being an impediment would not be established by a *pramāṇa*."

As dGe 'dun grub pa makes clear further on, an advocate of this position would give a quite different type of *prayoga* to prove imperceptible state of affairs. He would say (ibid. p. 271): *sbyin sogs chos can / spyad pa las bde ba 'byuṅ ba ste / spyad pa las bde ba 'byuṅ bar luṅ las gsuṅs pa'i phyir /.* "Take as the subject giving, etc.; happiness arises from their practice, because it is said in scripture that happiness arises from their practice." Dharmakīrti's own position on the actual formulation of the *prayoga* is not clear. In PV IV 98-100 his main point seems to be that words themselves can at most conflict or "impede" each other when there is no *pramāṇa*. There is no doubt that he does himself say in PV IV k. 95 that Dignāga thought that a treatise can an invalidator (*bādhaka*), but this does not necessarily mean that he would be partial to the second sort of *prayoga*.

Georges Dreyfus, in a chapter of his Ph.D thesis (U. of Virginia), will give an in depth account of the *luṅ gnod byed / luṅ gegs byed* debate in Indo-Tibetan Buddhism, with explanations of the respective positions of gSer mdog paṇ chen Śākya mchog ldan (i.e. *luṅ gnod byed)* and mKhas grub rje (*luṅ gegs byed*).

however, a rather special, indirect case in that it turns on an analogy which presupposes the use and correctness of direct perception and *vastubalapravṛttānumāna*.

B. Āryadeva, Dharmapāla and Candrakīrti

A remarkable point in this connection is that the Tibetan writer Tsoṅ kha pa blo bzaṅ grags pa (1357-1419) in his *Tshad ma'i brjed byaṅ chen mo* and *sṄags rim chen mo* noticed that Dharmakīrti's PV I k. 217cd resembles k. 280 in chapter XII of Āryadeva's *Catuḥśataka* (i.e. 'CS").[76] Tsoṅ kha pa was followed in this by rGyal tshab Dar ma rin chen (1364-1432), who also remarked that CS k. 280 was the same reasoning as found in Dignāga and Dharmakīrti (*phyogs glaṅ yab sras*); subsequently, the Mongolian, A lag śa Ṅag dbaṅ bstan dar (1759-1840)[77], in his *sTon pa tshad ma'i skyes bur sgrub pa'i gtam*, elaborated on the two verses, paraphrasing them into an identical formal reasoning (*prayoga*), and citing them in his proof that the Buddha is a "person of authority" (*tshad ma'i skyes bu*).[78] This latter author obviously follows Tsoṅ kha pa's thought, but — what is less obvious in Tsoṅ kha pa — Ṅag dbaṅ bstan dar markedly relies on Candrakīrti's commentary to CS k. 280 where the correctness of the Buddha's teaching on voidness is said to be an example (*dṛṣṭānta*) on the basis of which we can infer correctness in otherwise rationally inaccessible imperceptible matters, an argument which we saw was also implicit in PV IV k. 216-217.[79]

---

[76] See *Tshad ma'i brjed byaṅ chen mo* pp. 158-159 where Tsoṅ kha pa cites these two verses together and says that they show the same way (*tshul mtshuṅs pa*) to prove completely imperceptible states of affairs. For a similar discussion on these two verses, see *sṄags rim chen mo*, pp. 7, line 3 - 9, line 5 (ff. 4a-5a), transl. Hopkins (1977), pp. 88-90.

[77] Dates given by the Mongolian scholar, T. Damdinsüren.

[78] For rGyal tshab, see his *bŹi brgya pa'i rnam bśad*, p. 5: *spyi'i rnam gźag ni phyogs glaṅ yab sras kyis bśad pa daṅ / śiṅ rta chen po rnams 'dra bar yod do /*. Cf. also *rNam 'grel thar lam gsal byed*, Vol. I p. 179. For *tshad ma'i skyes bu*, see Steinkellner (1983) and the references therein. Cf. also M. Inami and T. Tillemans (1986) p. 128 and n. 12 for the triple division of *tshad ma* (= *pramāṇa*) into *śes pa* ("consciousness), *ṅag* ("speech") and *skyes bu* ("person").

[79] See *Tshad ma'i skyes bur sgrub pa'i gtam*, pp. 43-44: *de luṅ gis ci ltar sgrub ce na / saṅs rgyas kyis gtso bo'i don ṅes legs ji ltar gsuṅs pa ltar du mi bslu bar dṅos stobs rigs pas bsgrubs nas de mthun dper byas te phal ba'i don mṅon mtho gsuṅs pa la'aṅ mi bslu bar sgrub par byed pa yin pas / de yaṅ sbyin pa las loṅs spyod daṅ tshul khrims las bde ba 'byuṅ bar gsuṅs pa'i saṅs rgyas kyi gsuṅ chos can / raṅ gi bstan bya'i don la mi bslu ste / dpyad pa gsum gyis dag pa'i luṅ yin pa'i phyir / dper na saṅs rgyas kyis gaṅ zag gi bdag 'dzin zad pa'i ṅes legs ji skad gsuṅs pa ltar mi bslu ba bźin źes pa'i tshul gyis sgrub par byed pa'am / yaṅ na brjod bya gtso bo ṅes legs tshad mas grub nas / de daṅ rtsom pa po gcig yin pa'i rtags kyis brjod bya phal ba mṅon mtho ston pa la'aṅ mi bslu bar sgrub par byed de / gtso bo'i don gsuṅs pa la mi bslu ba'i tshad ma'i skyes bu phal ba'i don gsuṅs pa la bslu mi rigs pa'i phyir /* ***raṅ don le'u*** *las /*

blaṅ daṅ dor bya'i de ñid ni //

While it seems impossible to definitively establish lines of transmission here, it is not at all unlikely that Dharmakīrti was aware of Āryadeva's thought, and made use of certain elements via the commentary of Dharmapāla, a hypothesis which becomes even more seductive if we accept Tāranātha's account that Dharmapāla was a guru of Dharmakīrti.[80] The details of the external history will, no doubt, elude us, but the internal historian's approach of finding a common program between the Epistemologists and the Mādhyamikas is certainly insightful. However, are we to say that the Tibetans had a "flash of genius" (to use E. Steinkellner's term) in intellectually putting together two otherwise separate traditions, as they did with their notion of *tshad ma'i skyes bu*, combining the path-theory of the *Bodhipathapradīpa* with the *pramāṇa* tradition?[81] What seems more likely to me is that the members of the sixth and seventh century Epistemological and Madhyamaka schools were in fact very familiar with and referred to each other's works on these questions. Let us look at k. 280 with Dharmapāla's commentary.

After Dharmapāla has argued that the doctrines of the non-Buddhist Outsiders (*wài dào* 外道) contain various faults and untruths, the Outsider then objects:

---

thabs bcas rab tu ṅes pa yis //
gtso bo'i don la mi bslu'i phyir //
gźan la rjes su dpag pa yin // ***[PV I k. 217]***
źes daṅ / ***bźi brgya pa*** *las kyaṅ /*
saṅs rgyas kyis gsuṅs lkog gyur la //
gaṅ źig the tshom skye 'gyur ba //
de yi(s) stoṅ pa ñid bsten te //
'di ñid kho nar yid ches bya // ***[CS XII, k. 280]***
źes gsuṅs pa bźin no //.

Translation:

"How is the [Buddha's account of the cause of superior rebirths] proven by means of scripture? Having first proven by reasonings [functioning] through the force of reality (*vastubala*) that the principal matter, viz. what is supremely excellent [such as liberation, and enlightenment], is non-belying as the Buddha explained it, one takes this as a homologous example (*sādharmyadṛṣṭānta*) and proves that the explanation of the secondary meaning, i.e. superior rebirths, is also non-belying. Thus, taking as the subject [of the argument] the Buddha's statements asserting that wealth arises from giving and happiness from moral discipline, [these statements] are non-belying with regard to their expressed meaning, because they are scriptural citations which are [judged] immaculate through the three types of analysis, just as Buddha's explanation of the supreme excellence consisting in the elimination of grasping at the self is non-belying. In such a way is [the Buddha's account of superior rebirths] proven [by scripture.] Alternatively, when the principal explicandum, i.e. supreme excellence, has been proven by a *pramāṇa*, then using the reason that the author is the same, one proves that the teaching on the secondary subject, viz. superior rebirths, is also non-belying. For, it is logical that a person of authority who is non-belying in explaining the principal matters should be non-belying in explaining secondary matters. [The author then cites PV I, k. 217 and CS XII, k. 280]"

[80] See fn. 26. Other arguments in Dharmapāla seem to be taken up in Dharmakīrti too. See en. 44 . Furthermore, there is no doubt as to Dharmapāla's proximity to the Epistemological school.

[81] See Steinkellner (1983) p. 281.

"**(216c3)** [Objection:] In that case, the noble teaching in the Tripiṭaka of the Tathāgata [also] sometimes has statements which are scarcely believable, and so all the Insiders' and the Outsiders' texts would be untrustworthy; thus a gross absurdity (*tài guò shī* 太過失 = *atiprasaṅga*) would ensue. How so? [Because] in the Buddha's sūtras are mentioned various miraculous transformations (*shén biàn* 神變 = *vikurvaṇa; ṛddhi*) which are unimaginable. Or [these sūtras] speak about states of affairs which are extremely profound (*shèn shēn* 甚深 = *atyantaparokṣa(?)*) truths (*zhēn shí* 眞實 = *tattva*); no sentient beings fathom [these things]. [...]

(216c20) [Reply:] Phenomena, if they merely existed, could indeed give rise to [such types of] doubts. But phenomena are also void. Hence [Āryadeva] states in the following verse:

When someone entertains doubt concerning the profound (shēn 深 *= parokṣa; Tib. lkog gyur) things taught by the Buddha, then he can rely on the voidness which is free of all [defining] characters, and [can thus] gain sure faith.* **(k.280)**[82]

The point is that the correctness of the Buddha's teaching on voidness, which is accessible to ordinary inferential understanding, should lead one to believe that his teachings on matters inaccessible to such inferences are also correct. It is interesting to note that the Sanskrit of Āryadeva's verse employs the term *parokṣa*, which is translated into Chinese as *shēn* 深 "profound". In Dharmapāla's commentary we see him using the term *shèn shēn* 甚深 in this context, which might thus seem to be the equivalent here of *atyantaparokṣa*, although such an equivalent is not to my knowledge attested elsewhere and usually *shèn shēn* (and *shēn* 深 alone) translate *gambhīra*. At any rate, whether the equivalence is *gambhīra* or *atyantaparokṣa* is not of very great importance: it is clear that the *use* of *parokṣa* / *shēn* at stake in Āryadeva and Dharmapāla, just as in Dharmakīrti's k. 216 and Jinendrabuddhi's comment on PS II k. 5, does refer to propositions inaccessible to direct perception and ordinary inference.

The similarities between Dharmakīrti and Dharmapāla's approaches become even more striking when we look at the argumentation in the subsequent *kārikā* in the *Catuḥśataka* and Dharmapāla's commentary. Āryadeva gives a kind of contraposed version of the reasoning in CS k. 280, arguing that because the Outsiders are mistaken on objects which are accessible to inference, then they must also be mistaken on those which are not. Dharmapāla, at this point, launches into a long refutation of the Vaiśe-

---

82 Transl. according to the Chinese. Cf. the Skt. *buddhokteṣu parokṣeṣu jāyate yasya saṃśayaḥ / ihaiva pratyayas tena kartavyaḥ śūnyatāṃ prati.*

"When someone entertains doubt concerning the imperceptible [things] (*parokṣa*) taught by the Buddha, he should develop conviction in these very things on account of voidness (*śūnyatā*)".

Note that the Tibetan interprets *śūnyatāṃ prati* as "on the basis of voidness" or "relying on voidness": *de yis stoṅ pa ñid brten te // 'di ñid kho nar yid ches bya //.*

ṣika's metaphysical categories (*padārtha*) and the Sāṃkhya's theory of the Primordial Nature (*prakṛti*) and the three qualities (*guṇa*) to show that the Outsiders are indeed hopelessly mistaken in their accounts of rationally analyzable objects, and hence cannot be trusted in their accounts of what is unanalyzable and is essentially more difficult to comprehend. Not only is this completely consonant with Dharmakīrti's approach in PV I k. 215-16, but conspicuously, Dharmakīrti in the *Svavṛtti* to k. 215 explicitly mentions the three qualities and the Vaiśeṣika categories of substance, motion, universals, etc. as being prime examples of refutable objects.

C. Some final remarks on appeals to authority

It may be thought that in fact this Buddhist position, which is common to both the Madhyamaka and Epistemological schools, is not novel at all, but is already found in earlier Nyāya thought. It is true that elements of this approach to scriptural authority are no doubt also present in Nyāya-Vaiśeṣika, notably, the fact that a scripture's trustworthiness depends upon evaluative tests rather than on the eternalness of the words (as Mīmāṃsakas and Vaiyākaraṇas maintain)[83], and that accuracy in one area leads one to infer accuracy in others. Gautama and Vātsyāyana, for example, appeal to the observed trustworthiness of the Vedas on medicine (*āyurveda*) and spells (*mantra*): the authors of these texts are trustworthy in empirical matters in that we see that they have altruistic motivation and describe phenomena accurately; hence their words are trustworthy in all other matters too, empirical or not.[84]

Dharmakīrti, in PV IV's commentary on Dignāga's definition of the thesis (*pakṣa*), however, adds many more details to the Nyāya position from what we find in the *Nyāyabhāṣya*'s explanation of NS 2.1.69, with the result that the contrast between the Buddhist's orientation and the position of Nyāya-Vaiśeṣika is better brought out. The essential difference is that the Buddhist restricts scripture to only *atyantaparokṣa* phenomena, with the result that for all other types of phenomena he remains critical and does not accept any appeals to authority whatsoever; if we believe Dharmakīrti's characterization of the Naiyāyika, the latter fails to make this delimitation, thus mixing the domains of reason and dogma. And indeed this is not an unfair

---

[83] For Dharmapāla's criticisms of the Mīmāṃsakas see his commentary to CS XII, k. 294 and en. 124; for further criticisms of the Mīmāṃsakas and Grammarians (*vaiyākaraṇa*), see his commentary to CS XIII, k. 306cd. For Dharmakīrti, see PV I k. 213ff. See NS-bhāṣya to NS 2.1.69 for Vātsyāyana's arguments against the thesis that words are permanent and therefore trustworthy.

[84] Cf. NS 2.1.69: *mantrāyurvedaprāmāṇyavac ca tatprāmāṇyam āptaprāmānyāt* / NS-bhāṣya (p. 224): ... *evam āptopadeśaḥ pramāṇam / evam āptāḥ pramāṇam / dṛṣṭārthenāptopadeśenāyurvedenādṛṣṭārtho vedabhāgo 'numātavyaḥ pramāṇam iti / āptaprāmāṇyasya hetoḥ samānatvād iti* /. See the discussion in van Bijlert (1989) pp. 30-34 on Vātsyāyana (= Pakṣilasvāmin); ibid pp. 16-19 on the Naiyāyika *pramāṇa*, "testimony" (*śabda*), i.e. "the teaching of an authority" (*āptopadeśa*).

characterization: it is so that *Nyāyasūtra* 1.1.7 defines the *pramāṇa*, testimony (*śabda*) as the "teaching of an authority" (*āptopadeśa*) and then proceeds to say in 1.1.8 that it is of two sorts according to whether the object is empirical or not (*sa dvividho dṛṣṭādṛṣṭārthatvāt*) — scriptural statements are to be seen as specific cases of *śabda*.

Some representative elements of the discussion in PV IV where we see clearly that the general direction of Dharmakīrti's position (contrary to that of the Naiyāyika) is to eliminate the role of scripture in anything but *atyantaparokṣa* matters:

a) A treatise might ascribe various qualities to an entity, but it is only that quality intended by the proponent himself which is the proposition under discussion when he presents a reasoning. PV IV k. 42-47. The Nyāya-Vaiśeṣika, however, maintains that any and all properties put forth in his treatise are also under discussion; thus, when one argues about the thesis of sound's impermanence, one also must be arguing about sound's being a quality of space (*ākāśaguṇa*) because that is the way sound is characterized in the Nyāya-Vaiśeṣika treatises. Dharmakīrti rejects this completely: what one's own school's scriptures hold is simply irrelevant to the discussion.

b) PV IV 48-59. Dharmakīrti maintains that inferences which function due to the force of reality (*vastubalapravṛtta*) do not depend in any way on treatises. Naiyāyika: But if the proponent does not accept scriptural propositions, there would be no debate. Dharmakīrti: No, inferences are not engaged in because one accepts treatises; rather, they are themselves the *method* for deciding whether a treatise is valid or not. In short, Dharmakīrti wishes to avoid the circularity of relying on a treatise to examine whether that treatise should be accepted or not, and this he does by banishing all references to treatises from ordinary inference about rational matters.

c) PV IV k. 98-99. Scripture is no more authoritative in itself than one's own words. Unsubstantiated propositions, be they scriptural or otherwise, can only clash, but one does not refute the other. Thus, in the absence of a deciding *pramāṇa*, even if what one says is in contradiction with one's own scripture, this does not constitute a refutation. It is only when one proposition has a *pramāṇa* supporting it that it can refute the other.

Of course, Naiyāyika and Buddhist alike do accept some link between trustworthiness in one area and trustworthiness in another, but that is a relatively superficial and imprecise similarity. The Naiyāyika is allowing trustworthy scriptures to play a role in ordinary inferences about sound's impermanence, *ākāśaguṇatva*, etc., and in so doing he easily falls into circularity when he tests the scripture's truth, and risks refutation whenever the scripture conflicts with his own inferences. The Buddhist's approach, as we find it CS, PSV and PV, would avoid that circularity as well as the risk of refutation due to simple contradiction with dogma, in that it maintains the complete independence of *vastubala*-type inferences from scripture and relegates the use of scripture to a domain of objects where there can be no conflict with such inferences.[85]

[85] It seems to me that the Buddhist approach also differs significantly from that of Bhartṛhari in that the former maintains the adequacy and primacy of logical analysis independent of scripture, whereas Bhartṛhari seems to have little confidence in the adequacy of such inferences. Cf. *Vākyapadīya* I, k. 34:

A closing remark of a critical nature. Once one understands the Buddhist position as found in CS and the Epistemologists, it is difficult to resist the impression that the Buddhist, especially as explained by Dharmakīrti, sets his standards almost impossibly high. It should be apparent that no one, Buddhist or non-Buddhist, can in practice inferentially or empirically test for himself all rationally analysable propositions on which he must make a decision. The result to which a Buddhist philosopher is led, therefore, is that his stringent standards force him into a type of skepticism about much of what we would wish to term "justified true belief" or "knowledge", for inevitably the majority of our knowledge about matters which are not at all *atyantaparokṣa* (such as e.g. geography, history, etc.) is not due to our own personal observations or inferences. (We do not, for example, observe or infer the rationally analysable truth that Columbus sailed with three ships to America: we read about it. Nonetheless, is it not reasonable to claim that we know this fact?)

Interestingly enough, some later Buddhist philosophers seem to accept this skeptical consequence, saying that in non-*atyantaparokṣa* matters, reliance on testimony, books or any other type of information apart from one's own direct perception and *vastubalapravṛttānumāna*, does *not* yield real knowledge, but rather, "true presumption" (*yid dpyod*), to use the epistemic category elaborated upon in the Tibetan scholastic. The eighteenth century writer A kya yoṅs 'dzin clearly expresses this skepticism:

> "Understanding (*go ba*) which just comes from hearing is mostly true presumption and thus one says that its continuum is not solid (*brtan po min*)."[86]

---

yatnenānumito 'py arthaḥ kuśalair anumātṛbhiḥ / abhiyuktatarair anyair anyathaivopapādyate //
Transl. Biardeau: "Même si une chose a été inférée à grand labeur par d'habiles experts en inférence, elle peut l'être d'une autre manière par d'autres encore plus habiles." Cf., however, Hayes (1988), p. 253.

86 See A kya yoṅs 'dzin dByaṅs can dga' ba'i blo gros' *Blo rigs kyi sdom tshig blaṅ dor gsal ba'i me loṅ*, Collected Works, Vol. I, p. 518: *thos byuṅ tsam gyi go ba ni / phal cher yid dpyod yin pas na // de rgyun brtan po min źes gsuṅs //*. For definitions of *yid dpyod*, see ibid. p. 518: *de yaṅ raṅ yul bden pa la // gsar du źen pa'i tshad min blo // yid dpyod kyi ni mtshan ñid yin //*. "Now the defining characteristic of true presumption is that it is a cognition which is not a *pramāṇa*, but which newly conceives of its true object". *Yoṅs 'dzin blo rigs*, p. 53, folio 15a, line 5 et seq: *raṅ yul la źen pa'i* slu ba'i źen rig don mthun*. *Read *pa'i* instead of *pas*. The Tibetan Epistemologists classify true presumptions as based on contradictory reasons, unascertained reasons, or no reason at all apart from other peoples' say-so. The point, according to textbooks such as *Yoṅs 'dzin blo rigs*, etc., is that *yid dpyod* is a correct cognition in that it is in accordance with reality (*don mthun*). However, it is not real knowledge in that it is not *mi bslu ba* (= *avisaṃvādin*): it cannot bring forth any certainty which would conclusively eliminate error. To take my "Columbus" example, this would probably be what Yoṅs 'dzin phur bu lcog would term *rgyu mtshan med pa'i yid dpyod* "true presumption where there is no reason". This has to be understood as meaning that the person in question believes something true on the basis of no reasons; it does not mean that there *are no* reasons at all for anyone. Cf. *Yoṅs 'dzin blo rigs* p. 53, f. 15b: *daṅ po ni / sgra mi rtag ces pa'i ṅag tsam la brten nas sgra mi rtag 'dzin pa'i blo lta bu ste / sgra mi rtag ces pa'i ṅag des sgra mi rtag pa'i dam bca' brjod kyi / rgyu mtshan ma brjod pa'i phyir /*. "The first [sort] is like a mind which apprehends that sound is impermanent on the basis of the mere sentence 'sound is impermanent'. For, while the sentence 'sound is impermanent' does state the thesis that sound is impermanent, it does not state the reason."

Granted there is no specific technical term corresponding to our word "justified", but it is probably fair to say that the thrust of the Indian and Tibetan Buddhist system (as we see in Dharmakīrti as well as in the above quotation from a later writer) is that a belief is only justified for a person *X* if *X* himself has a *pramāṇa* which establishes that belief. If we take *that* understanding of "justification" coupled with the Buddhist account of *pramāṇas*, then most of what we "know" from simple hearing, reading, television or computer data-bases — cognitions which the A kya yoṅs 'dzin would have to call *yid dpyod* — could not be "justified true belief" for us. Certainly we do not personally have direct perception or *vastubalapravṛttānumāna* on most such matters. If, however, we say that it is not necessary for the person *himself* to have an inferential or perceptual *pramāṇa* on some matter in order to hold a justified belief, then it becomes rather hard to avoid something like a Nyāya account which would advocate reliance on trustworthy testimony, even in empirical matters.

"Knowledge", if we want Tibetan equivalents, would be *rtogs pa*, *rtogs pa'i blo*, which, as dGe lugs pas such as lCaṅ skya Rol pa'i rdo rje routinely point out, is a matter of "being able to elicit certainty which eliminates errors concerning the matter at hand" (*chos de la sgro 'dogs gcod pa'i ṅes śes 'dren nus pa*). Cf. *lCaṅ skya grub mtha'* p. 192: *de [= blo] la dbye na rtogs pa'i blo daṅ ma rtogs pa'i blo gñis su yod de / blo des chos de la sgro 'dogs gcod pa'i ṅes śes 'dren nus pa daṅ mi nus pa gñis su yod pa'i phyir /*. "If one divides [cognition] there are two, knowledge and non-knowledge, for there are two [sorts] according to whether the cognition can or cannot elicit certainty which eliminates errors on the matter at hand." As for *yid dpyod*, it is classified as *ma rtogs pa'i blo*, i.e. it is not knowledge. A kya yoṅs 'dzin op. cit. 517: *blo rigs bdun las mṅon rjes daṅ // bcad śes gsum po rtogs pa'i blo // gźan bźi ma rtogs blo yin la //*. "Among the seven sorts of cognition, perception, inference and subsequent cognition are knowledge (*rtogs pa'i blo*). The other four [viz. true presumption, erroneous cognition (*log śes*), doubt (*the tshom*) and inattentive cognition (*snaṅ la ma ṅes pa'i blo*)] are not knowledge."

Note that *rtogs pa'i blo* and *mi slu ba'i śes pa* are coextensive (*don gcig*) and span the same set of cognitions: if we adopt this dGe lugs pa position, they both will come to mean a cognition which is able to elicit sufficient certainty to eliminate error. It should be said, however, that this account of *yid dpyod* and *avisaṃvāda* is the prevailing dGe lugs textbook version, but was far from unanimously accepted; for intra-Tibetan debates about the meaning of *avisaṃvāda*, see the article by G. Dreyfus, "Dharmakīrti's definition of *pramāṇa* and its interpreters", forthcoming in the Proceedings of the Second International Dharmakīrti Conference, Vienna. It is difficult to find any Indian sources where *avisaṃvādakatva* would be clearly interpreted in terms of a cognition possessing sufficient *certainty* to eliminate error. Dharmottara's position in his *Prāmāṇyaparīkṣā* and in his *Pramāṇaviniścayaṭīkā* on PVin I 30, 17ff. (ed. Vetter) is, rather, to explain that a cognition which has *avisaṃvādakatva* makes one arrive at (*prāpaka*) the object in the real world to which it applies. See Durveka Miśra's *Dharmottarapradīpa* 17, 13: *avisaṃvādakaṃ pravṛttiviṣayavastuprāpakaṃ samyagjñānam iti*. See also note 54 for Dharmottara's explanation of *avisaṃvādakatva* as "reliability". The "reliability" of a cognition, then, seems to be grounded on *prāpakatva*. Cf. Steinkellner and Krasser (1989) pp. 75-76.

Finally, the term *yid dpyod* itself is probably due to the eleventh century thinker Phya pa Chos kyi seṅ ge who came up with so-called sevenfold classification of cognition (*blo rigs bdun du dbye ba*) in Tibetan Epistemology. See van der Kuijp (1978); on the latter author's translation of *yid dpyod* as "reflection-as-an-ego-act" in his (1978) and (1983), see n. 7 of my (1984a) review-article of van der Kuijp (1983).

III. CANDRAKĪRTI AND DHARMAPĀLA ON PERCEPTION

In what follows I intend to look at some aspects of Madhyamaka thought as seen via the perspectives of our commentators, namely, the status and role of direct perception (*pratyakṣa*) and the given. The subject of perception, which is extensively discussed in CS XIII and in the third chapter of Nāgārjuna's *Mūlamadhyamakakārikās* (MMK), is approached from differing standpoints by the commentators on CS. Dharmapāla here clearly concentrates his attention on refuting Vaibhāṣika and non-Buddhist philosophies of perception and on showing the general impossibility of the sense organs, their objects and the contact between them. Candrakīrti, however, besides fulfilling his commentator's duties in explaining the verses of Āryadeva, was obviously inspired by a subject on which Dharmapāla and Āryadeva said little, viz. the etymology, defining characteristics and epistemic status of direct perception, themes which recur in other writings of Candrakīrti, notably the first chapter of the *Prasannapadā*, and could be said to pervade much of his philosophy. Let us then first take up Candrakīrti's views.[87]

If Candrakīrti is to press forward his basic view — as we find it presented in texts such as *Catuḥśatakavṛtti* XII — that nothing whatsoever is established by its own nature (*svabhāva*), he not only has to refute naive realist views such as those of the Vaiśeṣika, but he equally must refute different idealist positions: these idealists refute external objects, but make a separation between perception and the conceptualization about what is perceived, the latter being the source of error. As we see in CSV XIII §9, Candrakīrti has a formidable adversary here in the Epistemological school, which holds that perception is *kalpanāpoḍha*, "free from conceptualization", and that it perceives inexpressible real particulars, or *svalakṣaṇa*.[88] The Epistemologist, in effect, takes a position which is common to many theorists East and West: he says that while

---

[87] I am indebted to articles by P. Williams (1979) and M. Broido (1988), who approach the problems from Tsoṅ kha pa's perspective. I have also profited from the recent book of D. Lopez (1987) on the dGe lugs account of Svātantrika. I have, however, in the following section deliberately kept my references largely to Indian material. For some of the problems seen from the dGe lugs pa approach, see also Tillemans (1982).

[88] On *svalakṣaṇa* see en. 366; for *kalpanā* see en. 367. Dharmakīrti subsequently elaborates the definition as *kalpanāpoḍha* plus *abhrānta* ("not mistaken"). In PV III, k. 123 he keeps simply *kalpanāpoḍha*: *pratyakṣaṃ kalpanāpoḍhaṃ pratyakṣeṇaiva sidhyati* /. But in NB I, 4 he adds *abhrānta* to insist upon the fact that the definition also eliminates all illusory cognitions: *tatra pratyakṣaṃ kalpanāpoḍham abhrāntam* /.

the ideas we have about our data may be false, at least the data which immediately appear as given to our perception, if taken only for what they are, must be real and unassailable. The implicit move is what R. Rorty would call the Doctrine of the Naturally Given: Knowledge is, or reduces to, cognitions of the sort of entity naturally suited to be immediately present to consciousness; the added metaphysical premise is that "the most knowable is the most real" (Rorty 1980 p. 105). The Epistemologist does indeed hold that the *svalakṣaṇa*, which is what is knowable, must be of the same nature as the mind and is real. It is a cardinal position of his Vijñānavāda, found clearly in Dignāga's *Ālambanaparīkṣā*, that the object of knowledge must be mental and that mind knows itself (see p. 61 and fn. 131 below). Indeed, there is a frequently used reasoning — which T. Iwata has called the "*saṃvedana* inference" — to the effect that a cognized object cannot be different from the consciousness which cognizes it, simply because it is cognized: only what is of same nature as the cognizing consciousness can be cognized (see n. 131 below).

Philosophically speaking, the prime candidate for an immediately given entity naturally suited to be present to consciousness is often thought to be some form of a sense-datum or phenomenon, and indeed B.K. Matilal in his 1986 study on Indian philosophies of perception repeatedly refers to the Buddhist positions as being various types of phenomenalism or sense-data theory. Alas, what exactly a sense-datum is turns out to be rather difficult for philosophers to specify, so much so that many contemporary writers, after comparing the contradictory accounts on such things, would say that sense-data and the like are no more than a muddle and do not exist. Such reservations aside, it is important to have a feeling for the seductiveness of postulating sense-data; the Western version of such entities comes through most clearly in the so-called "arguments from illusion". Here is how A.J. Ayer once put it:

> "Let us take as an example Macbeth's visionary dagger... There is an obvious sense in which Macbeth did not see a dagger; he did not see a dagger for the sufficient reason that there was no dagger there for him to see. There is another sense, however, in which it may quite properly be said that he did see a dagger; to say that he saw a dagger is quite a natural way of describing his experience. But still not a real dagger; not a physical object; not even the look of a physical object, if looks are open to all to see. If we are to say that he saw anything, it must have been something that was accessible to him alone, something that existed only so long as this particular experience lasted; in short, a sense-datum." (Ayer 1966, p. 90.)

In fact the key move, as Ayer points out further on (p. 96), is to pass from perfectly innocuous sentences like, "It now seems to me that I see a cigarette case" to the philosopher's rendition, "I am now seeing a seeming-cigarette case". To cite him again:

> "And this seeming-cigarette case, which lives only in my present experience, is an example of a sense-datum. Applying this procedure to all cases of

perception, whether veridical or delusive, one obtains the result that whenever anyone perceives, or thinks that he perceives, a physical object, he must at least be, in the appropriate sense, perceiving a seeming-object. These seeming-objects are sense-data; and the conclusion may be more simply expressed by saying that it is always sense-data that are directly perceived."

Let us then in what follows understand by the term "the given", the sense-data, i.e. the phenomena or seeming-objects, which present themselves to our perception immediately, without intermediary and without there necessarily being any real or external object which caused them or to which they correspond. These sense-data can be of various sorts. Generally, they are considered to be mental entities, but indeed, as H.H. Price once argued (1950, pp. 317-318), certain phenomenalists took them as being neither mental nor physical. For our purposes we shall put the emphasis on their being seeming-objects, stressing that they are wholly mind-dependent, but allowing the possibility (as in some Svātantrika positions) that they are not classified as *mental entities* in the way in which, for example, a feeling of pain is said to be mental. Some philosophers of a reductionist inclination, such as Bertrand Russell or R. Carnap (see p. vii in the preface to the second edition of his *Logische Aufbau*), would take them as being the sensations specific to the individual senses of vision, hearing, touch, etc. — particular patches of blue, tickings of the clock, feelings of heat, etc. — while gross objects are constructs out of these sensations. Others, as we saw above, would speak of "objects" like Macbeth's dagger as being a sense-datum: Bishop Berkeley, for example, was of this latter sort and maintained that trees and stones (*qua* impressions) were directly perceived. We shall understand the term "sense-data" or "phenomenon" as including both sorts; reductionists tend to use the term more along the first lines, but the other position where one speaks of a sense-datum of an object such as a rose is frequent too. The Epistemologists, with their notion of *svalakṣaṇa*, seem to have been reductionists and to have professed something like the first sort of sense-data.[89] Below

---

[89] Cf. Candrakīrti's arguments against the logicians in Pr. 58.14-59.4 and CSV XIII ad k. 301. In effect, a main theme of Candrakīrti's Madhyamaka is a type of anti-reductionism, in which the Epistemologists are, no doubt, his principal adversaries. Cf. Carnap (1967) p. vi on the reductionist approach: "[I]t is in principle possible to reduce all concepts to the immediately given." The Buddhist Epistemologist analyzes away common gross objects, which he considers to be unreal conceptual fictions, and reduces them to the only thing he accepts as real, the *svalakṣaṇa*, i.e. the particular, inexpressible, momentary entities which are what one *really* sees in direct perception — all the rest is mental fabrication coming from conceptualizing. See en. 366 on *svalakṣaṇa* and *sāmānyalakṣaṇa*.

A reductionist of this sort is clearly a redoubtable adversary, for he maintains that he accounts for the worldly truths while still being more sophisticated than the world. He can himself use the arguments showing inconsistencies in the gross entities accepted by the world to justify his own program; for him such arguments do not lead to the conclusion that *everything* is void or unreal, but rather that ordinary entities, as conceived by the world, are unreal. He will propose something more basic and unassailable in their stead. (It could perhaps be argued that Dharmapāla was a type of reductionist too, and indeed he was able to assimilate all Madhyamaka arguments to his own program.)

I will argue that certain Mādhyamikas, in particular the Svātantrikas, accept the other type of given when they speak of conventionally existing objects, which are in fact only "seeming-objects", like illusory daggers, and are nothing *real.*[90]

To the modern reader Candrakīrti's works can often seem to contain a large number of widely diffuse miscellaneous themes with no obvious interconnection or common goal. To be sure, a good portion of Candrakīrti's philosophy concerns the actual logical reasonings used to prove that things have no natures (*svabhāva*) whatsoever. But then there seem to be a number of other issues: the problems concerning *pratyakṣa*, its etymology and definition as discussed in CSV XIII; whether terms in arguments will be perceived similarly by both debaters; the rejection of self-awareness (*svasaṃvedana*; *svasaṃvitti*); the discussions in the *Madhyamakāvatāra* on "mere conventionality" (*saṃvṛtimātra*), on the erroneousness of ordinary beings' direct

---

Candrakīrti seems to have been implicitly aware of the fact that refuting a few details of his adversary's reductionist analyses was not enough; one must somehow show that the whole enterprise of providing such analyses is flawed. In the *Prasannapadā*, he shows a marked preference for the Naiyāyika's realism, which consists in uncritical description and schematization of worldly truths. See Stcherbatsky (1927) p. 140, n. 5. There his move was to characterize the Epistemologist's program as mere description of worldly truth, a description which the Epistemologist supposedly justifies on the grounds that other philosophers' descriptions, such as those of the Naiyāyikas, were bungled. In other words, the only justification for the Epistemologist's program would be if the Naiyāyika account of worldly truth was inadequate, but, argues Candrakīrti, such is not the case. Pr. 58, 14- 59,3: *atha syād eṣa eva pramāṇaprameyavyavahāro laukiko 'smābhiḥ śāstreṇānuvarṇita iti // tadanuvarṇanasya tarhi phalaṃ vācyam // kutārkikaiḥ sa nāśito viparītalakṣaṇābhidhānena tasyāsmābhiḥ samyaglakṣaṇam utkam iti cet // etad apy ayuktaṃ / yadi hi kutārkikair viparītalakṣaṇapraṇayanaṃ kṛtaṃ lakṣyavaiparītyaṃ lokasya syāt / tadarthaṃ prayatnasāphalyaṃ syāt / na caitad evam iti vyartha evāyaṃ prayatna iti //.*

In fact, this is a somewhat too facile and inaccurate characterization of what the Epistemologist is up to and blurs the fact of his reductionism: he is not trying to do a better inventory of the worlds' notions, he is explaining and criticizing them by reducing unrealities to more ontologically fundamental elements. A more profitable approach is to attack the notions of *svalakṣaṇa* and the privileged status which the Epistemologist confers on perception. In the *Prasannapadā* and *Catuḥśatakavṛtti* XIII, Candrakīrti frequently obfuscates things by providing too many arguments of uneven quality, but he is at his most persuasive when he uses the line of reasoning in Āryadeva's k. 301 and 304: if we reduce gross objects to *svalakṣaṇa* sense-data, such as form, colours, etc., the same argument which was used against the gross object will also apply to the *svalakṣaṇa*, for just as we never *see* the whole gross object, but only its parts, so we never see the whole form either. The conclusion is that the reductionist will never give us entities which are more coherent or ontologically fundamental than our ordinary unsophisticated notions.

[90] Note that some philosophers, such as the Sarvāstivādins, tried to maintain that these sense-data or collections of them *are* the external objects and are real. Thus, matter is analyzed into dharmas of color, shape, smell, tactile sensations, etc. — it is these latter data that exist really and externally. Such a position is, however, very difficult to maintain, as we see by the Buddhist counterarguments. See Kajiyama (1977), Hattori (1988) p. 34 et seq. on the Sarvāstivāda position. Cf. Matilal (1986) p. 246 on the Sarvāstivādin's "realistic phenomenalism": "The Vaibhāṣika view is that the objects of (external) perception are non-mental phenomena which are somehow 'out there', the gross sensibilia."

perceptions and on correct and false conventional truth, i.e. *tathyasaṃvṛti* and *mithyāsaṃvṛti*. Now, we can see these as a collection of miscellany — no more than *ad hoc* arguments against particular Buddhist opponents. But this is shortsighted. In fact, these issues are, broadly speaking, linked in constituting a philosophy of perception which harmonizes with and supports Candrakīrti's thoroughgoing rejection of *svabhāva*, for the opponents are introducing this given, or seeming-object, as an attempt to provide at least *something* which has *svabhāva*. I would argue, then, that a unity can be found among these themes in Candrakīrti's philosophy of perception by seeing them as supporting a common point: *there is no given at all.*

A. Candrakīrti on perception and the status of the given

While Western sense-data theorists would generally hold that the given is real, and would not quibble much about the sense of "real" involved here, Candrakīrti's adversaries' positions are more diverse on this latter point. Some would indeed hold that the given is ultimately and fully real, whereas others, of a Madhyamaka inclination, would say that the given has an unassailable conventional reality. At any rate, the opinion that the given is either ultimately real or possesses a *svabhāva* on at least a conventional level is shared by almost all of Candrakīrti's principal Buddhist adversaries. Most of the Vijñānavādins would subscribe to some form of this principle, depending upon their position on the status of the "aspects", or "images" (*ākāra*), which present themselves directly to perception. The Satyākāravādins (viz. Dignāga and Dharmakīrti) who, as their name implies, maintained the reality of these images, held that the raw sense-data which present themselves to perception, such as impressions of blue, etc., are real and possess dependent natures (*paratantrasvabhāva*) in that they are inseparable from consciousness, which is itself real.[91] These *ākāra* are then misinterpreted as external entities by conceptualization and thus subsequently, through the

---

[91] For *paratantra* and *parikalpitasvabhāva*, see the following section on "Dharmapāla on perception". This is one convenient way to characterize the Satyākāravādin's position and is to be found in Bodhibhadra's *Jñānasārasamuccayanibandhana*. See Mimaki (1976) pp. 202-203. In Bodhibhadra's text we see him dividing Yogācāra into *rnam pa daṅ bcas pa* (*sākāravādin*) and *rnam pa med pa* (*nirākāravādin*), the representatives of the first being Dignāga and Dharmakīrti, while the second school is that of Asaṅga. In fact, the terms *sākāra* and *nirākāra* in these Yogācāra contexts correspond to *satyākāra* (*rnam bden pa*) and *alīkākāra* (*rnam rdzun pa*) respectively. See Kajiyama (1978) p. 125. Cf. also *Blo gsal grub mtha'* ed. Mimaki (1982) pp. 99 and 100 which divides Yogācāra using these latter terms, Dignāga and co. being Satyākāravādin and Asaṅga and Dharmottara representing the Alīkākāravādins. See Moriyama (1984) for Haribhadra's arguments against these latter two schools; see also Kajiyama (1965) and Mimaki (1976) pp. 71-72; also Kajiyama (1978) for an explanation of the broad lines of the debate and Śāntarakṣita's arguments. Note that amongst later Vijñānavādins, Ratnākaraśānti becomes the principal representative of Alīkākāravāda, whereas Jñānaśrīmitra is probably the principal Satyākāravādin. See Ichigō (1985) p. lxxviii for a schematic diagram of the Vijñānavāda's positions on *ākāra* and those of Śāntarakṣita.

influence of a cognition different from simple perception, they acquire false or "thoroughly imagined natures" (*parikalpitasvabhāva*).[92]

Even amongst Candrakīrti's fellow Mādhyamikas, those of the Svātantrika school, while certainly not accepting real *ākāra*, and in fact refuting both Satyākāravāda and its opposite, Alīkākāravāda,[93] did hold that conventionally there must be something which appears similarly (*mthun snaṅ ba*) to both parties in a discussion, and without which logical discussion and communication in general would be impossible.[94] This object, if analysed, turns out to be impossible, but must at least exist as the

---

[92] The opposite Vijñānavāda position is that of the Alīkākāravādins, who profess that the given data, or *ākāra*, while conventionally existent, are themselves deceptive in that they are falsely of two sorts, subjective (i.e. *grāhakākāra*) and objective (*grāhyākāra*). Only the pure non-dual consciousness is real. See Moriyama (1984) pp. 12-14. This school is, no doubt, something of an exception to the Yogācāra tendency to attribute full reality to the given, and in that respect they are closer to those Svātantrika-Mādhyamikas who recognize an object-*qua*-appearance, one which is conventionally established, but is ultimately illusory. The major difference from the Mādhyamikas, however, is that the Alīkākāravādin, being a Vijñānavādin, wishes to say that the mind is still ultimately real. In particular, to take Bodhibhadra's explanation, the Alīkākāravādin maintains that the *ākāra* themselves are not *paratantra* but *parikalpitasvabhāva*: the raw given which one sees is itself unreal; it is only the self-awareness, or *svasaṃvedana*, which is fully real.

[93] See the refutations of both using the "neither one nor many" argument (*ekānekaviyogahetu*) in Haribhadra's *Abhisamayālaṃkārāloka*, transl. Moriyama (1984), and in Śāntarakṣita's *Madhyamakālaṃkāra*, transl. Ichigō (1985).

[94] The point occupies an important place in Śāntarakṣita's *Madhyamakālaṃkāra* and *vṛtti*, Kamalaśīla's *Madhyamakālaṃkārapañjikā* and Jñānagarbha's *Satyadvayavibhaṅga* and *vṛtti*. First of all, note that the requirements that the reason and subject be established for both parties (*ubhayasiddha*) were laid down by Dignāga in PS III, 11: *dvayoḥ siddhena dharmeṇa vyavahārād viparyaye / dvayor ekasya cāsiddhau dharmyasiddhau ca neṣyate*. Skt. found in PVBh 647,9; see Hattori (1958) fragment 8; Kitagawa (1973) p. 153. Indeed NM lb 11-12 (Tucci p. 13; Katsura 1977 §2.2, p. 122) makes it clear that this applies to all three characters of the reason (*rūpa*); see Tillemans (1984b) p. 80 and n. 21. Śāntarakṣita argues (*vṛtti*, pp. 73b6-74a3) that if there were not at least a datum of appearance which, *qua* appearance, would be understood by "scholars, women and children", then "the locus [i.e. the subject] of the reason would be unestablished (*gtan tshigs kyi gźi 'grub par mi 'gyur*). Kamalaśīla (*Pañjikā* 103b8), commenting on this problem of the locus being unestablished, argues: *chos can snaṅ ba 'di la raṅ bźin yaṅ dag par sgro btags pa dgag pa sgrub byed kyi / chos can gyi raṅ gi ṅo bo 'gog par ni ma yin pas* ... "although one refutes projections of a real nature to such an appearing subject, one does not refute the essence of the subject." See Jñānagarbha's *Satyadvayavibhaṅgavṛtti* D. 5b6: *rgol ba daṅ phyir rgol ba'i śes pa la snaṅ ba'i cha la ni rtsod pa su yaṅ med do // rtsod par byed na ni mṅon sum la sogs pas gnod par 'gyur ro //*. "Nobody has any debate about the element which appears to the consciousnesses of the proponent and opponent. If they did debate [about that], they would be refuted by direct perception and the like." Finally, in D. 5b4 we see Jñānagarbha using the words *mthun par snaṅ ba* in the context of showing that conventional truth "appears similarly to the consciousness of everyone, from children on up." *'di ltar byis pa yan chad kyi śes pa la mthun par don ji sñed rgyu las snaṅ ba de ni yaṅ dag pa'i kun rdzob yin par rigs te /*. See Tillemans (1982) pp. 105-112 on these topics; Lopez (1987) p. 78 *et passim* on *chos can mthun snaṅ ba* ("commonly appearing subjects"); also Hopkins (1989) on Tibetan explanations of *chos can mthun snaṅ ba*; Eckel (1987) for an edition and translation of the *Satyadvayavibhaṅga* and *vṛtti* along with a study of Jñānagarbha's thought. See also fn. 96, 107 below.

phenomenon on the basis of which our practical ordinary activity revolves. In effect, the Svātantrikas probably did make the reification, common to those who hold a perceptual given, that "seeming to see an *X*" implies "seeing a seeming-*X*"; this reification of appearances is well brought out in the Tibetan characterization of the Svātantrikas as holding that things are illusions, but that even *qua* illusions they do have an "objective mode of being" (*don gyi sdod lugs*). Part and parcel of this idea is the Svātantrika position that phenomena are "conventionally established by their natures" (*tha sñad du raṅ bźin gyis grub pa*) or "conventionally established from their own side" (*tha sñad du raṅ ṅos nas grub pa*). While the terms are not explicitly those of the Indian texts, but rather belong to the Tibetan doxographers, the ideas seem on the balance those of the Svātantrikas, at least from the point of view of what we are terming "internal history".[95] At any rate, the essential point for us, as we find it the Indian Svātantrika texts, is that what appears in non-conceptual direct perception is some type of an entity, a phenomenon about which we are undeceived so long as we do not give it anything more than conventional status: our mistake is to grasp it as having a real nature.[96]

What is important in this connection is that Candrakīrti's Buddhist adversaries, Svātantrika or not, generally seem to use the same definition of perception, that of the

---

[95] Cf. Tillemans (1982) n. 18 and 33 and the selection from Se ra rje btsun Chos kyi rgyal mtshan's *sKabs daṅ po'i spyi don* translated in Tillemans (1984c). Cf. the definitions of "Svātantrika" to be found in *Grub mtha' rin chen phreṅ ba*, ed. Mimaki (1977) p. 97: *raṅ gi mtshan ñid kyis grub pa tha sñad du khas len pa'i ṅo bo ñid med par smra ba de / raṅ rgyud pa'i mtshan ñid / ... ci'i phyir dbu ma raṅ rgyud pa źes bya źe na / tshul gsum raṅ ṅos nas grub pa'i rtags yaṅ dag la brten nas bden dṅos 'gog par byed pas na de ltar brjod pa'i phyir /.* "The defining characteristic of a Svātantrika is that he asserts that there is no nature while accepting that conventionally [things] are established by their own characteristics (*svalakṣaṇa*) ... Why does one say 'Mādhyamika-Svātantrika'? It is because they refute truly existent entities by means of valid reasons whose three characters are established from their own side". In *lCaṅ skya grub mtha'* p. 325, the author first defines what is meant by *svatantra* and then proceeds to explain "Svātantrika": *des na phyir rgol gyi khas blaṅs tsam la ma 'khris par gdams gźi'i ṅos nas don gyi sdod lugs kyi dbaṅ gis rgol gyi tshad ma ma 'khrul ba la chos can mthun snaṅ du grub ciṅ / chos can de'i steṅ du rtags kyi tshul rnams 'grub tshul ṅes par byas nas bsgrub bya rtogs pa'i rjes dpag bskyed pa źig raṅ rgyud kyi don yin la / de ltar dgos pa 'thad par khas len pa'i dbu ma pa la dbu ma raṅ rgyud pa źes zer pa yin no /.* "The subject (*dharmin*) is established as appearing similarly to the non-deceptive *pramāṇa* [i.e. direct perception] of the debaters by virtue of its objective mode of being (*don gyi sdod lugs*), a mode of being which belongs to the side of the locus in question (*gdams gźi*) and is not guided by the mere belief of the opponent. On the basis of such a subject the various characters of the reason are ascertained, and there arises an inference which cognizes the proposition to be proved. This is the meaning of *svatantra*. Those Mādhyamikas who agree that the above mentioned requirements are necessary are called 'Mādhyamika-Svātantrikas'." Cf. Lopez (1987) p. 294.

[96] Cf. Śāntarakṣita's *Madhyamakālaṃkāravṛtti*, P. 74a3: *kho bo yaṅ mig la sogs pa'i śes pa la snaṅ ba'i ṅaṅ can gyi dṅos po ni mi sel gyi /.* "As for us, we do not deny entities in so far as they are appearances to the eye and other sense consciousnesses." *Satyadvayavibhaṅgavṛtti*, D. 5a3: *rnam par rtog pa med pa'i mṅon sum gyi śes pas yoṅs su bcad pa'i ṅo bo'i dṅos po gzugs la sogs pa daṅ bde ba la sogs par rig par grub pa rnams ni kun rdzob kyi bden pa kho na yin no /.* "The establishment of cognitions of entities such as form, etc. and pleasure, etc., whose essences are discriminated by direct perceptions free of conceptualization, is conventional truth alone."

Epistemologists, to wit, a consciousness which is free from conceptualization.[97] In sum, be it in the Vijñānavāda schools where the *ākāra* are ultimately real, or in the Svātantrika school where the given is at least conventionally real and non-deceptive, there is a key separation between direct perception, on the one hand, and conceptualization (the source of error), on the other; the former is non-deceptive so long as it does not go beyond its legitimate bounds and is not influenced by the latter.

Now, first of all, in CS XIII we see that Candrakīrti does not accept the Epistemologist's definition of perception as always non-conceptual. The thrust of his argumentation on etymologies of *pratyakṣa* is, in effect, to eliminate the privileged status which perception has in his adversaries' systems, for once we grant a non-conceptual *pratyakṣa* which simply sees the given stripped of concepts about it, the road to *svalakṣaṇa*, real *ākāra*, "common appearances", etc. becomes dangerously open. By shifting etymologies Candrakīrti tries to make perception banal: any consciousness, conceptual or not, caused by a perceptible (*pratyakṣa*) object will be termed *pratyakṣa*.

This, however, is a skirmish, a small part of a larger combat against taking perception as being an unmistaken access to the given. In verse 23 in the sixth chapter of the *Madhyamakāvatāra*, Candrakīrti provides us with some clues about the main lines of his own position, saying that "the object of those who see correctly is called reality, and that of those who see mistakenly is called conventional truth" (*samyagdṛśāṃ yo viṣayaḥ sa tattvaṃ mṛṣādṛśāṃ saṃvṛtisatyam uktam*),[98] a passage which shows that what ordinary beings cognize, viz. conventional truth, is always in fact fundamentally mistaken, whether the cognition in question is a direct perception or not. Of course, as we shall see in more detail below, the subsequent verses of the *Madhyamakāvatāra* do show that, within this general misapprehension of things, we can find things which are "truths" for the world, and other things, like mirages, which are not even true in that limited sense. But what emerges is that the general misapprehension about the object's voidness will always be present for a non-Ārya, who has not realized voidness: even his direct perception is mistaken about the object and perceives it as having a *svabhāva* which it does not have at all.

Candrakīrti makes a number of points which tell particularly against the Yogācāra, rather than Svātantrika, version of the given. His refutations of the Yogācāra views on the ultimate reality of dependent nature (*paratantrasvabhāva*) are fairly accessible by now; suffice it to say that the arguments in *Madhyamakāvatāra* VI and

---

[97] Not only is this definition used amongst the Epistemologists, but also among the Svātantrikas. See e.g. TS(P)'s discussion of the definition of perception. Cf. the passage from the *Satyadvayavibhaṅgavṛtti* cited in fn. 96 where we see that Jñānagarbha qualifies *mṅon sum* (*pratyakṣa*) as *rnam par rtog pa med pa* ("without conceptualization").

[98] M. av. VI, 23: *samyaṅmṛṣādarśanalabdhabhāvaṃ rūpadvayaṃ bibhrati sarvabhāvāḥ / samyagdṛśāṃ yo viṣayaḥ sa tattvaṃ mṛṣādṛśāṃ saṃvṛtisatyam uktam //*. Cited in *Bodhicaryāvatārapañjikā* p. 174. Transl. LVP: "Les choses portent une double nature qui est constituée par la vue exacte et par la vue erronée. Le domaine de ceux qui voient juste est appelé 'réalité', de ceux qui voient faux, 'vérité d'erreur'." For Tsoṅ kha pa's discussion in *dBu ma dgoṅs pa rab gsal* and *rTsa še ṭīk chen* on this and related passages, see Broido (1988) pp. 34 et seq.; see also Williams (1979).

elsewhere[99] against *paratantra* will also refute the ultimate reality of *ākāra* in the Satyākāravādin's system. In *Madhyamakāvatāra* IV, 71cd he summarizes his main point of contention with the Yogācāra's idealism: Yogācāra holds that the subject and its states are real but that the object is unreal; this is impossible, for real subjective states must depend upon real objects. The Yogācāra philosopher, of course, seeks to avoid this dependence on objects by saying that the mind cognizes itself — hence, Candrakīrti's long arguments against such a "self-awareness" (*svasaṃvedana*).

While the arguments against the Yogācāra given are relatively clear, it is more difficult to see the difference, albeit subtle, between Candrakīrti and the Svātantrikas. The Svātantrika's given is perhaps best brought out by Jñānagarbha's famous dictum that "conventional truth is just as it appears" (*ji ltar snaṅ ba 'di kho na kun rdzob*). This is interpreted to show that conventional objects do not have any existence apart from the appearance to mind, typically to direct perception[100] — thus our depiction of the Svātantrika's conventional object as being a seeming-object, a reified appearance.

When confronted with the problem that there would be no difference, *qua* appearance, between illusions and conventional truth, Jñānagarbha agrees, but says that the difference comes out in their practical consequences, their possessing or lacking practical efficacity, i.e. *arthakriyā*.[101] Thus, for Jñānagarbha *et al.* the seeming-object which is given is itself no different in the case of error or conventional truth: that difference is discovered *a posteriori* by *praxis*. Nor was Jñānagarbha the first or only Svātantrika to hold such a theory: Bhāvaviveka, in his *Prajñāpradīpa* and *Madhya-*

---

99 See M. av. VI k. 47 et seq. Refutations of Yogācāra are also to be found in the *Śūnyatāsaptativṛtti* P. 318b-320b.

100 *Satyadvayavibhaṅga*, k. 3. *Vṛtti* D. 4a3: *ji ltar ba laṅ rdzi mo la sogs pa yan chad kyis mthoṅ ba de ltar kun rdzob tu bden pa rnam par gnas kyi yaṅ dag par ni ma yin te / mthoṅ ba daṅ mthun par dṅos po'i don ṅes par 'dzin pa'i phyir ro //.* "Just as something is seen by [people] from cowherds and the like on up, so is it conventionally established as true, but not ultimately, for they definitely apprehend an entity in accordance with what they see." Cf. *Madhyamakāloka* P. 254a6: *de'i phyir de dag gi bsam pa'i dbaṅ gis dṅos po brdzun pa'i ṅo bo thams cad ni kun rdzob tu yod pa kho na'o.* "So therefore, all entities which are deceptive [i.e. non-ultimate] natures because of [one's] thought about them, are just conventionally existent." Cf. Se ra rje btsun Chos kyi rgyal mtshan's comment in *sKabs daṅ po'i spyi don* f. 24b3-4: *blo la snaṅ ba'i dbaṅ gis bźag pa'i yod pa de kun rdzob tu yod pa'i don yin pa ...* "'An existence established in virtue of its appearing to the mind' is the meaning of 'conventional existence'." See Tillemans (1984c) pp. 360-361. See Lopez (1987) pp. 145-149. See also fn. 137.

101 *Satyadvayavibhaṅga* k. 12: *snaṅ du 'dra yaṅ don byed dag / nus pa'i phyir daṅ mi nus phyir / yaṅ dag yaṅ dag ma yin pas / kun rdzob kyi ni dbye ba byas /.* "Although their appearance is similar, one divides conventional [truth] into correct and false because of practical efficacity or inefficacity." *Vṛtti*: *śes pa gsal ba'i rnam pa snaṅ ba can du 'dra yaṅ / ji ltar snaṅ ba bźin du don byed pa la slu ba daṅ mi slu ba yin par ṅes par byas nas chu la sogs pa daṅ smig rgyu la sogs pa dag 'jig rten gyis yaṅ dag pa daṅ yaṅ dag pa ma yin par rtogs so //.* "Although the cognitions are similar in having appearances of manifest images, [still] after ascertaining whether or not [the objects] as they appear belie their practical efficacity, the world then understands that water, etc. and mirages and so forth are [respectively] correct and false." For *arthakriyā*, see Nagatomi (1967-68), Mikogami (1979); see also Katsura (1984) for *arthakriyā*'s general role in Dharmakīrti's theory of truth.

makārthasaṃgraha, had already similarly classified conventional truth (*saṃvṛtisatya*) into correct (*tathyasaṃvṛti*) and false (*mithyāsaṃvṛti*).[102] For the Svātantrikas, then, the given is a phenomenon, "something appearing to consciousness" (*śes pa la snaṅ ba'i cha*).[103] For Jñānagarbha and Bhāvaviveka, who accept conventionally existing external objects, a conventional external object "conforms to the appearance" (*śes pa la snaṅ ba daṅ mthun par dṅos po gnas pa*)[104] if the latter passes the tests of practical efficacity, otherwise there is only *mere* appearance, like a hallucination. Śāntarakṣita, and other Svātantrika-Mādhyamikas of his idealist-inclined faction (who do not conventionally accept external objects), hold that the appearance itself, if it passes the practical tests for *tathyasaṃvṛti*, simply *is* the object. But the difference between the two Svātantrika tendencies is not of great importance in this context. In effect, the essential point is that one always sees a seeming-object — it may subsequently be judged to be conventionally true, but that is a only matter of assigning a certain status to one and the same phenomenon: even for a Svātantrika like Jñānagarbha the external objects are unreal and are never anything but seeming-objects.

Candrakīrti, however, does not concede even this Svātantrika version of a minimal intersubjective "given" phenomenon which appears similarly to all, is *in itself* unassailable, and is the necessary condition for communication and rationality. There are a number of elements in the dossier which show Candrakīrti's distance from the key points of the Svātantrika position.

First of all, judging from CSV XIII §16 and *Madhyamakāvatāra* VI, 25, he seems to use two criteria for truth and error, both of which differ significantly from those of Jñānagarbha *et al.*: a) something is erroneous when the way it is and the way it appears are different (*rnam pa gźan du gnas pa'i dṅos po la rnam pa gźan du snaṅ ba*);[105] b) something is erroneous simply when there are causes for error present, like eye diseases and so forth.[106]

---

[102] See Lindtner (1981) pp. 200-201, n. 14.

[103] See fn. 94. At this point, though, one can imagine the objection that we have failed to make a distinction between the Svātantrika's version of appearances and his account of the objects which appear and that it is absurd to maintain that for a Svātantrika like Jñānagarbha the conventionally established *object* which appears is a given. In fact, I think that for a Svātantrika there can be very little difference between the two; it is a question of which label we confer on appearances after subjecting them to practical tests. As I shall argue below (see p. 64 et seq.), Mādhyamikas who accept external objects do so not because there *is* something external or something "behind" the seeming-object, but rather because they see no reason to revise our ordinary notions and assign *a preferred ontological status to mind.*

[104] *Satyadvayavibhaṅgavṛtti* D. 5b5.

[105] See CSV XIII §16.

[106] See M. av. VI, 25 quoted in *Bodhicaryāvatārapañjikā* p. 171: *vinopaghātena yad indriyāṇāṃ saṇṇām api grāhyam avaiti lokaḥ / satyaṃ hi tal lokata eva śeṣaṃ vikalpitaṃ lokata eva mithyā //*. Transl. LVP: "Ce que le monde considère comme perçu par les six organes exempts de trouble, cela est vrai du point de vue du monde; le reste, du point de vue du monde, est tenu pour faux." Cf. *Blo gsal grub mtha'* p. 156: *gźan dag skyon med skyon bcas ni / byis pa'i ṅor yin yaṅ log med //*. Transl. Mimaki (1982) p. 157: "Les autres (c.-à-d.

The first criterion is used to show that any perception by an ordinary being is erroneous, because something will appear as real or as having a *svabhāva*, whereas it is in fact void. The second criterion accounts for the difference between conventional truths and falsehoods simply in terms of agreed-upon causes for error: never is there question of an appearance or seeming-object being subsequently tested for *arthakriyā* so that, as was the case for Jñānagarbha, Bhāvaviveka and the other Svātantrikas, it can be found to be correct or false. In fact, in the *Prasannapadā*, Candrakīrti makes it clear that he does not even need an object appearing in common to both parties for logic and communication to function, and that especially in the case of arguments between Mādhyamikas and non-Mādhyamikas about voidness, such a common intersubjective appearance is, in any case, impossible.[107]

---

les Prāsaṅgika) [n'établissent la distinction de vrai et faux qu']eu égard aux gens ordinaires (*byis pa, bāla*) [dont l'organe est] sans défaut ou défectueux; [ils] n'[admettent] pas [la distinction entre] les vérités conventionnelles vraie [i.e. *tathyasaṃvṛti*] et fausse [i.e. *mithyāsaṃvṛti*]."

[107] See Pr. 28,4 - 30,14. Let me present a large excerpt, Pr. 29,6 - 30,8: *na caitad evaṃ / yasmād yadaivotpādapratiṣedho 'tra sādhyadharmo 'bhipretaḥ / tadaiva dharmiṇas tadādhārasya viparyāsamātrāsāditātma-bhāvasya pracyutiḥ svayam evānenāṅgīkṛtā / bhinnau hi viparyāsāviparyāsau / tad yadā viparyāsenāsat sattvena gṛhyate taimirikeṇeva keśādi / tadā kutaḥ sadbhūtapadārthaleśasyāpy upalabdhiḥ / yadā cāviparyāsād abhūtaṃ nādhyāropitaṃ vitaimirikeṇeva keśādi / tadā kuto 'sadbhūtpadārthaleśasyāpy upalabdhir yena tadānīṃ saṃvṛtiḥ syāt / ata evoktam ācāryapādaiḥ*

yadi kiṃ cid upalabheyaṃ pravartayeyaṃ nivartayeyaṃ vā /
pratyakṣādibhir arthaiḥ tadbhāvān me 'nupālambhaḥ //.

yataṣ caivaṃ bhinnau viparyāsāviparyāsau / ato viduṣām aviparītāvasthāyāṃ viparītasyāsaṃbhavāt kutaḥ saṃāvṛtaṃ cakṣur yasya dharmitvaṃ syāt / iti na vyāvartate 'siddhādhāraḥ pakṣadoṣa āśrayāsiddho vā hetudoṣaḥ / ity aparihāra evāyaṃ /.* *LVP has *'siddhādhāre pakṣadoṣa*. De Jong (1978) p. 31 reads *'siddhādhāraḥ pakṣadoṣa*.

Translation: "[Candrakīrti:] Now this is not so [i.e. it is not so, as Bhāvaviveka had argued, that the *dharmin* is simply the unqualified general term]. For, precisely when the negation of production is intended to be the property to be proved (*sādhyadharma*) here, then indeed this [philosopher, i.e. Bhāvaviveka] himself accepts the elimination of the *dharmin* which is the locus for this [*sādhyadharma*], viz. the self's possessions [such as the eye, etc.] which are found just because of error. Indeed, error and non-error are opposed. And so, when something inexistent is grasped as existent due to error, as in the case of the hairs and other such [illusions grasped] by those who have [the eye-disease known as] *timira*, then at this time how could there be a perception of even the slightest trace of a real entity? And when no inexistent thing is superimposed because there is no error, as in the case of the hairs and so forth when someone is free of *timira*, then how [too] could there be perception of even the slightest trace of an unreal entity, so that it would then have to be conventionally existent? It is precisely for that reason that the venerable Ācārya [Nāgārjuna] stated [in *Vigrahavyāvartanī* XXX]:

If, through perception or other [*pramāṇas*], I were to apprehend something, I would affirm or negate. But as such a thing is inexistent, I am without reproach.

Now, since error and non-error are thus opposed, then in the unerring state of the wise nothing erroneous can exist, so how would the conventional eye [i.e. the general unqualified term] be what is the *dharmin*? Therefore, [Bhāvaviveka] does not avoid the thesis-fault of an unestablished locus nor the reason-fault of an unestablished basis. And so this was not at all a reply [to our criticisms]."

This part of *Prasannapadā* I is greatly elaborated upon in numerous Tibetan texts such as mKhas grub rje's *sToṅ thun chen mo*, sGom sde Nam mkha' rgyal mtshan's *Thal bzlog gi dka' ba'i gnas*, etc. etc. and

The second criterion, then, is in accordance with a general thrust of Candrakīrti's philosophy: to dispense with the Svātantrika's and Yogācāra's postulation of seeming-objects as being *sine qua non* for our judgements of truth and falsity and our logical reasonings; truth, falsity and logic can be grounded simply on the conventions and rules of ordinary life, and *require nothing further* — no common intersubjective phenomena or data on which the world's practices would be based.

But to go back to the first criterion, however, let us look a bit more closely at what Candrakīrti seems to mean by things appearing different from the way they are and what the consequences are for the given taken in the Svātantrika way. A particularly interesting passage is to be found in Candrakīrti's *Madhyamakāvatārabhāṣya* to VI, 28, where we read that things which are conventional truths (*saṃvṛtisatya*) for ordinary beings, appear as just simply conventional (*saṃvṛtimātra*) for the Āryas, in that the latter *see* (*gzigs pa*) that conditioned things (*saṃskāra*) are false like reflections, and hence see them as artificial and not true.[108] What is important in this

---

forms the basis for the problem of "commonly appearing subjects" (*chos can mthun snaṅ ba*). See fn. 94; for remarks on the dGe lugs pa interpretation of the Bhāvaviveka-Candrakīrti debate, see my article "Tsoṅ kha pa *et al.* on the Bhāvaviveka-Candrakīrti debate" forthcoming in the proceedings of the 1989 Congress of the International Association of Tibetan Studies, Narita, Japan.

Finally, we should also mention Pr. 35,9 where Candrakīrti stresses that seeking agreement from both parties on an inference is generally pointless: *svārthānumāne tu sarvatra svaprasiddhir eva garīyasī / nobhayaprasiddhiḥ / ata eva tarkalakṣaṇābhidhānaṃ niḥprayojanam /.* "But in the case of an inference-for-oneself (*svārthānumāna*), it is always just one's own acknowledgment which is particularly important, not an acknowledgment by both [parties]. For this very [reason] the logical characterizations [of Dignāga and co.] are pointless." The passage is cited and discussed in *lCaṅ skya grub mtha'* pp. 407-408. For passages from Svātantrika texts which argue *for* commonly appearing subjects, see fn. 94; cf. also e.g. Kamalaśīla's *Sarvadharmaniḥsvabhāvasiddhi* P. 326b7 where he admonishes against reasons being established simply because one accepts them (*dam bcas pa tsam gyis 'dod pa'i don ma grub pa*), the latter absurd position being inevitable for him if reasons are established in the absence of anything objective and common to both debaters.

108 M. av. bhāṣya ad M. av. VI, 28 (LVP ed. 107,19): *de yaṅ ñan thos daṅ raṅ saṅs rgyas daṅ byaṅ chub sems dpa' ñon moṅs pa can gyi ma rig pa spaṅs pa / 'du byed gzugs brñan la sogs pa'i yod pa ñid daṅ 'dra bar gzigs pa rnams la ni bcos ma'i raṅ bźin yin gyi / bden pa ni ma yin te / bden par mṅon par rlom pa med pa'i phyir ro // byis pa rnams la ni bslu bar byed pa yin la / de las gźan pa rnams la ni sgyu ma la sogs pa ltar rten ciṅ 'brel par 'byuṅ ba ñid kyis kun rdzob tsam du 'gyur ro //.* Transl. LVP "Cette [*saṃvṛti*] — pour les śrāvakas, les pratyekabuddhas et les bodhisattvas, qui ont abandonné 'l'ignorance souillée' et qui voient les *saṃskāras* comme ayant le même mode d'existence que les reflets, etc., — est artificielle et non pas véritable, car il n'y a pas [dans ces Āryas] 'illusion sur la vérité' (*satyābhimāna*). Les [objets] qui trompent les sots (*bāla*) ne sont que *saṃvṛti* (*saṃvṛtimātra*) pour ceux qui ne sont point [des sots], parce que ces objets sont, tout comme une magie optique, etc., produits par l'enchaînement des causes."

Nagao (1954) p. 561 made an interesting hint at a rapprochement between the *saṃvṛtimātra* of Candrakīrti and the *paratantrasvabhāva* in Yogācāra, free of *parikalpita*. This is somewhat misleading if we think of *paratantra* as ultimately established, which is of course the way Vijñānavādins take it. Candrakīrti is clearly not advocating that. However, Mādhyamikas, such as Kamalaśīla in *Madhyamakāloka* P. 162b5-7, do also speak of a *paratantra* which is *not* ultimately established, and that might perhaps seem a better candidate for similarity with Candrakīrti's *saṃvṛtimātra*. Kamalaśīla writes: *dbu ma pa rnams kyaṅ ṅo bo ñid gsum rnam par bźag pa khas mi len pa ni ma yin te / gźan du na mthoṅ ba la sogs pa daṅ 'gal ba ji ltar spoṅs par 'gyur*

passage, is not that the Āryas and non-Āryas have exactly the same sense-datum and then conceptualize differently (as the other schools would have it); nor is the point at stake that Āryas have some of sort of radically different raw given from non-Āryas, as if we saw blue patches and they saw red patches. The upshot is that the Prāsaṅgika is probably not framing the problem in the context of there being uninterpreted sense-data, *ākāra*, "common appearances", etc. which are subsequently conceptualized. The various models of perception which turn around the definition of perception as *kalpanāpoḍha*, and which presuppose that one simply sees an uninterpreted brute datum are, in effect, being put in question in favour of perception of already interpreted data.[109]

/ de la dṅos po ma brtags na grags ji ltar snaṅ ba sgyu ma bźin du brten nas byuṅ ba gaṅ yin pa de ni gźan gyi dbaṅ gi ṅo bo ñid yin no // de yaṅ kun rdzob tu sgyu ma bźin du gźan gyi rkyen gyi dbaṅ gis skye'i /... "Mādhyamikas too do not fail to accept the presentation of the three natures, for otherwise how could they abandon contradictions with observation and the like. Here, that which is acknowledged so long as one does not analyse the entity, is just as it appears and arises dependently like an illusion is *paratantrasvabhāva*. It is produced conventionally, like an illusion, due to other conditions, ..." However, if we look at what Kamalaśīla is saying, the similarity with *saṃvṛtimātra* becomes more remote. He is obviously taking a position similar to that of Jñānagarbha, where conventional truth is, or corresponds to, simple appearance, the given which everyone has, whether Ārya or not. For Candrakīrti, *saṃvṛtimātra* only concerns the Āryas, and is their exclusive *way* of seeing objects; it is not also common to ordinary beings.

109 Part of the conceptual tool-kit of most contemporary analytic philosophers is the distinction formulated by Wittgenstein in his *Philosophical Investigations* between simply seeing an object — like seeing the lines on a page — and seeing an object *as* being something — one sees the lines as a picture of a duck or rabbit. Taken in the light of this distinction, one could say that Candrakīrti's point is to minimize or eliminate seeing in favour of seeing-as. His Svātantrika and Yogācāra opponents, by contrast, are saying that one sees something and then conceptualizes, or thinks, that it exists in a certain way. For Candrakīrti, however, the question of truth or falsity is not a matter of a given which first just simply appears and then is conceptually interpreted. The difference in the Ārya's and non-Ārya's perception is that the former "sees conditioned things *as* having a similar [illusory] mode of existence as reflections, etc."; the latter sees things as existing in reality.

A word on some of the numerous indigenous Tibetan debates on these matters. One could reasonably argue that it makes no sense to speak of the mere appearance of an object apart from its interpretation as true or false. Curiously enough, on Tsoṅ kha pa's point of view, it would be more accurate to say that it is the *ordinary person* who cannot make that difference between a mere appearance of X and the (erroneous) way in which X appears. *dBu ma dgoṅs pa rab gsal* p. 222: *...sṅon po raṅ gi mtshan ñid kyis grub par snaṅ ba na yaṅ / sṅon po'i steṅ nas raṅ bźin gyis grub par snaṅ mi snaṅ gi cha gñis dbyer med par snaṅ la* ... "Also in the case of blue, which appears as established by its own characters, then with regard to the blue, the element (*cha*) which appears as established by its own nature and that which does not appear [in this way] appear inseparably." Elsewhere in *dGoṅs pa rab gsal* (p. 175) he argues that to make that separation one must have realized voidness. In short, Tsoṅ kha pa's analysis detected two things, the appearance of a vase and its appearance as having a nature, and then argued that short of Āryahood we cannot make the distinction.

No doubt he had his reasons for this approach, not the least of which is his doctrine of the "identification of the object to be refuted" (*dgag bya ṅos 'dzin*) and his enormous effort to be able to somehow preserve *pramāṇas*. By saying that at least the Āryas could make such a separation, he could safely say that the appearance of the vase, (but not the appearance of it being established by *svabhāva*) is conventionally

Finally, a consequence of this rejection of uninterpreted data and of the fact that non-Āryas always erroneously *see* things as being real, or possessing *svabhāva*, is that Candrakīrti (in M. av. VI, 24-25) does not accept the Svātantrika idea of *tathya-saṃvṛti*, viz. that the appearances can correspond to, or be, the conventional object.[110] Instead, he makes a distinction between conventions of "truth" or "falsity" which presupposes that actually (in terms of the first truth-criterion which we gave above), all must be false. The only relevant element is the presence or absence of certain recognized causes for error, such as defective sense organs.

> "Those who see falsely are accepted as being of two sorts, those whose sense organs are clear [i.e. undefective] and those whose sense organs are defective. The consciousness of those with defective sense organs is held to be false relative to the consciousness of [those with] sense organs which are in good condition."[111]

Given that *svabhāva* / *svalakṣaṇa* is not even acceptable on a conventional level (cf. M. av VI, 36),[112] then the way in which we see can never correspond to anything. Thus, Candrakīrti rejects the Svātantrika's distinction between *tathyasaṃvṛti* and *mithyāsaṃvṛti*, and with that distinction also goes the Svātantrika's postulate of a minimal given which can *correspond to* the conventional object (as in the philosophy of

---

established by a *pramāṇa*. The debate on these subjects has a long development in Tibetan all the way up to the free-thinking twentieth-century scholar, dGe 'dun chos 'phel, who pertinently argued that because the two "elements" were, practically speaking, impossible to separate, it is best not to even attempt such a distinction, for the danger in speaking of *pramāṇas* is that one will surely reify conventional truth. See his *Klu sgrub dgoṅs rgyan*, f. 13a: *rje bla ma raṅ gi źal nas / stoṅ ñid ma rtogs bar du / yod pa tsam daṅ / bden par yod pa'i khyad par nam yaṅ phye mi srid ciṅ / de bźin bden par med pa daṅ / med pa tsam gyi khad par yaṅ 'byed mi nus źes gsuṅs śiṅ / thal raṅ la chos can mthun snaṅ ba med pa'i rgyu mtshan mthar thug kyaṅ de yin par gsuṅs pas / lta ba ma rtogs goṅ du bden grub zur du ṅos zin pa ga la srid / des na dgag bya ṅos 'dzin khul byas pa de la yid rton ga la yod /*. "The Holy Lama [Tsoṅ kha pa] himself stated: 'Before realizing voidness, one can never distinguish between mere existence and true existence and similarly one cannot make a difference between true inexistence and mere inexistence.' And he said that this [fact] is the ultimate reason why subjects [of reasonings] (*dharmin*) do not appear similarly to Prāsaṅgika and Svātantrika. Therefore, before realizing the view, how could one separately recognize 'true establishment' (*bden grub*)? So why should we have any confidence in those [followers of Tsoṅ kha pa] who pretend that they recognize the object to be refuted?" See Hopkins (1983) on the Sa skya-dGe lugs debate on these and related topics.

110 See fn. 106.

111 M. av. VI, 24: *mthoṅ ba brdzun pa'aṅ rnam pa gñis 'dod de // dbaṅ po gsal daṅ dbaṅ po skyon ldan no // skyon ldan dbaṅ can rnams kyi śes pa ni // dbaṅ po legs gyur śes bltos log par 'dod //*. Cf. LVP's translation, (1910) p. 300.

112 See M. av. bhāṣya to VI, 36: *de'i phyir raṅ gi mtshan ñid kyi skye ba ni bden pa gñis char du yaṅ yod pa ma yin no //*. Transl. LVP "Par conséquent, au point de vue des deux vérités, il n'y a pas naissance du caractère propre (*svalakṣaṇa*)." J. May emends: "Par conséquent, au point de vue de l'une et l'autre vérité

Jñānagarbha et al.), or which *is* itself the conventional object (as in Śāntarakṣita's system).

To resume Candrakīrti's view we could construct the following table showing the different positions on the given which we have examined:

Positions	**Schools which accept them**
1. *ākāra* are *paratantra* (ultimately real).	Satyākāravijñānavāda (Dignāga, Dharmakīrti)
2. *ākāra* are *parikalpita* but mind is real.	Alīkākāravijñānavāda (Asaṅga, Dharmottara, etc.)
3. *svasaṃvedana* is ultimately real	Satyākāravijñānavāda and most (if not all) Alīkākāravijñānavāda
4. Appearances (*snaṅ ba; snaṅ ba'i cha*) can conform to, or be the conventional object and are conventionally real.	All Svātantrikas

Svātantrika-Mādhyamikas all reject 1 and 3, but (at least according to Tibetan doxographical literature) those who accept Yogācāra on the level of conventional truth can lean towards Satyakāravāda or Alīkākāravāda on this level. E.g. in the first case *ākāra* are *paratantra* and are conventionally real; whereas in the second case it is only *svasaṃvedana* which is conventionally real.[113] At any rate, what is important for us is that *Candrakīrti rejects all four positions above.*

One final piece is necessary in the mosaic we have constructed. Although we see that Candrakīrti does not accept the Yogācāra's and Svātantrika's versions of the given, in the end does he, or could he, accept any kind of perceptual given at all? Paul Williams thinks he must:

---

[113] See e.g. the Mādhyamika classifications in 'Jam dyaṅs bźad pa's *Grub mtha' chen mo*, as well as in *lCaṅ skya grub mtha'* and *Grub mtha' rin chen phreṅ ba*. See Mimaki (1982) pp. 29-31. Śāntarakṣita and Kamalaśīla are Mādhyamikas who are "inclined towards Satyākāravāda" (*rnam bden pa daṅ mthun pa*), whereas Haribhadra, Jitāri and Kambala are Mādhyamikas "inclined towards Alīkākāravāda" (*rnam rdzun pa daṅ mthun pa*). At least in the case of Śāntarakṣita and Kamalaśīla, I can find some evidence that this classification is sound. See fn. 108 for the *Madhyamakāloka*'s position on *paratantra*. In the case of Kambala, his Alīkākāravāda seems probable, but it is not clear why he is to be classified as a Svātantrika-Mādhyamika rather than as a Vijñānavādin. Cf. his *Ālokamālā*, verses 19-21, 23-27. Text and translation in Lindtner (1985).

"Even the Prāsaṅgikas could not totally deny the given, and indeed to do so would be fatal to Buddhism for this would be to deny the basis for religious activity." (Williams 1979 p. 329.)

Any answer which we can present here will admittedly be somewhat speculative, but if we mean by the words "the given" the *entity* which, as we saw earlier, Richard Rorty and other contemporary philosophers describe as "the sort of entity naturally suited to be immediately present to consciousness" (Rorty 1980, p. 104), then I think Candrakīrti does not have a given at all. Undeniably, we do sometimes find uses of the term *ākāra* in Candrakīrti's works. In CSV XIII to k. 322 (§87) we find the words *jalākārasaṃjñā* ("a notion which has the aspect of water") used in describing cognitions of mirages, and in *Madhyamakāvatārabhāṣya* to VI, 37-38b he speaks of reflections being void, but that nonetheless "consciousnesses will arise in the aspect of these [reflections]" (*śes pa de yi rnam par skye 'gyur*). It is, however, far from clear as to whether *ākāra* is not just being used in a fairly loose sense where it just describes what the consciousness in question is like. As such, these passages give us little indication of Candrakīrti's stance. A perhaps more problematic case is to be found in the *Yuktiṣaṣṭikāvṛtti*, where Candrakīrti seems to flirt very briefly with what looks like a Sautrāntika Sākāravāda, i.e. the position that consciousness has *ākāra* which accord with those of the external object, or *svalakṣaṇa*.[113a] In fact, however, the reference to Sākāravāda here probably has little more than analogical value. Candrakīrti is seeking to answer a very specific objection, namely, how could one see anything at all when one realizes the truth of cessation? It is at this point that he says that it is like others' account of perceiving *ākāra*, but there is no evidence that he advocated *generalizing* a Sākāravādin account to apply to *all* perceptions. Indeed the Sākāravādin's explicit reliance on *svalakṣaṇa* here suggests that a literal acceptance of such a Sautrāntika position by Candrakīrti is impossible.

I would maintain that the simple talk about *ākāra*, even in an apparently more technical context, is not enough by itself to attribute to Candrakīrti an acceptance of a given. It is quite possible to use the terminology of *ākāra* merely to assert that consciousness has certain contents, without taking the additional step of reifying that content into something which is naturally suited to be the immediately present *entity*, like a seeming-object. That latter step, as I have tried to show, typically relies upon at least *some* acceptance of a constellation of other concepts, such as real *paratantra*, *svasaṃvedana*, common appearances, the non-deceptiveness of perception, *tathyasaṃvṛti*, etc., *all* of which Candrakīrti rejects. The same considerations apply *mutatis mutandis* to the not infrequent talk about "appearances" in Prāsaṅgika texts. Judging from the dossier which we have presented, Candrakīrti could reasonably speak of things

---

113a P 10a5-10a7: *gal te de'i tshe des ci mthoṅ na de'i tshe ci źig de la mṅon sum du 'gyur / bśad pa / ma mthoṅ du zin kyaṅ rnam par śes pas de'i rnam par rig pas mṅon sum du źes gdags so // gźan dag gis kyaṅ yul raṅ gi mtshan ñid kyi rnam pa daṅ mthun pas sṅon po la sogs par snaṅ ba'i rnam par śes pa gźan yaṅ mṅon sum du bstan to // 'di la yaṅ de daṅ mthun pa yod pas de mṅon sum źes bya ba de 'gal ba med do //.*
My thanks to C. Scherrer for this reference.

"appearing in a certain manner", or even of "appearances" and *ākāra*, without reifying them: "appearance" would mean no more than the way something looks, and not a type of phenomenal pseudo-object.

In sum, I think that Candrakīrti's position would have to be something like the following: *We seem to see objects such as vases, etc., are under the impression that we see such objects and certainly speak of seeing them, but no further explanations can or need to be given.* Firstly, Candrakīrti, by his thoroughgoing negation of all *svabhāva*, including the conventionally established *svabhāva* of the Svātantrika school, does, I believe, deny that "seeming to see *X*" implies seeing some determinate and definable phenomenon, i.e. an appearance of *X*, or a seeming-*X*. Disregarding the usual hyperbole which we find in Tibetan literature on how difficult it is to understand the Prāsaṅgika position of no *svabhāva*, I think we *can* venture two alternative interpretations: *a)* Svātantrikas and others reify the way an illusion appears into a determinate phenomenon with a nature; Candrakīrti says that *all* seeming-objects are impossible, because they have no natures. Thus, he would definitively block *any* move from "seeming to see *X*" to "seeing a seeming-*X*". *b)* The Svātantrika's version of the given, i.e. *his* type of seeming-object, is impossible, but there could be some type of seeming-object which nonetheless had no nature at all. I think *a)*'s rejection of all seeming-objects is the most readily defensible, and indeed some version of this rejection has been defended by quite a number of thinkers (e.g. R. Rorty, W. Sellars). The second alternative is extremely hard to imagine: we would on the one hand admit illusory "objects" like Macbeth's dagger, but on the other hand say that they had no illusory daggerness or any other nature at all. A second consideration: Candrakīrti's anti-reductionism (see fn. 89) and his positions on the functioning of logic and communication would tend to show that such a reified appearance is, moreover, quite unnecessary: without it he could still cogently say that there is a basis for religious activity. Indeed, Candrakīrti could appeal to ordinary usage, just as he does in CSV XIII §8-17, and maintain that he accepts "seeing objects" in just the way in which all non-philosophers do — pseudo-refinements like common intersubjective appearances of *X*, or even any kind of appearance which is not just the "way *X* looks", but is reified into an object, would be superfluous intellectual distinctions made by "logicians [who] become intoxicated through imbibing the brew of dialectics (CSV XIII §17)" and who are "completely unversed in mundane things" (CSV XIII §8).

B. Dharmapāla on perception

Turning now to Dharmapāla's philosophy of perception, let us provisionally adopt the usual formula and characterize it as idealism. This much will, no doubt, seem like a truism, especially if we refer to Dharmapāla's continual insistence on the refutation of external objects in his commentary on Āryadeva and in the *Chéng wéi shí lùn*, as well as his endorsement of the ultimate reality of the dependent natures (*paratantra*) and thoroughly established natures (*pariniṣpanna*) in the eighth chapter of his commentary on the *Catuḥśataka*. In fact, as we shall see below, while it is true that Dharmapāla's philosophy was a type of idealism, it is more complicated to say exactly what sort of an idealism it was. Complicating the picture is the fact that he is commenting on and using Madhyamaka arguments. But before taking up these questions, let us briefly look at some of the typical Yogācāra (= Vijñānavāda) elements in Dharmapāla's position.

We now have quite some material on the (written) debate which took place between him and the Mādhyamika, Bhāvaviveka: Dharmapāla put forward his position in the last chapter of his commentary on Āryadeva; Bhāvaviveka's critique of Dharmapāla's Yogācāra is set forth in the first and twenty-fifth chapters of the former's *Prajñāpradīpa* and in the fifth chapter of his *Madhyamakahṛdaya*; we also possess an account of the Bhāvaviveka-Dharmapāla debate by the Korean monk, Wŏnch'uk (Yuán cè 圓測) of Xī míng 四明 temple, a disciple of Xuán zàng.[114] It is impossible for me to go into many of the details of the debate and the interpretations of the various sūtra quotations, but the essential point of the debate concerns the interpretation of the *Prajñāpāramitāsūtra*'s pronouncements that dharmas are without natures (*niḥsvabhāva*), do not arise (*anutpāda*) or cease, have always been tranquil and by nature in nirvāṇa[115]; Dharmapāla took the *Prajñāpāramitāsūtra*'s statements as being of "interpretative meaning" (*neyārtha*) and opted for the *Saṃdhinirmocanasūtra*'s

---

[114] See Yamaguchi (1941) for an initial study. For research in European languages, see LVP (1933b) pp. 47-54 "Conflit Madhyamaka-Yogācāra" for an early but accurate presentation of the main issues and some quotes from Dharmapāla's commentary; see May (1979) *Hōbōgirin* s.v. *Chūgan*, pp. 484-486 for Chinese and Japanese sources on the "debate on voidness and existence" (*zhèng kōng yǒu* 諍空有), as the Indian debate came to be known; Hirabayashi and Iida (1977) on Wŏnch'uk's account; Iida (1980), especially pp. 259-269 on the *satyadvaya* and *trisvabhāva* theories plus excerpts from Tsoṅ kha pa's *Draṅ ṅes legs bśad sñiṅ po*; Iida (1973); Iida and Conze (1968); Kajiyama (1968) for a general account of the circumstances of the written debate and a few examples of Dharmapāla and Bhāvaviveka's interchanges in *Guǎng bǎi lùn shì lùn* VIII and *Prajñāpradīpa*; Eckel (1985) on Bhāvaviveka's critique of the Yogācāra in *Prajñāpradīpa* XXV plus a translation of the Appendix to Chapter XXV; Lindtner (1984) for an edition of the Appendix to Chapter XXV; Lindtner (1986) on Bhāvaviveka's critique of Yogācāra in the *Madhyamakaratnapradīpa* IV, plus a summary of his position in *Prajñāpradīpa*, *Madhyamakahṛdaya* and the commentary, *Tarkajvāla*. To complete and balance the dossier, we need a translation of the final chapter in the *Guǎng bǎi lùn shì lùn*, for as things stand the work on Bhāvaviveka is far more advanced than the work on Dharmapāla.

[115] Cf. *Aṣṭasāhasrikā Prajñāpāramitā* chap. 15, p. 148 and other citations in Lamotte (1935) p. 193, n.2.

explanation in terms of the three-nature (*trisvabhāva*) doctrine[116], while Bhāvaviveka took the statements about "non-arisal", etc. as definitive (*nītārtha*). For Yogācāra, the causally dependent phenomenon, i.e. *paratantra*, does really exist and does arise: it is the *parikalpitasvabhāva*, the misconceived or thoroughly imagined natures of *paratantra*, which have never existed nor arisen and which are without nature.

There are numerous *parikalpitasvabhāva* discussed in the Yogācāra school, but principally two take on major importance. In the *Saṃdhinirmocansūtra* and in Asaṅga's *Bodhisattvabhūmi* and *Mahāyānasaṃgraha*, the main fiction which we imagine is that words apply to their referents in virtue of the referents' own natures (*svabhāva*), and not simply due to our conceptualization. For Dharmapāla, however, the principal *parikalpitasvabhāva* which he stresses is the imagined difference between the subject which apprehends (*néng yuán* 能緣 = *grāhaka*) and the object which is apprehended (*suǒ yuán* 所緣 = *grāhya*); this is an unreality because in fact both subject and object are developments (*biàn yì* 變異 = *pariṇāma*) of the same karmic tendency.[117] At any

---

116 See Lamotte (1935) p. 193. See also *Siddhi* p. 556 note *b*. For the three-nature doctrine itself see *Saṃdhinirmocanasūtra* chapt. VI §3-7 (transl. Lamotte [1935] pp. 188-189); Vasubandhu's *Trisvabhāvanirdeśa*, transl. LVP (1933a); Asaṅga's *Mahāyānasaṃgraha* chapt. II, 16ff. (transl. in Lamotte [1973] pp. 108-124); *Siddhi* p. 514 et seq.; *Triṃsikā* k. 20-25, transl. Lévi (1932) pp. 114-119. Further references and explanations in *Siddhi* p. 514 n. *b*.; J. May and K. Mimaki (1979), *Hōbōgirin* s.v. *Chūdō* pp. 467-469. See also LVP (1933b) pp. 48-49 and the article by Liu Ming-wood (1982) on the three-nature doctrine in Indian and Chinese schools.

117 For Dharmapāla, see e.g. §229c11. For Asaṅga, see *Mahāyānasaṃgraha* chapt. II, 16 (p. 109 ed. Lamotte) which places the emphasis on language-based imputations of characteristics to objects. *Saṃdhinirmocanasūtra* chapt. VI §10 (Lamotte [1935] p. 190): "Le caractère imaginaire repose sur les noms attachés aux notions". See also Tsoṅ kha pa's *Draṅ ṅes legs bśad sñiṅ po* pp. 8, 30ff. *rJe btsun pa'i grub mtha'* f. 8a5-6 refers to both *parikalpita* in its presentation of the Yogācāra's notion of the subtle selflessness of dharmas (*dharmanairātmya*): *chos kyi bdag med phra mo'i mtshan gźi ni / gzugs daṅ gzugs 'dzin pa'i tshad ma rdzas gźan gyis stoṅ pa'i stoṅ pa ñid daṅ / gzugs gzugs źes pa'i sgra 'jug pa'i 'jug gźir raṅ gi mtshan ñid kyis grub pas stoṅ pa'i stoṅ ñid lta bu /*. "The illustrative examples of the subtle selflessness of dharmas are like the following: (a) the voidness [consisting in the fact] that form and the *pramāṇa* which apprehends form are void of any different substance; (b) the voidness [consisting in the fact] that form is void of any establishment by its own nature as being the referent for applying the word 'form'." Tibetans of Tsoṅ kha pa's school, in explaining Vijñānavāda, attempt a synthesis of these two sorts of *parikalpita*. See *lCaṅ skya grub mtha'* p. 238: *lugs 'dis ni gzugs sogs phyi rol don du ma grub pas phyi rol don snaṅ gi bag chags kyi dbaṅ gis don du snaṅ ba'i rnam par rig pa skye źiṅ / de la ni thog ma med pa nas 'di sṅon po'o 'di sṅon po'i skye pa'o źes sogs yaṅ daṅ yaṅ du mṅon par brjod pa'i bag chags kyi dbaṅ gis de lta bu'i tha sñad kyi gźir snaṅ ba 'byuṅ ṅo // de ltar snaṅ ba'i gzugs de ni naṅ śes pa'i bdag ñid tsam yin gyi de daṅ gtan nas 'brel ba med pa'i phyi rol gyi don ma yin pa'i phyir daṅ / de ñid miṅ gi tha sñad kyi gźir snaṅ ba yaṅ naṅ gi mṅon par brjod pa'i bag chags kyi dbaṅ gis snaṅ ba yin pa'i phyir / snaṅ tshul de miṅ brdas bźag pa la ma ltos pa'i yul raṅ gi gnas tshod kyi dbaṅ gis snaṅ tshul du mi rigs so //*. "According to this tradition [i.e. Vijñānavāda], form and so forth are not established as external objects, and thus, it is due to [karmic] tendencies (*bag chags* = *vāsanā*) for [things] to appear as external objects that a consciousness arises to which [form] appears. And here it is due to the tendencies [stemming] from saying again and again since beginningless [time], 'This is blue', 'This is blue's arisal', etc. that they [i.e. form etc.] appear as being the bases for linguistic designations such as ['blue', etc.]. The form, etc. which appear like this are just of the essence of the inner consciousness, but are not external objects which

rate, whether we follow the one account of *parikalpita* or the other, both Asaṅga and Dharmapāla would also say that there does exist a fact that *paratantra* lacks these *parikalpitasvabhāva*; this fact is itself real and is "thoroughly established" (*pariniṣpanna*).[118] Such was Dharmapāla's position, as can be seen from his adversary's depictions, those of Wŏnch'uk and his own statements in the last chapter of his commentary on Āryadeva. There is no doubt that for him both *paratantra* and *pariniṣpanna* exist really and ultimately (*paramārthatas*) and have natures (*svabhāva*). The former is inexpressible, directly perceived and, like the latter, must be classified as ultimate.[119] To take a representative quotation from the eighth chapter of Dharmapāla's commentary:

> "In reference to the thoroughly imagined natures (*biàn jì suǒ zhí xìng* 遍計所執性 = *parikalpitasvabhāva*[120]), he [i.e. the Buddha] said that they are void of nature, without arisal or cessation and so forth. Fools, on the basis of dharmas such as form, etc., which are developments of their own minds, have completely imagined understandings and grasp [these forms] as having various real natures. The Illustrious One, in reference to those [falsely imagined natures], said that the natures of dharmas such as form and the like are all void, without arisal, cessation, etc. As for the natures which arise in dependence on others [i.e. *paratantrasvabhāva*], because they lack the thoroughly imagined natures, they too are said to be void. [But] their own nature is not void, and they are not without arisal, cessation and so forth. The Tathāgata in various places has explained the three natures, always saying that the thoroughly imagined natures are void, but that the dependent (*yī tā* 依他 = *paratantra*) and thoroughly established (*yuán chéng* 圓成 = *pariniṣpanna*) natures both

---

would be completely unrelated to those [appearances]. Moreover, the [form's] seeming to be the basis for the linguistic designation, viz. the name, also appears [like this] due to inner speech-tendencies. Therefore, [for these two reasons,] this way of appearing cannot be a way of appearing which is due to the object's own mode of existence, independent of establishment through names and conventions."

118 Cf. *Madhyāntavibhāga* I, 13: *dvayābhāvo hy abhāvasya bhāvaḥ śūnyasya lakṣaṇam.* "The defining characteristic of voidness is the inexistence of duality [between subject and object][and] the existence of [that] inexistence."

119 T. 1571 x 247a6: 又現量證緣起色心言不能詮應非俗諦。"The dependently arising form and consciousness, which are established by direct perception, are inexpressible by words and cannot be conventional truth." Cf. fn. 2. The theme of the inexpressibility of the nature of dharmas is crucial in Yogācāra; cf. e.g. Asaṅga's *Bodhisattvabhūmi* chapt. IV p. 26, line 12 (ed. Dutt), who terms their nature *nirabhilāpyasvabhāvatā*. Cf. also Lamotte (1935) p. 182 and our §217a21, §221c7, en. 138. Candrakīrti in M. av. VI,47 represents his Yogācārin opponent as follows: *saṃvidyate 'taḥ paratantrarūpaṃ prajñaptisadvastunibandanaṃ yat / bāhyaṃ vinā grāhyam udeti sac ca sarvaprapañcāviṣayasvarūpam //.* Cited in the *Subhāṣitasaṃgraha*, f. 23. Transl. LVP: "Par conséquent existe le 'dépendant' (*paratantrarūpa*), qui est la condition de 'la chose existant en tant que désignée' (*prajñaptisadvastu*); il se produit indépendamment d'objet extérieur; il est; son être propre est inaccessible aux idées et aux paroles (*prapañca*)."

120 For various ways of translating the Skt. terms for the three natures, see Liu (1982) pp. 195-197.

exist. Therefore one knows that the teaching of voidness has another meaning."[121]

In reading Dharmapāla's commentary on Āryadeva, the question naturally arises as to how it is possible that Dharmapāla could write a seemingly Madhyamaka commentary, for just as it is sure that he accepted the reality of *paratantra* and *pariniṣpannasvabhāva*, it is equally sure that his Madhyamaka opponents, like Bhāvaviveka, did not accept these natures' reality.[122] Dharmapāla was not alone in performing this feat of doctrinal legerdemain: there were (at least) two Vijñānavāda commentaries on Nāgārjuna's *Mūlamadhyamakakārikās*, viz. those by Sthiramati and Guṇamati. The commentary by Guṇamati is no longer extant, but Sthiramati's commentary on MMK is conserved in Chinese. Tāranātha informs us that another commentator on MMK, Devaśarman, was supposedly a disciple of Dharmapāla; hence he would have been Vijñānavādin too, although this might seem to ill accord with Bhāvaviveka's apparent approval of Devaśarman's commentary.[123] At any rate, judging from the information

---

[121] T. 1571 x 248a25- b2: 此依遍計所執自性說自性空無生滅等　以諸愚夫隨自心變色等諸法周遍計度 執有眞實自性差別　世尊依彼說色等法　自性皆空無生滅等　依他起性由無遍計所執性故　亦說爲空　非自性空無生滅等　如來處處說三自性皆言遍計所執性空依他圓成二性是有故知空教別有意趣。

[122] See e.g. *Prajñāpradīpa* XXV, Lindtner (1984) p. 81 et seq. "*paratantrasvabhāva*" and p. 93 et seq. "*pariniṣpannasvabhāva*"; transl. Eckel (1985) p. 52 et seq. and p. 70 et seq. For a comparison between Dharmapāla and Candrakīrti's commentaries on CS, particularly on the question of the three nature doctrine and *niḥsvabhāvatā*, see Mitsukawa (1976).

[123] I.e. T. 1567 *Dà chéng zhōng guān shì lùn* 大乘中觀釋論 . In fact, we learn from Avalokitavrata's *Prajñāpradīpaṭīkā* that there were supposedly eight commentaries on MMK, viz. those of Nāgārjuna himself (the **Akutobhayā*), Buddhapālita, Candrakīrti, Devaśarman, Guṇaśrī, Guṇamati, Sthiramati and Bhāvaviveka. *Prajñāpradīpaṭīkā* P. 85a7-85b1 ... *bstan bcos 'di'i [i.e. MMK] 'grel pa byed pa maṅ ste / 'di lta ste / slob dpon gyi źal sṅa nas daṅ / gnas brtan buddha pā li ta daṅ / tsandra kīrti daṅ / de ba śarma daṅ / gu ṇa śrī daṅ / gu ṇa ma ti daṅ / sthi ra ma ti daṅ / slob dpon legs ldan 'byed ñid la thug pa'i bar dag yod pa las* ... See the discussion in Kajiyama (1963) pp. 37-38.

Yamaguchi (1947) p. 2 cites Tāranātha (transl. Schiefner p. 160, 174) to show that Guṇamati was a *disciple* of Sthiramati, but Frauwallner (1961) pp. 136-137 refers to Guṇamati as a *teacher* of Sthiramati, an opinion followed by Kajiyama (1963) and Ruegg (1981). Tāranātha himself (ed. Schiefner p. 123.16-20 states that Guṇamati was a follower of Sthiramati: *slob dpon yon tan blo gros ni rig pa'i gnas thaṅs cad la mkhas pa / mṅon pa mdzod kyi 'grel bśad byas / dbu ma rtsa ba la blo brtan gyi rjes 'braṅs te / legs ldan 'gog pa'i 'grel pa byas / legs ldan gyi slob ma saṃ pra du taḥ yaṅ 'di daṅ dus mñam du byuṅ / śar phyogs ba la pū rir rtsod pa yun riṅ du byas pas / yon tan blo gros rgyal lo źes grags so /*. "Ācārya Guṇamati was learned in all the sciences. He commented on the *Abhidharmakoṣa*. On the root text of the Madhyamaka [i.e. MMK] he followed Sthiramati and composed a commentary which was refuted by Bhāvaviveka. The disciple of Bhāvaviveka, Saṃpradutaḥ, also lived at this same time and debated [with him] for a long time in the East at Balapūri. It is generally said that Guṇamati won."

which we can glean, a common move in such Yogācāra commentaries may well have been to interpret the Madhyamaka's refutations of various entities as merely negating their *parikalpitasvabhāva* — certainly this tactic is very clear in the case of Dharmapāla. In other words, for Dharmapāla's Yogācāra the conclusion of a Nāgārjunian or Āryadevan argument is, in effect, that no entity exists different from the mind which apprehends it: there are no external objects (*wài jìng* 外境 = *bāhyārtha*). Naturally, the conclusion of virtually every Madhyamaka argument is phrased in terms of entities being void (*śūnya*) of nature (*svabhāva*), but the Yogācāra can turn this to his advantage by arguing that the ultimate nature of dharmas, their *parinispannasvabhāva* or thusness (*tathatā*), is "voidness" (*śūnyatā*) because these dharmas are void of all characters (*lakṣaṇa*), the latter all being *parikalpitasvabhāva* and without nature (*niḥsvabhāva*).[124] So long as the Yogācāra stresses exclusively the fact that *pariniṣpanna* is voidness and that all *lakṣaṇa* are purely imagined, he can make sense of most Madhyamaka argumentation. Indeed if one reads Dharmapāla's first seven chapters without reading the eighth, where he explains his standpoint on the three natures, his commentary on Āryadeva will, with a few exceptions, look like a Madhyamaka treatise. It is only when one arrives at the end that one fully realizes that one has to reinterpret all that came before in a Yogācāra light.

While the talk of voidness at least superficially concords with the Madhyamaka's use of terms, what clearly differentiates the usual Yogācāra position from the Madhyamaka is that for the former philosopher dharmas, when suitably purified of *parikalpita*, do really exist. Indeed the *Chéng wéi shí lùn* goes so far as to say that the ultimate nature of dharmas, or *pariniṣpannasvabhāva*, can also be said to be "existence" (*sattā*) in that dharmas, when we consider them free of these *parikalpitasvabhāva*, do exist purely as *paratantrasvabhāva*, as phenomena, dependent on causes and conditions,

---

As for Devaśarman, Tāranātha states (ed. Schiefner 133.17-19): *de'i dus na slob dpon chos skyoṅ gi slob ma de wa śar ma źes bya bas zla grags 'gog par bsam nas dbu ma'i 'grel pa dkar po rnam par 'char ba byas* / "At that time the disciple of Ācārya Dharmapāla known as Devaśarman composed the Madhyamaka commentary *dKar po rnam par 'char ba* in the intention of refuting Candrakīrti." See also Yamaguchi (1947) p. 2. Devaśarman's connection with Dharmapāla would however seem somewhat problematic in the light of the fact that Bhāvaviveka and Avalokitavrata apparently approved of his commentary. See *Prajñāpradīpaṭīkā* P. 225a7 et seq., Kajiyama (1963) p. 37, Ruegg (1981) p. 62, n. 187 and p. 67, n. 217.

If we accept Tāranātha's account, though, then of the eight commentators plus Dharmapāla, at least four would have been Vijñānavādins: Sthiramati, Guṇamati, Devaśarman and Dharmapāla. Asaṅga himself may have written such a commentary on MMK. T. 1565 on the eight negations in MMK's opening verse was translated by Gautama Prajñāruci and is attributed to Asaṅga; see *Inde Classique* §2138. See Ruegg (1981) p. 49 for these and other early commentaries on MMK.

[124] Cf. *Siddhi* p. 528: "Le Parinispanna est la perpétuelle privation (*rahitatā* = *śūnyatā*) de Parikalpita (première nature) du Paratantra (deuxième nature)." As for "*niḥsvabhāva*" ("no-nature"), the Yogācāra in fact has a doctrine of three *niḥsvabhāvatā*. See Lamotte (1935) pp. 193-196; *Siddhi* p. 556 et seq.; D. Shimaji, "Historique du système *vijñaptimātra*" in Lévi (1932) p. 38. What interests us here for the moment is the *niḥsvabhāvatā* which pertains to *parikalpita*, viz. *lakṣaṇaniḥsvabhāva*, no nature-qua-characters. See en. 50.

but free of the duality of subject and object.[125] The *Madhyāntavibhāga* and *Madhyāntavibhāgabhāṣya* arrive at the same result, in that their theory of voidness presupposes the real existence of something (i.e. *paratantra*) which is void of something else (*parikalpita*), the latter being inexistent, while the former exists.[126]

There is, however, an oddity in Dharmapāla's method: while he says that all *lakṣaṇa*, and especially existence and inexistence, are unreal fabrications of the imagination, he still, as a good Yogācārin, attributes existence to *paratantra* and *pariniṣpannasvabhāva*. But on numerous occasions he describes existence and inexistence as "proliferations (*prapañca*) of conceptualization" and says that ultimate nature, or thusness, is neither existence nor voidness. In the *Chéng wéi shí lùn* and in Kuī jī we find an attempt at differentiating between *śūnya* and *sat* on the one hand and *śūnyatā* and *sattā*, on the other, but if we look at Dharmapāla's commentary to CS XII k. 286cd (§219b20 et seq.), it is doubtful that he is invoking that point: instead he wants to give both existence and voidness the status of conventional truth — mere metaphorical descriptions used for methodological purposes as antidotes to grasping. This he justifies by the typical Madhyamaka assertion that even voidness is void — here he might seem to be

---

125 See *Siddhi* pp. 528-529.

126 See e.g. Vasubandhu's comment on *Madhyāntavibhāga* I,1: *evaṃ yad yatra nāsti tat tena śūnyam iti yathābhūtaṃ samanupaśyati yat punar atrāvaśiṣṭaṃ bhavati tat sad ihāstīti yathābhūtaṃ prajānātīty aviparītaṃ śūnyatālakṣaṇam udbhāvitaṃ bhavati*. Transl. Nagao (1978) p. 69: "Thus [in this verse] the characteristic of emptiness has been shown in an unperverted way as stated: 'It is perceived as it really is that, when anything does not exist in something, the latter is empty with regard to the former; and further it is understood as it really is that, when, in this place, something remains, it exists here as a real existent.'" In fact, as Nagao brings out, the Yogācāra are using a theory of voidness explained in the *Cūḷasuññatasutta*, where voidness is a lack of something unreal in something real: for the Yogācāra, the unreal is the *parikalpitasvabhāva* while the real is the *paratantra*. Thus the *paratantra* is "what remains" and exists after subtraction of all the *parikalpita*. As Nagao points out, this theory of voidness is explained in detail in Asaṅga's *Bodhisattvabhūmi*, *Tattvārtha* chapter p. 32 ed. Dutt: *kathaṃ punar durgṛhītā bhavati śūnyatā / yaḥ kaścic chramaṇo vā brāhmaṇo vā tac ca necchati yena śūnyam / tad api necchati yat śūnyam / iyam evaṃrūpā durgṛhītā śūnyatety ucyate / tat kasya hetoḥ / yena hi śūnyaṃ tadasadbhāvāt / yac ca śūnyaṃ tatsadbhāvāc chūnyatā yujyate / sarvābhāvāc ca kutra kiṃ kena śūnyaṃ bhaviṣyati / na ca tena tasyaiva śūnyatā yujyate / tasmād evaṃ durgṛhītā śūnyatā bhavati / kathaṃ ca punaḥ sugṛhītā śūnyatā bhavati / yataś ca yad yatra na bhavati tat tena śūnyam iti samanupaśyati / yat punar atrāvaśiṣṭaṃ bhavati tat sad ihāstīti yathābhūtaṃ prajānāti /*. "How then is voidness misconceived? It is said that when a śramaṇa or brahmin does not accept that of which something is void and does not accept that which is void, this sort of voidness is misconceived. Why is that so? For the following reason: When that of which the thing is void is inexistent and that which is void is existent, voidness is correct. Now since [according to this mistaken śramaṇa or brahmin] everything is inexistent, then what would ever be void of what? It is incoherent that the very thing be void of itself. So therefore, in this way voidness is misconceived. But how is voidness properly conceived of? [Reply:] One sees that *x* is void of the *y* which does not exist in *x*. [Lit. 'One sees that it is void of that which does not exist in it.'] However, one correctly acknowledges that the entity which remains here does indeed exist here." Cf. the transl. in LVP (1933b) p. 50. Finally note that in the Tibetan debate between advocates of "voidness of self" (*raṅ stoṅ*) and "voidness of other" (*gźan stoṅ*), the latter definition of Asaṅga is often invoked as the theory of voidness for the gŹan stoṅ pa. See e.g. Mi pham's *gŹan stoṅ seṅ ge'i ṅa ro*, pp. 366-367 (ff. 4b, 6 - 5a, 1), which cites this definition by Asaṅga.

leaning towards a more Madhyamaka than Yogācāra stance, in that he in effect dismisses these predications as not really true at all, but simply practical.

It is possible that Dharmapāla's Yogācāra side and his Madhyamaka were in something of an uneasy tension, the Yogācāra becoming dominant in the last chapter, while the other chapters were predominantly Madhyamaka. In fact, we see in his commentary to k. 323ab et seq. that he is also prepared to deny reality to consciousness (cf. §229a11), what is obviously a pleasing proposition for a Mādhyamika, but, at first sight, anathema for a Yogācārin. There is, however, a solution to these apparent conflicts: when Dharmapāla negates existence, inexistence, real consciousness and the like, he is negating characters which are essentially *parikalpita* and are misconceived; one can only regard such notions as conventional truths, void of *svabhāva*, but used for the sake of method in guiding disciples — even voidness, *qua parikalpita*, is no different on this score. On the other hand, when Dharmapāla subsequently affirms the existence of *paratantra*, *pariniṣpanna* and consciousness, he has changed perspective and is speaking of *paratantra*, etc. without distortions. In short, Dharmapāla's position seems to operate on two levels: a) his Madhyamaka-style critique is directed against misconceived notions of existence, inexistence, identity, difference, real consciousness and even voidness; b) his Yogācāra philosophy affirms the existence of consciousness and ultimate truth, what remains after misconceptions and errors are stripped away.[127] Taken in this light, it

---

[127] See *Siddhi* p. 523: "D'après Dharmapāla — Les Citta-caittas se développent (*pariṇam*) en deux Bhāgas par la force du parfumage (*vāsanā*). Ces deux Bhāgas, ainsi développés, naissent de causes et sont Paratantra au même titre que le Svasaṃvittibhāga. — Mais l'imagination (pien-ki, *vikalpa*), par rapport aux deux Bhāgas, conçoit les fausses notions de réelles existence, non-existence, identité, différence, existence plus non-existence, identité plus différence, ni existence ni non-existence, ni identité ni différence: les deux Bhāgas, conçus sous ces divers modes, prennent le nom de Parikalpita." Cf. also §225a10 and the verse in §229a11, which show that characters (*lakṣaṇa*) are unreal.

Kuī jī in the *Wéi shí èr shí lùn shù jì*, T. 1830 *shàng* p. 982c 12-16 brings out the *paratantra* nature of the parts of consciousness so long as they are not misapprehended due to grasping at externality. 若護法等以後聖説言内識生似外境現謂有依他自證見相三分而生不離識故名爲唯識　愚夫依此不離識法執爲離心有實境相此實所取心外二取體性都無。 "According to later Āryas such as Dharmapāla, it is explained that the inner consciousness gives rise to manifestations which resemble external objects. It is said that [the consciousness] arises having three parts which are dependent natures (*paratantra*), viz. the self-awareness, the perception and the characters — because [these parts] are not separate from the consciousness they are termed "just consciousness" (*vijñaptimātra*). Fools, in reference to these dharmas which are not separate from consciousness, grasp that there are real characters of objects separate from the mind [and that] these realities are what is apprehended. [These] natures [due to] dualistic apprehension of the mind and the exterior are completely inexistent." See fn. 25, 131.

Note that in fact this acceptance/rejection of existence from two different perspectives is nothing really new in Yogācāra. Asaṅga, whose theory of voidness demands the existence of *paratantra* (see fn. 126), also has many passages in the *Bodhisattvabhūmi* where he speaks pejoratively of "existence" as (mis)conceived by ordinary people, which is the root of all the world's conceptual proliferations. E.g. p. 26 ed. Dutt: *tatra bhāvo yaḥ prajñaptivādasvabhāvo vyavasthāpitaḥ / tathaiva ca dīrghakālam abhiniviṣṭo lokena / sarvavikalpaprapañcamūlaṃ lokasya /*. In the *Madhyāntavibhāga* and commentaries, the deliberate complexity of the various affirmations and denials of "existence" virtually precludes any attempt at detailed summary here. See

could perhaps be argued that there are even some advantages to his approach. He can safely deny all the lemmas of the *catuṣkoṭi*, for example, and not (like some Mādhyamikas) be prey to the frequently levelled charge of irrational nihilism, for he can maintain that the existence and inexistence which he is denying are *parikalpita* notions, and being fundamentally unreal, fictitious properties, they do not simply or in any combination qualify real entities like *paratantra*.[128]

Given this background on Dharmapāla's position, we can now make an attempt at answering our principal query, "In what sense is he an idealist?" The question, which on first sight seemed facile, now becomes considerably more complicated.

First of all, we should distinguish between epistemological and metaphysical arguments for Buddhist idealism.[129] The typical epistemological type of argument is what we find in Vasubandhu's *Viṃśatikā*, and is not far from Western idealists' "argument from illusion": since inexistent things, such as objects in a dream or hallucinations, appear qualitatively similar to objects which appear in the waking state, the latter are also mind-created, just like the former.[130] Another type of fundamentally epistemological argument is what we find in the *Ālambanaparīkṣā* of Dignāga. It goes like this: 1) the object of consciousness must satisfy two conditions, i.e. it must be causally related to the consciousness, and it must itself resemble the representation, or image (*ākāra*), which consciousness has of it. 2) External objects do not satisfy these criteria, in particular they do not satisfy the second criterion. 3) Therefore, external objects are not the objects of consciousness.[131]

Ruegg (1977) p. 22 et seq. Suffice it to make two remarks: a) As far as I can see, the conjunctions of seemingly contradictory affirmations and denials as in 1.3 (*sattvād asattvāt sattvāc ca madhyamā pratipac ca sā*) are not in fact contradictions. They are affirmations and denials of existence to different things, or to different aspects of the same thing, but never are we saying that the very same thing or aspect both exists and does not exist. The paradoxical way of expression is probably deliberate, but there is, I think, no real paradox. Cf. similar remarks of Ruegg on pp. 25-26; Nagao (1978) p. 75, however, does take 1.3 as saying that "one and the same entity is the subject of both 'is not' and 'is'." b) The most complicated case is that of the "unreal notion" (*abhūtaparikalpa*) which, as a notion, exists as *paratantra* and is the basis for voidness; it is inexistent, void or unreal in the sense that it is not as it seems. One has the nagging feeling that after the verbiage has been stripped away the point is fairly simple: the mistaken thought exists but the mistaken object it imagines doesn't. Cf. Nagao (1979), who is more charitable.

[128] See Appendix II.

[129] Matilal (1974) makes this distinction and summarizes most of the principal Buddhist arguments for idealism. A minor detail: he seems to include some arguments (such as those in the *Ālambanaparīkṣā*) under the rubric of "metaphysical" which I would say are more epistemological in nature.

[130] Cf. *Viṃśatikā*, k. 1: *vijñaptimātram evaitad asadarthāvabhāsanāt / yathā taimirikasyāsatkeśacandrādidarśanam //*. On the *Viṃśatika*'s response to four objections, see Hattori (1988) pp. 24-27.

[131] Note that *à la rigueur* this argument could also lead to what is commonly known as "representational realism", i.e. the position that what we perceive is not external objects but sense-data, but that there are external objects behind the "veil of perception". It does lead to idealism if we take the familiar idealist tack of saying that what is behind the "veil of perception", and is never itself perceived, does not exist. But while

These two sorts of argument are alluded to here and there by Dharmapāla in his commentary on Āryadeva, but are not of nearly as great an importance for him there as the metaphysical arguments, in particular, a variation on an argument which

---

it is perhaps not one hundred percent clear where exactly Dignāga made that supplementary move in the *Ālambanaparīkṣā* itself, it is abundantly clear that the *Ālambanaparīkṣā* gives external objects no role whatsoever in our cognition, and is explicitly arguing against different versions of *bāhyārtha* ("external objects"; Tib. *phyi rol gyi don*) being the object of cognition, as we already see from the introduction to k. 1. See Yamaguchi (1929) pp. 6 and 27.

Wayman (1979) p. 65 promulgates a confusion by writing: "Of course, if indeed the Yogācāra school denies the reality of an external object, it would hardly be possible to find its position attractive to the Buddhist logicians who were to follow, since Dignāga and his successors, especially Dharmakīrti, do not deny an external object; rather they call it a *svalakṣaṇa* (the 'particular') and even sometimes describe it as *paramārthasat* ('absolute existence'), to underscore the reality of this object of direct perception (*pratyakṣa*)." There is no reason to equate Yogācāra's *svalakṣaṇas* with external objects, nor would *svalakṣaṇa* necessarily be *unreal* in this school if they were of the same nature as the mind. In fact, contrary to Wayman, I have little doubt that Vasubandhu, Dignāga and Dharmakīrti were denying that external objects exist at all, just as was Dharmapāla. That is certainly the way their knowledgeable Hindu adversaries, like Uddyotakara and Kumārila, took them and it is also the way the Tibetan doxographers took them. See Matilal (1974) for Uddyotakara, Kumārila and Jayanta's arguments against these three authors. Dharmapāla in his commentary on the *Catuḥśataka*, of course, repeatedly denies that there are any external objects. See e.g. §217a2 and en. 36. (The case of Asaṅga in the *Yogācārabhūmi* is more complex. See Schmithausen [1987] p.32 n. 221 and 222.) Moreover, if we come up with the contrived interpretation that Yogācāra authors were not denying external objects, we have to say that Śāntarakṣita and the other Yogācāra-Mādhyamikas were also hopelessly confused on their interpretations of Yogācāra.

For Dignāga and Dharmakīrti's denials of external objects, we have to refer to the arguments from *svasaṃvitti* / *svasaṃvedana* (i.e. self-awareness) to get a balanced picture of how these authors proceed. See PVin I, k. 38 ≅ PV III, k. 327, which summarizes Dharmakīrti's idealism: *nānyo 'nubhāvyo buddhyā 'sti tasyā nānubhāvo 'paraḥ / grāhyagrāhakavaidhuryāt svayaṃ saiva prakāśate //*. "[Apart from consciousness itself] there is nothing else which is experienced by the mind. Nor does the [mind] have any other experience. As there is nothing apprehended and no apprehender, it is the [mind] itself which illuminates itself." Skt. found in Mokṣākaragupta's *Tarkabhāṣā*; see Kajiyama (1966) n. 413, Tosaki (1985) n. 31. Cf. PV III, k. 327 in Tosaki (1985) p. 10: *nānyo 'nubhāvyas tenāsti tasya nānubhavo 'paraḥ / tasyāpi tulyacodyatvāt svayaṃ saiva prakāśate //*. See also Mimaki (1980), p. 158 and n. 43.

Following Iwata (1984a) there seem to be two principal arguments turning on *svasaṃvedana*, however, the most well-known is the *sahopalambhaniyama* inference: "Blue and the consciousness of blue are not different, because they must always be apprehended together, just like when one [falsely] sees two moons." See Iwata (1981), (1984a), (1984b); Hattori (1988) pp. 50-51; Matilal (1974) and PV III k. 388-391 translated in Matilal (1974) pp. 159-160 as well as Tosaki (1985) pp. 71-75. The other inference, to be found in PVin I (p. 98. ed. Vetter [1966]) and called the "*saṃvedana* inference" in Iwata (1984a), is as follows: the object is not different from the cognizing consciousness, because it is being cognized (*saṃvedyamāna*); only what has essential identity (*tādātmya*) with consciousness is cognizable. (In short, external objects would be unknowable.) So, both of these arguments make it clear that ordinary objects, like blue, etc., are not external.

I am equally unconvinced by the arguments in Hall (1986) which maintain that Vasubandhu's *vijñaptimātratā* was not a metaphysical position, but "a practical injunction to suspend judgment: 'Stop at the bare percept; no need to posit any entity behind it.' (p. 18)" I fail to see why the practical aspects of the Abhidharmic Vasubandhu should have precluded him from taking metaphysical positions.

later writers would term the "neither one nor many" reasoning (*ekānekaviyogahetu*).[132] This is basically an argument which takes two forms: that any entity is neither one individual nor many different things, or that the part-whole relationship is impossible, for the parts are neither one with nor different from the whole. In fact, as I have argued elsewhere, the two forms of the argument are closely related, but the first usually turns on the second.[133]

Because the argument turns on the problem of the part-whole relationship, it can be generalized and used for a multitude of purposes, e.g. Vasubandhu used it to refute the relationship between a composite and the subtle atoms composing it, Dharmakīrti used it to show the impossibility of universals and their instantiations, space and time and their parts, and finally Mādhyamikas, such as Nāgārjuna and Candrakīrti, used it to show the incoherence of any relation between an ordinary object, like a cart, and its parts — indeed the reasoning is so wide in scope that the encyclopedic writer, Śāntarakṣita, was able to construct a treatise on the basis of this argument alone which would refute all entities, be they postulated by Buddhists or non-Buddhists.[134]

No doubt this is one of the most important, if not the principal reasoning which occurs in Dharmapāla.[135] He uses it to refute gross, external objects, universals,

---

132 Of course in his commentary on the *Ālambanaparīkṣā*, the *Guān suǒ yuán lùn shì*, T. 1625, Dharmapāla is using the Dignāgean argument. Indeed the arguments from the *Viṃśatikā* and *Ālambanaparīkṣā* seem to overlap, for the *Ālambanaparīkṣāvṛtti* ad k. 6a-c equally appeals to hallucinations to show that no external cause for perception is necessary.

133 See Tillemans (1983). The usual logic which we find in the *Madhyamakālaṃkāra*, Kamalaśīla's *Pañjikā*, and which is elaborated in Tsoṅ kha pa's *Draṅ ṅes legs bśad sñiṅ po* p. 137, is as follows: for an entity to be one individual thing, it would have to be one with or different from its parts, but both hypotheses are impossible. The entity cannot be many different things, because, by the previous reasoning, the individuals needed to make up a collection of many different things do not exist as ones. See also en. 37.

134 Cf. the opening "programmatic" verse of the *Madhyamakālaṃkāra*: *niḥsvabhāvā amī bhāvās tattvataḥ svaparoditāḥ ekānekasvabhāvena viyogāt pratibimbavat*. Cited in the *Bodhicaryāvatārapañjikā*, 173, 17-18. Transl. "Entities as asserted by ourselves and others, in reality, have neither the nature of oneness nor manyness. Therefore, they are without any nature, like a reflection." For some references to Vasubandhu, Dharmakīrti and Candrakīrti's uses of the argument, see Tillemans (1984c), n. 2.

135 In §229c11 he also uses the following reasoning: "the sense organs and their objects are all conventional, but not true [i.e. ultimate], in that they are objects of consciousness, like whirling firebrands' circles and other such [non-entities]." This could be variety of what T. Iwata (1984a) terms the *saṃvedana*-inference; see our fn. 131 and Iwata's p. 397. Note, however, that in TSP's introduction to the chapter on refutation of external objects we find a similar reasoning, and interesting enough, Kamalaśīla argues that the *vyāpti* ("implication"; "pervasion") holds in that nothing which is cognized can be an external thing, because it is neither one nor many, like a reflection. TSP p. 671: *tatra prayogaḥ yad yaj jñānaṃ tat tat grāhyagrāhakatvadvayarahitaṃ jñānatvāt pratibimbajñānavat / jñānaṃ cedaṃ svasthanetrādijñānaṃ vivādāspadībhūtam iti svabhāvahetuḥ / na cāvyāptir asya hetor mantavyā / tathā hi na tāvat pṛthivyādibāhyo 'rtho 'sya grāhyo vidyate tasyaikānekasvabhāvaśūnyatvāt /*. Transl. "Here there is the following reasoning: Every consciousness is free of the duality between apprehended and apprehender because it is a consciousness, like the consciousness of a

atoms, consciousness, etc., the conclusion being that since these would-be entities are contradictory, they do not exist externally, but are mind-created. But the very scope of the argument gives rise to the following qualm: "If Dharmapāla and other Yogācāras are using exactly the same arguments as the Mādhyamikas, do they in fact arrive at the same conclusions, and if not, what is the difference between the idealist and non-idealist conclusions of these arguments?"

There is a surprising vagueness in our definition of the term "idealism", a vagueness which becomes especially important in this discussion. If we follow dictionaries of philosophical terminology, we find statements like "the philosophical tendency which consists in reducing all existence to thought". And some authors have maintained that Yogācāra is idealist in this sense.[136]

While Yogācārins *are* indeed "idealists" in that sense, the problem is that in the Yogācāra vs. Mādhyamika discussion such a sense of "idealism" is too vague to be of much use in making the necessary distinction between the two schools: it seems to be trivially true of both. Indeed, a little reflection reveals to us that on *this* definition Mādhyamika writers — such as Candrakīrti, and what is really absurd, a Sautrāntika-Mādhyamika like Bhāvaviveka — might very well end up being idealists. After all, they too hold that all existence is, at least ultimately, mind-dependent or reducible to thought, for it is the mind which produces designations (*prajñapti*), and it is a cardinal tenet of Mādhyamikas that existents are only *prajñaptisat* or *upādāya prajñapti* ("dependent designations").[137] Moreover the recurring Madhyamaka theme is, of course, that nothing is substantially existent, but exists due to ignorance or error, like the illusions of a mesh of hairs for someone suffering from the eye disease, *timira*. A world existing

---

reflection. Now, the consciousnesses under discussion, viz. those of the healthy eye and other such [sense organs], are consciousness. The above is a reason which is an essential property (*svabhāvahetu*). Nor should it be thought that this reason has no *vyāpti*. For indeed, the [consciousness] has no external object, like earth, etc., which is apprehended (*grāhya*) because the latter is void of any nature of being one or many."

136 Cf. May (1971) pp. 265-266: "Les catégories qui gouvernent la pensée philosophique en Occident s'appliquent mal, en général, à la pensée indienne. Pourtant on peut admettre, sans trop forcer les choses, que le Vijñānavāda est un idéalisme. Encore faut-il s'entendre sur le sens de ce dernier terme, qui en a beaucoup. Il s'agit de l'idéalisme entendu comme 'la tendance philosophique qui consiste à ramener toute existence à la pensée'. Nous verrons que le Vijñānavāda peut être considéré comme tributaire de cette tendance." The definition quoted here is from André Lalande, *Vocabulaire technique et critique de la philosophie*, Paris, 1962, p. 435. Cf. also Schmithausen (1987) n. 222. Matilal (1974) p. 139: "Philosophical idealism is usually characterized as a denial of the common-sense view that material/external objects exist independently of the mind, i.e. independently of their being perceived. And this general character of idealistic philosophy was undoubtedly present in the Vijñānavāda theory of reality." In Matilal's definition, the problem is to define on which level of truth this denial takes place. All Yogācāras and Mādhyamikas would deny that the common-sense view is coherent from the point of view of ultimate truth. In short, in some sense they all make that denial.

137 See en. 40, 185, 363. Svātantrikas emphasize mind-dependence of all conventional entities. See p. 45 and fn. 100.

due to our ignorance, or like a dream — why isn't this idealism pure and simple? In brief, this definition commits the fault of *ativyāpti*: it includes too much.

In fact, Candrakīrti provides the basis for the differentiation between Madhyamaka and Yogācāra in his discussion of the dream example, arguing: "Because, in a dream, thought does not exist either for me, you have no [valid] example."[138] Tsoṅ kha pa elaborates on this solution in his *rTsa ba'i śes rab kyi dka' gnas brgyad*: the difference between the Mādhyamika (in particular, the Prāsaṅgika-Mādhyamika) and the Yogācāra is that the latter considers the mind to be more consistent and real than the imagined external objects.[139] Here is Tsoṅ kha pa's résumé of the fundamental point as to why a Mādhyamika like Candrakīrti is *not* an idealist:

> "So, from the point of view of convention, [external] objects and the mind are the same in being real. From the point of view of one contemplating the truth, object and mind are both the same in being unreal. Therefore, [for the Prāsaṅgika-Mādhyamika] it is incoherent that the object is unreal, while the mind is real."[140]

It is precisely this asymmetry or ontological hierarchy which Candrakīrti rejects, but which is crucial to the Yogācāra. Consequently, if we are to use the term "idealism" in the context of Buddhist philosophy, we have to redefine it so that the idealist is not just saying that objects are always dependent upon the mind, but rather that objects and the mind have a different ontological status. Both Yogācāra and Madhyamaka maintain that objects are reducible to mind, but the Yogācārin, in addition, maintains that the mind is more real than the object. For a Mādhyamika like Candrakīrti, however, the same arguments which he applies to objects are also applied to the mind, and hence both are on the same footing, neither is more real nor more logically consistent than the other and both have the same conventional existence.[141]

So in what sense is Dharmapāla an idealist given that, as we saw earlier, he also in some sense resists the tendency to reify mind? Applying our revised understanding of "idealism" we would have to say that Dharmapāla and other Yogācāras are idea-

---

[138] M. av. VI, 48cd: *svapne 'pi me naiva hi cittam asti yadā tadā nāsti nidarśanaṃ te //.*

[139] A more complicated case is that of the Yogācāra-Madhyamaka system of Śāntarakṣita and Kamalaśīla, who maintain that the mind is more real than the material on the level of conventional truth, but that ultimately both are unreal. (See Kajiyama [1978] p. 137 et seq. on Kamalaśīla's assimilation of the Yogācāra system as a stage in meditation to be subsequently transcended.) Candrakīrti makes no such distinction with regard to conventional truth.

[140] *rTsa śe dka' gnas brgyad* p. 17: *des na tha sñad pa'i ṅor don sems gñis ka yod par mtshuṅs la / de kho na ñid sems pa'i ṅor don sems gñis ka med par mtshuṅs pas / don med la sems yod par mi rigs so /.*

[141] For the point of view that early Yogācāra does *not* make such a difference in status between mind and external objects, see Nagao (1979) pp. 39-40. Unfortunately, like Candrakīrti, I do not see how the Yogācārin can deny duality and affirm mind *qua paratantra* without making *some* form of an ontological hierarchy.

lists *to the degree* that they do make the mind more fundamentally real than external objects. But curiously enough, while we see that Dharmapāla does accept the reality of mind *qua paratantra*, this is a very slim ontological commitment, for he is prepared to use Madhyamaka-style arguments to dismiss all its characters as mere *parikalpita*, and with these *parikalpitasvabhāva* goes not just the mind we conceive or talk about, but even our ordinary categories of existence and inexistence. The margin of difference between Dharmapāla's idealism and Candrakīrti's acceptance of external objects is thus fine indeed and turns on the acceptance or rejection of the mind *qua paratantra*, a mind which we cannot conceive of or say what it is, and whose mode of being we fundamentally do not understand. For Yogācārins the core of their position is that this inexpressible mind *qua paratantra* is a necessary condition for cognition, illusion and spiritual progress. In effect, then, their proofs of the reality of mind *qua paratantra* are transcendental arguments, and typically such arguments only show that something must be, but show nothing of its properties.

IV. A SUMMARY OF OUR ARGUMENTS IN CHAPTERS II AND III

A. The problem of scriptural authority

1. It is not only meaningful to speak of a common stance of the Epistemological school stance on questions of authority, but this same position is also found in Āryadeva and his two commentators. A connection between Dharmapāla and Dharmakīrti is very possible, even if we do not accept the account of Dharmapāla being a teacher of Dharmakīrti.

2. This common position on authority is developed further by Dharmakīrti. In theory at least, the role of authoritative people or scriptures is very limited: they can in no way challenge the results of inferences which function due to real states of affairs (*vastubalapravṛttānumāna*).

3. Indeed, the Buddhist logicians' rational orientation finally leads him to the position that most of our "knowledge", which inevitably depends on testimony, books, etc., is mere true presumption (*yid dpyod*), to use the category of the Tibetan scholastic.

B. Candrakīrti on perception and the status of the given

1. Candrakīrti, besides arguing logically against *svabhāva*, elaborated a complementary theory of perception directed against various versions of the given, viz. a type of *seeming-object* which, according to the adversaries, has a *svabhāva*.

2. Contrary to most of his Buddhist adversaries, Candrakīrti rejected perception as an immediate, non-deceptive form of knowledge. Whereas his adversaries used a definition of perception which would make a rigid separation between the latter and concepts, Candrakīrti was alone in rejecting such a definition and any such separation.

3. Most Yogācāras and Svātantrikas accepted some type of an unconceptualized, uninterpreted given which we perceive directly and which might then be misinterpreted by conceptualization. These are real *ākāra* in the case of the Yogācāras, and for the Svātantrika they are mind-dependent phenomena which we share in common

and which may be judged conventionally real (i.e.*tathyasaṃvṛti*) or unreal (i.e. *mithyāsaṃvṛti*) if they satisfy the tests of practical efficacity (*arthakriyā*).

4. Candrakīrti rejects such an uninterpreted given which appears similarly to everyone and which can then be judged as conventionally real or unreal. For him an object of perception is always interpreted, in particular, it is *seen* as real by those who have not realized voidness. Thus, the Svātantrika's distinction in terms of *tathyasaṃvṛti* and *mithyāsamvṛti* is rejected and with it their notion of a given.

5. Candrakīrti's works are best read as arguing for the position that there is no perceptual given at all.

C. Dharmapāla on perception

1. Dharmapāla, in spite of ostensibly commenting on a Madhyamaka text, adopts classic Yogācāra positions, construing Āryadeva's text as a refutation of *parikalpitasvabhāva*.

2. If we wish to satisfactorily answer the question as to whether Yogācārins, like Dharmapāla, were idealists, we must change our usual understanding of that term. A Buddhist idealist does not just accept mind-dependence or a reduction of existence to mind, but also that mind has a preferred ontological status and is more real than external objects.

3. While Dharmapāla's acceptance of the reality of mind *qua paratantra* does seem to make him an idealist in our revised sense, the structure of his system guarantees that any attempt to conceptualize or formulate what that mind is like or how it exists is impossible.

APPENDIX I: TEXTS AND TRANSLATIONS FROM PSV AND PST; A NOTE ON DHARMAKĪRTI'S AND DIGNĀGA'S APOHA

a) *PSV ad k. 5.*

The text is that of PSV(a) P. 29b6-30a1, unless otherwise indicated: *ji ltar de rjes su dpag pa ñid yin te / mtho ris la sogs pa'i sgra rnams kyis don tsam brjod pa ni ma yin no* // yid ches tshig kyaṅ mi slu bar / mtshuṅs phyir rjes su dpag pa ñid / yid ches pa'i tshig ñid gzuṅ nas kyaṅ mi slu bar mtshuṅs pa'i phyir de yaṅ rjes su dpag pa ñid du brjod do // de skad du yaṅ / miṅ gi las ni mṅon sum sṅon du 'gro ba can źes bya ba yin no** // phyogs 'dis ni gtso bo la sogs pa'i raṅ bźin rnams la rjes su dpag pa bkag pa yin no+ // de'i phyir rjes su dpag pa'i yul ni raṅ gi mtshan ñid ma yin no //.*

b) *Text-critical remarks and translation*:

* Based on PSV(b) P. 111a3. PSV(a) turns the whole sentence into an objection: *gal te mtho ris la sogs pa'i sgras don tsam brjod pa ni ma yin na ji ltar rjes su dpag pa ñid du 'gyur źe na*. This does not concord with PST which takes *mtho ris la sogs pa'i sgra ... ma yin no* as Dignāga's reply.

** Based on PSV(b) 111a4-5. PSV(a) reads *miṅ gi las rnams kyi sṅon du mṅon sum soṅ ba'i phyir ro źes 'byuṅ ṅo.*

\+ Based on PSV(b) 111a5. PSVa reads *de dag gis ni phyogs daṅ gtso bo la sogs pa'i raṅ bźin la yaṅ rjes su dpag pa dgag par bya'o*. As Hayes correctly pointed out (Op. cit. p. 250, n. 6), PSV(b)'s reading is supported by Jinendrabuddhi.

Hayes renders *don tsam brjod pa ni ma yin no* as "Words such as heaven *do not express any object at all*", which is, I think, a major cause of his problems. For the rest his translation is correct. What is also important is the conclusion, *de'i phyir ...raṅ gi mtshan ñid ma yin no* which figures in PSV(a) and (with some insignificant variants) in PSV(b): Hayes left it out.

My translation: "How can they [i.e. authoritative words] be inferences? [Reply:] Words such as 'heaven' and the like do not express *just the object* (*don tsam*) [consisting in the speech-intention]. Because authoritative words are also similar in not belying, they are an inference. When one apprehends authoritative words, they are similar in not belying, and therefore, they too are said to be inferences. Furthermore it is stated that the act of naming is preceded by a direct perception. This position refutes inferences with regard to natures such as *pradhāna* and so forth. Therefore the object of inference is not a *svalakṣaṇa*."

c) *PST P. 103b8-104a4*:

'o na yaṅ ji ltar yid ches pa ma yin pas rab tu sbyar ba'i sgra rnams ni brjod par 'dod pa'i mtshan ñid kyi don tsam gaṅ yin pa de tshig las rjes su dpag pa ñid yin gyi / phyi rol gyi don brjod par byed pa las ni ma yin pa de lta yid ches pas rab tu sbyar ba rnams kyaṅ 'gyur ro źe na bśad pa / ma yin źes pa la sogs pa ste / 'di ltar bsams pa ste / yid ches pa'i tshig ni brjod par 'dod pa'i don tsam la tshad ma ñid du 'dod par bya ba ma yin gyi

/ 'on kyaṅ phyi rol gyi don la yaṅ ste / rnam pa gźan du na de daṅ yid ches pa ma yin pa'i tshig la khyad par cir 'gyur / de'i phyir yid ches pas rab tu sbyar ba'i mtho ris la sogs pa'i sgra rnams kyis don tsam brjod pa ma yin gyi(s) / 'o na ci źe na 'jig rten pa'i sgra daṅ thun moṅ ma yin pa'i phyi rol gyi don yaṅ ṅo źes pa'o // raṅ gi mtshan ñid brjod par byed pa las luṅ rnams rjes su dpag pa ñid ma yin gyi (/) 'o na ci źe na / rnam pa de lta bu'i don la rnam par rtog pa tsam ñe bar skyed pa rnams kyi spyi'i rnam pas don gsal bar byed pa'i phyir /.

d) *My translation*:

"Objection: In the case of words employed by the unauthoritative, it is only the object which has the character of a speech-intention (*brjod par 'dod pa = vivakṣā*) which is inferred from the words, but the external object is not [inferred] from the expressions. So too, [words] used by the authoritative would be similar. [Reply:] 'No' (*ma yin*)* etc. That is to say, we should think as follows: Authoritative words should not be held to be valid just for the object which is the speech-intention, but also for the external object. Otherwise what difference would there be between it and unauthoritative words? Therefore the words "heaven" and so forth employed by authoritative [people] do not express *just the object* [consisting in the speech-intention], but rather, they also [express] the external object which is specific to the word [used] by the worldly people. Scriptures are not [classified as] inference because of [directly] expressing *svalakṣaṇa*. Rather, [they are classified as inference] because the [external] object is clarified by means of the universal aspects which are creations of mere conceptualization with regard to this type of object."

* *ma yin źes pa la sogs pa* refers to PSV's *mtho ris la sogs pa'i sgra rnams kyis don tsam brjod pa ni ma yin no*, and shows that Dignāga's reply starts at that point.

e) *PST P. 105a6-105b1*:

de skad du yaṅ smras pa / źes pa 'dis raṅ gi 'dod pa bstan bcos gźan der sgrigs par byed te / yid ches pa rnams mṅon sum du mtho ris la sogs pa rnams kyi raṅ bźin bzuṅ nas miṅ byed do // miṅ gi las ni ñe bar mtshon pa tsam du rig(s) par bya ste / de rnams ni thams cad du yaṅ don mthoṅ ba sṅon ma can kho nar tha sñad byed la / rnam pa gźan du na yid ches pa rnams kho nar mi 'gyur ro // de'i phyir de rnams kyi tshig thams cad mi bslu ba ste / des na rjes su dpag pa'o źes pa'o // phyogs 'dis źes pa ste / gtso bo la sogs pa rnams daṅ de rnams kyi rtags 'brel ba ma mthoṅ ba ñid kyi phyir / gtso bo la sogs pa rnams ni luṅ las ma grub pa kho na'o źes sṅar kyi rjes su 'braṅs nas brjod par bya'o //.*

* P. reads *grub pa* instead of *ma grub pa*. But note that PST is commenting on PSV's words *phyogs 'dis ni gtso bo la sogs pa'i raṅ bźin rnams la rjes su dpag pa bkag pa yin no*, which clearly imply a negation (= *ma grub*) rather than establishment (*grub*).

f) *My translation*:

"When it is said 'Furthermore it is stated', this lays out here another treatise which we accept. When authoritative people have directly apprehended the natures of things such as the heavens they give them names. The action of naming should be understood as simply pointing out. Indeed, the [authoritative people] in all cases apply designations to only those objects which have been seen before. Otherwise, they would not in fact be authoritative. Thus, all their words are non-belying and hence are said to be inference. 'This position' means that because a relation is not observed between *pradhāna*, etc. and their [linguistic] signs, then in keeping with what was [said] previously, one has to say that *pradhāna* and the like are not in fact established through scripture."

g) *A few remarks on R. Herzberger's view on Dignāga vs. Dharmakīrti on apoha.* Radhika Herzberger presents the position of M. Hattori and then argues for a frankly incredible counter-thesis to the effect that Dignāga did *not* maintain that words refer to conceptually created entities, but apply directly to the perceptual objects. For this she exhorts us to read the "details of Dignāga's text", and then proceeds to cite a passage from PS V k. 36c and PSV, in reconstructed Sanskrit, where Dignāga said that names apply directly (*sākṣādvṛtti*). See R. Herzberger (1986) p. 109; p. 138, note 4.; p. 163. Cf. the Tibetan text in Hattori (1982) pp. 136-137; p. 202, §49 for PST; Hayes (1988) p. 299. It seems to me, however, that Dignāga did not say that the name applies directly to the particular, but rather that it applies directly to the *apoha without reliance on other qualities.* Compare PST §49, Hattori (1982) p. 202, lines 33-35: *'dir ni yod pa ñid la sogs pa'i yon tan gźan la ma ltos par yod pa ma yin pa bsal ba'i dṅos po la sgra 'jug go //.* "Here without reliance on other qualities such as existence, etc., the word applies to the entity which is the exclusion of non-existence." This entity is an *apoha* and is conceptual. R. Herzberger also proposes an explanation of PS V, k. 1 which differs from that of the commentator, Jinendrabuddhi. See e.g. her p. 121 et seq.. For PS V k. 1, PST and PV IV k. 16, see Tillemans (1987) pp. 143-144. Now, it might be said that I'm not allowed to cite Jinendrabuddhi's PST because the author is too pro-Dharmakīrti. Let's say that the minimum which I should be able to uncontroversially claim is that R. Herzberger's citations of Dignāga give no hard evidence; they can and will be interpreted by Dharmakīrtians. It seems to me that for her controversial claims she needs much stronger evidence than the quotations which she gives, all the more so because her translation of PS V k. 36 is very doubtful. Cf. Hayes (1988) p. 299 and the article by S. Katsura, "Dignāga and Dharmakīrti on *apoha*", which gives a detailed critique of Herzberger's interpretation of *sākṣādvṛtti* and her translation of k. 36 (forthcoming in the proceedings of the Second International Dharmakīrti Congress, Vienna).

APPENDIX II: REMARKS ON THE *CATUṢKOṬI*

We see that in Dharmapāla's Chapter IV the true nature of things is said to be, in some sense, beyond existence and inexistence —— see e.g. §219c1. In Candrakīrti's CSV XII, too, we are repeatedly exhorted to avoid such extremes — see e.g. the quotations from the *Samādhirājasūtra* and *Ratnāvalī* in CSV XII §§13, 17. This is, of course, at the heart of Madhyamaka thought; its seemingly paradoxical aspects, therefore, merit some investigation here.

If we generalize this avoidance of extremes, we arrive at the four negations of the *catuṣkoṭi* ("tetralemma"), a classic statement of which occurs in k. 346 in Chapter XIV of the *Catuḥśataka*:

> *sad asat sadasac ceti sadasan neti ca kramaḥ / eṣa prayojyo vidvadbhir ekatvādiṣu nityaśaḥ //*. "Existent, inexistent, both existent and inexistent, neither existent nor inexistent, that is the method which the learned should always use with regard to oneness and other such [theses]."

Negating these four alternatives, we have denials that anything exists, is inexistent, is both or neither. The commentaries make it clear, however, that this fourfold negation also applies to other dichotomies, such as one /many, and so forth — in other words, it can be generalized to apply to any proposition *P*, and not just to the usual context of "...exists", "...is inexistent", etc. Ruegg (1977) p. 9 sums up the Mādhyamika use of this schema:

> "This type of analysis of a problem thus constitutes one of the basic methods used by the Mādhyamikas to establish the inapplicability of any imaginable conceptual position — positive, negative or some combination of these — that might be taken as the subject of an existential proposition and become one of a set of binary doctrinal extremes (*antadvaya*)."

Prima facie, it looks as if denying all four lemmas would lead to a deviant logic, a fact which, of course, has not gone unnoticed by Western interpreters — see Ruegg (1977) Appendix II for a history of the various modern attempts to interpret the tetralemma. See Haack (1974), Chapter I, for a precise specification of what is meant by the term "deviant logic". Roughly speaking, a deviant logic will have the same set of well-formed formulae (*wff*) and use the same vocabulary as classical logic, but will have a different set of theorems. Modal logic, for example, which uses additional "vocabulary", is not deviant, but intuitionist logic, which denies the laws of excluded middle and double negation, is.

In Tillemans (1989a) I looked at some versions of the *catuṣkoṭi*, the "Tibetan" version chosen being what we find in Se ra rje btsun Chos kyi rgyal mtshan's *sKabs daṅ po'i spyi don* f. 104a5-104b2 and 104b7-105a1 and in Tsoṅ kha pa's *rTsa śe ṭīk chen* p.

15 *et passim*. There are, it seems to me, two main approaches: the unqualified *catuṣkoṭi*, and the qualified one. The former is where one interprets the texts as denying existence, etc. and one does not add any qualifying phrases to the text. This approach is undoubtedly the most difficult to rationalize in that we need all our acumen to avoid violating some fundamental logical laws like double negation and excluded middle, or even the law of contradiction. In the latter approach, one adds qualifying phrases to the text and interprets "existence" as "true existence" (*bden par yod pa; raṅ bźin gyis yod pa*). As I tried to show in the above-mentioned article, the Tibetans' move to qualify "existence" as "true existence" leads to a type of modal logic which can handle the *catuṣkoṭi*'s fourfold denials in a relatively banal, non-paradoxical, non-deviant way. Its general exegetical disadvantage, however, is that it tends to strain credibility by making too many additions to the text.

B.K. Matilal (1986) suggests an approach which would also avoid deviancy, but which would not need recourse to the extensive qualification which we find in the Tibetan versions. He argues (on his p. 66) that

> "the [Mādhyamika] sceptic's use of negation, perhaps, can be better understood as an act of refutation, an illocutionary act where one negates some illocutionary force rather than a proposition."

In brief, the point (see his pp. 88-89) is that the Mādhyamika refuses to make *assertions* of P or of $\neg P$. If we represent assertion by the symbol "$\vdash$", then we get perfectly compatible denials: $\neg \vdash P$ and $\neg \vdash \neg P$, i.e. "I do not assert P"; "I do not assert not-P". This can, of course, be generalized to the *catuṣkoṭi* and yields a logic which is quite unproblematical.

Ruegg (1983) p. 236 et seq. suggests a similar approach to that of Matilal, using some concepts from J. Lyons *Semantics* Vol. 2 and other speech act theorists to take the negation in the *catuṣkoṭi* as denying the tropic ("it is so") and neustic ("I say so") illocutionary components of assertions, rather than the phrastic component, or propositional content, of the assertion. Ruegg's main reason for construing the negation in this way is that negation of the phrastic presupposes the existence of entities, and *that presupposition* is never accepted by Mādhyamikas. Ruegg (p. 237) writes:

> "...propositional negation is logically implicative and presuppositional; that is, in propositional negation (e.g. in the utterance: 'The grass is not red') just as much as in assertion (e.g. in the utterance: 'The grass is green') the producer of the utterance is committed to (the truth of the underlying proposition) presupposing the existence of an entity (e.g. the grass)."

From this presuppositional failure, Ruegg concludes:

> "It is in any case fairly clear that a form of 'external' negation of the assertion sign (Frege's $\vdash$) — i.e. negation of the tropic and negation of the neustic — rather than 'internal' negation — i.e. negation of the phrastic — is to be taken

into consideration when the subject of the embedded proposition (*bhāvas*, etc.) is empty (*śūnya*) and null, in other words when the existential presupposition fails or is not determinable in terms of the positions of the binary *vikalpa* and the quaternary *catuṣkoṭi*."

While this approach does have some advantages — e.g. it might be thought to account for the irenic aspect of the Madhyamaka, standing outside the fray conflicting assertions — it is certainly not the *only* way to handle presuppositional failure. Furthermore, I think that this approach has a serious philosophical drawback: the point about Nāgārjuna and Candrakīrti's argumentation is that they do not *just* refuse to commit themselves to certain positive or negative propositions, but they usually provide strong arguments (largely, but not exclusively, by *reductio ad absurdum*) as to why the propositions cannot be true. And if we look at these actual arguments, it does not seem to be just a matter of performing deconstructive therapy on the opponent, while one remains oneself uncommitted to the truth or falsity of it all. To take, for example, the case of the person being one with or different from the aggregates, both alternatives lead to absurdities and thus *cannot* be so — it seems difficult to maintain that Nāgārjuna and Candrakīrti did not themselves wish to assert that both positions were false. In short, this seems much closer to asserting *some form* of a negated proposition, i.e. $\neg P$, rather than simply being unwilling to assert P.

Our problem, then, is to see whether a plausible interpretation of the unqualified *catuṣkoṭi* can be formulated in terms of negated propositions, all the while remaining faithful to the Mādhyamika's view that existential presuppositions of statements must fail. The *catuṣkoṭi* as we find it in various places in Dharmapāla (especially in the last chapter) and Asaṅga would probably have to be classified as an unqualified version in that it does not add phrases like "truly" or "by its own nature" to the text. I would maintain that with some ingenuity it can also be made to avoid a deviant logic. Let me, therefore, add my contribution to the already numerous attempts to "rationalize" the *catuṣkoṭi*. To take Dharmapāla's system, suppose we grant that all *lakṣaṇa*, or predicates, are *parikalpita*, and that *paratantra* are all outside the range of language and concepts; no *paratantra* possesses any such *lakṣaṇa*. In that case, in constructing an artificial semantics (along usual logic-textbook lines), the domain of our models will contain no real entities (i.e. no *paratantra* or *pariniṣpannasvabhāva*), and will in fact be an empty domain. The Mādhyamika version can be accommodated too, if we simply speak of empty domains as domains with no *vastu*, no entities existing in themselves.

Take the fourfold negation in the *catuṣkoṭi* as the conjunction of four negated existentially quantified statements ($\neg$ = "not", $\&$ = "and", v = "or"):

> $\neg(Ex)Fx$; $\neg(Ex)\neg Fx$; $\neg(Ex)(Fx \,\&\, \neg Fx)$; $\neg(Ex)(\neg Fx \,\&\, \neg\neg Fx)$. Read: "There is not an x such that x has F; There is not an x such that x does not have F; There is not an x such that x has F and x does not have F; There is not an x such that x does not have F and does not not have F."

The fourth conjunct negates the possibility that something is neither F nor not F, viz. the possibility that $(Ex)(\neg Fx \,\&\, \neg\neg Fx)$. This conjunct could be equivalently presented as $\neg(Ex)\neg(Fx \vee \neg Fx)$ and would read "There is not an x such that x neither has F nor does not have F." In short, the third conjunct says there is no entity which combines the two lemmas, F and $\neg F$; the fourth conjunct says that there is no entity which combines the negations of the first two lemmas. Note that we can take F as any predicate we wish.

If we interpret quantification in the usual referential manner as ranging over entities in the domain, then we can deny all four lemmas without problem: the fourfold denial just shows that the domain is empty of objects, for any sentence beginning with an existential quantifier will be false in the empty domain. (A perhaps somewhat counterintuitive result which we have to live with is that if the domain is empty we would also have to assert the truth of the universally generalized statement $(x)Fx$. See W.V. Quine, "Quantification and the empty domain", *Journal of Symbolic Logic* 19, 1954, pp. 177-179.)

All Buddhists must, of course, find a way to preserve conventional designations. One way for us to do this is to make use of the fairly frequently used gambit of interpreting quantification substitutionally rather than referentially: on a substitutional interpretation, $(Ex)Fx$ does not mean that there is really some entity in the world which has F, but rather that there is a name a, such that substituting a for the free variable x in Fx yields a true atomic sentence, Fa. The domain of our interpretation will be a set of names, some of which may even be names for absurd pseudo-entities like rabbit's horns. In effect, we maintain conventional predication and existence-statements in saying, in accordance with the world's beliefs and practices, that certain atomic sentences are true and others false. The Buddhist's two truths then cease to be "things" or "objects", but are two different ways (i.e. referential *vs* substitutional) of interpreting the quantification in the one and the same sentence. The reconstructed *śūnyavādin* can, thus, use the world's language to communicate about whichever day-to-day affair the world concerns itself with: his *śūnyavāda*, however, dictates that he never accepts a referential interpretation of such language. To sum up, if we accept the Yogācāra's or Mādhyamika's position, then all fourfold denials of existentially quantified statements will be true on the referential interpretation. Most will be false on the substitutional, and that, I am prepared to argue, is about the best we can hope for as an unqualified interpretation of the *catuṣkoṭi* as a series of negated propositions. While substitutional quantification exhibits some fairly well-known deviant results when dealing with non-denumerably infinite sets (like irrational numbers), that is no doubt of little consequence for our purposes — let us say then that this interpretation would yield a logic which is not *significantly* deviant.

Finally, note that Nāgārjuna's famous phrase in the *Vigrahavyāvartanī*, "I have no thesis", is (as Ruegg 1986 and various Tibetan sources point out) probably better seen as not being a simple reluctance to assert anything whatsoever, but rather as a more nuanced statement: "I have no thesis which posits real entities". Ruegg (pp. 232-233) shows that in fact there are a number of places where the Mādhyamika *does* speak about his theses (*pakṣa*; *pratijñā*), e.g. that things are not produced from self, other, etc. On our reconstructed version, then, "not having a thesis" means that every existentially quantified proposition interpreted referentially will be false for a Mādhyamika-style philosopher. These subjects are further developed in my article, "La logique bouddhique est-elle une logique non-classique ou déviante? Remarques sur le tétralemme", appearing in the Felicitation Volume for Jacques May, *Etudes Asiatiques*.

A few references on substitutional interpretations of quantification: J. Michael Dunn and Nuel D. Belnap Jr., "The substitution interpretation of the quantifiers", *Noûs* 2, n°2, 1968 pp. 177-184. Ruth Barcan Marcus, "Interpreting quantification", *Inquiry* 5, n°3 1962 pp. 252-259 and "Quantification and ontology", *Noûs* 6, n°3 1972 pp. 240 - 250. Saul Kripke, "Is there a problem about substitutional quantification?" in M. Evans and J.H. McDowell eds., *Truth and Meaning; Essays in Semantics*. Oxford, Clarendon, 1976. For an introduction and summary, see D. Vernant, "Quantification substitutionnelle, contextes intensionnels et question d'existence", *Dialectica* 40, n°4, 1986 pp. 273-296.

APPENDIX III: RGYAL TSHAB RJE'S TOPICAL OUTLINES TO CATUḤŚATAKA-VṚTTI XII

1. *chos 'di la 'jig rten phal cher mi 'jug pa'i rgyu mtshan.* "The reason why the world for the most part does not apply itself to this Dharma".[142]

1.1. *ñan po'i mtshan ñid daṅ ldan pa rñed par dka' ba.* "It is difficult to find auditors which have the [required] characteristics [for understanding the Dharma]."

1.1.1. *ñan pa po'i mtshan ñid.* "The [required] characteristics of the auditors." (See §1-6; k.276)

1.1.2. *mtshan ñid ma tshaṅ ba'i ñes dmigs.* "The faults of not fulfilling [these] characteristics." (See §7-10; k.277)

1.1.3. *rtsod pa spaṅ ba.* "Rebutting objections."

1.1.3.1. *thub pa kun mkhyen du sgrub pa.* "Proving that the Sage is omniscient."

1.1.3.1.1. *sdug kun sun 'byin pa'i stoṅ pa ñid bstan pa la dga' bar rigs pa.* "One should rejoice in the doctrine of voidness which puts an end to all suffering." (See §11-17; k.278)

1.1.3.1.2. *ston pa'i bstan pa las gźan la thar pa med pa'i rgyu mtshan.* "The reason why there is no liberation apart from the doctrine of the Teacher [Śākyamuni]." (See §18-20; k.279)

1.1.3.1.3. *ston pa'i gsuṅs pa'i śin tu lkog gyur gyi don rnams ṅes par byed pa'i thabs.* "The way one ascertains the various completely imperceptible (*śin tu lkog gyur = atyantaparokṣa*) states of affairs spoken about by the Teacher." (See §21-23; k.280)

1.1.3.2. *gźan gyi ston pa ltar snaṅ du bstan pa.* "Showing that the other teachers are bogus." (See §24-27; k.281)

1.2. *gnas lugs kyi don rtogs dka' ba.* "The state of affairs of things as they are is difficult to realize."

1.2.1. *stoṅ pa ñid la skrag pa'i rgyu.* "The cause for fear of voidness."

1.2.1.1. *thar pa 'dod kyaṅ kha cig mu stegs byed kyi rjes su 'gro ba'i rgyu mtshan.* "The reason why some, even though they desire liberation, follow Outsiders." (See §28-31; k.282)

1.2.1.2. *stoṅ pa ñid la skrag pa'i gaṅ zag ṅos bzuṅ ba.* "Recognizing which people are afraid of voidness." (See §31-34; k.283)

1.2.1.3. *byis pa rnams stoṅ pa ñid la skrag pa'i rgyu mtshan.* "The reason why the infantile fear voidness." (See §34-36; k.284)

---

142 In fact, the first topical outline (*sa bcad*) in each chapter is: *le'u'i gźuṅ bśad pa daṅ le'u'i mtshan bstan pa* ("Explaining the text of the chapter and showing the title of the chapter"). But this division is trivial and I have left it out, presenting only the subdivisions of *le'u'i gźuṅ bśad pa*.

1.2.2. *stoṅ pa ñid rtogs pa la gegs byed pa'i ñes dmigs.* "The faults of impeding [others] in realizing voidness." (See §37-38; k.285)

1.2.3. *de kho na ñid kyi lta ba ma ñams pa la bag daṅ ldan par bya ba.* "One should be heedful that the view of the truth does not degenerate." (See §39-40; k.286)

1.2.4. *de kho na ñid la bkri ba'i rim pa.* "The stages in bringing [people] to the truth." (See §41-45; k.287)

1.2.5. *de kho na ñid ṅos bzuṅ ba.* "Recognizing what is the truth."

1.2.5.1. *gnas lugs ṅos bzuṅ ba.* "Recognizing the way things are." (See §46-51; k.288)

1.2.5.2. *dman pa skrag pa skye ba'i rgyu mtshan.* "The reason inferior [people] become afraid." (See §52-53; k.289)

1.3. *zab mo rtsod pa mdzad pa'i ched du gsuṅs pa min pa.* "The profound [i.e. voidness] was not explained for the sake of argumentation."

1.3.1. *chos 'di rtsod pa'i ched du ma gsuṅs kyaṅ smra ba ṅan pa mtha' dag bsreg pa chos ñid yin pa.* "Although this dharma [i.e. voidness] was not explained for argumentation, burning up the numerous wrong positions is its nature. (See §54-56; k.290)

1.3.2. *de'i rgyu mtshan.* "The reason for that, [i.e. why voidness destroys the numerous wrong positions]."

1.3.2.1. *dṅos.* "The actual [explanation]." (See §57-59; k.291)

1.3.2.2. *'phags pa rnams la skrag pa mi skye ba'i rgyu mtshan.* "The reason why the Āryas do not become afraid." (See §60-61; k.292)

1.3.3. *lam grol bar*[143] *źugs pa la sñiṅ rje bya bar rigs pa.* "One should have compassion on those who set out on the path to deliverance." (See §62-63; k.293)

1.4. *raṅ bźin gyi bstan pa'i phra rags bstan pa.* "Showing the [various degrees] of subtlety and coarseness of the [different] doctrines on nature (*raṅ bźin = svabhāva*)."

1.4.1. *blo dman pa gźan gyi bstan pa la gus śiṅ ston pa 'i bstan pa la mi gus pa'i rgyu mtshan spyir bstan pa.* "General explanation of the reasons why those of inferior intelligence respect rival doctrines and do not respect the doctrine of the Teacher [Śākyamuni]." (See §64-66; k.294)

1.4.2. *so sor bśad pa.* "Specific explanations."

---

143 rGyal (p. 10) reads *lam gol bar źugs pa*, which would necessitate the translation, "One should have compassion on those who set out on a *mistaken* path." This, however, would fit badly with the sense of k. 293 and CSV §63, which clearly says that we should have compassion for those who have seen the disadvantages of the Outsiders' paths and set out on the Buddhist path.

1.4.2.1. *lugs ṅan de dag thar 'dod kyi dpyad bya min pa.* "These wrong traditions are not worthy of consideration by those desirous of liberation." (See §67-68; k.295)[144]

1.4.2.2. *dbaṅ po dman pa gus pa skye ba'i tshul.* "How those of inferior faculties generate respect." (See §69-70; k.296)

1.4.2.3. *lugs de dag dam pa'i chos [mi] len pa'i rgyu mtshan.* "The reason these traditions do [not] obtain the Holy Dharma." (See §71; k.297)

2. *legs bśad mdor bsdus te bstan pa.* "Résumé of what was well explained [by the Buddha]."

2.1. *dṅos.* "The actual [résumé] (See §72-75; k.298)

2.2. *phyi rol pa'i chos la mi gus pa'i rgyu mtshan.* "The reasons for not respecting the Outsiders' Dharma." (See §76-77; k.299)

3. *grol ba don gñer legs bśad blaṅ bar gdams pa.* "The advice that those who strive for deliverance should accept what is well explained." (See §77-78; k.300)

---

144 rGyal tshab rje on p. 13 twice reads *dpyad bya ma yin pa / min pa*. It is clear that he must have read the text of CSV §68 as *thar pa 'dod pa rnams kyis dpyad par bya ba ma yin pa* ("is not to be considered by those who seek liberation"), instead of *...spyad par bya ba ma yin pa...*("is not be practised..."), and then commented accordingly.

APPENDIX IV: RGYAL TSHAB RJE'S TOPICAL OUTLINES TO CATUḤŚATAKA-VṚTTI XIII.

1. *bden grub 'gog pa'i rigs pa rgyas par bśad pa.* "Extensive explanation of the reasonings which refute that [the sense organs and their objects] are truly established."

1.1. *gzuṅ bya dbaṅ don bden pa dgag pa.* "Refuting that what is apprehended, viz. the objects of the sense organs, is true."

1.1.1. *spyir dgag pa.* "A general refutation."

1.1.1.1. *dṅos.* "The actual [refutation]."

1.1.1.1.1. *bum pa raṅ gi mtshan ñid kyis grub pa dbaṅ śes kyi mṅon sum du mthoṅ ba dgag pa.* "Refuting that vases established by their own defining characteristics are seen to be perceptible [objects] of the physical sense consciousnesses." (See §1-17; k.301)

1.1.1.1.2. *rigs pa de gźan la sbyar ba.* "Applying this reasoning to the other [constituents]." (See §18-19; k.302)

1.1.1.1.3. *gzugs raṅ mtshan mthoṅ bas gźan mthoṅ bar 'jog pa ha caṅ thal ba.* "The absurd consequence that by seeing the particular form one would see the other [constituents of vases, etc.]." (See §20-22; k.303)

1.1.1.1.4. *gzugs raṅ mtshan pa kho na la mṅon sum yin pa dgag pa.* "Refuting that only the particular form is perceptible." (See §23-24; k.304)

1.1.1.1.5. *sgrub byed bsgrub bya daṅ mtshuṅs par bstan pa.* "Showing that the *sādhana* [i.e. the reason] is similar [in being doubtful] to what is to be proven (*bsgrub bya daṅ mtshuṅs pa* = *sādhyasama*). (See §24-26; k.305)

1.1.1.2. *rigs pa gźan bstan pa.* "Showing other reasonings." (See §27-30; k.306)

1.1.2. *so sor dgag pa.* "Specific refutations."

1.1.2.1. *yul raṅ gi ṅo bos grub pa dbaṅ pos 'dzin pa dgag pa.* "Refuting that the sense organs apprehend objects which are established by their own essences."

1.1.2.1.1. *blta bya bden grub dgag pa.* "Refuting that the visible is truly established."

1.1.2.1.1.1. *yul dgag pa.* "Refuting the object."

1.1.2.1.1.1.1. *raṅ sde dgag pa.* "Refuting our co-religionists."

1.1.2.1.1.1.1.1. *kha dog daṅ dbyibs kyis bsdus pa'i gzugs raṅ mtshan mig śes kyi gzuṅ don du byed pa de gñis raṅ bźin gcig* *daṅ tha dad brtags la dgag pa.* "Refutation by examining the particular forms which serve as the objects apprehended by the eye-consciousness and which are included amongst colours and shapes, [i.e. examination] as to whether those two [sorts of form, viz. colour and shape] are of the same or different natures." (See §31-33; k.307)

1.1.2.1.1.1.1.2. *'byuṅ ba yod pa'i rgyu mtshan gyis gzugs gzuṅ don byed pa'i mig śes kyis gñis ka 'dzin par thal bas dgag pa.* "Refutation in that it would follow absurdly that if the eye-consciousness takes [particular] forms as its apprehended objects because the elements [which cause the forms] do exist, it would have to apprehend both [the form and the elements]." (See §34-37; k.308)

1.1.2.1.1.1.1.3. *'dod pa la gnod pa bstan pa.* "Presenting a refutation of [our co-religionists'] position [that the elements are the cause of form]." (§37-40; k.309)

1.1.2.1.1.1.2. *gźan sde dgag pa.* "Refuting the [non-Buddhist] rival schools." (See §41-44; k.310)

1.1.2.1.1.2. *yul can dgag pa.* "Refuting the subject."

1.1.2.1.1.2.1. *mig gzugs la lta byed du ṅo bo ñid kyis grub pa dgag pa.* "Refuting that the eye is established by its essence as something which sees form." (See §45-53; k.311)

1.1.2.1.1.2.2. *rnam śes byed pa po yin pa dgag pa.* "Refuting that consciousness is an agent." (See §54-57; k.312)

1.1.2.1.1.2.3. *mig byed pa po yin pa dgag pa.* "Refuting that the eye is an agent.

1.1.2.1.1.2.3.1. *mig gzugs la blta ba'i 'gros daṅ ldan na ha caṅ thal ba.* "There are absurd consequences if the eye moves to see the form." (See §58-60; k.313)

1.1.2.1.1.2.3.2. *gzugs mthoṅ nas lta ba'i ched du 'gro na dgos pa med pa.* "If [the eye] has [already] seen the form and then goes out to see it, there is no point [in such a movement]." (See §61-62; k.314)

1.1.2.1.1.2.3.3. *mig ma soṅ bar ṅo bo ñid yis gzugs 'dzin na yul kun mthoṅ bar thal ba.* "If the eye apprehends forms by its own essence, without going out [to the place of the object], then it would follow absurdly that it should see all objects." (See §63-65; k.315)

1.1.2.1.1.2.4. *mig de mig la ltos nas lta byed du thal ba.* "It would follow absurdly that the eye would [also] see the eye [itself]."[145] (See §66-67; k.316)

1.1.2.1.1.2.5. *rkyen gsum tshogs pa gzugs la lta byed yin pa dgag pa.* "Refuting that the collection of the three conditions is what sees form." (See §68-70; k.317)

1.1.2.1.2. *mñan bya bden grub dgag pa.* "Refuting that the audible is truly established."

1.1.2.1.2.1. *sgra smra ba'i byed pa po yin min brtags la dgag pa.* "Refutation by examining whether sounds are or are not the agents of speech." (See §71-73; k.318)

1.1.2.1.2.2. *sgra daṅ phrad nas 'dzin mi 'dzin brtags la dgag pa.* "Refutation by examining whether one does or does not apprehend [a sound] through [the ear's] contact with the sound." (See §74-75; k.319)

1.1.2.1.2.3. *sgra'i cha daṅ po mi 'dzin pa la gnod pa bstan pa.* "Presenting a refutation to [the idea that] one does not apprehend the initial part of the sound." (See §76-78; k.320)

1.1.2.2. *yid kyis 'dzin pa dgag pa.* "Refuting that the mind apprehends [objects which are established by their own essences.]" (See §79-83; k.321)

---

145 Literally, "It would follow absurdly that the eye would be a seer with reference to the eye."

1.2. *'dzin byed yul can bden pa dgag pa.* "Refuting that the apprehender, viz. the subject, is true."

1.2.1. *'du śes kyi phuṅ po'i mtshan ñid.* "The defining characteristics of the aggregate of notions (*'du śes kyi phuṅ po = saṃjñāskandha*)." (See §84-87; k. 322)

1.2.2. *de bden par grub pa dgag pa.* "Refuting that this [aggregate of notions] is truly established." (See §88-93; k.323)

1.3. *bden med mig 'khrul lta bu ṅo mtshar gyi rgyur bstan pa.* "Showing that things without truth, like optical illusions, are causes for astonishment." (See §94-97; k.324)

2. *bden pas stoṅ pa sgyu ma sogs daṅ mtshuṅs par bstan pa.* "Showing that [the sense organs and their objects] are similar to [magical] illusions and the like in being void of truth." (See §98-111; k.325)

ENGLISH TRANSLATIONS

DHARMAPĀLA'S COMMENTARY TO THE CATUḤŚATAKA

Chapter IV: Refutation of Heretical Views (*jiàn* 見 = *dṛṣṭi*)

(215c14) [Objection:] Now, if the nature and character of all dharmas (*zhū fǎ xìng xiāng* 諸法性相)[(1)], as they have been [previously] explained, is existence as things from the point of view of worldly convention and voidness from the point of view of the principle of ultimate reality (*shèng yì* 勝義 = *paramārtha*); [and if] the Tathāgata has unobstructed insightful vision (*zhì jiàn* 智見 = *jñānadarśana*)[(2)] into these matters, knows how to explain them in words and skillfully comprehends others' minds, then why is it that the world is still bewitched by various mistaken views and [thus] has thoroughly confused debates?

A. The qualities of the auditors of the teaching

(215c16) [Reply:] It is because the auditors [of the teaching] have [various] faults. What are termed "faults of the auditors"? As follows: attachment to one's own [wrong] views, not seeking zealous application (*shèng jiě* 勝解 = *adhimukti*) and not discriminating between good and bad teachings. [Accordingly,] if he does not have these three kinds of faults, then that [person] is said to be a vessel for hearing the true Dharma. In order to show this point, [Āryadeva] pronounces the following verse:

> *One who is naturally harmonious, aspires to zealous application*[(3)] *and is intelligent should be considered a vessel for the Dharma. Otherwise, even if he has the assistance of a master*[(4)], *that will not enable him to obtain excellent qualities (shèng lì* 勝利 = *guṇa).* **(k.276)**

(215c23) Commentary. [A person] needs to possess three qualities to be termed a vessel of the Dharma. First of all, [he should be] naturally gentle, without biases for factions; [he should] constantly examine things himself and not be attached to his own views. Secondly, he should always aspire to zealous application and untiringly seek the Dharma, not being satisfied with preserving his own lot. Thirdly, because he is naturally intelligent, he correctly perceives the different virtues and faults in good and bad explanations.

(215c26) If, however, he lacks the three qualities as they were just explained, then even if he has the assistance of a master, ultimately he will not [develop] any excellent qualities. "Excellent qualities" means the understanding and realizations (*zhèng dé* 證得 = *sākṣātkaraṇa*; *sākṣātkriyā*) [coming] from the assistance of a master, in their due order (*rú qí cì dì* 如其次第 = *yathākramam*).[(5)] Outsiders, like those six [heretical] masters[(6)] and others, realize nothing at all, even if they should [happen to] hear the true Dharma. It is not that the Buddha does not feel pity and wish to help these [Outsiders], or that the noble teaching falls short[(7)] of [the standards of] reason (*zhèng lǐ* 正理 = *nyāya*; *yukti*), for those in the world who were to be delivered have all been finally delivered by hearing the Buddha's noble teaching. To show this point, [Āryadeva] states in the following verse:

> *[If] the world itself does not understand when [the Buddha] explains existence, the cause of existence, purification and the means to purification*(8)*, then how could the fault lie with the Sage?* **(k.277)**

(216a5) Commentary. The unobstructed insightful vision of the tathāgata buddhas, in seeing which things benefit others, is of four sorts and no more, namely, what is to be abandoned (*suǒ shě* 所捨) and what is to be realized (*suǒ zhèng* 所證), as well as their [respective] two causes. The meaning (*tǐ yì* 體義) is completely true, [and so this] statement [of the Buddha] is free from any error. In other words, these four [noble] truths are a summary (*suǒ shè* 所攝 = *saṃgraha*) of the noble teaching. Although the Buddha extensively explains [this teaching], they [i.e. the world] do not understand; the fault [thus] lies with the world and not with the Sage. Because the Outsiders' intelligence (*jué huì* 覺慧 = *buddhi*) is mediocre, and because they lack the correct practice, they therefore do not attain any understanding. It is like when the fiery sun sends forth a thousand rays and yet the blind still cannot see: the fault is not with the sun.

B. The Outsiders' and Buddhist notions of liberation compared

(216a11) Now, these Outsiders, definitely have [their] minds ensnared(9) through ignorance (*wú míng* 無明 = *avidyā*), carelessness (*fàng yì* 放逸 = *pramāda*) and sloth (*shuì mián* 睡眠 = *middha*)(10), [with the result that] they do not place any confidence in what they themselves recognize. How so? Thus [in response], [Āryadeva] states in the next verse:

> *The heretical schools all accept that the abandonment of all existents is nirvāṇa. [So] why are they not pleased when voidness (zhēn kōng* 眞空 *= śūnyatā*(11)*) refutes all?* **(k.278)**

(216a16) Commentary. All the Outsider schools assert that what one terms "nirvāṇa" is the abandonment of the possessions of the self (*wǒ suǒ yǒu shì* 我所有事 = *ātmīya*), [so that] only the self remains, free from bonds, isolated, liberated, inactive and indifferent. [Now] voidness, which lacks any characters (*xiāng* 相 = *lakṣaṇa*), puts an end to all erroneous objects and is free from any [dichotomizing] conceptualization (*fēn bié* 分別 = *vikalpa*) which grasps at existence, etc. [i.e. existence or inexistence]. When one has insight into this [voidness], then all the objects of the mind will be eliminated, what [in fact] correctly comes down to the unexcelled great *parinirvāṇa*, and is not in contradiction with the liberation which you [heretics] seek. Why then are you hostile and not pleased [instead]?

(216a20) For us, nirvāṇa is not(12) just the elimination of the possessions of the self, but voidness also dispels the self: thus [we] know what is to be rejoiced in.(13) As for you [however], if the self exists in nirvāṇa, then necessarily it will not be free of the [self's] possessions. So how is [your type of] nirvāṇa possible? The self, which has been refuted, as previously(14) [shown], should not be clung to again; therefore, one should be pleased with this voidness which is free from self.

(216a23) If a thing exists it can accordingly be eliminated, but voidness never ceases (*qiǎn* 遣 = *vinivṛtti*). Grasping at existence gives rise to errors, but the insight into voidness is precisely what eliminates [these errors]. So the two paths of voidness and existence are far apart in [terms of their respective] merits and faults. Why then do you subscribe to existence and defame voidness? The pitiful followers of the heretics, are irrational, without any wisdom and do not accept the voidness which would bring them benefit. [Rather], continually attracted to heresies and seeking false existents which lack any benefit, they thus oppose the true teaching and generate anger. They are like those evil children who go to wild excesses of confusion(15), become addicted to forms and sounds, and on their rampage lack all propriety. They do not know how to respect and follow their mother's loving counsel, but themselves give rein to an unfortunate stubbornness, [so that,] on the contrary, they generate injury.

(216b1) Now, if one repudiates voidness, then there is absolutely no other method for the abandonments and realizations. Thus, [Āryadeva] states in the following verse:

> *He who does not know the causes(16) for the abandonments and realizations lacks the means to abandon [saṃsāra] and realize [nirvāṇa]. For this reason, the Sage has said that tranquillity (qīng liáng* 清涼 *= śiva(17)) is certainly not [found] elsewhere.* **(k.279)**

(216b5) Commentary. The Outsiders, even if they repeatedly apply themselves(18) and seek to realize nirvāṇa and to abandon saṃsāra, will in the end attain nothing with regard to what is to be abandoned and what is to be realized, for they do not know well [the requisite] method for abandonments and realizations. [Instead] they turn their backs on voidness and indulge in the pursuit of false existents. Hence, concerning the method, one says that they do not know it well. For apart from the insight into voidness, there is no other method for abandoning saṃsāra and realizing nirvāṇa. All who thirst after the Outsiders' views will not, in the end, obtain supramundane (*chū shì* 出世 = *lokottara*) tranquillity. [Here] the word "tranquillity" means the complete pacification of all suffering and the causes of suffering; it is only the insight into voidness which can cause this realization, for apart from such [an insight] there is no other method. [Now] such an insight into voidness is [to be found] in the Buddhadharma, and it is absent in all the Outsiders' heretical treatises. Thus the Sage stated, "The four fruits of religious practice (*shā mén guǒ* 沙門果 = *śrāmaṇyaphala*) are [to be found] in my Dharma and are certainly absent in that of others."(19) Because the Outsiders cling to their own views and defame the insight into voidness, they do not realize nirvāṇa.

(216b14) [Query:] How should one know that our [i.e. the Outsiders'] position is definitely not a correct method for the abandonments and realizations?

(216b15) [Reply:] It has already been stated earlier on [in previous chapters] that grasping permanent entities (*jù yì* 句義 = *padārtha*) and maintaining that there is really time is completely fault-ridden.[(20)] Later, [in the next chapter[(21)]] grasping at the sense organs and their objects, etc. is to be extensively refuted, and thus it will be understood that you hold an incorrect method.

(216b17) Furthermore, the Outsiders, in their [type of] state of nirvāṇa, do not really free themselves from such views as [grasping at] the possessions of the self, etc. But, nonetheless, they say that this state, when [just] their inner self exists, liberated from its possessions, is to be termed nirvāṇa. Why [would they be unable to free themselves]? It is because the self and its possessions are things which are completely mutually inseparable (*wú yǒu xiāng lí* 無有相離).[(22)] You cannot say that dharmas such as suffering, pleasure, etc. are absent in the self in [your so-called] state of nirvāṇa, for you yourself maintain that they are possessions of the self, just like the nature (*zì tǐ* 自體 = *svabhāva*) of the self which you accept.[(23)] And you cannot say that the nature of the self is not the possession of the self [and that] the homologous example (*tóng yù* 同喻 = *sādharmyadṛṣṭānta*) [in the previous reasoning] lacks the reason (*yīn* 因 = *hetu*).[(24)] Nor should [you say that] the self which you accept does not have an nature: it would then be like a flower in the sky, and you would commit the fault of contradicting [your own] thesis.[(25)] Therefore the position of you Outsiders does not finally [enable one to] abandon saṃsāra; nor does it [lead to] realizing final nirvāṇa. So it should be understood that [the Outsider's position] is not a correct method.

C. The problem of the authority of the Outsiders' and Buddhists' treatises and scriptures

(216b26) Now, the Outsiders and others set forth [various] treatises whose teachings are to some extent true. For instance, they say that giving, etc. (*shī děng* 施等 = *dānādi*), bring forth fortunate states of existence (*shàn qù* 善趣 = *sugati*) and other felicities, as it is their propelling cause (*qiān yǐn yīn* 牽引因 = *ākṣepa-hetu*).[(26)] Or they say that killing, etc. will bring forth unfortunate states of existence and other intense sufferings, as it is the propelling cause for that. However, [be this as it may,] their treatises' prior and subsequent [parts] are mutually contradictory. Also, [these treatises] advocate the taking of life [i.e. sacrifices] and such actions, or they give rise to evil heresies (*jiàn qù* 見趣 = *dṛṣṭigata* (?)) and adopt what results from these kinds of heresies. Just as there are blind men who [temporarily] happen to travel the correct path but at some time or another, through their confusion, revert to their mistaken course, so also the Outsiders' treatises are analogous to that [blind man]: there are some truths and some falsehoods, but one cannot trust [such treatises].

1. The Outsider's objection

(216c3) [Objection:] In that case, the noble teaching in the Tripiṭaka of the Tathāgata [also] sometimes has statements which are scarcely believable, and so all the Insiders' [i.e. Buddhists'] and the Outsiders' texts would be untrustworthy; thus a gross absurdity (*tài guò shī* 太過失 = *atiprasanga*) would ensue. How so? [Because] in the Buddha's sūtras are mentioned various miraculous transformations (*shén biàn* 神變 = *vikurvaṇa*; *ṛddhi* (27)) which are unimaginable. Or [these sūtras] speak about states of affairs which are extremely profound (*shèn shēn* 甚深 = *atyantaparokṣa* (?)(28)) truths (*zhēn shí* 眞實 = *tattva*); no sentient beings fathom [these things].

(216c7) [Objection continued:] Moreover, [the sūtras] state that the operation (*zuò yòng* 作用 = *kāritra*) of the three activities(29) of the Tathāgata cannot be understood by [those who follow] the vehicle of the hearers (*śrāvakayāna*), etc. [Specifically,] it is said that [the Tathāgata] effortlessly, everywhere in [each of] the immeasurable, infinite, extremely remote worlds of the ten directions, and according to each of the sentient beings' myriad(30) and innumerably different kinds of faculties, simultaneously manifests at will his magnificent body so that there is no end to the benefit. And even though he has eliminated all ratiocination, investigation (*xún sì* 尋伺 = *vitarkavicāra*) and conceptualizing (*fēn bié* 分別 = *vikalpa*)(31), to all those myriad sentient beings he preaches words of the infinite, extremely profound and vast Dharma, which is a truth of boundless splendour. [Moreover], in one moment he removes sentient beings' immeasurable and infinite stains of mind and conduct. Although his mind does not in reality arise or cease and lacks [any differentiation between] apprehender (*néng yuán* 能緣 = *grāhaka*) and apprehended (*suǒ yuán* 所緣 = *grāhya*), still in one moment he directly perceives absolutely all objects which can be known, and when he has [this] direct perception (*xiàn jiàn* 現見 = *pratyakṣa*), he is completely free of all conceptual discursive thought about what perceives (*néng jiàn* 能見) and what is perceived (*suǒ jiàn* 所見).

(216c16) [Furthermore] although [the Tathāgata] has eliminated all propensities [for passions] (*suí mián* 隨眠 = *anuśaya*) and all ensnarements (*chán fú* 纏縛 = *paryavasthāna*),(32) still he experiences death and birth in the three [forms of] existence. And although he has long since been free of desire, still he takes birth in the desire realm (*yù jiè* 欲界 = *kāmadhātu*), manifestly dwelling in the prison of one who is confined to live as a householder. He accumulates all varieties of riches, grains and precious treasures, and looks after wife, children, relatives and servants. As things such as these are all hardly credible, we harbour deep reservations about them.

2. The Buddhist reply appealing to voidness

(216c20) [Reply:] Phenomena, if they merely existed, could indeed give rise to [such types of] doubts. But phenomena are also void. Hence [Āryadeva] states in the following verse:

> *When someone gives rise to doubt concerning the profound (shēn* 深 *= parokṣa; Tib. lkog gyur) things taught by the Buddha, then he can rely on the voidness which is free of all [defining] characters, and [can thus] gain sure faith.* **(k.280)**

(216c24) Commentary. The thought behind this verse asserts(33) the following: The Tathāgata, in order to frighten the Outsiders, who are [like] a herd of deer, sets forth voidness with a great lion's roar. Accordingly, this state of affairs, voidness, is certain and is clearly proven through both scripture and logic. All the intelligent take [the teaching of voidness] as certain; no refined, difficult or clever thought surpasses it. When, by hewing to voidness, one practises without error, one will then be dignified with a host of virtues and will attain the unexcelled fruit [of buddhahood]. [So] one should generate sureness and conviction in that [i.e. voidness]. For only voidness is true; all else is not the truth, but is [just] the Tathāgata using skillful means (*shàn quán fāng biàn* 善權方便 = *upāyakauśalya*) to preach and publicize [the Dharma] in accordance with the desires of sentient beings.(34)

(217a1) Although the Buddha's teachings know no limit, they can be condensed into simply two sorts: voidness and non-voidness. When there are doubts regarding non-voidness [i.e. about the teachings concerning subjects other than voidness], one can, by relying on voidness, infer [the truth of] what is to be understood.

3. Voidness

(217a2) [Query:] But how can one see that all dharmas are void? [Reply:] Because neither the objects of consciousness nor those of words are established as [really] existent entities. When one resumes the nature and characters (*tǐ xiāng* 體相) of all dharmas, there are two types: what is understood by consciousness and what is expressed by words.(35) [Now] one object at the same time gives rise to many consciousnesses, and the object's character varies according to different perceptions. [Thus] these consciousnesses could not arise in conformity with an external object, for the nature of one object is not established as many [different] characters. Therefore we know that what is understood by cognition definitely does not exist.(36)

(217a7) As for words, they are designations (*jiǎ lì* 假立 = *prajñapti*) and only express universal characters (*gòng xiāng* 共相 = *sāmānyalakṣaṇa*). No universal characters are ever substantially existent (*shí yǒu* 實有 = *dravyato 'sti; dravyasat; asty eva*), because they are established in many [different] dharmas, just like armies, forests, etc.(37) Furthermore, universal characters will all depend on the particular (*bié* 別 = *viśeṣa*) dharmas [which are their instances]. As the particulars which are the bases [for the universal] are infinite in number, those [people] of limited insight cannot perceive them all. And since they do not perceive the particulars, then necessarily they [also] will not perceive the universal (*zǒng* 總).(38) It is like the case of "two", etc. (*èr xìng děng* 二性等 = *dvitvādi*), which are [qualities] depending on pairs, etc. of things: if we do not perceive the bases [for "two"], we can in no way perceive [the quality "two"].(39) So, since universal characters are not perceived, how could referring expressions (*néng quán* 能詮) be established in dependence on that [type of pseudo-entity]? Thus, universal characters are just designations(40); they should not be taken as substantially existent, [but] can be considered to be figures of speech (*yán quán* 言詮).

(217a13) Also, if universal characters substantially existed, they could not be established as either(41) wholly or partially existent in each individual dharma. If it were wholly existent in each individual dharma, then the universal character could never be established at all, being just like the particular dharmas. If [however] it were [only] partially existent in each individual dharma, then it would have to have many parts, and could not be one [unique] universal character. Moreover, in substance (*shí* 實 = *dravya*), etc. [i.e. in the six categories (*padārtha*) of the Vaiśeṣikas],(42) there cannot be a separately existing unique universal nature (*zǒng xìng* 總性)(43) of substance, etc., for [such a universal nature] would be an object [created] by the mind, just like something which is not a substance or other such [category]. [This type of] universal nature would be nothing less than a universal character of all dharmas [and hence could not be included amongst any of the six categories.](44) Thus [for the above-mentioned reasons], universal characters do not have substantial natures, but are [just] designated in common by the world. In this fashion, then, all dharmas reduce to two kinds, viz. either what is understood by consciousness or what is expressed by words, but neither [of these two sorts of dharmas] is substantially existent. And there are no other [kinds of] dharmas apart from these two [types of] objects. So therefore, one should be convinced(45) of the voidness of all dharmas.

(217a21) In this vein, the sūtra states the following: "The true nature (*shí xìng* 實性) of all dharmas is indescribable (*wú shì* 無示 = *anidarśana*), without resistance (*wú duì* 無對 = *apratigha*) and completely one in character; it is said to be without characters."(46) The existential character (*xìng xiāng* 性相 = *bhāvalakṣaṇa?*)(47) of all dharmas is not an object (*suǒ xíng* 所行 = *gocara*) of words, and words do not express it. Thus it is said to be "indescribable". Since it is not an object of minds and mental factors (*xīn xīn fǎ* 心心法 = *cittacaitta*) and since we do not perceive that it is either resisted by or is a resister of objects which [themselves] have resistance (*yǒu duì* 有對 = *sapratigha*), it is said to be "without resistance".(48) [Also,] [the true nature of dharmas] does not, in addition, have a different character over and above the characters of the two types of objects [viz. those of consciousness and those of words]. Thus one says that [the real nature of dharmas] is "without characters". Because voidness and characters are non-dual, it is said to be one in character.(49) When [people] are not afflicted by the poisoned arrows of erroneous grasping (*wàng zhí* 妄執 = *abhiniveśa*), desire and other such [passions], then voidness, which is to be realized by the correct view, can be clearly perceived; thus we say that it is "the [true] character".

(217a27) Furthermore, as the principle of voidness is free from all characters of dharmas, such as existence, [inexistence,] etc., we can say that it is without characters;(50) what is without [such] characters is non-dual; thus [voidness] is said to be one. That is to say, we take this type of lack of [imagined] characters as the [ultimate] character [of dharmas], and so we say that it can be considered to be a character, but not a character which is a distinct entity (*bié yǒu* 別有 = *bhāvāntara*).(51)

4. The Outsiders are untrustworthy

(217b1) Now, the Outsiders pose the following objection: All the Buddha's statements can be resumed as two sorts: [those concerning] voidness and [those concerning] non-voidness. [But] if the assertions of voidness are true (*shí* 實), then the other statements will necessarily be deceptive (*xū* 虛). [You argue that] when one part of the Buddha's assertions are true, then similarly the other part must also be non-deceptive; so our assertions must also be like that [given that you admit that some of them are true]. Why then are [our assertions] entirely rejected and said to be unworthy of belief?

(217b4) [Reply:] It is because you Outsiders err with regard to things of the present [world] that [your doctrine] is not trustworthy. Why? Hence, in the following verse [Āryadeva] states:

When [someone's] view on the present [world] (xiàn 現 *) has errors, then we know that [his account of] the next [world] will certainly be deceptive.* **(k.281ab)**

(217b8) Commentary. These Outsiders, due to their wrong understandings and confused minds, are mistaken about even simple phenomena; *a fortiori*, why would they not err in [their account of] the profound and difficult to understand principle of cause and effect concerning the next world. So their assertions are not trustworthy.

(217b10) [Objection:] Which simple things are we mistaken about?(52)

5. Arguments against the Vaiśeṣikas

(217b10) [Reply:] The Vaiśeṣikas think that limited universals (*tóng yì* 同異 = *sāmānyaviśeṣa*) and the like are objects of direct perception (*xiàn liáng* 現量 = *pratyakṣa*),(53) and the Sāṃkhyas think that *rajas*, *sattva*, etc. are objects of direct perception.(54) These types of phenomena are infinite in number, and all are erroneous. How so? [It is because] it is incoherent (*lǐ bù chéng* 理不成 = *na yuktaḥ; na siddhaḥ*) for limited universal natures, etc. to be objects of direct perception, as the Vaiśeṣikas hold. Cowness, horseness and the like, due to conceptual mental cognition (*yì shí* 意識 = *manovijñāna*), exist as designations (*jiǎ shī shè yǒu* 假施設有 = *prajñaptisat; prajñaptito 'sti*)(55) upon various dharmas such as colour, etc. (*sè děng* 色等 = *rūpādi*).(56) They are beyond the scope of the senses and hence are not apprehended by direct perception, because they are present everywhere in their bases (*suǒ yī* 所依 = *āśraya*) and without any difference, just like the nature of inherence (*hé hé* 和合 = *samavāya*). [Now] the [Vaiśeṣika] accepts that in the case of the sixth category (*jù yì* 句義 = *padārtha*), inherence, its nature is one and is present everywhere in its bases, [but] beyond the scope of the senses and *not* apprehended by direct perception. [But if we consider] natures such as the limited universals and so forth, these entities are also analogous [in these respects]. Why then does [the Vaiśeṣika] hold that they *are* objects of direct perception?(57)

(217b18) Moreover, when the [Vaiśeṣika's] treatise asserts that there is a category of substance (*shí* 實 = *dravya*) and that these [substances] are objects of direct perception, [this] is also incoherent. Why? [Because] things such as vases, cloths and so forth [i.e. substances], due to conceptual mental cognition, exist as designations upon various dharmas such as colour, etc. Why then hold them to be objects of direct perception?(58)

(217b21) However, the [Vaiśeṣika's] treatise asserts that things such as vases and cloths, etc. can be seen by the eyes and touched by the body due to connections (*hé* 合 = *yoga*) with qualities (*dé* 德 = *guṇa*), actions (*yè* 業 = *karman*)[(59)], substances [and] limited universals. Thus, they are sense objects and are known by direct perception.[(60)] But this could never be so.

(217b23) Firstly, it is clear that substance cognitions[(61)] which are brought about by qualities cannot be included among direct perceptions. In other words, a substance cognition which is brought about by such [colour] qualities as blue, etc. and such [tactile] qualities as warmth, etc. definitely cannot be included among visual or tactile direct perceptions; for [these cognitions] are not produced by action, limited universals or substances, but are produced through the connection with an another character [viz. qualities such as blue, warm, etc.], as in the case of substance cognitions brought about by [qualities such as] smell and taste. Substance cognitions which are brought about by action are also analogous. They can be duly (*rú qí suǒ yīng* 如其所應 = *yathā-yogam*) refuted by means of the following inference: substance cognitions which are brought about by action also cannot be included among visual or tactile direct perceptions, because they are not produced by limited universal natures and substances, but are produced through the connection with another character [viz. an action], just as [in the case of] substance cognitions which are brought about by smell and taste.

(217c1) All substance cognitions which are brought about by substances are like for example seeing a vase or knowing that such-and-such is a cow, and since we refute [the members of] the category of substance, such as vases, etc., [arguing that] they cannot be seen or touched, then we have in fact already refuted the substance cognitions which are brought about by these [substances]. For cognitions of vases, etc. can only arise through qualities and actions, and this has been refuted previously.[(62)] Hence [substance cognitions brought about by substances] also cannot be included among direct perceptions.

(217c4) Substance cognitions which are brought about by limited universal natures also cannot be included among visual or tactile direct perceptions, for they are produced through connections with characters other [than substances], just as are all cognitions of non-substances, etc. That is to say, cognitions of non-substances affirm with regard to qualities, actions, and the like that these [latter categories] are not substances, because they [, i.e. the cognitions of non-substances,] are produced through connections with other characters. [Therefore] they [, i.e. substance cognitions brought about by limited universals,] are definitely not included among visual and tactile direct perceptions.

(217c8) The other cognitions [, i.e. those of the remaining categories,] are analogous.[(63)] Thus, it should be understood that all categories give rise to [their respective] cognitions by virtue of [merely] designated connections (*jiǎ hé* 假合), but that [these cognitions] are all not, in reality, direct perceptions apprehending those [categories].[(64)] To elaborate: a cognition which apprehends a substance is not, in reality, a direct perception which apprehends [that] substance, because it arises by virtue of a [merely] designated connection, as [in the case of] cognitions of qualities, etc.

Similarly, the cognitions apprehending [the other categories] up to (*nǎi zhì* 乃至 = *yāvat*) inherence are also not, in reality, direct perceptions which apprehend these [categories], because they arise by virtue of [merely] designated connections, just like the cognitions of substances, etc. Therefore one should not hold that there are any objects of direct perception among the six categories, and thus the Vaiśeṣikas are also mistaken with regard to these simple phenomena of the present world.

6. *Arguments against the Sāṃkhyas*

(217c14) Next, turning to the Sāṃkhyas, they hold that dharmas such as form, etc. are established as composites of the three qualities (*dé* 德 = *guṇa*), but are real, are not [mere] designations and are apprehended by direct perception.(65) This is also incoherent, for they would be established in many dharmas, just like armies, forests and so forth, and thus form, etc. would have to be [mere] designations.(66) How could they be said to be real?

(217c16) Moreover, the triad, *sattva*, etc. (*lè děng* 樂等)(67) could never become one [thing such as a form], because they would have [mutually] different natures (*xìng* 性), just as they do in their untransformed state (*wèi biàn wèi* 未變位).(68) And also, if form and such dharmas [which are supposedly transformations of the three qualities] were to really exist, then they could never be composed of three [things] like *sattva*, etc. Or, in the case of the triad, *sattva*, etc., if their characters were each distinct, then how could they all become one character [such as form, etc.] by combining together? When they are combined they cannot turn into one character, because their substances (*tǐ* 體 = *dravya?*) do not differ from when they were not yet combined. Or, as the three natures, *sattva*, etc., are each distinct, then the character [existing when these natures are combined] could not be identical [i.e. it could not be one and the same thing, but would have to be many different things]. Because you maintain that the natures [i.e. the *guṇas*] and characters [such as form, etc.] are definitely the same(69), then the natures must [all] be identical, just like the character [into which they transform], or the character must be [many] different things, just like its natures.(70)

(217c22) Alternatively, [it might be argued that] *sattva*, etc. are particulars (*bié* 別), while form, and the others [viz. sound, taste, touch and smell(71)] are syntheses (*zǒng* 總 = *samudāya*?).(72) [But] since you maintain that the synthesis and the particulars must in fact be the same, then the synthesis would have to be three [different things], just like the particulars, and would not be one, or the particulars would have to be one, just like the synthesis and would not be three. How then could the three which are the particulars become the one which is the synthesis? Or, suppose that when the three qualities, *sattva*, etc., transform, they do not combine to establish one character. Then just as the [three qualities'] characters are different when untransformed, so also we could never perceive that they are one form, etc. If the three combine to establish one character, then they will have to lose their three types of particular characters, viz. *sattva*, etc: we can not say that the three qualities, *sattva*, etc., each have two characters, a synthetic one and a particular one.(73) Why? [Because] the synthetic character, if it were one, could never be three, and if the synthetic character were three[fold], then it could never be perceived as one.

(217c29) [Objection:] Suppose it is said that each of [the qualities], *sattva*, etc., has all three characters, i.e. *sattva*, etc., but that as the characters are mixed together, they can [only] be discriminated with difficulty. Therefore we perceive them as [making up] one thing.(74)

(218a1) [Reply:] This is also incorrect. If each [quality] had three characters, then we would still have to perceive three things. Why do we perceive [just] one thing? And how could we ever know that *sattva*, etc. are [in fact] different? Or if each [quality] had all three characters, then why should they combine together to establish form, etc.? In other words, each should [individually] establish the different sense objects such as form and so forth and bring about the enjoyment (*shòu yòng* 受用 = *bhoga*) of the self.(75)

(218a5) Also, if these three qualities each had three characters and [these characters] were mutually different, then why would a character such as form be one thing? Or suppose that *sattva* and the other [two qualities] all individually established dharmas like form, etc., but that the substance of each dharma was established through the combinations of all three [qualities]. Then, all dharmas would be without any differences, whether in nature or in character, for by the same three qualities the [same] three characters are established. In that case, all the differences between [things such as] the causes and effects of *mahat*, etc., the subtle elements (*wéi liáng* 唯量 = *tanmātra*), the gross elements (*dà* 大 = *mahābhūta*) and the organs (*gēn* 根 = *indriya*)(76), would be without exception unestablished, [with the result that] to the world's perception there would also be no difference between sentient beings and insentient [matter], pure and impure things and the like, and direct and inferential means of valid cognition (*liáng* 量 = *pramāṇa*), etc. Because this contradicts what all the world perceives, it would be an enormous absurdity.

(218a11) There are many such positions like the above sorts [which are put forth] by the Outsiders' heretical teachers; but they are all [in fact] incoherent. Who would ever bother with [such] a pile of crap? Since in the Buddhadharma many masters of the doctrine have already vanquished these opponents, I will not belabour the point.

7. Conclusions and rhetorical exhortations

(218a14) Thus [in conclusion], the Outsiders even manage to stumble in places which are simple, that is, level roads in broad daylight. Why then should they be free of error in the thick, dark, deep night of a dense forest which is profound and precipitous? Who with any intelligence at all would believe their mistaken words? So, to put a stop to reversion to error, [Āryadeva] states in the following verse:

All those who practise on the basis of their doctrines will be deceived forever. **(k.281cd)**

(218a18) Commentary. If sentient beings follow the doctrine explained in these Outsiders' stupid views and mistaken positions, then due to the influence of the heretical doctrines [espoused by] evil friends, they [themselves] will come to harbour tendencies (*xūn xí* 熏習 = *vāsanā*) towards these erroneous views; thus they will defame the Dharma which is produced from the Tathāgata's realizations and will obtain extremely bad karma whose measure is limitless. Given these causes and conditions they will fall into unfortunate states of existence, [with the result that] there will be no end to their experience of great suffering. So the intelligent should not, like fools, follow evil friends and thus deceive themselves; rather they should practise in accordance with the buddhas' true, irreproachable, noble doctrine which speedily realizes deliverance (*chū lí* 出離 = *niḥsaraṇa*).

(218a24) Now, the following had been stated above:(77) "In the Buddha's sūtras are mentioned various miraculous transformations which are unimaginable. Or [these sūtras] speak about states of affairs which are extremely profound truths; no sentient beings fathom [these things]", up until "things such as these are hardly credible." [All this] is indeed as it was depicted. As the virtues of the buddhas and the states of affairs mentioned [above] are all extremely profound, it is hard for one to be able to believe in them. [But] you fools, being of limited merit (*fú* 福 = *puṇya*) and scant wisdom, only seek your own interest and are unwilling to help others. Not having drunk in the flavour of the Dharma, the sweet nectar of great compassion, how then could you ever have conviction in such Dharma approaches (*fǎ mén* 法門 = *dharmaparyāya*) [as miraculous powers, etc.]? [But] if one has the light of wisdom one will dispel the darkness of ignorance and profoundly take compassion on all sentient beings. One will seek the buddhas' enlightenment, will come to have vast merit and so will have conviction in these types of Dharma approaches.

(218b2) To elaborate: In the case of the tathāgatas, throughout countless previous aeons the lineage (*zhǒng xìng* 種姓 = *gotra*)(78) of compassion and wisdom latently conditioned their minds. In order to uproot sentient beings' great sufferings of saṃsāra and in order to seek unexcelled perfect enlightenment (*wú shàng zhèng děng pú tí* 無上正等菩提 = *anuttarasamyaksaṃbodhi*), they paid homage and respect to the buddhas and so heard the true Dharma. Through being fully conscious and mindful (*xì niàn sī wéi* 繫念思惟 = *saṃprajānāḥ pratismṛtāḥ*)(79) they gained complete mastery of the limitless practices which are in keeping with the Dharma (*fǎ suí fǎ xíng* 法隨法行 = *dharmānudharmapratipatti*)(80), viz. the various difficult to practise and subtle perfections (*pāramitā*) such as giving (*dāna*), moral discipline (*śīla*), patience (*kṣānti*), vigour (*vīrya*), meditative trances (*dhyāna*), wisdom (*prajñā*), and so forth. [In these] they zealously and continuously trained until full accomplishment, and so they realized the unexcelled perfect enlightenment and acquired inconceivable masteries (*zì zài* 自在 = *vaśitā*) and miraculous powers.(81) The excellent action brought forth by their [bodhisattva] vow (*běn yuàn* 本願 = *praṇidhāna*) is inexhaustible. Why then do you not have conviction in such things?

(218b9) Things of the manifest world, such as implements, etc., move automatically after being set in motion by a previous force. Similarly, the Tathāgata's special miraculous powers operate automatically after having been brought forth by the [bodhisattva] vows. Also, in the world, if a practitioner of magical arts attains great accomplishment, his excellent action will be difficult to comprehend by the multitude of people. How then, in the case of the Tathāgatha, whose mastery of the long-practised various meditative absorptions (*shèng dìng* 勝定 = *samāpattiviśeṣa*; *samādhiviśeṣa*) is complete, could the operation of [his] miraculous powers ever be fathomed! So therefore you should generate conviction in these inconceivable qualities of the tathāgatas; you should sincerely strive for the masteries and miraculous powers from among the Buddha's perfections and not harbour carelessness (*fàng yì* 放逸 = *pramāda*). There are [inferior Buddhist practitioners] such as śrāvakas, who, when they have themselves completely understood the Buddha's limitless, inconceivable powers, pitifully cry out mournful lamentations, the sound of which arouses the three thousand [worlds] (*sān qiān* 三千).(82) How can it be that you, then, would denigrate [these powers] rather than having faith [in them]?

D. The fear of nirvāṇa

(218b18) Now, the intelligent proceed to nirvāṇa by themselves, but the dull of mind, [even if they] meet a teacher, do not learn [from him]. To show this point [Āryadeva] states the [following] verse:

> *The intelligent [proceed] by themselves to nirvāṇa; they accomplish what is difficult to do. Fools [however], even if they meet an excellent guide, lack the courage to follow.* **(k.282)**

(218b22) Commentary. The ensnarements of the passions (*fán nǎo* 煩惱 = *kleśa*) are ingrained from beginningless time, strong, resistant and difficult to break through. Nirvāṇa is empty, still and without characters or words; its qualities are limitless, it is profound and difficult to realize. The intelligent, by themselves, and not through another's doctrine, cross over the great ocean of saṃsāra and obtain the ultimate great *parinirvāṇa*. [Thus] these superior individuals accomplish what is difficult to do. Fools [however], who have long sunk into the mire of desires, are addicted to pleasure and do not seek deliverance. Like a dog who wants to gnaw on putrid blood and dry bones and will not give them up even when driven away with a cane, so too is the fool: he relishes desires, has contempt for the noble words [of the Dharma] and does not turn away [from saṃsāra]. The intelligent, thus, by themselves, bring forth understanding and realize *parinirvāṇa*. They accomplish what is difficult to do. But the fool, in his carelessness, understands nothing; even if he happens upon the [Dharma's] noble words, he is uninterested in the cessation [of suffering] (*jí miè* 寂滅 = *nirodha*; *śānti*).(83)

(218c2) Now, while saṃsāra is extreme suffering, nirvāṇa is great bliss — the [respective] faults and virtues are obvious and easily recognized. Why then are sentient beings blithely unwilling to turn their backs on saṃśāra and rejoice in proceeding to nirvāṇa? It is because they are afraid due to their bewilderment (*yú chī* 愚癡 =

moha), that is to say, they harbour self-cherishing (*wǒ ài* 我愛 = *ātmasneha*), so that when they hear that nirvāṇa is voidness, they fear that if one attains [a state of] no remainder (*wú yú* 無餘 = *aśeṣa*)[84], then the self will be destroyed. Hence they are afraid, and consequently they do not wish to turn their backs on saṃsāra or take pleasure in proceeding to nirvāṇa. In this manner does fear arise due to a little intelligence. Why is this? Hence, in the next verse [Āryadeva] states:

> *When one does not understand, one is without fear, and when one understands fully it is again like that [viz. one is unafraid]. It is certain that when one understands a little bit, one will become afraid.* **(k.283)**

(218c10) Commentary. If sentient beings are completely without any intelligence and fail to understand any dharmas, then they will not become afraid of nirvāṇa. If someone fully understands the correct principle of all dharmas, he will ascertain what saṃsāra as well as nirvāṇa are: when saṃsāra arises, there is merely a designated (*jiǎ* 假) arisal of suffering, and when saṃsāra ceases, there is merely a designated cessation of suffering. All dharmas, being fundamentally without self, are without exception void, and thus [one who knows this fact] is absolutely unafraid of nirvāṇa.

(218c14) If, however, someone only understands that at the time of *parinirvāṇa* all conditionings (*xíng* 行 = *saṃskāra*) completely cease and there is nothing at all, [but] he does not know that [at that time] the suffering due to conditioning (*xíng kǔ* 行苦 = *saṃskāraduḥkhatā*)[85] automatically ceases by itself and that lacking substance, nature and function, there is no self nor possessions of the self, then such [a person], due to his [false] view concerning the personality (*shēn jiàn* 身見 = *satkāyadṛṣṭi*)[86], will be gripped by self-cherishing, [and] on hearing that in nirvāṇa there is [just] voidness and nothingness, he will dread that the self is being destroyed and will become afraid. So in such a manner does fear arise due to a little intelligence. Therefore the [truly] intelligent should correctly reject [such misconceptions].

(218c18) Moreover, fear arises due to lack of training (*chuàn xí* 串習 = *abhyāsa*). Why is this? Thus [Āryadeva] explains in the following verse:

> *Fools have long trained in dharmas which are conducive to saṃsāra. Because they are untrained in what is in opposition [to saṃsāra], they are afraid.* **(k.284)**

(218c22) Commentary. It is the profane (*yì shēng* 異生 = *pṛthagjana*) who are termed "fools". They give themselves over to [their] passions (*fán nǎo* 煩惱 = *kleśa*) and [latent] propensities (*suí mián* 隨眠 = *anuśaya*)[87], and are thus attracted to birth, have aversion towards death and do not take pleasure in nirvāṇa. Since beginningless [time] they have repeatedly experienced desirable [karmic] retributions (*kě ài yì shú* 可愛異熟 = *iṣṭavipāka*), such as superior states of existence, but they have not trained in [i.e. are unfamiliar with] what is ultimately excellent (*jué dìng shèng dào* 決定勝道 = *niḥśreyasa*).[88] Effects of [karmic] retribution, such as superior states of existence, are [however] based upon propensities such as desire and the like. Although [a fool] gets burned for a long time by the fire of suffering, he does not comprehend [his situation] and enjoys himself in various amusements. Because he has so long trained in the suffering of saṃsāra, he does not know its misfortunes and [therefore] lacks any revulsion (*yàn lí* 厭離 = *nirveda*) [towards saṃsāra]; not knowing the flawless bliss of liberation (*jiě tuō* 解脱 = *mokṣa*), he takes no joy in practice or realizations. Just as in the world filthy pigs are addicted to enjoying dung and do not relish a pure, tranquil and attractive meal, so also the fool revels in saṃsāra's suffering and is without any inclination towards the bliss of liberation. Due to his lack of training, when he hears mention of the name of [liberation], he does not believe in it, but rather, is afraid. The intelligent, through their powers of discrimination (*sī zé* 思擇 = *nidhyāna*; *vicāra*) should correctly strive for the bliss of liberation and, contrary to the fool, should not be mistakenly distressed [by the idea of nirvāṇa].

(219a5) Now, all the faithful seek non-erroneous (*wú dào* 無倒 = *aviparīta*) liberation. [So] when through their virtuous characters or through their powers of wisdom they practise the method for perceiving the truth (*zhēn shí* 眞實 = *tattva*), then if [at that time one] impedes [them] in this, the bad karma obtained will be limitless in measure. In order to show this point, [Āryadeva] states the following verse:

> *People who, possessed of bewilderment (yú chī* 愚癡 *= moha), impede others in perceiving the truth will not [even] have fortunate states of existence as rebirths. So how could they ever realize nirvāṇa?* **(k.285)**

(219a10) Commentary. The perception of the truth, i.e. voidness, is the cause for realizing the perfect, unexcelled wisdom and is the method for [attaining] nirvāṇa, which is the complete absence of objects, i.e. permanent extinction.[(89)] This method is the source which gives rise to inconceivable qualities, and through it step by step (*zhǎn zhuǎn* 展轉 = *pāraṃparyeṇa*) one speedily attains enlightenment. When one does not dwell in nirvāṇa, then the benefit [for other sentient beings] is inexhaustible. One establishes various seeds (*zhǒng zi* 種子 = *bīja*), maturations (*chéng shú* 成熟 = *paripāka*),[(90)] etc. in accordance with the differences in faculties of the immeasurable [number of] sentient beings to be trained (*suǒ huà* 所化 = *vineya*), [and] the benefit is limitless.

(219a14) As for people who are possessed of bewilderment [however], the darkness of ignorance covers their eyes of wisdom (*huì yǎn* 慧眼 = *prajñācakṣus*)[(91)] with the result that they do not perceive voidness. Furthermore, due to their heretical explanations and other [wrong] methods, they place obstacles to what others practise, just as [they do] to previous virtues. The bad karma which such [people] obtain is immeasurable and limitless; only the Tathāgata knows its extent. Because this heavy bad karma defiles their minds, it will be extremely long for them to subsequently take birth in a fortunate state of existence, the continuity of the propensities and ensnarements remains firm, the various karmic causes pose grave impediments [to practice] and the patience of amenability (*shùn rěn* 順忍 = *ānulomikī kṣānti*)[(92)] to the method cannot arise either. [So] how could [such a person] realize the correct view or nirvāṇa? Knowing that the bad karma of impeding the true Dharma is profound, the intelligent should be on their guard not to commit downfalls [in this respect].

E. Moral and philosophical faults compared

(219a22) Now, all those who impede others' practice of the true Dharma themselves later cause heretical views to arise. The evil of these heretical views exceeds that of breaking moral discipline (*jiè* 戒 = *śīla*). To show this point, then, [Āryadeva] states the following verse:

It is better to break moral discipline than to destroy the correct view. **(k.286ab)**

(219a26) Commentary. As it is said in the sūtra, "It is better to break pure moral discipline than to destroy the correct view."[(93)] What does this mean? [Response:] Those who break pure moral discipline only harm themselves, whereas if one destroys the correct view, one harms oneself as well as others, leading to countless births where one experiences enormous suffering as a result as well as to the loss of immeasurable, limitless benefit. Furthermore, those who break moral discipline constantly harbour shame and guilt and upbraid themselves for their moral downfalls, but those who destroy the correct view are without shame or guilt; they commend heretical views and constantly vaunt themselves. While those who break moral discipline do not develop heretical views, if one destroys the correct view, the [as yet] unproduced evil of destroying moral discipline will be made to arise, and that which has already arisen will develop further and become entrenched so that it will be difficult to eliminate.

(219b3) In breaking pure moral discipline one only bars rebirth in the heavens, but he who destroys the correct view [also] rules out the bliss of nirvāṇa. Why? Thus in the next verse [Āryadeva] states:

By moral discipline one takes birth in a fortunate state of existence, by means of the correct view one attains nirvāṇa. **(k.286cd)**

(219b6) Commentary. Although breaking moral discipline and destroying the [correct] view both annul virtuous causes and block the effect [of such causes], i.e. happiness, still breaking moral discipline is [comparatively] light, while destroying the view is extremely heavy. How so? [Response:] When one has moral discipline, one will be born in the heavens, but will develop more and more attachment [to these states] and so experience the suffering of saṃsāra. Through the correct view [however] one realizes the enlightenment of the three vehicles (*chéng* 乘 = *yāna*)[(94)] and thus attains the bliss of nirvāṇa. Hence the intelligent should not destroy the correct view.

F. Selflessness

1. Debates

(219b10) [Query:] But what is the true nature (*zhēn lǐ* 眞理 = *tattva*) of all dharmas?[(95)] [Response:] It is the principle that all dharmas are without self (*kōng wú wǒ* 空無我 = *nairātmya*).[(96)] [Objection:] In that case, such a principle would also have faults. Why? It is like when some people (*yī lèi* 一類 = *ke cit*) people hear about selflessness, they say that dharmas are all inexistent, deny the rationality of any causality and so on and so forth until they [finally] sever all their roots of virtue (*shàn gēn* 善根 = *kuśalamūla*).[97]

(219b13) [Reply:] This is [because] their own views have faults; it is not a defect pertaining to selflessness. Due to their evil grasping at voidness they erroneously give rise to heretical views and engage in various evil practices. [But] as for the principle of selflessness, thought and words cannot fathom it, [and as such,] it is not something which can be realized by these [people]. The fool, when he hears it said that dharmas are all void, does not understand the noble meaning, and so he negates conventional (*shì sú* 世俗 = *vyavahāra*; *saṃvṛti*) causality as also inexistent, [with the consequence that] he eliminates all virtuous dharmas. How could this ever be a fault in selflessness?

(219b17) [Query:] What is the point then in the Noble One's explanation of the doctrine of voidness?[98] [Response:] It is in order to dispel all false (*xū wàng* 虛妄) grasping at existence. [Objection:] If that were the case, then he should also say that all dharmas exist in order to dispel erroneous grasping at the voidness of all dharmas. [Reply:] That is true. If someone grasps dharmas as void, then the Tathāgata also states that dharmas exist.[99]

(219b20) [Objection:] Since, to dispel grasping, he teaches existence and he teaches voidness, then is the true nature of all dharmas voidness or existence? [Reply:] The true nature of all dharmas is neither existence nor voidness; it completely transcends the proliferations of [dichotomizing] conceptualization (*fēn bié* 分別 = *vikalpa*; *xì lùn* 戲論 = *prapañca*).[100]

(219b22) [Objection:] Then why are the Noble One's statements not false? [Reply:] It is because they are destined to exclude mistaken grasping that [the Noble One's statements] are not false. [Objection:] The teachings of voidness and those of existence both exclude grasping, so why then does the Tathāgata more often preach the teaching of voidness? [Reply:] It is because sentient beings for the most part grasp at existence, [and] saṃsāra mostly comes about from grasping at existence. Therefore, the Tathāgata, in order to exclude grasping at existence and to extinguish the suffering of saṃsāra, mostly preaches the teaching of voidness.

(219b25) [Objection:] Whether [dharmas are] void or whether they are existent, this is all a [question of] teaching approaches. Why then was it previously stated [cf. §219b10] that voidness is the true nature [of dharmas]?

(219b26) [Reply:] Method and metaphorical description (*jiǎ shuō* 假說 = *upacāra*) are not contradictory (*xiāng wéi* 相違 = *viruddha*).[101] Besides which, this statement of voidness is a negation (*zhē* 遮 = *pratiṣedha*) and not a positive assertion (*biǎo* 表).[102] Not just is there voidness, but voidness is void too. By dispelling completely all grasping thoughts one brings oneself into conformity with the ultimate true nature of all dharmas which is neither existence nor voidness.[103] The true nature of all dharmas is not really voidness (*kōng xìng* 空性 = *śūnyatā*), but since one takes voidness as an approach (*mén* 門 = *paryāya*), then metaphorically [the true nature of dharmas] is taken to be voidness.

(219c1) [Objection:] If the true nature [of dharmas] is not voidness, but voidness is taken as the approach, then [similarly] given that the true nature [of dharmas] is not existence, existence should be taken as an approach. [Reply:] One explains [various] approaches according to [different] occasions [i.e. according to the disciples' capacities], so existence too is not wrong. Still, the essential point of the [Buddha's] approach accords with voidness. The [notions of] existence, existence of existence, etc. (*yǒu yǒu yǒu děng* 有有有等), are all in accordance with the grasping mind, while the [notions of] voidness, voidness of voidness, etc. (*kōng kōng kōng děng* 空空空等), are all opposed to erroneous grasping (*wàng zhí* 妄執 = *abhiniveśa*). Therefore, the intelligent, when they hear the word "voidness" said, should be free from all grasping at existence, inexistence and so forth, and come to understand that the true nature of dharmas is not existence nor is it inexistence. Thus they should not give rise to proliferations of [dichotomizing] conceptualization such as existence and inexistence.

2. Consequences of inappropriately teaching selflessness

(219c6) Now, in the presence of those of inferior intelligence one should never preach selflessness, [for] it will increase their evil views. Why? Thus in the next verse [Āryadeva] states:

> *It is better that he [i.e. one of inferior intelligence] gives rise to the conception of an I (wǒ zhí* 我執 *= ahaṃkāra) rather than the view of selflessness. In the latter case he will in addition go to an unfortunate state of existence, while in the former he will only turn his back on nirvāṇa.* **(k.287)**

(219c10) Commentary. "He" means those of inferior intelligence in the world. "The conception of an I" means their [erroneous] view with regard to the personality (*sà jiā yé jiàn* 薩迦耶見 = *satkāyadṛṣṭi*).(104) Such a [person's] view of the possessions of the self (*wǒ suǒ jiàn* 我所見 = *ātmīyadṛṣṭi*) also leads to the conception of an I, and hence the term "conception of an I" also refers to this [erroneous] view. Now, while the conception of an I is not said to be correct, still it is better that the [person of inferior intelligence] should give rise to it, for the fault is light. Although the view of selflessness is [in fact] said to be correct, nonetheless, he does not understand it correctly and thus negates all dharmas as inexistent. Because [such a] fault is serious, he had better not give rise [to the view of selflessness].

(219c14) Why are these two faults [respectively] light and serious? [Response:] In the former case, i.e. the conception of an I, he only turns his back on nirvāṇa, while in the latter, viz. when he misapprehends voidness, he will in addition go to an unfortunate state of existence. Those of inferior intelligence, when they misapprehend voidness, will also turn away from their roots of virtue.(105) What need to speak about [rejecting] sentient beings!(106) Because [those who misapprehend voidness] turn their back on virtue as well as the world, they will destroy [their] roots of virtue and harm [other] sentient beings. Not only will they cast away peace and nirvāṇa, but, in their egotism, they will also go to the fires of hell (*dì yù* 地獄 = *naraka*).

(219c19) These types of things [however] do not happen to those who give rise to the view of the self. Why? [It is because] they desire the self's happiness and wish that the self be free of suffering. So they do not commit the various evil actions (*zuì* 罪 = *pāpa*), but [instead] extensively cultivate merit; thus they abandon unfortunate states of existence and do not lose [their birth] as a man or god. However, as they fear nirvāṇa, they do not realize liberation. So [in this connection] it is said in the [*Kāśyapa-parivarta* of the *Ratnakūṭa-*] sūtra, "It is better to give rise to the view of the self, which is like Mount Sumeru, than to be conceited in misapprehending voidness."(107)

(219c22) [Objection:] In that case the principle of the selflessness of all dharmas is manifestly (*lín jìn* 隣近 = *sākṣāt*) a dangerous path (*qù* 趣 = *gati*), and the Noble One should not teach it. [Reply:] He should indeed not teach it in the presence of those of inferior intelligence, but superior intellects reap great benefit by practising in accordance with it, and hence he ought to teach it [to them]. Why? Thus [to explain this], [Āryadeva] states in the next verse:

The excellent principle of selflessness (kōng wú wǒ 空無我 *= nairātmya) is the true sphere of all the buddhas, the terror of evil views [and] the unrivalled door to nirvāṇa.*(108) **(k.288)**

(219c28) Commentary. For those who seek liberation, there is no other method to realize nirvāṇa apart from the excellent insight into voidness. When the intelligent wish to dispel the stains of evil views, then there is no other better method than this one. As the view of existence (*yǒu jiàn* 有見 = *astidṛṣṭi*; *bhavadṛṣṭi*) grasps the objects which it apprehends as an entity, then like other views of entities, it does not realize nirvāṇa, nor does it dispel the stains of evil views. Those who meditate on this sphere of voidness (*kōng xíng* 空行) to perfection realize the final fruit, unexcelled enlightenment. They then teach with skillful means everywhere for the sake of sentient beings, and thus bring about the complete realization of the excellent fruit which is sought after. For all which accomplishes the welfare of oneself and others, the insight into selflessness is the first and foremost cause. Therefore, knowing well the faculties of sentient beings, one should teach with skillful means and thus cause them to attain understanding.

(220a7) Now, the Tathāgata, in order to dispel the demon of evil views, explained the antidote (*ā jiē tuó* 阿揭陀 = *agada*), i.e. selflessness.(109) How so? [Because] those who have evil views all become afraid when they hear mention of voidness pronounced, and gradually, as they become subdued, naturally stop [holding such views]. To show this point [Āryadeva] states in the following verse:

Fools, when they hear mention(110) *of the doctrine of voidness, all become greatly frightened, just as those who see someone powerful, become cowardly and without exception run away.* **(k.289)**

(220a12) Commentary. "Fool" means that evil views blind [his] eye of wisdom (*huì yǎn* 慧眼 = *prajñācakṣus*).(111) If such [a person] hears mention of voidness, the life [force] of his evil views is automatically destroyed. Although voidness does not consciously wish to destroy evil views, still, because it is so powerful, [simply] hearing mention of it makes one desist of one's own accord. It is like the timid who believe themselves lost (*zì sàng* 自喪) when they hear [just a mere] mention of a tiger. Or, just as in the world there are tamed elephants across whose jowls flow impressive streams of sweat: although they do not consciously harm living beings, still, because such an elephant's awesome power is so great, he who sees or hears of him becomes wild with fear and runs away. The principle of voidness is also like that. As its awesome power is so great, it makes those who have evil views wild with fear on [simply] hearing mention of it, so that they naturally put an end [to such views].

3. Selflessness was not taught for the sake of argumentation

(220a18) [Qualm:] The principle of voidness, being unconscious, does not [itself] bring about harm to any beings, but those who realize such a principle will bring injury to others. [Response:] But if someone realizes voidness, then his mind will be pacified and his equanimity (*píng děng* 平等 = *samatā*) will be unrivalled; so how could he wish to injure others? Rather, in order to benefit all sentient beings, he teaches through skillful means the principle of selflessness, and those who harbour evil views, when they hear this [teaching], desist of their own accord. To show this point, then, [Āryadeva] states in the following verse:

The buddhas did not consciously state a doctrine which refutes rival assertions(112)*, but rival assertions are destroyed by themselves, just as a raging fire*(113) *burns up fuel.* **(k.290)**

(220a24) Commentary. The buddhas did not consciously wish to refute rival assertions, but instead, to benefit sentient beings who are to be trained, they taught the great path of all the previous buddhas, viz. that the nature and characters (*xìng xiāng* 性相)(114) of all dharmas are completely void. And thus the previous and subsequent tathāgatas are actively engaged (*wú bù yóu lǚ* 無不遊履)(115) in guiding the flock of the confused [sentient beings] from the cause to the fruit. The evil views and arguments of the heretical followers of the Outsiders cease naturally when confronted with this teaching of voidness. It is like the leaping flames of a raging fire in a mountain forest: when woodpiles of wet fuel have been dried by the hot sun, then even though no one [expressly] brings any fire near, still, when the fuel is in the vicinity of fire, it ignites, as if by itself. So similarly for the arguments of the heretical followers of evil views: they too collapse by themselves in the face of the power of the teaching of voidness.

(220b2) Now, the Outsiders' traditions all assert erroneous entities. [So] voidness is explained in order to dispel [their assertions]. Why? Hence the next verse states:

Whoever understands the true Dharma will certainly be unattracted to heretical traditions. [Thus] [the Tathāgata] taught the meaning of voidness so that others would leave behind [such] false teaching approaches. **(k. 291)**

(220b6) Commentary. The intelligent by themselves distinguish between truth and falsity, so that when they meet the true Dharma of the [Tathāgata], they are then unattracted to the heretical traditions, just as a connoisseur of jewels, on obtaining a priceless jewel, is never again attracted to other crystals (*shuǐ jīng zhū* 水精珠 = *sphaṭika*).[(116)] The Outsiders' traditions all invent erroneous entities and stray far from the true Dharma; like a deceptive method, they mislead sentient beings and deprive them of enormous benefit. Therefore we set forth the voidness [as found] in the Buddha's teaching in order to make these heretical followers turn to the truth and reject falsehoods.

(220b11) Now, why do the Outsiders relish heretical traditions and turn their backs on the noble doctrine? It is because of the strength of their [erroneous] view with regard to the personality (*shēn jiàn* 身見 = *satkāyadṛṣṭi*).[(117)] If they understood selflessness, then inevitably they would no longer have desire or aversion. Why? Hence the next verse:

If one understands the principle of selflessness explained by the Buddha, then one will not rejoice in what is favourable nor be afraid[(118)] *of what is unfavourable.*[(119)] **(k.292)**

(220b16) Commentary. If one understands the principle of selflessness in the Buddha's doctrine, one will dispel the [latent] propensities which are brought about by the [erroneous] view with regard to the personality, [and] one will see the world as like an empty dwelling: a cycle of saṃsāra whose conditionings (*xíng* 行 = *saṃskāra*) are false. [Thus] one will no longer rejoice in fortune nor fear misfortune, one will be without despondency, joy or fear, and hence, unperturbed. Should one [however] have the [erroneous] view with regard to the personality, then, because one thinks, "I will lose or profit", one will become despondent or joyful when misfortune or fortune present themselves. Because of this [view of the personality] one is then endlessly fearful. Thus the intelligent should dispel the conception of the I (*wǒ zhí* 我執 = *ahaṃkāra*).

(220b21) Now, the host of Outsiders, because of their attachment to the conception of the I, enslave themselves and enslave [other] sentient beings too. As many [beings] have been harmed, one ought to feel deeply compassion. To illustrate this point [Āryadeva] states:

Having seen that the host of the Outsiders are [just] many causes for misfortune, who[(120)] *will not [then] feel deep compassion for sentient beings attracted to the true Dharma?* **(k.293)**

(220b26) Commentary. The host of Outsiders, in their attachment to the conception of the I, make themselves and others commit immeasurable sins, for it is the [erroneous] view with regard to the personality which is the root for the arisal of all evil. As it is said, "All evil, unwholesome, dharmas without exception arise rooted in the view with regard to the personality (*satkāyadṛṣṭi*)."[(121)]

(220b28) Amongst beings those who have an attraction to the excellent Dharma do not of themselves necessarily grasp [at wrong views], but rather by following others. They are deceived because of the heretical words of the Outsiders, and are also attached to the view of self; thus they commit immeasurable sins. It is in this manner that the Outsiders make themselves and others alike give rise to various sorts of strong ensnarements. Who[(122)] among the intelligent would not be filled with compassion? Therefore, sentient beings of pure intention who are attracted to the true Dharma, when they generate the desire to be of aid, should feel deep compassion and diligently explain selflessness and voidness so that they will bring [beings] to practise the correct view and thus free them from bondage.

G. Arguments against the Brahmins and the Jains

(220c6) [Objection:] Now, buddhas and bodhisattvas have always resided in the world and truly have the pure wish to aid others. Why then does the world still have [an] immeasurable [number of] sentient beings who believe in heretical, perverted views and slander the Dharma? [Reply:] It is because the objects and cognitions expounded by the Buddha are extremely profound, subtle and difficult to comprehend. However, [those of] the Outsiders are not like that. How so? Hence in the next verse [Āryadeva] states:

> *The doctrines (suǒ zōng 所宗) of the three [traditions], i.e. of the Brahmins (pó luó mén 婆羅門 = brāhmaṇa), Jains (lí xì 離繫 = nirgrantha) and the Tathāgata, are [respectively] understood by the ears,[(122a)] the eyes and the mind. Therefore, the Buddhadharma is more subtle.* **(k.294)**

(220c12) Commentary. The Brahmins just have endless recitation of empty formulae as their path. The ear consciousness understands it; it is [thus] not profound or subtle. The Jain Outsiders merely take exposing their bodies' foulness and [inflicting] suffering on themselves through numerous cruelties as being the path. The eye consciousness understands it, and so it too is neither profound nor subtle. The Tathāgata's noble teaching, by its sword of undefiled (*wú lòu* 無漏 = *anāsrava*) wisdom which realizes voidness, permanently destroys all the thieving[(122b)] inner passions and leads to the attainment of unexcelled perfect enlightenment; it benefits and brings happiness to all sentient beings; [in this fashion] the thought (*yì qù* 意趣 = *abhiprāya*) behind its reasonings and scriptures is extremely profound and subtle.

(220c17) Those people who understand things correctly (*rú shí lǐ* 如實理) comprehend some of the Buddha's noble teachings and do not comprehend others. As the Buddhist reasonings and scriptures are so extremely profound and subtle, the Outsiders, fools that they are, do not understand them; most [people][(123)] believe in the coarse and superficial heretical words of the Outsiders, while [only] few believe in the profound and subtle noble teaching of the Tathāgata.

(220c20) The fact that the world mostly believes in the Brahmins is because the Brahmins largely practise deception: they recite spells (*zhòu* 呪 = *mantra*), worship fire and purify themselves through asceticism; they falsely establish auspiciousness and erroneously explain [what constitutes] fortune and misfortune. They [employ] various methods for [their own] livelihood: they trick women, Śūdras (*shù dá luó* 戍達羅) and the like to impress them with their status so that [the Śūdras, etc.] will provide them with the necessities of life and extend them veneration.

1. Refutation of the Vedas

(220c24) The ancient Brahmins, in their shrewdness, secretly invented the *Vedas* (*míng shū* 明書) and then said that they existed naturally (*zì rán yǒu* 自然有), that they just came to be incanted of themselves and were not acknowledged as dependent on anything else.(124) The Brahmins were commended as being the most worthy of veneration, while the Kṣatriyas (*chà dì lì* 剎帝利) and the rest were all [said to be] inferior; if [the latter] provided [the Brahmins] with the necessities of life, then they would obtain immeasurable merit. Fools, who lack intelligence, do not fathom [the Brahmins' various deceptions]; they wait upon [the Brahmins] with trust and respect, saying that they are a true field of merit (*fú tián* 福田 = *puṇyakṣetra*).(125)

(220c27) However, it is not so that these *Vedas* exist naturally, for they have been articulated, just like conventional speech. Moreover, these *Vedas* are not coherent (*chēng lǐ* 稱理 = *yukta*) at all, for they are not noble explanations, just like lies (*xū kuáng yán* 虛誑言). And the Brahmin caste is not in fact worthy of veneration, nor are they a true field of merit, for they continuously engage in asking for alms all the while that they support a wife and children, just as do greedy lepers.(126) So the intelligent should not take refuge [in such false teachers].

2. Jains and Brahmins compared

(221a2) Granted the Brahmins' doctrine is largely deception, what about the [teaching] which is studied by the Jain Outsiders? [Reply:] The doctrine studied by this [school] is by and large in keeping with bewilderment (*yú chī* 愚癡= *moha*). How so? Hence the next verse:

The Brahmins' doctrine by and large makes one practise deception, but the doctrine of the Jain Outsiders is for the most part [just] in keeping with bewilderment. **(k.295)**

(221a7) Commentary. The Jain Outsiders all fail to understand the truth. They just desire happiness in the next [world], but in the present [world] they subject themselves to intense suffering. Of all which is professed [by them], most is incoherent. Such sorts of bewildered [people], when they join together to form a group, [just] serve as a refuge for the bewildered of the world. How do we know for certain that they are [in fact] bewildered? Because they shamelessly expose their naked bodies, just like madmen, or like animals, or little different from babies.

(221a11) If the Brahmins are not actually worthy of veneration, then why do [people] esteem and revere them? [Reply:] It is because they recite the *Vedas* (*míng lùn* 明論). In fact, the Brahmins know nothing, but, for [their own] livelihood, they continually recite the *Vedas* and fraudulently present another character. As they sway men's hearts, the world esteems them but does not subject them to investigation, saying that one reveres the [Brahmins] because they have good qualities. Also, although there is nothing really true (*shèng yì* 勝義 = *paramārtha*; *pāramārthika*) in the *Vedas*, they do nonetheless have some few worldly rituals. So because of the world's esteem for learning, it also extends reverence [to the Brahmins] even though [the latter] are [in fact] without any good qualities. As for the other [Outsiders' traditions], which do not recite the *Vedas*, as they are of the same sort (*tóng lèi* 同類 = *sārūpya*) [i.e. as they also conform to the *Vedas*], worldly tradition does not subject them to investigation, and reveres them as well.

(221a18) [Objection:] The Jain Outsiders are [however] not like [these latter orthodox traditions]. Why then does the world for the most part also revere them? [Response:] It is because they know a little about astronomical calculations, and because they watch birds, interpret dreams and divine fortunes. Therefore, common fools by and large extend [them] reverence.

(221a20) Now furthermore, as the Brahmins' [way of] reciting the *Vedas* is difficult to execute, the world generally reveres them, and as the Jain Outsiders practise asceticism, the world generally feels pity for them: [but] none [of these traditions] gain liberation from saṃsāra. The intelligent should correctly understand [this fact] and not follow these views. Thus, in the next verse [Āryadeva] states:

> *[The world] respects the Brahmins for reciting the Vedas,*(127) *and it takes pity on the Jains for voluntarily inflicting suffering on their own bodies.* **(k.296)**

(221a26) Commentary. The Dharma of the Brahmins consists in diligently reciting the *Vedas*; because this is difficult, the world in general respects [the Brahmins]. However, the *Vedas* (*míng lùn* 明論) are not [in fact] a cause for liberation, for they just have empty words without truth. The Jain Outsiders voluntarily inflict extreme suffering on their bodies; as this is also difficult [to execute], the world takes pity on them.

3. Refutation of asceticism and high birth as means to liberation

(221a28) Why is self-inflicted suffering not a cause for liberation? [Reply:] Because such a retributive effect (*yì shú guǒ* 異熟果 = *vipākaphala*) is not a virtuous dharma.(128) These physical sufferings which are brought about by [such practices as] pulling out one's hair and so on are the consequences of evil actions in past lives. Such karmic retributions are not virtuous dharmas, and therefore, just like pleasurable retributions, they are not a cause for liberation.(129)

(221b2) [Objection:] Suppose it is said that these sufferings are the creation of a present effort (*gōng lì* 功力 = *prayāsa*) and are not retributive effects, [and thus] the reason [in the above argument[130]] is not established. [Reply:] This is also not the case. These sufferings which are experienced *are* retributive effects, because, without any benefit, they inflict pain on both the physical senses (*sè gēn* 色根 = *rūpīndriya*) and consciousness, just as do the physical sufferings which are experienced in hell. If among our coreligionists too there are those who do not recognize that these [self-inflicted] sufferings are retributive effects [of karma], they should ascertain this fact by means of such a *pramāṇa*.

(221b6) When physical sufferings are not retributions [of past actions], they also are not the direct (*qīn* 親 = *sākṣāt*) cause for realizing liberation, in that [such] defiled (*yǒu lòu* 有漏 = *sāsrava*) physical feelings arise through present conditions [viz. bewilderment], just as in the case of sexual pleasure.[131] Furthermore, these self-inflicted sufferings cannot be the cause for liberation, because they contradict the noble teaching, as does suffering due to self-destruction. What these [Jain] masters explain is not the noble teaching [at all], for it is something which no tathāgatas and the like would ever propound, just like treatises on erotica, etc. So, these self-inflicted sufferings are just consequences of evil actions in previous lives and products of present bewilderment. They certainly are not the cause for realizing true liberation.

(221b13) Now, some say the following: One attains liberation on the basis of a superior birth (*shēn* 身).[132] The superior [people] of the world are said to be the Brahmins, and therefore, Brahmins realize liberation, but other types [of people] cannot attain nirvāṇa. This assertion is not correct, and therefore, in the next verse [Āryadeva] states:

> *Just as suffering is a retribution (gǎn 感 = vi-PAC) of karma [and is therefore] not a cause for true liberation, so superior birth is a product of karma and does not lead to realizing liberation either.* **(k.297)**

(221b18) Commentary. Just as for the Jain tradition the physical suffering which they experience is not a cause for liberation because it is a karmic retribution, so too the Brahmins' birth, which is supposed to be superior, is [just] a retribution of karma and is not a cause for liberation either.

(221b20) [Objection:] Although birth does not directly lead to realizing liberation, still the virtues present in [certain types of] birth are a cause for liberation. [Reply:] If that were so, then the virtues of other births should be analogous in this respect too. Why do you only speak of the Brahmins? Moreover, the dharmas which serve as the sense organs, objects, etc. of Brahmins are all exactly the same as those of the other castes. Why then do [the Brahmins] themselves say that they are superior and that the others are inferior? Consequently, these assertions just [serve to] cheat fools; the intelligent should not believe them. The Brahmins are, on the contrary, *not* superior to the other castes, for they are people of this continent (*zhōu* 洲 = *dvīpa*), just as are the Śūdras. And the Śūdras, etc. are not inferior to this caste [i.e. the Brahmins], because they [too] are people of this continent, as are the Brahmins.

H. Résumé of the Buddhadharma

(221b26) It has by now been explained that the Outsiders' teachings are completely false (*xū* 虛 = *mṛṣā*), but it is not yet understood what truth the Tathāgata's Dharma might possess. So to dispel this doubt, [Āryadeva] states the following verse.

In brief (lüè yán 略言 *= samāsatas), the Buddha's teachings have two [features] setting them apart from other traditions: through non-violence one is born as a man or god, and through the insight into voidness one realizes liberation.*[133] **(k.298)**

(221c1) Commentary. The Buddha stated an immeasurable [number of] profoundly excellent approaches to the Dharma, but to benefit sentient beings, there need be just two sorts: firstly, through non-violence one experiences [birth as] a man or a god; secondly, through insight into voidness one realizes liberation. We collectively apply the term "violence" to the intentions to harm others as well as to both the physical and verbal karma which ensues [from such intentions]. If one eliminates these just-explained violent dharmas and practises the causes for virtue, then this is what is termed "non-violence". In other words: the ten virtuous actions (*shí shàn yè* 十善業 = *daśakuśalakarmapatha*), giving (*bù shī* 布施 = *dāna*), pleasant speech (*ài yǔ* 愛語 = *priyavacana*), beneficial conduct (*lì xíng* 利行 = *arthacaryā*), sameness of goal (*tóng shì* 同事 = *samānārthatā*) as well as the [four] trances (*jìng lü* 靜慮 = *dhyāna*) and the [four] formless meditative absorptions (*wú sè dìng* 無色定 = *ārūpyasamāpatti*), and so forth.[134] By means of these [practices] one obtains a birth in fortunate states of existence, such as those of a man or god, and experiences excellent, undefiled (*wú rǎn* 無染 = *akliṣṭa*) fruitions. Relying on these [practices], one eliminates all the passions and develops immeasurable causes for virtue.

(221c7) Thusness (*zhēn rú* 眞如 = *tathatā*), the true endpoint (*shí jì* 實際 = *bhūtakoṭi*) [and] the lack of characters (*lí xiāng* 離相 = *animitta*) are termed "voidness".[135] If one correctly has insight into this voidness, one will attain the bliss of nirvāṇa. The principle of selflessness is the lack of characters and inexpressibility of all dharmas[136] so that they all have the same taste of tranquillity and bliss: this, in other words, is nirvāṇa. It [i.e. nirvāṇa] must be an insight into voidness, for only [by such an insight] can it be realized.

(221c10) So in this fashion, the two causes for fortunate states of existence and liberation [respectively] are only fully attainable in the Buddhadharma. Although the Outsiders do speak somewhat about giving, etc. being the cause for birth as a man or god, still [their explanations] are incomplete. Why? Because these Outsiders do not have the intelligence to clearly explain cause and effect, do not explain that it is the mind (*yì sī* 意思 = *manas*) which gives rise to excellent merit, and lack the Dharma [to be found] in the *Prātimokṣasaṃvara* (*bié jiě tuō lü yí* 別解脫律儀),[137] they therefore do not yet really know the gross actions [necessary] for fortunate states of existence. As nirvāṇa has superior causes, it is ruled out [for them].

I. Conclusions

(221c15) If the reasonings and scriptures put forth by the Tathāgata are completely perfect, why do the heretical followers of the Outsiders not rejoice [in them]? [Reply:] As the true teaching of the Buddha is opposed to what is perversely coveted by these heretical positions, [the latter], as a result, have no liking [for the Buddhist teachings]. To illustrate this point, [Āryadeva] states the following verse:

Worldly people long for their own positions just as they love their native places.
[So] the heretical schools will not be pleased if the true Dharma defeats [them].
(k.299)

(221c20) Commentary. Even if one's native place is not fertile, nonetheless, when one has lived there a long time, one will be reluctant to abandon it. It is similar in the case of one's own [philosophical] position. Although it might be irrational, it was received from one's teacher, and hence one will not relinquish it. If one is even uninterested in other Outsiders' positions, what need to mention being attracted to the noble teaching which is the sweet nectar of the Tathāgata? The fire of the knowledge of voidness, i.e. the extremely profound true character [of things] (*shí xiāng* 實相 = *bhūtalakṣaṇa*)(138), burns up the accumulated fuel of the Outsiders' heretical graspings, but because such [knowledge] contradicts [worldly people's] own way of thinking, they have no liking [for it]. The intelligent should well direct their minds and not contradict the true Dharma by means of defiled heretical positions.

(221c26) Now, the Buddhadharma illumines all, just like the brilliant sun; people who seek superior understanding should rely on it. To show this point, [Āryadeva] states the following verse:

The intelligent person, who seeks excellent qualities, should accept true positions.
The true Dharma, like the sun, causes those with eyes to see. **(k.300)**

(222a1) Commentary. Here [Āryadeva] shows that one needs to possess two qualities to have faith in the Mahāyāna. The first is that one be intelligent.(139) The second is that one long for excellent qualities.

(222a2) The Mahāyāna eliminates all heretical positions. When one follows the Mahāyāna, those who are benefited are numerous: one realizes the unexcelled nirvāṇa [oneself] and causes other sentient beings to leave saṃsāra behind too. The true Dharma of the Mahāyāna is like the sun in that for the world, everywhere, it disperses the darkness of ignorance. Those who have the eye of wisdom will, by the light of this Dharma, clearly discern true and false appearances, turn their backs on the heretics and follow the truth, avoiding precipices and seeking safety, so that the benefit to self and others will in no way be incomplete (*chéng bàn* 成辦 = *abhiniṣpatti*).

(222a7) The intelligent should [thus] place their faith in the Mahāyāna and not hanker after heretical positions. He who defames the true Dharma will himself come to be drowned in the mire of saṃsāra and will deceive sentient beings, making them lose much benefit. The difference between intelligence and foolishness is said to be knowing what is and is not the case: the intelligent [then] should not, like fools, fail to distinguish true from false. If one really wishes to benefit others, one should, by means of the Mahāyāna, dispel heresies and establish the truth; diligently training in the insight into voidness one will speedily realize enlightenment and the benefit to sentient beings will exhaust the bounds of the [limitless] future.(140)

CATUḤŚATAKAVṚTTI XII: REFUTATION OF HERETICAL VIEWS (*dṛṣṭi*)

§1. Here, there is the following objection: You have very clearly and extensively explained selflessness. But if the Tathāgata understands this [principle] and commends it [to others], then why is it that the world for the most part does not follow this Dharma? Since this Dharma is purer [than the others] on account of the superiority of its founder, exponents and doctrine, then all those who aspire to liberation (*thar pa* = *mokṣa*) should follow it. How is it that there are differing assertions in the various traditions?

A. The qualities of the auditors of the teaching

§2. Reply: Although this Dharma does have superiority with regard to its promulgator, exponents and the very nature of the doctrine [expounded], nonetheless, it is extremely difficult to find auditors who are superior. Thus:

> *One says that an auditor who is impartial, intelligent and industrious is a vessel [for the Dharma].* **(k.276ab)**

§3. In this context, impartiality means not falling into factions. Now, who [is said to] have not fallen into factions? [Reply:] He who is free from attachment for his own faction and contempt for another's. Such [a person], because his mind-stream is undefiled (*ñon ma moṅs pa* = *akliṣṭa*), will indeed dedicate himself to seeking various precious excellent explanations; thus the root for abandoning the orientation towards the completely defiled (*kun nas ñon moṅs pa'i phyogs*) is impartiality. Therefore, in this fashion, the impartial auditor is the vessel for the supreme ambrosia of the sacred Dharma.

§4. If, in addition to being impartial, he is also intelligent, he will be skilled in differentiating what is sound and unsound in good and bad explanations. And such [a person], through his intelligence, will reject the unsound [doctrines] and embrace [only] what is sound. So, when the auditor is intelligent, he will [indeed] be a vessel [for the Dharma]. Thus he who is impartial as well as intelligent will strive to hear good explanations and will not, like a [mere] simulacrum (*ri mo'i skyes bu'i rnam pa ltar*), fail to exert himself. Therefore:

> "One says that an auditor who is impartial, intelligent and industrious is a vessel [for the Dharma]."

Now, if the auditor is [indeed] like that, then certainly,

> *the teacher's good qualities will not be anything other [than good] and nor will those of [his] auditor.* **(k.276cd)**

§5. In this context, the good qualities of the teacher are: impartiality, freedom from error, clarity and unconfused speech[(141)], [the ability] to understand the dispositions (*lhag pa'i bsam pa* = *adhyāśaya*) of [his] auditors, having a mind which is free from worldliness (*zaṅ ziṅ med pa = nirāmiṣa*) and so on and so forth. The auditor, on the other hand, has respect for both the Dharma and the teacher of the Dharma, he is concentrated, impartial, intelligent and industrious. One understands his "industriousness" as being his respect for the Dharma and its teacher, his concentration and the other such [above-mentioned] qualities.

§6. Now, in such a case [when teacher and auditor are as described above], then the teacher's good qualities will not be anything other [than good], and equally the auditor's good qualities will not be otherwise either.*(142)* When the auditor is as [described] above, the teacher's good qualities will not [seem to] turn into faults. It is because of the auditor's faults that the [teacher's] good qualities turn into faults and [his own] faults turn into good qualities. But when the auditor who possesses the above-described characteristics is a basis for the collection of non-erroneous good qualities which stem from listening and so forth [i.e. listening, reflection and meditation], then the teacher's good qualities will not be anything other [than good] and nor will the auditor's qualities become faults.*(143)*

§7. Thus, even though the teacher is much purer [than the auditors], the auditors do not reckon their own defects, but make [their teacher seem to] have faults.*(144)* Fools, praising themselves, will say,*(145)* "How could it be us who are without intelligence? There is no one who [could] understand." This can be known from the *Adhyāśayasaṃcodanasūtra*.*(146)* Therefore, the Illustrious One,

> *explained the [four noble truths]: existence, the means for existence, the means for peace and similarly, peace [itself]. When the world completely misunderstands something, they regard this [error] as if it were attributable to the Sage.(147)* **(k.277)**

§8. In this context, "existence" is the five appropriated aggregates which are the result [of conditionings]. The "means for existence" are the various conditionings (*'du byed = saṃskāra*) which are the cause [of the aggregates]. "Peace" means nirvāṇa, for its nature is free from anything which can harm. The "means for peace" is the noble eightfold path. Thus the Illustrious One taught the four noble truths to those desirous of liberation, for he taught what was to be realized (*blaṅ bar bya ba = upādeya*) and what was to be abandoned (*dor bar bya ba = heya*) along with their [resultant] effects.

§9. Now, the meaning taught by the Illustrious One is completely correct to the [mind-]streams of those who are endowed with listening, reflection and meditation and who themselves personally understand things as they really are. However, those who dislike (*sdaṅ ba*) exerting themselves in listening, reflection and meditation, being unaware that they are not [suitable] vessels, will think: "Since we don't understand the meaning correctly, surely it was not properly explained". And thus they will certainly take this error as if it were attributable to the Sage.

§10. [But] this much does not make the Illustrious Buddha also reproachable. By teaching the four noble truths he teaches all of man's goals without exception; so how could the teacher be at fault? Thus, it is said [in the *kārikā*] "as if it were attributable to the Sage", for these people did not correctly ascertain the truth (*de kho na ñid*

= *tattva*) of the things taught by the [Buddha]. The fact that the congenitally blind do not see is not the fault of the sun which is shining [on them], for those who are not blind do [in fact] see this [sun].

B. The Outsiders' and Buddhists' notions of liberation compared

§11. Here there is the following objection: While all the Tathāgata's account of [how to obtain] a good position [in the world] (*mṅon par tho ba* = *abhyudaya*) is very clear in its sense, [his] account of what is supremely excellent (*ṅes par legs pa* = *niḥśreyasa*) [i.e. liberation and buddhahood] is incomprehensible for people like us in that it seeks above all to teach that all entities are inexistent. The Illustrious One, thus, strives to refute the natures of all entities, and consequently we are repelled [by such a doctrine]. [Āryadeva's] reply:

The heretics (ya mtshan can = pāṣaṇḍin) all accept that nirvāna is [realized] through abandoning all [entities]. [So] why are they not pleased when all is refuted? **(k.278)**

§12. The heretics, such as Sāṃkhyas, Vaiśeṣikas and so forth, are all sure that liberation is obtained by the abandonment of all defiled entities such as pleasure, pain, etc. Since all the heretics [already] believe that nirvāṇa [is realized] through abandoning everything, we have not undertaken anything(148) unprecedented in this regard which might cause them to be repelled [by such a doctrine]. Indeed, we are [merely] cleansing the path leading to the city of nirvāṇa by means of this treatise which is designed to pull out the thorns of bad views and which seeks to teach the lack of nature of those very entities whose cessation [you] strive for in that [you hold that] they will not once again begin to function in [the state of] nirvāṇa.(149) So why, after etching an impious apprehension into your heart(150), are you thus afraid? Put great joy [in your heart]! Make this Dharma your own! Let the account of [how to] turn away defiled entities be firmly installed in your mind!

1. Citations and some grammatical remarks

§13. As the Illustrious One stated [in the *Samādhirājasūtra*]:

"In extinction dharmas are without dharmas (*nivṛtti dharmāṇa na asti dharmā*). Whatever is inexistent in this [state] does not exist at all. For those who imagine 'existence' and 'inexistence' and practise accordingly, suffering will not cease."(151)

§14. Nirvāṇa, or passing beyond suffering, is the realm of nirvāṇa without the aggregates remaining; it is like the extinction of a lamp when the wick and butter are used up. We think that for those who understand correctly, the force of the fire of the wisdom of thusness (*de kho na ñid* = *tathatā*) causes the attachment to the possessions of the self (*bdag gi ba* = *ātmīya*)[152] to cease, and thus attachment, aversion, bewilderment, conceit, pride and the other [passions] become absolutely inexistent. As you heretics all accept [this], you should be pleased by the Illustrious Buddha's explanations. However, the Outsiders (*mu stegs byed pa* = *tīrthakara*) do not ascertain that this is true. Here [in the words *nivṛtti dharmāṇa na asti dharmā* of the *Samādhirājasūtra* quotation] the seventh case [i.e. the locative] does not appear [in *nivṛtti*][153], in accordance with the [grammatical] sūtra [of Pāṇini], "[the following elements are substitutes] for the case-endings (*sup*) [in the Vedas]: *su* [i.e. the nominative singular *s*], *luk* [i.e. suppression of the ending] ..., etc.".[154]

§15. In this vein, the Illustrious One states:

"Now, that which is extinct is non-existent. Just as the [mesh of] hair (*skra śad*)[155], the flies, and so forth, which are observed by those suffering from [ocular problems such as] *timira* (*rab rib can* = *taimirika*)[156], [do not exist] when there is no more *timira*; or just as when there is a light and one thinks that there is [just] empty space in the house, this will dissipate the doubt that one is going to be infected with the poison of something which one saw, [a doubt which arose] because of the fear at having seen a [striped] rope as being a snake; so too these [illusory entities], which in no way [really] appear or exist, are like the hair, flies, etc. of the *taimirika*s when they [actually] suffer from [the disease,] *timira*. And, just as when there is light there are no 'snakes', and one therefore no longer thinks that the rope is a snake, so too [one realizes that] in the dark there was no real snake [either], and hence one does not think that there was a snake at all. Analogously, the state of saṃsāra is also completely inexistent."[157]

§16. [Objection:] Well then how could saṃsāra arise from the defilements (*kun nas ñon moṅs pa* = *saṃkleśa*) and karma? Reply: saṃsāra is like the collection of mind-created entities, i.e. the hair and so forth which are perceived by those who are suffering from *timira*, and is like mistakenly fearing the snake when it is dark. It [i.e. saṃsāra] too pertains to those infantile people whose eye of intelligence is blinded by the darkness of mistakes about unrealities. To explain this it was said:

"For those who imagine 'existence' and 'inexistence' and practise accordingly, suffering does not cease."

[Further grammatical remarks on the *Samādhirājasūtra*'s use of *nivṛtti dharmāṇa na asti dharmā*:] Correctly speaking, one would say *rnams yod min* [i.e. *na santi* instead of *nāsti*]. But in accordance with the [*Mahābhāṣya*'s] rule (*mtshan ñid* = *lakṣaṇa*) to the effect that "it should be said that verbal endings (*tiṅ*) are [substituted] for [other] verbal endings", [the *Samādhirājasūtra* passage cited above] states *chos yod min* [i.e. *nāsti dharmā*].[158] *dharmāṇām* is what ought to be stated, but here [in the *Samādhirājasūtra*] the letters *ā* and *m* did not appear [and one finds *dharmāṇa* instead of the normal genitive plural *dharmāṇām*].

§17. "Those who imagine 'existence'" refers to you Sāṃkhyas, Aulūkyas, Kaṇāda, Kapila and the Vaibhāṣikas, while "those who imagine 'inexistence'" refers to the Vaiśeṣikas(?), the Sautrāntikas and the Vijñānavādins.(159) Those who practise accordingly, i.e. those possessed by the demons of "existence" and "inexistence", are like the *taimirikas* when under the influence of *timira* and like those who think that a rope in the dark is a snake: the suffering of these [individuals] with mistaken views — i.e. the sufferings, sorrows, etc. of birth, old age, sickness, and death in the saṃsāra [composed of] five states of existence — will not cease. The analysis of these things has already been taught here in various places, so we have not explained it [again]. Thus it is said [in the *Ratnāvalī*]:

> "Ask the world as well the Sāṃkhyas, Aulūkyas, Nirgranthas [and] those who assert that the person is the aggregates if they assert [a doctrine] that is beyond existence and inexistence."
>
> "Thus, know that the ambrosia of the buddhas' teaching, which is termed 'profound', is the 'present of the Dharma' beyond existence and inexistence."(160)

2. *The Outsiders do not know the method for liberation*

§18. Objection: If this very same thought is also shared by all the heretics, that is to say, that by abandoning everything one [realizes] nirvāṇa, then, I ask you, what is the difference between you [Buddhists] and the Outsiders? [Reply:] The difference is that for the Outsiders abandoning everything is no more than an idea; they do not, however, state a method for abandoning everything. Now, when the method for abandoning all is not taught,

> *how will he who does not know the method for abandoning effectuate [this] abandon?* **(k.279ab)**

§19. Even if he should wish to abandon all, how will one who relies on the Outsiders' opinions, and who [hence] does not know the method for abandoning, ever effectuate [this] abandon when he does not know the method for abandoning all, viz. the ultimate truth, which is characterized as the voidness of nature of all dharmas? Thus,

> *it is assuredly for this [reason] that the Sage has said that peace is not [found] elsewhere.* **(k.279cd)**

§20. It is certainly with this very intention in mind that the Sage spoke as follows [in the *Mahāparinirvāṇasūtra*]: "Here is the one who is the first mendicant, here is the second" and so on up to the fourth [mendicant]. "The opponents' systems are void of [true] mendicants."(161) Now, it is precisely on account of this complete explanation of the method to abandon everything that one realizes that the Illustrious

Buddha is a true teacher in that his wisdom functions everywhere without any impediment. Also, the fact that the Outsiders have false understandings on other sorts of things too need not be proven, for it has already been established by their inability to give a complete explanation of the method for abandoning everything.(162)

C. The problem of the authority of the Outsiders' and Buddhists' treatises and scriptures

§21. Objection: But, given that there is no limit to what is knowable, then with regard to the suprasensible things which are explained, surely, since these [things] are unobservable, the doubt must also occur to you [Buddhists] as to whether this thing really is as it was explained or whether it is otherwise. Indeed, there is no way to be certain concerning such [things]. [Reply:] To this also [Āryadeva] says:

When someone entertains doubt concerning the imperceptible [things] (parokṣa) taught by the Buddha, he should develop conviction in these very things on account of voidness (śūnyatā). **(k.280)**

§22. Indeed, not all entities are cognizable by means of perceptual consciousness; there are also those which are cognizable by inference. Now, with regard to these [imperceptible things], we are able to make an inference because there does in fact exist an example. In this context, the means for abandoning [everything] is the voidness of nature of all dharmas. This [voidness] is such that nothing can cause it to be otherwise, and this state of affairs, although always at hand, is subtle, for no [ordinary] people can observe it. However, its truth is proven through reasoning in that it stops one from believing in the nature of any dharmas. [So] it is on precisely this [point] that one should first of all ground [one's] certainty. But if in this matter there is any reason at all for uncertainty as to whether this [state of affairs, viz. voidness,] is actually so or otherwise, then let this [reason for uncertainty] be stated, providing it has not [already] been dissipated by the certitudes established in the [previously] taught chapters or in those to come. Now, the [adversary] cannot state even the slightest reason for any uncertainty, and thus this example [viz. voidness] is indeed proven. Therefore, you should understand by means of your own principles that the other statements of the Illustrious One, which establish unobservable states of affairs, are also true, for they were taught by the Tathāgata, just as were the statements setting forth [that] state of affairs which is the voidness of nature. How then could there be any place for doubt concerning the imperceptible things taught by the Buddha?

1. Citations

§23. States the Illustrious One [in the *Samādhirājasūtra*]:
"The sūtras which I have preached in the thousands of worlds have differing letters, but the meaning is the same; it cannot be widely proclaimed."

"When one has contemplated one single phenomenon, one is acquainted with them all. However many [different] dharmas were taught by all the buddhas,

all [such] dharmas are selfless. Whichever people are experienced, they will find the Buddha's dharmas without any difficulty when they have trained in this matter."

Similarly, as was stated [by the Buddha in the *Samādhirājasūtra*]:

"Just as one has understood the notion of the self, so one should direct the mind in precisely the same way with regard to everything [else]. Now, all dharmas are of that nature: pure, like the sky."

2. The untrustworthiness of the Outsiders

§24. Moreover, one cannot be sure that the Outsiders also speak about non-erroneous states of affairs, as does the Tathāgata, for they are mistaken with regard to what is in fact empirical (*dṛṣṭa*). Thus, for example, they teach that the origin of this world has an antecedent cause which is [itself] permanent. Now, such an [origin] cannot be advocated, it being in contradiction with both experience and reason. And so:

He who has difficulty observing this world will [inevitably] be completely confused about the next one. **(k.281ab)**

§25. Indeed, one can suppose that he who cannot see the full moon well will not see the North Star (*dhruva*) or Alcor (*arundhatī*).(163) Analogously, when this Outsider, being confused about the causality of the world — in other words [about the causality] of the living beings and the "receptacle" —, does not [even] correctly view what is actually just a gross [type of] state of affairs, then one can wonder how he will ever understand a state of affairs which is extremely subtle, is far away in space and time and is highly diversified. Therefore,

those who, **(k.281d)**

wishing to drink the pure waters of the understanding of the true nature [of reality] in order to relieve their fatigue and weariness on the path of saṃsāra,

follow this **(k.281d)**

Outsider, who himself has a completely erroneous view and who, like the water in a mirage, does not merit any attention at all,

will be deceived for a very long time. **(k.281c)**

§26. Those who reject the true teacher, the Illustrious Buddha, and then, in their desire for liberation, follow an Outsider, who is thoroughly confused about the natures of both empirical (*dṛṣṭa*) and non-empirical (*adṛṣṭa*) entities, will, alas, be deceived in an interminable saṃsāra which is without any endpoint.

§27. Here the following is stated:
"Just as on Ratnadvīpa some bad merchants who are ignorant about jewels, desire precious stones, but in their confusion end up choosing rhinestones after rejecting a very valuable jewel, so similarly those on Jambudvīpa who are of poor intelligence [and] who are ignorant about [philosophical] systems, have hopes for liberation, but in their confusion end up choosing the Outsiders' system after casting aside the Buddha's system."(164)

D. Fear of voidness and nirvāṇa

§28. [Query:] But why do those desirous of liberation follow an Outsider who has a view which is mistaken in this way? [Reply:] Because they are afraid to hear the teaching of the Dharma on the voidness of nature. This fear comes from the terror [which they feel] due to [the idea] (165): "The I does not exist, nor will I exist; the mine does not exist, nor will it exist."(166) Now, this fear stems from longstanding habituation to the conceptions of the I (*ahaṃkāra*) and the mine (*mamakāra*). Thus,

those who of themselves go to nirvāṇa, **(k.282a)**

after having, thanks to the care of a spiritual friend, cast aside [their] defiled attachment to the nature of entities, all be [this attachment] a longstanding habit,

they accomplish what is extremely difficult to do. **(k.282b)**

§29. Having himself become a buddha, an Illustrious One, he proceeds of himself alone to the city of nirvāṇa.

The mediocre person [however] lacks the courage in his heart(167) *to go [to nirvāṇa], even following a guide,* **(k.282cd)**

who, in this respect, accomplishes [an action] which is so difficult to do.

§30. Mediocre people, who remain fixed in their conceptions of the I and the mine, not only lack the courage in their hearts to go alone by themselves to nirvāṇa, but, what is more, even when he follows a guide as was previously described, the mediocre person does not exhibit the courage in his heart to go to nirvāṇa.

§31. But why does the mediocre person lack the courage in his heart to go to nirvāṇa, even when he follows this [sort of] guide? It is because he is afraid of voidness. And who has a fear of this [voidness]? To show this [type of person] who has [such a fear], [Āryadeva] states:

When one has not seen [anything], fear does not arise, [and] when one has seen [it], the [fear] completely vanishes. So therefore, certainly, it is when one understands a little bit that fear will occur.(168) **(k.283)**

§32. Indeed, those who are unversed in scientific conventions, viz. cowherds and other such [illiterates], even if one explains voidness a hundred times [to them], they will not enter into it at all, and thus they will have no fear of it, in that they will not have seen the point of voidness, just as with regard to momentary destruction (*kṣaṇabhaṅga*), he who understands nothing about this [is also unafraid], or just as he whose [mind-]stream is supported by wrong views [is unafraid] of the fires of the hells.

"When one has seen [it], the [fear] completely vanishes."

§33. Indeed, when they have seen the dharma known as "voidness", this terror [of which we spoke] will completely vanish for those who are experts in this [voidness], for they will be free of the attachment to the self and its possessions which is the cause for fear. Similarly, someone who came to mistake a rope for a snake will cease to fear [that it is actually] a snake once he sees the rope [for what it is]. However, fear will certainly, i.e. inevitably, occur to him who knows [just] a little bit [about voidness]. Indeed, one who is well-trained in driving elephants in rut will not be afraid when he is carried off on an elephant(169). And nor will the stupidest of stupid villagers, who is eager for a ride on that [animal],[be afraid]. As he does not see the harm [which would come] from [accidents such as] falling off and so forth, he values [the elephant] just as a ride and is not afraid of it. But he who understands a little bit [about the dangers] will be extremely afraid when he thinks about discovering(170) himself sitting there on the [elephant]. Now then, it is certain that a person who [only] understands a little will be afraid in every action [he might undertake] when he does it under such conditions (*evam*). But it is not so for someone who knows the matter at hand, for he is confident, nor is it so for someone who is completely ignorant, for he is thoroughly in the grip of bewilderment. Rather, it is he who understands a little [about what could happen] who is afraid, for he wonders whether this thing could occur or not.

§34. [Query:] But why do those who understand a little not strive for a higher level until they fully attain what they need to know? Response: Because of fear. And what causes the fear? — No training. And what is the cause of that? — Wrong training. To show this very [point] [Āryadeva] states:

> *The infantile definitely have a training in the dharma which activates (pravartaka) [saṃsāra]. [But] they are afraid of the dharma which quietens (nivartaka) [saṃsāra] because they are untrained [in it].* **(k.284)**

§35. "Dharma which activates" [refers to] the one which is conducive to developing saṃsāra. Now, beings who reside on the level belonging to the profane (*pṛthagjana*)(171) are trained in only the dharma which activates. "Dharma which quietens" [refers to] the voidness of nature, for it is that which is conducive to the cessation of saṃsāra.(172) What stops one from training in this is self-cherishing (*ātmasneha*). Because their mind-streams are in keeping with this [self-cherishing], the profane are all the more afraid of the dharma which would put an end to this latter [attitude]. They regard the voidness of nature as something similar to a precipice, and [hence] cannot bear to understand it as it is.

§36. Thus, suppose that some or another person, having lost the proper path(173) in the great jungle forest of saṃsāra whose outer limit cannot be seen and where the true nature of things is enveloped in the thick darkness of ignorance, then devotes himself to the account of the voidness of nature. Just as this [person] acquires faith in voidness because conditions conducive to such [faith] are realized, so [he too] should act in the same fashion: he who is compassionate and grateful (*kṛtajña*) to the Illustrious Tathāgata and who wishes to abandon acts which cause obstacles to the true Dharma [and] are the cause of great downfalls for himself,(174) should teach this true Dharma to those who are its vessel, gathering [disciples] by means of the four ways of gathering (*saṃgrahavastu*) after having [himself] plunged into even the impassable and given even what is difficult to give.(175)

§37. On the other hand, he who not only has no esteem [for the Dharma] as it has been taught, but, what is more,

> *who, obscured by some form of bewilderment (moha), would create an impediment to the truth, such a person will not [even] have a fortunate state of existence. What is the point in speaking about liberation?* **(k.285)**

§38. He who "by some form of bewilderment" — i.e. by jealousy, miserliness, laziness, fear, hatred towards [his] auditor, and so forth —, impedes someone in listening [reflecting,] etc. to an explanation of the truth when [that latter] person is [indeed] a vessel for the teaching on the truth, this [bewildered person] will certainly go to an unfortunate state, and therefore already has not even the possibility of a fortunate state of existence, be it divine or human. All the more so then, why would there be any occasion to speak about liberation for him? Indeed, has he not done harm to his own and others' [mind-]streams? For, he seeks to obstruct the lamp of wisdom when it arises in the [mind-]stream, [a lamp] which pervades all directions without exception, whose light is extremely brilliant, whose force goes forth unweakened throughout the three times, whose amount of light is ever-increasing in order to destroy day by day the obscurities of ignorance, [and] whose power consists in revealing all the thought-processes of beings.

E. Moral and philosophical faults compared

§39. It is precisely in this vein that the Illustrious Tathāgatā, seeing fully the extreme harm to self and others, stated:

> *It is better to fall from moral discipline than [to fall] in any way from the view.* **(k.286ab)**

The sūtra states: "It is better to have failed in moral discipline than to have failed in the view".(176) Therefore, the Master [Āryadeva] brings out the correctness of these words of the Tathāgata by saying the following:

> *By moral discipline one goes to heaven, by means of the view one attains the supreme state.* **(k.286cd)**

§40. Indeed, a failure in moral discipline for those who accumulate minor, middling and major degrees [of such a failure] will lead to its result — i.e. birth as a hungry ghost (*preta*), an animal or a hell-being according to the measure of the magnitude of the retribution (*vipāka*) [for such a failure] — provided that it does not come to perish in Noble Ones (*ārya*) who have attained the correct view. For the profane, who have not yet attained the correct view, purity of moral discipline will, however, at its best, have [birth in] paradise as its result. But a failure with regard to the view, no matter how minor it might be, cannot be even equalled, much less surpassed, in the magnitude of its retribution (*vipāka*)[(177)], albeit by uncountable hundreds of thousands of failures in moral discipline. But if a person, through conviction (*pratyaya*)[(178)] [gained] in one way or another, happened to perfect the correct view by giving rise to the noble path (*āryamārga*), then he would definitely shake off the obscurities of ignorance existing in beginningless saṃsāra and would reach nirvāṇa, honoured by the whole realm of sentient beings. Thus, having understood the immense importance of this [correct] view on the true nature [of reality], the learned should strive to abolish [all] impediments [to this view].

F. Selflessness

1. Consequences of teaching selflessness

§41. Furthermore, this [learned person], who sees the danger of impediments to the [correct view], should not teach this view of selflessness (*nairātmyadarśana*) everywhere, to those who are not [fitting] vessels [to receive it], and without having first ascertained [that his auditor is] an excellent vessel. Indeed, for one who is not a [fitting] vessel this teaching would be just calamitous. As it is said [in the *Pañcatantra*]:

> "For fools, teaching is [just] agitating rather than calming. For snakes, drinking milk just increases their poison."

§42. Also the Illustrious One said [in the *Kāśyapaparivarta*]:
"Kāśyapa, the view that there is a personality, [a view] which is as gross as Mount Sumeru, is indeed better than a self-conceited person's view on voidness. Why is that? Voidness, Kāśyapa, is what delivers one from all views. He who has a view on voidness, him I declare incurable."[(179)]

§43. Therefore:
For a mediocre person, the conception of an I (ahaṃkāra) is better than the view[(180)] *of selflessness.* **(k.287ab)**

§44. One calls "mediocre" him who is lacking in zealous application towards the Dharma of selflessness, is attached to self-grasping [and] seeks the impenetrable thicket of [heretical] views because he bases himself on something other than the true Dharma. To this mediocre person it is better to teach [that there is a] self in that such [a teaching] will be conducive to [his] ceasing bad actions. For indeed, due to his self-cherishing, he desires his own welfare and thus will place great importance on ceasing bad actions: one who has stopped evil conduct will easily obtain a fortunate state of existence. The teaching of selflessness will [however] definitely harm his mental and physical continuum in that he will mistakenly understand [such a teaching] or cast it aside. Therefore:

The first just goes to an unfortunate state of existence, while the one who is out of the ordinary (netara) goes to only peace. **(k.287cd)**

§45. Indeed, an unlearned person who errs with regard to the view of selflessness will just simply go to an unfortunate state of existence, and not to peace. However, he who is out of the ordinary will go to only peace, and not to an unfortunate state. The word *itara* ("ordinary") means someone who is not superior. And who is "not superior"? He who mistakenly understands the meaning of voidness or who casts it aside. Negating ["ordinary"] yields "out of the ordinary" (*netara*)(181); "out of the ordinary" [thus] means "superior" (*utkṛṣṭa*). The very teaching on voidness on account of which an ordinary person ends up in an unfortunate state of existence, that same teaching on voidness is what enables a person who is out of the ordinary to attain nirvāṇa. He who is conditioned by the view of voidness and conquers the horde of the passions and karma in that he completely abandons attachment, is certain to reach cessation (*nirvṛtti*).(182) Alternatively, [it could be said that] a mediocre person who listens to the Dharma of selflessness will cast it aside or misunderstand it, and thus he will go to just an unfortunate state. He who does not listen [to such a teaching] will, due to [his] meritorious karma, go to a fortunate state.

2. Explaining what selflessness is

§46. [Query:] But what is this so-called "selflessness" which one is not supposed to teach to the mediocre and which one is supposed to teach to the excellent? To set it forth [Āryadeva] states:

Selflessness is said to be the unrivalled door to peace, the terror of evil views [and] the sphere of all the buddhas.(183) **(k.288)**

§47. Selflessness is "the unrivalled door to peace". Selflessness is "the terror of evil views". Selflessness is said to be "the sphere of all the buddhas." Now, what one terms "self" is entities' nature (*svabhāva*), or essence (*svarūpa*), which does not depend on anything else; the absence of this ["self"] is selflessness.(184) Moreover, this [selflessness] is understood to be of two sorts on account of its division in [terms of] dharmas and in [terms of] the person, namely, the "selflessness of dharmas" (*dharma-nairātmya*) and the "selflessness of the person" (*pudgalanairātmya*) [respectively]. In this vein, what one terms the "person" is the appropriator (*upādātṛ*) of the five aggregates (*skandha*), which are said to be "the appropriated object" (*upādāna*); it is designated in dependence upon the [five] aggregates (*skandhān upādāya prajñapyate*).(185) If one searches for it amongst the aggregates by means of the five ways (*pañcadhā*)(186), it cannot exist. Dharmas, on the other hand, are the entities which we term the aggregates, the domains (*āyatana*)(187) [and] the elements (*dhātu*).(188) So, because these dharmas, as well as the person, arise [each] according to their individuality in dependence upon their causes and conditions, and are dependently designated (*upādāya prajñapyamānatva*), they do not have an uncreated essence which would be dependent on [only] itself, independent of anything else [and] innate. Dharmas and the person are, thus, established as lacking natures.

§48. Now, when an object is not established by its essence, by what other nature might it then be established? So, entities, whose own proper characters (*svalakṣaṇa*) are never actually in any way established, exist dependently (*pratītya*) or [in other words] on account of [other things] (*upādāya*), and according to a nature which is deceptive for fools(189); they become the focus of foolish minds' attachment. However, when [such entities] are scrutinized according to their [actual] nature by those who have the correct [philosophical] vision(190), they set in motion the complete destruction of [all] attachment to the dharmas and the person. And [this] complete destruction of attachment is the cause for attaining nirvāṇa. There is no [other] Dharma, apart from the view of no nature, which is the cause for completely destroying attachment in this manner.(191)

§49. Therefore, this selflessness, which is characterized as the lack of nature, is the "unrivalled door to peace".(192) For entering the city of nirvāṇa, this alone is the one and only door. Although there are three "accesses to liberation" (*vimokṣamukha*), namely "voidness" (*śūnyatā*), the "lack of characters" (*ānimitta*) and the "no focusing [on objects]" (*apraṇihita*), nonetheless, it is the view of selflessness which alone is the essential.(193) For indeed, he who has understood selflessness [and] whose attachment to entities is [thus] destroyed, will have absolutely no wishes for anything whatsoever; or [what is more], how could he ever perceive any characters (*nimitta*) [of things]?(194) Therefore, this selflessness is indeed the unrivalled door to peace.

§50. And so the **Bodhisaṃbhāra* states:

> "Since [dharmas] lack nature they are void; and being void, how could they ever have characters? As all characters have ceased, why would the wise seek anything?" (195)

§51. Furthermore, this [selflessness] is the "terror of evil views". "Evil views" means views which are reprehensible. Indeed, no entity is perceived at all in selflessness, and thus this selflessness is a "terror" in that it is a vision(196) of the complete destruction of evil views, since they are wholly based on imagining essences of entities.

Selflessness is the "sphere of all the buddhas": "all the buddhas" means the hearers (*śrāvaka*), solitary realizers (*pratyekabuddha*)(197) and unexcelled perfectly enlightened ones (*anuttarasamyaksaṃbuddha*). It is said to be the "sphere of all the buddhas" because it is established as being the sphere of [their] special wisdom. Or alternatively, to show all the perfectly enlightened ones' condition of not being distinct from the Body of the Dharma, he said "the sphere of all the buddhas".(198) [Thus] the Master [Āryadeva] described selflessness by means of the [above-explained] series of qualifications.

§52. Now, this selflessness should not be taught by the superior person to one who is dull of mind, since

even mention(199) of this doctrine frightens the mediocre. **(k.289ab)**

So unfathomable and profound is this doctrine that the mediocre [person] is afraid to even hear the word "selflessness". Indeed,

what powerful being can we see that does not frighten others? **(k.289cd)**

§53. The view of selflessness is powerful in that it is able to uproot all mediocre views. A mediocre view is weak in that it can be uprooted. Now, it is inevitable that one who is weak is afraid of one who is strong. And therefore, this doctrine [of selflessness] should not be taught to a weak person whose mind-stream is possessed by evil views, for it is [just] a cause for fear.

3. *Selflessness was not taught for the sake of argumentation*

§54. Objection: But, in fact, shouldn't this doctrine be taught [to him], since it extirpates all [his] evil views? For indeed, rival teachers (*parapravādin*)(200) are certainly to be defeated with the Dharma. So therefore, one who seeks out arguments and who wishes to vanquish the opposing position should teach this doctrine even to unworthy vessels. Reply: No, this is not so, for

the tathāgatas did not state this doctrine for the sake of argument. **(k.290ab)**

§55. Now, if this doctrine had been taught for the sake of argument, then it would be as you say. But it was not taught for the sake of debate, for it was taught as an access to liberation (*vimokṣamukha*). Even so,

nonetheless, it burns up rival assertions, just as fire [burns up] fuel.(201) **(k.290cd)**

§56. Although it was not taught for the sake of argument, this doctrine does indeed dispel rival assertions. The use of fire is for the sake of such actions as cooking and so forth, but not for the sake of burning up fuel. Nonetheless, because its nature is to burn, it accomplishes the desired actions and burns up the fuel. When the consciousness arises in the [mind-]stream of the faithful that all dharmas are by nature selfless, this should also be understood just as [the example of] fire, for [such a consciousness] has a nature which is to burn up all the bonds of the passions.

§57. [Query:] But how will this doctrine, when it has arisen in the [mind-] stream of the faithful, burn up rival assertions? Reply:

Whoever understands this doctrine will be unattracted to another(202) **(k.291ab)**

§58. He who has tasted the nectar of the excellent Dharma's vision of the true nature [of reality] will not relish(203) the taste of views other than this one, and therefore will be unattracted to any other views. The Master [Āryadeva] states [the following] *pādas* to gratify intelligent people such as those who have tasted the nectar of the excellent Dharma:

Therefore, it seems to me that this doctrine is like the door to destruction [of rival views]. **(k.291cd)**

§59. To the Master [Āryadeva] it seems that this doctrine is the cause for the destruction of all the mediocre views [there might be] in a [mind-]stream which realizes the doctrine of selflessness, for one observes the destruction [of these views] in that they do not once again arise. According to some people, because this [selflessness] is of the nature of a non-perception (*mi dmigs pa = anupalabdhi*), it is not a cause for destruction, and hence was said to be "like the door to destruction". Or alternatively, [Āryadeva] meant the doctrine which is stated [in the scriptures] and then [in that sense] said that [the doctrine of selflessness] is "like the door to destruction". The point is as follows: nirvāṇa is complete destruction, and the access for entering it, i.e. the voidness which is the access to liberation, is of the nature of a realization. But the stated doctrine also seems like this [i.e. like the door to destruction of rival views] to the Master, [for] just as the faithful are unattached to rival views once they have understood in their hearts the nature of the noble doctrine, so too when they understand the doctrine in the scriptures they will be unattracted to rival [doctrines].(204)

§60. Objection: But why does this [doctrine] not also cause fear in the Noble Ones (*'phags pa = ārya*)? [Reply:] It is because they are free from attachment to the self. Whoever has attachment to the self will accept realist views (*dṅos po'i lta ba*)(205) which are in accord with this [attachment], but not the view of selflessness, as it is in disaccord with this.

How could

a Noble One,

who [firmly] abides in the thought that in reality there is no self, rejoice in existence, [and] how could he be afraid in the face of inexistence? **(k.292)**

§61. He who [firmly] abides in the thought that no entities exist by their natures in that he does not imagine any essences of external and internal entities, what does he see as inexistent so that he becomes afraid that it is selfless? [And] how could he delight in seeing something as existent? Therefore, one says that he is free of the attachment and aversion to these two [i.e. existence and inexistence], for he is without attachment to the view of existence and he is without aversion to the view of selflessness. So, one who does not engage in either of these two [i.e. attachment and aversion] and is without arguments will easily go to the city of nirvāṇa. Thus, as [a Noble One thinks that] nirvāṇa is a superior state, this selflessness will not cause him fear.

§62. The Outsiders, who are attached to realist views and consider nirvāṇa to be a [dangerous] precipice, take the world as being annihilated by nirvāṇa and provide people with realist views which cause infinite suffering; in so doing they are the seed for endless suffering for sentient beings. Therefore:

> *When he has seen that the Outsiders, who are seeds for misfortune, are many, who would not feel compassion for people who are attracted to the Dharma?* **(k.293)**

§63. This world is diverted off the excellent path by the extremely thick tangle of thorns which are the Outsiders' impious views on illusory entities and non-entities. Once one has entered the tangle of thorns of [such] views, day by day [these views] kill by eliminating the virtuous vital faculty (*dge ba'i srog gi dbaṅ po* = *kuśalajīvitendriya*), which is conducive to liberation.(206) Whoever in some way by human effort saves himself from this [condition] and then relies on the excellent path, this [person] — i.e. one who frees himself from resorting to problematic and superficial friendships —, should be pitied by friends, whose hearts melt on hearing the account of [his] previous misfortunes (*rgyud pa* = *vipatti; vyasana*). So equally, who of the lineage of bodhisattvas would not feel compassion for such kinds of people? Because of [the bodhisattvas'] compassion, [such people] will respect [the bodhisattvas], with the result that [these people], who will never again be robbed by the illusory words of the Outsiders, can be taught the path of no nature.

§64. Objection: Now, why is it that although sentient beings have virtuous intentions, they mostly follow the Outsiders' traditions rather than that of the Buddhists?(207) [Reply:] Because the latter is more subtle. Indeed, [people] who have erroneous views after observing [just] gross [aspects] and after having focused chiefly on the Buddhists' temples, food, monk's robes and the like, do not fathom the depths of the profound meaning of the Tathāgata's speech, [depths] which should be understood by the wise and learned, but [rather] they are deceived by mere observation and hearsay, and [thus] come to respect the traditions of the [various] Outsiders.

G. Arguments against the Brahmins and Jains

§65. To show how the Buddhists' Dharma is subtle and its rivals are gross, [Āryadeva] states:

> *The doctrines of the three [traditions], i.e. of the Buddha, the Jains and the Brahmins, are [respectively] apprehended by the mind, the eyes and the ears.*(208) *Therefore, the tradition of the Sage is more subtle.* **(k.294)**

§66. The Brahmins take recitation as being essential; this [practice] of theirs is an object for the ears. As for the Jains — who lack any practice of hygiene and are hence clothed [only] by the ever-increasing filth of their foul-smelling bodies(209), their bodies lacking [even] a bathing cloth — they support various sufferings such as cold, wind, the sun and the plucking out of their hairs. Their tradition can be understood by [mere] observation; as such, their doctrine is understandable [simply] by the eye-consciousness. [However, turning to] the Buddha, the fact that his mind-stream has been illuminated by the sun[light] of the view that all entities are without nature, that the thick and dense darkness of ignorance stemming from false views has been overcome, that conditioned [phenomena] are seen as being like a dream, like Indra's net(210), like an illusory young girl, a reflection, or a being created by magic, [and] that his mind-stream has become immaculate through eliminating all the passions' stains — [all these things] can only be ascertained as such through meditative equipoises. Therefore, the [Buddha's] virtuous thought must be understood by means of the mental-consciousness; in that sense the Sage's tradition is more subtle. So, although [people] might wish for merit, still because they do not understand with certainty, they do not apply themselves to the Dharma of the Buddhists.

1. Jains and Brahmins compared

§67. Here there is the following objection: If the world, due to coarse intelligence, applies itself in reliance on the Outsiders, then in this case you should comply [with them] too.(211) [Reply:] The Outsiders' actions are not in compliance [with their doctrines]. So:

Just as the Brahmins' doctrine is said to be mostly outward show (phyi 'chos)(212),
so too the Jains' doctrine is said to be mostly stupidity. **(k.295)**

§68. The Brahmins, through recitation of formulae, fire offerings (*sbyin sreg = homa*), auspiciousness (*bkra śis = maṅgala*), penitence and other such similar activities, seek profit, respect and such [worldly benefits] from others. Thus, they are held to be hypocrites. Their doctrine being "mostly outward show" means that it is primarily like this. This doctrine is opposed to those people who seek liberation. Because it accords with saṃsāra and because it is a cause for increasing depraved [practices] such as the obtention [of things] through vaunting oneself (*kha gsag = lapanā*), it [i.e. the Brahmins' doctrine] is not taught to Buddhists. Just as the Brahmins' doctrine, which is mostly outward show, is not to be practised by those who seek liberation in that it impedes liberation, so too the Jains' doctrine, which stupefies the mind, is also not to be practised, for it is largely stupidity. Therefore, [its] teaching is also not to be complied with.

§69. As the Brahmins' doctrine is mostly outward show, the world for the most part *respects the Brahmins for their acquisition of knowledge. Similarly it takes pity on the Jains for their acquisition of passions.* **(k.296)**

§70. Just as the world, whose minds are coarse, respects the Brahmins for their acquisition of knowledge simply because [the latter] recite [the *Vedas*], so similarly it takes pity on the Jains for their acquisition of passions, that is to say, for mortifying their bodies in various ways such as plucking [the hairs off] their heads.

2. *Refutation of asceticism and high birth as means to liberation*

§71. The [Jains'] experience of the suffering of their thoroughly defiled bodies cannot be for the sake of the Dharma, as it is the effect of [past] evil actions. To explain this [Āryadeva] states:

Just as suffering is a retribution (rnam smin = vipāka) of karma(213) *and is therefore not the Dharma.* **(k.297ab)**

Just as for those who practise nakedness, the experience of such a type of suffering is not for the sake of the Dharma any more than is an experience of the suffering of hell,

so too the [superior] birth **(k.297c)**

of the Brahmins

is a retribution of karma and is therefore not the Dharma either. **(k.297cd)**

H. Résumé of the Buddhadharma

§72. [Objection:] If suffering and [superior] birth, being retributions of [past] karma, are not the Dharma any more than are the eyes [which are also just karmic retributions], then what is the Dharma? Reply:

In brief, the tathāgatas taught that the Dharma is non-violence. **(k.298ab)**

§73. Violence, being the harming of others, is the intention to harm sentient beings, as well as the physical and verbal actions arising due to that [intention]. Non-violence is the path of the ten virtuous actions [attained] by turning away from this. Whatever benefits others, even slightly, is all included in the category of non-violence. The tathāgatas taught that the Dharma, in brief, is simply non-violence.

Voidness is nirvāṇa. Here [in the Buddhadharma] these two [principles] are pure ('ba' źig = kevala).(214) **(k.298cd)**

§74. What we explained as the voidness of nature is precisely what the illustrious buddhas termed nirvāṇa. The complete pacification of the suffering which is of the nature of the five aggregates is nirvāṇa. When one sees that there is no production by nature, one understands that suffering does not arise by its nature [either]. Therefore, as error is eliminated and because it [i.e. suffering] cannot be once more imagined as existing in some other way, one thinks that suffering has definitively ceased. And in this sense the Tathāgata said that it is the vision that entities are void of nature which is nirvāṇa, but he did not mean that it is nirvāṇa because [suffering] will not once again arise in the form of an entity's nature, for natures do not cease. Therefore, nirvāṇa is only the vision that there is no arisal by nature.(215)

§75. The two doctrines termed "non-violence" and "voidness" lead [respectively] to one's attainment of heaven (*mtho ris* = *svarga*) and emancipation (*byaṅ grol* = *apavarga; vimukti*). Thus,

"Here [in the Buddhadharma] these two [principles] are pure (*'ba' źig* = *kevala*)."

"*kevala*" means "pure" (*yoṅs su dag pa* = *pariśuddha*). Those who wish to correctly bring about the happiness of heaven and emancipation for themselves and others should understand that it is only in the Tathāgata's teaching that one apprehends these two [principles] extremely purely, but not elsewhere.

I. Conclusions

§76. Query: Now, why is it that Outsiders, inspite of the fact that they are aware of the Sugata's teaching, have no respect for these two doctrines? [Reply:] It is because they are attached to their own positions. Thus:

When all worldly people hold their own positions dear just like their native places, then how will something which causes the defeat of this [position of yours] be pleasing to you?(216) **(k.299)**

§77. Attachment to one's own positions is something which we have trained in since beginningless saṃsāra. The worldly person is unable to relinquish this [attachment] just as [he cannot relinquish attachment] to his own native place. Thus, the infantile do not apply themselves to this Dharma of the Tathāgatha, because they grasp at their own views. As for the learned [however], even in the case of their own native place, when it is destined to ruin(217), they should abandon hope and then rely upon [another] country which is prosperous.(218) So similarly, [the learned] should abandon attachment to their own positions and commit themselves to what has excellent qualities, even be it the position of a rival. Thus, since in this way he is without sectarianism,

the intelligent person, who seeks excellence, accepts things which are correct, even from rivals. [After all], is not the sun common to all those on earth who have eyes? **(k.300)**

§78. The intelligent person should accept whatever he perceives to be well explained from whoever it may be by thinking that it is as if it were his own. This Dharma does not jealously exist for [just] some, for it is the same for everyone. For example, just as the sun's illuminating action is common to all who have eyes in that [the sun] is free of attachment or anger towards anyone, so too this Dharma, if it is [indeed] perfect because of being [logically] proven, will benefit all our coreligionists and rivals [alike]. Therefore, having understood this, the respectful should then take this Dharma for their own.

§79. [Here ends] the commentary to the twelfth chapter, entitled "Training in the refutation of [heretical] views", from the Master Āryadeva's *Bodhisattvayogācāra-catuḥśataka*.

Chapt. V: Refutation of the sense organs and their objects (*gēn jìng* 根境 =*indriyārtha*)

(222a21) Now, as had been stated above [in §216b15 of the previous chapter], viz. "later we shall extensively refute the sense organs, their objects and so forth," I shall at this time explain [this refutation]. The sense organs are the bases for cognizing (*liǎo bié* 了别 = *vi-JÑĀ; pari-CHID*) objects. When one wishes to refute [these] sense organs, one should first of all refute their objects. Once one has refuted the objects, the sense organs will accordingly be eliminated too.

PART I: SENSE OBJECTS

A. Against Sāṃkhya. Refuting sense objects because one never sees the whole.

(222a23) [The Sāṃkhya philosopher] Kapila asserts [the following]: Things such as vases and cloths are established simply as [visual] forms (*sè* 色 = *rūpa*) and other such [properties]; the natures (*tǐ* 體 = *svabhāva; dravya?*), which are the objects of the sense organs, do really exist.(219) To refute this opinion [Āryadeva] states the following verse:

> *Amongst the parts of the vase, it is only the form which can be seen. Which [person] who knows the truth would say that the vase is visible in its entirety?* **(k.301)**

(222a28) Commentary. According to your own tradition, you yourself say that the eyes and the other sense organs each apprehend their own objects: they do not mix up [such objects]. The eye [for example] just sees [visual] form. [Now] a vase is composed of four objects (*chén* 塵 = *artha; viṣaya*) [viz. form, smell, taste and tactile sensations].(220) How then can one see the vase's nature (*píng tǐ* 瓶體) in its entirety when one sees [only] its form? This indicates that the vase's nature is not seen by the eyes, for it is not merely a [visual] form, just as sounds and other [invisible] things [are not seen] either.

(222b1) [Objection:] But surely the vase's nature is also [visual] form! [Reply:] I do not say that the vase's nature is absolutely not form, but rather I say that the vase's nature is not established as being only form. Therefore, the reason for the [proposition] to be proved (*suǒ lì* 所立 = *sādhya*) does not have the fault of being unestablished (*bù chéng* 不成 = *asiddha*). Since you make errors concerning present states of affairs and still say that [you] understand the truth, why should we believe this [assertion of yours to the effect that vases *are* visual forms]?

B. All sense objects are to be similarly refuted

(222b4) Just as it is only the [visual] form which is seen by the eyes, and not the vase, so too for smells and the like [which are experienced by their respective sense organs]. Thus in the next verse [Āryadeva] states:

By means of the points explained earlier those people of supreme intelligence should refute everything, viz. smells, tastes, and tactile sensations. **(k.302)**

(222b8) Commentary. The nose, tongue and corporal sense organs all have their different objects, [so that] they too do not establish an object [such as] the vase's nature apprehended in its entirety. The vase is [therefore] not apprehended by these three organs: the individual inferences (*bǐ liáng* 比量 = *anumāna*) [in question] should be understood along the lines of what was explained previously [i.e. one should use, *mutatis mutandis*, the same argument which showed that the eyes do not see the whole vase]. As sound is not always [present in objects] it is not said to be of the same sort as these [visual] forms and so forth. But sound too must be analogous [in that when one perceives it one does not perceive the whole object].

(222b10) All these things, such as vases, cloths, carts and the like, are not objects apprehended by the physical sense organs (*sè gēn* 色根 = *rūpīndriya*). Nor must the mental consciousness (*yì shí* 意識 = *manovijñāna*) apprehend an external object; [*manovijñāna*] must follow upon the physical sense organs. Since vases and so forth are not objects of the physical sense organs, they can not be [objects] of the mind either. If this were not so, then blind and deaf people should also cognize external objects such as [visual] forms and the like [for they would perceive them solely by means of *manovijñāna*]. Thus vases and the like are not objects of the [physical or mental] organs, but are completely produced by the [dichotomizing] conceptualizations of one's own mind.

(222b15) [Objection:] Suppose one argues that because the natures of the vases, etc. are not different from the dharmas such as [visual] form and so forth, the sense organs such as the eyes, etc. also apprehend the vases, etc., just as they do their own objects [viz. form, etc.], and that therefore the sense organs also indirectly apprehend objects such as vases.

(222b17) [Reply:] If that were so then vases, etc. would have to be objects of all the physical sense organs. This would contradict [the fact] that the sense organs each apprehend their own object. Either one nature such as a vase would have to be many [different things], or you must accept that the sense organs do *not* apprehend vases and the like because it is only the natures such as [visual] form and so forth which are the objects of the senses. As the form, [smell, taste] etc. are each different, they are not the vase. How then could they be a real vase-nature when they combine together?

C. One cannot see the whole object by merely seeing its visual form

(222b20) It might be said that vases and the like are established as the combination of their various parts so that when you see one part it is said that you see the vase, just as when you see one part of a city it is said that you see the city [itself]. [Reply:] This is also incorrect, for a city is not real. The city's nature is established as a designation (*jià* 假 = *prajñapti*) on the combination of its various parts, [but] when you see one part it is not said that you see the whole. Vases and so forth, if they are like that [viz. combinations of their parts], are designations and [hence] not real. Why do you hold that they really can be seen?

(222b24) Now, if someone sees one part and then says that he can see [the whole], this is irrational. Thus [Āryadeva] states in the following verse:

Suppose you said that you saw the vase by merely seeing the [visual] form. Then, as you did not perceive the smells and so forth, you ought to say that you did not see the vase. **(k.303)**

(222b28) Commentary. Suppose [you argue] that in a collection (*hé hé* 和合 = *saṃghāta; sāmagrī*) there are many parts and that the whole receives its name in virtue of one part. In other words, one vase has parts such as [visual] form and so forth, and because you see the form you say that you see the vase. [Reply:] As the other [parts] such as smell and so forth are not visible, then on account of the many parts [which you do not see], you should say that you do *not* see the vase.

1. Discussion as to whether the visual form itself is indeed perceptible

(222c2) Nor should it be said that the form-nature is special, for it is [simply] one part of the vase, just like smells and other such [constituents]. As [visual] form and the other [constituents] do not have any hierarchy in the vase, one ought to say that due to [the invisible constituents such as] the smell and so forth one cannot see [the vase]. The world's application of terms either conforms to [objects'] many parts or conforms to the principal [part], but there is nothing superior in [visual] form: smell and the other [constituents] are equal. Therefore one should say that vases and the like, in keeping with [their invisible constituents such as] smells, etc., cannot be seen. That being the case, external form cannot be real either, for it is [supposedly] visible and it is included as one constituent amongst invisible dharmas of [imperceptible things] such as vases, cloths, etc., just like the smells and so forth.

(222c7) [Objection:] But the world commonly knows that a vase's form can be seen! How can you prove that it cannot be seen? [Reply:] What the world knows is based on the transformations of their own minds and is metaphorically designated (*jiǎ shuō* 假說) as visible, but is not an external real form. Since we deny that there is really anything visible external to the mind, there is no contradiction [with what the world knows].

(222c10) [Objection:] Invisible dharmas do not exist at all (*wú suǒ yǒu* 無所有 = *nāsti kiṃcit*), so they could not be spoken about. Why? One says that [something] is invisible because it lacks anything visible. Absences of dharmas are all inexistent, so how could they be spoken about? It is because dharmas which are visible have natures (*tǐ* 體) that they can be spoken about to others.(221)

(222c12) [Reply:] This is also not correct, [for] dharmas which are without natures are also causes for descriptions. If that were not so, then the word "invisible" would obviously have to be inexistent [given that you hold that invisible dharmas do not exist at all and that what is inexistent cannot be spoken about].

(222c14) Moreover, the fact of seeing [visual] form is absolutely inconsequential. Why say that form is considered to be visible and not that it is invisible? How so? It is not because one sees or does not see it that the form [itself] will be any different. So why should one say that form is visible because one sees it and not say that it is invisible because one does not see it?(222) Just as one says that a vase is visible because the form of the vase is visible, so too one should say that the vase is invisible because the smell, etc. of the vase are invisible: the logic is the same. When the eyes see it one says that the form is visible. So when the eyes do not see it, one should also say that the form is invisible: the logic is the same.

(222c20) [Objection:] Since the vase and the [visual] form are [both] visible and invisible objects, then why at this point do you completely refute that they are visible and establish that they are invisible? [Reply:] [Thinking that] they are visible leads to grasping, [and so] I refute visibility, and therefore I state that they are not visible, [but] I do not *establish* that the vase and the form are invisible.(223)

2. *The whole form cannot be seen*

(222c22) Furthermore, [visual] form is also such that the whole nature cannot be seen. How can one say that one sees the vase on account of the form? Why? Thus [Āryadeva] states:

> *All forms, which are resistant (yǒu zhàng ài* 有障礙 *= sāvaraṇa),(224) cannot themselves be seen in their entirety. Their parts and center are blocked by this [outer] part.* **(k.304)**

(222c27) Commentary. Forms, which are resistant, cannot be seen in their entirety. Their parts and center are blocked by this [outer] part, just like all the forms of things such as walls and the like: although you see one part you do not see the others, and so, just like the vase, you have to say that [the form] cannot be seen. Amongst the various parts, this [outer] part [which you see] is not special. The other parts are many, [so that] in keeping with [its] many [invisible parts] you would have to say that this [form] cannot be seen.

D. Against Buddhist Vaibhāṣikas and other realists. Part-whole arguments used against various positions on the reality of atoms

(223a1) When the gross [visual] form is divided step by step, one does not arrive at [indivisible, subtle] atoms (*jí wēi* 極微 = *paramāṇu*), for there are always many parts. If one did arrive at atoms, they would not be objects of the physical sense organs, and therefore forms would all be invisible.(225)

(223a3) [Objection:] But surely when atoms' outer sides are laid out(226) without obstruction and exist bordering on each other, the whole is visible? [Reply:] The universal character (*zǒng xiāng* 總相 = *sāmānyalakṣaṇa*) of the collection of the atoms is a designation and is not substantial. The individual particular characters [of the atoms] are not objects of the physical senses. The sides of resistant atoms [also] have the one and the other [features]. How can one establish that the dharma, [visual] form, substantially exists [and that] the whole nature can be seen?

1. Sādhyasama

(223a6) [Objection:] Although the universal character of the atoms is a designation, and each particular state is substantial but not visible, nonetheless the atoms cooperate together in a collection which is indivisible. Their sides [also] have the one and the other [features]. So, this [collective] nature of the individual atoms does substantially exist and is wholly visible.(227)

(223a9) [Reply:] This is also incorrect. Thus, in the next verse [Āryadeva] states:

One should analyse as to whether atoms do or do not have parts. One cannot finally prove a state of affairs which is to be proved by invoking something which is not proven. **(k.305)**

(223a12) Commentary. Atoms are also connected with other things and hence, just like gross things, they too must have parts and are designations. In the chapter on refuting permanent entities [i.e. Chapter I = CS IX] we have already explained that atoms have parts and are not substantial. Since atoms cannot be seen one by one, then why should they be visible when they cooperate together in a collection? If they do not lose their original characters when they cooperate together, then they can not cooperate [to form a visible whole]. If [however] they do lose their original characters, then they cannot be atoms. When they cooperate together, then if they are [still] minute, as they were originally, they should not be able to cooperate and thus should be invisible. If they transform into gross [objects], they cannot be atoms and must be designations rather than substantial [things].

(223a17) When one analyzes atoms, then, because they are resistant, they have parts, are not substantial and cannot be seen in their entirety. Therefore, you cannot prove that forms are substantial and visible. Just as in the case of form, which, by the previously explained reasoning, had parts, was not substantial and was not an object of the physical sense organs, so it is analogous for all resistant dharmas: they are established through their parts and are not objects of the physical sense organs. To show this point [Āryadeva] states in the following verse:

All resistant dharmas are established through [their] parts. **(k.306ab)**

(223a23) Commentary. All resistant dharmas can be intellectually divided; as they all have parts, they are dependently established. If the division is not completed, then just like gross things, the collections of the parts will always be designations and not substantial. If [however] the division is complete, then [the entities] revert to space: just like something absolutely inexistent, they are outside the realm of the physical senses.[(228)]

(223a25) The world commonly knows that visible things are all established on account of their parts — so they are entirely designations and not substantial. As for the minute parts, they are resistant and cannot be seen in their entirety. The atoms' cooperating is also incoherent: all resistant things can be divided, and when the incomplete [division] is completed, the [objects in question] which revert to space are [seen to be just] designations and therefore all without any real, substantial, dharmas of form [= matter][(229)] which could be seen, heard, smelled, tasted and so on.

2. *Atoms and akṣara are analogous*

(223a29) Now, because the dharmas of form which are referred to [by words] are not sense objects, so also the referring expressions are not either. Thus [in this vein], the following verse states:

Utterances of syllables (zì 字 = akṣara) are also like that. Thus, they are not apprehended by the sense organs. **(k.306cd)**

(223b3) Commentary. When you divide step by step all the utterances of words which you hear, you arrive at the individual syllable. And this is also just like [the atoms discussed] previously [in that] it still has minute parts. When you again divide these parts step by step until the atoms, these [atoms] will not be audible and will still have minute parts. You in turn divide [these] parts until they are all no more: [this] division proceeds without end, for as the [parts] have resistance, they always [in turn] have minute parts. They are [thus] designations and not substantial.

(223b6) The minute parts of words do not form a sequence of previous and subsequent states; their nature is not composite, they do not really refer (*quán biǎo* 詮表 = *pratyāyaka*) nor are they really audible. In order that this logic [i.e. the parallel with the discussion concerning atoms] be clear, [Āryadeva] explained it separately again [in the verse]. If [however, it is argued that] the minute parts of words come into being simultaneously and do not exist as previous and subsequent states like the minute parts of form, then syllables such as *sa*, *ra*, (*saras* = "lake") [and] *ra*, *sa* (*rasa* = "taste") could be heard simultaneously [without any difference in their order], [and thus] the meanings [of *sara* and *rasa*] would have to be without any differences.(230) Thus [in conclusion] we have now refuted that the natures of the five [sense] objects such as [visual] form, etc. are substantially existent and are attainable by the physical senses.

E. Examination of the Abhidharma's notion of the domain of visual form (rūpāyatana): the relationship between shape and colour

1. Shape is not different from colour

(223b12) Now, it might be said that shape (*xíng sè* 形色 = *saṃsthāna*) is seen by the eyes. Here one should inquire: So is shape considered to be different from colour (*xiǎn sè* 顯色 = *varṇa*) or identical with colour? If it were different from colour, then the eyes would not see it, for it would be different from [colours such as] blue, etc., just like music and other such things [which the eyes do not see either.] If it were identical with colour, then it would be like colours [rather than shapes] and the eyes would not see it either. This has been extensively discussed previously [?] and now [Āryadeva] states in the following verse:

> *If the shape were different*(231) *from the colour, then how would one apprehend the shape?* **(k.307ab)**

(223b17) Commentary. If shape existed separately as something different from colour, then how would one apprehend the shape by means of [an apprehension of] colour [as does seem to occur]? Just as in the case of [sounds such as] music, etc., which are different from colours, so too when one's own sense organs apprehended [shape], this would not be by means of the colour. However, if [shape were different from colour and] one did apprehend shape by means of colour, then it would be like seeing fire in the distance and then [inferentially] understanding its universal character (*zǒng xiāng* 總相 = *sāmānyalakṣaṇa*), heat.(232) Thus, certainly [in such a case], shape would not be apprehended by the physical senses nor seen by the eyes.

(223b20) [Objection:] It might be argued that one does apprehend shapes without relying upon [colours such as] blue, etc. [Reply:] This should be refuted in the following way: when a cognition of a shape does not act upon the domain of colour(233), it must be preceded (*wéi xiān* 爲先 = *pūrvaka*) by a cognition of an object of the physical senses, for it does apprehend the shape (*xíng xiāng* 形相 = *saṃsthāna*). Apprehensions of shapes must be preceded by cognitions of physical sense objects, just like a cognition of the shape of a circle which was traced by a whirling firebrand (*shī huǒ lún* 施火輪 = *alātacakra*) or like the cognition of a shape in the dark [and as such they are indirect, conceptual, understandings].(234)

(223b24) Some say the following: The natures of the two [sorts of] form, viz. shape and colour, *are* each different, for their cognitions are different, just like smells, tastes and other such things [which are substantially different and have different cognitions]. In the perceptible world cognitions of [shapes] such as length, etc. and those of [colours] such as blue and so forth are different.(235)

(223b26) [Dharmapāla's reply:] If that were so, then for the world the [colours, shapes, smells, tastes which are] [matter] derived (*zào sè* 造色 = *bhautika*) from the elements (*dà* 大 = *mahābhūta*) and [the objects] such as gold and silver [which are composites of the elements](236) would necessarily have different natures, because their cognitions are different. Since the reason is inconclusive (*bù dìng* 不定 = *anaikāntika*) how can your thesis be established?(237) Or, again, how does one apprehend shape? If shape substantially existed it should [just] be seen by the eyes.(238) How could one apprehend shape by means of the sense of touch [eg. in the dark]? When one does not see [colours] such as blue and so forth, but apprehends [a shape] by means of touch, then since shapes are cognizable by means of touch, they cannot be seen by the eyes, just like roughness.(239)

(223c2) [Objection:] If, through this reasoning, you asserted that you must necessarily cognize shapes [only] by means of touch, then you could not cognize shapes in reliance upon colours [at all]. If you asserted that by touch you must necessarily cognize shapes, then when you touched air, water, and other [such shapeless things] you should also cognize shapes.

(223c4) [Reply:] This difficulty is illogical. My point is merely to assert that shapes *are cognizable* by touch, and therefore that they are not [really] seen by the eyes. I do not say that shape-cognitions' dependence on touch is necessary.(240)

(223c5) [Opponent's rejoinder:] If [what you just said] were true, then colour is [in fact] also cognized by means of touch and [according to your reasoning] it could not be seen. For example, on account of the [sense of] touch one does know the colour, etc. of fire.(241)

(223c6) [Reply:] This [i.e. the colour of fire which is known via the sense of touch] can only be cognized when it is mediated by various [shapes such as] length and so forth. Therefore, the reason [viz. "... is cognizable by the sense of touch"] for what is to be proved [viz. "...cannot be seen by the eyes"] does not have the fault of being inconclusive. Why is this so? If you know [colours such as] blue, etc. by means of touch, this [cognition] must necessarily be an inference (*bǐ zhī* 比知 = *anumāna*): [the colour] is not seen by the eyes. The universal characters (*gòng xiāng* 共相 = *sāmānyalakṣaṇa*) [which one infers], viz. blue and so forth, must be mediated by various [shapes such as] length, etc., but are not [cognized] directly (*qīn* 親 = *sākṣāt*) by means of touch.

(223c10) You cannot criticize [our position] by saying that shape must also be analogous [to colour in that cognition of shape by means of vision must also be indirect], for shape has no necessity with regard to touch [viz. it is not only touch which apprehends shapes.] Colour does have necessity [with regard to vision, in that it is only visual perception which directly apprehends colour], and thus [the two] are not similar.(242)

2. *Shape is not the same as colour*

(223c11) In this manner we have now refuted that shape exists different from colour. It is also not identical with colour. Thus, the following verse states:

If [shape] were identical with colour, then why wouldn't the apprehension of colour be by means of the body? **(k.307cd)**

(223c14) Commentary. If shape were identical with colours such as blue and the like, then the colours, just like the shapes, would have to be apprehended by means of the body. In that case colours would have to be cognized by the body's sense of touch, for they are identical with shapes, just like shape [itself]. The body's sense of touch cognizes shapes, but does not cognize their colours, and therefore, we know that colour is not identical with its shape. This means that shape is not identical with colour, for they do not have the same cognitions, just as music [is not identical with colour].*(243)*

(223c17) If shape were neither identical with colour nor different from it, then its nature could not be real, just like that of a cart, etc. [which is neither identical with nor different from its parts.]*(244)* If shape's nature were substantial [i.e. real], then like blue colours, etc., it should be either identical with the colours or different from them.

3. *Shape, colour and atoms*

(223c19) Moreover, the various sorts of shapes do not have separate atoms, for each individual atom is without [shapes such as] length, etc.*(245)* If, apart from colour atoms, there separately existed atoms of [shapes] such as length, etc., then their nature (*zì xìng* 自性 = *svabhāva*) would be hardly comprehensible. The size (*liàng* 量 = *parimāṇa*) of the atoms for colours and shapes would not differ, so how could there be a separately existing substantial shape different from colour? Nor can it be said that each individual atom has characters such as length and so forth: length, etc., just like gross objects, can be divided, so why say that they are atoms?

(223c24) Now, the size of atoms is not different — this is commonly accepted. But here you say that atoms do have characters such as length and so forth, and thus you contradict your own tradition. The [Abhidharmic] tradition which you study accepts that there is no difference in the size of atoms. So you also must accept that there is no shape apart from colour.

(223c26) Suppose it is said that although atoms are without length and other such [shapes], still the collection [of such atoms] establishes shapes such as length and so forth, and it will be atoms identical with the colours which will collectively establish length and the like. Then [we reply], why should one separately hold that there are atoms of shape?

(223c28) Also, shapes such as length, etc. are not like [colours] such as blue and so forth in that when one divides the atoms [of colour] into minute parts, their original character still remains. Therefore, length, etc. are not objects of the physical senses, for they do not have any substantial nature, like flowers in the sky. If the atoms are not really long, etc. then how can their collection be long, etc.?[(246)] You hold that atoms in their nature are not massive (*cū dà* 麁大), so how could their collection be massive? So therefore, length and other such [shapes] are not substantially existent, but are established by the collection of [coloured atoms such as] blue and the like.

F. Critique of Vaiśeṣika positions

(224a5) Now, in the Vaiśeṣika tradition they establish that there really are limited universal natures (*tóng yì* 同異 = *sāmānyaviśeṣa*)[(247)] and other such [categories] distinct from colour (*sè* 色 = *rūpa*) and such [qualities].[(248)] These [limited universals], due to relying on colour and other such [visible qualities], are [themselves] objects of the physical senses. [Reply:] This is also incoherent: since it has been previously explained [by us in this chapter, §§222c2-223b6,] that form, etc. are not apprehended by the physical senses, these [limited universals] will not be objects of the physical senses either.

(224a7) This tradition [i.e. the Vaiśeṣikas] asserts that one can only see substances, etc. when they are connected with the quality, "large", and with the quality, "colour".[(249)] If these two qualities are lacking, [the substance] will be like atoms and the air in space: even though they exist, one does not see them. [Reply:] This is equally incoherent. "Large", just like length and such [shapes], reverts to inexistence when divided and colour cannot be seen. Furthermore, as we previously discussed [in chapter four §§217b21-217b23], how does one see substances and the like because of these [qualities]?

(224a11) Some of the [Vaiśeṣikas] say the following: Bases such as substances, etc. must be visible by depending on colour, just as in the case of hot water where [the substance], water, covers up the colour of fire — although the substance, fire, is present, it cannot be seen.

(224a13) Then in this [Vaiśeṣika] tradition there are those who refute this latter [Vaiśeṣika view] by saying that when blue dye-colour dyes a white cloth, you do not see the white colour, and [as a result] you should not see the cloth [,which is absurd]. [They continue by arguing that] you cannot say that by seeing the dye-colour you see the [substance] which is the basis of the dye and that because there is a connexion between the substance which is the basis of the dye and the cloth, you therefore also can see the cloth. Why [shouldn't this be said]? Since the two substances, water and fire, are in contact together, then by seeing the colour of water, one would then see water, and for this reason one should also see the substance, fire.

1. Refuting the Vaiśeṣika views on colours and their causes: substances are not the cause for colour

(224a17) [Dharmapāla:] The two teachers of this [Vaiśeṣika] tradition are both wrong. First of all, if we suppose that first [teacher's views], we take the [second teacher's] refutation of his theses as refuting his position. Next, [Āryadeva] states the following verse [against the Vaiśeṣika's general position]:

If there were a cause for colour distinct from colour [itself], it could not be seen by the eyes. Since both dharmas' natures are different then why doesn't one see them separately? **(k.308)**

(224a22) Commentary. The substances which are the bases of colour are termed "the causes of colour". Thus, if the causes of colour were distinct from [colours such as] blue, etc., then, just like tastes and other such [invisible] things, they could not be seen by the eyes. If colour and the causes of colour had different natures and characters, then, just like [distinct qualities] such as blue and yellow, one should be able to see them separately [too]. Since substances cannot be seen separately, distinct from colours, then just as colours have no separate substanceness (*shí xìng* 實性 = *dravyatva*), so colour could not[(250)] be separately seen from substances. Since [you say that] the two cognitions are separate, like seeing blue and yellow, then in this way the two cognitions cannot be physical sense consciousnesses, for they arise through [merely] designated connections, just like awarenesses of non-substances.[(251)]

(224a28) Now some Vaiśeṣikas say the following: Colours really exist, but because collections of colours do not really exist, [these collections of] colours cannot be seen. If you were to hold that one [and the same] locus (*chù* 處 = *āśraya; adhikaraṇa(?)*)[(252)] had a collection of many [different] colours, then these faults [as described above] could occur [viz. the fault that one would not directly see coloured substances.] [But] we say that loci of same kinds (*tóng lèi* 同類 = *samānajāti*)[(252a)] cannot be identical, and thus, in one locus there is only one colour: we do not have these faults.

(224b2) [Dharmapāla:] This is also incoherent. If colour really existed, then it could not be visible, for it would be without minute parts, just like space and other such [partless] things.

(224b3) [Vaiśeṣika:] This reason is inconclusive (*bù dìng* 不定 = *anaikāntika*) due to the fact that colourness (*sè xìng* 色性 = *rūpatva*) and such [universals] do not have minute parts either, but can nonetheless be seen.

2. Refuting the Vaiśeṣika views on colours and their causes: colourness is not the cause for colour.

(224b4) [Dharmapāla:] How do you know that there separately exists a [universal,] colourness, distinct from the colours themselves? And how do you know that colourness can be seen? In order to refute these positions, [Āryadeva] said:

"If there were a cause for colour distinct from colour [itself]," etc., etc. [i.e. "it could not be seen by the eyes"].

(224b6) Here colourness is taken to be the "cause for colour" in that cognitions of colour and the words for colour [supposedly] arise in reliance on this [universal]. If this colourness were different from colours themselves and were one [indivisible, partless thing], then it would completely pervade all loci which are without [any colours such as] blue, etc, and one should also be able to see loci which do not have blue, etc. [,given that colourness is visible.] Since [such loci] cannot be seen, colourness would have to be something which the eyes do not see at all [, which is absurd].

(224b9) A [Vaiśeṣika] may say: If you hold that the nature of colourness is all-pervasive, then this fault would perhaps occur. We say that colourness conforms to its own bases [i.e. loci] and is thus not the same in each [locus]: we do not have these faults [which you attribute to us].

(224b11) [Dharmapāla's reply:] This is incoherent too. If colourness and other such [universals] conformed to their own bases and their natures were not uniform [everywhere], then loci without blue and such [colours] would abruptly become blue, etc., and in the case of loci which did have blue and so forth, the blue, etc. would abruptly disappear.(253) So in such a case, colourness as well as the colour [qualities] which are its bases would have loci which are not uniform and each [colourness conforming to a specific locus] would have to be established as different. But you do not accept that, so how are you without faults?

(224b14) Suppose it is said that colourness has mobility: it moves to other loci or it newly arises. [Reply:] In that case this [universal] nature is not one [and the same] thing, nor is it permanent. Since you maintain that [universals] are unique and permanent natures, they must be all-pervasive, and so again we return to the same fault as before: one would also have to be able to see loci which are without blue and such [colours]. Since [such loci] cannot be seen, the [universals] cannot be objects of the eyes.

(224b17) [Objection:] But surely something is [only] invisible insofar as there are no causes for cognition in it or in the other dharmas?

(224b18) [Dharmapāla's reply:] What do you term a "cause for cognition"? [Adversary's answer:] Particular shapes and sizes. [Dharmapāla:] In that case, colourness would be invisible, for the colours which are its basis are without shape or size.(254)

(224b20) This colourness can not be seen by the eyes because its nature is all-pervasive, just like soundness (*shēng xìng* 聲性 = *śabdatva*) and other such [universals]. If colours as well as colourness were different in nature and character, then you should be able to see them separately, like blue, yellow and so forth, but you cannot see these two kinds of things separately, [and know that] one is the colour and the other is the universal. Therefore, they are not different. Nor can you say that you see but do not understand the two characters' difference, viz. that one is the colour and the other is the universal. The difference in character between colours and the universal would have to be like [that between] blue and yellow, because in order for perception to occur it must resemble what is seen.(255) Since the perception [of colour and colourness] is the same, the perceived object(s) must be identical, and thus there is no separate colourness existing apart from colours.

(224b25) [In sum:] Since there is no colourness which can be seen as distinct from colours, then why should the reason in the inference [that colour qualities are invisible because they are without minute parts, like space] be inconclusive? As for the other [universals] such as soundness and the like, when you in due order investigate them one by one, [these] examples are like the previous refutation [of colourness].

3. The Vaiśeṣika view that the eye and the body apprehend earth, water and fire

(224b28) Now, in the Vaiśeṣika tradition the following is said: Earth, water and fire have [both] colour and touch-sensations (*chù* 觸 = *sparśa*) and thus can all be apprehended by the eye and corporal sense organs, for the world commonly acknowledges that [these] three elements, viz. earth, etc., can be seen by the eyes and cognized by the body. Air is only apprehended by the body, for it is colourless.

(224c1) [Reply:] This is not correct either. We have already refuted the eyes' seeing [such things]; now it remains to refute cognition by the body [i.e. the sense of touch]. If we follow what the world commonly acknowledges, then the body only cognizes touch-qualities and no others. Why is this? Thus [Āryadeva] states the following verse:

> *The bodily feelings (jué 覺 = sparśana) of hardness, etc. are commonly termed "earth", etc. Therefore, it is just to [these] touch-sensations that one ascribes qualifications such as earth, etc.* **(k.309)**

(224c6) Commentary. The world, when the body feels hardness, wetness, heat and motion, commonly designates [these touch-sensations as] earth, water, fire and air.(256) Thus, it is just touch-sensations which are termed "earth", etc: apart from touch-sensations there are no four substances of earth, etc. which are separate bases. To explain this point: The four substances, earth, etc., are not distinct from touch-sensations, because they are felt by the body, just like touch-sensations such as hardness, etc. If you hold that earth, etc. are not included amongst touch-sensations, then it would follow that they are not felt by the body, just like tastes, [colours, sounds], etc. If [however] you apply names such as "earth", etc. to hardness and so forth, then this is not disputed (*zhēng* 諍 = *vivāda*), for the natures are not different. If you maintain that earth, etc. are bases for touch-sensations but are not identical with hardness and such [touch-sensations], then you contradict the [above-described] inference [viz. the inference proving that earth, etc. are *not* distinct from touch-sensations, because they are felt by the body, just like hardness.]

(224c12) In the verse, the first half shows that the bodily feelings which are the particular characters (*zì xiāng* 自相 = *svalakṣaṇa*) of earth and the other elements are the same as what is included amongst the touch-sensations. The latter half shows that their universal characters (*gòng xiāng* 共相 = *sāmānyalakṣaṇa*), viz. earth, etc., are not included amongst touch-sensations; the body does not feel [such universal characters]; [rather] they are only cognized by conceptual mental consciousness. The particular and universal characters of colourness, etc. [discussed] previously [in §224b3 et seq.] would respectively be analogous to [the sensation of hardness and the universal character, earth.]

4. Substances like earth, etc. are in fact imperceptible

(224c16) Now, the elements, such as earth and the others, do not become different in character when they are heated (*shāo* 燒), etc.(257), and thus they are not objects of the senses. [Example:] When, for example, one heats a vase and other such [gross, perceptible objects], they *do* become different in character in their heated state, namely red in colour, etc.(258) These different characters are included in the category of qualities (*dé* 德 = *guṇa*); apart from these [qualities], no different characters belonging to the category of substances ever arise. How then could one assert that apart from qualities, there is a separate category of substances, such as earth and so forth, which can be felt by the corporal organ? To show this point [Āryadeva] states in the following verse:

> *When a perceptible [quality, such as the colour red] arises, one does not see that [,apart from the new colour, etc,] the vase has some different quality [so that the state of the substance itself would be different]. A [separately existing] entity [such as a vase] would have to become [different during heating] just like perceptible [qualities]. So, [such a substance] must be completely without reality.*(259) **(k.310)**

(224c23) Commentary. When vases and the like are heated there arise qualitative characters such as red colours and so forth, and one perceives them as being other than before (*yì qián* 異前 = *anyathātva*). Except for those [qualities], in the category of substances there are no vase-entities which become different from [what they were in] the non-heated state. If things belonging to the category of substances, such as vases and so forth, were separately existing entities, they would have to have different characters which would arise [during heating], just like the category of qualities. In states such as that of contact between a heating [object] and something being heated, no different characters of [things belonging to] the category of substances arise, and thus, just like space, etc., they would not be really existent. Also [these supposed substances] are not objects apprehended by the physical senses, but are cognized by conceptualizing mental consciousness. They are accepted as conventional truths (*shì sú dì* 世俗諦 = *saṃvṛtisatya*), are designations, but are not real.

5. General refutation of the Outsiders and the other Buddhist vehicles

(224c29) Next, after having summarily refuted the characters of gross objects as they are accepted in various different ways by the Outsiders and the other [Buddhist] vehicles, we shall, in general, refute all the characters of the objects thoroughly imagined (*biàn jì suǒ zhí* 遍計所執 = *parikalpita*) by the Outsiders and the other [Buddhist] vehicles by saying that these objects' characters are, in brief, of two types: having resistance and not having resistance. Objects which have resistance are all divisible because of their having resistance, just like a house or like a forest. When divided they revert to space or there is the fault of an infinite regress(260), and therefore one cannot hold that [resistant objects] are substantially existent. Objects which do not have resistance are not substantially existent either, for they are without any resistance, like flowers in the sky.

(225a5) Also, the objects which are accepted can be resumed as being of two types: those that are conditioned (*yǒu wéi* 有爲 = *saṃskṛta*) and those that are unconditioned (*wú wéi* 無爲 = *asaṃskṛta*). Conditioned dharmas(261), because they come into being from causes, are like illusions (*huàn shì* 幻事= *māyā*) and are not substantially existent entities. Unconditioned dharmas(262) are not substantially existent either, for they do not come into being [at all], like for example the hairs of a tortoise.

(225a8) What is more, each dharma of the objects which [the Outsiders] accept has many [different] natures according to the various accesses to the entity (*yì mén* 義門). If these [natures] substantially existed, they would be mutually contradictory.(263) And when one again divides [dharmas] they either revert to space or there will be the fault of an infinite regress.

(225a10) Moreover, the colours which [the Outsiders] accept can not be real colours, for they are objects of cognition (*suǒ zhī* 所知 = *jñeya*), just like sound, etc., and so on and so forth until [we assert that] all the dharmas which they accept cannot be real dharmas, for they are objects of cognition, just like colours, etc. By these reasonings, then, everything which they accept, be it existent or inexistent, is unreal. The wise should correctly understand that existents, inexistents, and other such objects all depend on worldly convention, are metaphorically termed characters, but are not ultimate.

PART II: SENSE ORGANS

A. Refuting other Buddhist schools' positions on the reality of the sense organs

1. All sense organs are alike in being derivatives from the elements. Why then do only the eyes see?

(225a15) Next, having refuted the objects of the [sense organs], we now refute the sense organs [themselves], and to do this we first of all refute the other [Buddhist] vehicles [i.e. the Śrāvakayāna]. Thus, [Āryadeva] states the following verse:

The eye and the other [sense organs] are all derived from the elements (dà zào 大造 = bhautika). Why then does the eye see, but the other [sense organs] do not? **(k.311ab)**

(225a18) Commentary. The five sense organs, such as the eyes and so on, all have subtle matter (*jìng sè* 淨色 = *rūpaprasāda*) derived from the four elements (*dà zhǒng* 大種 = *mahābhūta*) as their nature.(264) Thus, the sūtra says that the subtle matter derived from the four elements is termed the eyes and other such sense organs.(265) These [however] are conventional statements, but not ultimate assertions. If one holds them to be true, then their meaning will not be established. Why? The [sense organs] are the same derived matter, so why does the function of vision only belong to the eyes and not to the others? One does not observe that two dharmas in the world can be identical in character, but that the functions to which they give rise are dissimilar.

(225a22) [Opponent's objection:] But surely the characters of the sense organs are different, that is to say they each act as the basis of their respective consciousnesses.

(225a23) [Dharmapāla's reply:] Their effects [viz. the consciousnesses] being different does not constitute a difference in their characters. As the characters are not different, then how could the effects differ [because of them]?

2. The view that the sense organs' characters are the same but their functions differ

(225a24) [Opponent:] The effects of the [sense organs] differ because the [sense organs'] functions (*yòng* 用) differ. In the perceptible world functions may differ while the character is the same, as in the case of [certain] medicinal plants whose harmful and beneficial functions may differ but whose characters of hardness and so forth are the same.

(225a26) [Dharmapāla:] If the characters were the same the functions could not possibly differ. Now, [according to you] the sense organs would have to be identical with the elements, but the difference in functions to produce consciousnesses would be termed the eye and other such senses. [Your example is:] just as things whose [characters] such as hardness, etc. are identical but whose functions differ get different sorts of names for medicinal plants. This cannot be correct, for the [plants'] characters and functions would be identical, but it would [just] be the names which differ. As vision and other such functions are [indeed] different, then it is apparent that the characters of the eyes and other [senses] are different: differing functions do not depend on non-differing characters.

3. Could the eyes and other organs have different characters because they exist separately from the elements?

(225b1) [Opponent:] Since the functions are not the same, then [I acknowledge that] the characters must be different. Therefore, [the eyes, etc.] are established as separate entities existing distinct from the elements.

(225b2) [Dharmapāla:] If that were so, then since the functions of the medicinal plants are not the same, [the plants] should also have separately existing natures distinct from the elements.

(225b3) [Opponent:] If we accept that they do have separate natures, what is the contradiction in [such] entities?

(225b4) [Dharmapāla:] If, like vision and other such [mental entities], the [sense organs] were completely distinct from the elements, then [these] entities could be non-contradictory. But they are not completely distinct [from the elements], so how could they be non-contradictory?

(225b5) If you argue that although the natures (*xìng lèi* 性類) of the eyes and so forth are identical, their characters (*xiāng* 相) differ, then this would contradict your own [Abhidharmic] tradition. In your tradition the nature [of an entity] equals the characters of [its] dharmas: since the natures are identical how could the characters be different?(266) One thing cannot be both the same and not the same. Two different characters are not both substantially existent,(267) just as one form does not have the two different characters blueness and yellowness. If one dharma-nature could be divided into two characters, then here each [character] should once again be divisible, and like this step by step you would divide until you arrived at [just] space, or you would continue infinitely: there still is nothing substantially existent.

(225b10) Now, why should the sense organs, such as the eyes and the others, actually be different? [Opponent:] It is because the causes for vision, [hearing], etc. differ.

(225b11) [Dharmapāla:] How is it that vision and so forth are not the same in using the elements? Why should [vision, etc.] be different on account of their causes? If, because of the differences among the elements, the vision and so forth produced [from such elements] were to be different, then the eye consciousness and the other [such sense consciousnesses] should arise [simply] in dependence upon these different elements. What use are the eyes and other such [organs]?(268)

4. The view that it is the combination of karma and the elements which produces the different effects, such as vision, hearing, etc.

(225b14) [Opponent:] It is not just the elements which cause vision and so forth. How can you say that because they [i.e. the elements] are not different, vision, etc. would not be different [either]? [Dharmapāla:] What other causes are there? [Opponent:] Good and bad acts (*yè* 業 = *karman*). These karmas, due to various conditions such as desiring pleasant sights and so forth, come into being as mutually different, and because of these [distinct] karmas, vision and so forth are different.

5. Does one karma cause different effects?

(225b17) [Dharmapāla:] If many different accomplishing karmas (*mǎn yè* 滿業 = *paripūrakakarman*)[(269)] [each] individually projected (*gǎn* 感 = *ā-KṢIP*) vision and the other [sense perceptions], then this point could be so.[(270)] If [however] it is just one karma that completely projects one [whole] birth, then how could there be any differences [between the sense perceptions]?

(225b19) Now, the karmas for birth in the realm of form (*sè jiè* 色界 = *rūpadhātu*) are not different,[(271)] and [thus] the sense organs in this realm, which are elicited by just one karma, such as disgust [at saṃsāra] and so forth, could not be different. If you say that one karma has many different powers (*gōng néng* 功能 = *śakti; sāmarthya*) and that therefore the sense organs of the birth which is projected do differ, then [we reply that] the karma and the power are both functions, so how can one function also have many different functions?

(225b22)[Opponent:] We do not say that one function also has many different functions, but rather say that the one entity (*tǐ* 體) has many different powers. Thus the powers produce many different effects; just as in the case of the eye which has its own proper activity (*tóng fēn* 同分 = *sabhāga*)[(272)], the entity is one but it gives rise to consciousnesses as well as giving rise to things of its own kind [i.e. the subsequent moments of the eye organ].

(225b24) [Dharmapāla:] Metaphorically speaking, this could be so. But really, how is it possible? For, it is incoherent (*lǐ xiāng wéi* 理相違 = *ayukta*) when one [thing] is many. Should you maintain that one karma has many powers and projects the many different sense organs, then why not maintain that the karma just projects one sense organ which [in turn] gives rise to many different consciousnesses? Such [consequences] are irrepressible; so logically what value is there [in this view]?

(225b27) Also, when one sense domain (*gēn chù* 根處 = *indriyāyatana*)[(273)] is impaired or aided, the other senses should also be equally impaired or aided [due to the force of the same karma].[(274)] And if one sense organ [is inferior], the [whole] body would have to be inferior. We do not force upon you that there is just one [identical] sense organ(?),[(275)] but rather we seek to refute your [position that] one karma has many different functions.

(225c1) Now, the sense organs are not impaired or aided at the same time due to the force of karma, just as in hell sentient beings' sense organs are not destroyed even though fierce fires may burn their bodies. Also, on account of [certain] sense domains the body's features may be well-formed, just as in the case of a youthful blind person whose physical form is not inferior.

(225c3) If one karma produced many effects, then when you prove that there are different sense organs because they produce different consciousnesses, such an inference could not be established. When one exists, the other does too [and] when one does not exist, the other does not either. But [according to you] we can establish different powers without having to prove that there are different characters [so why would the sense organs have to be different in order to have differing functions to produce their respective consciousnesses]?(276)

6. Could the powers of karma alone produce the different effects?

(225c6) [A hypothetical debate:] Now why don't the different powers of this karma alone (*jí* 即 = *eva*) produce the different consciousnesses? At the time the consciousnesses arise the karma has already ceased, and therefore it does not have the function to produce.(277) Then in that case the eyes and other [sense organs] could not arise because of these karmic functions. If the tendencies (*xí qì* 習氣 = *vāsanā*) produced by the karma still exist they will produce the eyes and so forth.(278) Why then should not the [sense] consciousnesses arise because of those karmically produced tendencies?

(225c10) [Dharmapāla's reply:] This could not be so. [There would be the absurdity that] when one is born in the formless realm (*wú sè jiè* 無色界 = *ārūpya-dhātu*), the five [sense] consciousnesses, such as the eye [consciousness] and so forth, would also have to operate, for they are consciousnesses which depend on karmic tendencies. When it is established that there are physical sense organs, then there is no fault of this sort, but when one is born in the formless realms the elements are inexistent, and so the matter which is derived [from the elements, viz. the sense organs] is also inexistent. How is it that one takes birth in this [realm] without elements?

(225c13) [Opponent:] It is because one is without any craving for form that one therefore destroys the seeds (*zhǒng* 種 = *bīja*) for [sense] consciousnesses, and thus the eye and other such [sense's] consciousnesses do not arise here. [Dharmapāla:] [But] this cannot be correct. It is not so that just because one is free of desire towards objects, the seeds of the consciousnesses which apprehend [these objects] will also be destroyed. When someone has become desireless with regard to the realm of desire (*yù jiè* 欲界 = *kāmadhātu*), or when he has become desireless with regard to all three realms, his consciousness which apprehends [objects] does not completely fail to arise!

(225c17) Suppose it is said that the bases [i.e. the sense organs], by being produced by karma of their own realm, produce the consciousnesses.(279) [Dharmapāla's reply:] Then, when the body is born in the form realm there could be no apprehension of objects in the desire realm. And if that were so, then one would have to say that when one is born in the formless realm, then because there are no objects [at all in this realm], consciousnesses of them do not arise [either].(280) Why should they not arise as apprehending objects of lower realms?

(225c20) If it is asserted that they do not apprehend [these objects] because they are free of craving for them, then this has already been replied to before [and was shown in §§225c13-225c17 to be absurd]. What was replied before? It was said [in §225c17] that when born in higher realms one would not apprehend the objects of lower realms [with the consequence that consciousness would not arise in the formless realm.]

(225c22) [Dharmapāla's own position:] If karmic seeds alone produce the five [sense] consciousnesses, then the consciousnesses do not have to be respectively impaired or aided because of impaired or aided [conditions of] sense domains. Why? The karmic tendencies do not take the [sense organs] as bases, since the [sense organs themselves] are *developments* (*biàn yì* 變異 = *pariṇāma*)(281) [of karmic tendencies]. The consciousnesses conform to [these] developments, for [the latter] manifest their consciousnesses as impaired or aided. On account of karmic tendencies, [consciousness] is then also impaired or aided. How can all this be? The [causal] condition (*yuán* 緣 = *pratyaya*) for the world's manifest existents is only one's erroneous conceptual cognition of mental objects; it makes other dharmas established as impaired or aided things, just as in dreams when one erroneously views(282) the mind.(283)

(225c27) [Opponent:] If you do not know that the sense domain has been impaired or aided, then the impairment or aid to the consciousness which depends [on the sense organ] cannot exist. [Reply:] Here there must be a subtle experience. These sorts of debates are endless, so as I fear that one will tire of my loquacity, I must stop for now.

7. Conclusion: Karma is responsible for the sense organs, but is unanalysable and inconceivable

(225c29) The nature and character of dharmas (*zhū fǎ xìng xiāng* 諸法性相) is subtle and extremely profound and the host of [people with] superficial minds understand it [only] with extreme difficulty. Now, first of all, one has to say, in accordance with [worldly] conventions, that there are sense organs. Ultimately, [however,] if one investigates thoroughly, one will not adopt [such] entities as real. Thus, [Aryadeva] states in the following verse:

> *Consequently, the Sage rightly said that the effects of karma are difficult to imagine.* **(k.311cd)**

(226a4) Commentary. The meaning of this verse is as follows: The retributive causes and effects of karma, such as in the case of the eyes and the other [sense organs], is inconceivable. Only the Tathāgata understands it profoundly; it is not an object of the intellectual powers of the other superficial minds. In keeping with the world, one must to that degree (*qiě* 且 = *tāvat*) say that [karmic cause and effect] does exist,but [this] provisional analysis does not understand its true nature.The true thusness (*shí xìng* 實性 = *bhūtatathatā*) of dharmas is known by an inner realization and is not an object understandable by the world's ratiocination and investigation (*xún sī* 尋思 = *vitarkavicāra*).(284)

(226a7) Should one hold [karmic retributions such as the sense organs] to be substantially existent, this [position] must be incorrect. Why? Because it contradicts the following inference: the eyes do not [in fact] see, just as the ears and other [organs do not see]; the ears do not hear either, just as the eye organ, etc.; the nose does not smell, just as the tongue and other such sense organs [do not smell]; the tongue does not taste, just as the nose and other such organs; the body does not feel, just as the above sense organs [do not feel either]. [Reason:] For all of these [sense organs] are derived from the elements, or they are the elements, or they are the effects of karma.

(226a12) Moreover, the eyes and the other [sense organs] all have resistance and can thus be divided, so that they either completely revert to space or there occurs the fault of an infinite regress. In conclusion, one should not hold them to be substantially existent, but rather, they are one's own mind's false (*xū jiǎ* 虛假) conjurings (*biàn xiàn* 變現)(285) due to the influence of causes and conditions, just like illusions and such things. They are conventionally existent but ultimately inexistent.

B. Refutation of the Sāṃkhyas' view that form, etc. are apprehended by the sense organs and the inner mind

(226a16) Now, the Sāṃkhya Outsiders say the following: Objects such as [visual] form and so forth are all apprehended by two organs, i.e. the eyes, etc. see [these objects] and the inner mind (*nèi zhì* 内智) understands them.(286) This should be examined at this time. Do sight(287) and the mind act simultaneously with regard to the object or do they act sequentially?(288) Supposing that one accepts [that they act] sequentially, then which comes after and which comes before? Sequential or simultaneous, both are incoherent. Why? Thus in the next verse [Āryadeva] states:

> *Because the condition for the mind would not yet exist, the mind would not exist before sight. But if it existed after [sight], then the mind would be pointless (táng juān* 唐捐 = *vyartha). If they were simultaneous, then sight would be useless.* **(k.312)**

(226a22) Commentary. Sight is the condition of the mind; the mind arises on account of sight. If sight did not yet exist, then the mind could not come into being, just as a congenitally blind person does not have a mind which understands form. Therefore, the mind definitely does not arise before sight.

(226a24) If it existed after the sight, then the mind would be pointless: sight has already cognized the form, so what further use would there be for the mind? In your [Sāṃkhya] tradition, the production of dharmas must be for the needs of the self, for they do not arise automatically, simply on account of causes.[(289)] If one who had already cognized something needed to again give rise to the mind [which cognizes the same thing], there would have to be an infinite number of cognitions of cognitions with regard to one [and the same] object.

(226a26) If the two [viz. the mind and sight] were simultaneous, then sight would be useless. When two dharmas coexist they are not established as causes or effects [of one another], just as two horns of an ox [are not causally related], or like *rajas, sattva* and so forth. [So] you could not hold [the Sāṃkhya position] that sight is the cause of the mind.

(226a28) If the mind cognized an object without sight occurring, then the blind or deaf and other such people [with defective sense organs] should also clearly cognize the object. Also, there would not be any blind or deaf people, for all would clearly cognize form and other such [sense-data, inspite of their defective senses.] Nor would the five sense organs of sentient beings exist, for the mind and touch [alone] would cognize objects such as form and so forth.

C. Refuting prāpyakāritvavāda — contact between the object and the sense organ

(226b3) Now, some argue that cognition only occurs when there is contact between the eye or the ear and their objects.[(290)] This is [also] mistaken. Thus, [Āryadeva] states in the following verse:

> *It would take a long time for the eye to see a form far away, if it were to go out to [its] object. And why wouldn't it clearly illuminate forms whether they were very far or near?* **(k.313)**

(226b7) Commentary. "Eye" means the eye's light-rays (*yǎn guāng* 眼光). Because they constitute the functioning of the eye and are not distinct from the eye, they are also termed "the eye".[(291)] If these light-rays of the eye went out to the place of the form, then why wouldn't it take a long time to see a far away form? How is it that the [distant] moon and nearby forms are all seen at the same speed by glancing at them? One does not observe that in the world something mobile can in the same time go to two [different] places, far away as well as nearby. For this reason, the following inferences must be established: Sight which illuminates a far away form does not go out to the far away form, because the time taken is no different from that of sight which illuminates a nearby form. [Example:] Just like the sight of a nearby form. Sight which illuminates a nearby form does not go out to the nearby form, because the time taken is no different from that of sight which illuminates a far away form. [Example:] Just like the sight of a far away form.[(292)]

(226b13) Furthermore, if sight only occurred when the light-rays of the eyes went out to the form, then one would clearly see forms whether very far away or nearby,(293) and there would be no difference from seeing equidistant things. Since there is [such] a difference, [the eye] does not go out to its object.(294) The nose and the other sense organs [,which are said to function by contact(295),] do not have such differences of clarity vs. distance with regard to smells, tastes and touch sensations. Thus it is inferred that the eye does not go out to its object, for it functions differently with regard to nearby and far away objects, just like a magnet.(296)

(226b17) Now, when the eye goes out to the form, does it first see it or does it not see it? Both [hypotheses] are absurd, and thus [Āryadeva] states in the following verse:

If [the eye] only went out [to the form] after having seen it, then there would be no advantage in going. If it went without seeing [the form], then it would not be so that one would definitely [see] what one wished to see. **(k.314)**

(226b21) Commentary. The fundamental [position in the discussion] is that in order to see a form, there is movement to the object. When this form has already been seen, what would going again accomplish?

"[The eye] only went out [to the form] after having seen it".

Also, there would be a contradiction with the earlier position that it is only when there is contact with the eye's and ear's objects that there can be cognition, [for the eye would first cognize its object without contacting it and *then* would go out and come into contact with its object.]

(226b23) Nor could it be said that [the eye] goes without seeing [its object]. How could it move [anywhere] vaguely and without any indications? Like a blind man, it could never reach its desired destination. There would also be the following consequence: If [the eye] went without seeing, it would either not stop, or it would meet a form in the middle [of its journey] and then stop. If the [sense] basis (*qī xīn* 期心 = *āśaya*) moved, it would either attain its goal or its force would be used up and it would then stop along the route.(297) Since these two types of cases are not established and there is no third, [the eye] therefore does not come into contact with its object.

D. Refuting aprāpyakāritvavāda — no contact between the object and the sense organ

(226b28) Now, it might be asserted that the eye organ sees without coming into contact [with its object]. This is also absurd. Thus in the next verse [Āryadeva] states:

If the eye apprehended [its object] without going out [to it], then it would see all forms. Since the eye is without any movement, there is nothing which is far away or hidden. **(k.315)**

(226c3) Commentary. If there were no contact, then things (*tǐ* 體) would be without characters and without differences, with the result that one would see everything or one would see nothing at all. Why? [Response:] The perceptions would not differ, and in keeping with the [undifferentiated] perceptions, there could not be any differences amongst the dharmas.

(226c5) [Objection:] But surely one would not see forms when they were far away or hidden?

(226c5) [Reply:] Since the eye does not go [anywhere], how could being far away or being hidden prevent one from seeing? If the eye sees without coming into contact with the form, there would be no differences such as far away, near, hidden or unhidden, for the factor*(298)* of not coming into contact [with the object] would be no different. So seeing and not seeing could not be established.*(299)*

(226c8) Moreover, the term "very far away"*(300)* would lack any real meaning. How could there be any impediment which would prevent sight from occurring? Two dharmas which are set apart (*zhōng jiàn* 中間 = *antara; sāntara?(301)*) would not be termed "far away", for this would pose no impediment to the functioning of sight. If [however] it were held that set apart dharmas were termed "far away" and impeded the functioning of sight, then being far away and being hidden would have to be the same [, for in neither case would the eye be prevented from seeing].

(226c11) If one asserts that the eye does go out to the form there will also be this fault, viz. the term "very far away" will lack any real meaning and so on and so forth. When one holds that the eye is permanent and goes out to the form, there will really be this fault. Why? [Because] if one held that the eye was *impermanent* and went out to the form, then one could say that the force [of the eye's motion] was used up and [hence] that it did not reach the far away place. [But] if one holds that the eye functions *permanently*, without any degeneration [in its force], and goes out to the form, then the fault will be the same as before [i.e. there would be no reason for anything to be far away]. Going and not going are both faulty, and therefore when the eye sees form it neither goes nor does it not go.

(226c15) [Objection:] But surely the light-rays do aid the eye to see. Because the light-rays are blocked one does not see.*(302)*

(226c16) [Reply:] During the night one gazes far away at the forms of various lights*(303)*, but since they are separated [from us] by the obstacle of darkness, one ought not to see them.

(226c17) [Objection:] Suppose one says that the eye organ, although it does not go out to the form, is nonetheless just the same as a magnet in that it functions differently according to what is near or far.*(304)* [Reply:] This is also not correct, for [the example has faults] such as being doubtful. [Opponent's rejoinder:] The world commonly observes [this], so why is it doubtful?

(226c19) [Dharmapāla's reply:] This is incorrect too on account of the difference between the ultimate (*zhēn* 眞 = *paramārtha*) and the conventional (*sú* 俗 = *vyavahāra; saṃvṛti*). What the world observes is conventional, but you hold it to be ultimate. Nor does the world know that one sees without coming into contact [with the object]: how can you say that it is just the same as a magnet?

(226c22) In the previous verses, although one does correctly refute the eye [organ], one equally refutes the ear [organ], for it is similar.[305] To elaborate: If the ear organ were to cognize its object by coming into contact with it, then it should not hear things which are far away and near both at the same time. Sounds come [to our ears] from substances: since [the latter] have farness or nearness, [sounds] should not all equally reach the ear organ in one moment. The ear does not have any light-rays and so could not go out to its object, but if it did go out to its object, the faults would be the same as those for the eye organ. Moreover, if sound came without any substances [causing it], entered the ear and was heard, this would also be absurd in that the sounds of things such as bells and drums are clearly not without [such] substances, and [these things] can be heard as far away. If there were no [relation of] hearing between the ear and the sounds, but still apprehension occurred,[306] then like odours and other [directionless] things, so too one would not distinguish the direction[307] [of the sounds]. If the ear apprehended without coming into contact with sound, it would hear everything as neither far away nor near, for if there were no contact, the objects would be without characters [such as nearness and farness] and without differences. [Either that,] or it would not hear anything at all. Consequently, whether [one says that] the ear organ really apprehends its object by coming into contact or by not coming into contact with sound, both [positions] are unestablished.

E. Refutation of the Sāṃkhyas' position that the eye and its object are fundamentally identical

(227a3) Now, if one holds that the eye organ does see form, then it should see its nature. Why? Thus, [Āryadeva] states in the following verse:

The svabhāva, characters and functions of dharmas would, of necessity, be constantly the same. Why then would this eye organ not see the eye's [Primordial] Nature?[308] **(k.316)**

(227a7) Commentary. Dharmas' *svabhāva* (*tǐ* 體), characters and functions would constantly have to be the same, for they would have a mutually undifferentiated Primordial Nature (*xìng* 性 = *prakṛti*). If the eye saw, then it would always have sight as its *svabhāva*, just like the conscious principle, the Spirit (*wǒ* 我 = *ātman; puruṣa*).[309] In that case, even in the situation where it was not confronting an object, the eye organ would always have to see, just as [it sees] when it does confront an object. In such a situation, if [the eye still] had its function of sight even in the absence of form, then it would have to be the *svabhāva* of the eye which is being seen by the [eye]. If [however] the eye did *not* see in the absence of form, then in a situation where there was form, it would not see either.

(227a11) Furthermore, if the eye organ had sight as its *svabhāva*, it would have to see itself, just as [it sees] its light-rays. This would contradict your own thesis that the sense organ is not the object of the [same] sense organ.[310] If [however] it did not see itself, it would not see other things, just as absolutely nothing is seen by a person who is born blind.

(227a14) Now, your [Sāṃkhya] tradition asserts that the characters and functions of dharmas such as the eye, etc. and form, etc. are established by *sattva* and the other [*guṇas*];[(311)] while the characters and functions may differ, their *svabhāva* (*tǐ* 體)[(312)] remains undifferentiated. [Reply:] Then when the eye sees the *svabhāva*, form, it is just seeing itself, and this too contradicts your own thesis that the sense organ is not the object of the sense organ. Now, with regard to the eye's seeing form, if you say that this is true and that it does see, then the *svabhāva* of the form and that of the eye organ [must] really be identical: just as [the eye] sees form it would have to see the eye organ. Since it does not see the organ [however], it could not see the form. Nor can the *svabhāva* of the eye and that of the form be truly different: don't contradict your own thesis that their Primordial Nature (*xìng* 性 = *prakṛti*) consisting in [the three *guṇas* such as] *sattva* and so forth is the same![(313)] You cannot reply that you do not say that [the eyes] truly see: don't contradict your own thesis that they are included among perceptual *pramāṇas*![(314)]

(227a20) If you say that [the eye] seeing itself is in contradiction with worldly states of affairs, this will not be correct either, for the *svabhāva* (*tǐ* 體) is undifferentiated.[(315)] If you say that the function of sight is just *sattva* and the other [*guṇas*], then [objects such as] blue, etc. are also similar [in being just simply the *guṇas*], and [hence, as there is nothing which sees itself] they could not be seen. If you say that the *svabhāva* of the sense organs and of their objects differs, then this would contradict your own thesis that both are the Primordial Nature consisting of *sattva*, etc.

(227a23) It is not possible that the one Primordial Nature has many different *svabhāva*; the transformations [of *prakṛti*] are also like that [viz. they could not be many different *svabhāva*], in that they are not distinct from the Primordial Nature. If it is asserted that their *svabhāva* are both different and the same, who would say such a thing apart from clever talkers like you! This sort of thesis to the effect that the sense organs and their objects are the same *svabhāva* but that [the sense organ] perceives the object and does not [perceive] the sense organ [itself] is extremely difficult to believe in. Just as we refuted that the eye could see, the ear and the other [sense organs] would be similar, for [on the Sāṃkhya view] the sense organs and their objects are all of the same Primordial Nature consisting of *sattva*, etc. One [and the same] object would become all the sense spheres and one sense sphere would become all objects. In that case, the [respective] states of being sense organs and objects would not be possible; thus [the Sāṃkhya] cannot assert that the sense organs [as he conceives them] truly exist.

F. Refutation of the Aulūkyas (Vaiśesikas)

(227a29) Now, the followers of Ulūka (*xiū liú* 鵂鶹)[(316)] say: In our tradition the natures of the sense organs and those of their objects are different. We are not the same [as the Sāṃkhyas] in having this fault. Why? [Because] the five sense organs, i.e. the eyes and so forth, respectively consist in the substances, fire, space, earth, water and air.[(317)] The eye sees three substances, i.e. fire, earth and water, and also sees colours. The body feels four substances, i.e. all except space, and also feels touch-sensations. The ear only hears sound, the nose only smells odours and the tongue only tastes flavors. Thus our Master's tradition is not the same [as the Sāṃkhyas'] in having this fault.

(227b4) [Reply:] In that case the sense organs and their objects are different and the same. Being different is indeed possible, but being the same is like the [Sāṃkhya's] fault. The eyes and the other [organs] and fire and the other [elements] do not have the same characters.[(318)] Why then should the five sense organs have the five substances as their natures? Because substances such as earth, water and fire are different from [qualities] such as blue, they would not be seen by the eyes. As for earth, water, fire and air, if their natures were different from touch-sensations, then the body would not feel them.[(319)] So therefore [in conclusion], your tradition too has many faults.

1. Refuting the Vaiśeṣikas' four conditions for vision

(227b8) Moreover, this [Vaiśeṣika] tradition holds that one sees colour (*rūpa*) because of the contact between four dharmas, viz. the eye, the *rūpa*, the mental organ (*yì* 意 = *manas*) and the self (*wǒ* 我 = *ātman*).[(320)] This is also absurd. Thus [Āryadeva] states in the next verse:

The eye has no rūpa and no consciousness[(321)]*, consciousness has no rūpa nor eye and rūpa has neither the one nor the other. How can they see when in contact [with each other]?* **(k.317)**

(227b13) Commentary. The three[(322)], viz. the eye, *rūpa*, and consciousness, because they each individually lack the two [other necessary factors] and are not in contact, do not give rise to the function of sight. [But] when the three dharmas are in contact, they are no different from [when they were] apart, so how could one maintain that they [then] have the function of sight?

2. Buddhist Hīnayāna views also refuted by the same arguments

(227b15) Some Hīnayānists say: This difficulty is absurd. Who would say that when they are in contact they are no different from when they were apart? Although the individual dharmas are each powerless, when they are in contact, they have the function [of sight] in dependence upon each other.

(227b16) [Reply:] If, in their state of contact, they arose as different characters and were not the same as before, they would not be [things] such as eyes, [*rūpa* and consciousness]. But if, in their state of contact, they did not arise as different characters, then since they would be the same as before, they would not have the function of sight.

If it is said that the same kind [of thing] (*lèi* 類 = *jāti*) arises as different characters, this is also absurd, in that it is contradictory: the nature of a kind is not different from that of a character, so how can you say that the kind is the same, but the characters are different? The two things, sameness and difference, are mutually contradictory, and yet you say that the nature [of the eyes, etc.] remains identical — this cannot be coherent.

(227b21) If the three [factors], viz. the eyes [*rūpa* and consciousness], gave rise to the function of sight, then at the same time the function of sight would also give rise to the three [factors]. It is impossible that cause and effect exist simultaneously and that the three produce sight, but that sight does not produce the three. If at one moment the former [i.e. the cause] and the latter [i.e. the effect] both existed, then why would they have [the relationship of] cause and non-cause relative to each other? Also, if simultaneous, [the three] would have to be without causality (*yīn guǒ yì* 因果義 = *hetuphalabhāva; kāryakāraṇabhāva*): if the effect's nature already existed, then why would it again need a cause?(323) If they were not simultaneous, then you would have to admit a temporal sequence. And when simultaneity is not established, how could the temporal sequence come about? [For,] at the time of the effect, there is no cause: so the effect is the effect of what? At the time of the cause, there is no effect: so the cause is the cause of what?(324) In that case, there would be no causes or effects at all. Yet if you do not accept that they exist, how could you admit that they are inexistent and still say that the various causes and effects are not the same?(325) This [difference between cause and effect] is a conventional assertion but is not ultimate.

3. Conclusions

(227b29) When one correctly refutes the [Vaiśeṣika] Outsiders one also refutes the Hīnayāna. So in this verse there is just a refutation of the eye and the other [factors, viz. *rūpa* and consciousness]; the self has already been refuted [in Chapter II] and hence will not be discussed anew.(326) Just like the refutation [showing] that one does not see form because the eye and the other [factors] enter into contact [with each other], so too the ear and the other [factors, viz. sound and consciousness] should be similarly refuted.

G. Critique of sounds and words

(227c3) Now, sounds heard by the ear make it so that names (*míng* 名 = *nāman*) and phrases (*jù* 句 = *pada*)(327) refer to (*quán biǎo* 詮表)(328) states of affairs (*fǎ yì* 法義 = *artha*) and objects such as particular forms. Consequently, here again we should analyze [things] so that we understand that reference conventionally exists but ultimately does not exist. Do the sounds which we hear refer to entities or not? What would be wrong if they did? To show that the first [hypothesis] is absurd [Āryadeva] states in the next verse:

If what is heard did refer, then why wouldn't it be a non-sound? **(k.318ab)**

(227c8) Commentary. *Suǒ wén* 所聞 ("what is heard") and *yīn* 音 ("sound") are synonyms of *shēng* 聲 (= *śabda*; "sound"); they both describe entities. *Biǎo* 表 ("state"; "describe"; "show") is the same as *quán* 詮 : here it is shown that a sound does not refer [to anything]. Suppose it did refer, then it would lose its nature of being a sound, for the particular character (*zì xiāng* 自相 = *svalakṣaṇa*), sound, could not possibly refer, as it is cognized by a non-conceptual consciousness, just as other particular characters [are also cognized by non-conceptual consciousnesses.](329) Also, the sounds *qua* particular characters could not possibly refer to the entities which one wishes to describe, for there would be no homologous examples [in arguments], just like when a [logical] reason is [too] exclusive (*bù gòng yīn* 不共因= *asādhāraṇahetu*).(329a)

(227c12) The universal characters (*gòng xiāng* 共相 = *sāmānyalakṣaṇa*) of sound [however] are not things which are heard by the ears, for they each are established in dependence upon many [different] dharmas and have subtle parts, just like non-substances, etc.(330) If they referred, they would lose their nature of being sounds, for they would be inaudible, like pleasure, and other [feelings]. [But] there are no audible things existing separately without the nature of sound, for, like forms and so forth, they would have the nature of being non-sounds.

(227c15) The latter [alternative mentioned above, viz. that sounds do not refer,] is also absurd. Thus [Āryadeva] says in the following verse:

If sound did not refer, then why would it produce knowledge? **(k.318cd)**

(227c18) Commentary. If the sounds which are heard did not refer, then understanding could not arise on account of these names and phrases. It is because only phrases and names refer to states of affairs that in this context we do not mention the collection of letters (*wén shēn* 文身= *vyañjanakāya*).(331)

(227c20) Now if sentences (*yǔ* 語 = *vākya*) and sounds [i.e. words] did not refer, then, just like [any] other noises, they would not be causes for understanding states of affairs. In that case, we would not listen to sounds to understand states of affairs, but since hearing does lead to understanding states, [sounds] must refer.

1. Critique of sound's universal characters

(227c21) [Objection:] But surely the mental consciousness (*yì shí* 意識 = *manovijñāna*) arises after the ear consciousness and designates a universal character in reliance upon the sounds which are heard. This is the reference which brings forth understanding of states of affairs.

(227c23) [Reply:] When the mental consciousness arises, the sound and the ear consciousness have both already ceased, so what does the universal character rely upon? As the sound's nature is no more, then of what is there a universal character?

(227c24) Should it be said that by the force of memory (*niàn* 念 = *smṛti*) one recalls (*zhuī yì* 追憶 = *SMṚ*) the previous sound and that the mind and the other [mental factors] designate the universal character in reliance upon this [remembered sound], then [we reply that] the minds and mental factors (*xīn xīn fǎ* 心心法 = *cittacaitta*) would have separate objects (*suǒ yuán* 所緣 = *ālambana*). But an apprehension which is not in accordance with the *citta* would not be a *caitta*.(332)

(227c26) If it is said that the universal character does not need to depend upon sounds, but is a [false] notion (*jiǎ xiǎng* 假想 = *saṃjñā*) constructed simply by the conceptual mind, then why should this character only belong to sounds? And if it is said that [the universal character] does come into being because of sounds, then why shouldn't the ear organ, consciousness and so forth [also] be its causes?(333)

(227c28) Moreover, when the ear consciousness arises it does not perceive universal characters, so how could we establish with certainty what causes the universal character? It might be replied that [the case] is like [that of] form: after [form] has been seen it then predominates [in causing the universal character]. But this is equally doubtful and cannot be demonstrated. If it is retorted that the various [causal] powers of dharmas are difficult to imagine, then since that is so, how can you say that [sound] does definitively establish the universal character?

(228a2) It might be said that both characters [viz. the universal and the particular] equally depend upon one [and the same] sound: the particular character is heard first, and then subsequently the mind (*yì* 意 = *manas*) cognizes both. Then, because the characters of the sound would be different, how can you say that its nature is the same? As the cognitions and characters differ, the nature [of the sound] must differ too. It is impossible that the mental consciousness would apprehend the two characters together, for memory just recalls a previously apprehended character; if the memory of the sound's universal character was not due to hearing [this universal character], then the particular character would equally be remembered without hearing it. [In sum] if the two [characters] were previously cognized separately, they could subsequently be apprehended together, but since [such] separate cognitions do not exist [because only the particular character is heard], how can there be a joint apprehension [of the particular and universal characters]?

(228a7) Therefore in conclusion, the universal character [of the sounds] does not in fact refer. Nor is it possible that non-sounds refer. Although there are extensive debates [on these questions] and hardly any end to the arguments, I must stop these digressions (*bàng yán* 傍言 = *atiprasaṅga*)(334) and push forward the investigation of the fundamental points in question.

2. Refuting prāpyakāritvavāda and aprāpyakāritvavāda with regard to sound

(228a10) Next, whether one holds that hearing [occurs] when sound and the ear come into contact or without coming into contact, the refutation is for the most part the same as in the case of form. Hearing being due to contact between sound and the ear is absurd. Thus [Āryadeva] states in the following verse:

If sound is heard after it has reached the ear, then how does one cognize the origin (běn 本)(335) *of the sound?* **(k.319ab)**

(228a13) Commentary. "Origin" (*běn* 本) means the speaker in that he is the source (*yuán* 源) of the sound's arising. If the sound left its origin, came to the ear and was heard, then how could one know what produced the sound? As one does [in fact] know from where [the sound] is produced, the sound cannot come [to the ear]. Nor could one say that the ear goes out to the locus of the sound; it functions without light-rays or matter, so how could we know that it goes [anywhere]?(336)

3. Sounds cannot be cognized in their totality

(228a15) Next, referring sounds cannot be cognized in their totality. Why? Thus, [Āryadeva] states in the following verse:

If sound is not spoken all at once (dùn 頓)(337)*, then how could one know it in its totality?* **(k.319cd)**

(228a18) Commentary. The subtle parts of names and phrases are produced in stages [with the result that] the ear does not hear them all at once. How then does one know them in their totality? Nor can you say that you know them because of memory: a memory must resemble what was earlier and be completely(338) like the initial discernment.

(228a20) But it is not possible to know [a sound] without memory and randomly (*shuài ěr* 率爾): [otherwise] the mind would separately cognize [the sound] without relying on hearing, and if that were the case, then the deaf would spontaneously cognize sounds. Or alternatively, the sounds of the speaker's speech would become useless [in that one would understand even without hearing anything].

(228a22) If it is said that hearing a sound [in its totality] is brought about through the influence of the immediately preceding condition (*cì dì yuán* 次第緣 = *samanantarapratyaya*),(339) and that one therefore cognizes the whole [sound], this is also absurd, for the subsequent cognition of the whole [sound] could not arise. Suppose it is said that the cognition of the whole must arise right after hearing [the parts of the sound]. This too cannot be so [for the following reasons:] *(a)* after the super-knowledge known as the "divine ear" (*tiān ěr tōng* 天耳通 = *divyaśrotrābhijñā*), the mind in meditative trance (*dìng xīn* 定心 = *dhyānacitta; samāpatticitta*) would necessarily be interrupted, but it is only then that one would cognize the whole [sound];[340] *(b)* the different mental consciousnesses which follow after one has heard the sound(s) would *also* stretch out over a considerable time, and it is only then that one would cognize the whole.[341]

(228a25) [In conclusion:] It is impossible to maintain that real referring sounds exist and that the ear hears them first and the mind cognizes them afterwards. Rather, it is sounds which are manifestations of false conceptual (*xū wàng fēn bié* 虛妄分別 = *abhūtaparikalpa*) consciousness which are thought to refer.

4. Temporal arguments against the reality of sounds

(228a28) Next we should examine as to which dharmas are being termed sound: its nature is [supposedly] substantially existent and it is heard by the ear. To show that in that case there would be absurdities, [Āryadeva] says in the next verse:

> *Insofar as [something] is not heard, it will not be of the nature of sound. Being first inexistent and then later existent is definitely absurd.* **(k.320)**

(228b3) Commentary. The nature of a future sound is not heard by the ear, for the five sense organs, such as the eyes and so forth, apprehend present objects. In that case, a future sound would not be of the nature of sound (*shēng xìng* 聲性 = *śabda-tva*) in that it is not heard, like forms and other objects.

(228b5) Suppose that because future sounds are similar to present ones and the present [sounds] can be heard, they [i.e. the future sounds] are also termed sounds. Then because the present sound and the [future one] are similar and the latter is not a sound, it would follow that the present one is not a sound either.

(228b6) Moreover, if [sounds] passed over (*liú rù* 流入 = *saṃ-CAR*) to the present from the future, then the present [sound] could accordingly be said to be a non-sound. The future [sounds] do not pass over from the present, so why, on account of the present [sound], do you say that the [future one] is a sound [too]?

(228b8) If [just] what can be heard in the present is of the nature of sound (*śabdatva*), then it would follow that this *śabdatva* was originally inexistent but came into being, and that would contradict your own position that *śabdatva* existed from the first [i.e. the opponent's position that the future sound already had *śabdatva*]. If *śab-datva* did exist from the first, then it would not begin to come into being, and since it would not begin to come into being, it would not later cease. A *śabdatva* which neither comes into being nor ceases would have to be permanent.

(228b11) A past sound would not be of the nature of sound, because it is not heard, just like a future sound. Suppose that because a future sound[341a] passes over to the present and the present [sound] is a sound, we therefore say that the former is a sound. Then because the present sound passes over to the past and the past [sound] is not a sound, it would follow that the present one is not a sound either. If that is the case, then it follows that in the three temporal realms [i.e. past, present and future] (*sān shì* 三世 = *tryadhvan; trikāla*) none of what is established in dependence on *śabdatva* is ever really a sound.

(228b15) If the present sound came from the future and could be said to come into being, then the past sound which came from the present would also be said to come into being. Hence, the past sound would be said to be present [because what is produced is present] and would subsequently have to cease once again. If the past sound came from the present and could be said to have ceased, then the present sound coming from the future would also be said to have ceased, and in that case the present sound would be termed past and could not subsequently cease.[(342)] The future, which lacks both [coming into being and cessation], must be said to be permanent, while that which has cessation and that which has coming into being (*yǒu shēng* 有生 = *jātimant*) must [respectively] be termed past and present. If we examine in this way, the nature of sound (*śabdatva*) crumbles to pieces (*sàn huài* 散壞 = *vi-SṜ*). Form and other such [entities] should be considered analogously.

H. Critique of some Sāṃkhyas' views on the mind (manas)

(228b22) Now some Sāṃkhyas make the following assertion: It is only when the mind goes to the locus of the object that there is cognition. [Reply:] This is just like the previous refutation of the sense organs going out to their objects. One cannot say that the mind, alone, without the sense organs, cognizes the object, and thus in the following verse [Āryadeva] states:

If the mind were without sense organs, its going would also be useless. **(k.321ab)**

(228b26) Commentary. If the mind without sense organs definitely does not cognize dharmas such as form and so forth, then its going would also be pointless. Should the mind, alone, without relying on the sense organ, cognize its object, then the blind, deaf and other such sorts [of people who have deficient sense organs] would cognize the various objects. [Either that,] or there would be no people who are blind, deaf and so forth. This was already examined previously [in §§222b10 and 226a28 of this chapter] and will not be discussed again.

(228b29) When one cultivates the senses, the mind becomes keen (*míng lì* 明利= *paṭu*); thus it is certain that the mind cannot be separated from the sense organs. Some [Sāṃkhyas] maintain that the inner mind's nature is all-pervasive, but that its operation (*yòng* 用 = *vṛtti*) depends on individually going out to the objects which are cognized.[(343)]

(228c1) "Operation" is that the mind manifests aspects (*xíng xiāng* 行相 = *ākāra*) of the objects.[(344)] But the functioning (*qǐ* 起 = *pravṛtti?*)[(345)] of the mind consists in its cognizing the object. So again what does the going accomplish? You cannot maintain that the manifestations are one thing and cognitions are another. Let it not be [said] that when [the mind] manifests form and so forth it cognizes objects such as sound! Also, the mind would not uselessly go out to its object. If you held that [the mind's] nature was everywhere, then to which place would it go?

(228c4) Now, this [hypothesis that the mind goes out to its object] is absurd, and so [Āryadeva] states in the next verse:

In that case the living being in question would be forever mindless. **(k.321cd)**

(228c7) Commentary. If the mind went out to the object, then its nature would not be everywhere, and if the mind was constantly going out to its object, the self would remain without a mind. However, [in fact] the subtle mind is always present in the body. It is constantly active when one is in states such as sleep and unconsciousness (*mēn* 悶 = *mūrchā*), for there are [animal functions] such as breath, there can be dreams, fatigue grows, [the subtle mind] causes one to awaken, it controls the body and experiences physical sensations.

(228c10) If there was constantly no mind in the body (*nèi shēn* 内身 = *ātmabhāva*), then, as in the case of [inanimate things] such as corpses (*sǐ shī* 死屍 = *kuṇapa*), killing would not be reprehensible, nor would respect be meritorious. In that case the view of voidness and that of the Outsiders would be just the same.

(228c12) Some [Sāṃkhyas] maintain that the nature of the mind is not everywhere and that it does not go out [to its object], but that the operations (*yòng* 用 = *vṛtti*) do go. [Such a view] has the same fault, for [in the Sāṃkhya view] the operations of the mind and the mind's nature are not separate from each other.(346)

(228c13) If the mind's nature did go out to an object in front, then when [someone or something] touches one's body, one would feel nothing, and even if one concentrated intensely [on the sensations] the inner mind would be unperturbed.

(228c15) If one holds that this mind does not come into contact with its object, then, just as [it does not cognize] the objects of others, it would not cognize [its own object] either. Each individual mind would cognize all objects or each object would be cognized by all minds. So, these positions, which hold that there are real objects of the senses, are all illogical and must be taken to be untrue.

I. Discussion of "notions" (saṃjñā)

(228c17) [Objection:] But surely the Mahāyāna also has these same faults. [Reply:] If one accepts the slightest substance, then these faults will be the same.

(228c18) [Opponent:] In that case [if there are no substances], there would be no worldly entities, for [the world's] notions (*xiǎng* 想 = *saṃjñā*) would become erroneous (*diān dǎo* 顛倒 = *viparīta*). [But] it is said that these [worldly entities] are not inexistent. What then are these so-called "notions" so that error causes one to say that worldly things are existent and not inexistent?

(228c20) [Reply:] "Notions" means the aggregate of notions (*xiǎng yùn* 想蘊 = *saṃjñāskandha*), and thus in the next verse [Āryadeva] states:

The object which causes the mind to apprehend erroneously is based upon a previous perception, just like a mirage (yàn 焰 *= marīci). This should be understood to be the aggregate of notions for the [different] erroneous determinations of all dharmas.*[(347)] **(k.322)**

(228c24) Commentary. When the mind first arises, it apprehends characters such as blue and so forth. Just as one uses symbols (*biāo zhì* 標幟) to later recall [something], so one apprehends characters of an object which is [now] outside the range of the physical sense organs, and therefore one terms [these representations] *saṃjñā*.[(348)] Due to these notions, at a later time [after the perception] one recalls a representation (*fēn míng* 分明) of the object's character. Although every mind has these notions, still, [Āryadeva] says "based on a previous [perception]" to insist upon the state of being an effect; the subsequent representation shows what existed previously.

(228c28) These notions erroneously determine the characters of all states of affairs, be they the worlds' sentient beings or its insentient [matter], just as when due to a mirage (*yáng yàn* 陽焰 = *marīci*) a notion arises that there is water — it tricks one's mind and one then tells others [about the "water"]. Thus, erroneous notions establish the senses, their objects and the various other different things in the world. In order to show that these notions are established in dependence upon many [different] dharmas, and are hence designations and unreal, [Āryadeva] speaks of "the aggregate of notions". Also, to show that the different states of affairs in the world are all established by notions, he says "should be understood".

(229a3) [Objection:] But surely the five [sense] consciousnesses perceive substantially existing objects. The mental consciousness (*yì shì* 意識 = *manovijñāna*), which follows upon the five [sense] consciousnesses, would be similar [in apprehending substantially existent objects]. Notions and the objects of the consciousnesses must be similar, so how can you say with certainty that notions are erroneous?

J. The unreality of consciousness

(229a5) [Reply:] Who says that the [sense] consciousnesses perceive substantially existent objects and that [their] erroneousness is hardly possible? Thus in the next verse [Āryadeva] states:

The consciousnesses arise in dependence upon the eye, form, etc., like an illusion (huàn 幻 *= māyā).* **(k.323ab)**

(229a8) Commentary. Just as in the case of illusions, their natures do not really exist, and yet [these illusions] produce various erroneous consciousnesses, so also in the case of the eyes and the other such [causes of consciousness]: their nature and characters are all false (*xū* 虛 = *mṛṣā*). Notions arise due to these [causes], just as they do when an illusionist induces erroneous consciousnesses in others. How could the objects be real? Sense objects are all false. As we explained before [?], the consciousnesses which arise due to these [objects] are not real either. All which is perceived is false, just like illusions. The natures of the consciousnesses are not identical with the objects perceived: unlike their objects, consciousnesses cannot be without ideation (*yuán lù* 緣慮).[(349)] Nor do the natures of consciousness exist separately, different from the objects; the characters of consciousnesses equally do not exist as different from the objects which are perceived. So how can you say that the natures of consciousnesses really exist? As was said in the [following] verse:

> "These perceiving consciousnesses are not identical with the objects which are perceived. Nor are they different from their objects. Therefore they have no characters which can be apprehended."[(350)]

1. Debates about illusions

(229a17) Some argue as follows: Illusions are all real and not false. The powers of spells (*zhòu shù* 呪術 = *mantra*), when applied to [things] such as wood and stones, make them appear to have the characters of chariots, horses and so forth. These characters either have the sounds [of the incantations] and the other [materials] as their nature, or their nature is identical with one part of the consciousness. To refute this reply (*jiù* 救 = *parihāra*), [Āryadeva] states in the following verse:

> *If it were held that they were really existent, then the comparison with an illusion would not be established.* **(k.323cd)**

(229a21) Commentary. If an illusion really had sounds and other such things as its nature, then, like other sounds, etc., it could not be termed "an illusion". If it is said that the illusion is fleeting and does not remain, like something created by magic (*huà* 化 = *nirmāṇa*), and that therefore it is termed "an illusion", this is also not correct. Since the [illusion's] nature really exists, like other sounds and so forth, then why not say that it is true? What is fleeting and does not remain does not have the character of an illusion either: don't say that lightning and such things must also be called "illusions"!

(229a25) If it is said that what deceives the world is termed "an illusion", but that the character of the illusion is not false, then why say that it deceives! If it is said that it is because it gives rise to errors such as [belief in] permanence and so forth, then other dharmas must also be termed "illusions".

(229a26) Nor should it be said that the illusion is a part of consciousness: if it does not have the nature of cognition how can it be mind? [There are two possibilities:] *a)* ["illusion"] would be a synonym (*yì míng* 異名 = *paryāyaśabda*) for saying "an object of consciousness alone". One must accept that all dharmas whatsoever are not different from mind: how then could the one mind really have many parts? *b)* One has to accept that the nature of consciousness is unreal.

(229a29) If consciousness were real and was accepted as having many parts, then all dharmas would be of that same nature. If the nature of the consciousness were one, but it appeared as dual, then just as in a mirage there [merely] seems to be water, so one could not say that the illusion *is* a part of consciousness, for the real consciousness which is its nature is non-dual. The "water" which one apprehends is not a part of the mirage, so how does it illustrate consciousness' nature being one and the parts many?

2. *Dharmapāla's position*

(229b4) [Objection:] In that case, what does the Mahāyāna explain as being an illusion? [Reply:] The illusion which we speak about is like what is commonly understood by the world. When one analyzes with intelligence, no natures to illusions are to be found in fact. How [could] words [for them] be referring [to anything]? So thus all dharmas are likened to illusions: in them not the slightest substance whatsoever can be found. As was said in the verse:

> "When one analyzes with intelligence, the natures of dharmas are inexistent. Thus, they are said to be without natures and are not referred to by [conceptual] proliferations (*xì lùn* 戲論 = *prapañca*)."(351)

Thus, dharmas are produced by causes and conditions; their natures are all void, like an illusion.

K. Replying to the charge that the Madhyamaka is simply counterintuitive

(229b10) [Objection:] If the natures of dharmas are void and yet they appear to exist, how do they differ from [absurdities, such as] snares capturing space?

(229b12) [Reply:] Why are you amazed that natures of dharmas are [conventionally] established? Worldly states of affairs are hard to fathom (*nán cè* 難測): their varieties are in fact complex. To establish this assertion [Āryadeva] states in the following verse:

> *Nothing in the world is not hard to fathom. The sense organs and their objects are similar [in that respect], so why should the wise be amazed?* **(k.324)**

(229b16) Commentary. One mental karma ripens into endless different sorts of inner and outer effects in the future, something an extremely skilled craftsman could not perform: this is said to be the first "hard to fathom thing in the world". An external seed grows into a sprout and stalk and [then] immeasurable [numbers of] branches, twigs, flowers, leaves, roots and fruit with all sorts of shapes, as if they were ornaments: this is said to be the second "hard to fathom thing in the world".

(229b19) The body of a libidinous woman is like a manure pit, its nine orifices constantly flowing with all sorts of filth. Nonetheless, someone filled with desire will see [her] and become sexually aroused: this is said to be the third "hard to fathom thing in the world". Flowery trees are said to be without [feelings of] love[(352)], and yet when a libidinous woman touches them, the flowers vie to develop and the branches brush near her as if [the tree] were in love: this is said to be the fourth "hard to fathom thing in the world". Flowery trees are said to like music; when they hear pleasant sounds, they raise themselves up and sway back and forth, their branches curving gracefully, just like dancers. This is said to be the fifth "hard to fathom thing in the world". Flowery trees are said to like the singing of birds; when they hear the sounds of the birds' songs, they immediately sway back and forth, their branches waving gracefully, like people joyfully clapping. This is said to be the sixth "hard to fathom thing in the world".

(229b27) In previous lives one has passed through innumerable births. When one dies and is reborn, one seeks the mother's breast, frolics about, plays, sleeps, eats and has desires: this is said to be the seventh "hard to fathom thing in the world". If one rejoices in unsurpassed enlightenment, one should correctly practise the subtle, excellent, Dharma. But [in fact] one practices carelessness (*fàng yì* 放逸 = *pramāda*) and denigrates (*bō* 撥 = *apavāda*) the Dharma as being nothing at all: this is said to be the eighth "hard to fathom thing in the world". Someone renounces the confines of the home and sets out for the seat of enlightenment (*dào chăng* 道場 = *bodhimaṇḍa*), but still engages in everyday affairs, coveting wealth without any scruples: this is called the ninth "hard to fathom thing in the world". The excellent operation of the miraculous powers developed in the pure meditative trances (*jìng dìng* 淨定 = *śuddhakadhyāna*)[(353)] are without limit and unobstructed; anything and everything is established by the mind's [mere] wishes. This is said to be the tenth "hard to fathom thing in the world".[(354)]

(229c5) Thus there is no end to hard to fathom worldly states of affairs. The existence or inexistence of the sense organs and their objects is a convenience of method: from the point of view of worldly conventions they exist; from the point of view of the ultimate they are void. The wise should not be amazed [at this].

L. Similes for dharmas' mode of existence

(229c7) In order to show that dharmas are conventionally existent but in truth void, [Āryadeva] at the end of the chapter now states the following verse:

> *Dharmas are like the circle of a whirling firebrand, a magical being, a dream, an illusion, the moon [reflected] in water, a comet (huì xīng 彗星), an echo, a mirage or floating clouds.*[(355)] **(k.325)**

(229c11) Commentary. A circle of a whirling firebrand, a magical being, a dream and so forth, although they appear to exist, are all, nonetheless, actually void. So too for dharmas: the fool, due to conceptual grasping, says that they exist, but their natures are actually inexistent. When one is free of grasping then none of them are seen at all, just as someone whose eyes are healthy does not see flowers in the sky. The unconditioned (*wú wéi* 無爲 = *asaṃskṛta*)[(356)] is seen by the noble wisdom and is true (*zhēn* 眞) in that the aspects (*xíng xiāng* 行相 = *ākāra*) of apprehender (*néng yuán* 能緣 = *grāhaka*) and apprehended (*suǒ yuán* 所緣 = *grāhya*) have ceased. This conforms well with the sūtra's statement: "Conditioned consciousnesses and objects are not real." Thus the sense organs and their objects are all conventional, but not true [i.e. ultimate], in that they are objects of consciousness, like whirling firebrands' circles and other such [non-entities].[(357)]

(229c16) What the Outsiders establish is untrue due to their grasping at existence and inexistence, as in the case of someone with [eye diseases] such as *timira* (*xuàn yī* 眩醫) [who grasps at illusory appearances]. If one wishes to strive for the noble wisdom, exclude falsities and adopt the truth, one should conform to the Tathāgata's immaculate teaching of the Dharma.

CATUḤŚATAKAVṚTTI XIII: REFUTATION OF THE SENSE ORGANS AND THEIR OBJECTS (*indriyārtha*)

PART I: SENSE OBJECTS

§1. Here, when it is stated [in k. 300],

"The intelligent person, who seeks excellence, accepts things which are correct, even from rivals."

it might then be said, "What are these 'things which are correct' which are to be accepted by the intelligent?" Reply: It is seeing that all entities, outer or inner, are by nature (*raṅ bźin gyis* = *svabhāvena*) selfless.

A. Refuting sense objects because one never sees the whole

§2. Objection: One cannot establish this [statement] that all entities are without natures, for while things such as donkey's horns and the like, which are inexistent, are not perceptible (*mṅon sum* = *pratyakṣa*), vases and the like, as well as [patches of] blue, etc., are perceptible.(358) Therefore, entities such as vases and so forth do in fact all have natures. [Reply:] This is incorrect, for

when one sees the [visual] form, indeed, one will not see the whole vase. Which [person] who knows the truth would also say that the vase is perceptible (pratyakṣa)? **(k.301)**

§3. By the word *api* ("also") [Āryadeva means,] "Which [person] who knows the truth would say that the blue [colour] and the other [eight substances](359) which are the substrata (*ñer bar len pa* = *upādāna*) of the [vase] are also perceptible?" In this regard some say that the vase is established as being essentially a transformation of the three *guṇas*, while others say that what one terms the vase is a substance which is a whole (*yan lag can* = *avayavin*) that is seen separately from its parts and [that the vase] is established as something apprehendable by the sense of touch. These [philosophers, viz. the Sāṃkhya and Nyāya-Vaiśeṣika schools respectively](360) are also refuted by [the verse which states]

"How could something produced from a permanent entity be impermanent? Never does one see a disparity of character between causes and [their] effects."(361)

Thus, as there is nothing which is simply the vase itself, how could it be perceptible?

§4. Objection: If [the vase] were thus impossible, then how could one know that such-and-such a vase is established? Reply: The vase is designated in dependence (*brten nas 'dogs pa* = *upādāya prajñapti*) upon the eight substances (*rdzas* = *dravya*), i.e. the four elements (*'byuṅ ba chen po* = *mahābhūta*) and the four [types] of form which depend upon [the elements].(362) Just as fire is designated in dependence on fuel, houses in dependence upon grass and wood, and the self in dependence upon the aggregates, but if one searches [for these entities] among their causes by means of the fivefold [reasoning] one will not perceive them, so too a vase, which is something perceptible for the world because it is understood by the sense faculty which sees that it can scoop up honey, water and milk, is established in dependence on its causes as being the appropriator (*ñe bar len pa po = upādātṛ*) [of the eight substances].(363) However, rival conceptions, which do not hold that [things] are dependently designated as just explained, are unable to establish [anything] as being a vase.

§5. It might be thought that because the vase is not perceived separately from its form, etc., therefore a cognition of a vase is only of the relevant form and the like, but that there is absolutely no entity which one terms a vase. According to such a proponent, because absurdities such as [fire's having to] burn forever and so forth would [otherwise] follow, fire does not exist without an object (*las = karman*) [and] apart from fuel, and thus it is just completely imagined by the mind.(364) [Reply:] But, similarly, because the elements as well as the mind and mental factors (*sems daṅ sems las byuṅ ba = cittacaitta*) cannot arise without the other [elements and mental factors], they would [also] be merely imagined by the mind, just as the vase, and would be unestablished by their natures. This [consequence] is not accepted by these [philosophers]. Therefore, why don't they accept that vases, just like the mind and the mental or the elements, are dependent arisings or [in other words] are dependently designated? So the vase, which has the eight substances as substrata, is the appropriator of what it appropriates, and the agent of the action of appropriation (*ñe bar len pa'i bya ba*); the whole, which is something perceptible for the world, exists in this manner, [but] should one analyse it [then],

"when one sees the [visual] form, indeed, one will not see the whole vase,"

for the vase is of the nature of the eight substances.

§6. The eye sees only the [visual] form, but not odours and other such [substances], for they are different objects. Thus, as the whole vase is not seen by the eye, then, making no analyses of the nature of the entity, we take the world's own conceptions as valid, whatever they might be, and so we can then say that for us the vase is perceptible. But whoever analyzes, knows the nature of entities [and] does not take it to be possible that one sees the whole by [merely] seeing one side [of it] cannot say things such as "the vase is perceptible".

1. Debate with the logicians on pratyakṣa

§7. On this point the logicians (*rtog ge ba = tārkika*) argue as follows: The vase is not at all *pratyakṣa*;(365) the particular characters (*raṅ gi mtshan ñid = svalakṣaṇa*) of [visual] form and the other [eight substances] are inexpressible and are designated as "*pratyakṣa*" because they are the objects of the visual consciousnesses, etc., which is what is [really] said to be *pratyakṣa*.(366) Because the vase is merely something completely imaginary, it does not exist as a particular character, and whatever lacks a particular character cannot in reality be *pratyakṣa*, not only that but it cannot even be metaphorically designated as *pratyakṣa*. Therefore, as there is no need to refute [the vase's] being *pratyakṣa*, then just like refuting [an obviously false proposition, such as] that sound is apprehendable by the eyes, so too it is incorrect to refute the vase in this regard.

§8. This logician, because he is completely unversed in mundane objects, must be instructed from the very beginning just like a young child. Therefore, in order to teach him he should be questioned, "What is *pratyakṣa* for you?"

§9. He answers: Consciousness is *pratyakṣa*. What sort of consciousness? One which is free from conceptualization (*rtog bral* = *kalpanāpoḍha*). But what is "conceptualization"? Any clear and distinct notion (*'du śes g.yer po*) which superimposes names and kinds on objects. Because they are free from such [conceptualizations], the five sense consciousnesses apply to nothing but the inexpressible particular character of the object, and thus they are to be termed *pratyakṣa* in that they "occur in connection with the various individual sense organs" (*dbaṅ po daṅ dbaṅ po la gnas pa* = *akṣam akṣaṃ prati vartate*).(367)

§10. [Candrakīrti:] But how could one momentary instant of a sense consciousness be a perception (*pratyakṣa*)? It cannot occur in dependence on various individual senses, for it is specific (*thun moṅ ma yin pa* = *asādhāraṇa*) [to one sense],(368) and [what is more,] the momentary instants of the sense organs and consciousnesses perish as soon as they have arisen.

§11. It might be argued: The fivefold collection of consciousness has bases [i.e. sense organs] and objects which are assemblages (*bsags pa*).(369) Thus the atoms constituting the sense organs and those constituting the focus of perception are not *each* established as being the bases and objects, for one who suffers from [the eye disease known as] *timira* (*rab rib can* = *taimirika*) does not separately see the individual strands of hair [which would be the objects of his perception. He just sees a pile of hair.](370) Just as the individual [hairs] in the collection are causes [for the perception of the collection], so too the collected atoms making up the eyes and other [sense organs] are each individually causes [for sensory perception].

§12. [Candrakīrti:] The example [of the person suffering from *timira*] is not similar. Since one who is free from *timira* does [in fact] see individual hairs, it is when the eyes are damaged that he does not see [separate strands of hair]. But in the case of the atoms constituting the sense organs, then apart from their collected state, one does not see that individually each atom is a basis for its consciousness. Therefore it is incorrect to imagine that the [atoms] forming the collection are individually bases [for the sensory consciousness in question].

§13. When one observes absolutely no [causal] efficacity in the parts, then although [the parts] might form a collection, one should conceive [of that collection] as being similar to its [parts in that it too must be causally inefficacious]. Thus, for instance, one observes that one blade of grass has the power to bind the legs of gadflies (*śa sbraṅ*), mosquitoes (*sbraṅ bu mchu riṅs*) and the like,(370a) and then [one supposes that] a collection of these [blades of grass] can go so far as to bind up elephants. Similarly, each sesame seed can individually yield a little oil and the collection can yield a vase full of oil. But because the sense organ's atoms, independent of the collection, are not thus each and individually bases for the consciousness, then although [the collection] depends on the atoms, it cannot be efficacious.(371) Thus, "the eye organ", which depends on the organ's atoms, which is void of any conceptions of identity or difference from the atoms, which is the basis of its [corresponding] consciousness, [and] which is a worldly [notion existing] through dependent designation, does not [itself] possess the action of seeing an object. And since this [object] is momentary and hence ceases along with its consciousness, how could it [in fact] be capable [of producing a perception?](372) In conclusion, it is incorrect to say that a consciousness which occurs in connection with the various individual sense organs is *pratyakṣa*.

§14. But suppose it is objected that the collection of the [various] consciousnesses does occur in connection with the sense organs which are of the corresponding sorts and that [*pratyakṣa*] can thus be etymologically explained in this manner. [Reply:] This is not the case either. Why? Because it is impossible to etymologically explain one moment of an eye consciousness in this fashion, and [moreover] a collection, which is insubstantial, [can] not [in fact] depend on the sense organs. The establishment of form and so forth should be understood as being analogous to the establishment through dependent designation of the eye organ which is the basis for the [eye] consciousness, for these [objects of consciousness, such as form, etc.], when dependently designated, also become bases for consciousness. So therefore it is incorrect to understand consciousness as being *pratyakṣa*.

2. *Candrakīrti's view: it is the object which is pratyakṣa, rather than the mind*

§15. It is [however] correct [to understand] the object [as being *pratyakṣa*]. The crescent moon and other such things are all seen to be sense objects for people from many [different] extractions.(373) In the case of worldly things, it is illogical to abandon the world's vision and then rely on something else. So, in the world it is just the object which is directly termed *pratyakṣa*; the consciousness is [so termed] metaphorically.(374) But according to the opponent [i.e. the logician], the word "*pratyakṣa*" directly [refers] to the consciousness and metaphorically to the object. This is not in accordance with the world, for in the world there is no such [linguistic] convention (*kun tu tha sñad* = *saṃvyavahāra*). So then, as there is a worldly convention [for objects being *pratyakṣa*], then just because of the world it is correct to say that a vase is *pratyakṣa*. But should one look for any nature, then he who understands the truth cannot make this type of an assertion, for in no respect is any nature of a vase perceived. For a worldly consciousness vases are *pratyakṣa* [i.e. perceptible], [visual] form and the like are also *pratyakṣa* and the material causes (*ñe bar len pa* = *upādāna*) of such [things] are *pratyakṣa* too. Thus there is no fault [here].

§16. He who fabricates the notion that this sense consciousness is *pratyakṣa* and then also imagines that it is a means of valid cognition (*tshad ma* = *pramāṇa*) is completely beside the point. While a non-belying (*mi slu ba* = *avisaṃvādin*) consciousness is regarded as being a *pramāṇa* in the world, the Illustrious One said that consciousness, since it is conditioned (*'dus byas* = *saṃskṛta*), is false and deceptive and is like an illusion (*sgyu ma* = *māyā*).(375) Whatever is false and deceptive and is like an illusion is not non-belying, for it is an entity which exists in one way and appears in another. Something like that should not be imagined to be a *pramāṇa* in that [if it were] it would follow that every consciousness would also have to be a *pramāṇa*.(376)

3. Conclusions

§17. In conclusion, when this logician becomes intoxicated through imbibing the brew of dialectics, then, in his madness, he abandons the excellent path known as dependent origination and dependent designation, and completely fails to see through the collection of bad jokes propounding entities which is set forth in the Outsiders' treatises. He considers this world as being generally inferior too, and then this [logician], who is confused about the states of both worldly and transcendent entities, uses simply his own conceptions, blocks the path to heaven and liberation and totally meaninglessly embarks on the path of dialectics. Thus, just like one who has imbibed intoxicating drink, he cannot turn away from senseless jokes. But enough of these digressions (*spros pas chog* = *ity alaṃ prasaṅgena*)! It should be understood that this [logician], who denies that vases are perceptible (*pratyakṣa*), will [end up] denying that any entity which is a visible sense object is perceptible at all.

B. All sense objects are to be similarly refuted

§18. Just as [Āryadeva] had previously explained [in k.301] that it would be incorrect [to consider] that vases and the like are [really] perceptible, so too he states the following in order to deny the perceptibility of things which are distinguished by other sense organs, i.e. the dependently designated [entities] which are smelled, tasted or felt.

> *By means of this very same analysis those of supreme intelligence should refute everything, viz. the fragrant, the sweet and the soft.* **(k.302)**

§19. By saying "the fragrant" he indicates all the objects of the olfactory organ, such as [the fragrances of] nutmeg blossoms (*sna ma'i me tog* = *jātikusuma*), lotuses, *utpalas* and sandalwood, which are [all] distinguishable by means of the nose; even in darkness one apprehends the smells alone without seeing the [visual] forms. Similarly, by saying "the sweet" he indicates all the objects of the gustatory organ, such as sugar, salt and Nimb.(377) By "the soft" he indicates all the objects of the corporal organ, such as cotton, sand and stones. As these also have the eight substances as their material causes (*ñe bar len pa* = *upādāna*), the corresponding appropriate sense organs apprehend each of their [respective] objects, but they do not apprehend all aspects [of the whole entity]. Therefore, which [person] who knows the truth would say that nutmeg blossoms, sugar, cotton and so forth are perceptible (*pratyakṣa*) for him? The refutation of sounds will be explained *in extenso* later on.

C. One cannot see the whole object by merely seeing its visual form

§20. Objection: But, the vase is not different from its [visual] form (*rūpa*); given that it is pervaded by [this] form one will see the whole vase by [merely] seeing the form. [Reply:] To show that this [position] is also inconsistent [Āryadeva] states:

> *Suppose you were to see the whole [vase] by seeing the form. Then why not [think that] the form which you [supposedly] saw was not [actually] seen as you did not [in fact] see [the whole vase]?* **(k.303)**

§21. Suppose that by merely seeing the [visual] form you were to see the whole vase, although [in fact] it is unseen. Then as you did not [in fact] see the vase, why not [think that] the form which you [supposedly] saw was not [actually] seen? Or alternatively, this [verse] has another meaning: the vase has the eight substances as its material cause, but if you think that you see the entire [eight substances] by seeing [just] one substance, viz. form, then equally, why not think that because you have not seen the other seven substances you have not [really] seen the form itself, which does not exist apart from those [other seven]? In the world too one observes that things are described in an approximate fashion, as [for example] when one calls what is actually something like *mudga*-beans a heap of *māṣa*-beans.(378)

§22. In conclusion, because you do not observe such things, i.e. because you do not distinguish the smells, etc., then the form must also be unseen, and thus because the form is not perceptible, the vase cannot be perceptible either.

D. Part-whole arguments applied to visual form and atoms

§23. Objection: Following the above-described analysis it is surely impossible that the vase be perceptible, but the [visual] form of the vase is indeed perceptible. Therefore, indirectly the vase will also be perceptible. [Reply:] This is not so. If the form were perceptible then this [type of indirect perception of the vase] would be the case as described, but [Āryadeva] states the following to show that form cannot possibly be perceived:

> *Form by itself is not perceptible, for it too has distant (pha rol = para), near (tshu rol = apara) and central parts.* **(k.304)**

§24. Form by itself, i.e. [form] when one does not intend to describe it as related with smell and other such [sense domains], is also observed as always having near, middle and distant parts, and thus it cannot properly be perceptible. The near, distant and central parts again have other near, distant and central parts. When one makes divisions in this way, thinking "these too have other [parts] and these in turn have others", then this form will end up being atoms. But these atoms which one imagines also have divisions into front and back parts as well as divisions into near, central and distant parts so that

the analysis as to whether the atoms do or do not have parts will apply there too. **(k.305ab)**

1. Sādhyasama

§25. If they have divisions into front and back parts, then, just like a vase, they [too] will lose their quality of being atoms. But if they do not have [such divisions], then in that case such an invisible and unapprehended thing will not exist either. So how could they ever be perceptible?

It is thus not proper to establish something which is to be proved (bsgrub bya = sādhya) by means of something [else] which is to be proved. **(k.305cd)**

§26. As the perceptibility [of atoms] is unestablished, it is not correct. So, because perceptibility is unestablished and is [itself] to be established, it is something to be proved. Entities which are [just] established by the opinions of our adversaries as having natures are not proper [for proving that vases and the like are perceptible].(379)

§27. Furthermore, if we examine the object apprehended by the physical sense organs, then

given that everything is a part, it will also be a whole. **(k.306ab)**

§28. A vase is a whole relative to its parts, the potsherds. These potsherds will also be wholes relative to their parts. One should equally apply [this line of analysis] up to and including the atoms: they too will again be wholes relative to their eight substances or relative to their front, back and central parts. So, nothing is ever a part or a whole by virtue of its essence (*raṅ gi ṅo bo = svarūpa*). Consequently, [wholes] such as vases and the like are not perceptible.(380)

2. Atoms and akṣara are analogous

§29. The same type of analysis which was applied to atoms also applies to syllables (*yi ge = akṣara*), which are the ultimate components of words, in that just like the atoms they [too] are unestablished.

Thus, in such a case, utterances of syllables are also inexistent. **(k.306cd)**

§30. The point is that utterances of syllables are also impossible. In other words, if vases and so forth are inexistent, then the utterances of syllables which describe such things are also impossible, for when the object is inexistent consciousness and speech cannot function:

"In such a case, utterances of syllables are also inexistent."

E. Examination of the Abhidharma's notion of rūpāyatana: the relationship between shape and colour

§31. To those who posit a domain of [visual] form (*gzugs kyi skye mched = rūpāyatana*) having two natures, viz. colour (*kha dog = varṇa*) and shape (*dbyibs = saṃsthāna*),(381) and who imagine that vases are perceptible because of this [domain of form], one says the following: When you imagine this shape here, do you imagine it as being different from the colour or not different? Now first of all,

if the shape were different from the colour, then how would one apprehend the shape? **(k.307ab)**

§32. Supposing that colours, such as blue and the like, are objects of the eye organ, then if the shape were different from these [colours], it would not be apprehended by the eyes, for it would be something different from the colours, just like sounds and so forth [which are also different from colours and are not apprehended by the eyes.] But because the eyes do also apprehend [shapes], just as they do colours, [shapes] are not different from the [colours]. Contrary to the way in which [the eye] apprehends some or another [colour] from among various distinct colours, such as blue, yellow and so forth, and then also apprehends the others, it does not apprehend a [visual] form which is different from the colour.(382)

But if [shape] were not different [from colour] then why wouldn't the body also apprehend colour? **(k.307cd)**

§33. If, in the intention of avoiding the above-described faults, one imagines that shape is not different from colour, then just as in the dark the body apprehends [shapes] such as length and so forth, so too why wouldn't it also apprehend colours just like shapes, for [the colours] are not different from the [shapes]? Although they ought to be apprehended, they are not. Therefore, because [the body] does apprehend shapes but not [colours], shapes are not non-different from colours. One cannot [however] posit another conception apart those of identity and difference. Thus, shapes are also incoherent, just as are colours, and given that they do not [in fact] exist, it is then proven that nothing is ever perceptible.

F. Critique of visual form and its causes, i.e. the elements

§34. Here it might be argued as follows: The domain of [visual] form does in fact exist because its causes exist. Here the causes of form are the four elements, and they do indeed exist.[(383)] Because they exist, their effect, viz. the domain of form, will also exist. [Reply:] In order to show that this is not correct either [Āryadeva] states:

The causes for form [viz. the elements] do not appear apart from the sight of a form.[(384)] **(k.308ab)**

§35. One does not perceive a [visual] form apart from the four elements which must necessarily arise together with the eight substances.[(385)] One does not perceive the causes of form apart from the domain of form. Now the domain of [visual] form is apprehendable by the eye organ, but the causes of form [viz. the elements] are apprehended by the corporal organ [i.e. the sense of touch].[(386)] Therefore, if the so-called "causes of form" had been in the slightest established in their natures, form would also have been established in its nature, but it is impossible that the causes of form be established as something other than form. Consequently, when the causes of form are inexistent, it is proven that the form, which would be causeless, cannot exist either.

1. The view that form and its causes are not different

§36. The [opponent] might think: Well then let us grant that form is obtained from causes of form which are not different [from their effects, viz. form]. [Reply:] This too is impossible.

If [form and its causes] were like this [i.e. not different], then why wouldn't both be apprehended by the eye alone? **(k.308cde)**

§37. Since [according to the opponent] the causes for a form are also not different from the form, then the eye organ would have to apprehend both the causes and [their] effects. But this is also impossible in that the [causes and their effects] are objects of different sense organs and have differing [defining] characters (*mtshan ñid = lakṣaṇa*). To express this fact [Āryadeva] states:

We see that the earth [element] is said to be hard.[(387)] *Now, the body apprehends this [hardness].* **(k.309ab)**

§38. Due to its action of supporting, [the earth element] exists as a basis.[(388)] Thus, being a basis, it is hard and so [as Āryadeva says],

"We see that the earth [element] is said to be hard. Now, the body apprehends this [hardness],"

because the solidity of the [earth element] is something which is to be apprehended by the corporal organ. [Thus,] as the [earth element] is of such a nature, *therefore, it is just this touch-sensation which one calls "earth".* **(k.309cd)**

§39. The domain of [visual] form is what is to be apprehended by the eye organ. Thus, in this way the cause [of form, viz. the elements] and [their] effects [viz. form itself] cannot be without difference, for their defining characters are different and the [organs] which apprehend them are different.

2. *The view that form and its causes are different*

§40. But when [one says that] they are different one will end up asserting that [form] has no cause, [for as shown in k.308ab and §35 the elements do not exist apart from their effect, form.] One cannot reasonably imagine that entities which are neither identical nor different could ever exist by their own essences, and therefore, the causes of form do not [in fact] exist. It is however shown that if the causes for form are inexistent then form cannot exist by its own essence. And thus for precisely this reason, the Illustrious One stated [in the *Vajracchedikasūtra*]:

> "Whoever has seen me as a form, whoever has been guided by my voice, such people who have set out upon a mistaken course of action will not see me [at all]."

Well then how is [the Buddha] to be seen? It is stated [in the same sūtra]:

> "It is by the Dharma that the buddhas are to be seen, for it is the Dharma-bodies (*dharmakāya*) which lead one. The nature of things (*dharmatā*), being beyond [our] understanding, cannot be known."(389)

G. Refuting perceptibility (draṣṭavyatva)

§41. Here some say the following: The vase is not perceptible by its own essence, but it is nonetheless certainly not imperceptible either. Rather, it becomes perceptible due to its connection with perceptibility (*lta bar bya ba ñid = draṣṭavya-tva*).(390) Thus, being perceptible, it is *pratyakṣa*. To show that this [position] is also incorrect, [Āryadeva] says:

> *The vase, in this case, would have absolutely no [special] quality due to its production as perceptible. Therefore, just like the [absurd] production of perceptibility [in imperceptible things], [the vase] does not have existence either.*(391) **(k.310)**

§42. Whether perceptibility is a manifestation (*mṅon par gsal ba = abhivyakti*) [of the object itself] or whether it is distinct [from the object], in both cases there is no need here for [the entity,] perceptibility. When one imagines this "perceptibility", does one think of it as being the perceptible object's own essence or as being the essence of something imperceptible? In the first case, if it is the perceptible object's own essence, then what is the point in imagining it? Whatever might be the purpose for imagining [perceptibility], that [purpose] is in fact realized even without it. Thus it is illogical to imagine [an entity, perceptibility].

§43. But if one imagines that perceptibility belongs to something which is imperceptible, then this too is illogical in that: *(a)* it would follow absurdly that non-physical things would also be perceptible; *(b)* there is a contradiction with the fact that perceptibility is not produced [in the thing in question as it is imperceptible].

§44. [Now] perceptibility is not produced [in such things],

"therefore, just like the [absurd] production of perceptibility",

i.e. just as [perceptibility] could not be produced in that it is absurd for perceptibility to ever belong to vases which are [according to you, in essence] imperceptible, so too, the vases, which would not be perceptible, would not have existence either. And because one cannot imagine perceptibility as belonging to vases which do not even exist, this [entity] is illogical.

PART II: SENSE ORGANS

A. Refuting other Buddhist schools' positions on the reality of the sense organs

§45. At this point [the opponent] may say: Perceptible things (*mṅon sum* = *pratyakṣa*), such as objects like [visual] form and so forth, do really exist, because the sense organs, such as the eyes, etc., which apprehend these [objects] do exist. These sense organs which exist must necessarily function with regard to their own objects; the objects like form, etc. to which these [sense organs] can apply are [thus] perceptible.

1. All sense organs are alike in being derivatives from the elements. Why then do only the eyes see?

§46. Reply: If the sense organs did have the power to discriminate (*yoṅs su gcod pa* = *pariccheda*) [objects], then they would have [visual] form and so forth as their objects, but they do not have [this power]. Why? Here it is taught that the five [sense organs], such as the eye, etc., are all derived from the elements; it is their actions which differ according to the different objects. Thus, for example, the eye sees only [visual] form but does not hear sound, while the ear hears sound but does not see form.

§47. Since

the eye is derived from the elements ('byuṅ 'gyur = bhautika), like the ear, [and] the eye sees [form] but the other [sense organs] do not, **(k.311ab)**

then, given that there cannot be an action [like vision, etc.] which is in contradiction with reason, how could one conceive of the eyes and other [sense organs'] own essences? Just as the [sense organs] are all the same in being derived from the elements, so one cannot reasonably imagine that they apprehend their objects differently. If the existence of the eyes and other [sense organs] is inferred from the [different] apprehensions of objects, then this is contradictory and hence impossible. Therefore, it is illogical [to say that] objects are perceptible because the sense organs exist.

§48. Objection: If the eyes and so on thus cannot exist, then how can one establish that sense organs such as the eyes, etc. are retributions of [past] acts (*las* = *karman*)? [Reply:] Why should we deny that they are retributions? The [opponent] retorts: By proving that the [existence of the] eyes, etc. is negated, why wouldn't you have thereby denied [that they are retributions of karma?] [Reply:] It is because our analysis is primarily concerned with seeking out the natures of objects. In this context we are denying that entities exist by their [own] essences, but with regard to the eyes and the like, we do not deny that they are karmic retributions which dependently arise. Thus, the eyes and so forth do exist, for we say that they are retributions due to the existence of the [karma].

2. *Karma is responsible for the sense organs, but is unanalysable and inconceivable*

§49. Objection: In that case, would there not be the very faults which [were expressed in the verse,]

> "The eye is derived from the elements, like the ear, [and] the eye sees [form] but the other [sense organs] do not"?

§50. These faults do not ensue, for the retributions (*rnam par smin pa* = *vipāka*) of the various karmas are inconceivable.(392) Karmic retributions cannot be understood by applying reasonings, in that karma itself is not in fact established by its own essence. If [karma] were established by its essence, then it could never cease, and a karma whose retribution had already occurred would once again yield a retribution, or alternatively, [karma] would not yield any retribution [at all] because its nature could not change into anything different.

§51. The effects of karma are not [however] unobserved either. Consequently, the wise do not apply this sort of [logical] analysis, which pertains to the vision of the truth (*de kho na ñid* = *tattva*)(393), to worldly states of affairs [such as karma and other such conventional truths]. [Instead] they accept that karmic retributions are inconceivable: everything worldly is to be thought of as [one] illusion proceeding from [another] illusion.

§52. When one observes something, one cannot then disavow it. Now, when it was said [above in §46] that the eye, albeit derived from the elements, sees only [visual] form but does not hear sound, this is also something which is observed. So

> *consequently, the Sage said that the retributions of karma are definitely inconceivable.* **(k.311cd)**

§53. Because entities, while lacking natures, do have definite effects which will be produced, the Illustrious One, in the following passages, said that the retributive effects of the various karmas are inconceivable:

> "Due to the inconceivable retributions of sentient beings' karma this world arises from the winds (*rluṅ* = *vāyu*). The seeds of the oceans, mountains and of the divine palaces, which have been made majestic with jewels, are scattered about. Rain falls because of the clouds which originate from the winds, and then the winds again dispel the clouds. Because of the winds the world's crops grow; thus the winds bring happiness to all beings."(394)

And similarly,

> "Those who exist but are free from the faults of existence do not also cast aside the effects of karma when they profess voidness. Those who have burned away stains by means of knowledge but who are moistened by compassion and whose actions are governed by selflessness, they are also subject [to karma]."

B. The view that the eyes, etc. must exist because we observe their effects, viz. the sense consciousnesses

§54. Here there is the following objection: The eyes and the other [sense organs] do exist by their natures because we observe their effects, namely, the consciousnesses. Reply: If their effects, viz. the consciousnesses, did [in fact] exist, then the eyes and so forth would exist — but this is impossible. Why? First of all,

> *because the conditions (rkyen = pratyaya) would be incomplete, the consciousness could not exist before sight. But after [sight], the consciousness would be pointless. In the third case [viz. simultaneity], the instrument (byed pa = karaṇa)*(395) *would be pointless.*(396) **(k.312)**

§55. First of all, the eye consciousness does not exist before [the organ of] sight, for eye-sight , i.e. the dominant condition (*bdag po'i rkyen* = *adhipatipratyaya*) [for the consciousness], is incomplete.(397) If, however, one thought that [the eye consciousness existed] after [the organ of] sight, then the consciousness would be pointless, [for] if the eye could see form without there being consciousness, then there would be no point in imagining that there is a consciousness.

§56. "In the third case [viz. simultaneity], the instrument (*byed pa* = *karaṇa*) would be pointless"

That is to say, the third conception is that [the organ of] sight and the consciousness occur simultaneously: in that case the [eye being a] cause is pointless. [In other words,] in that case, [the organ of] sight, or the instrument (*byed pa* = *karaṇa*), would be pointless. If [the organ of] sight and the consciousness both existed simultaneously, then the consciousness which exists at the same time as [the organ of] sight could not arise in dependence upon that [organ of] sight. The right and left horns of an ox exist concurrently and one cannot come into being in dependence upon the other. Similarly, the consciousness which exists concurrently with [the organ of] sight does not come into being in dependence upon [the organ of] sight. And thus, [the organ of] sight would be completely pointless.

§57. Objection: But, although they are simultaneous, [consciousness] does exist in dependence upon [the organ of] sight, just like a lamp and [its] light. [Reply:] This is not so either, for the issue (*brgal źiṅ brtag pa* = *paryanuyoga*) [concerning the relation between cause and effect] is the same here too. By means of a worldly understanding [such as the example of the lamp and its light] one cannot elucidate the understanding of the truth, because [the former understanding] is a *pramāṇa* only from the worldly point of view and the state of affairs which it apprehends is proven to be false and deceptive (*brdzun pa bslu ba'i chos can* = *mṛṣā moṣadharmaka*). Since the consciousness is thus [in reality] impossible, then the idea that the eyes and other [sense organs] exist because it exists is incorrect.

§58. Objection: The eye is not in fact the instrument (*byed pa* = *karaṇa*) [of the consciousness]. What is it then? It is the agent (*byed pa po* = *kartṛ*). Because we maintain that it is an entity which is an agent, it is incorrect to say,

"In the third case [viz. simultaneity], the instrument would be pointless."

C. Refuting prāpyakāritvavāda — contact between the object and the sense organ

§59. [Reply:] Even if one imagined things as being like this, the eye would lack the action of seeing. Why? When the eye sees this [visual] form, would it see it by going to the place of its object or by not going? To show that both cases are faulty [Āryadeva] states:

> *It would take a long time for this eye to see far away, if it were to move. And why wouldn't this form be clear whether very near or far away?* **(k.313)**

§60. If the eye operated by contact (*prāptakāritva*) and therefore went out to the place of the object, then it would not apprehend [distant] things such as the moon and the stars by a mere glance.(398) Something possessed of movement could not apprehend a nearby object and at the same time apprehend an object which is far away, for the times needed for the movement would differ. In fact, by a mere glance the eye does also see what is far away just as well as what is close by, so this [view that the eye moves] is incoherent. Furthermore, if the eye did operate by contact, then it would see the ointments or lancets applied to the eye, although they be very near, and it would see [things] clearly far in the distance. Now this cannot be, and thus this [position] is incoherent.

§61. Moreover, if the eye sees its object by going [to it], then does it go to the place of the object after having seen [that] object or without having [first] seen it? To show that both [hypotheses] are faulty [Āryadeva] states:

If the eye went out to the form after having seen it, then there would be absolutely no advantage in going. Or alternatively, [if the eye went out to the object without having first seen it], then it would be false that one would definitely [see] what one wished to see.[(399)] **(k.314)**

§62. If it was thought that the eye goes out to the place of the [visual] form after having seen the form, then the eye would have absolutely no need to go [to the form] by means of this movement.[(400)] Indeed, the eye would move in order to see its object, but this object was already seen earlier by the [sense organ] which remained here; so there would be absolutely no need for [the eye] to move. But if [the eye] went [out to its object] without having first seen it, then it definitely would not manage to see the object which it wished to see. For, given that it had not first seen [the object], it would be going to an unindicated place, just like a blind man. Therefore it definitely would not manage to see what it was supposed to see.

D. Refuting aprāpyakāritvavāda — no contact between the object and the organ

§63. However, wishing to avoid this fault, if [one then said that]
the eye apprehends [its object] without going out [to it], then it would see the whole universe. There is nothing which is far away or hidden for something which is without any movement. **(k.315)**

§64. When someone thinks that the eye does not come into contact with its object because the scripture says, "The eye, ear and mind do not come into contact with their objects", we reply to him that there is in fact no contradiction with scripture, for [the scriptural passage] is above all concerned with negating the mere [proposition] that [these sense organs] operate by contact.[(401)] Affirmation (*vidhi*) is predominant wherever it is not contradicted; negation (*pratiṣedha*) is predominant wherever it is not contradicted. So, given that affirmation is not possible here, then the proposition that [these sense organs] do not come into contact with their objects (*aprāptaviṣayatva*) is established as just simply negating that they operate by contact (*prāptakāritā*).

§65. If, however, one construes "not coming into contact with the object" (*aprāptaviṣayatva*) as an affirmation, then [we reply that] the eye, which just remains here [immobile], would see the whole universe. Indeed, how could anything be far away for it when it does not move? For, without going [anywhere], it ought to see an object far in the distance just as well as one which is nearby. So though [the object] might be far away, there would be no difference. Since [the eye] sees without going [anywhere], it would see [things] far in the distance just as if they were right here. Similarly, it would see hidden things too.[(402)] For indeed, if there is movement, then when something is hidden, there are obstacles to movement, and thus it would be coherent to say that one does not see what is hidden. However, since things are to be seen without [the eye] going [anywhere], then there would be no obstacle to movement when something is hidden, and thus it would be seen just as when it is not hidden.

E. Sight is not the nature (svabhāva) of the eye

§66. Now, if the eye had sight as its nature (*svabhāva*), then it would also see itself, for nowhere would the nature be impeded. Indeed, in the world,

the nature of all entities is first seen in [the entities] themselves.[(403)] *Why then would the eye itself not apprehend the eye?*[(404)] **(k.316)**

§67. Just as the fragrance of yellow magnolia[(405)], jasmine or other such [flowers] is first of all perceived in their own loci [i.e. in the flowers themselves] and is then later also [perceived] in oils and such things in which it is mixed, and just as fire's heat [first] exists due to [the fire] itself and is [then] also perceived in other things because they come into contact with it, so similarly if the eye had sight as its nature, then it would first of all see itself. Why then does the eye itself not apprehend the eye? Now, since the nature of entities is first and foremost in [the entities] themselves, the eye itself ought to apprehend the eye. [However] the eye does not [in fact] see itself, and thus it is also inconceivable that it sees other things, just as [for example] lumps of earth and so forth [do not have sight as their natures and cannot see other things either.]

F. Refuting the Buddhist's three conditions for vision

§68. As for the opinion that it is not just the eye alone which has the power to see form, but that one sees form when the three [factors], the eye, form, and the eye consciousness, come together[(406)], this is also inconsistent. Since

the eye has no consciousness, consciousness no [organ of] sight[(407)] *[and] form has neither the one nor the other, how can these [three] see form?* **(k.317)**

§69. First of all, the eye has no consciousness. For, the eye does not cognize an object, as it is unconscious in essence. Indeed, the eye is derived from the elements (*bhautika*).[(408)] Since it is inert matter (*jaḍa*), it cannot have any comprehension of an object. Thus,

"the eye has no consciousness."

§70. Nor does consciousness have [an organ of] sight either.[(409)] It is not physical (*gzugs can* = *rūpavat; rūpin*), so how could it have [an organ of] sight? Lacking an [organ of sight], then like a blind man, it does not see.[(410)] As for form it has neither the one nor the other: it does not have consciousness in that it does not have comprehension as its own essence; nor does it have [an organ of] sight, for it does not [itself] perceive form.[(411)] Now, when the sense organs, objects and consciousnesses are thus defective with regard to their mutual purpose, then it can be supposed that even if they are brought together, they still will not see form. The point is that [they will not see even when brought together] because their [necessary] factors for seeing form are defective, just like a group of blind men [will not see either].

G. Critique of sounds and words

§71. Now, when seeing form is thus impossible, then which person who knows the truth could ever say that form is seen or could see it himself? Just as the person who knows the truth cannot see form, he will also be equally unable to hear sound, for in the same way as [it is impossible] to see form, it is impossible to hear sounds.

§72. In this vein, if sound is heard, then would it be heard after having reached (*saṃprāpta*) the locus of hearing [i.e. the ear], or without having reached it? On the first [hypothesis], if [a sound] is heard when it has reached [the ear], then when it is going to the locus of hearing would it make sounds[(412)] or would it go soundlessly? Taking the former idea, then

> *if sound went while speaking, why wouldn't it become a speaker (vaktṛ)? On the other hand, if it went without speaking, then how would there be any knowledge (pratyaya)*[(413)] *of it?* **(k.318)**

§73. So because it is a speaker, like Devadatta, it is not a sound. However, if it went without speaking, then who could have the certainty that it was a sound, as this sound would go soundlessly? Nor could something unapprehended exist, and thus this [hypothesis] is absurd.

§74. What is more,

> *if sound is apprehended after it has reached [the ear] then what apprehends the beginning (ādi)*[(414)] *of the [sound]? Moreover, sound does not go alone (kevala)*[(415)]*; how could it be apprehended alone?* **(k.319)**

If sound is apprehended after it has reached the locus of the ear organ, then

"what apprehends the beginning of the [sound]?"

Since sound is apprehended after contact [with the ear], there would be no apprehension of a sound's beginning. Nor could any other sense organ serve to apprehend it — thus its beginning would not be apprehended by anything at all.[(416)] Consequently, being unapprehended, this [beginning moment] would not be a sound at all — such is the point [of the verse].

§75. Moreover, since an atom of sound has nine substances,[(417)]

"sound does not go alone."

Now, you say that it is just sound, and nothing else, which is apprehended by the ear; smells and so forth are not. This is incoherent. Either sound must be unapprehended, or smells and the other [substances] must be apprehended too. But such is not the case, and thus sound is not the object which is contacted.

§76. [Objection:] But as for what you said [in k.319], viz.

> "If sound is apprehended after it has reached [the ear] then what apprehends the beginning of the [sound]?"

what fault is there then if the beginning of the [sound] is not apprehended? [Reply:] The fault is that its very nature of being a sound is destroyed. Indeed,

> *insofar as a sound is not heard, it will not be a sound. And that a non-sound also ends up being a sound is absurd.* **(k.320)**

§77. What is not heard is not a sound at all, for it is not being heard, like smells and other such [inaudible] things. Suppose you think that *when* it is heard, then *at that time* it will be a sound. This also must be considered to be impossible. For, smells and the like are not observed to become sounds later, and in precisely the same fashion, it is absurd that this non-sound too [viz. the beginning moments] would later become a sound.

§78. As the Illustrious One stated [in the *Upālipariprcchā*]:

> "Also, when one hears an agreeable sound, it never penetrates inside. Nor does one perceive its movement. Rather, it is due to conceptualization (*kalpa*) that sound arises."(418)

And similarly [in the *Lalitavistara*]:

> "E.g. in reliance upon strings, wood and manual effort, then by the conjunction of [these] three [factors], musical instruments such as *tuṇa* and *vīṇā* ("lutes") issue a sound which arises due to these [factors]. But should a wise person search as to where it comes from and where it goes, then when he searches in all directions and intermediate directions, he does not find sound's going nor its coming."(419)

H. Critique of the mind (manas)

§79. After having thus first of all shown that the sense organs are incapable of apprehending objects, [Āryadeva] now states the following to show that the mind (*manas*) is also incapable of apprehending objects:

> *Even having gone out [to the object], what will the mind (citta) accomplish without the sense organs?* **(k.321ab)**

§80. If it is thought that the mind goes out to the locus of the object and then discriminates this object, this [idea] is absurd. In that case, the mind in question would go to the locus of the object either accompanied by the sense organs or alone. Now, first of all, it does not go accompanied by the sense organs, for sense organs always remain only in the vicinity of the body, and if they were to go [with the mind], it would follow absurdly that the body would be missing its sense organs.

§81. However, if [the mind] goes out [to its object] alone, then again, "even having gone out [to the object], what will the mind accomplish without the sense organs?"

Indeed, when the [mind] has been deprived of the sense organs such as the eyes, which are its means of access(420), it is incapable of seeing form and the like, for [otherwise] it would follow absurdly that the blind and other [people whose sense organs are damaged] would also in fact have sight and the other [types of perceptions].

§82. Moreover, if it was thought that the [mind] in one way or another perceives an entity by going out to the locus of the object, then too, given that [the mind] would never stop [going out] because the cognition of entities has no end,(421)

in that case, why wouldn't the living being in question be forever mindless? **(k.321cd)**

§83. The self would become perpetually insentient. Now, it is not reasonable to suppose that something insentient has a self, for it is insentient, like pillars and other such [material] things. So in conclusion, the sense organs, objects and consciousnesses, if they are examined by means of logical reasonings, cannot be real, and hence their essences are not established.(422) If the essences of these [sense organs, objects, etc.] were established, then when [these entities] are examined by reasonings, they would be perceived perfectly clearly according to their essences as [these essences] are. But they are not so perceived. Therefore, it is shown that they are void of nature.

I. Discussion of "notions" (saṃjñā)

§84. Objection: In that case, if the [sense organs, the objects and the consciousnesses] did not have anything which could be called a nature, then how could one teach that the notion (*saṃjñā*), which has as its nature their specific individuations (*pariccheda*), is the cause for establishing the various entities. Reply: If entities existed, then a notion, which has as its nature the specific individuation of the [entity] would exist. Now, since it is shown that these entities do not exist, then how could the essence [of this notion](423) be established through them?

§85. Objection: So then is there absolutely no individuation of objects? [Reply:] No, we can say that it is not inexistent, for things exist without natures. Indeed,

the object which is apprehended by the mind is [in fact something which was] seen earlier [and is] like a mirage.(424) This [consciousness] is termed the 'aggregate of notions' (saṃjñāskandha) for the [different] determinations of all dharmas. **(k.322)**

§86. In this regard, when visual consciousness ceases, after having arisen in dependence upon the eye and form, it ceases along with the sense organs and the objects. This [consciousness] having ceased, the very object which had been seen earlier is [then] apprehended later by the mind.(425)

§87. Objection: But how could one admit that something which is not present is being apprehended? [Reply]: 'Like a mirage', says [Āryadeva]. Although there is not the slightest amount of water in a mirage, still, through the influence of causes and conditions, a notion which has the aspect (*ākāra*) of water does in fact occur. Similarly, even though the object which was apprehended earlier has no essence, like a mirage, the conceptual consciousness (*vikalpakaṃ vijñānam*) which arises is the cause of the [different] determinations of all the dharmas.(426) Now, because [the conceptual consciousness] is the cause of the determinations of all dharmas, it is called the "aggregate of notions", for it has the [fivefold] association (*saṃprayoga*) with the various corresponding notions.(427) It should be understood that the determination of any dharma is due to the notion, but is not caused by the essence of the entity [in question], for [entities' own] nature (*svabhāva*) is absurd in all cases whatsoever.(428)

J. The unreality of consciousness

§88. Objection: If that were so, then the aggregate of notions would exist by its nature, for if it did not exist, then one could not determine any dharmas. Reply: The notion is itself also associated with the consciousness, and thus does not exist without the [corresponding] consciousness, while the consciousness, in turn, is unestablished without the notion, and so does not exist by its essence. Also, for the following reason [consciousness] does not exist: because

the mind arises in dependence upon the eye and form(429), like an illusion (māyā). **(k.323ab)**

§89. Indeed, before [its] arisal, there is no consciousness which would function as the basis of the action of production. Even when conditions such as the eyes [and form] are present, consciousness, as it has no essence, cannot arise, for the action of production cannot be set in motion.(430) Now, this consciousness does [nonetheless] arise. So what can we ascertain other than that it has the quality of an illusion?

§90. The Illustrious One, indeed, said [in the *Saṃyuttanikāya*]:

"Monks, it is just as if an illusionist or an apprentice illusionist, at the crossroads of four great avenues, exhibited various sorts of magic, such as a corps of elephants, a cavalry corps,(431) a corps of chariots or an infantry corps. Should a man endowed with vision see that [magic], reflect upon it and properly analyse it, then when he sees it, reflects upon it and analyses it properly, it will appear to him as inexistent (*asat*), empty (*rikta*), insignificant (*tuccha*) and insubstantial (*asāra*). Why is that? Because he wonders, 'Is there anything substantial in this magical creation?' In precisely the same fashion, whatever consciousness one takes, be it past, future, present, inner or outer, gross or subtle, low or high, be it far away or nearby, should a monk see that [consciousness], reflect upon it and properly analyse it, then when he sees it, reflects upon it and analyses it properly, it will appear to him as inexistent, empty, insignificant, insubstantial, as a sickness (*roga*), an abscess (*gaṇḍa*), a splinter (*śalya*), as an impurity (*agha*), impermanent (*anitya*), painful (*duḥkha*), void (*śūnya*) and selfless (*anātman*). Why is that? Because he wonders, 'Is there anything substantial in this aggregate of consciousness?'"(432)

§91. When one examines(433) it in just the way in which it is perceived, then it can be ascertained that consciousness resembles a young girl [created by magical] illusions in that it [too] does not have any essence. So therefore it was completely accurate [to assert that]

"the mind arises in dependence upon the eye and form, like an illusion."

If, however, the [mind] did have an essence, then

what has true existence **(k.323c)**

essentially,

could not be said to be an illusion. **(k.323d)**

§92. Indeed, in the world one could not say that a woman, who is not void of nature [and] exists, is an illusion. Similarly, as consciousness would also exist by its essence, it would not be comparable to an illusion. But it is [in fact] taught that consciousness *is* comparable to an illusion. So consciousness [must] be without any nature. And when consciousness has no nature, it is then established that a notion associated with a consciousness which lacks nature [must itself] be without any nature.

§93. The Illustrious One said [in the *Samādhirājasūtra*]:

"The notion is taught to be an apprehension which has knowledge as its aim. But this notion does not apprehend anything; it is shown to have separation as its aim."

"The notion consists in separation; [its] indication consists in separation. Now, when one knows the nature of notions, then accordingly the notion will not occur."(434)

"He to whom the notion 'We will abandon such a notion' occurs, is engaged in the proliferation of notions, [but] will not be delivered from notions."

"Of what does the notion arise? By what is a notion produced? By what is the notion perceived? By what is it stopped?"

"The Buddha has not found any dharma of which a notion arises. You should think of this point and thus notions will not occur."

K. Replying to the charge that the Madhyamaka is simply counterintuitive

§94. Objection: It is astonishing that on the one hand sense faculties can in no way apprehend objects and that on the other hand consciousness is produced in dependence upon the eye and various forms.

§95. Reply: Is this the only astonishing thing that you have observed? Aren't the following astonishing: a sprout cannot reasonably arise from a seed which has ceased, nor from one which has not ceased, and yet the sprout does [indeed] arise in dependence upon the seed; similarly, an act (*karman*) which has been performed and accumulated, once it has ceased cannot abide anywhere, but nonetheless, from an act whose cessation happened hundreds of thousands of eras ago there does manifestly arise an effect; furthermore, vases and such [objects], if examined as to whether they are identical with or different from their causes, cannot possibly exist, but still, due to dependent designation (*upādāya prajñapti*), they are suitable for performing actions such as containing and scooping honey, water and other such [liquids]? So therefore,

when there is nothing astonishing on earth for the wise, then what is so amazing about the sense organs' comprehension?(435) **(k.324)**

§96. It is seen that effects conform to their causes, i.e. in cases such as a cow [being born] from a cow, a horse from a horse, rice from rice. But for the elements (*bhūta*), as well as for the [*bhautikas* such as] form, sound and the like, this rule is not seen [to hold]. Thus, because they are apprehended by the corporal sense organ,(436) the elements are neither visible nor audible, [and yet] due to them visible forms and audible sounds arise. This is supremely astonishing. The same thing applies to the objects of smell, etc. and also to the eyes and the other organs.

§97. Alternatively, [it could be said that] this fact that the sense organs comprehend objects is *not* a cause for amazement. For, if this strangeness only applied to just the sense organs' comprehension of objects, then it would be a source of amazement. But when absolutely the whole world, as we have said, is amazing for the wise, like Indra's net (*indrajāla*)(436a), then this [one thing, viz. sense perception] is not [especially] astonishing. What is amazing is when some exceptional, inconceivable thing is perceived, but not something which is uniform everywhere: the fact that fire is hot is nothing amazing at all!

L. Similes for dharmas' mode of existence

1. Explanations

§98. On account of this very reason,

existence,

for the wise,

is like the circle of a whirling firebrand, a magical being, a dream, an illusion, the moon [reflected] in water, mist, an echo in [the mountains], a mirage or clouds(437) **(k.325)**

in that, being without any fixed essence, it transforms in various manners in accordance with conditions.

§99. Just as when one quickly turns a flaming piece of wood, one perceives the aspect of a circle, the sight of the [wood's] movement being the cause of an error, but [nonetheless] there is not the slightest essence of a circle in that [aspect];

§100. Just as magical beings, which are made to come forth by means of special trances (*samādhi*), perform various types of actions and thus produce, by an error of sight and mind, the notion of a truly existent *yogin,*(438) but for the *yogins* [themselves] these [magical beings] are not really existent in that they are without minds, mental factors and sense organs;

§101. Just as a body in a dream, which is conditioned by a body which has a consciousness associated with [the mental factor] sleep, causes the error of attachment to the self, as does a body in an awakened state,(439) but this [body] is not really existent because someone who is awake does not see it like that;

§102. Just as the magically created young girls caused by the illusionist's talismans only have the purpose of bewildering the minds of those unaware as to what these ['girls'] are and come into being void of any really existent women;

§103. Just as the moon [reflected] in water, but void of any really existent moon, is produced as [a moon] because of dependent arising, and causes the erroneous perception of a moon for infantile people;

§104. Just as the mist which is produced simply due to dependent arising in reliance upon the appropriate times, places and causal factors will cause an erroneous perception of really existent smoke for those who are far away;

§105. Just as an echo in [places] such as mountain caverns and hollows arises dependently and gives rise to ignorant people's presumption of a really existent sound;

§106. Just as a mirage, conditioned by the rays of the sun which are concentrated together at a particular place and time, lacks any essence of water but gives rise to erroneous perception of water for those who are far away;

§107. Just as clouds in the distance produce an erroneous perception which has the aspect of mountains and such things;

§108. So, similarly, for the wise, who are well-versed in the nature of dependent arising as it is, the ocean of births — which starts with consciousness, which is conditioned by the karma projected by errors of ignorance, which arises along with the external receptacle, and which, like a whirling firebrand's circle and such things, is false and deceptive (*mṛṣā moṣadharmaka*) and completely void of nature — seems like a trick for the infantile. Now, those who know the nature of dharmas come to rely on deliverance, thanks to the complete elimination of attachment to anything whatsoever. Thus it is established that saṃsāra is without any nature, like a circle of a whirling firebrand and other such [illusory things].

2. *Citations*

§109. As it was said [in the *Ratnāvalī*]:
"Just as the eye, due to error, apprehends the circle of the whirling firebrand, so the sense organs apprehend objects as if they were present."(440)

And,

§110. According to the *Ratnakūṭa[sūtra]*, while the Sage was not yet in *parinirvāṇa,* two monks, who were without the quality of being true monks, dispelled the darkness of bewilderment of the five hundred monks by the sunlight of the excellent doctrine stated by the Great Sage.(441)

Similarly [in the *Samādhirājasūtra*],

§111. "Just as in a dream a young girl sees her son born and die and when he was born she was extremely joyful but when he died she was in a state of sadness, so you should know all dharmas."(442)

"Just as an illusionist magically creates forms such as various chariots [drawn by] elephants and chariots [drawn by] horses, but no chariot whatsoever is [in fact] observed there, so you should know all dharmas."

"Just as with a clear sky the moon's reflection is seen in a limpid lake, but the moon does not move into the water, so you should know that all dharmas have that character."

"Just as echoes of inaccessible mountain streams in rocky hollows dependently arise, so you should understand all conditioned phenomena; all the world is like an illusion and a mirage."

"Just as at midday in the hot season a man might wander consumed by thirst [and] see a mirage as a pond, so you should know all dharmas."

"In a mirage there is not [actually] any water, [but] this confused person wants to drink it. One cannot drink unreal water. So you should know all dharmas."

"Just as when there is not a single cloud in the sky and yet in an instant a circle of clouds appears and one should understand where they came from originally, so you should know all dharmas."

"Just like a city of Gandharvas, a mirage, like an illusion or like a dream, characters created mentally but empty of nature, so you should know all dharmas."

§112. Thus ends the thirteenth chapter in the *Bodhisattvayogācāracatuḥśataka*, entitled "The Refutation of the Sense Organs and [their] Objects".

NOTES TO THE TRANSLATIONS

(1) *zhū fǎ xìng xiāng* 諸法性相 — a term with many uses. See en. 47 for extensive explanations. Note that while the term can be used to refer simply to the ultimate character of dharmas, as we see in en. 47 *b)*, in Vijñānavāda contexts it frequently means the ultimate nature *plus* the conventional "character". It is this use of *xìng xiāng* that we find for example in Chapter VIII of Dharmapāla's commentary, T. 1571 x 245b17: *zhū fǎ xìng xiāng sú yǒu zhēn wú* 諸法性相俗有眞無 "The nature and character of all dharmas is to exist conventionally but to be ultimately inexistent." See en. 114 and §220a24.

(2) Cf. AK viii, LVP p. 193 and n. 2. According to the *Vyākhyā*, *jñāna* is a conceptual (*vikalpa*) type of discernment (*prajñā*) associated with mental consciousness (*manovijñānasaṃprayuktā*), whereas *darśana* is a non-conceptual discernment. In the extensive references given in the remainder of de la Vallée Poussin's n. 2, *jñānadarśana* is explained in terms of its worldly dimension (viz. understanding the past, the present and the future as well as previous lives) and in terms of enlightenment or deliverance (*vimukti*). In its latter use *jñānadarśana* is understood as part of the "super-knowledge which realizes an understanding [capable of] destroying defilements" (*āsravakṣayajñāna-sākṣātkārābhijñā*). Cf. AK vii, p. 100, n. 2 (*Vyākhyā*): *vimuktasya vimukto 'smīti jñānadarśanaṃ bhavati / kṣīṇā me jātir yāvan nāparam asmād bhavaṃ prajānāmīti / iyam ucyate āsravakṣayajñānasākṣātkārābhijñā*. Cf. also the *Yogācārabhūmi*, transl. Xuán zàng, xii, 15; found in *Fǎ xiāng dà cí diǎn*, p. 903, (*xiū dìng wéi dé zhì jiàn* 修定爲得智見). As for the interpretation of the compound, AK and the Tibetan equivalents in Mvyut (*ye śes mthoṅ ba; ye śes gzigs pa*) give no real clues. We have, however, followed Nakamura, *Bukkyō-go dai jiten* p. 947, who takes it as an instrumental *tatpuruṣa*. For the "unobstructedness of the Buddha's thought" (*apratihatacitta*), cf. *Traité*, I Chapt. XII.

(3) Following Dharmapāla's commentary, *shèng* 勝 = *shèng jiě* 勝解 (*adhimukti*).

(4) *shī zī* 師資 . Lang (Thesis) p. 435, n. 2, following Tucci, translates this as "the teacher's assistance", which is probably the most plausible interpretation. (The Tibetan translation of the *kārikā* has no correlate to these characters.) However, cf. Nak. p. 544, where the compound is taken in the sense of "master and disciple": *shī zī* 師資 = *shī dì* 師弟. Other uses: *shī zī xiāng chéng* 師資相承 "master-disciple transmission".

(5) This may refer to AK vii (LVP pp. 108 and n. 2), where we find a discussion of three super-knowledges (*abhijñā*) which are characterized as *sākṣātkriyāvidyā*, and which come about "in [their proper] order" (*yathākramam*). In brief, according to AK, the point is that the *abhijñā* known as the "remembrance of past lives" (*pūrva-nivāsānusmṛtijñānasākṣātkārābhijñā*) dispels errors relative to the past, the *abhijñā* consisting in the understanding of birth and death (*cyutyupapādajñānasākṣātkārābhijñā*

or *divyacakṣus*, "divine eye") dispels errors relative to the future, and the *abhijñā* consisting in the understanding which eliminates defilements (*āsravakṣayajñānasākṣāt-kārābhijñā*) dispels the errors relative to the present. By the first one sees the suffering of self and others, by the second, one experiences disgust at such suffering, and thus on the basis of these two *abhijñā*, one produces the third and comes to understand the bliss of nirvāṇa. For references for the usual sixfold classification of *abhijñā*, in which these three are included, see Dantinne (1983) pp. 271-272, note *z*.

(6) Namely, Pūraṇa Kāśyapa, Maskarin Gośālīputra, Ajita Keśakambalin, Kakuda Kātyāyana, Nirgrantha Jñātiputra, Saṃjayin Vairaṭīputra. See *Inde classique* §§2241-2. See Vogel (1970) for a translation of the relevant portions in the Tibetan and Chinese versions of the *Mūlasarvāstivāda Vinaya* concerning the doctrines of the six heretics.

(7) *zhòng* 中 "hits", "attains".

(8) As Dharmapāla's commentary makes clear, Āryadeva is referring here to the four noble truths.

(9) See en. 32 on *paryavasthāna*.

(10) *avidyā*, *pramāda* and *middha* are mental factors (*caitta*). *pramāda*: see AK ii, LVP p. 162, and p. 157 for *apramāda*; also AK iv pp. 45, 85. *middha*: AK ii p. 168; v pp. 99-100. *avidyā*: see e.g. May (1959) n. 586.

(11) The Tibetan of k. 278 differs here and does not speak about *śūnyatā* (*stoṅ pa ñid*). Tucci (1925), p. 546 as well as Lang (Thesis) p. 436, n. 10, translate *zhēn* 眞 separately as *vero* / "true"; this, however, seems unnecessary in light of the fact Hirakawa (p. 272) attests that Xuán zàng renders *śūnyatā* by *zhēn kōng*, and that Paramārtha apparently also followed suit, rendering *śūnyatā* by *zhēn kōng lǐ* 眞空理 .

(12) Following the Japanese translation, I have added *bù* 不 in front of *wéi* 唯 . See Kyik *Chūgan-bu* iii, 314.13 and n. 12.

(13) Cf. LVP (1932) on Āryadeva and Dharmapāla's conception of nirvāṇa.

(14) In Chapter II (= CS X) on the refutation of the *ātman*.

(15) *yín* 淫 — or with the radical for "woman", as in our text — has a sexual sense often translating Skt. *maithuna* or *kāma*, a sense which seems unlikely if we are speaking about children. It does, however, also mean "excessive", and can be taken as a verb meaning "to go to excess", "to indulge in" or "to be addicted to", as we see in its Modern Japanese use as "*insuru*". This meaning is very similar to *dān* 耽 , and hence

would give us a parallelism between the two groups of four characters *yín luàn mí xīn* and *dān miǎn sè shēng*.

(16) As Tucci (p. 547, n. 1) points out, *yīn* 因 "cause" is explained by Dharmapāla as meaning *fāng biàn* 方便 = *upāya*, i.e. "method", "means".

(17) Cf. Skt. k. 279. *Qīng liáng* literally means "coolness", which does, however, concord with the well-attested Buddhist image of nirvāṇa, or peace, as being a cool respite from the fire of the passions (*kleśa*). Cf. *Vinaya* i, 34: *sabbam ādittam* ("all is aflame"); and Pr. 497.6-7, May (1959) p. 232, where nirvāṇa without remainder *(nir-upadhiśeṣanirvāṇa)* is characterized as a rainfall which puts out the fire of suffering.

(18) *Fā xīn* 發心 is usually *cittotpāda* ("generating the mind of enlightenment"), which makes little sense given Dharmapāla's contempt for the Outsiders. More likely, it is translating something like *samārambha*. Cf. Nak. p. 1257a.

(19) Quotation unidentified. The four fruits of religious practice are "stream enterer" (*srotaāpanna*), "once returner" (*sakṛdāgāmin*), "non-returner" (*anāgāmin*) and *arhat*. See LVP's "Note sommaire sur le chemin" in AK v, pp. iv-xi, in particular pp. vi-vii, ix-x; also Lamotte, *Traité* I p. 130, n. 1 for the steps leading up to "stream entering" (*srotaāpatti*); AK vi pp. 194-277 for *srotaāpanna*, etc. and pp. 241-2 for *śrāmaṇyaphala*; Nak. 514b; Pr. 484.6-7, 485.8-487.4; May (1959) pp. 216-218 and n. 739.

(20) I.e. in chapters I (= CS IX) and III (= CS XI) respectively.

(21) Cf. §222a21, p. 123.

(22) More common is *bù xiāng lí* 不相離 = *aviyukta*, or *avinābhāva* ("necessarily connected"). It would seem that it is especially the Vaiśeṣika school which is being singled out here. The argument is similar to that in PV II k. 220 et seq. where Dharmakīrti argues against the Vaiśeṣika's idea of the *ātman* existing separately by saying that "necessarily when one is attached to the self, one will not be free of its possessions". *niyamenātmani snihyaṃs tadīye na virajyate* /. Cf. PVV ad k. 222 (= 220 in Miyasaka's edition): *yady apy ātmani snehavān tathāpy ātmīye sukhasādhane vairāgyān na saṃsaratīti cet / naitad yuktaṃ yata ātmani snihyan prīyamāṇas tadīya ātmīye sukhasādhane niyamena na virajyate 'bhiṣvajaty eva, tat katham ātmīyavirāgān muktiḥ / ātmasnehasyātmīyavairāgyavirodhitvāt*.

(23) Cf. for example Praśastapāda (p. 70.10-12), who holds that intelligence, pleasure, suffering, desire, hate, effort, merit, demerit, conditioning, number, size, separateness, contact and disjunction are all qualities belonging to the self. *tasya guṇāḥ buddhisukhaduḥkhecchādveṣaprayatnadharmādharmasaṃskārasaṃkhyāparimāṇapṛthaktva-saṃyogavibhāgāḥ* /.

(24) A valid homologous example should possess both the property to be proved (*sādhyadharma*) and the property which constitutes the reason (*hetu*). Failure to possess these properties leads to a fallacy of the example (*dṛṣṭāntābhāsa*). Cf. NP 3.3.1 for the five possible fallacies of the homologous example. See also Vidyābhūṣaṇa (1921-1971) pp. 296-297 and NM, k. 11 pp. 36 et seq. in Tucci and pp. 62 et seq. in Katsura (1981).

In Dharmapāla's reasoning, the subject (*dharmin*) would be "qualities such as suffering, pleasure, etc.", the *sādhyadharma* would be "not being absent in the self in nirvāṇa" and the reason would be "being a possession of the self". The opponent could not try to assert that there is a *dṛṣṭāntābhāsa*, for the example, "the nature of the self", would indeed not be absent in the self in nirvāṇa and would also be a possession of the self. Cf. the subsequent argumentation, where it is said that if the self at any time lacked its nature, it would simply be inexistent.

(25) If the adversary asserts that the self has no nature — which is tantamount to saying that it is inexistent — this statement will obviously contradict his previous position. NM gives five ways in which the thesis (*zōng* 宗 = *pakṣa*) can be contradicted: by one's own words; by one's previous position; by generally recognized statements; by direct perception or by inference. See NM, T. 1628 p. 1a, 15-21; Tucci pp. 6-7; Katsura (1977) pp. 113-115. NP 3.1 has roughly the same five and then adds four other fallacies to come to a total of nine *pakṣābhāsa* in all. For a thorough study, see the article by Masahiro Inami, "On *pakṣābhāsa*", forthcoming in the proceedings of the Second International Dharmakīrti Conference, Vienna.

Note that there are various formulations of the requirement that the thesis must be free from contradiction. Cf. PSVa 43a6-b2. NM k. 1 defines the thesis as: *svayaṃ sādhyatvenepsitaḥ pakṣo viruddhārthānirākṛtaḥ.* ("The thesis is something which [the proponent] himself intends to be proven [and which is] not negated by a contradicting proposition.") Skt. found in PVV ad PV IV, k. 86. Dharmakīrti in PV IV k. 86 et seq. shows that this formulation is not essentially different from the definition of the thesis in PS III, k. 2; see our fn. 49. For the argumentation in PV IV on these definitions, see Tillemans, "*Pramāṇavārttika* IV and its commentaries", forthcoming in the *Encyclopedia of Indian Philosophies*, volume on Mahāyāna Buddhism, Motilal Banarsidass, Delhi.

(26) For the use of the term *ākṣepahetu*, cf. MAV ad 11cd, ed. Nagao 22.5. Other references found in Nak. p. 326d and *Fǎ xiāng dà cí diǎn*, vol. 1, p. 1037, which gives references from the *Yogācārabhūmiśāstra*. The term is usually understood in the context of the ten causes, and means the latent karmic seeds (*bīja*) which will "propel" or "project" forth their results when other conditions are also present. Cf. *Siddhi* II, pp. 453-463, and p. 456 in particular. See also LVP (1913), p. 66: "*ākṣepahetu*, a. semences actuelles d'*avidyā*, etc., qui 'projettent' la renaissance [...]." In the passage from Dharmapāla, however, it seems that it is not strictly speaking the

latent *bījas* which are being discussed, but rather various *actions*, and hence the term is probably being employed in a less rigorous and technical fashion.

(27) For *vikurvaṇa*, see AK vii, p. 112, n. 3 and references therein: *vikurvaṇa* is classified as one of the ten sorts of *ṛddhi*. Cf. Mvyut section XXVI (*bodhisattvabalāni*) where *vikurvaṇabala* is classified as one of the ten powers of a bodhisattva. See also BHSD p. 481 s.v. *vikurvaṇa* and *Siddhi* II p. 633. Note that *shén biàn* can also equal *shén tōng* 神通 (*ṛddhi*). Cf. Nak. p. 795b. For *ṛddhi*, see AK vii p. 98, n. 1; pp. 112, 122; *Siddhi* II, pp. 792-4; *Traité* I p. 382, n. 2a.

(28) In k. 280 *parokṣa* is rendered into Chinese by *shēn shì* 深事. Thus, *shèn shēn* 甚深 could reasonably translate *atyantaparokṣa* here, although the usual equivalence is *gambhīra*. See Chapter II, B. p. 31 and Tillemans (1986a), pp. 37-38 and n. 21.

(29) Viz. those of body, speech and mind.

(30) To avoid an irritating over-repetition of the same hyperbolical superlatives, I have had to translate *wú liáng* 無量 in different ways: "immeasurable", "myriad".

(31) On these terms, see May (1959) n. 89, 581 for their general sense and numerous references to AK, *Siddhi* and *Traité*. Note that the Epistemological school, to which Dharmapāla very probably belonged, had a special position on *vikalpa*, understanding it as a process of associating a name with a thing, and thus creating distinctions such as substance, universals, etc. See en. 367.

(32) For *anuśaya* and *kleśa* ("passions"), see en. 87. The *Abhidharmakośa* speaks of eight and also ten ensnarements (*paryavasthāna*); see AK v, LVP p. 90 et seq.; see PSP p. 137.18-26 and Lamotte, *Traité* I p. 424 for the ten: anger (*krodha*), hypocrisy (*mrakṣa*), torpor (*styāna*), sloth (*middha*), regret (*kaukṛtya*), frivolity (*auddhatya*), disrespect (*āhrīkya*) impudence (*anapatrāpya*), avarice (*mātsarya*) and envy (*īrṣyā*). While the Vaibhāṣika accept ten *paryavasthāna*, there are also references to five hundred! See *Hōbōgirin*, s.v. *Bonnō*, p. 124 and *Traité* I p. 424, n. 3. Edgerton and others tend to translate the term as "possession", "obsession", which is a sense of the Skt., but is not clearly reflected in the Tibetan and Chinese. Lamotte translates *paryavasthāna* as *enveloppements*, which captures the sense of the Chinese ("bind"; "fetter") and the Tibetan *kun nas dkris pa* ("wrap up completely"; "ensnare"), but is perhaps a bit anomalous in formulae such as "the strong envelopings of the passions". I opt for "ensnarements", which seems to me closer to the Tibetan and Chinese. Finally, note that, following PSP and *Traité*, any passion can be termed *paryavasthāna* in that it ensnares or fetters the mind and thus makes an obstacle to virtue. PSP p. 137.18-19: *kun nas 'khri śiṅ sems la thams cad du dkris nas gnas pas kun nas dkris pa ste / dge ba'i phyogs la 'jug pa'i bar chad byed pa ñid do //.*

(33) Japanese transl. (Kyik p. 317.1) has *rú* 如 instead of *yán* 言

(34) For *quān fāng biàn* and *shàn quān fāng bián*, see Nak. pp. 434b and 849c respectively; see Lamotte (1962) n. 68 for two sorts of *upāyakauśalya*. The idea that only voidness or nirvāṇa is really true and that all else is false is supported by numerous references. Cf. *Majjhima* III 245.19-21: *etaṃ hi bhikkhu paramaṃ ariya saccaṃ yadidaṃ amosadhammaṃ nibbānaṃ*. Sanskrit in Pr. 41.4-5: *etad hi bhikṣavaḥ paramaṃ satyaṃ yad uta amoṣadharma nirvāṇaṃ sarvasaṃskārāś ca mṛṣā moṣadharmāṇaḥ*. Transl.: "Indeed, Monks, this is the ultimate truth: what is non-deceptive in character, nirvāṇa. Now, all conditionings are false and deceptive in character." Cf. M. av 119, 17-19 ed. LVP for the same passage with a few variants. MMK XIII, 1: *tan mṛṣā moṣa-dharma yad bhagavān ity abhāṣata / sarve ca moṣadharmāṇaḥ saṃskārās tena te mṛṣā //*. Elaboration on the above sūtra passage in Pr. ad MMK XIII, 1. My thanks to C. Scherrer-Schaub for references.

(35) The Japanese translator (Kyik p. 317.8) preferred to read *shì suǒ shì* 識所識 and *yán suǒ yán* 言所言 as conjunctive compounds, i.e."consciousness and what is known", "words and what they express". This version fits less well with the preceding statement and with the subsequent argumentation, where Dharmapāla only refutes what is understood *by* consciousness and what is expressed *by* words.

(36) The argument here is reminiscent of Dignāga's refutation of the Vaiśeṣika position that one and the same substance can be grasped by means of two different sense perceptions. See PSVa 19b3 (PSVb 100b2) et seq: *gal te yaṅ rdzas gcig pa dbaṅ po du ma'i gzuṅ bya yin no že na...* transl. Hattori (1968a) p. 44 et seq. In brief, Dignāga argued that the different senses, like sight, touch, etc., apprehend different objects, viz. colour, warmth and so forth. If the object of these different perceptions was the same then various absurdities would follow: there would be no difference between visual qualities such as colour and tactile qualities such as warmth; visual perception should be able to grasp tactile qualities; the variety of the senses would be pointless, etc. etc. In Dharmapāla's argument, the "object" of perception (*jìng* 境) which he is investigating and refuting is an external object (such as a vase, etc.). He then argues that because such an "object" would absurdly be many different and contradictory things according to the sense perceptions, it is unreal.

(37) *a)* The terms *shí* 實 and *shí yǒu* 實有 admit of numerous Skt. equivalents in H., just as the Chinese itself has various nuances ("real"; "substantial"; "true"; "in fact existent", "actual") according to the different contexts. I also translate *shí* according to context. Be all this as it may, it should be borne in mind that for the Buddhist, "substantially existent", "real", "true", etc. are synonyms.

b) For Buddhist Epistemologists the meaning of a word (*śabdārtha*) is always a conceptually created fiction, because it is a type of universal applying to several distinct things, and is thus not a particular (*svalakṣaṇa*) which has its own unique essence (*svarūpa*). Cf. PV III 287: *śabdārthagrāhi yad yatra taj jñānaṃ tatra kalpanā / svarūpaṃ ca na śabdārthas...* "Wherever it apprehends a word-meaning, that consciousness is a conceptualization. Nor does a word-meaning have its own essence..." Now, Dharmapāla is using a variety of the "neither one nor many" reasoning (*ekānekaviyoga-hetu*), where it is argued that a whole, such as a forest, cannot be identical to, or in some in way exist in the parts (viz. the trees), because it is one thing and the parts are many different things. See Chapt. III, B. pp. 63-64 and fn. 133, 134. In the Epistemological school, this style of reasoning is adapted to refute the reality of universals by treating the universal as a kind of whole and its instances as being analogous to parts. Thus, the universal, which is one thing, cannot be present in many instances (*anekavṛtti*). See PVV ad PV IV, k. 12 translated in Tillemans (1986b) pp. 156-159 and n. 62 for the corresponding PVin passages (i.e. P. 286a4-8). Prajñākaragupta's PVBh ad PV IV k. 12 gives a long elaboration of this style of argumentation in the Epistemological school, using it to refute, *inter alia*, the Naiyāyika's notion of time (*kāla*) and universals. Finally, see Tillemans (1982), (1983), (1984c) for Indian and Tibetan Mādhyamika uses of the different varieties of the "neither one nor many" reasoning, and in particular, its use in Śāntarakṣita's *Madhyamakālaṃkāra*, where it serves to refute all types of entities, be they espoused by Buddhists or non-Buddhists.

(38) Usually *zǒng* would mean "the whole" or "the collection" (*samudāya*), but here the use of this term is somewhat different as witnessed by the subsequent discussion. What is at stake are universals rather than wholes or collections. Cf. Nak. p. 876: *zǒng* = *sāmānya* and Tib. (Mvyut. 4443) *spyi* ("universal"). See also en. 43, 72.

(39) Taking the Vaiśeṣika standpoint, number (*saṃkhyā*) is one of the qualities (*guṇa*); "two and all the rest" (*dvitvādi*) is cited as an example of qualities inhering in their bases, i.e. substances. See VS 1.1.23 and *Praśastapādabhāṣya* p. 111 (ed. V.P. Dvivedin): *ekādivyavahārahetuḥ saṃkhyā / sā punar ekadravyā cānekadravyā ca / ... anekadravyā tu dvitvādikā parārdhāntā /*.

(40) *jiǎ shī shè* 假施設 = *jiǎ shè* 假設 = *jiǎ lì* 假立 = *prajñapti*. The term is used to indicate that some expression or notion has no objective counterpart in the world and is in that sense just an invention of language or thought. See en. 363. For the use of *prajñapti* in Madhyamaka contexts, see *Hōbōgirin, Chūdō,* p. 462. (There the Chinese term *jiǎ míng* 假名 [= *upādāya prajñapti*] is translated as "nom d'emprunt", "nom provisoire". While *jiǎ* does have a secondary sense of "borrow", its primary sense is "false", "untrue", and it seems to me that this sense might better capture the very frequent and important contrast which we find in Dharmapāla between *jiǎ* versus *shí* 實 ["real"; "true"; "substantial"].)

The Epistemologists, like the Mādhyamikas, also use the term *prajñapti* as meaning a notion or expression with no objective counterpart, although their general doctrinal position obviously differs. See PSVb, P. 97a7, trans. Hattori (1968a) p. 34 and n. 17 for *prajñaptisat* (*btags pa yod pa*) and *dravyasat*. The prime example of a designation in this system is a universal, whereas the only things which are substantially existent are particulars.

Note that subsequently the Tibetan dGe lugs pa epistemologists went so far as to incorporate this idea of mere invention, or mere designation (*btags pa tsam*), by language or thought in their definition of *sāmānyalakṣaṇa* (i.e. *spyi msthan*): *sgra rtog gis btags tsam yin gyi raṅ mtshan du ma grub pa* (see *bsDus grwa chuṅ* p. 7b, ed. T. Kelsang and S. Onoda [1985]). Transl.: "Something which is not established as a particular, but is merely designated by words and thought". A *svalakṣaṇa* (*raṅ mtshan*; "particular") is defined as a "dharma which is not merely designated, but exists due to its nature".

Finally, see also the **Upādāyaprajñaptiprakaraṇa* (*Qǔ yīn jiǎ shè lùn* 取因假設論 T. 1622) translated in Kitagawa (1973). This text, attributed to Dignāga, speaks of three sorts of designations: wholes (*yǒu fēn* 有分 = *avayavin*) continua (*xiāng xù* 相續 = *saṃtāna*) and different states / qualities (*fēn wèi chā bié* 分位差別 = *avasthāviśeṣa*). These "entities" do not themselves have any objective existence or *svabhāva* ("nature"), but are designated in dependence upon other things — probably *svalakṣaṇa* — which do have *svabhāva*. See Hattori (1988) pp. 42-44.

(41) Japanese translation (Kyik p. 317.16) reads *gòng* 共 instead of *jù* 俱 .

(42) Viz. substances (*dravya*), qualities (*guṇa*), actions (*karman*), the genus or universals (*sāmānya*), species or particulars (*viśeṣa*) and inherence (*samavāya*). See Frauwallner (1953-56), Vol. II, Potter (1977), Ui (1917), Foucher (1949) and Matilal (1977) for general accounts of the Vaiśeṣika categories. For the nine substances, see en. 61. For *sāmānya* and *viśeṣa*, see en. 53.

(43) The term is used in two primary senses and has many Sanskrit equivalents: *a) sāmānya*, a "universal" as opposed to particulars (*viśeṣa*) — this is what is at stake in the present context; *b) samudāya, samuccaya*, "collection"; "synthesis". See en. 38, 72.

(44) The argument is directed specifically against the Vaiśeṣikas, who held that all reality was subsumable under six categories of entities. A word can designate a number of entities only in virtue of some feature existing distinctly from the entities themselves and serving as grounds (*nimitta*) for applying that word. A problem then arises when we try to find the grounds for applying the most general terms like "*padārtha*": If there is some general nature of *all padārtha*, and if it is indeed something separate from *padārtha*, then it cannot itself be in one of those six categories, and by implication, must be unreal. It is interesting to note that Dharmapāla's argument seems to recur in Dharmakīrti's *Pramāṇavārttika* III (*pratyakṣa*) k. 158: *padārthaśabdaḥ kaṃ hetum anyaṃ ṣaṭsu* samīkṣate //*. Tib.: *drug rnams la ni tshig don sgra // rgyu gźan gaṅ la ltos par mthoṅ*. *Miyasaka ed.: *ṣaṭkaṃ*. D. Shāstrī reads *ṣaṭsu*, which seems preferable in view of Tib. *drug rnams la*. Cf. Tosaki (1979) Vol. I, pp. 256-7, cf. n. 128. Manorathanandin comments: *kiṃ cānuyāyī padārthaśabdaḥ ṣaṭsu padārtheṣu kam anyaṃ*

hetuṃ nimittaṃ pravṛttau samīkṣate / na hi ṣaṭpadārthātiriktaṃ kiṃcid asti //. lCaṅ skya grub mtha' (p. 56 Sarnath ed.) gives a good characterization of this argument against the Nyāya-Vaiśeṣika: *du ma la sgra gcig 'jug pa rgyu mtshan don gźan gyis khyab pa yaṅ mi 'thad de / tshig gi don drug la dṅos po źes pa'i sgra gcig 'jug pa yaṅ tshig gi don drug las gźan pa'i dṅos po la bltos par thal bar 'gyur pa'i phyir / ci ste de yaṅ yod do źe na / tshig gi don drug las gźan pa'i śes bya med par smras pa mi 'thad par 'gyur ro // 'di ni rnam 'grel le'u gsum pa'i rigs pa'o /.* "It is also incorrect [to say] that one word's being applied to many [things] must imply grounds [for the designation in question] which are separate objects. For, the same word "entity" applies to [all] six *padārtha*, but it would follow [absurdly] that [the word "entity"] would depend on an entity distinct from the six *padārtha*. [Objection:] Suppose one says that this exists too. [Reply:] Then it would be incorrect to assert that there are no knowables apart from the six *padārtha*. This is an argument in the third chapter of *Pramāṇavārttika*."

(45) *xìn jiě* 信解. The term figures repeatedly in this chapter (cf. 216c4, 28; 218a29; 218b2, 9, 14), and judging by the contexts, we conclude that it is probably being used in a general, relatively non-technical sense of "belief" or "conviction", rather than in its normal use as a translation of *śraddhādhimukti* ("faithful application") or *adhimukti* ("zealous application"). What is at stake in 216c4, for example, is simply belief or conviction in the statements found in the scriptures of the Tathāgata, and not *śraddhādhimukti*. Cf. Nak. p. 776a, which does attest the occasional use of *xìn jiě* for *pratyaya* and *saṃpratyaya* in MAV. Note too that in §215c16, k. 276 and §215c23 that, at least in this chapter, Xuán zàng seems to prefer *shèng jiě* 勝解 for *adhimukti*. For the use of *xìn jiě* in a technical sense as *śraddhādhimukti*, see AK vi LVP p. 196 and 274. The *Abhidharmakośa* makes a difference between two sorts of disciples, an inferior one who applies himself primarily through faith, and a superior one who is possessed of philosophical vision (*dṛṣṭiprāpta*).

(46) Similar passages in the *Pañcaviṃśatisāhasrikā Prajñāpāramitā*. T. VIII 223 vi 259c20-21; Skt. ed. N. Dutt p. 225, 23-24. Cf. *Śatasāhasrikā Prajñāpāramitā*, T. V 220 lxvi 309c5.

(47) *a) xìng xiāng* 性相 probably has to be taken here in the sense of *bhāvalakṣaṇa* ("the character of existence"; "the existential character"); see Nak. p. 714. In our en. 1 we saw instances of the term being used to refer to both conventional characters and ultimate natures. Here, however, *zhū fǎ xìng xiāng* 諸法性相 seems to be used much in the same way as the sūtra's use of *zhū fǎ shí xìng* 諸法實性 ("the true nature of all dharmas"), i.e. the ultimate nature of dharmas.

b) zhū fǎ xìng xiāng figures in Vijñānavāda literature with a number of different senses: Nak. p. 714bc gives four different uses, the principal three of which treat the compound as conjunctive, i.e. the nature (*xìng* 性) and the character (*xiāng* 相); see Takakusu (1947), chapter on the Hossō doctrine (i.e. Vijñānavāda), which is also known as *shōzōgaku* (= *xìng xiāng xué* 性相學), "the study of the nature and the characters"; see also D. Shimaji, *Historique du système Vijñaptimātra*, p. 34 in S. Lévi (1932), who explains that the term *xiāng* 相 in such phrases as *xìng xiāng bié guān* 性相別觀 ("separate inspection of the nature and the characters") means the conventional phenomena, while *xìng* is their ultimate nature. As these writers make clear, the conjunctive interpretation of the term is the usual one in Vijñānavāda contexts. We do also find conjunctive uses in this chapter of Dharmapāla; see en. 69, 114 and §220a24.

c) The term does also figure often in the *Guǎng bǎi lùn shì lùn* — eg. T. 1571 iii 198b25; iv 206a17; iv 215c14 (see en. 1), v 211b25, viii 230a3 —, but it is unlikely that it must always be taken in a conjunctive sense. Tucci (1925) pp. 529-530 n. 1, in translating Dharmapāla's commentary to CS k. 221, takes the Chinese compound as the equivalent of *bhāvalakṣaṇa*.

d) Finally note that *zhū fǎ shí xìng* and the present usage of *zhū fǎ xìng xiāng* seem to be close to that of the term *zhū fǎ shí xiāng* 諸法實相 , which figures again and again in Kumārajīva's translation of the *Mahāprajñāpāramitāśāstra* (*Dà zhì dù lùn* 大智度論 , and is, as Lamotte remarks, the pivotal term in this text's explanation of voidness. See *Traité* III, xlii and ibid. p. 1501 (quoted below in our en. 138) for a description of this "true character of things". In our text, Dharmapāla, as rendered by Xuán zàng, also uses this term to refer to voidness; see §221c20. It should be noted that the Japanese translator (Kyik p. 318.2) had qualms about our text's use of *xìng xiāng* and chose to read *zhū fǎ fǎ xiāng* 諸法法相, a reading which seems less plausible. At any rate, *dharmāṇāṃ dharmalakṣaṇa*, which literally ought to be rendered as *zhū fǎ fǎ xiāng*, is attested in Nak. 691a as a Sanskrit equivalent, amongst others, of *zhū fǎ shí xiāng*.

(48) For *apratigha* and *sapratigha*, see May (1959) n. 195, 670. *sapratigha*, "having resistance" is a characteristic of form (*rūpa*), i.e. matter. See AK i, LVP p. 51. The point, then, is that voidness, or the true nature of dharmas, is not in any way obstructed or blocked by material things, nor does it itself block them — it is neither *suǒ duì* 所對 nor *néng duì* 能對 .

(49) Cf. §217a28, *wú xiāng wú èr gù shuō wéi yī* 無相無二故說爲一 Cf. *Traité* V p. 2345 which speaks of "le Nirvāṇa de caractère unique (*ekalakṣaṇa-nirvāṇa*)".

(50) Here Dharmapāla's thought corresponds quite well to the third of the three "absences of nature" (*wú xìng* 無性 = *niḥsvabhāvatā*) which figure as negative counterparts in connection with the Vijñānavāda doctrine of the three natures (*svabhāva*) or three characters (*trīṇi lakṣaṇāni*) of dharmas. The canonical source for the three absences of nature is *Saṃdhinirmocanasūtra,* Chapt. VII §2-13 (ed. and transl. Lamotte [1935]; see also *Siddhi* II p. 556ff for the three *niḥsvabhāvatā*s, viz. the absence of nature concerning characters (*lakṣaṇaniḥsvabhāvatā*), concerning production (*utpattiniḥsvabhāvatā*) and the absence of nature concerning the ultimate (*paramārtha-*

niḥsvabhāvatā). The first *niḥsvabhāva* pertains to *parikalpitasvabhāva* and is the unreality of the thoroughly imagined (*parikalpita*) characters themselves; the second is the unreality of any self-production of dependent phenomena (*paratantra*); the third *niḥsvabhāva* is the ultimate status of dharmas and is the negative correlate of *pariniṣpannasvabhāva* ("the nature which is thoroughly established") — this *niḥsvabhāvatā*, then, equals the real nature of dharmas, a nature which is free of duality, characters and other thoroughly imagined natures (*parikalpitasvabhāva*). Cf. D. Shimaji p. 38 in Lévi (1932). On the three natures, viz. *parikalpita, paratantra* and *pariniṣpanna*, see our Chapter III B. "Dharmapāla on perception", and *Siddhi* II p. 514ff.

(51) Equivalence attested in H. 423. *bhāvāntara* has the sense of a "reality sui generis". See Stcherbatsky (1930) vol. II, p. 93, n. 4. Dharmapāla is presumably refuting that voidness could be something existing in its own right, over and above the things which are void.

(52) In what follows, Dharmapāla's argumentation against the Vaiśeṣikas and Sāṃkhyas shows many points of similarity with his discussion of these two schools in the *Chéng wéi shí lùn*. Cf. T. 1585 i 2b23-2c22 for the Sāṃkhyas (transl. in *Siddhi* I pp. 23-26) and 2c22-3b7 (transl. *Siddhi* pp. 26-29) for the Vaiśeṣikas.

(53) For the usual six Vaiśeṣika categories, see en. 42. To examine what perception is in general for the Vaiśeṣika, in the *Vaiśeṣikasūtras* we have a somewhat more complex explanation of perception than the classic definition which can be found in the *Nyāyasūtras* of Gautama. In Book III, Kaṇāda speaks of cognitions proceeding from a contact between the mental organ, the self, the sense organ and the object. (Gautama in NS 1.1.4 had just spoken of perception [*pratyakṣa*] as a contact between the object and the sense organs.) VS 3.1.13: *ātmendriyamano'rthasannikarṣād* yan niṣpadyate tad anyat.* *Sinha's text leaves out *manas*; see Hattori (1968a) p. 135, n. 4.4. for some textcritical remarks. Note that Candrānanda's *vṛtti* (ed. Jambuvijayaji p. 27.12) speaks of a "fourfold contact" (*catuṣṭayasannikarṣa*), as does Dharmapāla in his discussion below (his Chapter V §227b8 et seq.) of the Vaiśeṣika theory of perception. See also en. 60 for Śrīdhara and Praśastapāda on the fourfold contact.

Translation of VS 3.1.13: "That [cognition] which is produced from the contact between the self, the sense organ, the mental organ and the object is other [than fallacious]." Praśastapāda (p. 186) speaks of four sorts of knowledge (*vidyā*): perception, inference, memory and what stems from authority. Perception (*pratyakṣa*) is defined as a knowledge arising in dependence on one or more of the organs, including the mental organ: *tatrākṣam akṣaṃ pratītyotpadyata iti pratyakṣam / akṣāṇīndriyāṇi ghrāṇarasanacakṣustvakchrotamanāṃsi ṣaṭ /*. See also Ui (1917) pp. 152-153; cf. Matilal (1977) pp. 65-66 for a comparison between Candramati and Praśastapāda's accounts of cognition. For further details concerning the Vaiśeṣika account of perception, see also en. 60.

The first five of the six Vaiśeṣika *padārtha* are said to be perceptible, but inherence (*samavāya*) is not. See Ui (1917), pp. 67-68. Cf. also Kuī jī, T. XLII 1830 i (*mò*) 261a15:

> 有彼本許六句義者前之五句現量所得
>
> "In this work, for those who maintain six categories, the first five categories are accessible to direct perception."

For the ways in which universals are perceived, see Potter (1977) p. 137. Note however that not *all* entities which fall under these five categories are perceptible, i.e. there are, for example, substances such as subtle atoms which are simply too small to be perceptible. Cf. VS 4.1.6. Praśastapāda (pp. 328-329) explains that inherence is one, i.e. an indivisible thing, and that because it has a relation of identity (*tādātmya*) or self-occurrence (*svātmavṛtti*) with its relata, it cannot be perceived but must be inferred: *ata evātīndriyaḥ sattādīnām iva pratyakṣeṣu vṛttyabhāvāt svātmagatasaṃvedanābhāvāc ca / tasmād iha buddhyanumeyaḥ samavāya iti.* Cf. Potter (1977) pp. 302-303; p. 683 in the translation of G. Jha (Chaukhambha, Varanasi, reprinted 1982).

Interestingly enough, Dignāga, in the *Nyāyamukha*, discusses the Vaiśeṣika position that vases, etc. (i.e. substances), number, etc. (i.e. qualities), going upwards, etc. (i.e motions), existence (i.e. the genus) and vaseness, etc. (i.e. species) are directly perceived, arguing that these "perceptions" are fallacious in that they would involve conceptualization. Conspicuously, he leaves out inherence. T. XXXII, no. 1628, i, 3b28-3c1:

> 如是一切俗有中瓶等數等舉等有性瓶性智皆似現量
> 於實有中作餘行相假合餘義分別轉故
>
> "Thus as regards conventional existents, the cognitions of vases, etc., number, etc., upward motion, etc., existence [and] vaseness are all fallacious direct perceptions, for there is conceptualization which, with regard to what really exists, fabricates other [different] characters and imputes connections with other things."

(Note that Tucci's translation [pp. 51-52] is unsatisfactory in that, *inter alia*, he did not translate *yǒu xìng* 有性 , which is important here because it shows that Dignāga probably understood *sāmānya* as being only "existence".)

In translating and explaining Dignāga, it is probably preferable to render *sāmānya* as "genus" and *viśeṣa* as "species". This is in keeping with Hattori's style of translation in his work on Dignāga, and makes good sense in that Dignāga, like the author of the *Vaiśeṣikasūtra*, seems to have taken *sāmānya* in Vaiśeṣika contexts to be the all-embracing universal, viz. existence, and took *viśeṣa* as meaning a lesser universal, such as substanceness or vaseness. When, for example, Dignāga cites VS 8.1.6, his commentator Jinendrabuddhi explains *sāmānya* as meaning *mahāsāmānya* (i.e. existence) and *viśeṣa* means the other *sāmānyas* such as substanceness (*dravyatva*). See Hattori (1968a) p. 137, n. 4.15. Thus, in Dignāga *sāmānya* is understood as what Praśastapāda would term a "higher" (*para*) universal, and *viśeṣa* is taken as a lower universal. Cf. Praśastapāda (p. 11): *sāmānyaṃ dvividhaṃ paramaparaṃ ca...*

H. Ui (1917), however, pointed out (pp. 69-71 et seq.) that the term *tóng yì* 同異 in Dharmapāla is being used to mean *sāmānyaviśeṣa* much in the same way as Candramati used it in the *Daśapadārthaśāstra*, i.e. as a limited universal, such as potness. (From this he deduced various conclusions about the history of Vaiśeṣika thought.) Candramati had, in addition to *sāmānya* (= existence) and *viśeṣa* (= ultimate particular, i.e. *antyaviśeṣa*), introduced a category termed "both" (*jū fēn* 俱分): on the basis of an occurrence of *tóng yì* near the end of Candramati's text, Ui argued that this must be *sāmanyaviśeṣa*, where this compound is to be taken as meaning just one type of thing, i.e. the "limited universal", and not two categories, viz. *sāmānya* + *viśeṣa*. This odd sense of the term seems to be attested in other texts of the same general period, such as Śaṅkarasvāmin's *Nyāyapraveśa*, (cf. Tachikawa [1971] transl. p. 126, Sanskrit: 3.2.3 example #3 in Tachikawa's text). Note that the term *sāmānyaviśesa* may very well also be used in a similar sense in the *Vākyapadīyavṛtti* ad Chapter I (*Brahmakāṇḍa*) k. 23: *sā ceyam ākṛtiḥ śabdatvasāmānyaviśeṣād anyā* /. See Biardeau (1964) pp. 52-53.

Now, Ui gave a number of references to the *Chéng wéi shí lùn* of Dharmapāla / Xuán zàng, citing in particular page 2b of an older edition of the canon. As far as I can tell, the *Chéng wéi shí lùn* section at stake must be T. 1585 i 2c22 - 3b7 (transl. *Siddhi* I pp. 26-29), but here Dharmapāla / Xuán zàng definitely does not explicitly state a neat list of the six categories, including the problematic *sāmānyaviśeṣa*. Rather, as de la Vallée Poussin had already pointed in *Siddhi* p. 28 n. 1, Ui frequently cited the commentary by Kuī jī, viz. the *Chéng wéi shí lùn shù jì* 成唯識論述記 T. 1830. And in fact, it is there in Kuī jī's commentary, which is giving a kind of introduction to the discussion in *Chéng wéi shí lùn* 2c22ff, that we find a nicely numbered list of the categories. T. 1830 i (*mò*) 255c15-17:

> 一實二徳三業四有五同異六和合　此依百論及此本破唯有六句義法
>
> "The first is substance, the second is quality, the third is action, the fourth is existence, the fifth is limited universal (*sāmānyaviśeṣa*), the sixth is inherence. These are refuted by the *Śataśāstra* [i.e. here 百論 = 廣百論, the text on which Dharmapāla comments] as well as by the present work [viz. the *Chéng wéi shí lùn*]. There are just six categories."

To conclude from this mass of data, we shall prudently follow Kuī jī (and Ui's) lead in taking the fifth category in Dharmapāla as being *sāmānyaviśeṣa*, understood as a limited universal — the various "reasons for" seem more convincing than those "against". Nonetheless, the following reservations are in order: the issue is not clear-cut, and certainly cannot be decided just by a quotation from a later Chinese commentator such as Kuī jī; in contrast to Candramati, it is clear that the Vaiśeṣika system which Dharmapāla is discussing has only six categories, and in the context of the argumentation in his fourth chapter (= CS XII), he enumerates them (viz. *shí, dé, yè, tóng, yì, hé hé*) but never seems to speak of two separate categories, i.e. *yǒu* 有

(*sattā* ="existence") and *tóng yì* 同異 (*sāmānyaviśeṣa*). Finally, it may be worthwhile to note that Louis de la Vallée Poussin was faced with a similar problem as to how to translate *tóng yì* in the passage 故同異性唯假施設 T. 1585 i 3a25-25; *Siddhi* I p. 28. He opted for the conjunctive rendering of the compound: "Concluons que tous ces genres ou espèces n'ont qu'une valeur de désignation."

(54) For the Sāṃkhya's definition of perception (*pratyakṣa*) or "what is seen" (*dṛṣṭa*), see SK k. 5, *prativiṣayādhyavasāyo dṛṣṭam...* Gauḍapāda's *Bhāṣya: prativiṣayeṣu śrotrādīnāṃ śabdādiviṣayeṣu adhyavasāyo dṛṣṭaṃ pratyakṣam ity arthaḥ.* "*Dṛṣṭa* or perception is the apprehension of the respective objects of the [senses such as] the ear, etc., viz. the objects, sound and so forth". Cf. §217c14 and en. 65. Dignāga, however, in criticizing the Sāṃkhya theory of perception, used a definition mentioned in the *Yuktidīpikā*, p. 3.20-21 (ed. Pandeya) : *śrotrādivṛttiḥ pratyakṣam* ("The operation of the [senses such as] the ear, etc. is perception"). See PS I, Hattori (1968a) p. 52 and n. 5.1. This latter definition is that of Vārṣagaṇya = Vṛṣagaṇa. See Frauwallner (1958) on the Sāṃkhya epistemology of Vṛṣagaṇa as can be gleaned from PS and PST. The full definition of Vṛṣagaṇa as found in PST and in the *Nyāyāgamānusāriṇī Nayacakravṛtti* of Siṃhasūri (see Frauwallner [1958] p. 124 and Hattori [1968a] pp. 148-149, n. 5.2) is as follows: *śrotratvakcakṣurjihvāghrāṇānāṃ manasādhiṣṭhitā vṛttiḥ śabdasparśarūparasagandheṣu yathākramaṃ grahaṇe vartamānā pramāṇaṃ pratyakṣam*. Transl. Frauwallner (1958) p. 127: "Die vom Denken geleitete Tätigkeit des Gehörs, der Haut, des Auges, der Zunge und des Geruchs, welche sich der Reihe nach beim Erfassen des Tones, der Berührung, der Form, des Geschmacks und des Geruchs betätigt, ist das Erkenntnismittel sinnliche Wahrnehmung." Dharmapāla seems to allude to this position in the next chapter, viz. his commentary on CS XIII. See §228b29 and en. 343.

For a general account of the Sāṃkhya system, its history and its twenty-five elements (*tattva*), see Frauwallner (1953-56), Vol. I, p. 275 et seq., Hulin (1978), Larson (1969), Garbe (1894). The three qualities (*guṇa*), viz. "ontological excellence" (*sattva*), "agitation" (*rajas*) and "dullness" (*tamas*), are inherent in and are the ontological constituents of the Primordial Nature (*prakṛti*), which, according to the different combinations of these qualities, makes up the various coarse objects in the world. For the process of "evolution" of *prakṛti*, see en. 68. In effect, then, when one perceives an object, one must perceive (in some fashion or another) the qualities; note that this position is stated in its various forms and is subjected to intense scrutiny by Dignāga in PS I. To take an example of one Sāṃkhya position:. "Since *sattva*, etc. are not [essentially] different from sound and other such [objects of the senses], they are apprehended [by the senses] like sound, etc." (transl. Hattori 1968a, p. 55).

Finally note that *lè* 樂 in this portion of Dharmapāla's text refers to *sattva* (one of the qualities) and *kǔ* 苦 refers to *rajas*, although literally they, of course, mean pleasure (*sukha*) and suffering (*duḥkha*) respectively. Cf. Nak. p. 1406 *raku* 樂 . Dharmapāla, or perhaps Xuán zàng, seems to have chosen to call the qualities by the terms for their corresponding feelings: *sattva* is associated with pleasure, *rajas* with suffering and *tamas* with bewilderment (*moha*). Cf. SK k. 12: *prītyaprītiviṣādātmakāḥ ... guṇāḥ.*

Gauḍapāda: *tatra prītyātmakaṃ sattvaṃ prītiḥ sukhaṃ tadātmakam iti / aprītyātmakaṃ rajaḥ aprītir duḥkham / viṣādātmakaṃ tamaḥ viṣādo mohaḥ /*. The same indirect way of referring to the qualities also occurs also in PS and PV's discussion of the Sāṃkhyas. Cf. the *Jīn qī shí lùn* 金七十論 (**Suvarṇasaptati*) k. 13, where Paramārtha uses *xǐ* 喜 ("joy"), *yōu* 憂 ("suffering") and *àn* 闇 ("stupor") for the terms *sattva*, *rajas* and *tamas* respectively. See also Takakusu (1904) p. 996, n. 1 for other Chinese renditions of the three *guṇas*. So, *lè děng* 樂等, which in fact more precisely corresponds to *sukhādi*, does refer to *sattvādi*, i.e. the three qualities; for the sake of convenience I will therefore generally translate by "*sattva*, etc.", instead of saying something like "[the three qualities which are of the nature of] pleasure, etc." Cf. §217c16.

(55) See en. 40 and 363.

(56) In Vaiśeṣika contexts it makes better sense to translate *sè* = *rūpa* as "colour", which is one of the *guṇas*. This is borne out in other chapters of CS where the Vaiśeṣika theory is discussed (e.g. CS XIV). In Buddhist and Sāṃkhya contexts, the usual translation, viz. "form", is to be maintained.

(57) Dharmapāla is arguing that inherence and universals are similar, according to Vaiśeṣika philosophy, in being unique entities, present indistinguishably in all their bases. Thus, if they are alike, then it should also follow that universals are not perceptible, just as inherence is not perceptible. But this runs counter to the Vaiśeṣika position on the perceptibility of universals. For the "oneness" and the imperceptibility of inherence, see the references to Praśastapāda in en. 53. For *sāmānya*, see e.g. Annambhaṭṭa's *Tarkasaṃgraha*: *nityam ekam anekānugataṃ sāmānyam* ("Genus /universal is permanent, one [and] inherent in many [instances]"); see Foucher (1949) pp. 164-165. Note that Annambhaṭṭa follows Praśastapāda's understanding of *sāmānya* as including higher and lower universals, viz. existence and substanceness, etc. respectively. See also en. 53 for indications on the Vaiśeṣika's position that universals *are* perceptible.

(58) Dharmapāla had previously argued that universals, which are designated upon various dharmas, cannot be directly perceived. So analogously for vases, cloths, etc.

(59) In the Vaiśeṣika system the action at stake is movement. Cf. *Tarkasaṃgraha*: *calanātmakaṃ karma* ("Action is movement"); Foucher (1949) p. 163.

(60) Dharmapāla is referring to the Vaiśeṣika's position that perceptions of substances depend on the other categories. Cf. §224a7. For example, the *Vaiśeṣikasūtra* states that "[cognition] in respect of substances, qualities and actions, depends on the *sāmānya* ('genus' / 'universal') and *viśeṣa* ('species' /'particular')" (VS 8.1.6: *sāmānyaviśeṣāpekṣaṃ dravyaguṇakarmasu*) and that "[cognition] with regard to substance depends on substance, qualities and action" (VS 8.1.7: *dravye dravyaguṇakarmāpekṣam*).

In the latter case, for example, the point is that in cognitions of states of affairs such as when "a white cow, possessing a bell, goes", there is a quality (viz. white), a substance (viz. the bell) and an action (viz. going) which must be apprehended along with the substance, the cow. (Cf. Śaṃkara Miśra's commentary ad VS 8.1.7 in N. Sinha's ed. and transl.)

Dharmapāla's strategy in attacking the Vaiśeṣika's position is to consider the various possibilities where a cognition of a substance would depend on other categories. In each case his argument seems to be the same: if a cognition of something in category *A* is brought about by a non-*A*, then this cognition is not a *direct perception* of *A*. The underlying thought would be that if we directly perceive *A*, then it must be *A*, and not something else, which is responsible for our perceptions, an idea which would seem to be implied by the Vaiśeṣika's own explanation of perception as being dependent on the contact between the sense organ and its object. Cf. VS 3.1.13, en. 53.

Note that Praśastapāda speaks of two kinds of perception (*pratyakṣa*) of substances: (1) the mere perception of the substance in its own nature; (2) perception arising from contact between the mental organ and the self and depending on qualifiers (*viśeṣaṇa*) such as *sāmānya*, *viśeṣa*, substances, qualities and actions. As Hattori (1968b) p. 162 et seq. points out, Praśastapāda's formulation of (1) is based on VS 4.1.6 and (2) is clearly based on VS 8.1.6-7. Cf. Schmithausen (1970) n. 7. It may well be this second type of perception which Dharmapāla has in mind too. See *Praśastapādabhāṣya*, pp. 186.14-19: *dravye tāvad trividhe* mahaty anekadravyavattvodbhūtarūpaprakāśacatuṣṭayasannikarṣād dharmādisāmagrye ca svarūpālocanamātrakam / sāmānyaviśeṣadravyaguṇakarmaviśeṣaṇāpekṣād ātmamanaḥsannikarṣāt pratyakṣam utpadyate sad dravyaṃ pṛthivī viṣāṇī śuklo gaur gacchatīti /*. *Read *trividhe* rather than *dvividhe*; see Hattori (1968b) n. 2. "Firstly, with regard to three sorts of substance: in the case of a large [substance], then due to the fourfold contact, a manifestation of a distinct colour and the fact that [the substance] possesses many [component] substances, and given that there exists the collection [of causes] such as merit and so forth, there is then [perception] which is just a representation of [the substance in] its own nature. [Also] perception arises from the contact between the self and the mental organ, and in dependence on qualifiers [such as] *sāmānya*, *viśeṣa*, substances, qualities and actions, as [when one thinks] 'The existent substance, which is earth and is a horned, white cow, is going'". Śrīdhara (*Nyāyakandalī*, pp. 188 et seq.) glosses the "fourfold contact" as between the self, *manas* ("mind"; "mental organ"), the sense organs and their objects. He terms the first sort of perception *nirvikalpaka* ("non-conceptual") and the second sort *savikalpaka* ("conceptual") and explains that in Praśastapāda's example of *savikalpakapratyakṣa*, the words "existent substance", "earth", "what has horns", "white cow", "goes" show that the perception is qualified (*viśiṣṭa*) by the *sāmānya*, by earthness (i.e. a *viśeṣa*), by a substance, by a quality and by an action respectively. *Nyāyakandalī* p. 190: *...tasmāt sad dravyam iti sāmānyaviśiṣṭaṃ pṛthivīti pṛthivītvaviśiṣṭaṃ viṣāṇīti dravyaviśiṣṭaṃ śuklo gaur iti guṇaviśiṣṭaṃ gacchatīti karmaviśiṣṭaṃ pratyakṣaṃ syāt.* (Note that my translation of Praśastapāda's example is closer to that of Potter [1977] p. 294 and Jha p. 391 than to Hattori [1968a] p. 138, n. 16, who translates by a series of small sentences:

"'[this] substance exists,' '[this substance is] earth,' '[this is] the horned,' '[this is] white,' or '[this] cow goes.'" Cf. Schmithausen op. cit. n. 7). Schmithausen (1970) brings some important modifications to Hattori's general stance in (1968b), notably the idea that *nirvikalpaṃ pratyakṣam* does *not* see the object as an undifferentiated composite of the categories, but rather sees the substance.

Finally, note that in the *Pratyakṣa* chapter of the *Pramāṇasamuccaya*, Dignāga also argues against VS 8.1.6-7, citing them explicitly, and also arguing that perceptions in which the object is cognized as dependent on other categories are impossible given the Vaiśeṣika's view that perception is produced from the contact between the object and the sense organ. See Hattori (1968a) pp. 43-44 and n. 15 and 16. Jinendrabuddhi's *Pramāṇasamuccayaṭīkā* here gives a similar example to that found in Praśastapāda.

(61) I.e. cognitions of substances. Of the nine kinds of substance recognized by the Vaiśeṣika — viz. earth (*pṛthivī*), water (*ap*), heat (*tejas*), air (*vāyu*), space (*ākāśa*), time (*kāla*), direction (*diś*), selves (*ātman*) and mental organs (*manas*) (cf. VS 1.1.4) —, the first three are grasped by the senses, whereas the latter six can only be inferred. Cf. Potter (1977) p. 87, Hattori (1968a) p. 144, n. 54. Praśastapāda p. 24: *trayāṇāṃ [= pṛthivyaptejasāṃ] pratyakṣatvarūpavattvadravatvāni.*

(62) The refutation seems to turn on the previously mentioned point that one does not perceive substance alone, but in dependence upon, or via, other *padārtha* such as actions and qualities. See en. 60. But then if a substance cognition which is brought about by substances also depends on non-substances such as qualities, etc., then the situation is indeed similar to what was discussed in connection with substance cognitions brought about through qualities or actions. Just as these latter substance cognitions could not be direct perceptions, so also cognitions of vases, etc. cannot be direct perceptions.

(63) Dharmapāla has refuted that substance cognitions are direct perceptions because they depend on other categories. He now wants to apply the same line of argument to cognitions of qualities, actions, universals and inherence.

(64) Although one classifies a cognition of a pot, for example, as a cognition of a substance, in fact it must also be connected with, or conditioned by, non-substances such as qualities, etc. Dharmapāla would seem to be referring to this point when he speaks of "[merely] designated connections": the cognition of *A* is only thought to be connected with *A*; in fact it is also connected with non-*A*'s.

Note that we find the same argument in the *Chéng wéi shí lùn*, i 3b3-7:

又緣實智非緣離識實句自體現量智攝假合生故　如德智等
廣說乃至緣和合智非緣離識和合自體現量智攝假合生故　如實智等
故勝論者實等句義 亦是隨情妄所施設

LVP translates (*Siddhi*, p. 29):

> "Inversement, la connaissance (*jñāna*, savoir) qui porte sur les *dravyas* n'est pas comprise dans une connaissance immédiate qui porterait sur une nature propre de *dravya* existant à part du Vijñāna, parce qu'elle naît d'un complexe de causes, comme la connaissance des *guṇas*, etc. Et de même jusque: la connaissance qui porte sur le *samavāya* n'est pas comprise dans une connaissance immédiate qui porterait sur une nature propre de *samavāya* existant à part du Vijñāna, parce qu'elle naît d'un complexe de causes comme la connaissance des *dravyas*, etc.
>
> Conclusion: les *padārthas* des Vaiśeṣikas n'existent qu'en opinion (*ruci*); ce sont de simples dénominations."

As for the phrase *jiă hé shēng* 假合生 , LVP translates this non-literally as "naître d'un complexe de causes". He is partially justified by Kuī jī's commentary, T. 1830 i (*mó*) 261c20: 先假合生者顯藉多法 . "Above, '*jiă hé shēng*' shows reliance on many [different] dharmas." And indeed, Kuī jī's commentary develops the details of this explanation. However, it seems to me that the point is not that *jiă hé shēng* itself *means* "production from various causes", but rather that since there are various different causes involved, the link between the cognition of *A* and *A* itself is unreal, and mind-invented. Note that this conclusion that substance cognitions are not of an external object but of something essentially mind-invented is clearly the thrust of the *Chéng wéi shí lùn* passage cited above. Most likely, in our chapter of the *Guăng băi lùn shì lùn*, Dharmapāla's argument is ultimately trying to arrive at the same conclusion; in the Epistemologist's system, if something is not an object of direct perception, it must be mind-invented, i.e. by *vikalpa*.

(65) See en. 54. Parallel passages in *Siddhi* pp. 23-26. See T. 1585 i 2b23ff. The discussion seems to turn on the Sāṃkhya principle *guṇasaṃdrāvo dravyam* "substance is a composite of the *guṇas*." See en. 219 and Wezler (1986).

(66) There seems to be a deliberate parallel with the earlier discussion of *sāmānyalakṣaṇa*. See §217a7.

(67) See en. 54.

(68) In the Sāṃkhya system, the Primordial Nature, which is composed of the three qualities, undergoes a series of transformations (*biàn* 變 = *pariṇāma*) to become the diverse objects in the world. From the Primordial Nature evolves the intellect (*buddhi*) or "great one" (*mahat*), which in turn evolves into the ego (*ahaṃkāra*), and then the five subtle elements (*tanmātra*), and these in turn into the five gross elements (*bhūta*), the five sense organs, the five organs of action and the mind. See Frauwallner (1953-56) Vol. I, p. 348 et seq. Note that because of the Sāṃkhya's doctrine of *satkār-*

yavāda (i.e. the doctrine that an effect already exists in a hidden fashion in the cause prior to its appearance), there is no difference between the diverse objects which are the effects and the *guṇas* or Primordial Nature which is the cause. The effect is a manifesting of what was, in fact, already there. On *satkāryavāda*, see SK k. 9 and Gauḍapāda; for elements of Āryadeva's critique in CS XI and *Bǎi lùn* see Honda (1974), p. 489. For the process of transformation from unmanifest (*avyakta*) to manifest, see SK k. 16 and 22.

(69) Note that here understanding the argumentation in Dharmapāla's commentary presupposes that *xìng xiāng* 性相 be interpreted as a conjunctive compound. Cf. en. 1, 47, 114.

(70) Cf. *Siddhi*, p. 24 for the same argument about the nature (i.e. the *guṇas*) and the characters. In PS I's refutation of the Sāṃkhyas, we find a somewhat similar dialectic of one object versus many qualities.

(71) See Gauḍapāda's *bhāṣya* to SK k. 38.

(72) Cf. *Siddhi*, p. 25: "Les trois Guṇas sont 'particuliers' (*bhinna* ...) ayant chacun une nature à part; le Mahat (et les autres Tattvas) est 'synthétique' (*tsong* ... *sāmānya*)*, car il constitue un seul et indivisible Dharma. Cependant le Mahat = les trois Guṇas (comme l'or et les joyaux): le 'synthétique' est 'les particuliers'. — Vous devez donc ou nier l'unité du Mahat ou nier la triplicité des Guṇas." Neither in the *Siddhi* and its commentary (see Kuī jī, T. 1830 i 254b12 et seq.), nor in our text is it clear, however, which historical Sāṃkhya, if any, Dharmapāla is arguing against.

*See LVP's note on p. 25 for the numerous Skt. equivalences of *zǒng* 總, amongst which we find *samudāya* ("collection") and *samuccaya* ("synthesis"). Cf. en. 38, 43. The term seems to be used here in a fashion which is somewhat different from that of the Buddhists and the Vaiśeṣikas, where it means a "universal" (*sāmānya*) or a "general nature". Furthermore, for the Sāṃkhyas, it is usually the Primordial Nature and the *guṇas* which are *sāmānya* and the elements which are *viśeṣa*, the cardinal tenet being the non-difference of the two. (See Frauwallner [1953-56] Vol. I, pp. 398-400 for the Sāṃkhya's adaptation of Vaiśeṣika categories.) However, here the situation seems to be contrary: the *guṇas* are being termed "individual", "distinct", "particular", while form and so forth are "synthetic". What seems to be at stake is the part-whole relation, rather than that between particulars and universals. Once again, the view invoked seems to be that things are *guṇasaṃdrāva*, or what is equivalent, *guṇasamudāya*. See en. 219.

(73) Japanese transl. (Kyik p. 320.14) reads *yī zǒng yī bié* 一總一別 instead of *yī zǒng èr bié* 一總二別.

(74) Cf. *Siddhi* p. 25: "Le Sāṃkhya dira que la nature de chaque Guṇa comporte trois caractères (c'est-à-dire les caractères des trois Guṇas): nous voyons des

choses unes, parce que ces caractères, amalgamés (*houo* ... *tsa*...), sont difficiles à reconnaître." What follows in our text is also more or less mirrored in *Siddhi*. Cf. *Yuktidīpikā ad* SK k. 13 which also discusses the problem: *eko guṇas trirūpaḥ / sarve vā sarvarūpāḥ* (ed. Pandeya p. 60, line 24). "One *guṇa* has three characters. Or, all have all characters." The answer is that the *guṇas* mutually beget each other (*anyonya-jananavṛttayaḥ*), but do not have "mixed natures". *Yuktidīpikā* p. 61, line 9: *tasmād yuktam etat anyonyajananavṛttayo guṇāḥ na ca saṃkīrṇasvabhāvāḥ*.

(75) A reference to the key theme in Sāṃkhya philosophy that the Primordial Nature (*prakṛti*), which is "blind", exists for the benefit of the Spirit (*puruṣa*), who is the enjoyer (*bhoktṛ*) of the diverse objects exhibited by the Primordial Nature (cf. SK k. 17), but who will finally come to realize his separateness from this nature and thus attain liberation. See SK k. 21, 56, 58, 60.

(76) See en. 68. Cf. Paramārtha's terminology in Takakusu (1904) pp. 1062-1064.

(77) I.e. as an objection leading to Āryadeva's answer in k. 280. See §216c3-216c20.

(78) T. reads *zhǒng xìng* 種姓 = *vaṃśya*, *gotra* (which is correct), but gives *xìng* 性 as variant. The interchange of the two characters is frequent; see Demiéville (1987), p. 39, n. 6.

(79) For Sanskrit equivalents, see Nak. p. 302. The term is one which is used in the *Vinaya*. Cf. the entry in *Mahāparinirvāṇasūtra*, ed. E. Waldschmidt, p. 173 ("Vinaya Chinesisch") which refers to T. XXIV 1451 xxxvi 386a4. Other variations on this term, such as *smṛtimān saṃprajānan* and *smṛtisaṃprajanya*, are also to be found. For the former term, see *Traité* II, pp. 1024-5 (note), where the term is used in connection with the third level of "trances" (*dhyāna*). For the latter, see BHSD, s.v. *saṃprajanya*. In *Traité* I, p. 7, n. 6 the quality *smṛtaḥ saṃprajānaḥ* characterizes the Buddha at the moment of his birth. Cf. also May (1959) n. 925.

(80) The understanding of this term is problematic: I have taken it as a *karmadhāraya*. Cf. Nak. p. 1234: *dhamma-anudhamma-patipanna*. Mvyut. 1124: *chos daṅ rjes su (')mthun pa'i chos la źugs pa* = *dharmānudharmapratipanna*. See May n. 749 and index: *dharmānudharmapratipatti, chos daṅ rjes su mthun pa'i chos kyi nan tan*, "application aux dharma conformes à la loi". BHSD p. 27, s.v. *anudharma*.

Hayashima (1976) gives a detailed discussion on the different ways to render the compound, i.e. taking *dharmānudharma* as a *dvandva* compound and the whole as a *tatpuruṣa*, "the practice of the Dharma and the *anudharma*", or taking the whole compound as a *karmadhāraya*, "the practices which are in keeping with the Dharma". He gives the following example of the first version: In the *Vivṛtagūḍhārthapiṇḍāvyākhyā* on Asaṅga's *Mahāyānasaṃgraha*, *dharma* is interpreted as being the path of no more learning (*aśaikṣamārga*) whereas the *anudharma* ("secondary *dharma*") is the path of learning. Let me translate the Tibetan text which Hayashima gives in n. 7, p. 13: *chos kyi rjes su mthun pa'i chos śes bya ba la chos ni bden pa mthoṅ ba'o // rjes su mthun pa'i chos ni de'i sbyor ba'i lam mo // rnam pa gcig tu na chos ni mi slob pa'i lam mo // rjes su mthun pa'i chos ni slob pa'i lam mo // rnam pa gcig tu na chos ni don dam pa mya ṅan las 'das pa'o // rjes su mthun pa'i chos ni zag pa med pa'i las thams cad do* (P. 390a4-6). "In the term *dharmānudharmapratipatti*, *dharma* is the seeing of the truth [and] *anudharma* is the path which brings one to that [vision]. Or, *dharma* is the path of no more learning [and] *anudharma* is the path of learning. Or again, *dharma* is the ultimate, viz. *nirvāṇa*, [while] *anudharma* consists in all the non-defiled actions." As for the second version, Hayashima cites *inter alia* a passage from the *Gaṇḍavyūhasūtra*: *teṣāṃ ca tathāgatānāṃ dharmadeśanāṃ śṛṇomi dharmasya cānudharmaṃ pratipadye.* "I both listen to these tathāgatas' teaching of the Dharma and practise in accordance with [that] Dharma." (P.L. Vaidya, *Gaṇḍavyūhasūtra*, Buddhist Sanskrit Texts, no. 5, p. 296). The second version seems to apply better when *dharmānudharmapratipatti* is taken as belonging to the practice of meditation (*bhāvanā*) in the three trainings of hearing, reflection and meditation.

Finally, note that Dharmapāla actually lists the six *dharmānudharmapratipatti*; they are simply the six perfections. These then may very well be the six *anudharmas* (or dharmas) which are referred to in Mvyut. 9320-1 and about which Edgerton puzzled on p. 27 of BHSD.

(81) For the ten *vaśitā*, see BHSD p. 474 and Mvyut. 770-780. "Miraculous powers" (*shén lì* 神力 ; *shén tōng* 神通 = *ṛddhi*) is one of the ten.

(82) *sān qiān* = *sān qiān shì jiè* 三千世界 or *sān qiān dà qiān shì jiè* 三千大千世界 . Cf. H. p. 161 and Nak. p. 479.

(83) See Nak. p. 618 for the various Sanskrit equivalents.

(84) See en. 215.

(85) One of the three sorts of suffering, viz. suffering qua suffering (*duḥkha-duḥkhatā*), the suffering of change (*pariṇāmaduḥkhatā*) and *saṃskāraduḥkhatā*. Cf. AK vi LVP 125 et seq.; M. av. I, LVP (1907b) p. 259 and 260 n. 2.; Mvyut. 2228, *traya-duḥkhatā*; May (1959) n. 694; and BHSD p. 265 s.v. *duḥkhatā*. Edgerton sums up *saṃskāraduḥkhatā*: "this means particularly experience in itself, not painful or pleasurable, but, because impermanent and so undependable, still a cause of misery." AK vi LVP p. 128: "Mais, fût-elle accompagnée d'agréable, l'existence (*bhava*) dans sa totalité a la même saveur de *saṃskāraduḥkhatā*: les Āryas la considèrent donc comme douleur."

(86) The belief in the reality of the self and what belongs to the self (*ātmīya*). It is one of the five wrong views (*dṛṣṭi*) and admits of innate (*sahajā*) and speculative (*vikalpitā*) forms — the latter often being classified into twenty sorts. For canonical references, see *Traité* II, p. 737, n. 3. Other references, see May (1959), n. 720. See also BHSD p. 553, AK v LVP p. 15: "Croire au moi et au mien (*ātmātmīyagrāha*), c'est la *satkāyadṛṣṭi*." Cf. parallel formulations in M. av. VI and *bhāṣya*, 234.1 LVP (1911) p. 282 and Se ra rje btsun Chos kyi rgyal mtshan's *dBu ma'i spyi don* for debates on the fine points of this part of M. av. (ff.151a-157b). AK v p. 15 n. 3 explains that the Sautrāntikas take *satkāya* (*shēn* 身) as referring to "the accumulation (*kāya*) of perishing things" (*sat*), viz. the aggregrates (*skandhas*). Cf. Tib. *'jig tshogs la lta ba.* (literally "the view with regard to the collection of the perishable") as translation of *satkāyadṛṣṭi*. Vaibhāṣikas, however, take *sat* in the normal sense of "existent / real" and *kāya* as collection. Thus, "the view with regard to the existent collection". At any rate, the self is said to be designated here by the term *satkāya* (viz. the aggregates) for quasi-pedagogical reasons: if one simply spoke of the view of the self (*ātmadṛṣṭi*), it might be thought that the self, as object of cognition, must exist.

(87) For the passions and their various different classifications, see *Hōbōgirin*, s.v. *Bonnō* and May (1959) n. 226. For the six *anuśayas* (attachment, hatred, pride, ignorance, doubt and wrong views), see AK v LVP p. 1ff, PSP pp. 130-135 §29. Often *kleśa* is used synonymously with *anuśaya* as when the six *anuśayas* are referred to as the six *kleśas*. Cf. AK v p. 1, n. 4. This usage was adopted by Tibetans, who rarely use the term *phra rgyas*, but instead speak of the "six principal *kleśas*" (*rtsa myon drug*). Cf. *Yoṅs 'dzin blo rigs*, ff. 21a and 22a, ed. T. Kelsang and S. Onoda. Note however that strictly speaking the *anuśayas* are the latent *kleśas*; see Stcherbatsky (1923), p. 35 and Lamotte, KSP, p. 167. For the classification of *anuśayas* into ninety-eight sorts, see Lamotte, *Traité* I p. 424, n. 4.

(88) I.e. enlightenment or liberation.

(89) Japanese transl. (Kyik p. 324.14) reads *yì lǐ* 義理 instead of *wú yì* 無義 Taking his reading we would have to translate the passage as: "...and is the method for [attaining] *nirvāṇa*, which permanently extinguishes all objects (*yì lǐ* 義理 = *artha*)."

(90) See *Siddhi* pp. 100-123 and Lamotte, KSP, for the Vijñānavāda theory of karmic seeds (*bīja*) and Nak. p. 745b for *paripāka*.

(91) One of the five powers of insight (literally "eyes"); see *Traité* I p. 439; for canonical references see ibid p. 439, n. 1. The five are: the eye [made] of flesh (*māṃsacakṣus*), the divine eye (*divyacakṣus*), the eye of wisdom (*prajñācakṣus*), the eye of the Dharma (*dharmacakṣus*) and the eye of a buddha (*buddhacakṣus*). The *prajñācakṣus* is said to see the true character of the *dharmas*. Note that these five are spoken about

in the first chapter of *Abhisamayālaṃkāra*, verses 21-22; cf. Se ra rje btsun Chos kyi rgyal mtshan, *Don bdun cu*, p. 21.

(92) For a detailed account of the complicated problem of the threefold, tenfold and fivefold classifications of *kṣānti* ("patience", "receptivity" or sometimes even "conviction"), see Lamotte (1965) pp. 160-162, n. 119. See also Nak. 373c on the fivefold classification and BHSD s.v. *kṣānti*. Lamotte (ibid. n. 119) translates the *Avataṃsaka*'s definition of *ānulomikī kṣānti* as follows: "Qu'est-ce que l'*ānulomikī kṣānti* des bodhisattvas? Le bodhisattva examine (*vitarkayati*) et apprécie (*vicārayati*) ces mêmes dharma [prêchés par le Buddha]; il les assimile et ne les contredit pas (*na virodhayati*); il les intellige graduellement si bien que sa pensée se purifie; il s'installe correctement dans leur culture et les possède (*pratipadyate*)."

(93) Unidentified. For Skt. see CSV §39 ad k. 286ab.

(94) Viz. that of the hearers (*śrāvaka*), solitary buddhas (*pratyekabuddhas*) and bodhisattvas. For the three sorts of enlightenment (*bodhi*), see *Hōbōgirin*, s.v. *bodai*, p. 87. Dutt (1930) p. 26; see also Dayal (1931) p. 11 and Lamotte, *Mahāyanasaṃgraha*, p. 63* for the corresponding vehicles (*yāna*). Tibetan *grub mtha'* (*siddhānta*) texts and commentaries on *Abhisamayālaṃkāra* teach that for the Vijñānavāda, as well as for the Svātantrika branch of the Madhyamaka school, these three vehicules have different sorts of realizations, and that it is only the *bodhisattvayāna* which realizes the definitive type of voidness of all phenomena. However, for the Prāsaṅgikas there is said to be no difference in their realizations. Cf. Tsoṅ kha pa, *rTsa ba'i śes rab kyi dka' gnas brgyad* p. 28 et seq. (the "sixth point" of the eight) for the similarity of realization according to the Prāsaṅgikas. Tsoṅ kha pa seems to rely on the *Yuktiṣaṣṭikāvṛtti* in this connection. *lCaṅ skya grub mtha'* pp. 403-404 gives an explanation of the Svātantrika position on the three vehicules' differing realizations. Page 404: *chuṅ ṅu gaṅ zag gi bdag med thun moṅ ba rtogs pa daṅ / 'briṅ po gzuṅ 'dzin rdzas tha dad kyis stoṅ bar rtogs pa daṅ / chen po chos thams cad bden med du rtogs pa'o /*. "The inferior [stage, viz. that of the *śrāvakas*] is the realization of the common lack of self of the person; the middle [stage, i.e. that of the *pratyekabuddhas*] is the realization that the [object] which is grasped and the [subject] which does the grasping are void of any difference of substance; the great [stage, i.e. that of the bodhisattvas] is the realization that all dharmas are not truly existent."

(95) Read *yé* 耶 rather than T. *xié* 邪. The former was used by the Japanese transl. (Kyik p. 325.17) and is a variant in T.

(96) Cf. k. 287, where the Sanskrit corresponding to *kōng wú wǒ* is simply *nairātmya* rather than *śūnyānātman* (see H. 102) or something of that sort.

(97) The *Abhidharmakośa* speaks of three roots of virtue: absence of desire (*alobha*), absence of aversion (*adveṣa*) and absence of bewilderment (*amoha*), the latter being equivalent to *prajñā* ("wisdom / intelligence"). Obviously, these three are the contraries of the basic *kleśas*. See AK ii LVP p. 160; iv, 34; PSP pp. 124-125 §24.

(98) In what follows, the characters *kōng* 空 and *yǒu* 有 can, according to the context, be translated by "voidness" or "void" and "existence" or "existent" respectively. *kōng*, for example, can be a translation for *śūnyatā* as well as *śūnya*; cf. H. p. 101.

(99) Cf. CS VIII k. 195: *sad asat sadasac ceti nobhayaṃ ceti kathyate / nanu vyādhivaśāt pathyam auṣadhaṃ nāma jāyate //*. "Existence, non-existence, [both] existence and non-existence, and neither [existence nor non-existence] are taught. Surely, isn't it in accordance with the illness that the medicine becomes salutary?" Transl. by Lang (1986) p. 85. See her n. 20 for the question as to whether one should read *pathyam auṣadhaṃ nāma* (as she does) or *sarvam auṣadhaṃ nāma*.

(100) "Proliferation" or "elaboration" of phenomena and the creation of difference is a feature of all conceptualization. The result of this essentially erroneous process is the constitution of objects with distinct characters corresponding to the concepts which we have created. Entities constituted in this manner, i.e. by conceptual elaboration, only have a nominal existence qua designations (*prajñapti*). Cf. Lamotte's transl. of *prapañca*: "vains bavardages", in other words, not far from "blah, blah" and with all its pejorative connotations. See *Siddhi* II, p. 607 as well as May (1959) n. 562 for numerous references. Cf. *Madhyāntavibhāga* I, 3-4; see chapter III, B pp. 59-61 on this argumentation concerning existence and inexistence.

(101) In other words, for teaching purposes it is permissable to state something which is not literally true.

(102) It seems plausible to take *biǎo* 表 here as the equivalent of *vidhi*, which makes for the contrast between *pratiṣedha* and *vidhi*. LVP in *Siddhi* p. 529 took 遮表 as *pratiṣedhavijñapti* which he translated as "par voie de negation." This is unlikely. Admittedly, the more usual equivalent (see H. pp. 401-402) is *vijñapti*, which has the banal sense of "information" or "report" in addition to its technical use in the Vijñānavāda system, and this is clearly what influenced LVP. But we see other example of *zhē biǎo* 遮表 used in Dharmapāla's commentary where the sense clearly must be the contrast between negation and affirmation. E.g. in Dharmapāla's commentary to CS XVI k. 395 （有非眞有故　無亦非眞無　既無有眞無　何有於眞有）, he cites an objector (T. 1571 x 245b20): 此中一類釋此難言我說眞無是遮非表 "Here some make the following objection: 'We assert that true inexistence is a negation and not an affirmation.'"

Dharmapāla's strategy in saying that statements about voidness are just negations resembles Bhāvaviveka and Candrakīrti's style of argumentation, where statements about voidness are taken as non-implicative negations (*prasajyapratiṣedha*) and do not assert any positive quality or phenomenon. For this development of two sorts of *pratiṣedha* in connection with Buddhist Madhyamaka philosophy, see Kajiyama (1973), Ruegg (1977) p. 4, n. 10 and (1981) pp. 37-38, 65 and n. 94, Matilal (1971) pp. 163-164.

(103) Cf. *Siddhi* pp. 528-529: "...en effet, la Tathatā est à part de l'existence et de l'inexistence". T. 1585 vii 46b 17-18: 眞如離有離無性故 . See Chapt. III, B. p. 59 et seq.

(104) See en. 86.

(105) Note that the general line of argumentation is a recurrent one in Buddhist texts; cf. e.g. *Ratnāvalī* II, 19-25.

(106) The passage is translated in Tucci (1925), pp. 547-548, n. 2. However, Tucci translates *hán shì* 含識 as *ālayavijñāna*, the "store-consciousness" of the karmic seeds; this makes no sense at all. *hán* ("hold"; "contain") *shì* ("consciousness") just means "sentient beings"; see Nak. p. 199b, who gives *yǒu qíng* 有情 = *prāṇin; sattva* as a gloss for *hán shì*.

(107) Cf. *Kāśyapaparivarta* 64, ed. A. von Staël-Holstein pp. 95-96. My translation follows the Chinese of Dharmapāla's commentary. Cf. the different versions presented in Staël-Holstein. Same sūtra passage quoted in CSV XII §42.

(108) Cf. *Traité* I p. 69. In IV pp. xiii-xiv, Lamotte revises his previous identification of this verse as well as its translation:

"La non-dualité, la porte de la félicité,
La destruction des vues fausses,
Le domaine parcouru par tous les Buddha:
Voilà ce qui est appelé Non-moi."

Cf. also ibid. p. xiv for Lamotte's translation of the Sanskrit; this translation is only very slightly different substituting "épouvantail des vues fausses" for "la destruction des vues fausses". However, Lamotte's "la non-dualité" should probably be rejected: both the Sanskrit (*advitīyaṃ śivadvāram*) and Tibetan (*źi sgo gñis pa med pa*) can easily be read as taking *advitīyam* / *gñis pa med pa* as being an adjective modifying *śivadvāram* / *źi sgo*. And moreover, this understanding of the verse is the one which is borne out by both Candrakīrti's and Dharmapāla's commentaries. Cf. Skt. of CSV ad k. 288: *nairātmyam advitīyaṃ śivadvāraṃ bhavati / nirvāṇapurapraveśāya ekam evāsahāyam etat dvāram* /. It seems that apart from differences of word-order and the absence of *iti* ... *ucyate* the grammar in Dharmapāla's text is similar to that of the Sanskrit which we possess, although he reads "nirvāṇa" instead of *śiva*. Hence my rendition of *niè pán bù èr mén* 涅槃不二門 by "the unrivalled door to nirvāṇa."

(109) Cf. Nak. pp. 2d-3a and Japanese transl. Kyik p. 328, n. 88. Monier-Williams, *Skt.-English Dictionary*: "*agada* mfn. free from disease, m. freedom from disease; a medicine, drug, (especially) antidote."

(110) Literally "the name" (*míng* 名).

(111) See en. 91.

(112) *lùn* 論 = *vāda* and *tā lùn* 他論 is probably *paravāda* = *parapravāda*. See en. 200 and 201. I understand the syntax differently from Tucci and the Japanese translator. The former (cf. p. 548) understands the passage as: "Although the buddhas did not expressly speak to refute the dharma of the opposing doctrine..." This would seem to me syntactically improbable and would also deviate too radically from the Skt., in that "dharma" would not be the doctrine of selflessness, but rather the position of the opponent.

(113) Tucci translates *yě huǒ* 野火 as "a fire in a field", but I have taken *yě* 野 in the sense of "wild" or "raging", which accords better with Dharmapāla's commentary about the "raging fire in the mountain forest". The Sanskrit is lost, and the Tibetan just speaks of "fire".

(114) See en. 1, 47, 69.

(115) More literally: "not unengaged" (?). See Nak. p. 1387d.

(116) See Nak. p. 804c. *shuǐ jīng* 水精 = *shuǐ jīng* 水晶 .

(117) See en. 86.

(118) *yàn bù* 厭怖 is attested as an equivalent of *udvega*, "fear" (Cf. H. p. 60); *yàn* 厭 can equal *ud-VIJ*.

(119) Quoted in Lamotte, *Traité* III p. 1686 and IV p. xv. However, the text in Kumārajīva's translation is somewhat different. The Skt. is lost but the Tibetan also differs considerably from the two Chinese versions.

(120) I read *shéi* 誰 ("who") instead of *wéi* 唯 ("only"), as does the Japanese translator (see Kyik p. 330.4).

(121) Numerous parallel passages. Cf. *Tathāgataguhyasūtra* quoted in Pr. 361.12-13 and translated in De Jong (1949) p. 20: *tadyathāpi nāma śāntamate vṛkṣasya mūle chinne sarvaśākhāpattraphalāni śuṣyanti / evam eva śāntamate satkāyadṛṣṭyupaśamāt sarvakleśā upaśāmyante /*. See May (1959) n. 720 for other citations from treatises showing that *satkāyadṛṣṭi* is at the root of all passions (*kleśa*), heresies (*dṛṣṭigata*) and faults (*doṣa*). E.g. *Siddhi* p. 348: "Cette vue a pour action d'être le support de toutes les opinions fausses (*dṛṣṭigata*)." Finally, cf. M. av. p. 234.1 and also PV I k. 222: *sarvāsāṃ doṣajātīnāṃ jātiḥ satkāyadarśanāt.*

(122) See en. 120. Read *shéi* 誰 instead of *wéi* 唯 . Cf. Kyik p. 330.9.

(122a) Chinese reads: ..."[respectively] understood by the eyes, the ears and the mind". I have deliberately changed the word order here in keeping with Dharmapāla's (and Candrakīrti's) interpretation that the Brahmin's doctrine is understood by the ears, the Jain's by the eyes and the Buddhist's by the mind.

(122b) For a similar comparison between the passions and thieves (*caura*), see AK vi ad k. 28ab, LVP 190 n. 3, which speaks of *kleśacaura*.

(123) Following Japanese transl. (Kyik p. 331.1) read *duō* 多 ("most"; "many") instead of T. *wài* 外 ("outside").

(124) Dharmapāla is probably alluding to the Mīmāṃsaka's "proof" that the *Vedas* are eternal, and hence non-belying, because they are not man-made (*apauruṣeya*). See *Mīmāṃsāsūtra* I, 1, 6-23, 27-32; see Frauwallner (1961) p. 120 on the relation of this argument in 27-32 to the general Mīmāṃsaka position that words are permanent. Cf. Dharmapāla's explanation and refutation of the Mīmāṃsaka's proofs of the Vedas' permanence in T. 1571 i 187c16-188a7, and in particular, pp. 187c16-19:

> 復次有偏執明書聲常切不待緣後無壞滅性自能顯越諸根義爲決定量會不差違　現比等量依士夫見　士夫有失見是疑因　故能依量皆難信受
>
> "Now, other factions hold that the words of the *Vedas* are permanent, that their beginning was never perceived, that they will never subsequently come to an end, that their nature is self-manifested and is beyond all sense objects, [and] that they can never fail to be a sure *pramāṇa*. *Pramāṇas* such as direct perception, inference and so forth depend upon the views of a person, and when the person has faults, his views are a cause for doubt. Therefore, reliance on [such] a *pramāṇa* is completely unconvincing."

Dharmapāla replies that if, as the adversary maintains, all man-made views and *pramāṇas* which depend upon human beings are faulty, then it follows that the adversary's own views and texts as well as those of his teacher should also be faulty (in that they are also man-dependent). And thus the adversary's statements become self-refuting (*zì hài* 自害). Another counter-argument: "The words of the *Vedas* and other sorts of words are similar in nature. So why say that only the *Vedas* are permanent? You should not be able to assert that other words are impermanent." Note that Dharmakīrti in PV I k. 224 et seq. argues at length against the same Mīmāṃsaka position on *apauruṣeyatva*, which he introduces as follows in k. 224: *girāṃ mithyātva-hetūnāṃ doṣāṇāṃ puruṣāśrayāt / apauruṣeyaṃ satyārtham iti kecit pracakṣate //.* "Some say, 'As faults [or] causes for the verses being erroneous depend upon man, it is [statements] which are not man-made which have true meaning.'" Manorathanandin (PVV p. 367) specifies that the opinion is that of the Jaiminīyas, i.e. the followers of Jaimini's *Mīmāṃsāsūtra: girāṃ vācāṃ mithyātvasya hetūnāṃ doṣāṇām ajñānavisaṃvādābhiprāyādīnāṃ vā puruṣasyāśrayād āśrayaṇatvāt apauruṣeyaṃ vākyaṃ mithyātva-hetoḥ puruṣadoṣasyābhāvāt satyārtham iti kecit jaiminīyāḥ pracakṣate //.*

(125) See *Śūraṃgamasamādhisūtra* §133 et seq. in Lamotte (1965) p. 231ff and n. 266 for four sorts of *puṇyakṣetra*; Van den Broeck (1977) pp. 86, 91; Nak. p. 1187cd. The image behind the term is that of a source of merit or happiness, i.e. the "field" in which virtuous "seeds" (*bīja*) can be planted.

(126) Read *tān lài zhě* 貪癩者 ("greedy lepers") instead of T. *pín lài zhě* 貧癩者 ("poor lepers"). Japanese transl. (Kyik p. 331.10) also reads *tān*.

(127) Tucci (p. 549) translates: "Si onora il brāhmano perchè ha penetrato la scienza...". However, the context and Dharmapāla's commentary make it clear that *wèi sòng zhū míng gù* 爲誦諸明故 means "because they *recite* the *Vedas*": *zhū míng* does not refer to knowledge, but rather to the *míng lùn* 明論, the *Vedas*. As for *sòng* 誦, H. gives as equivalences *ā-MNĀ* and *PAṬH* "read, recite". Bhattacharya (p. 161), probably basing himself on Tucci, takes the Chinese as corroborating his reconstruction, *vidyāgrahaṇataḥ* ("for the acquisition of knowledge"), but in fact the Chinese and Tibetan seem different.

(128) The underlying argument is that suffering is the result of a previous unvirtuous action, and that, *qua* retribution, it is neither virtuous nor unvirtuous and is "not defiled and not defined" (*anivṛtāvyākṛta*). Cf. AKBh ad ii, k. 57ab: *anivṛtā-vyākṛto hi dharmaḥ vipākaḥ /* (Pradhān ed. p. 95, 10; LVP p. 289). Liberation (*mokṣa*), however, is itself virtuous and must depend upon previous virtuous causes: thus suffering is not the cause for liberation because it is not virtuous.

Vipākaphala, or the effect of virtuous or unvirtuous actions, is one of five types of effects spoken about in the *Abhidharma*'s elaboration of the law of karma. See Mvyut 2272-4 and 2276-7 and AK ii p. 287ff for the five. *Siddhi* p. 97 (LVP transl.)

describes it as: "le 'fruit de rétribution' des actes bons ou mauvais qui projettent (*Ā-KṢIP*) une existence dans une certaine sphère d'existence, dans une certaine destinée, par une certaine matrice." *Vipākaphala*, as its name implies, is the effect of *vipākahetu* (i.e. virtuous or non-virtuous actions which will "ripen" as fortunate or unfortunate types of existences), one of six sorts of causes; see AK ii p. 244ff for the six and ii, p. 271ff for *vipākahetu* in particular. See also de la Vallée Poussin (1913) pp. 54-55 for the six causes. Finally, note that when *vipākaphala* is the result of virtuous actions, the causal virtue is one which is "defiled" or "impure" (*sāsrava*) in that it is under the influence of ignorance (*avidyā*) and craving (*tṛṣṇā*). Cf. AK ii (LVP p. 271) k. 54cd: *vipākahetur aśubhāḥ kuśalāś caiva sāsravāḥ* (ed. Pradhān p. 89). Transl. LVP "Sont cause de rétribution les *dharmas* mauvais et les *dharmas* bons qui sont impurs." (AKBh ad k. 54cd adds the word *dharmāḥ*.) Cf. also the definition of *rnam smin gyi rgyu* (= *vipākahetu*) in *bsDus grwa briṅ* p. 20a4 : *mi dge ba daṅ dge ba zag bcas gaṅ ruṅ gis bsdus pa / rnam smin gyi rgyu'i mtshan ñid / mtshan gźi ni / srog gcod kyi las lta bu /*. "The defining characteristic of *vipākahetu* is: 'What is classed as either unvirtuous or as defiled virtue.' The illustrative example (*mtshan gźi*) is the karma of killing and so forth."

(129) A formal reasoning (*prayoga*) which can be reworded as follows:

Thesis (*pakṣa*): The various self-inflicted physical sufferings of the Jains are not a cause for liberation.
Reason (*hetu*): Because, such karmic ripenings are the consequence of past evil actions and are not virtuous *dharmas*.
Example (*dṛṣṭānta*): Just like pleasurable ripenings.

Cf. the Japanese translator's note 105, Kyik p. 332. The example must refer to ripenings which are pleasurable in the saṃsāric sense of "defiled" or "impure" (*sāsrava*) pleasure. See the preceding note.

(130) See en. 129.

(131) The subsequent commentary makes it clear that the "present conditions" are *moha*.

Note that there are sufferings or pleasures which are *not vipāka* of past virtuous or non-virtuous actions. In particular, as AK ii k. 60-61 and *bhāṣya* make clear, no mind (*citta*) or mental factor (*caitta*) which is defiled (*kliṣṭa*), or unvirtuous, can be the effect of a *vipākahetu*. It can easily be seen that this principle is a direct consequence of AK ii, k. 57ab, which states that a ripening (*vipāka*) is always a non-defined dharma, i.e. it is neither virtuous nor unvirtuous. See en. 128. Cf. AK ii, LVP p. 298: "La pensée et les mentaux [...] lorsqu'ils sont souillés, naissent de cinq causes à l'exclusion de la cause de rétribution [i.e. *vipākahetu*]." The example which Dharmapala presents, viz. sexual pleasure, is a defiled state of mind, and as such cannot be a *vipākaphala*.

(132) *shēn*, of course, usually means "the body" (= *deha*; *kāya*; *śarīra*, etc.), but it can also translate *janman* ("birth"; "origin"; see Nak. p. 770c), and that is the sense at stake in this discussion.

(133) *lüè yán* 略言 = *lüè shuō* 略說 = *samāsatas*. Lang (Thesis) n. 27 p. 444 translates from the Chinese as follows: "In brief, what the Buddha said: 'These two things are distinct from other schools, viz., non-harming produces [rebirth as] men and gods, and the view of emptiness verifies Nirvāṇa'." But this does not account for *jù* 具, which has the sense of "to have" as the Japanese translator (Kyik p. 333.17) also brings out clearly. Nor is there reason to suppose that this is a quotation from the Buddha.

(134) See *Traité* II pp. 782-784 ("note préliminaire") for a summary of morality in the Sarvāstivādin-Vaibhāṣika system; see also Lamotte (1962) pp. 413-415.

For the ten virtuous and ten non-virtuous actions, see BHSD p. 170 s.v. *karmapatha*, Lévi (1929) pp. 268-271 for a work on the *daśa akuśalakarmapatha*, a text attributed to Aśvaghoṣa; *dāna*, see *Traité* II chapter 19, pp. 662 et seq; *priyavacana*, BHSD p. 394; *arthacaryā*, BHSD p. 66; *samānārthatā*, Dayal (1931) pp. 255-257, BHSD p. 569. Dayal p. 256 cites the *Bodhisattvabhūmi*'s gloss of *samānārthatā*: "Here the bodhisattva himself pursues the same Ideal or Aim and the same Good (Root of Good) as he exhorts others to follow". The latter four are known as "the four ways of gathering [disciples]" (*catvāri saṃgrahavastūni*); see Lamotte (1962) p. 116, n. 67, Dayal op. cit. pp. 251-259, Mvyut section XXXV, 925-928, *Dīgha* iii 232, *Dharmasaṃgraha* 19. For the four *dhyāna*, see *Traité* III pp. 1233-1238; for the fourfold *ārūpyasamāpatti*, see *Traité* III pp. 1274-1279. These *samāpatti* are: *(a)* the sphere of the infinity of space (*ākāśānantyāyatana*), *(b)* the sphere of the infinity of consciousness (*vijñānānantyāyatana*), *(c)* the sphere of nothingness (*ākiṃcanyāyatana*), *(d)* the sphere of being neither conscious nor unconscious (*naivasaṃjñānāsaṃjñāyatana*). See Dayal (1931) p. 230 on five *samāpattis* — the four *dhyānas* and five *samāpattis* go to make up the nine *anupūrvavihāras* ("states following one another in regular succession"). The difference between *samādhi* and *samāpatti* is a subject of some controversy. Edgerton opined in BHSD (s.v. *samāpatti*) that the term in other contexts signifies "attainment", but in Buddhism it comes to mean the same as *samādhi*. (Cf. Lamotte's translation as "receuillement" and the frequent use, in Chinese, of *dìng* 定 for both *samādhi* and *samāpatti*.) But cf. Dayal op. cit. pp. 229-231 on the *ārūpyasamāpattayaḥ*; he translates *samāpatti* as "attainments"; May (1959) translates as "obtentions"; see his n. 436 for further references. Tib. *sñom par 'jug pa* is just a completely literal translation of *samāpatti* and does not (as Edgerton would have it) specially emphasize "entering into equanimity".

(135) On the term *tathatā* ("thusness"), see *Siddhi* II pp. 743ff. For *bhūtakoṭi*, see ibid. II pp. 750ff. for explanation and canonical references. On the etymology of the latter term, *Siddhi* p. 750: "La Tathatā est *bhūta-koṭi* parce qu'elle est l'objet du savoir exact, donc *bhūta*, vraie; parce qu'elle est l'extrémité: il n'y a rien à trouver plus loin que le *nairātmya*, donc *koṭi*, extrémité." MAV 1, k. 15 gives *tathatā, bhūtakoṭi* and *animitta* in its list of synonyms for voidness: *tathatā bhūtakoṭiś cānimittaṃ paramārthatā / dharmadhātuś ca paryāyāḥ śūnyatāyāḥ samāsataḥ //*."Thusness, the true endpoint, what is without characters, the ultimate truth and the sphere of the Dharma are, in short, synonyms for voidness". Cf. T. 1600 (transl. Xuán zàng) i 465c 13-14:

略說空異門　謂眞如實際　無相勝義性　法界等應知

The points behind saying *tathatā*, *bhūtakoṭi* and *animitta* respectively are, according to MAV 1, k. 15, *bhāṣya* and *ṭīkā*, that voidness is never different (*ananya*), is non-erroneous (*aviparyāsa*) and is the cessation, or absence, of all characters, be they conditioned (*saṃskṛta*) or unconditioned (*asaṃskṛta*). Cf. MAV-*bhāṣya* ad k. 16: *ananyathārthena tathatā nityaṃ tathaiveti kṛtvā / aviparyāsārthena bhūtakoṭiḥ viparyāsā-vastutvāt / nimittanirodhārthenānimittaṃ sarvanimittābhāvāt /*. Translations of the relevant passages from the *bhāṣya* and *ṭīka* in Stcherbatsky (1936) reprinted (1970), pp. 81-83.

(136) See p. 55, fn. 117, §217a21, en. 138.

(137) Literally, "the disciplinary code of individual liberation", the name of the code of precepts for monks in the *Vinaya*. *Prātimokṣasaṃvara* can also refer to the text in which this code is contained. Cf. BHSD s.v. *saṃvara*, *prātimokṣa*.

(138) See §217a21 & en. 47. See *Traité* III p. xlii for a list of the occurrences of this term in the *Dà zhì dù lùn*. See ibid. p. 1501 for a good example of the way the term is used in the *Prajñāpāramitā* literature: "Ce [vrai] caractère [des *dharma*] est non-né (*anutpanna*) et non-détruit (*aniruddha*), ni souillé (*asaṃkliṣṭa*) ni purifié (*avyavadāta*), ni existant ni non-existant (*naivasan nāsat*), ni pris (*anupātta*) ni rejeté (*aparityakta*), toujours apaisé (*śānta*), parfaitement pur, pareil à l'espace (*ākāśasama*), indéfinissable (*anirdeśya*), inexprimable (*anabhilāpya*); il est destruction de tous les chemins du discours (*sarvavādamārgoccheda*), il dépasse le domaine de toutes les pensées et de tous les mentaux (*sarvacittacaitasikadharmagocarasamatikrānta*); il est pareil au Nirvāṇa: c'est la Loi des Buddha."

(139) Read *zhì* 智 instead of T. *zhī* 知. Japanese translation (Kyik p. 335.4) and T. variant: 智 .

(140) Nak. p. 1292a explains that as the future has no end, this idiom, "bounds of the future" (*wèi lái jì* 未来際), is used to say that something is eternal.

(141) I follow Red mda' ba p. 143.11-12: *smra ba po'i yon tan tshig zur dad pa / don phyin ci ma log pa / ṅag sṅa phyi ma 'khrugs pa brjod pa blo gsal ba.* "The teacher's good qualities are that [his] words are impartial, the meaning is non-erroneous, the speech does not state confusions between [what came] before and [what comes] after and [his] mind is clear." Note that both Lang and Bhattacarya understand *ma 'khrugs pa* in the sense of *akopa* "without anger". (See Lang, Thesis p. 418. Her understanding of the syntax differs too.) This is one possible sense, but I have taken *'khrugs pa* in the sense of *saṃkula / ākula*, "confusion", which accords with Red mda' ba's understanding. Cf. also Lokesh Chandra s.v. *'khrugs pa.*

(142) *smra ba po la yon tan* literally means "the good qualities, in the case of the teacher, ..." Following Red mda' ba, rGyal and Kaḥ thog, however, I understood the *la don* as essentially possessive: *smra ba po'i yon tan.* Similarly for *ñan pa po* ***la***. Cf. B's reconstruction: *vaktur guṇaḥ.*

(143) The point of the argument is not that good qualities *actually* change into bad ones, but rather that they *seem* to be bad to a disciple or master who is himself riddled with faults. Cf. Kaḥ thog's summary of the argument (pp. 190b5-191a2): *snod mtshan ñid tshaṅ na smra ba po'i yon tan zur dod pa daṅ gsal ba daṅ ma 'khrugs pa daṅ / ñan po'i lhag pa'i bsam pa khoṅ du chud la / sems la zaṅ ziṅ med pa sogs de las rnam pa gźan du skyon du snaṅ bar mi 'gyur ba yon tan kho nar snaṅ la / ñan pa po la'aṅ yon tan skyon gyi ṅo bor 'gyur ba min te / ñan pa pos smra ba po'i yon tan la de ñid du śes pas de las gźan skyon du go bar mi 'gyur la / ñan po'i yon tan la smra ba pos yon tan du śes pa las gźan skyon du mi 'gyur ro /.* "When the vessel satisfies the definition, then the teacher's good qualities, viz. impartiality, clarity, not being confused ... and so forth will not appear to be anything other than this, i.e. as faults, but will [instead] appear to be only good qualities. And the good qualities of the auditor, too, will not become faults. Since the auditor correctly understands the teacher's good qualities, he will not understand them as otherwise, i.e. as faults. And because the teacher will comprehend the auditor's good qualities as [in fact] being good qualities, they will not become otherwise, i.e. faults."

(144) Cf. Red mda' ba p. 143.15-16: *ñan pa po raṅ gi ñes pa mi brtsi ba rnams kyis smra ba po skyon daṅ ldan pa ñid du brtsi bar byed de /.* The exact sense of the word *'dzud par byed* (usually: "guide; impose; insert") is unclear in CSV, although Lokesh Candra does give *pravartaka* ("set in motion"; "causing"; "effecting") as a possible equivalent.

(145) Following Bhattacharya's amendment to the text we would have "teaching" instead of "praising".

(146) Unidentified. B reconstructs: *abhiprāyopadeśasūtra.* But see Lokesh Chandra s.v. *lhag pa'i bsam pa bskul ba'i mdo.* The *Adhyāśayasaṃcodanasūtra* is a

medium length sūtra of the *Ratnakūṭa* group — *Ratnakūṭasūtra* #25 in the *Ōtani Kanjur Catalogue*.

(147) Literally: "They regard this as if of the Sage".

(148) Following Tib. one would translate: "we have not said anything..."

(149) The length and complexity of the Skt. and Tib. forces me to significantly alter the word order in the English translation. I begin with the main verb, which is at the end of the Skt. sentence.

(150) Following Tib. and B. we would translate: "So why, after imagining an impious apprehension in your heart, ..."

(151) Note that the Sanskrit is hybrid here, with the result that we have *dharmāṇa* instead of *dharmāṇām*, *dharmā* instead of *dharmāḥ*, the use of the singular *asti* where one would expect the plural, as well as *astī* with a long *ī* instead of the final *i*. See Edgerton (1953) p. 59 §8.117, p. 55 §8.78, p. 129 §25.4 and p. 131 §26.2 respectively for explanations of these phenomena. As we shall see below in CSV, Candrakīrti also gives a grammatical commentary on some of these particularities of hybrid Skt. In particular, he shows that *nivṛtti* has to be interpreted as if it were the locative *nivṛttau*; this concords nicely with Tib. *mya ṅan 'das la*. Stcherbatsky (1965) did not take this into account, and as a result his translation of the passage is quite different. Cf his p. 188.

Finally it should be remarked that in what follows the discussion in CSV is largely parallel to that in Pr. 522.10 - 523.13; see en. 159.

(152) I.e. principally the body.

(153) See en. 151.

(154) The sūtra which is partially quoted is Pāṇini's *Aṣṭādhyāyī* VII 1.39: *supāṃ sulukpūrvasavarṇāccheyāḍāḍyāyājālah*, a sūtra describing phenomena in Vedic Sanskrit. Transl. Renou (1966). Candrakīrti, interestingly enough, uses the part of this sūtra which speaks of substituting *luk* (i.e. "suppression"; "dropping out") in order to justify the elimination of the locative singular and thus explain why we find *nivṛtti* rather than *nivṛttau*. See en. 151. This elimination of the locative ending does frequently occur in Vedic locative singulars, notably in nouns in *-an* — e.g. *carman*. Nonetheless, it is curious that in connection with the *Samādhirājasūtra* Candrakīrti repeatedly (cf. en. 158) invokes considerations about Vedic in order to explain Buddhist Hybrid Sanskrit: while Candrakīrti in other works often makes reference to grammatical sūtras to explain classical Sanskrit, I know of no other instance where he invokes Pāṇinian sūtras or Vedic Sanskrit forms to explain hybrid Sanskrit phenomena. Cf. the

discussion of *tiṅ* below in §16. On *sup* and *su* see Abhyankar (1977)'s entries for these Pāṇinian terms.

(155) On *skra śad*, cf. *Zidian* p. 54: *mgo nas lhuṅ ba'i skra'i miṅ ste...* "A word for the hairs which have fallen from one's head." *skra śad 'dziṅs* = *keśoṇḍuka* "tangled hair", "a mesh of hair".

(156) On the use of this example, see en. 370. *Timira* is often thought to be some form of ophthalmia. However, J. Filliozat, who was both an ophthalmologist and an orientalist, has argued that this translation is mistaken. See Filliozat's explanations in May (1959), n. 779: "*Timira* ne peut se traduire valablement par 'ophtalmie'. Ce dernier terme désigne des conjonctivites qui ne donnent pas les symptomes de *timira*. *Timira* = 'obscurite' ou plus généralement 'trouble visuel' dû à des opacités et altérations de réfringence à l'intérieur des milieux transparents de l'oeil." Note that when the *timira*, or "opacities of one's vision" develop further, they often lead to advanced cataracts.

(157) Quotation unidentified; the snake-rope and *timira* themes, however, are very common in Madhyamaka discussions. Cf. e.g. the opening verses of the *Hastavālaprakaraṇa* and its *vṛtti* (attributed by Tibetans to Āryadeva), pp. 276-277 in F.W. Thomas and H. Ui (1918).

(158) The rule is from the *Mahābhāṣya* of Patañjali (ed. Kielhorn III p. 256, line 14): *tiṅāṃ ca tiṅo bhavantīti vaktavyam*. This is a qualification to Pāṇini VII 1.39 and again concerns Vedic Sanskrit. What is at stake is of course Candrakīrti's continuing attempt to explain why the *Samādhirājasūtra* says *nivṛtti dharmāṇa na asti dharmā*. Previously he had explained the fact that *nivṛtti* should be taken as being in the locative, although the case-affix does not appear. Subsequently he will explain that *dharmāṇa* means *dharmāṇām*. Now he is again invoking considerations about Vedic to explain why we find *asti* instead of *santi*. Unfortunately such a distinction does not come out clearly in the Tibetan because there is no distinction between singular and plural verb forms.

As for the key term *tiṅ*, it figures in Pāṇini as a *pratyāhāra* for the eighteen personal endings for verbs, i.e. *tip*, *tas*, etc. for the Active, and *ta*, *ātām*, etc. for the Middle. See Pāṇini's *Aṣṭādhyāyī* III 4.78; Renou (1966) vol. 1, pp. 273-274; Abhyankar s.v. *tiṅ*. My thanks to J. Bronkhorst for identifying the two grammatical citations in CSV XII.

(159) It is very odd to classify Kaṇāda (= *gzegs zan*) on one side and the followers of Kaṇāda, viz. the Vaiśeṣikas (= *bye brag pa*), on the other! We can reasonably assume that the Tibetan text is corrupt here. Cf. Pr. 523.9-13 which gives a more elaborate account: *astīti bhāvasadbhāvakalpanāvatāṃ jaiminīyakāṇādakāpilādīnāṃ vaibhāṣikaparyantānāṃ, nāstīti ca kalpanāvatāṃ nāstikānām apāyagati-*

niṣṭhānāṃ, tadanyeṣāṃ cātītānāgatasaṃsthānāṃ avijñaptiviprayuktasaṃskār[āṇāṃ] nāstivādināṃ tadanyad astivādināṃ, [pari]kalpitasvabhāvasya nāstivādināṃ paratantra-pariniṣpannasvabhāvayor astivādinām evam astināstivādinām evaṃ caratāṃ na duḥkhaṃ saṃsāraḥ śāmyatīti* //. *Read *avijñapti°* instead of Pr. *vijñapti°*; cf. Tib. *mam par rig byed* ***ma*** *yin pa*. Translation: "Those who think 'it exists' and thus imagine that entities really exist, [are] the followers of Jaimini [i.e. the Mīmāṃsakas], Kaṇāda [i.e. the Vaiśeṣikas], Kapila [i.e. the Sāṃkhyas] etc. up to and including the [Buddhist] Vaibhāṣikas. And those who imagine 'inexistence' [are] the nihilists, who end up in unfortunate states of existence. And the others — viz. those [Sautrāntikas] who say that the past, the future, unmanifest [karma] and conditionings which are neither [mental nor physical] are [all] inexistent, but say that apart from these [things] there is existence, as well as those [Vijñānavādins] who say that imagined natures (*parikalpitasvabhāva*) are inexistent but say that dependent (*paratantra*) and thoroughly established (*pariniṣpanna*) natures exist — [these philosophers] in such a fashion assert both existence and inexistence. For [all] them who practice in this way, suffering, i.e. saṃsāra, will not cease." Note that I have replaced LVP's half-*daṇḍas* with commas. Also, because of the length of the Skt. sentence, I have had to alter the syntax a bit by rendering the series of genitive plurals into complete English sentences.

(160) Cf. the translation of these verses from the *Ratnāvalī* in Tucci (1934) pp. 321-322, Hopkins (1975) pp. 25-26.

(161) See *Mahāparinibbānasuttanta* 5.27, *Dīgha* II 151.20-22: *idh' eva subhadda samaṇo, idha dutiyo samaṇo, idha tatiyo samaṇo, iddha catuttho samaṇo. suññā parappavādā samaṇehi aññe.* Cf. Skt. in *Mahāparinirvāṇasūtra* (ed. Waldschmidt) III, 378: *iha prathamaḥ śramaṇa upalabhyata iha dvitīya iha tṛtīya iha caturtho ... śūnyāḥ parapravādāḥ śramaṇair vā brāhmaṇair vā*.

(162) Tib. understands the syntax slightly differently: "Now the Outsiders, because of their inability to teach the method for abandoning all, are established as having faulty understandings with regard to other sorts of entities too, and thus [this] need not be established."

(163) Monier-Williams *Dictionary* p. 88: *arundhatī...* "the little and scarcely visible star Alcor (belonging to the Great Bear, and personified as the wife of one of its seven chief stars, Vasiṣṭha, or of all the seven, the so-called seven *ṛṣis*;...)."

(164) Unidentified. On *mchiṅ bu* ("rhinestones"), cf. *Zidian* p. 240. *mchiṅ bu: rin po che bcos ma'am rdzun ma'i miṅ.*

(165) Following Tib. (*brtags nas*) we would translate: "having imagined [the idea] that ...".

(166) Quoted in the *Bodhicaryāvatārapañjikā*, p. 212.20-21: *nāsty ahaṃ* na bhaviṣyāmi na me 'sti na bhaviṣyati / iti bālasya saṃtrāsaḥ paṇḍitasya bhavakṣayaḥ //*. Cf. B. p. 146 n. 1. *Ed. Vaidya: *nasmy ahaṃ*.

(167) A somewhat non-literal rendering of *notsahate... asato manaḥ*. Literally, "The mind of the mediocre person does not have the courage ...".

(168) Cf. *Ratnāvalī* 1.39 (ed. Hahn): *sarvaduḥkhakṣayaṃ dharmaṃ śrutvaivam aparīkṣakaḥ / saṃtrasyaty aparijñānād abhayasthānakātaraḥ //*. "Thus, after hearing the Dharma that removes all suffering, someone who does not examine it, [and] who is afraid of the fearless state, is terrified due to not thoroughly understanding." Cf. the translations of this verse from the *Ratnāvalī* in Lang (Thesis) p. 440 and Hopkins (1975) p. 22.

(169) Tib. has "when he is lifted up *by* the elephant" (*glaṅ po ches spar ba na*).

(170) *parijaya* = Skt. *paricaya* ("acquaintance, knowledge of"). See BHSD p. 322.

(171) Skt. has literally: "the profane who reside on the level belonging to the profane." To avoid this pleonasm I have followed Tib. in reading "beings" (*sems can* = *sattva*).

(172) Tib. has: "The quietening dharma is what opposes that training, [in other words,] the voidness of nature of entities, for it is conducive to the cessation of saṃsāra."

(173) I use the formulation "having..." purely out of convenience to handle the long Skt. sentence. The Skt. does not have an absolutive, but rather has the *bahuvrīhi*, *pranaṣṭasanmārgasya*.

(174) Tib. seems to take *mahāprapātahetu* as the "cause for great precipices / abysses" (*g.yaṅ sa chen po'i rgyu*), perhaps in keeping with the preceding mention of precipices (cf. §35) (*prapāta*). "Cause for great precipices", however, is not clear, and I prefer to take *prapāta* here in the sense of "downfall".

(175) The passage is translated on the basis of the Skt. text. Tib. has some differences; see Bhattacharya's notes to his p. 148. For the four *saṃgrahavastu*, see en. 134.

(176) Unidentified.

(177) See en. 128.

(178) Tib. translates *pratyayāt* in this context by *rkyen las* ("by conditions"), but it is not clear what the point would be. Hence I have taken *pratyaya* in its sense of "belief", "firm conviction", etc.

(179) My translation follows the Tibetan; I have placed in parenthesis those words in Staël-Holstein's Skt. text which do not have any correspondent in the Tibetan. *Kāśyapaparivarta* §64 (ed. Staël-Holstein): *varaṃ khalu (punaḥ) kāśyapa sumerumātrā pudgaladṛṣṭir (āśritā) na tv evādhimānikasya* śūnyatādṛṣṭi(mālinā) / tat kasmād dhetoḥ /.* Ibid. §65: *sarvadṛṣṭigatānāṃ śūnyatā niḥsaraṇam yasya khalu (punaḥ) kāśyapa śūnyatādṛṣṭis tam aham acikitsyam iti vadāmi** /.* *Bhattacharya reads *evābhimānikasya*; cf. his reconstructed Skt. text on p. 150; cf. also the virtually identical passage from the *Ratnakūṭasūtra* cited in Pr. p. 248.9-11 where we find *evābhāvābhiniveśikasya*. ***iti vadāmi*, while it has no correspondent in CSV, is translated in the Tib. found in Staël-Holstein's edition: ... *gsor mi ruṅ ṅo <u>źes ṅas bśad do</u>*. Finally note that in the Tib. of Staël-Holstein's text the last lines of §65 are the same as those for the last lines of §64. The Skt. differs however.

Nāgārjuna develops the same thought in MMK XIII, 8: *śūnyatā sarvadṛṣṭīnāṃ proktā niḥsaraṇaṃ jinaiḥ / yeṣāṃ tu śūnyatādṛṣṭis tān asādhyān babhāṣire //.* "The Victors have explained that voidness is the deliverance from all views. But, they have said that those who have a view on voidness can never be healed."

(180) Tib. takes *darśana* here in the sense of "teaching", rather than "view". Cf. Tib. *ston pa*. However, the Chinese takes it as "view" (*jiàn* 見).

(181) Cf. the Tibetan translation of *netara* by *tha mal pa ma yin pa* ("uncommon").

(182) *nirvṛtti* is frequently indistinguishable from *nirvṛti*, *nivṛti* and *nivṛtti*. *nirvṛti* is synonymous with *nirvāṇa*. See May (1959) n. 682.

(183) See en. 108.

(184) "the absence ...selflessness" is not in HPS and has been translated on the basis of the Tibetan.

For the use of the term *svabhāva* ("nature"; "own-being"; *svabhāva* = *svarūpa* = *svalakṣaṇa*) in Madhyamaka philosophy, see e.g. De Jong (1972) pp. 2-3, Ames (1982), (1986) pp. 321-322. Note that the definition which Candrakīrti gives here in CS XII is frequently cited in Tibetan explanations as to what *svabhāva* is. In both Indian and Tibetan Madhyamaka, however, the term often used in a more banal sense where it is simply a way of saying what something is conventionally, and where it does not have the technical sense of a "mode of being independent of causes and conditions." Note that the Epistemological school's idea(s) of *svabhāva* and *svalakṣaṇa* differ from those of the Madhyamaka in that they define *svalakṣaṇa* in terms of momentary existence and causal efficacity, uniqueness of location in space and time, etc., but certainly not as something independent. See en. 366; see also Steinkellner (1971), (1973a) on the Epistemologists' understanding of *svabhāva*, *svabhāvapratibandha* and *svabhāvahetu*. These subjects would need a separate study to be treated adequately, and in fact until we are clearer on the differences in the various schools' conceptions of these terms, it is difficult to evaluate and interpret the debates which they had amongst each other.

(185) Cf. Pr. 212.18: *tatropādīyata ity upādānaṃ pañcopādānaskandhāḥ / yas tān upādāya prajñapyate sa upādātā grahītā niṣpādaka ātmety ucyate /*. "Here, *upādāna* means what is appropriated, i.e. the five appropriated aggregates. The appropriator, the holder, the effectuator, which is designated in dependence upon those [aggregates], is said to be the self." Transl. Schayer (1931). See May (1959) index, s.v. *upādāna* and n. 467 for a distinction between a wider and narrower sense of *upādāna* in this sort of discussion, that is, the word can mean the process of appropriation or the object of appropriation. In our discussion, it is the narrower sense which is at stake, a sense where *upādāna* means virtually the same as *upādeya*. Thus, the aggregates are the object; they are what is "taken up" or appropriated by the self, which is the agent, i.e. that which effectuates the "taking" or "appropriation".

Note that the absolutive *upādāya* has the sense of "on the basis of", "in dependence upon", as Candrakīrti later brings out in CSV XII §48 by means of his gloss *pratītya*. See en. 40 and 363 for *upādāya prajñapti*. Other senses of *upādāna*: (1) material cause or basis, as in the discussions of fuel and fire, where fuel is termed the *upādāna*; (2) appropriation in the sense of a fourfold type of grasping or clinging, as in the context of the twelve links of *pratītyasamutpāda* (cf. Pr. 555-556, transl. May pp. 262-263 and LVP [1913] pp. 26-29).

(186) See en. 363.

(187) The six sense organs including the mind (*manas*) are known as the *ādhyātmikāyatana* ("internal domains"); their respective objects are the *bāhyāyatana* ("external domains). We find in Mvyut the list of twelve; see also PSP pp. 144-145 on *dvadāśāyatana*; frequently one simply speaks of the group of six organs, terming them *ṣaḍāyatana*. Edgerton also mentions the use of *ṣaḍāyatana* in the context of *pratītyasamutpāda* as applying to the six pairs of organs and their respective objects. See BHSD s.v. *āyatana* and Mvyut 2027-2039, 2246, LVP (1913) pp. 18-20, AK iii, p. 63, May (1959) n. 505 and 938.

(188) Various uses: (1) three *dhātus* in the sense of worlds, viz. the realms of desire, form and no-form; (2) eighteen *dhātus* or phenomenal constituents, viz. the six organs, six objects and six consciousnesses; (3) six *dhātus* or psycho-physical elements, viz. earth, water, fire, air, space, consciousness. See BHSD s.v. *dhātu*; Stcherbatsky (1923) pp. 9-10; Myvut. 2040-2058; PSP p. 145 for the eighteen; AK iii, pp. 1-12 for the three *dhātus*; AK i, pp. 34ff. for a general discussion of the *skandhas*, *āyatanas*, *dhātus*

and the purpose in introducing these schemata. It might seem as if it must be the six *dhātus* which are at stake here in our text. Pr. chapter V is consecrated to the "examination of the dhātu" (*dhātuparīkṣā*), while chapters III and IV are devoted to the *āyatanas* and *skandhas* respectively, all with the general aim of refuting the scholastics' version of what the person is. In Pr. chapter V the sense of *dhātu* being examined is indeed that of the six *dhātus*. However, note that it is also equally possible that it is the eighteen *dhātus* which are at issue in our text: AK i, LVP p. 40 speaks of how the doctrine of the *skandhas*, *āyatanas* and *dhātus* is supposed to counter grasping at the self; in this context, there are eighteen.

(189) "For fools" (*mūrkhajanasya*) is missing in the Tibetan.

(190) I take *darśana* here as "vision" in keeping with Tib. *mthoṅ ba*.

(191) "There is no [other] ... in this manner" is missing in Skt. and has been translated on the basis of the Tibetan.

(192) "Therefore" and "which is characterized ... nature" are missing in Skt. and are translated following the Tibetan.

(193) For the three *vimokṣamukha*, which are types of meditative trances (*samādhi*), see especially AK viii, pp. 184-187 and p. 184 n. 1. To resume the discussion in AK: (1) *śūnyatāsamādhi*, which is directed towards the void and selfless aspects (*ākāra*) of the truth of suffering, is the opponent to the wrong view with regard to the personality (*satkāyadṛṣṭi*). (2) *ānimittasamādhi* is directed towards the lack of ten sorts of marks or characters. These *nimitta* are the five *āyatanas*, such as form, sound, etc. plus the genders, male and female, plus the three characters of what is conditioned (*saṃskṛtalakṣaṇa*), viz. arisal, duration and destruction. *ānimittasamādhi* is linked to the truth of cessation (*nirodhasatya*) and has its four aspects. (3) *apraṇihitasamādhi* has the aspects of the other noble truths, and is a meditation where one does not direct the mind towards any dharma in the three worlds, viz. anything impermanent, ridden with suffering, etc. Other references: Dayal (1931) p. 234 and n. 489 for scriptural references to *Samādhirājasūtra*, etc.; Pr. 246.6 and n. 1; De Jong (1949) p. 21 and n. 59; May (1959) n. 436; *Traité* I, p. 163, and especially pp. 321-325 for a Mahāyānist version of the three; Van den Broeck (1977) for the *Amṛtarasa*'s explanations; Dantinne (1983) pp. 267-269 for further references and translations of pertinent passages from the *Yogācārabhūmiśāstra*.

(194) The point is that perceiving selflessness will automatically imply the acquisition of *apraṇihitasamādhi* and *ānimittasamādhi*.

(195) From the **Bodhisaṃbhāra* = *Byaṅ chub kyi tshogs*, attributed to Nāgārjuna; on this text see Lindtner (1982)'s *Introduction* as well as his Chapter XIII

for further remarks and a translation from the Chinese. The text is inexistent in Sanskrit, but was translated into Chinese by Dharmagupta as the *Pú tí zī liáng lùn*.
A few quotations survive here and there in Tibetan translation. My translation here is based on Tib. Cf. the Chinese (T. XXXII, 1660 iv 532a 19-20):

菩提資糧論　無自性故空　已空何作相　諸相既寂滅　智者何所願

Cf. also Lindtner's translation on p. 235. Note, however, that he splits *jí miè* 寂滅 into "extinct·(*śānta*) and abolished (*niruddha*)". This hardly seems justified, especially as *jí miè* often just translates *nirvṛta* (H. *nivṛta*) and the Tib. just has *log pa*.

(196) Tib. *mthoṅ ba*.

(197) Very common terms. Indeed they are now part of the English language — see Jackson (1982). *śrāvaka* = the followers of Hīnayāna. *pratyekabuddha*: "one who has won enlightenment but lives in solitude and does not reveal his knowledge to the world" (BHSD p. 379). See en. 94.

(198) Instead of *dharmaśarīrāvyatirekavartitāṃ*, the Tibetan seems to read °*vartināṃ* (*chos kyi sku las tha mi dad par bźugs pa*), which would necessitate the following translation: "Or alternatively, to show that it belongs to all the perfectly enlightened ones, who abide inseparably from the Body of the Dharma (*dharmaśarīra*), he said 'the sphere of all the buddhas'."

What is invoked here is the schema of the three "bodies" (*kāya*) of the Buddha; see *Siddhi* II, pp. 762 et seq. In much of the Indo-Tibetan *Prajñāparamitā* literature and that centred around the *Abhisamayālaṃkāra*, selflessness or voidness (i.e. the *dharmadhātu*) is regarded as the "naturally abiding buddha-nature" (*prakṛtistha-gotra*); the *dharmakāya* (= *dharmaśarīra*) is in effect this "buddha-nature" once it has been cleared of adventitious (*āgantuka*) defilements (*mala*). Cf. Tsoṅ kha pa's explanations in *Legs bśad gser phreṅ* 208a5-210a6 translated in Ruegg (1969) pp. 118-122. Note that in *Abhisamayālaṃkāra* VIII, the *dharmakāya* is of two sorts: the wisdom-*dharmakāya* (*jñānadharmakāya*) and the essential-body (*svābhāvikakāya*; *svabhāvakāya*). See Obermiller (1932) pp. 46, 83 and 45, 83 respectively. Roughly speaking, the former is the omniscient mind of the buddhas; the latter has two aspects (1) voidness and (2) the mind free from adventitious defilements. See *rJe bstun pa'i don bdun cu* (ed. Onoda) pp. 56-57, where the two *kāya* are treated as topic 61 and 64 in the seventy topics on the *Abhisamayālaṃkāra*: *dag pa gñis ldan gyi dbyiṅs mthar thug de ṅo bo ñid sku'i mtshan ñid / de la dbye na / raṅ bźin rnam dag gi char gyur pa'i ṅo bo ñid sku daṅ / blo bur rnam dag gi char gyur pa'i ṅo bo ñid sku gñis yod /... ji lta ba daṅ ji sñed pa la ltos te gzigs pa mthar thug pa'i mkhyen pa de / ye śes chos sku'i mtshan ñid.* "'The ultimate sphere endowed with the two purities' is the defining characteristic of the *svābhāvikakāya*. Here there are two divisions: the *svābhāvikakāya* consisting in the fact of essential purity and the *svābhāvikakāya* consisting in the fact of adventitious purity. ... 'The wisdom which is the final vision on how things really are (*ji lta ba*) and how they appear (*ji sñed pa*)' is the defining characteristic of the *jñānadharmakāya*." Note that *ji lta ba* in this context means basically *paramārthasatya* and *ji sñed pa* here means *saṃvṛtisatya*; see Lokesh Chandra s.v. *ji lta ba* and *ji sñed pa*. Finally, see also *Siddhi* II's appendix, "Les corps du Bouddha", as well as Ruegg (1969) *passim* for numerous different precisions.

(199) Literally "the name" (*nāman*).

(200) See BHSD s.v. *parapravādin*: "false teacher, one who promulgates false doctrine". *parapravāda*: "rival (false, heretical) doctrine". See en. 112, 201.

(201) Quoted on p. 232 of M. av. *bhāṣya* ad M. av. verse 118cd. See LVP transl. p. 281. De la Vallée Poussin gives *paravādin* ("les contradicteurs") as the equivalent of *gźan smra rnams*. However, CSV previously used *phas kyi rgol ba*, rather than *gźan smra rnams*, in that sense of *parapravādin* ("rival assertors"); when it subsequently glosses *gźan smra rnams* it uses *pha rol po'i smra ba*, which equals the term *parapravāda* ("rival assertions") in Yamaguchi (1974) *Index to the Prasannapadā part II*. Cf. also Lokesh Chandra, *gźan smra ba* = *paravāda* while *phas kyi rgol ba* = *parapravādin*; *paravādin*; Mvyut 2730. Lang (1986) p. 115 translates: "Nevertheless, it destroys other theses, just as fire destroys fuel". See en. 112 and 200.

(202) Lang (1986) translates: "An opponent (*para*) dislikes anyone who has understood this teaching". It is syntactically impossible to take *gźan la* as the subject. The verb *dga' ba* in Tibetan has its object with the particle *la* (*la don*). The subject does not take the instrumental (*byed sgra*); thus *de* is the subject of *mi dga'* and *gźan la* is the object.

(203) *mnog* = *āsvāda* in Lokesh Chandra.

(204) The argument seems to turn on the division of the Dharma into two: statements or scriptures (*bstan pa; luṅ*) and realizations (*rtogs pa*). The real refuge of the Dharma is the latter, but the former is a facsimile. See e.g. Pr. 487.6 et seq., May (1959) p. 219 and n. 744; Stcherbatsky (1923) p. 2, n. 2; AK iii p. 87, n. 3, AK viii pp. 218-220; *sKabs daṅ po'i spyi don*, the chapter on the three refuges, i.e. *kun mchog gsum gi rnam bźag*.

(205) B. reconstructs as *vastudṛṣṭi*. However the equivalence, *bhāvasadbhāvadarśana*, is also plausible as this is the entry in Yamaguchi (1974) for *dṅos por lta ba*.

(206) On *jīvitendriya* see AK ii k. 45 and AKBh, LVP p. 214 et seq. *jīvita* = *āyus* ("life") and is held, by the Vaibhāṣikas, to be a distinct dharma which is the basis for warmth and consciousness and is the cause for the duration (*sthiti*) of the continuum (*saṃtāna*). The Sautrāntikas do not recognize this *jīvitendriya*. As for

"tangle"/ "thicket" (*tshaṅ tshiṅ*). Cf. *Zidian*: *(rgyan tshig) rtsi śiṅ sogs stug ciṅ 'dziṅs pa ste...*

(207) The Tib. syntax in *bde bar gśegs pa pa'i daṅ ma yin* is somewhat weird, but probably has to be understood as an ellipsis for *bde bar gśegs pa pa'i lugs daṅ rjes su 'brel ba ma yin*. At any rate, that seems to be the way rGyal and Kaḥ thog took it. rGyal p. 12: *...saṅs rgyas kyi bstan pa daṅ min źe na*. Red mda' ba (p. 154) chose the solution of simply eliminating the problematic genitive: ... *bde bar gśegs pa daṅ ma yin źe na*.

(208) Lang (1986) understands *śākya* as Śākyamuni, *gos med* as *nagnaka* and *bram ze* as *vipra*. One could perhaps argue that *śākya* in the *kārikā* and CSV should be taken in the sense of "the Buddhists" in keeping with CSV's reference to *bde bźin gśegs pa pa*. Cf. the commentaries of rGyal tshab (p. 12) and Kaḥ thog (p. 405), which speak of *śākya pa*; Bhattacharya also seems to take *śākya* in CSV in the sense of "the Buddhists". Nonetheless, the Chinese version of k. 294 must be read as referring to the Buddha /Tathāgata, and thus supports Lang. Finally note that *gos med* could also be *acelaka* or *nirgranthika*, while *bram ze* is more usually simply *brāhmaṇa*. Cf. the Chinese of k. 294, which uses *pó luó mén* = *brāhmaṇa*.

(209) My understanding of the syntax differs from B. and follows Red mda' ba (p. 154): *de yaṅ 'di ltar gcer bu pa rnams ni gtsaṅ sbra spyod pa daṅ bral ba'i phyir lus dri ma'i 'dam gyis gos śiṅ khrus ras med ...*

(210) *mig 'phrul*. Literally, "illusion", but the equivalence *mig 'phrul* or *mig 'khrul* = *indrajāla* is attested; cf. Yamaguchi (1974) p. 173 and Lokesh Chandra. *Indrajāla*, in Buddhism, becomes an image for the vast phantasmagoria of the world which holds people captive and is, in fact, more or less synonymous with *māyā* ("illusion"). The term has a long history, but is first found in *Atharvaveda* VIII.8.8, a hymn which is a charm for vanquishing enemies: *ayaṃ loko jālam āsīc Chakrasya mahato mahān / tenāham Indrajālenāmūṃs tamasābhidadhāmi sarvān //* "This vast world was the net of the great Indra. With this net of Indra, I encircle all those with darkness."

(211) Cf. rGyal p. 13: *...khyod kyis kyaṅ de ltar bsgrub rigs so źe na /*.

(212) Lang (1986) translates *phyi 'chos* as "outward show". Note that rGyal p. 13 glosses *phyi 'chos* as *phyi tshul 'chos pa* ("hypocrisy"). Cf. *Zidian* s.v. *tshul 'chos*: *yon tan med bźin du yod pa ltar byas nas gźan gyi mgo skor ba'i bya spyod kyi miṅ* "A practice to cheat others where one pretends to have good qualities which one does not in fact have".

(213) See en. 128.

(214) Transl. De Jong (1949) p. 13, Ruegg (1969) p. 447 n. 3 and Lang (1986). However, De Jong, Ruegg and Lang take *kevalam* as simply meaning "only". De Jong: "Dans leur doctrine il n'y a que ces deux concepts". Ruegg: "ici [dans leur enseignement] il n'y a que ces deux [choses]". Lang: "Here [in our system] there are only these two". I prefer to follow CSV's gloss of *kevalam* as *pariśuddham* (*yoṅs su dag pa*).

(215) Cf. the discussion of these themes in *Yuktiṣaṣṭikā*, k. 9-11, transl. in Lindtner (1982). Red mda' ba (p. 156) has an interesting comment in this regard: *'di lhags bcas daṅ lhag med kyi myaṅ 'das kyi raṅ sde pa gźan dag ñon moṅs ma lus pa spaṅs śiṅ phuṅ po ma 'gags pa daṅ / phuṅ po ma lus pa 'gags pa la 'dod pa ltar 'dir mi bźed de / ñon moṅs ma lus pa ma spaṅ yaṅ mthoṅ nas mya 'das mṅon sum du byed de / rigs pa drug cu pa las / de ñid mthoṅ chos mya ṅan las // 'das śiṅ bya ba byas pa'aṅ yin // źes bśad pas so //*. "Here it [i.e. nirvāṇa] is not to be taken in the way in which our other coreligionists, who [accept] nirvāṇa with remainder (= *sopadhiśeṣaṃ nirvāṇam*) and without remainder (= *nirupadhiśeṣaṃ nirvāṇam*)*, accept that [in the former case] the passions are all abandoned but the aggregates have not [yet] ceased and [in the latter] the aggregates have all ceased. Although all the passions have not [yet] been abandoned, still, when one has seen [voidness] one directly realizes nirvāṇa, for as it is said in the *Yuktiṣaṣṭikā***: 'This is extinction [nirvāṇa] in this very life (*dṛṣṭadharmanirvāṇa*) and one's task is accomplished (*kṛtakṛtya*).'" *For these two concepts in the Yogācāra school, see the passages from the *Viniścayasaṃgrahaṇī* of the *Yogācārabhūmi* in Schmithausen (1969) pp. 46ff et passim. **k. 11ab. The translation of the *kārikā* is that of Lindtner (1982) p. 107.

(216) Cf. Lang's translation: "All people love their own thesis, just as they love their own birth-place. Yet why should a reason that defeats it distress you?" She has taken *sdug pa* in two opposite senses, viz. love and distress. Now admittedly *sdug pa* is an odd word and does have these opposite senses, but it would be strange to have both in one verse. Cf. Bhattacharya, who used *priyaḥ* in both occurrences. Finally, cf. Red mda' ba's commentary (p. 158): *'di phyir rol pa khyod la rgyu gaṅ gis na sdug par 'gyur te mi 'gyur ba kho na'o* "For what reason would this be pleasing to you, the Outsider — it would not be [pleasing] at all". On this interpretation then *sdug pa mi 'gyur ba kho na'o* is being rhetorically expressed by the verse's words *gaṅ gis sdug par 'gyur*. This would fit nicely with the *bù shēng xīn* 不生欣 of the Chinese translation.

(217) Literally, "when there is a cause for perishing / declining".

(218) Cf. Red mda' ba p. 158: *ji ltar mkhas pas ran gi skyes sa yin yaṅ rgud pa'i rgyur mthoṅ na / de la re ba spaṅs nas 'byor pa'i yul gźan la brten pa de bźin du ...*

(219) Kapila, who is traditionally recognized as the founder of the Sāṃkhya system, is nonetheless a historically obscure personage. See Mainkar (1972) p. 14 and Frauwallner (1953) p. 282, 286.

tǐ 體 is most commonly the equivalent of *svabhāva,* but also has the less usual equivalents *dravya* ("substance") or *artha* ("entity"). See H. p. 320 and en. 308. At any rate, whatever the Skt. might be, it is clear that what is being meant is the object itself; the thing or substance which we perceive. While Dharmapāla's Sāṃkhya terminology may be somewhat unorthodox, it seems that he is arguing against the basic Sāṃkhya conception of what a material object, or substance, is, viz. a collection of qualities.

A. Wezler (1986) has shown on the basis of the reference in *Mahābhāṣya* II 366.26 to the Sāṃkhya position, *guṇasaṃdrāvo dravyam,* as well as on the basis of other sources, that the Sāṃkhyas held a fundamental position to the effect that substances (such as vases, etc.) are simply composites or collections of the *guṇas*. Wezler p. 23: "...according to Sāṃkhya a *dravya* consists of *guṇas*, or, to be more precise, is nothing but a *guṇasamudāya*, an "aggregate/integrated whole of *guṇas*." Ibid p. 11: "There can indeed be hardly any doubt that *guṇasamudāyo dravyam* is but another formulation of *guṇasaṃdrāvo dravyam*, or *vice versa*, and that the expressions *samudāya* and *sandrāva* are hence considered here to be practically synonymous."

Following Mallavādin and Siṃhasūri's explanations, the *guṇas* mentioned in the phrase *guṇasaṃdrāvo dravyam*, can be understood as being the qualities or properties of the *tanmātras* ("subtle elements") of sound, tactile sensations, form, taste and smell, viz. *śabdatanmātra*, *sparśatanmātra*, *rūpatanmātra*, *rasatanmātra*, *gandhatanmātra*. Here, in Dharmapāla, we see what looks like the same Sāṃkhya position, although our author speaks of "objects" or "dharmas" (rather than *guṇas*) making up "natures", i.e. *tǐ* 體 , but judging from the enumeration which he gives in the course of the argumentation (cf. §§222a28, 222b4 and k. 302), he seems to be speaking about *rūpa*, *gandha*, *rasa* and *sparśa*, leaving out *śabda* (see §222b8). It is not at all impossible that he means these terms in the Sāṃkhya sense of the properties of *rūpatanmātra*, etc., although as the discussion proceeds it is clear that he is *also* arguing against Buddhist Abhidharma based positions.

It is, however, worth stressing Wezler's point that, according to Siṃhasūri, *guṇa* in the phrase *guṇasaṃdrāvo dravyam* is equally explained as referring to the three constituents of the primary matter or Nature (*prakṛti*), viz. *sattva*, etc. And in fact, it seems that Dharmapāla in the previous chapter's discussion on Sāṃkhya did take up this understanding of *guṇasaṃdrāva*, *guṇasamudāya*. See §217c14 et seq. and en. 72. In short, he seems to have taken up — in different chapters — both interpretations of what it means to say that a thing is a composite of the *guṇas*. In both chapters we see that the Sāṃkhya's weak point, for Dharmapāla, is his problematic position that the entity itself is not different from the *guṇas*, and that hence there is the absurdity that predicates pertaining to some or all of these *guṇas* — e.g. invisibility, the manyness of the *guṇas* — should also apply to the entity itself.

(220) See en. 219 and k. 302, §222b8.

(221) While it seems that in this section Dharmapāla's adversary is still the Sāṃkhya, the argument about the inexpressibility of non-entities is primarily a Buddhist-Nyāya controversy. The general tactic of the Buddhist is to hold that words for non-entities refer to a mentally created fiction, i.e. a *sāmānyalakṣaṇa*. See Matilal (1970), Mimaki (1976) p. 60, Tillemans (1982) p. 112 et seq. and (1984c) for some aspects of the discussion in PS, PV IV, *Madhyamakāloka* and other texts. Cf. also PV IV k. 222-236 summarized in our article, "*Pramāṇavārttika* IV and its Commentaries", forthcoming in K. Potter (ed.), *The Encyclopedia of Indian Philosophies*, Motilal Banarsidass.

(222) If "visibility" were a property belonging to the form itself, then the form should always be visible. But in fact, it is sometimes visible and sometimes not. If the act of seeing *X* gives *X* itself the property of visibility, then not seeing *X* should equally make it have the property of invisibility. Ultimately the argument seems to turn on the hypothesis that visibility or "being seen" is a property belonging to the nature of form, and that this nature cannot change. Finally note that in this and the following arguments, "visibility" is not taken in a dispositional sense (i.e. *Y* is visible because if a person looked at *Y*, he would see *Y*), but in a more ordinary sense: "*Y* is visible now" means we *do* see *Y* now.

(223) The Madhyamaka tactic of negation without affirming the contrary. See en. 102.

(224) See en. 48.

(225) The hidden premise is that if *X* is composed of atoms (which alone are fully real), and none of the atoms have a property *P*, *X* does not have *P* either. Cf. en. 246.

(226) *páng bù* 傍布 = *SPHAR; spharitvā* (H. p. 432), Tib. *khyab par byed pa*, "spread out", "distribute". Note that this is a possible sense of *bù* 布, besides its usual sense, "cloth". Cf. the occurrence of these characters in AKBh iii ad k. 65-68, T. 1558 xi 60a 7. LVP (p. 162) translates by "cover". Cf. AK ed. Pradhan p. 168.13: *pañcāśat yojanāni śākhāpatrapalaśaṃ spharitvā* tiṣṭhati* /. *Pradhan reads *skaritvā*, which is a misprint.

(227) For the interpretation of k. 305 as showing the fallacy of *sādhyasama*, see en. 379.

Dharmapāla's argument seems to be against a position described in the *Chéng wéi shí lún*, T. 1585 i 4b 16-18:

有執色等一一極微不和集時非五識境　共和集位展轉相資有麁相生為此識境彼相實有為此所緣

"Certain people hold that the individual atoms of form, etc., when they are not combined, are not objects of the five [sense] consciousnesses. But in their combined state, when they mutually interact, there arises something gross in character. It is this which is the object of the consciousnesses; its character is substantially existent and it is this which is perceived."

See *Siddhi* I p. 45. Kuī jī in T. 1830 ii 271 a 10 attributes this view to *Zhòng xián* 衆賢 (Saṃghabhadra). a "Neo-Sarvāstivādin" (*xīn sà pó duō* 新薩婆多); cf. Sthiramati's *Triṃśikāvijñaptibhāṣyam* p. 16.26-27 (in S. Lévi's edition): *anyas tu manyate / ekaikaparamāṇur anyanirapekṣyo 'tīndriyo bahavas tu parasparāpekṣā indriyagrāhyāḥ /*. "But another thinks that the individual atoms which do not depend on anything else are beyond the range of the senses. However, many [such atoms] which depend upon each other are apprehendable by the senses."

Saṃghabhadra seems to have postulated a collective character of atoms which would be the objective condition (*ālambanapratyaya*) for consciousness. In this way he hoped to avoid Dignāga's critique that individual atoms could not serve as objects of consciousness because they do not resemble the representation which consciousness has of its objects. Note that Yamaguchi and Meyer (1929) n. 11, basing themselves on Kuī jī, are of the opinion that the third opponent being refuted in *Ālambanaparīkṣā* — i.e. k. 3ab et seq. — is Saṃghabhadra, in spite of the fact that Vinītadeva's commentary speaks only of "Vāgbhaṭa, etc.". This seems to be borne out in reading Kuī jī. Dignāga and Vinītadeva describe this view as holding that the collection of atoms, rather than the individual atoms themselves, is perceived, although the atoms themselves can still be said to cause the perception via the intermediary of the collection. (Cf. the similar views of Vasubandhu and Yaśomitra described in en. 370 as well as Candrakīrti's discussion [in CSV XIII §11-13] of the *timira/keśa* example used in this regard.) The opponent avoids Dignāga's critique by arguing that in general things have several characters — form, smell, etc. — but that for any given perception only one is perceived. Similarly, we perceive only the collective aspect and never that of the individual atoms.

Kuī jī in T. 1834 xià 992c 25- 993a 4 gives the following explanation on Saṃghabhadra's view as found in the Abhidharma commentary, the *Nyāyānusāra*:

其正師恐違自宗眼等五識不緣假法異於經部　若順於古即有陳那五識之上無微相故非所緣失　遂復說言色等諸法各有多相於中一分是現量境故諸極微相資多有一和集相　此相實有各能發生似己相識故與五識作所緣緣如多極微集成山等相資各有山等量相　眼等五識緣山等時實有多極微相資山相五識並得故成所緣　不爾即有非所緣失。

"The teacher of the *Nyāyānusāra*, fearing [the Sautrāntika view that the whole is unreal] would contradict his own [Sarvāstivādin] theses, [said that] the five consciousnesses, such as those of the eyes, etc., do not apprehend dharmas which are designations, and [thus] he differed from the Sautrāntikas. If one follows the older [Sarvāstivādins], then Dignāga [argues in the *Ālambanaparīkṣā*] that because the character of atoms is not found in the five sense consciousnesses, there is the fault [that the atoms] are not what is apprehended. So then [Saṃghabhadra] replied that dharmas such as form and the like each have several characters. Amongst them, one part is the object of perception. Thus, the atoms' interactions each have one collective character. This character substantially exists. Each [such character] gives rise to a consciousness which resembles [the collection's] own character, and therefore, they serve as the objective conditions (*suǒ yuán yuán* 所緣緣 = *ālambanapratyaya*) for the five consciousnesses. For example, when the interactions of many atoms become [gross objects] such as mountains, etc., the interactions each have the dimension of the mountain, etc. When the five consciousnesses of the eye and so forth apprehend the mountains, etc., there substantially exists a character of a mountain which consists in the interaction of many atoms; the five consciousness obtain [i.e. cognize] it. Therefore, it is established as what is apprehended. Were it otherwise, there would be the fault of not being what is apprehended."

(228) Below and in §224c29 Dharmapāla formulates this dilemma somewhat more clearly: *a)* either the division of matter goes on forever and one incurs the fault of an infinite regress, never arriving at anything indivisible and hence real; or *b)* the division is carried through to an end where there are no more material characteristics and the object is then unfindable like space.

For a Vijñānavādin's account of atoms, cf. *Chéng wéi shì lún*, T. 1585 i 4b 28-4c 4:

爲執麁色有實體者佛說極微令其除析　非謂諸色實有極微
諸瑜伽師以假想慧於麁色相漸次除析至不可析假說極微
雖此極微猶有方分而不可析　若更析之便似空現不名爲色故
說極微是色邊際

"To those who hold that gross forms exist substantially, the Buddha taught about [subtle] atoms to dispel [this view]. But he did not say that forms are really atoms. The Yogācāryas, by means of the concepts of their intellect, step by step divide gross forms to arrive at what is indivisible. They metaphorically term this 'atoms'. Although these atoms still have directional parts, they are indivisible: if one continues to divide them it will be like looking at space: one cannot call them forms. Therefore, it is said that the atoms are the extreme limit of form."

Cf. *Siddhi* pp. 46-47. In n. 3 on p. 47 de la Vallée Poussin gives the citation from AK alluded to in the final line above. Note however that my translation differs in a number of places from that of LVP, who, in all due respect, translates oddly here. E.g. "Les Yogācāryas, non pas avec un réel couteau mais par la pensée [=... *yǐ jiǎ xiǎng huì*! 以假想慧]"; "à cette extrême fraction, d'existence toute fictive, ils donnent le nom d'atome [= *jiǎ shuō jí wēi* 假説極微]"; but *jiǎ shuō* is better taken as meaning *upacāra*, i.e. "metaphor(ically)".

(229) As is often the case, *rūpa* has two senses in these discussions. In the previous paragraphs *rūpa* referred to the visual characteristics of an object — similar to *rūpa* in the Buddhist notion of *rūpāyatana*. But now "form" is used in its equally frequent sense as a synonym of matter, and includes not just visual form, but also sounds, smells, tastes, the elements and other tactile sensations.

(230) The position being attacked is probably that of the Mīmāṃsā. See *Mīmāṃsāsūtra* 1.1.6-23; Frauwallner (1961). Note that Dharmakīrti was familiar with this argument about *saras* vs. *rasa* and alludes to it in PV I k. 301: *ānupūrvyām asatyāṃ syāt saro rasa iti śrutau/ na kāryabheda iti ced asti sā puruṣāśrayā //.* "Suppose it is said that when there is no [objectively existing] order, then the words *saras* and *rasa* would not have any different effects. [Reply:] This [order] depends upon the person." In PVSV to this section of PV I Dharmakīrti identifies his opponents as "Jaiminīyas", i.e. Mīmāṃsakas. See PVSV's introduction to PV I k. 283cd; p. 150, 6 in Gnoli's edition. The basic conceptions at stake are, however, also common to Bhartṛhari's notion of *sphoṭa*. Cf. *Vākyapadīya* I, 49 ed. Rau (48, ed. Biardeau): *nādasya kramajātatvān na pūrvo na paraś ca saḥ / akramaḥ kramarūpeṇa bhedavān iva jāyate //* "As it is the resonance which occurs successively, the [word itself, i.e. the *sphoṭa*] has neither before nor after. It [i.e. the *sphoṭa*] is without any successive order, but appears to be divided due to the successive nature [of the resonances]." See Biardeau (1964), p. 91.

(231) Taishō reads *suī xiǎn sè* 雖顯色 and gives no variants, but we should read *lí xiǎn sè* 離顯色, as does the Japanese translator (Kyik p. 340, 18). This not only concords with Tib. but also is the reading commented upon by Dharmapāla.

(232) *sāmānyalakṣaṇa*, in the Epistemologist's system, are only cognizable by inference (*anumāna*) and not by perception. Cf. Dignāga's PSV ad PS I k. 2, quoted in PVBh 169, 9-10: *svalakṣaṇaviṣayaṃ hi pratyakṣaṃ sāmānyalakṣaṇaviṣayam anumānam iti pratipādayiṣyāmaḥ /.* Transl. Hattori (1968a) p. 24. See also en. 366, 367.

(233) I.e. when it does not also perceive colour, e.g. a cognition of a shape in the dark.

(234) If the opponent tries to maintain that shapes are understood independently of other understandings, Dharmapāla replies that understanding of shapes, such

as those of a whirling firebrand, must nonetheless rely on initial sense perceptions (e.g. the perceptions of the fire on the torch which twirls around). As such it is inferential or conceptual.

(235) LVP AK i p. 16: "Le visible est couleur et figure. La couleur (*varṇa*) est quadruple: bleu, rouge, jaune, blanc... La figure (*saṃsthāna*) est octuple: long, court, carré, rond, haut (*unnata*), bas (*avanata*), égal, inégal."

(236) The elements (*bhūta*) are fourfold: earth, air, fire and water and are considered as being only perceptible by the sense of touch. The derivatives from the elements (*bhautika*) include all the various visual, olfactory, gustatory, and auditory sensa of colours, shapes, etc. Other tactile sensations such as roughness, heaviness and so forth are also classified as *bhautika*, so that in effect the sense of touch is the only sense that perceives both *bhūta* and *bhautika*: the others perceive only *bhautika*. It should be mentioned there are other *bhautika*, such as the invisible subtle matter (*rūpa-prasāda*) making up the sense organs (*indriya*)(see en. 264 below) and the unmanifest (*avijñapti*) forms. A commonly invoked classificational schema is to take the elements, plus the other sensa as constituting the "outer domains" (*bāhyāyatana*) of consciousness, while the sense organs *qua* subtle matter are the "inner domains" (*ādhyātmikāyatana*). See AK i, k. 12, 23, 24; LVP AK i pp. 21-23, 43-46, 63-66; May (1959) n. 184, 198; de la Vallée Poussin (1913) pp. 18-20. For a summary presentation of the *bāhyāyatana* according to the Tibetan scholastic, see *Yoṅs 'dzin bsdus grwa chuṅ* ff. 3a6-4a4 ed. T. Kelsang and S. Onoda. See also en. 237, 256, 264, 386, 387.

(237) Colour, smells, etc., which are derived from the four elements, are perceived by the eyes, nose and so forth. The four elements (earth, air, fire, water) themselves, however, are perceived by the sense of touch. While these entities are perceived by different faculties, the world does not make such a differentiation between object itself (viz. the elements) and its derivative properties. In that sense, the reason in the argument, viz. "having different cognitions", does not conclusively prove the thesis, viz. that the *bhautikas* and the *bhūtas* are taken as different *by the world*. Cf. in this vein AK i, k. 13: *pṛthivī varṇasaṃsthānam ucyate lokasaṃjñayā*. "What one terms 'earth' according to worldly convention is a colour and a shape."

(238) Dharmapāla here invokes the orthodox position of AK where shape is said to be seen by the eyes.

(239) Thesis: Shapes are not seen by the eyes.
Reason: They are cognizable by means of touch.
Example: Like roughness.

The equivalences in H. (p. 222) show that Xuán zàng often used the character *sè* 澁 ("astringency"/ "roughness") in the sense of *karkaśatva* ("hardness"; "roughness"). Cf. Nak. p. 668a. Dharmapāla's argument is that if shape really exists, it must comply with the Abhidharmic division of phenomena: what is seen by the eyes is not felt by the body and vice versa. Thus if shape is real and is felt, it is not seen. The implicit conclusion seems to be that because shape is conventionally thought to be both felt and seen, it cannot be real.

(240) The argument is turning on the use of the restrictive particle *eva* ("only") which is supposedly present, implicitly or explicitly, in every assertion and which provides for different sorts of restriction or necessity (*jué dìng* 決定 = *avadhāraṇa; niyama*) between the terms in the sentence. See Kajiyama (1973) and Gillon and Hayes (1982). Thus, Dharmapāla's opponent is in effect construing the argument as saying that shapes are only cognized by means of touch: in that case they cannot be cognized by seeing colours. Or, it is only shapes which are cognizable by touch: in that case shapeless things couldn't be felt. But Dharmapāla replies that his point is that shapes, *inter alia*, are *indeed* cognized by touch. The difference is between *saṃsthānaṃ spraṣṭavyam eva, saṃsthānam eva spraṣṭavyam* (the opponent's two versions) and *saṃsthānaṃ spraṣṭavyam asty eva*, the latter being Dharmapāla's version. Similar types of arguments about *eva* and *avadhāraṇa* are found in *Pramāṇaviniścaya*'s *Svārthānumāna* chapter concerning the *pakṣadharmatva* in the triply characterized reason (*trirūpaliṅga*): see PVin ed. Steinkellner (1973) p. 30 et seq.; transl. Steinkellner (1979) pp. 32-35. See also the discussion in PV IV (k. 171-172) about whether one must understand the definition of the thesis as *sādhyanirdeśa eva pratijñā* or *sādhyanirdeśaḥ pratijñaiva*. Dharmakīrti is known to have systematized the uses of *eva* as *ayogavyavaccheda* ("exclusion of non-connection"), *anyayogavyavaccheda* ("exclusion of connection with something else") and *atyantāyogavyavaccheda* ("exclusion of absolute non-connection"). See Kajiyama, Gillon and Hayes, op. cit. To put things in Dharmakīrtian terms, Dharmapāla's opponent is construing *eva* as *ayogavyavaccheda* and *anyayogavyavaccheda* respectively, while Dharmapāla would be taking it as *atyantāyogavyavaccheda*. I have summarized PV IV k. 190-194 dealing with these three uses of *eva* in my article "*Pramāṇavārttika* IV and its Commentaries". Note that *dìng* 定 does occasionally translate *eva*, especially in logical contexts, as we see in Xuán zàng's Chinese translation of the *Nyāyapraveśa*, T. 1630. See Katsura (1986c) and my remarks in Tillemans (1988b), pp. 156-158.

(241) The term here is *sè* 色 = *rūpa*, but the subsequent explanation which speaks of "blue, etc." makes it clear that *here rūpa* is to be taken as having its meaning, "colour". Cf. also Japanese transl. p. 341, n. 29: "The cognition of colour (色彩 *shikisai*) by means of touch must necessarily have shapes such as length, roundness, etc. as its intermediary (媒介 *baikai*), and is an inference."

(242) See en. 240 . *jué dìng* 決定 = *avadhāraṇa; niyama*, "necessity", "restriction".

(243) Previously, in §223b26, Dharmapāla had argued that one cannot prove that shape and colour are *different* by invoking the reason that their respective

cognitions are different. But now he says that they are not *identical*, and here he himself gives the reason that their cognitions are different. The conclusion which he draws in §223c17 is that shape and colours are neither identical nor different, and are hence unreal.

(244) See en. 243. A variation on the *ekānekaviyogahetu*. See Chapt. III, B. pp. 63-64, fn. 133, 134, en. 37.

(245) Shape, according to AK iv k. 3, does not exist in the individual atoms, and there are no "atoms of length" and so forth. See AK iv LVP p. 11: ... "mais l'existence de ces atomes [de figure] n'est pas établie comme est établie l'existence des atomes de couleur..."

(246) The recurrent principle that if none of the atoms (which are alone are substantial) have a property *X*, then the collection (which is insubstantial) cannot have *X* either. See en. 225.

(247) See en. 53.

(248) See en. 56 for the Vaiśeṣika use of the term *rūpa*, viz. colours, which are in the category of qualities (*guṇa*).

(249) Note that the character *cū* 麁 here is probably being used for the Vaiśeṣika technical term, *mahattva*, rather than its more usual Buddhist equivalent, *audārika* ("coarse"). Size (*parimāṇa*), one of the seventeen qualities in Kaṇāda's Vaiśeṣika system, is subdivided into five: largeness (*mahattva*), smallness (*aṇutva*), longness (*dīrghatva*), shortness (*hrasvatva*) and sphericity (*pārimaṇḍalya*). See VS 1.1.5 and 7.1.15-26 as well as p. 213, §9 and 218, §66 in Hattori's summary in Potter (1977). Cf. also Śaṃkara Miśra's commentary ad VS 7.1.15 (ed. Sinha, 7.1.8; transl. Sinha p. 221): "Moreover, in the perceptibility of Substance, Measure or Extension [i.e. *parimāṇa*] also is a cause, like colour; for, without magnitude, substance cannot be perceptible."

(250) The text reads 實之與色亦可別觀 which has little sense. I would emend to 實之與色不可別觀

(251) The argument is reminiscent of the discussion of the Vaiśeṣika's theory of perception in the previous chapter. If the cognition of the colour is different from that of the substance, then these cognitions are not direct perceptions caused by substance. In a direct perception really caused by the substance, one could make no distinctions like, "here is substance", and "here is the colour".

(252) This equivalence is not attested in H. and Nak., but these are the usual Sanskrit terms in Nyāya-Vaiśeṣika contexts. See Potter (1977) p. 49: "The best a Naiyāyika can do to explain what a locus is [is] to say that it is that which we say things reside 'in' or 'on' or 'at'. It is not spatiotemporally conceived, although spatiotemporal difference implies different loci."

(252a) The "same natural kind" is that of colourness, the *jāti* or lower universal (*aparasāmānya*) in virtue of which the different individual colour qualities are all said to be colours. Cf. *Praśastapādabhāṣya* p. 103: *rūpādīnāṃ sarveṣāṃ guṇānāṃ pratyekam aparasāmānyasaṃbandhād rūpādisaṃjñā bhavanti.*

(253) The point seems to be that if the nature of the universal varied in keeping with the different particulars, then ascribing a universal would become haphazard. The reason there is colour is because of the presence of the property colourness, which is always the same. If such a universal did not exist, then particular colours could equally arbitrarily come into being or go out of being.

(254) The Vaiśeṣika position is that the colours, being qualities, do not have other qualities such as size. Rather it is the substance in which the colour inheres which would have these other qualities.

(255) See Chapter III, B. p. 61, fn. 131.

(256) See en. 236, 264, 386, 387 on the elements. Cf. *Yoṅs 'dzin bsdus grwa chuṅ*'s definitions of the elements (f. 4a): "hard and resistant" (*sra źiṅ 'thas pa*) = earth; "wet and liquid" (*brlan źiṅ gśer ba*) = water; "hot and burning" (*tsha źiṅ sreg pa*) = fire; "light and moving" (*yaṅ źiṅ g.yo ba*) = air. While this approach might perhaps seem to lead to idealism, in fact the definition of the elements in terms of touch sensations is already fundamental in the (realist) philosophy of the Abhidharma. See AK i k. 12 and AKBh and other references in en. 387, 388. See also fn. 90 for the Sarvāstivādin's (unstable) position that sense-data *are* external objects.

(257) A reference to the Nyāya-Vaiśeṣika theory that the qualities of a substance may alter while the substance itself continues to exist. This whole process of qualitative change is known as *pāka*, "cooking", the prototypical example being that of a pot, which changes colour and other such qualities when it is baked, but whose atomic constituents persist. See Potter (1977) pp. 84-86.

(258) The example here is a *vaidharmyadṛṣṭānta*, i.e. something which has neither the reason-property (*hetu*) nor the property to be proved (*sādhyadharma*). Vases, etc., according to the Vaiśeṣikas, are perceptible and they do become qualitatively different when heated. Thus this example is used to establish the con-

traposition of the implication in question (*vyatirekavyāpti*): whatever is an object of the senses does become different when heated.

(259) My translation is based on Dharmapāla's interpretation. It can readily be seen that Candrakīrti's interpretation is completely different, taking k. 310 as being a refutation of the general term, perceptibility (*draṣṭavyatva*). It is interesting to note that following Candrakīrti's interpretation, the second half of k. 310 has a rather unobvious connection with the first half. Dharmapāla has no such problem. Finally note that my translation differs significantly from that of Tucci (1925) p. 553, n. 1, who seems to have taken k. 310 as expressing a similar point to a passage in *Băi lùn* VI. I presume that this must be T. 1569 *xià* 176c 12-15; see Tucci (1929) p. 56 for a generally accurate translation. The point however is not very similar as far as I can tell. At any rate, neither Dharmapāla's nor Candrakīrti's interpretations of k. 310 seem to concord with this argument from the *Băi lùn*. Dharmapāla's argument seems to be an appeal to empirical observation and to the Buddhist theme that only changing and impermanent things are real: if substances existed we would have to be able to see that they undergo change, but in fact we see nothing of the sort.

(260) Cf. §223a 24-25 and en. 228.

(261) T. has *yǒu wú fǎ* 有無法, which is clearly an error for *yǒu wéi fǎ* 有爲法. Japanese transl. (Kyik p. 346.11) reads *yǒu wéi fǎ*.

(262) See AK i k. 5 for the three unconditioned dharmas, viz. space (*ākāśa*) and the two sorts of cessations (*nirodha*). Cf. *Siddhi* p. 72 et seq. for the Vijñānavādin's refutation.

(263) For the term *yì mén* 義門, see Nak. p. 219c. The argument may be a similar point as expressed in §217a2 of the previous chapter: "One object at the same time gives rise to many consciousnesses, and the object's character varies according to different perceptions. [Thus] these consciousnesses could not arise in conformity with an external object, for the nature of one object is not established as many [different] characters."

(264) Cf. AK i k. 9cd: *tadvijñānāśrayā rūpaprasādāś cakṣurādayaḥ*. Cf. T. 1558 i 2b 12:

彼識依淨色　名眼等五根

"The bases of the consciousnesses of these [objects], i.e. the subtle matter, are [the five sense organs such as] the eye and so forth."

Cf. LVP AK i p. 15, where *rūpaprasādāḥ* is translated as "des éléments matériels subtils". See also LVP AK i p. 65 ; *Traité* I p. 332; May (1959) n. 131, 199. As for the difference between the eye organ *qua* subtle matter and the eye *qua* "ball of flesh" (*māṃsapiṇḍa*) the former is just derived from the elements (*bhautika*), is invisible and is an "inner domain" (*ādhyātmikāyatana*), while the latter is an "outer domain" (*bāhyāyatana*) and is composed both of the elements, earth, etc., themselves (*bhūta*) as well as the colours, shapes, etc. derived from them (*bhautika*). See en. 236, 268 and cf. AK i LVP p. 65.

(265) See AKBh ad AK i k. 9cd: *yathoktaṃ bhagavatā cakṣur bhikṣo ādhyātmikam āyatanaṃ catvāri mahābhūtāny upādāya rūpaprasāda iti vistaraḥ*. Identified in Y. Honjō (1984) pp. 4-5 as *Saṃyuktāgama* (*zá ā hán jīng* 雜阿含經) 322, i.e. T. I 99 xiii 91c 5. Same quotation in longer form in AKBh ad AK i k. 35, transl. LVP p. 65.

(266) The opponent accepts the cardinal tenet of Abhidharmic philosophy that entities are nothing other than the collection of their constituent dharmas.

(267) T. has: 二相差別俱非假有 "Two different characters are both not designations". It would seem to make better sense to read 二相差別俱非實有 .

(268) Dharmapāla's argument turns on the highly simplistic physics of his time where matter was thought to be composed of four elements: the organs would therefore be all the same in that each is composed of the four. If, however, one argues that there is some difference in the collections of elements constituting the causes for consciousness, then it should be possible for the consciousness to be produced directly from the elements — e.g. from an object which has the necessary collection of elements — and thus bypass the sense organs. It is probably fair to say that these anomalies and the remedies proposed in the subsequent argumentation by both Dharmapāla and his opponents just occur within the context of a now outmoded conceptual framework. It is interesting, however, to see that the scientific framework of the period leads to all sorts of *ad hoc* postulates, and finally to the fundamentally anti-theoretical standpoint that perception is simply inexplicable, as we find in k. 311cd. Curiously enough, the physical theory itself was never put in question, no doubt partially because, as we see in k. 311cd, the Buddhist sūtras endorsed the inconceivability of karmic processes. Thus the paradoxes were not at all taken as constituting a *reductio ad absurdum* of any initial physical assumptions; rather they were further proof of the veracity of the sūtras' assertions of inconceivability.

(269) The scholastic speaks of two sorts of karma: *a)* "propelling karma" (*yǐn yè* 引業 = *ākṣepakakarman*), which is responsible for one's taking birth in a particular realm, viz. as a god, man, hell-being, etc; *b)* accomplishing karma, which takes care of the details of one's existence in that realm, viz. whether one is rich, poor, has defective senses, etc. See AK ii LVP p. 273, n. 1; AK iii LVP p. 43; AK iv, k. 95b LVP p. 199-200; Nak. 1288a.

(270) In other words, if each sense organ were produced from a different karma.

(271) Cf. Japanese translator's n. 58 on p. 348: "Because the retributive cause for the realm of form is just virtuous karma."

(272) See H. p. 349 for the equivalence. For the terms *sabhāga* ("having [its own] share") and *tatsabhāga* ("that which is analogous to a *sabhāga*"), see AK i, LVP pp. 75-78. AKBh ad AK i k.39d (ed. Pradhan p. 28.2): *yaḥ svakarmakṛt sa sabhāga iti* /. "What performs its own action is *sabhāga*". Objects, sense organs and consciousnesses can all be *sabhāga*. In the case of the sense organs, they are *sabhāga* when intact and functioning, but *tatsabhāga* when they are not functioning. As LVP (p. 78 n. 2) notes, the Mādhyamikas make use of this terminology arguing that the eye organ which is *sabhāga* does not in reality see the visible objects because it is an organ just like the eye organ which is *tatsabhāga*. Cf. Bhāvaviveka's *Prajñāpradīpa* D. 76b7-77a1: *don dam par brten pa mtshuṅs pa'i mig ni gzugs la lta bar mi byed de / mig gi dbaṅ po yin pa'i phyir dper na de daṅ mtshuṅs pa bźin no.* Cf. Tib. and Skt. in Pr. 32.9 and n. 8.

(273) The domains are of two sorts, outer and inner, the outer being the objects and the inner being the sense organs. See en. 236. Here what is meant are the domains which are the sense organs.

(274) *sŭn yì* 損益 = *kārāpakāra*; Tib. *phan pa daṅ gnod pa* has been translated here as "impaired /impairment" and "aided/ aid" rather than the more usual "harmed/harm and benefited/benefit". What is at stake is the defective and the improved functioning of the senses, as when the eye is damaged or when collyrium or medication is applied.

(275) Translation unsure.

(276) In other words, there must be an *avinābhāvaniyama* ("necessary connection") between the terms of the inference: when there are different consciousnesses there must be different sense organs and when there are no different sense organs there are no different consciousnesses. The opponent accepts this, but he also argues that one and the same entity can have several different powers. In that case the *avinābhāvaniyama* in the inference would not hold: it would not necessarily be so that there must be different sense organs to produce different consciousness, for one and the same sense organ could have several different powers. For the development of the notions of *avinābhāvaniyama*, *vyāpti* ("pervasion") and other such related concepts, see the historical study on this subject by Katsura (1986a) and its English summary in (1986b); see also Stcherbatsky (1926), Chapt. XV; Mookerjee (1935) Chapt. XXIV.

(277) Cf. TS k. 488: *saṃkṣepo 'yaṃ vinaṣṭāc cet kāraṇāt kāryasaṃbhavaḥ / pradhvastasyānupākhyān niṣkāraṇam idaṃ bhavet //.* "To summarize: if the effect were produced from a cause which had perished, it would be causeless, for what is destroyed is indiscernible."

(278) On *vāsanā* ("tendencies"; more literally, "residues"), see Lamotte (1974). They are likened to the smell of a flower which remains after the flower itself is gone. Note that *vāsanā* ≅ *bīja*. The theory of karmic production from *vāsanā* is in opposition to the theory of the Sarvāstivādin, who maintains that the past karma itself produces the result. For Vijñānavāda and most other schools the karma perishes immediately after its production but leaves *vāsanā* or *bīja* which will produce the effect. See *Siddhi* p. 475 and en. 283.

(279) The opponent is seeking to maintain that karma is responsible for the production of the sense consciousnesses, but at the same he wishes to avoid the absurd consequence that the very same karma should also produce sense consciousnesses in the formless realm. He therefore argues that the karma produced in realm *X* only produces the sense organs in the same realm *X*. These organs in turn produce the consciousnesses which cognize objects in *X*. Thus it is impossible that a karma produced in realm *X* would eventually lead to a sense consciousness in another realm *Y*.

(280) An appeal to the principle that any consciousness, being a subject (*viṣayin*), must have an object (*viṣaya*). If mind in the formless realm could not perceive objects in the other realms, it could not perceive any objects at all, and thus it could not exist.

(281) If there were real, externally existent, sense organs, and consciousness were produced by karma, then the absurdities mentioned in the previous paragraphs would ensue. But Dharmapāla and the Vijñānavādin's theory is that karmic tendencies *develop* into the various conditions of the sense organs which then affect consciousness: everything (be it object, sense organ or consciousness) is thus a development of a karmic tendency; the problem of the relationship between the karma and the sense organ is to be resolved by saying that the organ is not a distinct external object, but is itself a manifestation of the karma. See en. 283 for the Vijñānavāda account of the sense organs. As for *pariṇāma*, it is the key term in Vijñānavāda, signifying in general the various transformations which consciousness undergoes to manifest objects. See our en. 283; *Siddhi* pp. 6, 92-93 and *passim*; p. 140 for *pariṇāma* by the influence of conceptualizations (*vikalpabala*).

(282) Cf. H. *wàng wèi* 妄謂 = *dṛṣṭi*. Cf. also *Zuì xīn shí yòng hàn yīng cí diǎn* (ed. Liang Shih-chiu et al, Taipei, The Far East Book Co., 1972), p. 1028 s.v. *wèi*: "1.to tell; to say 2. to name...3. to think; to be of the opinion; to assume."

(283) After having shown the incoherence and unreality of the different ways in which consciousness could be caused (viz. by the sense organs, by the sense organs + karma, by karma alone) Dharmapāla here seems to be stating his own position, viz. that everything, be it consciousness, the sense organs or the objects, is caused by karmic tendencies in an illusory fashion, like dream phenomena. At any rate, such is his and the other commentators' account as described in the *Chéng wéi shí lùn*.

To elaborate: The usual Vijñānavādin account (Cf. *Siddhi* I pp. 41-42 and p. 229 et seq.) is that karmic seeds produce both the sense organs and their objects, although nothing exists externally and all is a development (*pariṇāma*) of consciousness. The sense organs themselves are simply "powers" (*gōng néng* 功能 = *śakti*), but not external things constituted of derived matter. *Siddhi* p. 42: "Comme l'indique leur nom d'*indriya* (*Kośa*, ii, p. 103), ils sont seulement des "puissances" (*śakti*), non pas des choses extérieures constituées par de la matière dérivée des quatre grands éléments (*upādāyarūpa*, bhautikarūpa, Kośa, i, p. 21)." Dignāga himself also held that the sense organ was a power and, in keeping with his idealist position, explicitly denied that it was constituted of matter. Cf. *Ālambanaparīkṣā* k. 7cd: *lhan cig byed dbaṅ nus pa yi / ṅo bo gaṅ yin dbaṅ po'aṅ yin //*. "That which is in essence a power capable of acting simultaneously [with the object for producing consciousness] is the sense organ". The *Ālambanaparīkṣāvṛtti* comments: *dbaṅ po ni raṅ gi 'bras bu las nus pa'i ṅo bo ñid du rjes su dpag gi 'byuṅ ba las gyur pa ñid du ni ma yin no /*. "The sense organs are inferred from their effects as being in essence powers, but they are not derivatives from the elements". Cf. the translations of Yamaguchi and Meyer (1929); Tola and Dragonetti (1982) p. 128 seem to have forgotten to translate k. 7cd. Dharmapāla himself certainly must have endorsed this position as he wrote a commentary on the *Ālambanaparīkṣā*, but unfortunately the text of his commentary (only available in Chinese translation) abruptly ends before this point. In the present context, however, Dharmapāla does not devote more than a few lines to such a theory. Instead he seems to wish to insist on the inconceivability of karma and causation, and thus tries to demonstrate that the various theories of *real* sense organs and karma do not withstand logical analyses. See §225c29 below. Note that Dignāga and Jinendrabuddhi also accepted that the karmic production of the sense organs was ultimately inexplicable. See en. 284.

(284) The Epistemological school equally subscribed to the inconceivability of the karmic production of the sense organs. See Hattori (1968a) n. 5.6 for quotations from the *Pramāṇasamuccayaṭīkā* to this effect. On Buddhist assertions of the inconceivability (*acintya*) of karmic retribution, see LVP (1913) p. 64 and references in his n. 1: *Aṅguttara* ii, 80; M. av. vi, k. 42 (LVP [1910] p. 321); *Bodhicaryāvatāra*, ix, 4, 100 for the inconceivability of dependent origination.

(285) On this term, see Nak. p. 1215c. "showing a change of appearance." Skt. *prātihārya* in the *Bodhisattvabhūmi*.

(286) The allusion is to the Sāṃkhya theory that when a sense object is perceived, four elements are involved: *a)* the sense organ; *b)* the intellect (*buddhi*); *c)* the ego (*ahaṃkāra*); *d)* the mental organ (*manas*). See SK 30: *yugapac catuṣṭayasya tu vṛttiḥ kramaśaś ca tasya nirdiṣṭā / dṛṣṭe tathāpy adṛṣṭe trayasya tatpūrvikā vṛttiḥ //.* The latter three are collectively known as the internal organs (*antaḥkaraṇa*) and have differing functions (see Gauḍapāda ad SK 29); the mental organ (*manas*), which is considered to be an *indriya*, is responsible for reflection (*saṃkalpa*; cf. SK 27) and distinguishing one thing from another. Dharmapāla / Xuán zàng's use of *nèi zhí* 内智 in this context can not mean simply *buddhi*, but rather should be referring primarily to *manas*, as amongst the *antaḥkaraṇa* it is only *manas* which is termed an *indriya* — Dharmapāla makes it clear that he is speaking about two sorts of *indriya* here. Cf. Dignāga's refutation in PS I k. 8-9 of the Sāṃkhya view that the object apprehended by means of *indriyavṛtti* ("the operation of the senses") is then apprehended by means of *manovṛtti*. See Hattori (1968a) p. 157, n. 5.58 for PST's description of this position.

(287) Here we have to take "sight" in the sense of the perception which arises from the function of the eye. In Candrakīrti's interpretation, however, *darśana* means "the organ of sight", i.e. the eyes. This we can see by Candrakīrti's references to *adhipatipratyaya*. See en. 397. Dharmapāla, by contrast, makes no references to *adhipatipratyaya* ("the dominant condition"), i.e. the eyes, but rather takes the verse as refuting the Sāṃkhya's theory of "double perception", where one is supposed to see something first and then apprehend it by means of the mind.

(288) Cf. SK 30 and *Bhāṣya* where it is said that in certain cases the sense organ and the *antaḥkaraṇa* act simultaneously (e.g. when things are seen in a flash) and in others they act sequentially (e.g. when one slowly discerns more and more about a distant object.)

(289) An allusion to the cardinal tenet of Sāṃkhya philosophy that the Primordial Nature (*prakṛti*) undergoes its various manifestations for the benefit of Spirit (*puruṣa*). See SK 21: *puruṣasya darśanārthaṃ kaivalyārthaṃ tathā pradhānasya / paṅgvandhavad ubhayor api saṃyogas tatkṛtaḥ sargaḥ //.*

(290) In what follows Āryadeva and Dharmapāla take up the question of *prāpyakāritvavāda* ("the position that [sense organs] operate by contact") versus *aprāpya-kāritvavāda*, i.e. the problem as to whether sense organs function by "going out" to their object or not. The Sāṃkhyas, Naiyāyikas, Vaiśeṣikas, Mīmāṃsakas and Vedāntins held that this "operation by contact" was necessary; Dignāga denied it and was hence an *aprāpyakāritvavādin*. See Mookerjee (1935) chapter XVIII for a résumé of the Indian philosophical debate on *prāpyakāritvavāda*. See also TS and TSP chapter XXIV k. 2518 et seq. (transl. Jha Vol. II, pp. 1164-1170).

As for the Buddhists' position, they generally held that the eye, ear and *manas* ("mind"; "mental organ") function without contacting their objects; if they did have to contact the object, then, as Dignāga argues in PS I, they could not apprehend things at a distance (*sāntaragrahaṇa*), nor could they apprehend objects bigger than the sense organ itself (*adhikagrahaṇa*). See PS I k. 1cd, Hattori (1968a) p. 37 and especially pp. 124-126, n. 3.33 for further details and Uddyotakara's counterarguments in the *Nyāya-vārttika*. The Buddhists held that the nose, tongue and corporal sense organs function by contact and can only perceive objects which are of their same size. Cf. AK i k. 43cd-44ab (ed. Pradhan pp. 32-33; transl. LVP pp. 87, 93): *cakṣuḥśrotramano 'prāptaviṣayaṃ trayam anyathā / tribhir ghrāṇādibhis tulyaviṣayagrahaṇaṃ matam //*. Finally, however, in what follows it becomes clear that, in contrast to Dignāga and AK, Dharmapāla takes a more Madhyamaka stance arguing that both the theory of *prāpyakāritva* and that of *aprāpyakāritva* lead to absurdities. Cf. the parallel discussion in *Bǎi lùn* T. 1569 xià 175c 28- 176a15; Tucci (1929) pp. 51-52.

(291) Note that Dharmapāla seems to provisionally adopt the Naiyāyika view that the eye is not the fleshy organ or the pupil, but rather the light-ray (*raśmi*) which goes out to the object. Cf. NS 3.1.34: *raśmyarthasaṃnikarṣaviśeṣāt tadgrahaṇam //*. "Their apprehension is due to a particular contact between the light-ray and the object". Vātsyāyana's NS *bhāṣya*: *tayor mahadaṇvor grahaṇaṃ cakṣūraśmer arthasya ca sannikarṣaviśeṣād bhavati yathā pradīparaśmer arthasya ceti* / "The apprehension of these two, viz. the gross and the minute, is due to a particular contact between the eye's light-ray and the object, just like that between the light-ray of a lamp and an object." It would be all too easily refutable to hold that the actual fleshy organ comes into contact with the object. As Dignāga argued in PSV I (p. 194, 6-7): *dbaṅ po ni rten gyi yul ñid na gnas pa ste der gso ba la sogs pa rab tu sbyor ba'i phyir* (transl. Hattori p. 38: "The sense remains at the very place of its [physical] basis, since it is to this [basis] that medical treatment and so on is directed.")

(292) Cf. TS XXIV, k. 2522 (Jha 2523) and TSP. Kamalaśīla's commentary gives a good idea of the debate and the subsequent replies to Uddyotakara (Vol. II p. 830): *kiṃ punar atra pramāṇam / sannikṛṣṭaviprakṛṣṭayos tulyakālagrahaṇāt / yo hi gatimān sa sannikṛṣṭam āśu prāpnoti viprakṛṣṭaṃ cireṇa yathā devadatto grāmād grāmāntaraṃ gacchan / śākhācandramasos tu tulyakālam unmeṣasamanantaram eva grahaṇaṃ dṛṣṭam / tasmād aprāpyakāri cakṣur iti gamyate /*

atroddyotakaraḥ prāha jñānānām āśūtpatteḥ kālabhedasyāgrahaṇān mithyā pratyaya eṣa utpalapatraśatavedhavad iti / tad etad asamyak / evaṃ hi saro rasa ityādāv api kramavyavasāyo na syāt / āśūtpattes tulyatvāt / tataś ca pratītibhedo na syāt / sarvāsāṃ ca buddhīnām āśūtpattir astīti na kadācit kramagrahaṇaṃ syād iti prāg nirloṭhitam etad vistareṇa /.

"But what *pramāṇa* is there for this [position that sense organs operate without contact]? [Kamalaśīla's reply:] It is because there is simultaneous apprehension of what is near and what is far away. Indeed, something mobile reaches a nearby thing quickly and a far away thing with a longer delay, just as when Devadatta goes from one village to another. However, we observe that the apprehension of branches [in a nearby tree] and that of the moon is simultaneous, immediately after opening one's eyes. Therefore it is understood that the eye operates without any contact [with its object].

To this Uddyotakara replies: 'Because the consciousnesses are produced quickly, no difference in time-lapse is apprehended. Consequently, the idea that [the cognitions occur] like the [simultaneous] piercing of a hundred-petal lotus is mistaken.' [Kamalaśīla:] This is not correct. For in that case then there would be no ascertainment of any order in [words] such as *saras* and *rasa* as they are the same in being produced quickly. Therefore there would be no difference in our understanding [of such words]. Now, all cognitions are produced quickly, so there could never be any apprehension of order: this has already been thrashed out extensively earlier on."

(293) Literally: "the sight of very far away and nearby forms would have to be clear."

(294) The argument is as follows: *prāpyakāritva* implies no differences in clarity when the object is far or near. Sight and hearing do exhibit such differences, therefore we infer *aprāpyakāritva* in their cases. Cf. TS(P) XXIV, k. 2522: *dūrāsannādibhedena spaṣṭāspaṣṭam yathekṣyate / rūpaṃ tathaiva śabdo 'pi tīvramandādivid bhavet //*. "[In spite of their being no contact between the objects and the sense organs], just as form is seen clearly or unclearly due to such differences as being far away or near, so too would there be cognitions of intensity and weakness, etc. of sound as well."

(295) See en. 290.

(296) Mookerjee (1935) p. 307 summarizes the prevailing physical view of that time: "A magnet attracts a piece of iron from a considerable distance and no physical relationship between the two is observable." Thus, the magnet is thought to possess the property to be proved, viz. *aprāpyakāritva*, as well as the reason, that is, like the eyes, its force varies with distance. Cf. TS XXIV, k. 2518 (Jha k. 2519): *aprāptimātrasāmye 'pi na sarvasya graho yathā / ayaskāntena lohasya sāmarthyaniyamasthiteḥ //*. "Although the simple absence of contact is [always] the same, one does not apprehend anything and everything [irrespective of distance], for the power [of things] remains restricted, just as between a magnet and iron." Interestingly enough, Śaṅkarasvāmin (see TSP ad TS k. 2519) argued that the magnet *did* send out "light-rays which penetrated the iron" and were responsible for attracting it. But Kamalaśīla and Śāntarakṣita appealed to "empirical" evidence and said that this "light" was unobservable and hence couldn't exist.

(297) *Taishō*: *tú* 塗 = "smear"; "erase". The Japanese translator (Kyik p. 352. 7) reads *tú* 途 = "road". Note that on p. 182 of *Zuì xīn shí yòng hán yīng cí diǎn*, it is specified that 塗 is sometimes used with the sense of 途 .

(298) *yīn* 因 . Lit. "cause"; "reason".

(299) Ironically, here Dharmapāla / Āryadeva are using a variation on the basic argument of the Prāpyakāritvavādins, one which is developed by Kumārila in SV *śabdanityatādhikaraṇam*, 119 and 120: *yeṣāṃ tv aprāpta evāyaṃ śabdaḥ śrotreṇa gṛhyate / teṣām aprāptitulyatvaṃ dūravyavahitādiṣu // tatra dūrasamīpasthagrahaṇāgrahaṇe same / syātāṃ na ca kramo nāpi tīvramandādisaṃbhavaḥ //.* This is the argument which Śāntarakṣita, a confirmed *aprāpyakāritvavādin*, was seeking to answer in TS XXIV, k. 2522 (Jha, k. 2523). Basically, Dharmapāla / Āryadeva's strategy is to first use the Aprāpyakāritvavādins' arguments against the Prāpyakāritvavādin and then to proceed vice versa. Not surprisingly, the Madhyamaka conclusion of using both adversaries' arguments is that real perception is impossible.

A final point worth mentioning is that Dignāga used the impossibility of phenomena being hidden as an absurd consequence of *prāpyakāritvavāda*, and hence as an argument *in favour* of *aprāpyakāritvavāda*. Cf. PS I section 3, k. 2b.

(300) Japanese translator reads *jìn yuǎn* 近遠 ("near and far") instead of T. *jí yuǎn* 極遠 ("very far").

(301) The theme that distance and obstruction would be impossible is frequent in this sort of discussion, both in the present chapter and in other texts such as PS. A frequent way of expressing distance in these sorts of debates on *(a)prāpyakāritvavāda* is *sāntara*, lit. "having an interval". See en. 290 for Dignāga's use of the term; *sāntaragrahaṇa*, e.g. means "perception at a distance". Be this as it may, *sāntara* is usually *yǒu jiàn* 有間, leading us to suppose that either *zhōng jiàn* 中間 is being used oddly or that it is an error for *yǒu jiàn*.

(302) Cf. *Bǎi lùn xià* 176a 23-24:

外曰：光意去故見色眼光及意去故到彼能取色

"Outsider: Because the light-rays and the mental organ (*manas*) go out, one sees form. As the eye's light-rays and the mental organ go out, then when they reach that [object] one apprehends form."

Cf. Tucci (1929) p. 52, who mistakenly takes *yǎn guāng* 眼光 as "the eye and the light".

(303) T. has *zhū dēng* 珠燈 (*zhū* = *ratna*; "jewel"), but gives *shū dēng* 殊燈 ("various lights") as a variant.

(304) The typical Aprāpyakāritvavādin argument. See en. 296.

(305) As we see in the verses cited from TS and SV the two are generally treated as analogous. See en. 294, 299.

(306) T. reads *ruò ĕr yŭ shēng wú wén ér qŭ* 若耳與聲無聞而取 (Lit. "If the ear and sound were without hearing, but still there was apprehension"). Perhaps *ruò ĕr yú shēng* 若耳於聲 . . . would make better sense. At any rate, the point is that if the ear is not what hears sounds, then turning one's head and ears in the direction of a particular sound would be inexplicable.

(307) *fāng wéi* 方維 . Paramārtha translates AK's *koṇa* ("angle"; "intermediate point of the compass") and *vidiś* by *wéi* 維 .

(308) Dharmapāla commentary (in e.g. §227a14) makes it clear that he interprets "nature" (*xìng* 性) in this verse as the Primordial Nature or Primordial Matter (*prakṛti*) in Sāṃkhya philosophy. See en. 68. Obviously Dharmapāla interprets k. 316 very differently from Candrakīrti: in effect, the last half of the verse, on Dharmapāla's interpretation, asks "Why would not the eye organ see the Primordial Nature making up the eye?" Note that while the Skt. just speaks of *svabhāvaḥ sarvabhāvānāṃ* ("the nature of all entities"), the Chinese speaks of the *tĭ* 體 , *xiāng* 相 , *yòng* 用 of all dharmas. Dharmapāla's commentary in §227a14 shows that these are three separate terms: "...while the characters (*xiāng*) and functions (*yòng*) may differ, their *svabhāva* (*tĭ*) remains undifferentiated. The character *tĭ* in this context poses a problem as to its potential Skt. equivalent: viz. *dravya* / *svabhāva*. Given that *svabhāva* does occur in the Skt. and *dravya* does not, it might seem more reasonable to opt for *svabhāva*. At any rate, be it *svabhāva* or *dravya* here, the basic idea is much the same: the entity itself composed of the *guṇas*. See en. 219. I leave the term *svabhāva* ("nature"; "own-being") in Sanskrit here to avoid confusion with *prakṛti* (*xìng* 性), i.e. the Primordial Nature.

(309) See en. 75. *puruṣa* = the consciousness; the self. "Conscious principle" = *caitanya*, a frequently used synonym of *puruṣa*. See e.g. CSV X, HPS 488, 2 et seq.

(310) A generally held thesis in Indian philosophy: *svātmani kriyāvirodha* ("the contradiction of there being an action [directed] to itself"). See May (1959) n. 135; M. av. 166, 7 (LVP [1910], p. 349 and n. 2); K. Bhattacharya (1973), p. 53 n.

(311) See en. 54, 68, 72, 219.

(312) Viz. the Primordial Nature (*prakṛti*). Cf. en. 308.

(313) However, cf. Gauḍapāda ad SK 16, who argues that although the Primordial Nature is one, it does not follow that everything ends up the same, because this Nature is transformed according to the predominance of the different *guṇas*. *yasmād ekasmāt pradhānād vyaktaṃ tasmād ekarūpeṇa bhavitavyam / naiṣa doṣaḥ pariṇāmataḥ salilavat pratipratiguṇāśrayaviśeṣāt / ekasmāt pradhānāt trayo lokāḥ samutpannāḥ tulyabhāvā na bhavanti /*.

(314) The Sāṃkhya recognizes three *pramāṇas*: perception (*dṛṣṭa* = *pratyakṣa*), inference (*anumāna*) and authoritative speech (*āptavacana*). See SK 4.

(315) We should probably read *tǐ wú bié gù* 體無別故 instead of *tǐ yòng bié gù* 體用別故 ("because the substance and functions are different"), which makes no sense in this context. The former reading would correspond to the Sāṃkhya's own principle, which Dharmapāla is using against him to draw absurd consequences.

(316) The equivalence *xiū liú* 鵂鶹 = *ulūka* is attested in H. "Ulūka" ("owl") is a very common appellation of Kaṇāda, the author of the *Vaiśeṣikasūtras*. The Aulūkyas (*xiū liú zǐ* 鵂鶹子), thus, are the Vaiśeṣikas.

(317) In other words, the eye organ has fire as its material cause, the ear organ space, the nose earth, the tongue water and the body organ the air element. Ui (1917) pp. 78-79, in discussing this passage from Dharmapāla, pointed out that the Vaiśeṣika position described is that of Praśastapāda. Ui argued that the *Vaiśeṣikasūtra* itself does not assert that space is the material cause of the ear organ; see op. cit. pp 194-195. Now, it is true that in the *Padārthadharmasaṃgraha* passages describing earth and the other elements we do find the view which Dharmapāla discusses. See pp. 26 et seq. in V.P. Dvivedin's edition. However, the same theory is also presented in Candramati's *Daśapadārthaśāstra* (see Ui p. 103) and indeed also in the *Nyāyasūtra*.

(318) Dharmapāla does not argue for this, but presumably he is asserting that from a common sense point of view the eye does not resemble fire, the ear does not resemble space and so forth.

(319) The Buddhist holds that the elements are just touch sensations. See k. 309 and commentaries.

(320) Cf. Praśastapāda pp. 189-90; see en. 60 for translations of the relevant sections. Cf. VS 3.1.13, which speaks of the fourfold contact: *ātmendriyamano'rthasannikarṣād yan niṣpadyate tad anyat*. See en. 53 for translation and remarks.

(321) Dharmapāla comments on the verse as being a refutation of the Vaiśeṣikas and of the Hīnayāna. So because the term *rūpa* means different things for the Vaiśeṣika (i.e. "colour") and for the Hīnayāna (viz. "form"), I leave it here in the Sanskrit. See en. 56. Note that Tucci (1925) translated *sè shì* 色識 as *rūpavijñāna*, i.e. probably "consciousness of *rūpa*" and *sè yǎn* 色眼 as "visione del *rūpa*". This seems unjustified as a translation: *a) sè yǎn* 色眼 = *rūpa* + *cakṣus* and not *rūpadarśana*. *b)* Dharmapāla's interpretation of the verse makes it clear that he takes the verse as talking about three things, the eye, the *rūpa* and the consciousness, and that because each of them lacks the other two, they cannot individually produce sight. *c)* Finally his introduction to the verse and subsequent commentary (§227b29) make it clear that he

takes the verse as actually refuting the Vaiśeṣika's *four* factors, but that Āryadeva did not talk about the self because it had already been refuted. See en. 53 and 60 for the four in VS and Praśastapāda. In short, the "consciousness" spoken about in the verse is, according to Dharmapāla, the *manas* of the Vaiśeṣika.

(322) T. reads *èr* 二 ("two") rather than *sān* 三 ("three") but gives *sān* as a variant in two editions. The Japanese translator (Kyik p. 355.9) read *sān*, which is no doubt correct, as we see by the subsequent discussion about the "three dharmas".

(323) A widely used argument against the idea of the effect existing at the time of the cause (*satkāryavāda*). See MMK I,1; M. av. VI 8cd; TS I, k. 17-18. MMV p. 11: *'di ltar dṅos po bdag gi bdag ñid du yod pa rnams la yaṅ skye ba dgos pa med do.* "So there is no need for entities which exist in themselves to arise again."

(324) Cf. MMK I, 6, MMV (p. 20) and Pr., as well as TS IX k. 488-489 for similar reasonings involving the impossibility of a temporal sequence in causation.

(325) If causes and effects are inexistent, it makes no sense to speak of identity or difference.

(326) The Vaiśeṣika had argued that four factors were necessary to see colour: the eyes, the colour, the mental organ and the self. See §227b8. The self was refuted already in Chapter II = CS X. Note that this allusion to the four factors shows clearly that Dharmapāla interpreted Āryadeva's use of "consciousness" as meaning the mental organ or *manas* of the Vaiśeṣika. See en. 321.

(327) Cf. AK ii k. 47ab and AKBh (LVP pp. 238-240) classification of expressions in terms of three "collections" (*kāya*): names, phrases and letters (*vyañjana*). In what follows, "sound" (*śabda*), as is often the case in Indian philosophy, has often to be understood as meaning "linguistic expressions" or "words".

(328) Alternatively, "describe", "express". H. *quán biǎo* 詮表 = *pratyāyaka* ("making known"; "causing to understand").

(329) The point of the preceding argument seems to be that the particular character could not be responsible for reference, in that reference depends on conceptually created entities, viz. *apoha*, and not on something perceived in direct perception. Cf. Chapter III, Appendix I, §g.

(329a) The argument here is very brief and may have eluded us. Nonetheless, the point probably turns on a theme frequently found in the Epistemologists: in reasonings the terms must be universals, failing which we cannot give homologous examples (*tóng yù* 同喻 = *sādharmyadṛṣṭānta*) which are different from the *dharmin* and possess the *hetu* and *sādhyadharma*. Cf. en. 24. Suppose we are proving that sound is impermanent because it is produced. In that case, if the *sādhyadharma* and *hetu* are particulars (e.g. sound's impermanence or sound's producthood), we cannot give any *sādharmyadṛṣṭānta*, like a vase, which has these properties: a vase does not have sound's impermanence; it simply has the universal property, impermanence. This much is standard fare. In Dharmapāla's argument there is presumably a hidden premise that particular sounds uttered at specific times and places could not refer to universal properties, but why this is so is left unexplained.

If no homologous examples can be given, the reason is classified as an *asādhāraṇānaikāntikahetu* — "a reason which is inconclusive because it is [too] exclusive". To take the usual case, "sound is impermanent because it is audible", no example different from the *dharmin*, "sound", can be given. Thus the pervasion *(vyāpti)* between *hetu* and *sādhyadharma* cannot be ascertained and the reason is inconclusive. See Tillemans (1990) on the Indo-Tibetan debates concerning the *asādhāraṇānaikāntika-hetu*.

(330) I.e. *sāmānyalakṣaṇa* are not heard because they are mental creations without reality. On *sāmānyalakṣaṇa*, see en. 366, 367.

(331) See en. 327 above.

(332) An allusion to one of the five similarities (*samatā*) which must hold between minds and their mental factors. *Inter alia*, they must have the same object (*ālambana*). See en. 427 for explanation of the fivefold similarity.

(333) This would be absurd because, according to the ontology of the Epistemologists, *sāmānyalakṣaṇa* are not effects, but are mental constructions or designations. If they were subject to causation by the sense organs and so forth, they would be no different from real entities (*vastu*) or *svalakṣaṇa*. See en. 330, 366, 367.

(334) Cf. H. p. 432 *bàng lún qiě zhǐ* 傍論且止 = *alam atiprasaṅgena*.

(335) Note that CSV and Dharmapāla take k. 319 differently, the former understanding the verse as speaking of "the beginning of the sound", the latter "the origin". Tucci translated *shēng běn* 聲本 as "il principio del suono", but this is not borne out by Dharmapāla who glosses *běn* 本 as *yuán* 源, "source".

(336) The idea seems to be that if sounds came to the ear and were then heard, one would never actually hear the speaker emitting the sound, but only the sound which had entered the ear. It might be thought that the ear would indeed have to go out to where the speaker was to make the correlation between sound and its source, but this is not in any way observed. Note that some later authors such as Dharmarājādhvarīndra, the writer of the *Vedāntaparibhāṣā*, did actually hold that the

ear organ had to make the journey to the actual place of the object, failing which it would be impossible to know the connection between sound and its source. See Mookerjee (1935), p. 303.

(337) H. *dùn* 頓 = *yugapad.*

(338) T. *jù* 具 . Japanese transl. (Kyik p. 358.5) *jù* 俱 is preferable.

(339) One of the four conditions for consciousness. See Mvyut. §CXV, *catvāraḥ pratyayāḥ* for equivalents. The *samanantarapratyaya* of a consciousness *A* is that consciousness which immediately precedes *A* and ensures that *A* is a consciousness, and not matter. See AK ii k. 61c, LVP pp. 299-306 and *Siddhi* II pp. 437-444. Cf. *Yoṅs 'dzin bsdus grwa briṅ* pp. 20b 6-21a 1 for a concise, textbook-style definition: *bźi pa ni / sṅon 'dzin mṅon sum myoṅ ba gsal rig tsam du gtso bor dṅos su skyed byed kyi rig pa / sṅon 'dzin mṅon sum gyi de ma thag rkyen gyi mtshan ñid / mtshan gźi ni / sṅon 'dzin mṅon sum gyi sṅa logs de ma thag tu byuṅ ba'i sṅon po yid la byed pa'i śes pa lta bu /.* "As for the fourth [condition], the defining characteristic of the immediately preceding condition of a perception which apprehends blue is: the consciousness which principally and directly produces the perception of blue *qua* clear and knowing experience. The illustrative example is: a consciousness directed at blue which arises immediately before the perception of blue."

(340) For *divyaśrotrābhijñā*, which is one of the six super-knowledges and depends on meditative trances, see AK vii, k. 42ad, LVP pp. 98-100. It is said to perceive sounds irrespective of whether they are near, far, subtle, etc., just as the "divine eye" (*divyacakṣus*) perceives all forms. See AK vii, k. 54cd, LVP pp. 123-124. Dharmapāla seems to be giving a counterexample to the opponent's view that one cognizes the whole sound only after hearing the parts. In the case of the *divyaśrotra*, one hears sounds in their totality; it would follow absurdly from the opponent's view, however, that only the subsequent mind which arises right after the *dhyāna* could cognize whole sounds.

(341) The moments t_1, t_2, t_3 of hearing, which correspond to the moments of the sound, would be followed by three successive mental consciousnesses. Thus, the apprehension of the whole could not follow immediately after one hears the parts.

(341a) T. and Kyik 359.5 read *wèi fēi shěng* 未非聲 ("something which is not a non-sound"), but the context clearly demands that we read *wèi lái shěng* 未來聲 ("a future sound").

(342) The argument turns on the notion that "coming into being" is the defining characteristic of the present, while "having ceased" is the characteristic of the past. This is more or less generally accepted, the differences amongst the schools being

whether the future and past do or do not in some sense exist. Cf. for example AKBh ad AK v k. 26 for the Vaibhāṣika view: *yadā sa dharmaḥ kāritraṃ na karoti tadānāgataḥ / yadā karoti tadā pratyutpannaḥ / yadā kṛtvā niruddhas tadātīta iti /* "When this dharma is not executing its activity it is future; when it is executing, then it is present; when it has executed [its activity] and has ceased, it is past". This position accepts that there is something existing in the three times which is past, present or future in terms of its activities. The other schools, especially the Sautrāntikas, deny this. For definitions of the three times from the Tibetan scholastic standpoint see *Yoṅs 'dzin bsdus grwa briṅ* ff. 21b6- 22a2.

(343) This was the position of the Sāṃkhya philosopher criticized in PS and PST (cf. en. 54) — Frauwallner (1958) identifies him as Vṛṣagaṇa. Cf. PST cited in Frauwallner p. 110: *bstan bcos su rna ba la sogs pa rnams kyi* raṅ gi yul la rnam par 'jug pa daṅ / da ltar ba'i dus la 'jug pa ñid du bsgrubs nas 'di skad bśad do // de bźin du yid ni don thams cad la dus gsum pa ñid du rab tu 'jug ste /...* Transl. Frauwallner: "Das Śāstram (*bstan-bcos*), d.h. das Ṣaṣṭitantram, hatte also gelehrt, dass die äusseren Sinne, das Gehör usw., sich auf das ihnen entsprechende besondere Objekt richten und dass sich ihre Tätigkeit nur auf die Gegenwart erstreckt. Anschliessend daran hiess es: 'In entsprechender Weise richtet sich das Denken auf alle Gegenstände und auf alle drei Zeiten...'" *We should read *kyis* instead of *kyi*.

(344) Cf. Vidyābhūṣaṇa (1913) p. 84 on NS 3.2.4: "The Sāṃkhyas affirm that knowledge is a mode of the permanent intellect [i.e. *buddhi*] from which it is not different. Knowledge, according to them, is nothing but the permanent intellect modified in the shape of an object which is reflected on it through the senses." Vātsyāyana's *Nyāyabhāṣya* to NS 3.2.2-3 and 3.2.9 describes their position that the *buddhi* or "inner organ" (*antaḥkaraṇa*) is one, but has *vṛtti* ("operations"; "functioning") which differ just in the way in which a glass put over differently coloured substances will *seem* to have different colours. Cf. *Nyāyabhāṣya* ad NS 3.3.9: *ekam antaḥkaraṇaṃ nānā vṛttaya iti saty abhedavṛtter idam ucyate/*

sphaṭikānyatvābhimānavat tadanyatvābhimānaḥ (9)

tasyāṃ vṛttau nānātvābhimāno yathā dravyāntaropahite sphaṭike anyatvābhimāno nīlo lohita iti evaṃ viṣayāntaropadhānād iti.

See also the description of this process in *Bǎi lùn* T. 1569 *shàng* 171c 22-25:

"The one can have various forms, like crystal. As one crystal becomes blue, yellow, red and white according to the colors (of things near by), just so one *buddhi* becomes various according to its objects. At one time it perceives misery, at another time pleasure and so on. Although *buddhi* has various forms (actually) there exists only one *buddhi*." (Translation in Honda 1974, p. 487).

Note that *vṛtti* in the context of the Sāṃkhya theory of perception means that the sense or mind "transforms" so that it has the aspects (*ākāra*) of the object. Cf. *Yuktidīpikā*'s explanation, *viṣayākārapariṇāmātmikā vṛttir...* ("the operation is in essence a transformation into the aspects of the object"), quoted in Hattori (1968a) p. 148, n. 5.1.

Following Jinendrabuddhi's explanation of Vṛṣagaṇa's Sāṃkhya definition of perception discussed in *Pramāṇasamuccaya* (see en. 54 and Hattori [1968a] n. 5.1, 5.2), the term *manasādhiṣṭhitā* ("controlled by the mind") was interpreted by some Sāṃkhyas to mean that the mind went together with the senses, while others took it as meaning that the mind apprehends the initial sense perception. Dharmapāla seems to be refuting the former position now, but also discussed something very similar to the latter view in connection with k. 312.

(345) The equivalence is amply attested in H. and Nak. Note that Vṛṣagaṇa also seems to have made a difference between *'jug pa* = *vṛtti* and *rab tu 'jug pa* = *pravṛtti*, the former term applying to the senses and the latter term applying to the mind. See en. 343. Dharmapāla seems to reject the distinction.

(346) See en. 344.

(347) Tucci (1925) mistakenly translates *chén* 塵 as *āyatana* which renders the passage perfectly incomprehensible. *chén* 塵 = *artha* is attested in H. p. 275, and *artha* is what occurs in the Skt. of k. 322. Although the Skt. does not have a separate word for "erroneous" in the verse, the nuance seems to be important to Dharmapāla's interpretation. As a result, although the Skt. is simply *vyavasthā*, I translate the Chinese *wàng lì* 妄立 as "erroneous determinations".

(348) One of the usual senses of *saṃjñā* is indeed "sign", "signal".

(349) Nak. p. 121a: "The fact of mental reflection. In the Vijñānavāda, it is the sixth consciousness reflecting upon the phenomenon."

(350) Unidentified.

(351) Unidentified.

(352) Read *ài* 愛 rather than *yōu* 憂 (= *daurmanasya*; "despondency"). Cf. the immediately following line (229b23) in the Chinese text: *ài xīn* 愛心 .

(353) See AK viii k. 17ab, LVP pp. 168-173.

(354) An inhabitual, and so far untraceable, tenfold schema.

(355) See en. 437 for references to other works. Instead of "comet" one more usually finds "mist".

(356) A key Indian Buddhist notion — lit. "what is not made (*kṛta*) by bringing together parts or conditions", or "what does not depend on causal conditioning". See Bareau (1951). The Chinese term, lit. "without activity", has a long history, serving *inter alia* as the early Buddhist translation of *nirvāṇa*. AK i k. 5 gives the traditional three *asaṃskṛtas*: space (*ākāśa*) and the two cessations (*nirodha*); for the Vijñānavāda interpretation of these three as being ways of designating the ultimate "thusness" of dharmas, the *bhūtatathatā*, see *Siddhi* pp. 72-78. Note that some philosophers, e.g. the Vātsīputrīyas, held that only *nirvāṇa* was *asaṃskṛta*; others, as discussed in Pr. 176.9-10, held that voidness, which is defined as "thusness" (*tathatālakṣaṇa*), is *asaṃskṛta*. See AK i, LVP's p. 7 n. 2. Nāgārjuna maintained that when one has shown that there can be no conditioned things, there cannot be any unconditioned things either. MMK VII, k. 33: *utpādasthitibhaṅgānām asiddher nāsti saṃskṛtam / saṃskṛtasyāprasiddhau ca kathaṃ setsyaty asaṃskṛtam //*.

(357) Cf. Kamalaśīla's reasoning in TSP's introduction to TS Chapter XXIII (*bahirarthaparīkṣā*) (p. 670). See fn. 135.

(358) The discussion below alternates between two meanings of *pratyakṣa*: *a)* perceptible or evident objects; *b)* direct perception, viz. the consciousness which perceives such objects.

(359) Cf. the discussion below in §4. See also en. 362.

(360) For the Sāṃkhya, see en. 54, 68, 219. The Nyāya-Vaiśeṣika held that the whole was different from the parts but linked to them by "inherence" (*samavāya*). Cf. Śāntarakṣita's TS k. 560 (Jha, k. 561): *vibhinnakartṛśaktyāder bhinnau tantupaṭau tathā / viruddhadharmayogena stambhakumbhādibhedavat //*. "Similarly, the threads [i.e. the parts of the cloth] and the cloth [i.e. the whole] are different in that they have different makers and different powers, just as pillars, vases and so forth [differ] due to their contradicting dharmas". For the Buddhist critique of the inherence relation between parts and wholes, see TS and TSP chapter XV, k. 822 et seq., *samavāya-padārthaparīkṣā*. See also Udayana's *Ātmatattvaviveka* pp. 617 et seq. (résumé in Potter [1977] pp. 541-544) and Potter (1977) pp. 74-86 for the Buddhist-Nyāya debate on wholes and parts.

(361) CS IX k. 211, translated in May (1981) p. 88. The point according to the CSV ad k. 211 is that the cause cannot be permanent while the effect is impermanent: such differences of character between cause and effect are not to be found. In the Sāṃkhya system the Primordial Nature (*prakṛti*), i.e. the three *guṇas*, which are the essence of all phenomena, is permanent, while the phenomena themselves are

impermanent. In the Nyāya-Vaiśeṣika system, the ultimate constituents of objects, viz. the atoms, are permanent.

(362) For the Vaibhāṣika the eight substances are: the four elements, viz. earth, air, fire and water, plus their four derivatives (*bhautika*), i.e. the four domains (*āyatana*), those of (visual) form (*rūpa*), smell, taste and tactile sensations. See AK i LVP pp. 144-149. PSP p. 114, 26-28: *de la rdzas brgyad ni 'di lta ste / 'byuṅ ba chen po bźi daṅ / gzugs daṅ / dri daṅ / ro daṅ / reg bya'o //*. On the elements and their derivatives, see en. 236, 256, 264.

(363) For the "fivefold" (*pañcadhā*) reasoning, see e.g. MMK XXII,1: *skandhā na nānyaḥ skandebhyo nāsmin skandhā na teṣu saḥ / tathāgataḥ skandhavān na katamo 'tra tathāgataḥ //*. "He is not identical with the aggregates; he is not different from the aggregates; the aggregates are not in him; nor is he in them; the Tathāgata does not possess the aggregates. Who then is the Tathāgata?" See Pr. 432.12-13; De Jong (1949) pp. 73-75; Pr. 454.14-15; May (1959) pp. 183-184. The five lemmas, if generalized are as follows: *X* is identical with *Y*; *X* is different from *Y*; *Y* is in *X*; *X* is in *Y*; *X* possesses *Y*. They apply to various relationships, such as that between parts and wholes as well as cause and effect. In other words, not finding one of the five possibilities shows that the entities in question are without nature (*svabhāva*), are impossible and cannot exist as anything more than mere designations (*prajñapti*). In M. av. VI, 151 Candrakīrti adds two lemmas to come up with the sevenfold reasoning: *X* is not the collection of *Y*'s; *X* is not the shape of the *Y*'s. To take the part-whole relationship, the result is that *X* is designated in dependence upon *Y* (*upādāya prajñapti*) as what appropriates (*upādātṛ*) its substrata (*upādāna*), but neither conventionally nor ultimately does it have any of the possible relations with *Y*: it is a mere "designation" in that its name is without any real denotation. Cf. M. av. VI, 158, transl. LVP "Sans doute, le char n'est établi, ni au point de vue de la réalité, ni au point de vue du monde, d'aucune de ces sept manières [identité avec les membres, etc.]: mais le monde, abstraction faite de la critique (*avicāratas*), le désigne en raison de ses membres." Note that *upādāya prajñapti* is glossed by commentators like Avalokitavrata as *upādānam upādāya prajñapti*. *Prajñāpradīpaṭīkā* P. vol. 97, f. 277; see Nagao (1979) p. 33. However, *upādāna* need not mean just the material cause (like a seed) of an effect (like a sprout), it can also be the substrata, i.e. the parts. See also en. 40, 185.

(364) Here and in what follows the argumentation is largely directed against the Epistemological school or "logicians" (*rtog ge ba* = *tārkika*), who held that it is only the particulars (*svalakṣaṇa*) such as a form, a colour, etc. which exist and which are cognized through direct perception without the intermediary of any conceptualization (*vikalpa*; *kalpanā*). See en. 366, 367. The present argument is that if gross objects like fire or vases were independently real, they would be independent of their *upādāna*, viz. their causes or parts, and would thus exist unaffected by changes in the latter.

Candrakīrti subsequently retorts that the same logic can be universally applied; no entity has any preferential status in this regard.

(365) CSV XIII §7-9 and §15 and *Prasannapadā* pp. 71-72 (see en. 374), show us that there two ways to understand the word *pratyakṣa*: *a)* "what is present before (*prati*) the sense organs (*akṣa*)", i.e. something perceptible or visible; *b)* "what is in connection with the sense organs", i.e. direct perception. See en. 367. Candrakīrti clearly takes the first etymology, while the Epistemologists opt for the second. The result is that for Candrakīrti the word *pratyakṣa* is to be taken in the sense of an evident, or perceptible, object and that the corresponding cognition is metaphorically termed *pratyakṣa* because it has an object which is *pratyakṣa* (i.e. perceptible) as its cause. This etymology would seem like a matter of word-play were it not for the fact that it permits Candrakīrti to include under "perception" any and all consciousnesses, conceptual or not, for which the object is one which is perceptible; it is, for example, possible to have a perceptual judgment about a vase; in other words, one can have a perception which is *also* conceptual, because the vase which causes such a judgment is itself a perceptible object. See en. 428.

(366) Dignāga characterizes *svalakṣaṇa* as inexpressible (*avyapadeśya*). See PSV ad PS I, k. 2c-d, Skt. quoted in PVBh p. 236.13-14. Dharmakīrti gives what became the standard characterization of *svalakṣaṇa* in four points: *a)* they have practical and causal efficacity (*arthakriyā*); *b)* they are unique (*asadṛśa*); *c)* they are not objects of words (*śabdasyāviṣaya*); *d)* their cognitions do not rely on any other causes (*anyanimitta*) but them. Universal characters (*sāmānyalakṣaṇa*) are the exact opposite. See PV III, k.1-2:

mānaṃ dvividhaṃ viṣayadvaividhyāc chaktyaśaktitaḥ /
arthakriyāyāṃ keśādir nārtho 'narthādhimokṣataḥ //
sadṛśāsadṛśatvāc ca viṣayāviṣayatvataḥ /
śabdasyānyanimittānāṃ bhāve dhīsadasattvataḥ //

Text in Tosaki (1979) pp 58-59. Note that the insistence on *arthakriyā* seems to be Dharmakīrti's development; see Hattori (1968a) n. 1.14 and Tosaki (1979) p. 60; on diverse aspects of *arthakriyā* see Mikogami (1979), Nagatomi (1967-68), May (1982) n. 35. Note also Dharmakīrti's pronouncement in PV III k.53cd: *meyaṃ tv ekaṃ svalakṣaṇam.*"It is the *svalakṣaṇa* alone which is [really] cognized." See Stcherbatsky (1926), Chapt. VII on *svalakṣaṇa* and *sāmānyalakṣaṇa*. See also en. 40, 184.

For Tibetan explanations see en. 40 and the definitions in Tsoṅ kha pa's *sDe bdun la 'jug pa'i sgo don gñer yid kyi mun sel* p. 8: *raṅ mtshan gyi mtshan ñid / don dam par don byed nus pa / dper na sṅon po lta bu'o // yaṅ na yul dus ma 'dres par gnas pa'i dṅos po / spyi mtshan gyi mtshan ñid don dam par don byed mi nus pa'i chos / yaṅ na rtog* pa la yul dus 'dres par snaṅ ba'i snaṅ yul / dper na rtog pa la lto ldir źabs źum snaṅ ba lta bu'o /.* * Text has *rtogs.* Transl.: "The defining characteristic of a *svalakṣaṇa* is being ultimately efficacious; or alternatively, [it is] being an entity which exists without combining [different] places and times. For example, like [a patch of] blue. The defining characteristic of a *sāmānyalakṣaṇa* is being a dharma which is not ultimately efficacious; or alternatively, [it is] being an appearing object which seems to combine [different] places and times. For example, like the appearance to conceptualization of [a vase] which bulbous and splay-bottomed." Cf. also *lCaṅ skya grub mtha'* pp. 98-99, where *sāmānyalakṣaṇa* is said to be equivalent to conventional truth (*kun rdzob bden pa* = *saṃvṛtisatya*) for the Epistemological school, and *svalakṣaṇa* equivalent to ultimate truth (*don dam bden pa* = *paramārthasatya*).

(367) For *g.yer po*, see Mvyut *g.yer po* = *paṭu*, *Bod rgya tshig mdzod chen mo* vol. III, which gives the primary meaning as "intelligent", but also gives uses of the word where it means "clear" (e.g. *gnam g.yer po*) or "luminous".

On *pratyakṣa* and *kaplanāpoḍha*, see NM k. 15ab et seq. (T. 1628 3b 14-17):

現量除分別　餘所說因生　此中現量除分別者謂若有智於色等境
遠離一切種類名言假立無異諸門分別　由不共緣現現別轉故名現量。

"Direct perception is free of conceptualization; the other [cognition, i.e. inference] arises from the reason as just explained. Here *pratyakṣaṃ kalpanāpoḍham* means: that cognition which does not conceptualize through imposing an identity between qualifiers and linguistic expressions upon objects such as form, etc.; it occurs in connection with the individual sense organs because they are its specific cause (*bù gòng yuán* 不共緣 = *asādhāraṇahetu; asādhāraṇakāraṇa*), and thus it is [named] *pratyakṣa*."

Skt. fragments given by Katsura (1982) p. 84: *pratyakṣaṃ kalpanāpoḍham* (=PS I, 3c, Vibhūticandra, p. 174); *tatrāyaṃ Nyāyamukhagranthaḥ yaj jñānam artharūpādau viśeṣaṇābhidhāyakābhedopacāreṇāvikalpakaṃ tad akṣam akṣaṃ prati vartata iti pratyakṣam* (TSP ad TS k. 1236; p. 456). See also PS I, k. 4ab: *asādhāraṇahetutvād akṣais tad vyapadiśyate*. Transl. Hattori (1968a): "it is named after the sense-organs because they are its specific cause". NP 4: *tatra pratyakṣaṃ kalpanāpoḍhaṃ yaj jñānam arthe rūpādau nāmajātyādikalpanārahitaṃ tat / akṣam akṣam prati vartata iti pratyakṣam /*. "Perception is free of conceptualization; it is that cognition which does not conceptually construct proper names, classes and so forth upon objects such as form, etc. As it occurs in connection with the various individual sense organs it is [named] *pratyakṣa*."

See Hattori op. cit. n. 1.27 for the Buddhist Epistemologist's use of the term *kalpanā*; see also Stcherbatsky (1926), Chapter VI. The basic point for Dignāga is that conceptualization is the association of a proper name, a class, a quality, action or substance with the inexpressible *svalakṣaṇa* which one perceives, so that the resultant combination becomes describable. See PSV and PS I, k. 3d: *atha keyaṃ kalpanā nāma / nāmajātyādiyojanā //*. Dharmakīrti adds *abhrānta* ("unmistaken") to *kalpanāpoḍha* in NB I,4 and redefines *kalpanā* as "a cognition of a representation which is fitting to be associated with words" (PVin P. 252b4: *rtog pa ni brjod pa daṅ 'drer ruṅ ba snaṅ ba'i śes pa*. NB I,5: *abhilāpasaṃsargayogyapratibhāsapratītiḥ kalpanā*). Dharmakīrti introduced the specification "fitting" (*yogya*) to allow for the fact that infants and illiterates still have *kalpanā*, i.e. consciousnesses of representations which *would* be fitting to be associated with words, if the person could use language. For Śāntarakṣita's interpretation of *kalpanā*, see TS(P) k. 1212 et seq., Franco (1984) and Hattori (1968a) n. 1.27. The Tibetan scholastic generally adopts an abbreviated and somewhat different version of Dharmakīrti's definition: *sgra don 'dres ruṅ tu 'dzin pa'i źen rig* "A consciousness which apprehends words and objects as fitting to be associated". One interpretation is that *sgra* here means *sgra spyi* (lit. "word-universals"; i.e. images dependent upon language) and *don* means *don spyi* (lit. "object-universals"; i.e. images dependent upon perceptions of the objects). See *lCaṅ skya grub mtha'* pp. 100 et seq., where the author has an interesting discussion explaining why he disagrees with this widespread Tibetan definition.

(368) Cf. PS I, k. 4ab quoted in en. 367.

(369) Cf. *Ālambanaparīkṣā* and *vṛtti*, k. 1-5, where after refuting that the individual atoms are the objects of perception, Dignāga then shows that the collection (*'dus pa*) is not the object and nor is the combined aspect of the atoms (*'dus pa'i rnam pa*). The argument there, and perhaps in CSV, seems directed against the Neo-Sarvāstivādins, such as Saṃghabhadra. See en. 227. Vasubandhu is also clearly the target of CSV's arguments. See en. 370.

(370) On *timira*, *taimirika* and the illusion of a "mesh of hair" (*keśoṇḍuka*) — a recurrent example of an illusion used as a simile to describe conventional truth — see en. 155, 156; Pr. 373, transl. De Jong (1949) pp. 29-30; M. av. 102,109, transl. LVP (1910) pp. 300, 306; *Saṃdhinirmocanasūtra* VI,7, transl. Lamotte (1935), p. 189 and n.7.

The opponent's use of the example in the present context is, however, not the usual case of a purely *illusory* perception of a "mesh of hair" (*keśoṇḍuka*). Rather, the example is designed to show that one can see a collection (i.e. a pile of hair) without in fact seeing the individuals (i.e. the strands): a person suffering from *timira* does not have the visual acuity to see anything but a collection of hair. Note that the debate has some clear echoes in Abhidharmic literature. Cf. Saṃghabhadra's position as outlined in en. 227. As Kajiyama (1971) p. 1003 (21) points out, Vasubandhu himself, in debating on the meaning of *skandha* in AK i, k. 20 et seq., asserted that a collection of atoms is a cause for perception, for each individual atom contributes causally to the collections (*ekaśaḥ samagrāṇāṃ kāraṇabhavāt*), all be the contribution minute. (It is this latter point which Candrakīrti will attack in §13.) As for the use of the *timira/keśa* example in this context, interestingly enough, Yaśomitra in his *Sphuṭārthā Abhidharmakośavyākhyā* (ed. D. Shāstrī I, p. 61, 18-21) to AK i, k. 20, gives the same example of a pile of hair: single strands are not visible to the *taimirika*, but are nonetheless causes for perceiving the whole pile: *yathā vā keśāḥ pṛthag pṛthag avasthitā na samarthās taimirikacakṣurvijñānakaraṇe, samuditās tv asaṃyuktāpi samarthāḥ / tadvac cakṣurādīn-*

driyaparamāṇavo rūpādiviṣayaparamāṇavaś ca cakṣurādivijñānotpādane pratyekam asamarthāḥ, samuditās tu samarthāḥ /. "Just as the separately existing hairs are incapable of causing a *taimirika*'s eye consciousness, but when assembled together, even the disjoint [hairs], become capable, so too the atoms of the eye organ and the atoms of the objects such as form, etc. are each individually incapable of producing the eye consciousness, but when assembled together are capable."

(370a) An entomological aside: *śa sbraṅ* are various sorts of *méng* 虻 ("gadfly") according to *Bod rgya tshig mdzod chen mo*. E.g. *śa sbraṅ* can be a *niú méng* 牛虻 — a cattle-fly. In other words, it is some type of gadfly rather than a "blue-bottle fly", as Jäschke had erroneously speculated in his *Tibetan-English Dictionary* s.v. *śa*. The latter is just the common house and garden variety of fly ("a large buzzing fly with a blue body", *Concise Oxford Dictionary*), but the former is something distinctly more sinister, as its name "flesh-fly" (*śa sbraṅ*) would seem to suggest. As for the *sbraṅ bu mchu riṅs* ("long-lipped fly"), the *Bod rgya tshig mdzod chen mo* s.v. *mchu riṅ* once again comes to our aid specifying that *mchu riṅ* = *dug sbraṅ mchu riṅ* ("the long-lipped poisonous fly"): the Chinese translation tells us that this is "a synonym for a long-mouthed mosquito" 長觜蚊的異名.

(371) The text reads *gnod pa mi srid do* —"even when it depends on the atoms, there cannot be any harm / refutation / impairment". This makes no sense in terms of the line of argument. It seems more likely that *gnod pa* is a mistake for *nus pa*. A similar problem occurs in the next line where we encounter *gnod pa ga la srid*. Cf. Kaḥ thog's (f. 210a) explanation of the point at issue: *so sor phye ba la raṅ gnas pa'i rdul phran re re źiṅ śes pa de sñed bskyed na ma dmigs pa de'i phyir nus pa cuṅ zad kyaṅ yod pa ma yin na tshogs pa la yaṅ ji ltar yod de med do* //. "One does not observe that when separated, the atoms existing by themselves individually produce a corresponding number of consciousnesses. Thus, given that they have absolutely no efficacity, then how could the collection [of the atoms] have any [efficacity] — it would not have any at all."

(372) See preceding note.

(373) Translating *rgyud du ma las skyes pa'i dbaṅ po'i yul ñid* as a relative clause yields little meaning: "The crescent moon, etc. are all seen to be objects of senses which arise from many extractions." One could however take *skyes pa'i* as equalling *skyes bu'i* and thus the problematic phrase would mean "sense objects of (for) persons from many [different] extractions". This would accord with rGyal tshab's interpretation of *rgyud du ma las skyes pa* as being a backhanded way to say *skyes bu du ma* ("numerous people"). rGyal p. 2: *'jig rten na yaṅ zla ba tshes pa sogs skyes bu du mas mṅon sum du grub pa'i yul mṅon sum du grags kyi yul can la ma grags pa'i phyir* /. "For, in the world, things such as the crescent moon and so forth, which are objects established by numerous people as being perceptible (*mṅon sum* = *pratyakṣa*), are acknowledged as perceptible.

But the subject (*yul can* = *viṣayin*) is not so acknowledged." Cf. also Lokesh Chandra, who gives *nara* and *puṃs* ("man") as possible equivalents of *skyes pa*.

(374) Cf. Pr. 71.10- 72.1: *api cāparokṣārthavācitvāt pratyakṣaśabdasya sākṣād abhimukho 'rthaḥ pratyakṣaḥ / pratigatam akṣam asminn iti kṛtvā ghaṭanīlādīnām aparokṣāṇāṃ pratyakṣatvaṃ siddhaṃ bhavati / tatparicchedakasya jñānasya tṛṇatuṣāgnivat pratyakṣakāraṇatvāt pratyakṣatvaṃ vyapadiśyate //.* Note that my translation of *pratyakṣakāraṇatvāt* differs from that of Stcherbatsky (1927) p. 159: I follow the Tibetan in reading it as a *bahuvrīhi*. Cf. Tib.: *de yoṅs su gcod par byed pa'i śes pa ni rtsa daṅ sogs ma'i me bźin du mṅon sum gyi* **rgyu can** *yin pa'i phyir mṅon sum ñid du rjod par byed do.* "Now, moreover, because the word *pratyakṣa* means objects which are not imperceptible, an object which is clearly in front [of us] is *pratyakṣa* [i.e. perceptible]. Vases, blue [patches] and other such non-imperceptible things are established as being *pratyakṣa* in that the senses accede to them. The consciousness which discriminates such things is taught to be a *pratyakṣa* because it has a *pratyakṣa* [i.e a perceptible object] as cause, just like grass and chaff fires [which are so-called because grass and chaff are their causes]."

(375) Cf. *Daśabhūmikasūtra* (ed. Rahder) 43.6: *[sarvasaṃskṛtaṃ] riktaṃ tucchaṃ mṛṣā moṣadharma visaṃvādakam.* Note that *bslu ba'i chos can* = *moṣadharman* or, as we find in CSV XIII §108, *moṣadharmaka*; cf. Mvyut. 7314: *bslu ba'i chos can* = *moṣadharmiṇaḥ.* See also en. 34 for canonical references. Note that *bslu ba / mi bslu ba simpliciter* are not *moṣa / amoṣa*, but are almost always some variant on *visaṃvādin / avisaṃvādin*. This is especially so in the definition of *pramāṇa*. Hence, I have translated the two uses of *bslu ba* differently.

(376) The argument seems to turn on the combination of scriptural citations plus the logician's definition of *pramāṇa* as being *avisaṃvādin* (i.e. *mi bslu ba*). Cf. PV II, k. 1: *pramāṇam avisaṃvādi jñānam.*

(377) Monier-Williams p. 551: "nimba, m. the Nimb or Neemb tree, Azadirachta Indica (its fruit is bitter and its leaves are chewed at funeral ceremonies)."

(378) The point of the aside seems to be that if one analyzes, one cannot say that one really sees the vase. The world, of course, says that it sees the vase, but this is just an approximate, conventional description — like the world's habit of inaccurately labelling beans and so forth. Some botanical remarks: In fact, the *mudga* and *māṣa* are two closely resembling species. Monier-Williams: *mudga* = Phaseolus mungo; *māṣa* = Phaseolus radiatus. Cf. *Hobson-Jobson* ss. vv. Mash and Moong and the quotation there (s.v. Moong) from the observer Ibn Batuta: "The munj is a kind of māsh, but its grains are oblong and the colour is light green ..."

(379) Note that my translation of k. 305 differs significantly from that of Lang (1986). She translates (p. 119): "The investigation of whether or not an atom has parts also occurs in the system [of our opponents]. Therefore, it is not logically possible to establish that [atom] to be established (*sādhya*) by means of [an atom] that remains to be established."

First of all, the words "system [of our opponents]" seem unjustified. Secondly, it seems to me unlikely that one is seeking to establish atoms by appealing to considerations about atoms. Cf. rGyal p. 4: *de'i phyir dṅos po raṅ mtshan pa ma grub bsgrub par bya ba yis bsgrub bya bum pa raṅ gi ṅo bo ñid kyis grub pa mṅon sum gyi gźal byar 'gyur bar mi 'thad do /.* "So, by means of something which is to be proved, i.e. unestablished particular entities (*dṅos po raṅ mtshan pa*), it is improper to [prove that] something [else] to be proven, viz. a vase which exists in virtue of its nature, would be the object of a direct perception." In short, one is appealing to considerations about atoms to establish the perceptibility of gross objects such as vases, but both are equally in doubt. Kaḥ thog (f.212a) makes it clear that what is at stake here is the fallacy of *sādhyasama*, where the reason is itself as much in doubt as the proposition to be proved: *de'i phyir sgrub byed (b)sgrub bya daṅ mtshuṅs par ma grub bo.* See also rGyal tshab's topical outline §1.1.1.1.5 to k. 305, translated in our Appendix. Cf. NS 1.2.8 for the logical fallacy of *sādhyasama*. See MMK IV, k. 8 and Pr. translated in May (1959) for *sādhyasama* in Madhyamaka method; cf. also K. Bhattacharya (1978) p. 22, n. 3.

(380) For whole objects to exist really and hence be perceptible in truth, they would have to be wholes in virtue of their own nature (*svabhāva*). But this is not the case: they are only wholes relative to something else, but cannot be wholes simply in themselves.

(381) Cf. en. 235 and AK i k. 10 and AKBh: *rūpaṃ dvidhā varṇaḥ saṃsthānaṃ ca*. "Form is twofold, viz. colour and shape."

(382) One can see different colours individually and separately, but one cannot see shape and colour in this manner. So in what sense would they be different?

(383) Visual form (i.e. colour and shape) is a derivative (*bhautika*) of the elements (*mahābhūta*) and is in that sense caused by them. See en. 236.

(384) Lit. "distinct from a seeing form"

(385) See AK ii LVP p. 145 which mentions that in the *Kāmadhātu* every molecule must have at least the eight substances, viz. the four *mahābhūta* and four *bhautika*. One cannot perceive the causes of form (viz. the elements) and the form itself separately, for the latter is simply a type of manifestation or derivative (i.e. *bhautika*) of the former.

(386) Cf. AK i LVP pp. 64-65: "Or le solide, l'humide, etc. sont tangibles et seulement tangibles: la solidité n'est pas perçue par l'organe de la vue." See en. 236, 256, 387, 388.

(387) Cf. *Traité* I p. 367: "Ainsi la terre (*pṛthivī*) a pour caractère la solidité (*khakkhaṭatva*)..." See May (1959) n. 197 for references in Pr. and secondary literature. For canonical references concerning the nature of the four elements see *Traité* I, p. 367, n. 2. and en. 386, 388.

(388) Cf. AK i k. 12cd: *dhṛtyādikarmasaṃsiddhāḥ kharasnehoṣṇateraṇāḥ*. "The solid, the viscous, the hot and the moving consist in actions of supporting and the like." Cf. Tib. of AK i k.12 (*'dzin pa la sogs las su grub*) and AKBh ad i k. 12: *dhṛtisaṃgrahapaktivyūhanakarmasv ete yathākramaṃ pṛthivyaptejovāyudhātavaḥ* /. "The earth, water, fire and air elements consist respectively in the actions of supporting, cohesion, 'cooking' and expansion."

(389) Translated according to the Sanskrit. Transl. by De Jong (1949) p. 84.

(390) rGyal tshab rje (p. 7) takes the opponents here as being Vaiśeṣikas (*bye brag pa*) and understands "perceptibility" as being a universal (*spyi* = *sāmānya*). However, as J. Bronkhorst points out to me, this is problematic in that perceptibility would then have to inhere in a substance, quality or motion. But in fact, "perceptible" is not a member of any of these three categories, so (at least strictly speaking) perceptibility does not satisfy the requirements for being a universal. Cf. *Praśastapādabhāṣya* p. 17: *dravyādīnāṃ trayāṇām api sattāsambandhaḥ sāmānyaviśeṣavattvaṃ* ... "The three, viz. substance and [qualities and motions] are also connected with existence, have *sāmānya* and *viśeṣa* ..." Ibid. p. 19: *sāmānyādīnāṃ trayāṇāṃ ... asāmānyaviśeṣavattvaṃ* ... "The three, viz. *sāmānya*, *viśeṣa* and inherence (*samavāya*) do not have *sāmānya* and *viśeṣa* ..." In short, *if* Candrakīrti is speaking about a Vaiśeṣika universal, it is in a loose and unorthodox way: in fact, it is not clear whose ideas are being refuted.

(391) Lang (1986) p. 120 seems to have understood *skyes pa* as "genus (*jāti*)". She translates as follows: "There is no quality in this pot here having the genus (*jāti*) perceptibility. Therefore, there is no such truly existent thing as [the genus] perceptibility." Not only does this seem to me unjustifiable on syntactical grounds, but *jāti* in the technical sense of "genus" (or natural kind) is not rendered by *skyes pa* or *skye ba*, but rather by *rigs*. Admittedly the commentary of Candrakīrti is tortuous here, but at any rate it does not support Lang's rendering, nor do the indigenous Tibetan commentaries take *skyes pa* in the technical sense of "genus"/natural kind.

In the second half of the verse, she does not adequately render the word *ltar*, which is clearly showing a parallel: in §44 Candrakīrti glosses *ltar* by ... *ji ltar* ... *de bźin du* .... I would tentatively propose that we understand Candrakīrti's explanation of k. 310cd in CSV §44 as follows: *1)* the hypothesis of §43 is that the vases are essentially imperceptible but become perceptible due to their connections with another entity, perceptibility; *2)* perceptibility cannot be produced in vases which, on the hypothesis of §43, are essentially imperceptible; *3)* existence would be parallel to perceptibility in that the object would be existent only on account of some other entity, existence. *4)* Like perceptibility's absurd production in essentially imperceptible things, so too things such as vases, which would not have existence as their own essence, could not acquire existence either.

(392) *bsam gyis mi khyab pa* = *acintya* ("inconceivable"). The term should be taken in the sense of something being too subtle for us to understand, and not in the sense of something being impossible or inconsistent.

(393) The equivalence could also be *tathatā*, "thusness".

(394) This and the next citation remain unidentified. For a similar account of the creation of the world from the primordial wind *(prāgvāyu)*, see AK iii k. 90cd et seq. LVP pp. 185-186.

(395) *byed pa* = *kartṛ, kāraka, karaṇa*, etc. in Lokesh Chandra. But it seems likely that it is *karaṇa* ("instrument") at stake here. Further on, in CSV §58, the opponent tries to argue that the perception is not the *byed pa*, but rather the *byed pa po* (= *kartṛ*), "the agent" — this pair of terms *karaṇa* / *kartṛ* (= *byed pa* / *byed pa po*) is frequent in Indian and Tibetan grammatico-philosophical discussions. See Tillemans (1988a), p. 493, n. 8, 9 and Tillemans and Herforth (1989) p. 6, n. 10 and p. 40.

(396) Cf. *Bǎi lùn* T. 1569 *xià* 175c 11-28; Tucci (1929) pp. 50-51. Cf. also MMK IX, 12 and Pr., where Candrakīrti gives a similar argument against the relationship between the person and the senses.

(397) The introduction to the verse and Candrakīrti's conclusion suggest that we probably have to understand "sight" as meaning the "organ of sight", "the faculty of sight", i.e. the eye. Cf. en. 287. Lang seems to be in disagreement, taking *darśana* here as meaning "perception" (Lang 1986) or "the act of perception" (Thesis). In connection with the conditions for consciousness, the term *adhipatipratyaya* usually refers specifically to the sense organs, the objects or to *manas*, as we shall see below. But on p. 467, n. 21 of Lang's thesis, she invokes a definition of *adhipatipratyaya* in Pr. 77.4 which perhaps justifies a looser use, so that, according to her, it is the "act of perception" (*darśana*) (see her p. 454) which would be the *adhipatipratyaya*: *yasmin sati yad bhavati tat tasyādhipateyam iti.* "That, which being existent, something else comes into existence is the dominant [condition] of that [latter thing]." (Transl. Lang.)

However, if we say that Candrakīrti is speaking about the conscious phenomenon, sight or perception, rather than the eye, then it is not clear that the verse has much connection with what Candrakīrti is trying to prove. The opponent's point was essentially a *kāryahetu*: the eyes exist because the consciousness which is their effect exists. Candrakīrti's conclusion is that "since the consciousness is thus [in reality] impossible, then the idea that the eyes and other [sense organs] exist because [consciousness] exists is incorrect (§57)." What he in fact wants to show is that consciousness cannot exist because it cannot stand in any possible temporal relationship with the sense organs. Cf. also §58, where the opponent refers to k. 312 and concedes that the *eye* is not the instrument for consciousness, thus clearly showing that the instrument referred to in the so-called "third case" mentioned in the *kārikā* is *not* sight *qua* conscious phenomenon, but rather the eye.

Lang is, however, not alone in taking the *kārikā*'s use of *darśana* as meaning perception: rGyal tshab's topical outline §1.1.2.1.1.2.2. reads *rnam śes byed pa po yin pa dgag pa* ("Refuting that consciousness is an agent"), indicating that he took k. 312 as speaking about the conscious phenomenon, and not the eyes. He then gives *mig byed pa po yin pa dgag pa* ("Refuting that the eye is an agent") as a heading starting with §58 and introducing a new hypothesis which will be treated in the subsequent verses (k. 313 et seq.) on the organs' movement or non-movement. This seems an improbable interpretation. There can be little doubt that it clashes with §58's obvious reference to k. 312, for §58 is the opponent's attempt to say he avoids the problems in k. 312 because the *eye* is an agent, not an instrument. If the opponent were really changing subjects from consciousness to the eye (as rGyal tshab would have it), this parry of the "third case" would be incoherent.

The *adhipatipratyaya* is routinely taken as being one of four conditions (*catvāraḥ pratyayāḥ*), i.e. the [general] causal condition (*hetupratyaya*), the objective condition (*ālambanapratyaya*), the immediately preceding condition (*samanantara-pratyaya*) and the dominant condition; (*adhipatipratyaya*); see BHSD p. 13, Pr. 76.5 et seq., AK ii LVP pp. 299-313. The *adhipatipratyaya* ≅ the "effective cause" (*kāraṇahetu*); see AK ii k. 62d, LVP p. 307. Thus, for example, in the case of the production of a sprout, it is the seed (AK ii LVP pp. 247-248). In the case of a sense consciousness, however, the dominant condition is usually taken to be the sense organ, but even the objects are included so that we end up with the ten *āyatana* being dominant. See AKBh ad AK ii k. 56c (LVP p. 288): *tadyathā pañcasu vijñānakāyeṣu daśānām āyatanāṃ ... ādhipatyam*. The Tibetan scholastic manuals such as the *Blo rigs kyi sdom tshig* of A kya Yoṅs 'dzin dByaṅs can dga' ba'i blo gros (18th C) stress that the sense organs and *manas* are the dominant conditions for sense consciousnesses, but do not seem to mention the objects under this particular rubric. See A kya Yoṅs 'dzin op. cit. p. 524: *thun moṅ thun moṅ ma yin pa'i // bdag rkyen gñis yod daṅ po ni // de yi bdag rkyen yid daṅ ni // gñis pa mig dbaṅ lta bu'o //*. "There are two dominant conditions: the common and the exclusive. The first is the *manas* which is that [consciousness'] dominant condition. The second is [the sense organ] such as the eye organ."

The inescapable impression is that Candrakīrti's interpretation of k.312 in terms of *adhipatipratyaya* is less elegant than that of Dharmapāla. In order to make sense of Āryadeva's thought he seems to be forced to appeal to an ambiguity in the term *lta ba* = *darśana*, viz. "vision" or "sight" vs. "the eye organ"; "the organ of sight".

Cf. May (1959) n. 131, 524 on this ambiguous use of *darśana*. Note that a similar problem for Candrakīrti arises in connection with k. 317, and here *darśana* in CSV clearly has to mean "the faculty of sight", i.e. the eyes. Finally note that Dharmapāla has a rather different interpretation from Candrakīrti, one which does not speak of *adhipatipratyaya* and which takes k. 312 in the context of a refutation of the Sāṃkhya's philosophy of perception. See en. 287.

(398) See en. 292, 294.

(399) Lang (1986) translates: "Alternatively, [if the eye moves without having perceived anything,] it is false to maintain that [the visible form] is necessarily perceptible (*draṣṭavya*)." But this does not concord with CSV, which glosses k. 314cd as *athādṛṣṭvā gacchati tadā didṛkṣitaviṣayadarśanaṃ niyamena na prāpnoti*.

(400) Tib. "...the eye would have absolutely no need to go, i.e. to move."

(401) AK i k. 43cd: *cakṣuḥśrotramano 'prāptaviṣayaṃ trayam anyathā //*. The verse in AK specifies that the eye, ear and mind operate without any contact with their objects, while the other three senses do contact their objects. Candrakīrti's comment in §64, which explains the AK passage as being only a negation (*pratiṣedha*) of "operation by contact", seems to neglect, somewhat disingenuously, the last part (*trayam anyathā*) of the verse, which clearly is an affirmation. See AKBh ad k. 43 (LVP pp. 87-93) for the Abhidharmic arguments on these points.

(402) This sentence does not figure in Skt., but is translated on the basis of Tib. It is nonetheless necessary for the reasoning in the passage, especially if the following sentence *gatau hi satyām*, etc. is to have any connection.

(403) Lang (1986): "[You claim that] the own-nature of all things must first be seen in the things themselves. [We reply:] ..." There is, as far as I can see, no textual justification in CSV for taking the first half of the verse as being specifically a *pūrvapakṣa*. It seems to represent a generally accepted view of how things behave in the world. Āryadeva and Candrakīrti, in typical Mādhyamika fashion, provisionally accept this worldly truth, and then show that it leads to absurdities.

(404) See *Bǎi lùn* T. 1569 *xià* 176a15-21; Tucci (1929) p. 52. Cf. MMK III, 2: *svam ātmānaṃ darśanaṃ hi tat tam eva na paśyati / na paśyati yad ātmānaṃ kathaṃ drakṣyati tat parān //*. Transl. May (1959) p. 79. CS k. 316 is quoted in PP; see D. 78b3.

(405) *campaka*. See *Hobson-Jobson* s.v. *Chumpuk*: "a highly ornamental and sacred tree, a kind of magnolia, whose odorous yellow blossoms are much prized by the Hindus, offered at shrines, and rubbed on the body at marriages."

(406) Lang (Thesis) p. 469, n. 28 cites *Majjhima* I, p. 111: *cakkhuñ ca paṭicca rūpe ca uppajjati cakkhuviññāṇam.* "The eye-consciousness arises in dependence upon the eye and form." Cf. Pr. 6.3; Stcherbatsky (1923) p. 55; the canonical references cited in LVP's n. 5 to Pr. 6.3; MMK III, 7. See also *Traité* II, p. 747, n. 1 for Skt. sūtra reference (= *Saṃyutta* II, p. 72): *cakṣuḥ pratītya rūpāṇi cotpadyate cakṣurvijñānam, trayāṇāṃ saṃnipātaḥ sparśaḥ, sahajātā vedanā saṃjñā cetanā.* "The eye consciousness arises in dependence upon the eye and the forms. The coming together of the three is contact; feelings, notions and attention are produced together with [the consciousness]." Cf. k. 323 below.

(407) Here too "sight" has to be taken as meaning "the organ of sight", i.e. the eyes. See en. 397. Cf. the Chinese which clearly speaks of "the eyes". See also §68, 70 and en. 409.

(408) See en. 236, 264.

(409) Cf. Tib: "Nor does consciousness have eyes (*mig*) either". This would tend to corroborate my point that *darśana* in this context in CSV has to be taken as "the organ of sight", "the eyes". See en. 397, 407.

(410) Translated on the basis of the Tibetan. The argument is not very clear in the Skt.: "For consciousness cognizes but does not see. If, however, consciousness saw, then it would also have the sight of form*, as the consciousness would really exist." *Or perhaps, "sight and form".

(411) Cf. Tib: "Nor does it have [the organ of] sight, for it has as its nature something which is not [the faculty of] sight."

(412) Some remarks on Candrakīrti's possible adversary. In the Vaiśeṣika conception of *prāpyakāritvavāda*, sounds can be produced from sounds — they travel by means of a series, like waves in water, one engendering the other until the ear organ is reached. Cf. VS 2.2.36: *saṃyogād vibhāgāc ca śabdāc ca śabdaniṣpatteḥ.* "For sound is produced from conjunction, disjunction and from [another] sound." *Praśastapādabhāṣya* p. 288.4-6: *...śabdāc ca saṃyogavibhāganiṣpannād vīcīsantānavac chabdasantāna ity evaṃ santānena śrotrapradeśam āgatasya grahaṇam.*

(413) Lang (1986) translates: "how can any *confidence* be placed in it?" But the Tibetan takes *pratyaya* as *śes pa*, so this translation seems unlikely.

(414) Candrakīrti's commentary to k. 319 and his introduction to k. 320 make it clear that he understands the verse as discussing the beginning moments of the sound and not the "origin" or "speaker". He argues, in effect, that this "beginning" is a sound, an insistence which would obviously be absurd if he were, like Dharmapāla, construing

k. 319 as talking about the "origin" of sound, i.e. the speaker. Cf. also Tib. *ādi* = *daṅ po* ("first"; "beginning").

(415) Lang (1986) translates *kevala* as "whole": "If the sound does not come as a whole, why is it apprehended as a whole?" This is fairly improbable as a translation of *kevala*, which Tib. *rkyaṅ par* / *reṅ bu* clearly takes in the sense of "alone". What is more it runs counter to CSV's interpretation which speaks of the impossibility of sound being alone in that it must be accompanied by other *dravya*. Interesting enough, though, the Chinese of CS does have *quán* 全 ("whole"; "totality"), but Dharmapāla's understanding of the verse is completely different from that of Candrakīrti and it is perilous to mix the two perspectives here.

(416) Tib: "Thus it would not be apprehended by any sense organ at all." The idea of the argument seems to be that sound *A* which begins at time t_0 is heard when the sound reaches the ear at t_1, t_2, t_3, which are times later than t_0. What one hears is thus sound at t_1, etc., but never the sound which existed at t_0. The assumption is that if one hears *x* at some time *t*, *x* must exist at *t* and not at some time before. Cf. rGyal p. 12, 1-2: *gal te rna ba'i dbaṅ po daṅ phrad de sgra 'dzin na phrad pa'i sṅa rol gyi sgra yi daṅ po gaṅ gis 'dzin...* "If one apprehended sound when it came into contact with the ear organ, then what would apprehend the sound's beginning, which is before the contact?"

(417) An allusion to the "atoms which are aggregates", or the molecules (*saṃghātaparamāṇu*), spoken about in texts such as AK ii k. 22, LVP pp. 144-149. A molecule, as opposed to the atom properly speaking (i.e. the *dravyaparamāṇu*), is supposed to be composed of at least eight substances (*dravya*): the four elements and the four *bhautikas*, viz. (visual) form, smell, taste and tactile sensations. However, in case it also has sound, then there is a ninth substance.

(418) Cf. transl. in Python (1973) p. 125; May (1959) p. 87.

(419) Translated according to the Sanskrit in Vaidya's ed. of the *Lalitavistara* and the Tibetan version found in M. av. *bhāṣya*. Cf. LVP's transl. p. 314. It is unclear to me as to what sort of instrument a *tuṇa* is. BHSD and Kern (see LVP p. 314 n. 5) hypothesize that it is some sort of drum, but the Tibetan has *gliṅ bu* = "flute".

(420) *dvāra*: lit. "doors".

(421) Cf. Red mda' ba p. 169: *de'i tshe yul mtha' yas pas don rtogs pa yaṅ mthar thug pa med pa'i* phyir 'ldog par mi 'gyur la* /. "Then, because there is an infinite number of objects, the cognition of entities would also be without end, and hence [the movement of the mind] would not stop." *Text reads *med pas*; cf. Tib. of CSV, *med pa'i phyir*.

(422) Literally, "there is no establishment of their own essences". Following Tib. *raṅ gi ṅo bos grub pa*, however, we would have to take the compound *svarūpasiddhi* as meaning "establishment *by* their own essences" rather than "establishment / proof *of* their essence." While this Tibetan reading is a possible interpretation, it seems to fit less well with the rest of the passage.

(423) Adding "of this notion" can be justified on the basis of the Tib.: *bstan pa de'i tshe de rnams kyi sgo nas 'du śes de raṅ gi ṅo bos grub par ga la 'gyur.*

(424) While it might at first sight seem that *yo ...sa* in k. 322 were correlated, this is not borne out by Candrakīrti's commentary, nor would it make much philosophical sense, because the *artha* would then have to be the aggregate of notions. Cf. the Chinese version of k. 322.

(425) See en. 428 for the Epistemologist's and Mādhyamika's use of mental perception (*mānasapratyakṣa*). It should be remarked, however, that there is one significant difference here from the Dharmakīrtian view. Whereas Dharmakīrti had maintained that the object of mental perception and that of sensory perception are qualitatively identical but must exist at different moments, Āryadeva and Candrakīrti say that it is the very same object which is subsequently apprehended by *manas* (*sa eva paścān manasā gṛhyate*).

(426) One might very well translate *avidyamānasvarūpe 'pi pūrvagṛhīte 'rthe* as "with regard to the object which had been apprehended earlier, but whose own nature does not exist either", instead of as a locative absolute. Although the locative absolute seems the more plausible interpretation of the Skt., it does not concord with the Tib. *de bźin du smig rgyu la bya ba ltar yod pa ma yin pa'i raṅ bźin can gyi dṅos po bzuṅ zin pa la yaṅ gaṅ rnam par rtog pa can gyi rnam par śes pa skye ba de ni chos thams cad rnam par 'jog pa'i rgyu yin no.* If we translated in keeping with the Tibetan translator's interpretation of the Skt. text, we would have something like, "In this same fashion, the cause for the [different] determinations of all dharmas is the conceptual consciousness which arises with regard to an object which had been apprehended earlier, but whose own nature does not exist, like a mirage."

(427) Tib. translates *°saṃprayoga* as *daṅ mtshuṅs par ldan pa* ("having similarity"). What is at stake is the *saṃprayuktakahetu*, ("associated cause"; Tib. *mtshuṅs ldan gyi rgyu*) which is included in the Vaibhāṣikas' sixfold classification of causes (*ṣaḍvidho hetuḥ*). See LVP (1913) pp. 54-55. Minds (*citta*) and mental factors (*caitta*) must have a fivefold set of similarities (*samatā*): *a)* basis (*āśraya*), i.e. they depend upon the same sense organs; *b)* object (*ālambana*), i.e. they apprehend the same object; *3)* aspect (*ākāra*), i.e. they both adopt the likeness of their object [AKBh ad ii k. 34, Pradhan ed. p. 62.6: *sākārās tasyaivālambanasya prakāraśa ākaraṇāt*] ; *d)* time (*kāla*), i.e. they are simultaneous; *e)* substances (*dravya*), i.e. they have the same substantial

cause or substratum (*upādāna*). Cf. AK ii, k. 34bcd, LVP pp. 177-179: *...cittacaitasāḥ / sāśrayālaṃbanākārāḥ saṃprayuktāś ca pañcadhā //*. AKBh ad k.34: *pañcabhiḥ samatāprakārair āśrayālambanākārakāladravyasamatābhiḥ*. Any mind (*citta*), conceptual or not, must have at least ten mental factors (*caitta*) associated with it (cf. AK. ii, k. 24, LVP pp. 153-155), one of which is the notion (*saṃjñā*). Candrakīrti's point about the *vikalpakaṃ vijñānam* being termed "*saṃjñā*", then, is that while the conceptual consciousness is not strictly speaking the notion and is not actually the "aggregate of notions" in the traditional classification of five *skandhas*, it is so intimately associated with the notion that it is termed "*saṃjñā*". For the five aggregates (*skandha*), see e.g. Stcherbatsky (1923) pp. 6-7; Takakusu (1947) p. 72.

(428) K. 322 and CSV are interpreted by Tibetans as showing that Āryadeva and Candrakīrti postulated a conceptual mental perception (*mānasapratyakṣa*), a claim which is plausible. Let us look briefly at the details as presented in the *Tshig gsal stoṅ thun gyi tshad ma'i rnam bśad* of 'Jam dbyaṅs bźad pa Ṅag dbaṅ brtson 'grus (1648-1722), his work on the Prāsaṅgika use of *pramāṇas*. The point is also briefly explained in a section of Se ra rje btsun Chos kyi rgyal mtshan's (1469-1546) textbook (*yig cha*) on the *Madhyamakāvatāra*, the *dBu ma'i spyi don*, f. 147b, which I have translated as an appendix to an article, "Indian and Tibetan Mādhyamikas on *mānasapratyakṣa*", i.e. Tillemans (1989b).

First of all, for the notion of mental perception (*mānasapratyakṣa*) in the Epistemological school, see Stcherbatsky (1930) vol. II, appendix III; Mookerjee (1935) chapter XIX, pp. 311-314. Mookerjee summarizes Dharmakīrti's basic view; Stcherbatsky translated a number of passages, among them one from 'Jam dbyaṅs bźad pa's *Blo rigs* which describes and criticizes the Sa skya pa's description of the three Indian traditions on the matter, viz. those attributed to Prajñākaragupta, Saṃkarānanda and Dharmottara. See also: Nagatomi (1980); Kajiyama (1966) pp. 45-47 for Mokṣākaragupta's account in his *Tarkabhāṣā*.

The basic idea for the Epistemologists is that there is a type of perception which has the mind as its dominant condition (*adhipatipratyaya*), which is free of conceptualization (*vikalpa*) and which perceives an object which had initially been perceived by a sense perception. In fact, the explanation is somewhat more complicated if we take the Dharmakīrtian position. Dharmakīrti maintained that the object of mental perception was qualitatively identical to that of sense perception, but that the two sorts of perceptions apprehended objects which existed at different moments. The point in saying the object of mental perception was a facsimile, but not identical with that of sensory perception, was to avoid Kumārila's charge that if the mental perception apprehended the exact same object as the sensory perception, the former would be redundant and would not give any new experience. See NB I, 9: *svaviṣayānantaraviṣayasahakāriṇendriyajñānena samanantarapratyayena janitam tan manovijñānam*. "*Manovijñāna* is that which is produced by the immediately preceding condition, i.e. the sense cognition, which is coactive with the object which immediately follows [the sense cognition's] own object."

Why there must be such a mental perception is a thorny point. Jñānagarbha seems to have considered it to be a necessary intermediate stage between sense perception and conceptualization, but Dharmottara and his followers felt that there really was no argument which could be given except an appeal to the scripture which stated: "O monks, form is apprehended by two [sorts of cognition], i.e. by the visual consciousness and by the mind (*manas*) which is induced by this [visual consciousness]." *dvābhyāṃ bhikṣavo rūpaṃ gṛhyate cakṣurvijñānena tadākṛṣṭena ca manasā.* Quoted in Durveka Miśra's *Dharmottarapradīpa* ad *Nyāyabindu* I, 9 (ed. Malvania 62, 21). Dharmottara went so far as to say in his *ṭīkā* to NB I, 9 that there is absolutely no means of valid cognition (*pramāṇa*) which proves its existence. *etac ca siddhāntaprasiddhaṃ mānasaṃ pratyakṣam / na tv asya prasādhakam asti pramāṇam /.* "This mental perception is recognized by [our] philosophical system, but there is no *pramāṇa* which proves it." In short, for many non-Prāsaṅgika schools, *mānasapratyakṣa* was postulated because it was mentioned in the scriptures, but it had little or no philosophical import. dGe lugs pa Epistemologists, such as dGe 'dun grub pa (1391-1474) in his *Tshad ma rigs pa'i rgyan*, accept Dharmottara's characterization but assimilate the problem to an "inference based on [scriptural] authority" (*yid ches pa'i rjes dpag*). See his p. 63 of *Rigs rgyan*. This is also implicitly the line of defense found in Mokṣākaragupta.

Candrakīrti's revised definition of *pratyakṣa* (see en. 374) is used as a key step in reinterpreting this theory of mental perception (*mānasapratyakṣa*) to Madhyamaka purposes, for it allows one to postulate perceptions which are also conceptual. For the other schools, mental perception, like all direct perceptions, was free of conceptualization, but Candrakīrti relied on CS k. 322 to postulate a type of *conceptual* mental perception. It would always be associated with sense perceptions and would be responsible for the genesis of the notions (*saṃjñā*) by means of which we impose natures on objects; because it is conceptual, one can claim that these notions are mind-invented and do not correspond to anything in the object.

Here then is 'Jam dbyaṅs bźad pa's Prāsaṅgika definition of perception. Folio 581: *mṅon sum tshad ma'i mtshan ñid yod de / raṅ gi rten rtags yaṅ dag la dṅos su ma brten par raṅ gi 'dzin staṅs kyi yul gyi gźal bya mṅon sum pa la mi slu ba'i śes pa de de yin pa'i phyir /.*

> "A consciousness which, without directly relying on a valid reason as its basis, doe not belie with regard to the perceptible (*mṅon sum pa*) discriminable object apprehended by it."

After having given a definition of mental perception which omitted mention of *kalpanāpoḍha* (= *rtog bral*) and which simply specified that such a perception must have *manas* as its dominant condition, he says that this is the defining characteristic because:

> "While this much [i.e. the dependence on *manas*] is common to all philosophical systems (*grub mtha'* = *siddhānta*), here the fact that most mental perceptions in sentient beings' [mind]-streams are pervaded by being conceptual

cognitions is a Prāsaṅgika position which is not common to the Svātantrikas and on down. According to these [Prāsaṅgikas], amongst mental perceptions there are many conceptualizations, such as where one thinks [something is] "such and such" [a thing], and thus one definitely has to give up the [specification] "free from conceptualization" in the defining characteristic of perceptions which are *pramāṇas*. Thus, the reason for negating [*kalpanāpoḍha*] is of such a sort."

Text on f. 586: *...yid kyi mṅon sum tshad ma'i mtshan ñid yin te / de tsam grub mtha' kun mtshuṅs kyaṅ 'dir ni sems can rgyud kyi yid mṅon phal cher la źen rig gis khyab pa ni raṅ rgyud pa man chad daṅ thun moṅ ma yin pa'i thal 'gyur ba'i lugs yin no // 'di pas yid mṅon la 'di'o sñam pa lta bu'i rtog pa maṅ bas mṅon sum tshad ma'i mtshan ñid du rtog bral ṅes par 'dor dgos pas bkag pa'i rgyu mtshan de ltar yin pa'i phyir.*

For 'Jam dbyaṅs bźad pa this type of *mānasapratyakṣa,* which would be responsible for our thinking that something is "such and such" (*'di'o sñam pa*), is already to be found in Nāgārjuna's *Ratnāvalī* 4,53. (In fact it is especially Ajitamitra's commentary which is important here for 'Jam dbyaṅs bźad pa.) But what is significant for us is that 'Jam dbyaṅs bźad pa leans heavily on CS and CSV and cites CSV ad k. 322 in this connection. The interpretation is plausible, for what is especially noteworthy is that Candrakīrti's commentary, in speaking of *vikalpakaṃ vijñānam,* lends credence to the Tibetan's idea that the Prāsaṅgikas were speaking about a *conceptual* mental perception in these contexts. In short, the rather complicated mechanism of mental perception apprehending a previous, and now inexistent, point-instant of the object is being used to reinforce the Mādhyamika's position that the object itself has no nature; indeed by the time it is apprehended as being something or another, the object itself has ceased to exist. See Tillemans (1989b) on these subjects.

(429) See en. 406.

(430) An action must have a basis (*āśraya*), or subject to which that action occurs. However, in the case of the action of production, that which is undergoing the action does not yet exist, and so cannot serve as the basis. In general terms, production of *X* is impossible because *X* does not yet exist at the time of its production. See en. 324 for references in MMK, MMV, etc. Cf. Dharmapāla's commentary, 227b26-27: "[For,] at the time of the effect, there is no cause: so the effect is the effect of what? At the time of the cause, there is no effect: so the cause is the cause of what?"

(431) Tib. adds "a cavalry corps". In fact, Indian armies would classically have four corps: the "cavalry corps (*rta'i tshogs* = *aśvakāya*)" should thus be included. See Mvyut 3638-3641; *Inde Classique* §1596.

(432) Cf. *Saṃyutta* iii, 142. For the cliché *asato, ṛktato* (= *riktato*), *tucchato ... anātmato*, cf. *Śālistambasūtra*, ed. LVP pp. 89-90, quoted in Pr. 593; May (1959), p. 296.

See also *Traité* II, p. 641 and n. 1 for canonical references from *Majjhima* and *Aṅguttara*. AKBh viii ad k. 4cd applies the same images to the *saṃjñā*; see LVP p. 144 and n. 2. Contemplating that everything is impermanent, painful, void, selfless, like a sickness, an abscess, a splinter and an impurity constitutes the eight sorts of contemplation (*anupaśyanā*)(see *Traité* p. 641); the first four are the aspects (*ākāra*) of the truth of suffering.

(433) *vicāryamāṇasya*, although a passive, is to be taken in an active sense. See Renou (1975) §342, p. 464 n.: "A basse époque, on rencontre des passifs avec valeur active-transitive,...notamment en bouddh[ique]."

(434) *na bheṣyati* = Tib *'byuṅ mi 'gyur*. *bheṣyati* is a Hybrid Sanskrit future for *bhaviṣyati*, the stem *bhe* being used for *bhavi*. See Edgerton (1953) p. 224 column 1.

(435) Lang translates *indriyāṇāṃ gatau* as "in the *movement* of the sense faculties". This, however, does not fit the context (which is no longer discussing movement), nor does it concord with Tib., viz. *dbaṅ rtogs*.

(436) See en. 386.

(436a) See en. 210.

(437) Cf. *Ratnāvalī* 1,36; *Śūnyatāsaptati*, verse 66; *Yuktiṣaṣṭikā*, verse 28. See *Traité* I chapter XI on the ten examples used to illustrate the illusory nature of dharmas.

(438) Translated on the basis of the Sanskrit. The Tibetan would give: "Just as magically created women which come forth by means of trances are causes for passions in the desirous, as are really existent women, [and just as] there does not exist any nature to the 'sages' magically created due to the power of sages'* [own] magic trances, but the [magical creations] which lack the nature of real sages can vanquish the mental darkness of all beings, as can real sages, and can be causes for sentient beings' paths to higher states and salvation;" *I read *thub pa rnams kyi* instead of *thub pa rnams kyis*, which is incomprehensible for me. Cf. Kaḥ thog p. 449: *de bźin du thub* ***pa'i*** *tiṅ ṅe 'dzin las sprul pa'i thub pa rnams raṅ gi ṅo bos med kyaṅ* ... Note that here I translated on the basis of the actual Tibetan text, rather than B's restitution of the Tibetan into Sanskrit.

(439) *ātmabhāva* means simply "the body". Cf. BHSD. Note that Tibetan translators sometimes translates the term as *bdag gi dṅos po* and sometimes as merely *lus*. See May (1959) n. 1017. Candrakīrti adopts the formula "associated with sleep" (*middhasaṃprayukta*) no doubt in keeping with the Abhidharma's theory of *citta* and *caitta* being associated. See en. 427. *middha* is a mental factor (*caitta*).

(440) *Ratnāvalī* 4, 57. Cf. transl. in Tucci (1936) p. 429 and Hopkins (1975) p. 70.

(441) Translation unsure. This passage is clearly destined to support the second simile, viz. magical beings (*nirmāṇa*) which, although unreal, aid people in their practice of the Dharma. The passage, which refers to the *Ratnakūṭasūtra*, seems to allude to the story of the two magically created monks in the *Kāśyapaparivarta* §§138-149 (ed. Staël-Holstein) of the *Ratnakūṭa*. Cf. in particular *Kāśyapaparivarta* §141.

(442) Cf. transl. May (1959) p. 142 and 258.

VOLUME II: TEXTS AND INDEXES

PREFACE TO THE TEXTS AND INDEXES

Three texts are presented here:

a) a critical edition of the Tibetan of the *Catuḥśataka* (CS) and *Catuḥśataka-vṛtti* (CSV) to chapters XII and XIII as found in the Peking, sDe dge, Co ne and sNar thaṅ editions of the Tibetan *bsTan 'gyur*.

b) a transcription of the Sanskrit fragments of CS and CSV found in Haraprasād Shāstrī (1914). At the present time, there is only one manuscript available, although we can hope that further manuscripts might still be findable in Beijing or perhaps in Sa skya Monastery. There is, however, to our knowledge at this time, no evidence or even rumour of the existence of a Sanskrit manuscript of CS or CSV in these two collections, nor in the Nepalese-German collection. I have compared Bhattacharya's emendations in his (1931) edition, have altered Shāstrī's punctuation here and there and made a number of minor corrections, but essentially the text is as found in Shāstrī. For methodological remarks see Vol. I, Chapter I, A.

c) a reproduction of the Chinese text of Dharmapāla's *Guǎng bǎi lùn shì lùn*, chapters IV (= CS XII) and V (= CS XIII), as found in *Taishō* 1571.

For the Sanskrit and Tibetan of CS I have also compared the edition of Vaidya (1923) and Lang (1986). In editing the Tibetan of the *kārikā*s, the other Tibetan version of the CS (viz. the text of the *kārikā*s alone) has been consulted in all four editions of the *bsTan 'gyur*. However, I have given preference to the readings of the *kārikā*s to be found in CSV, as explained in my remarks in Vol. I, Chapter I, A. Finally, for the sake of completeness, I have also compared the edition of the Tibetan of CS published in 1974 by the Pleasure of Elegant Sayings Press in Sarnath, U.P.; with very few exceptions, this latter text is a reproduction of the Co ne version of CS (*kārikā*s alone). David P. Jackson, in a letter, has made me aware of the existence of a potentially significant old edition of the Tibetan of the CS *kārikā*s printed by a certain nobleman "Goṅ dkar bźi 'dzom in c. 1415-1420 at the request of the Phag mo gru ruler Grags pa rgyal mtshan (1374-1432)". The text is to be found in the Library of Tibetan Works and Archives, and will, hopefully, one day be published.

I have generally indicated both the adopted and rejected readings in the usual manner, i.e. separating them by means of a colon. However, given the number of texts consulted for the Tibetan (especially for the *kārikā*s), it was impractical and unnecessary to follow this procedure in the case of some trivial divergences. In those case my notes only indicate the rejected readings. Paragraphs of the Sanskrit, Tibetan texts and the translations are correlated by the same numbers prefixed by the symbol "§". In the case of the Chinese text, the references are to the *Taishō* page-number given in the margin of each third folio in Chinese characters, the folio (a,b,c), and finally the lines of the *Taishō* text.

Some other conventions to be noted. Bhattacharya's edition of the Sanskrit and Tibetan, which haphazardly leaves out various portions of the Tibetan text, can be retraced by means of the following two symbols which occur in our text and in the margins: "°" in the Sanskrit and Tibetan shows that what follows was left out by Bhattacharya; "*" shows that what follows was edited by Bhattacharya. The symbol "#" in the Tibetan text shows the place in the Tibetan which corresponds to the beginning of a Sanskrit fragment in Shāstrī; "##" indicates the end of the relevant fragment. "<...>" indicates Sanskrit fragments found in sources other than Shāstrī.

Four indexes have been compiled, namely, an index of proper names, Sanskrit terms, Tibetan and Chinese. Translations of the terms are included, although I naturally have not intended to give all their possible senses, only the ones which figure in our work. When a term is used in two or more significantly divergent senses — as for example in the case of the word *pratyakṣa* ("perceptible"; "perception") — I give sub-references to each use. On the few occasions when it is simply the *term itself* which is being talked about, the references follow immediately after the main entry. Thus, to take the entries for *pratyakṣa*, we find the following:

pratyakṣa 40, 44, 176, 177, 178, fn. 71, en. 358
— "perceptible" 26-28, 44, 175, 179, 180, fn. 71, en. 373, 374
— "perception" 37, 44, 91, 94, 177, fn. 37, 49, 97, en. 53, 60, 314, 365, 367, 428

The numbers immediately following *pratyakṣa* (viz. 40, 44, etc.) indicate the pages where the term fits into neither sub-heading — for example, when Candrakīrti is debating as to whether we should understand *pratyakṣa* as meaning "perception" or "perceptible".

The Sanskrit equivalents which I have given for the Tibetan and Chinese terms are those which were given in the translation or notes: here again I have not attempted to give *all* equivalents which one might find in glossaries, but only the ones which we have used. The page references following the equivalences show where these Sanskrit terms were cited. Finally, note that in the *Index of Proper Names*, we have given a number of sub-classifications under the different authors: for example, "Dharmapāla, debate with Bhāvaviveka". These subject sub-headings concern largely the introductory chapters and the notes — for the translations, the *Table of Contents* should provide sufficient indications of the subject matter discussed. The works cited in the *Index of Proper Names* are the primary sources which figure in our introductory chapters, translations, and endnotes.

Remarks added in 2006:

The Chinese page numbers in the margins of the Taisho text have been rendered into English. The repunctuation of the Chinese texts has been omitted.

Tom J.F. Tillemans
Lausanne, Switzerland

TABLE OF CONTENTS

PREFACE TO THE TEXTS AND INDEXES iii

ABBREVIATIONS AND SIGLA vi

SANSKRIT AND TIBETAN TEXTS OF CATUḤŚATAKAVṚTTI XII: REFUTATION OF HERETICAL VIEWS (*dṛṣṭi*) 1

SANSKRIT AND TIBETAN TEXTS OF CATUḤŚATAKAVṚTTI XIII: REFUTATION OF THE SENSE ORGANS AND THEIR OBJECTS (*indriyārtha*) 59

CHINESE OF DHARMAPĀLA'S COMMENTARY 129

Chapter IV 131
Chapter V 138

INDEXES 147

Sanskrit terms 149
Tibetan terms 160
Chinese terms 165
Proper names 180

ABBREVIATIONS AND SIGLA USED IN THE EDITIONS

B	V. Bhattacharya's edition of CS and CSV.
C	CSV in the Co ne edition of the Tibetan Tripiṭaka, bsTan 'gyur, microfiches made by the Institute for the Advanced Study of World Religions, Stony Brook, N.Y., 1974.
C_k	CS (kārikās alone) in Co ne edition.
CS	Catuḥśataka of Āryadeva.
CSV	Catuḥśatakavṛtti (or ṭīkā) of Candrakīrti.
D	CSV in the sDe dge edition of the Tibetan Tripiṭaka, bsTan 'gyur, published by the University of Tokyo, 1981-.
D_k	CS (kārikās alone) in sDe dge edition.
Ego	reading proposed by the present editor.
HPS	edition of Sanskrit fragments of CS and CSV published by Haraprasād Shāstrī.
k	kārikā(s).
L	K. Lang's edition of CS.
N	CSV in the sNar thaṅ edition of the Tibetan Tripiṭaka, bsTan 'gyur, conserved in the Musée Guimet in Paris.
N_k	CS (kārikās alone) in sNar thaṅ edition.
P	CSV in the Peking edition of the Tibetan Tripiṭaka, bsTan 'gyur.
P_k	CS (kārikās alone) in Peking edition.
S	edition of CS published in Sarnath.
Skt	Sanskrit.
Tib	Tibetan.
V	P.L. Vaidya's edition of CS.
°	end of Bhattacharya's text.
*	start of Bhattacharya's text.
#	start of Tibetan text corresponding to HPS.
##	end of Tibetan text corresponding to HPS.
§	paragraph sign.
<...>	Sanskrit fragments found in sources other than HPS.

SANSKRIT AND TIBETAN TEXTS

SANSKRIT AND TIBETAN TEXTS OF

THE CATUḤŚATAKAVṚTTI, CHAPTER XII:

REFUTATION OF HERETICAL VIEWS

CATUḤŚATAKAVṚTTI XII: TIBETAN TEXT

* **§1. [P.206a6; D.183a6; C.180a4; N.202b7]** * 'dir smras pa / khyod kyis bdag med pa 'di ches gsal[1] źiṅ rgyas par bstan la / de bźin **[N.203a]** gśegs pa yaṅ 'di thugs su chud pa po daṅ / ñe bar 'doms pa po yin na / de ci'i phyir chos 'di la 'jig rten phal cher 'jug par mi 'gyur / gaṅ gi phyir chos 'di ni mdzad pa po daṅ rnam par 'chad pa po daṅ chos kyi che ba'i bdag ñid rnams kyis ches dkar ba źig ste / de'i phyir thar **[D.183b]** pa 'dod pa thams cad kyis 'di la 'jug par rigs na[2] / lugs kyi khyad par ñe bar bśad pa gźan rnams ci ste 'byuṅ /

§2. bśad par **[P.206b]** bya ste / chos 'di la rab tu gsuṅ pa po daṅ rnam par 'chad pa po daṅ / chos kyi raṅ gi ṅo bo'i bdag ñid chen po dag yod mod kyi / de lta na yaṅ ñan pa po'i che ba'i bdag ñid śin tu rñed par dka'o // 'di ltar /

gzur gnas blo ldan don gñer ba'i //
ñan po snod ces bya bar bśad // **(k.276ab)**

§3. de la gzu bor gnas pa ni gaṅ phyogs su ma ltuṅ[3] ba'o // phyogs su **[C.180b]** ma lhuṅ ba yaṅ gaṅ źig ce na / gaṅ źig raṅ daṅ gźan gyi phyogs dag la rjes su chags pa daṅ rgyab kyi phyogs pa daṅ bral ba'o // de ni de ltar sems kyi rgyud ñon ma moṅs pa'i phyir[4] legs par bśad pa rin po che'i khyad par tshol[5] ba lhur byed pa kho na yin pas kun nas ñon moṅs pa'i phyogs 'dor ba'i rtsa ba ni gzu bor gnas pa ñid yin no // de'i phyir de ltar na ñan pa po gzu bor gnas pa ni dam pa'i chos kyi bdud rtse phul du byun ba'i snod yin no //

§4. gzu bor gnas par gyur kyaṅ gal te blo daṅ ldan par 'gyur na ste / legs par bśad pa daṅ / ñes par[6] bśad pa dag gi sñiṅ po daṅ sñiṅ po med par rnam par dbye ba[7]

---

[1] DC ches gsal: P ches bsal; BN chos bsal.

[2] BN ni.

[3] PDC ltuṅ: BN lhuṅ.

[4] DN ñon ma moṅs pa'i phyir: PC ñon moṅs pa'i phyir; B ma ñon moṅs pa'i phyir.

[5] B tshul.

[6] DCNB ñes par: P ñe bar.

[7] PDCN dbye ba: B dpyod pa.

la mkhas pa'o[1] // de ni blo daṅ ldan pa ñid kyis sñiṅ po med pa btaṅ nas sñiṅ po len no // de ltar gal te ñan pa po blo daṅ ldan par gyur na ni de de ltar snod du 'gyur ro // de ltar gzu bor gnas **[N.203b]** śiṅ blo daṅ ldan par gyur kyaṅ legs par bśad pa ñan pa don du gñer bar 'gyur źiṅ ri mo'i skyes bu'i rnam pa[2] ltar mi brtson pa ma yin te / de ltar na /

gzur gnas blo ldan don gñer ba'i //
ñan po snod ces bya bar bśad do[3] //

ñan pa po rnam pa[4] de lta bu yin na ni ṅes par /

smra po'i[5] *yon tar rnam*[6] *gźan du* //
mi 'gyur ñan pa po la'aṅ[7] *min* // **(k.276cd)**

§5. de la smra ba po'i yon tan dag ni zur dod pa daṅ phyin ci ma log pa daṅ /**[P.207a]** gsal ba daṅ ma 'khrugs par brjod pa daṅ / ñan pa po'i lhag pa'i bsam pa khoṅ **[D.184a]** du chud pa daṅ / sems la zaṅ ziṅ med ñid de / de lta bu la sogs pa dag go // ñan pa po yaṅ chos daṅ chos smra ba po gñis la gus pa daṅ / yid gtod pa ñid daṅ / gzu bor gnas pa ñid daṅ / blo daṅ ldan pa ñid daṅ / don du gñer ba ñid do // de'i don du gñer ba ñid ni chos daṅ chos smra ba dag la gus par byed pa daṅ yid gtod pa ñid la sogs pa dag gis rtogs par byed do //

§6. de lta yin daṅ smra ba po la yon tan rnam pa gźan du mi 'gyur la / ñan pa po la'aṅ[8] yon tan rnam pa gźan du mi **[C.181a]** 'gyur ro // ñan pa po rnam pa de lta bu yod na ni smra ba po la yon tan skyon gyi ṅo bor mi 'gyur ro // ñan pa po'i

---

[1] DCB mkhas pa'o: PN mkhas na'o.

[2] P par.

[3] PNB do: DC omit.

[4] DC rnam pa: PNB rnams.

[5] DC smra po'i: D_kC_kPNBLS smra po; N_kP_kV smra por.

[6] DC$D_kC_kN_k$BLS rnam: PN rnam pa; P_kV rnams.

[7] PDCNB ñan pa po la'aṅ; $P_kD_kC_kN_k$VLS ñan po la yaṅ.

[8] D la yaṅ.

skyon las ni yon tan yaṅ skyon gyi ṅo bor rnam par 'gyur la / skyon yaṅ yon tan gyi ṅo bor rnam par 'gyur gyi / bśad zin pa'i mtshan ñid can gyi ñan pa po thos pa las byuṅ ba la sogs pa'i yon tan phyin ci ma log pa'i tshogs kyi gźir gyur pa yod na ni / smra ba po la yon tan rnam pa gźan du mi 'gyur la / ñan pa po la yon tan skyon gyi
° ṅo bor mi 'gyur ro //°

§7. de'i phyir smra ba po ches yoṅs su dag pa yin yaṅ ñan pa po raṅ gi ñes
* par mi brtsi ba rnams kyi[1] skyon daṅ ldan pa ñid du 'dzud par byed de / * blun po bdag la bstod[2] pa na ci **[N.204a]** bdag cag la śes rab med dam ci źig bya / rtogs[3] par byed pa po med do źes de skad du gaṅ smra ba kho na yin no[4] // 'di ni ***lhag pa'i bsam pa bskul ba'i mdo*** las rtogs par bya'o // de ñid kyi phyir bcom ldan 'das kyis /

srid daṅ srid thabs źi ba yi //
thabs daṅ de bźin źi[5] *gsuṅs te //*
'jig rten yoṅs su mi śes gaṅ //
de ni[6] *thub pa'i lta bur mṅon //* **(k.277)**

§8. de la srid pa[7] ni 'bras bur 'gyur[8] ba'i **[P.207b]** ñe bar len pa'i phuṅ po lṅa'o // srid pa'i thabs ni rgyur gyur pa'i 'du byed rnams so // źi ba ni mya ṅan las 'das pa ste ñe bar 'tshe ba thams cad log pa'i raṅ bźin yin pa'i phyir ro // źi ba'i thabs ni 'phags pa'i lam yan lag brgyad do // de ltar bcom ldan 'das kyis thar pa 'dod **[D.184b]** pa rnams la 'phags pa'i bden pa bźi ñe bar bstan te / blaṅ bar bya ba daṅ dor bar bya ba'i 'bras bu daṅ bcas pa dag ñe bar bstan pa'i phyir ro //

---

[1] PDCN kyi. But cf. Red mda' ba (p. 143): raṅ gi ñes pa mi brtsi ba rnams *kyis*...

[2] PDCN bstod ("praise"): B bstan ("teach").

[3] B rtogs: PDCN rtog. Cf. Kaḥ thog, rtogs.

[4] PDCN gaṅ smra ba kho na yin no: B gaṅ smra ba po ma yin no.

[5] PN$P_k$$D_k$$C_k$$N_k$BVLS źi: DC bźi.

[6] V na.

[7] PNB srid pa: DC srid par.

[8] B gyur.

§9. de la thos pa daṅ bsam pa daṅ sgom pa daṅ ldan źiṅ yaṅ dag pa jı lta ba so so raṅ gis[1] khoṅ du chud pa rnams kyi rgyud la ni bcom ldan 'das kyis ñe bar bstan pa'i don ji lta ba bźin kho na yin gyi / thos pa daṅ bsam pa daṅ sgom pa la mṅon par brtson pa la sdaṅ ba[2] rnams ni bdag ñid snod ma [C.181b] yin par ma 'phrigs pa na[3] gaṅ gi phyir kho bo cag gis don ji lta ba bźin mi rtogs pas ṅes par 'di yaṅ dag par ma bśad do źes 'khrul pa de thub pa'i yin pa ltar ṅes par byed do //

§10. de tsam gyis ni saṅs rgyas bcom ldan 'das noṅs pa daṅ ldan pa yaṅ ma yin no // 'phags pa'i bden pa bźi ston par mdzad pa ñid kyis skyes bu'i don ma lus pa ñe bar ston pa'i mdzad pa po yin pa'i phyir smra ba po'i skyon ga la yod / de'i phyir na thub pa'i lta bur[4] źes bśad de[5] / kha cig dag gis des ñe bar bstan pa'i dṅos po'i de kho na ñid ji lta [N.204b] ba bźin ṅes par ma zin pa'i phyir ro // dmus loṅ gis ma mthoṅ ba ni snaṅ bźin pa'i ñi ma'i skyon ma yin te ma loṅ ba rnams kyis de mthoṅ ba'i phyir ro //

§11. 'dir smras pa / de bźin gśegs pa'i[6] mṅon par mtho ba'i gtam thams cad ni ches don gsal ba yin na / ṅes par legs pa'i gtam ni dṅos po thams cad med par ston pa lhur [P.208a] len pa ñid kyis kho bo cag lta bu[7] rnams kyis rtogs par mi nus te / 'di ltar bcom ldan 'das dṅos po thams cad kyi raṅ gi ṅo bo sun 'byin par źugs pa'i phyir kho bo cag gi yid mgu bar mi mdzad do // bśad par bya ste /

---

[1] PBN gis: DC gi.

[2] Ego sdaṅ ba ("dislike"): (The text is corrupt) P brdar ba; DC sdar ba; B dor ba; N illegible (sdaṅ ba?). The Tibetan commentaries all express the sense of *sdaṅ ba* by explaining: thos bsam sgom pa la mi brtson pa'i 'jig rten.

[3] PDCN 'phrigs pa na: B 'phags pa ni.

[4] PDCN lta bur: B lta bar.

[5] PNB de: DC do.

[6] B de'i.

[7] P bur.

thams cad btaṅ bas mya ṅan las //
'das par[1] *ya mtshan can kun 'dod //*
kun sun 'byin la[2] *de dag ni //*
mi dgar 'gyur ba'i[3] *rgyu ci źig //* ° **(k.278)**

§12. graṅs[4] can pa daṅ bye brag pa la sogs pa ya mtshan can thams cad kyis bde ba daṅ sdug bsṅal ba la sogs pa dṅos po kun nas ñon moṅs pa mtha' dag **[#]** log pas[5] thar pa 'thob bo źes bya bar khas **[D.185a]** blaṅs so // gaṅ gi tshe de ltar ya mtshan can thams cad kyis thams cad btaṅ bas mya ṅan las 'das par mṅon par 'dod pa de'i tshe gaṅ źig rgyab kyis phyogs pa'i rgyur 'gyur ba sṅon[6] chad ma byuṅ ba gsuṅs pa cuṅ zad tsam yaṅ med do // ya mtshan can rnams kyis dṅos po gaṅ dag mya ṅan las 'das par slar mi 'byuṅ bas mya ṅan las 'da' bar 'dod pa de dag kho na bdag gis[7] raṅ bźin med par ston pa lhur **[C.182a]** byed ciṅ dam pa ma yin pa'i lta ba'i tsher ma 'byin pa'i bdag ñid can gyi bstan bcos kyis mya ṅan las 'das pa'i groṅ khyer du 'gro ba'i lam yoṅs su sbyoṅ[8] bar bsgrubs pa yin te des na khyod yod pa ma yin pa'i 'jigs pa sñiṅ la brtags nas / ci'i phyir 'jigs / yid la yoṅs su dga' ba bskyed pa daṅ / chos 'di bdag tu 'gyur bar **[N.205a]** gyis śig / bdag ñid la kun nas ñon moṅs pa'i dṅos po thams cad mya ṅan las zlo[9] ba'i gtam yaṅ khoṅ cig //**[##]**

---

[1] DC 'das par: $PNP_kD_kC_kN_k$BVLS 'da' bar.

[2] $PNP_kD_kC_kN_k$BVLS kun sun 'byin la: DC kun sun 'byin pa.

[3] PDCNB mi dgar 'gyur ba'i: V mi dka' 'gyur ba; $P_kD_kC_kN_k$LS mi dga' 'gyur ba.

[4] From here (B p. 142) on until the end of HPS Sanskrit to CSV XII (B p. 154), Bhattacharya does not edit the Tibetan of CSV, but only gives some indications in his notes. He does, however, edit the Tibetan of the kārikās.

[5] PN log pas: DC log par. Cf. Skt [ni]vṛttyā.

[6] DC sṅon: PN sṅan.

[7] Ego gis: PDCN gi. Cf. Skt mayā.

[8] PN sbyoṅ: DC sbyaṅ.

[9] DC zlo: PN bzlo.

CATUḤŚATAKAVṚTTI XII: SANSKRIT TEXT

§12....[HPS.494] [ni]vṛttyā[1] mokṣāvāptir iti niścayaḥ / yadā caivaṃ sarvatyāgena sarvapāṣaṇḍināṃ nirvāṇam abhimataṃ tadā na kiṃcin mayātrāpūrvam upacaritaṃ[2] yad vaimukhyakāraṇaṃ bhavet / yeṣām eva[3] hi padārthānāṃ nirvāṇe punar apravṛttyā nirvṛttir abhisamīhitā teṣām eva mayā naiḥsvābhāvyapratipādanapareṇa śāstreṇāsad-darśanaka[ṇṭakoddharaṇātmakena][4] nirvāṇanagaragāmimārgapariśodhanam anuṣṭhitam / tat kim iti hṛdi bhayam asad ālikhya[5] bhavān bibheti / ādhīyatāṃ manaḥparitoṣaḥ kriyatām ātmasād ayaṃ dharmo niveśyatāṃ cetasi sāṃkleśikavastunivāraṇakathā /

---

[1] HPS ...vṛttyā. B restitutes nivṛttyā. Cf. Tib. log par.

[2] HPS upacaritaṃ: B uktaṃ.

[3] HPS yeṣām eva: B pāṣaṇḍikair yeṣām eva.

[4] HPS śāstreṇāsaddarśanakaṭā + + + + + + + +. Restitution follows B. Cf. Tib dam pa ma yin pa'i lta ba'i tsher ma 'byin pa'i bdag ñid can gyi bstan bcos kyis.

[5] HPS ālikhya: B kalpayitvā.

§13. ji skad du bcom ldan 'das kyis /
mya ṅan 'das la[1] chos rnams chos yod min[2] //
'di na gaṅ med de dag gźar yaṅ med //
yod daṅ med **[P.208b]** ces rtog pa daṅ ldan źiṅ //
de ltar spyod rnams sdug bṅal źi[3] mi 'gyur //
źes gsuṅs so //

§14. mya ṅan las 'das pa ni mya ṅan las rgal ba phuṅ po lhag ma med pa'i mya ṅan las 'das pa'i dbyiṅs te sdoṅ bu daṅ mar yoṅs su zad pas mar me śi ba bźin no // raṅ ñid kyis yaṅ dag pa ji lta ba bźin rtogs pa rnams la de kho na ñid kyi ye śes kyi me'i stobs kyis bdag gi ba la chags pa log pas 'dod chags daṅ źe sdaṅ daṅ gti mug daṅ rgyags pa daṅ ṅa rgyal la sogs pa rnams kyi yod pa ñid rnam pa thams cad du med pa ñid yin no sñam du[4] khyed[5] cag ya mtshan can thams cad kyis mṅon par 'dod do źes saṅs rgyas bcom ldan 'das kyis bśad pa rnams kyis yid yoṅs su dga' bar 'gyur gyi / mu stegs byed rnams kyis 'di de kho na ltar yin no źes bya bar ṅes par ni ma zin to // 'dir

sup rnams kyi[6] su **[D.185b]** mi mṅon par byas so

źes bya ba la sogs pa'i mdor byas pa bdun pa mi mṅon par byas pa'o //

§15. 'di la bcom ldan 'das kyis /

da ltar gaṅ dag mya ṅan las 'das pa 'di ṇi med pa ste / rab rib med pa'i gnas skabs na rab rib can rnams kyis dmigs pa'i skra śad daṅ sbraṅ bu la sogs pa lta bu'am / sgron ma'i[7] gnas skabs na khyim na nam mkha'o zer gyur bas[8] thag pa

---

[1] C las.

[2] The sūtra is also quoted in Pr. The Tibetan of Pr. reads mya ṅan 'das la chos rnams yod ñid med /. See Pr 522, n. 2.

[3] DC źi: PN źiṅ.

[4] DC sñam du: PN źes bya bar.

[5] PN khyed: DC khyod.

[6] Ego kyi: PDCN kyis. Skt. has the genitive plural, supām.

[7] PN sgron ma'i: D sgrol ma'i; C sgrol ba'i.

[8] PN nam mkha'o zer gyur bas: DC nam mkha' 'od zer gyur bas.

§13.

<nivṛtti dharmāṇa na asti dharmā
ye neha astī[1] na te jātu asti /
astīti nāstīti ca kalpanāvatām
evaṃ carantān na duḥkha śāmyati //>[2]

<supāṃ sulukpūrvasavarṇāccheyāḍāḍyāyājālaḥ>[3]

---

[1] In keeping with Pr. and Tib. read *neha*; Vaidya has *yeneti nāsti* and LVP's mss. (cf. Pr. 522, n. 3) has *ye neha nāsti*.

[2] *Samādhirājasūtra* chapt. 9, verse 26 (p. 48 ed. Vaidya); Skt. also quoted in Pr. 522.11-14.

[3] Pāṇini's *Aṣṭādhyāyī* VII.1.39. Candrakīrti quotes simply *supāṃ suluk* and designates the rest by *...ityādi*.

la sbrul du mthoṅ ba'i **[C.182b]** 'jigs pas mthoṅ ba'i dug 'phog pa'i[1] dogs pa log pa bźin rnam pa thams cad du mi snaṅ bar gyur ciṅ yod pa ma yin pa de dag ni rab rib can gyi gnas skabs na rab rib can rnams **[N.205b]** kyi skra śad daṅ sbraṅ bu la sogs pa dag lta bu daṅ (/) ji ltar snaṅ ba'i gnas skabs na sbrul med pas thag pa la sbrul gyi blo med pa de bźin du mun pa'i gnas skabs na yaṅ bden **[P.209a]** par[2] gyur pa'i sbrul med pas sbrul gyi blo gaṅ yin pa de yaṅ med pa bźin gźar yaṅ ste / 'khor ba'i gnas skabs 'ga' yaṅ yod pa ma yin no /

źes gsuṅ bar gyur to //

§16. 'o na ji ltar 'khor ba kun nas ñon moṅs pa daṅ las las[3] byuṅ źe na / bśad pa / 'khor ba ni rab rib can gyis dmigs pa'i skra śad la sogs pa'i blo'i ṅo bo'i tshogs daṅ 'dra ste mun pa'i gnas skabs na sbrul gyis 'jigs pa phyin ci log bźin no // 'di yaṅ yod pa ma yin pa'i phyin ci log gi mun pas blo gros kyi mig ldoṅs par byas pa'i byis pa'i skye bo rnams kyi yin no / źes bśad pa ni

yod daṅ med ces rtog[4] pa daṅ ldan źiṅ //
de ltar spyod rnams sdug bsṅal źi mi 'gyur //

źes bya ba'o // legs par bśad pa las ni rnams yod min źes bya bar 'gyur mod kyi[5] /

tiṅām ni tiṅ ṅor gyur ro[6] źes bya ba brjod par bya'o

źes bya ba'i mtshan ñid las na chos yod min źes gsuṅs so // dhar mā ṇā am źes

---

[1] Ego dug 'phog pa'i: PDCN dug 'phos pa'i. 'phos pa = "to move"; "to transfer". 'phog pa = "to be hit"; "to be infected". Cf. *Zidian* p. 493: nad byuṅ ba'i don te: ... śa rul zos na śa dug phog ñen che lta bu. dug phog simply means "to get poisoned".

[2] DC bden par: P don bden par; N de na bden par.

[3] DC las: PN la.

[4] PDC rtog: N rtogs.

[5] Ego legs par bśad pa las ni rnams yod min źes bya bar 'gyur mod kyi /: DC legs par bśad pa las ni rnams yod rnams za min // źes bya bar 'gyur mod kyi /; PN legs par bśad pa las ni rnam pa yod min źes bya bar 'gyur mod kyi /. The text is corrupt. I would, however, hypothesize that what is being said here is that in classical Sanskrit we should find na santi = rnams yod min. See en. 158.

[6] Ego tiṅām ni tiṅ ṅor 'gyur ro: PN tiṅ ṅan ni tiṅ ṅor 'gyur ro; D ti ṅan ni tiṅ ṅor 'gyur ro; C tiṅ nan tiṅ ṅor 'gyur ro. Cf. the Sanskrit of the quotation from the *Mahābhāṣya*. The Tib. is trying to transliterate the Skt. tiṅām.

<tiṅāṃ ca tiṅo bhavantīti vaktavyam>[1]

[1] *Mahābhāṣya* III p. 256, line 14 (ed. Kielhorn) on Pāṇini's *Aṣṭādhyāyī* VII.1.39. See en. 158.

bstan par bya ba la[1] / 'dir yi ge ā daṅ ma[2] mi mṅon par byas so //

§17. de yod ces rtog pa daṅ ldan pa ni khyed cag graṅs can pa daṅ 'ug pa pa daṅ / gzegs zan daṅ / ser skya daṅ / bye brag tu smra ba pa rnams yin la / med ces **[D.186a]** rtog pa daṅ ldan pa ni bye brag pa daṅ mdo sde pa daṅ rnam par śes pa smra ba rnams te / de ltar spyod pa yod pa daṅ med pa'i gdon gyis zin pa rab rib kyi gnas skabs na[3] rab rib can rnams lta bu daṅ mun khuṅ du thag pa la sbrul gyi blo can rnams bźin du lta ba phyin ci log tu gyur pa rnams kyi sdug bsṅal te / 'gro ba lṅa'i 'khor bar skye ba daṅ / rga ba daṅ **[C.183a]** na ba daṅ[4] 'chi ba'i sdug bsṅal daṅ mya ṅan la sogs pa źi bar mi 'gyur ro // de dag gi rnam par dpyad pa ni gnas daṅ gnas su 'di ñid las **[N.206a]** bstan zin **[P.209b]** pa'i phyir ma bśad do // de ñid kyi phyir

gaṅ zag phuṅ po[5] smra ba yi[6] //
'jig rten graṅs can 'ug phrug daṅ //
gos med bcas[7] la gal te źig //
yod med 'das pa smra na dris //

de'i phyir saṅs rgyas rnams kyi[8] ni //
bstan pa 'chi med yod med las[9] //
'das pa zab mo źes[10] bśad pa //
chos kyi khud pa yin śes gyis[11] //

źes gsuṅs so //

---

[1] N bstan par bya la.

[2] PN yi ge ā daṅ ma: DC yi ge a daṅ yi ge ma.

[3] DC na: PN omit.

[4] PN na ba daṅ: DC omit.

[5] PDCN phuṅ po: *Ratnāvalī* (ed. Hahn) 1.61, phuṅ por.

[6] DC + Ed. Hahn yi: PN yin.

[7] DC + Ed. Hahn bcas: PN bca'.

[8] PN + Ed. Hahn (*Ratnāvalī*, 1.62) kyi: DC kyis.

[9] PN + Ed. Hahn las: DC pas.

[10] PDCN źes: Ed. Hahn, 'di.

[11] Ed. Hahn śes gyis: DC źes gyis; PN źes kyis. Cf. Skt. viddhi.

§17.

<sasāṃkhyaulūkyanirgranthapudgalaskandhavādinam /
pṛccha lokaṃ yadi vadaty astināstivyatikramam //>

<dharmayautakam ity asmān nāstyastitvavyatikramam /
viddhi gambhīram ity uktaṃ buddhānāṃ śāsanāmṛtam //>[1]

[1] *Ratnāvalī* 1.61-62 (ed. Hahn p. 26). Both verses are cited in Pr. p. 275.

§18. gal te gaṅ 'di lta ste / thams cad btaṅ bas mya ṅan las 'das pa[1] źes bya ba 'di ñid ya mtshan can rnams kyi yaṅ bsam pa yin na ni **[#]**khyod daṅ mu stegs can rnams la khyad par ci yod ce na / khyad par ni mu stegs can rnams la thams cad gtoṅ ba'i bsam pa tsam źig tu zad kyi thams cad gtoṅ ba'i thabs brjod pa med pa gaṅ yin pa 'di yin no // thams cad gtoṅ ba'i thabs ma bstan na yaṅ /

gaṅ źig gtoṅ thabs mi śes de //
ci źig gtoṅ bar byed par 'gyur // **(k.279ab)**

§19. thams cad gtoṅ ba'i bsam pa la gnas kyaṅ mu stegs can gyi lugs la brten źiṅ btaṅ ba'i thabs mṅon par mi śes pas ci źig gtoṅ bar byed par 'gyur te / gaṅ gi phyir thams cad gtoṅ ba'i thabs don dam pa'i bden pa'i chos thams cad raṅ bźin gyis stoṅ pa ñid mtshan ñid can mi śes pa'i phyir ro // de ñid kyi phyir /

des na ṅes par thub pa yis[2] //
gźan du źi ba med ces gsuṅs // **(k.279cd)**

§20. 'di ñid la dgoṅs nas thub pas dge sbyoṅ daṅ po ni 'di ñid du'o // gñis pa daṅ gsum pa ni 'di ñid **[D.186b]** du'o // bźi pa ni 'di ñid du'o // pha rol po smra ba ni dge sbyoṅ dag gis stoṅ pa'o źes gsuṅs so / źes bya bar ṅes so // thams cad gtoṅ ba'i thabs yaṅ dag par bstan pa 'di las ni saṅs rgyas bcom ldan 'das kyi ye śes kyi 'jug pa thams cad la thogs pa med pas **[P.210a]** don ji lta ba bźin du ston pa po ñid du rtogs so // **[C.183b]** mu stegs **[N.206b]** can rnams ni thams cad gtoṅ ba'i thabs ston pa'i nus pa daṅ bral bas dṅos po'i rnam pa gźan du yaṅ śes pa'i phyin ci log pa ñid du grub pa'i phyir bsgrub[3] par mi bya'o //

---

[1] DC 'das pa: PN 'da' ba.

[2] $P_k D_k C_k N_k$VBLS yis, which is better grammatically: PDCN yi.

[3] Ego bsgrub: PDCN sgrub. Grammatically, a *ba*-prefix is probably preferable for bsgrub par mi bya.

§18. nanu ca yadi sarvapāṣaṇḍinām apy ayam evābhiprāyo yad uta sarvatyāgena nirvāṇam iti kaḥ punar bhavatas tīrthikānāṃ ca viśeṣaḥ / ayaṃ viśeṣo yat tīrthikānāṃ sarvatyāgābhiprāyamātraṃ na tu[1] punaḥ sarvatyāgopāyākhyānam / anupadiṣṭe ca sarvatyāgopāye

kiṃ kariṣyati sa tyāgaṃ tyāgopāyam na vetti yaḥ / **(k.279ab)**

§19. sarvatyāgāśaye 'pi sthite[2] tīrthikamatāvalambī tyāgopāyānabhijñaḥ kiṃ tyāgaṃ kariṣyati / yan na jānāti sarvadharmasvabhāvaśūnyatālakṣaṇaṃ sarvatyāgopāyaṃ paramārthasatyam / ata eva /

śivam anyatra nāstīti nūnaṃ tenoktavān muniḥ // **(k.279cd)**

° **§20.** °ihaikaḥ prathamaśramaṇa[3] iha dvitīyo yāvac caturthaḥ / śūnyāḥ parapravādāḥ śramaṇair ity amunaivābhisandhinā muninaivam uktam iti niścīyate / asmād eva ca sarvatyāgopāyasamākhyānāt sarvatraiva bhagavato buddhasya jñāna-pravṛttyavyāghātena yathārthaśāstṛtvaṃ pratīyate / tīrthikānāṃ ca sarvatyāgopāya-samākhyānasāmarthyavaikalyenetaratrāpi padārthajāte viparyastavijñānatā siddhatvān na sādhyā /[4]

---

[1] HPS tu: B omits.

[2] B sthite: HPS sthita. Cf. Tib gnas kyaṅ.

[3] Ego śramaṇa: HPS repeatedly has śravaṇa. But cf. Tib: dge sbyoṅ = śramaṇa. See B p. 280, n. 2.

[4] HPS here has the marginal note: aniṣṭa siddheḥ. The whole of the preceding paragraph was not edited in B.

§21. gal te khyod kyi ltar na yaṅ mṅon sum ma yin pa'i phyir na śes bya mtha' yas pa dbaṅ po las 'das pa'i don ñe bar bstan pa dag la ci don 'di ji skad du[1] bstan pa de kho na ltar yin nam 'on te gźan du yin źes de rnams the tshom skye bar 'gyur ba ñid ma yin nam / de'i yul can gyi ṅes pa'i rgyu ni yod pa ma yin no // de la yaṅ bśad par bya ste /

saṅs rgyas kyis gsuṅs lkog[2] gyur la[3] //
gaṅ źig the tshom skye 'gyur ba //
de yis[4] stoṅ pa ñid bsten[5] te //
'di ñid kho nar yid ches bya // **(k.280)**

§22. dṅos po thams cad mṅon sum du śes pas go bar bya ba ni ma yin gyi rjes su dpag pas rtogs par bya ba yaṅ yod do // rjes su dpag par bya bar nus pa yaṅ yin te /[6] dpe yaṅ[7] yod pa'i phyir ro // 'dir thams cad gtoṅ ba'i thabs ni chos thams cad raṅ bźin gyis stoṅ pa ñid yin te / de ni gaṅ gis kyaṅ gźan ñid du bsgyur bar mi nus so // don 'di ni rtag tu ñe yaṅ skye bo thams cad kyis mṅon sum ma yin pa'i phyir phra ba yaṅ yin la de ni 'thad pas chos thams cad la raṅ bźin du 'dzin pa bzlog pa'i sgo nas ji lta ba bźin du'aṅ bstan to // re źig 'di ñid la 'di ṅes par gyis śig // ci ste 'di la ci 'di ni de kho na ltar yin nam / 'on te rnam pa gźan du yin sñam du mi ṅes pa'i rgyu cuṅ zad cig yod ciṅ gal te bśad zin pa daṅ 'chad pa'i rab tu byed pas bstan pa'i ṅes pas de ma bsal na ni de smros śig // 'dis ma ṅes **[P.210b]**pa'i rgyu cuṅ zad kyaṅ brjod par nus pa ni ma yin te / de'i phyir dpe 'di[8] grub **[D.187a]** pa kho na'o //

---

[1] DC du: PN omit.

[2] N_k sgrog.

[3] DC pa.

[4] PDCN$D_k C_k$BLS yis: $P_k N_k$V yi.

[5] $P_k D_k C_k N_k$BVLS bsten: DC bstan; PN brten.

[6] PN nus pa yaṅ yin te /: DC nus pa ma yin te /.

[7] DC yaṅ: PN omit.

[8] PN 'di: DC omit.

* §21. * nanu ca tavāpy aparyantatvād jñeyasyātīndriyeṣv artheṣūpadiṣṭeṣv asamakṣatvāt teṣāṃ saṃśaya eva jāyate kim asāv artho yathopadiṣṭas tathaivāhosvid anyatheti / na hi tadviṣayaṃ niścayakāraṇam astīti / tatrāpy ucyate /

buddhokteṣu parokṣeṣu jāyate yasya saṃśayaḥ /
ihaiva pratyayas tena kartavyaḥ śūnyatāṃ prati // **(k.280)**

§22. na hi sarve bhāvāḥ pratyakṣajñānagamyā anumānagamyā api vidyante / śakyaṃ cātrānumānaṃ kartuṃ dṛṣṭāntasadbhāvāt / iha tyāgopāyaḥ[1] sarvadharma-svabhāvaśūnyatā / sā cāśakyā kenacid anyathātvam āsādayitum / sūkṣmaś cāyam artho nityasaṃnihito 'pi sarvajanāsamakṣatvāt / tasya copapattyā sarvadharmasvabhāva-grāhavinivāraṇamukhenopapāditā yathāvattā / atraiva tāvad āsthīyatāṃ niścayaḥ / kim evam[2] evaitad utāho 'nyatheti athātrāsti[3] kiṃcid aniścayakāraṇaṃ tad upadiśyatāṃ yadi tan na nirākṛtam uktavakṣyamāṇaprakaraṇapratipāditaniścayena / na ca śakyam anena svalpam apy aniścayakāraṇaṃ kiṃcid abhidhātum iti siddha evāyaṃ dṛṣṭāntaḥ /

---

[1] HPS tyāgopāyaḥ: B sarvatyāgopāyaḥ.

[2] HPS kim evam: B athātra kim evam.

[3] HPS athātra: B omits. B placed athātra at the beginning of the sentence.

de'i phyir de las gźan pa'i bcom ldan 'das kyi gsuṅ[1] mṅon sum ma yin pa'i don ston par byed pa yaṅ raṅ ñid kyi tshul gyis don ji lta ba bźin no źes bya bar rtogs par bya ste / de bźin gśegs pa'i **[N.207a]** bstan pa'i phyir raṅ bźin gyis stoṅ pa ñid kyi don rjod[2] par byed pa'i gsuṅ bźin no // de'i phyir saṅs rgyas **[C.184a]** kyis gsuṅs pa'i lkog tu gyur pa dag la the tshom gaṅ[3] la za //**[##]**

§23. bcom ldan 'das kyis /
'jig rten khams ni stoṅ rnams su //
ṅa yis mdo rnams gaṅ gsuṅs pa //
yi ge tha dad don gcig ste //
yoṅs su bsgrag par nus ma yin[4] //

dṅos po gcig ni bsams[5] byas na //
de dag thams cad bsgoms 'gyur te //
saṅs rgyas kun gyis[6] chos[7] maṅ po //
ji sñed rab tu bstan pa rnams //

chos rnams kun gyi bdag med yin //
mi gaṅ don la mkhas rnams kyis //
gnas 'di la ni bslab byas nas[8] //
saṅs rgyas chos rnams rñed mi dka'[9] //

---

[1] DC gsuṅ: PN gsuṅs.

[2] DCN rjod: P brjod.

[3] DC gaṅ: PN ga.

[4] DC bsgrag par nus ma yin: PN bsgrag pa nus pa yin. Cf. Skt na śakyaṃ parikīrtitum.

[5] PN bsams: DC bsam. (bsam =future form; bsams =past).

[6] DC gyis: PN gyi. Cf. Skt sarvabuddhehi, where the *ehi* is a hybrid form of the instrumental plural.

[7] PN chos: DC ches. Cf. Skt dharmāḥ.

[8] PN nas: DC na. Cf. Skt śikṣitvā.

[9] DCN dka': P dga'.

tataś cānyad apy asamakṣārthapratipādakavacanaṃ bhagavato yathārtham iti pratīyatāṃ svanayenaiva tathāgatopadiṣṭatvāt svabhāvaśūnyatārthābhidhāyakavacanavad iti kuto buddhokteṣu parokṣeṣu saṃśayāvakāśaḥ /

§23.

<lokadhātusahasreṣu ye mayā sūtra[1] bhāṣitāḥ /
nānāvyañjana ekārthā na śakyaṃ parikīrtitum //>

<ekaṃ padārthaṃ cintetvā sarve te bhonti bhāvitāḥ /
yāvantaḥ sarvabuddhehi bahu dharmāḥ prakāśitāḥ //>

<nairātmyaṃ sarvadharmāṇāṃ ye narā arthakovidāḥ /
asmin pade tu śikṣitvā buddhadharmā na durlabhāḥ //>[2]

---

[1] A hybrid plural form. Cf. Tib. mdo rnams.

[2] *Samādhirājasūtra*, 32, verses 5-7 (ed. Vaidya p. 195).

źes bya ba daṅ / de bźin du /

ji ltar bdag gi 'du śes śes gyur pa //
de bźin thams cad la ni blo sbyar bya //
chos rnams thams cad de yi raṅ bźin te //
rnam par dag pa nam mkha' lta bu yin //

źes ji skad du gsuṅs pa lta bu'o //

§24. **[#]** de bźin gśegs pa ltar mu stegs can rnams kyaṅ phyin ci ma log par brjod pa ñid du ṅes par ni mi nus te[1] / de rnams ni mthoṅ ba'i chos ñid la phyin ci log tu gyur ba'i phyir ro // 'di ltar de rnams kyis ni 'jig rten 'di'i 'jug pa rgyu rtag pa sṅon du 'gro bar ston na mthoṅ ba daṅ 'gal ba daṅ 'thad pa daṅ 'gal ba de ni bstan par mi nus so // de ltar na /

gaṅ gis 'jig rten 'di mthoṅ **[P.211a]** *dka'*[2] //
de ni gźan la[3] *blun pa ñid* // **(k.281ab)**

§25. zla ba ña ba la mthoṅ ba'i[4] nus pa ñams pa 'ga' źig gis skar[5] ma dhru va daṅ a run dan ti[6] mthoṅ ba ni ma yin no // de bźin du mu stegs can 'dis kyaṅ gaṅ gi tshe re źig sems can daṅ snod ces bya ba'i 'jig rten 'di'i rgyu daṅ 'bras bu la rmoṅs pas don rags pa[7] yaṅ dag par mi mthoṅ ba de'i **[D.187b]** tshe don ji ltar don śin tu phra ba yul daṅ dus riṅ pos chod ciṅ rab tu dbye ba **[N.207b]** daṅ bcas pa śes par 'gyur / de'i phyir 'khor ba'i lam gyi ṅal dub bsal bar bya ba'i phyir de kho na ñid mthoṅ ba'i chu dri ma med pa btuṅ bar 'dod pa / *gaṅ dag*[8] mu stegs can raṅ ñid lta ba śin tu phyin ci log ciṅ smig rgyu'i chu ltar bsten **[C.184b]** par bya ba ma yin pa /

---

[1] DCN ṅes par ni mi nus te: P ṅes par ni nus te.

[2] N_k dga'.

[3] $DCND_kC_kBLS$ la: P_kN_kV ma; P pa.

[4] DC mthoṅ ba'i: PN mthoṅ ba yi. PN turn this passage into a verse.

[5] PN skar: DC skad.

[6] N a run dan ti: DC a nu dan ti; P a dun dan ti.

[7] PDN rags pa: C rigs pa.

[8] This is the word *gaṅ dag* which should figure in k. 281cd.

<yatha jñātvātmasaṃjñās tathaiva sarvatra preṣitā buddhiḥ /
sarve ca tatsvabhāvā dharma viśuddhā gaganakalpāḥ//>[1]

§24. na ca tathāgatavat tīrthikānām api śakyam aviparītārthābhidhāyitvam avasātuṃ teṣāṃ dṛṣṭa[2] eva viparyastatvāt / tathā hy asya lokasya tair nityakāraṇapūrvikā pravṛttir upadiśyate / sā cāśakyapratipādyā[3] dṛṣṭaviruddhā copapattiviruddhā ceti[4] / evam / [HPS.495]

loko 'yaṃ yena durdṛṣṭo mūḍha eva paratra saḥ / **(k.281ab)**

§25. na hi saṃpūrṇe candramasi vyāhatadarśanasāmarthyo dhruvam arundhatīṃ vā paśyatīti[5] saṃbhāvyam / tadvad ayaṃ tīrthiko lokasya sattvabhājanākhyasya hetuphalavyāmūḍhatvāt sthūlam evārthaṃ tāvad yadā na samyag īkṣate tadā katham ayam atisūkṣmaṃ vidūradeśakālavyavahitaṃ saprabhedam arthaṃ jñāsyatīti saṃbhāvayituṃ śakyam / tad imaṃ tīrthikaṃ svayam atyantaviparyāsitadarśanaṃ mṛgatṛṣṇājalavad anupāsanīyaṃ tattvadarśanāmalajalapipāsavaḥ saṃsārādhvapariśramaklamāpanodanāya

---

[1] *Samādhirājasūtra*, 12, verse 7 (ed. Vaidya p. 77).

[2] HPS dṛṣṭa: B dṛṣṭadharma.

[3] HPS °pratipādyā: B °pratipādanā.

[4] Ego ceti / evam /: HPS cety evam /; B ca / evam /.

[5] B vā paśyatīti: HPS vāpaśyatīti.

de'i[1] *rjes 'gro de dag* //[2]
śin tu yun riṅ[3] *bslus par 'gyur* // **(k.281cd)**

§26. gaṅ dag saṅs rgyas bcom ldan 'das kyis don ji lta ba bźin ston pa la mi brten par[4] thar pa 'dod pa ñid kyis mthoṅ ba daṅ ma mthoṅ ba'i dṅos po'i raṅ bźin la rnam par rmoṅs pa'i mu stegs can gyi[5] rjes su 'gro ba de dag ni phyi ma'i mtha'i[6] mur gtugs pa med pa can gyi 'khor bar bslus par 'gyur ro //**[##]**

§27. 'dir /

'ji ltar nor la mi mkhas tshoṅ pa ṅan pa rin chen gliṅ du soṅ rnams rin po che //
'dod pas rmoṅs las nor bu rin thaṅ chen po btaṅ nas nor bu mchiṅ bu[7] len pa ltar //
de bźin gźun lugs dag la mi mkhas blo gros ṅan źiṅ 'dzam[8] bu gliṅ du soṅ ba[9] rnams //
thar pa'i re ba bcas[10] pas rmoṅs las[11] saṅs rgyas gźuṅ lugs dor nas mu stegs gźuṅ lugs len //

źes bśad do //

---

[1] $P_kD_kC_kN_k$VBLS all read de rjes 'gro. However I have preferred to keep the reading in PDCN (de'i); judging from the commentary it seems that rjes su 'gro ba takes the genitive.

[2] k. 281c: gaṅ dag de'i rjes 'gro de dag //.

[3] PDCNC_kBLS riṅ: $P_kD_kN_k$V riṅs.

[4] DC mi brten par: PN mi bsñen par.

[5] DC gyi: PN gyis.

[6] PDC mtha'i: N omits.

[7] DC mchiṅ bu: PN 'chiṅ bu.

[8] DC 'dzam: PN dzam.

[9] DC soṅ ba: PN son pa.

[10] PN bcas: DC bcad ("cut"; "eliminate"). PN has re ba bcas pas, which seems to be a shortening for metrical reasons of re ba daṅ bcas pas.

[11] PDC las: N pas.

vañcitās te bhaviṣyanti suciraṃ ye 'nuyānti tam // **(k.281cd)**

§26. aparyavasānāparakoṭike saṃsāre te vata vañcitā bhaviṣyanti ye yathārtha-śāstāraṃ buddhaṃ bhagavantam avadhūya dṛṣṭādṛṣṭapadārthasvabhāvavyāmūḍhaṃ mokṣakāmatayā tīrthikam anugacchanti /

§28. **[#]**yaṅ ci'i phyir / thar pa 'dod pa de dag phyin ci log tu mthoṅ ba mu stegs can gyi rjes su 'gro źe na / raṅ bźin gyis stoṅ **[P.211b]** pa ñid kyi chos bstan pa ñan pa la 'jigs pa'i phyir ro // 'jigs pa de ni / bdag yod ma yin 'byuṅ mi 'gyur / bdag gi yod min 'byuṅ mi 'gyur / źes brtags nas skrag pa las so // skrag pa de yaṅ śin tu yun riṅ por bdag tu 'dzin pa daṅ bdag gir 'dzin pa goms pa las so // de ñid kyi phyir śin tu yun riṅ por goms par byas kyaṅ dge ba'i bśes gñen gyis yoṅs su bzuṅ bas dṅos po'i raṅ bźin la mṅon par źen pa'i dri ma dor nas /

mya ṅan 'das par raṅ 'gro gaṅ //
de dag[1] *śin tu bya dka'*[2] *byed //* **(k.282ab)**

§29. raṅ ñid saṅs rgyas bcom ldan 'das su gyur nas raṅ ñid kho na mya ṅan las 'das pa'i groṅ **[N.208a]** khyer du ñe bar gśegs te / de ltar dka' ba **[D.188a]** mdzad pa thugs rje chen po mṅa' ba /

'dren slad bźin du'aṅ dam pa ni[3] *//*
ma yin yid 'gror[4] *spro ma yin //* **(k.282cd)**

§30. dam pa ma yin pa bdag tu 'dzin pa daṅ bdag gir 'dzin pa la rnam par gnas pa'i yid raṅ ñid mya ṅan las 'das par 'gro bar[5] mi spro ba 'ba' źig tu ma zad kyi / 'on kyaṅ dam pa ma yin pa'i **[C.185a]** yid ni mdzad dka' ba mdzad pa'i 'dren pa po'i[6] slad bźin du yaṅ[7] mya ṅan las 'das par 'gro bar mi spro'o //

§31. yaṅ ci'i phyir dam pa ma yin pa'i gaṅ zag gi yid 'dren pa po de'i rjes bźin du yaṅ mya ṅan las 'das par 'gro ba mi spro źe na / stoṅ pa ñid la skrag pa'i phyir ro // yaṅ gaṅ źig 'di la skrag par 'gyur źe na / gaṅ źig 'gyur ba de bstan pa'i phyir bśad pa /

---

[1] PDCN de dag: $P_kC_kD_kN_k$VLBS de ni. Cf. Skt te.

[2] N_k 'ga'.

[3] PDCNB 'dren slad bźin du'aṅ dam pa ni: $P_kD_kC_kN_k$VLS 'dren pa'i slad bźin dam pa ni.

[4] PDCNB 'gror: $P_kD_kC_kN_k$VLS 'gro.

[5] DC 'gro bar: PN omit.

[6] PN 'dren pa po'i: DC 'dren pa'i.

[7] PN yaṅ: DC omit.

§28. kasmāt punar ete mokṣakāmās tam evaṃ[1] viparyastadarśanaṃ tīrthikam anugacchanti / svabhāvaśūnyatādharmopadeśaśravaṇabhayāt / tad bhayaṃ nāsty ahaṃ na bhaviṣyāmi na me 'sti na bhaviṣyatīty ālambyottrāsāt / trāsaś cāyaṃ[2] suciram ahaṃkāramamakārābhyāsāt / ata eva kalyāṇamitraparigrahāt sucirābhyastam api bhāvasvabhāvābhiniveśaṃ malavat[3] tyaktvā /

svayaṃ ye yānti nirvāṇaṃ te kurvanti suduṣkaram / **(k.282ab)**

§29. buddho bhagavān svayaṃ bhūtvā svayam eva nirvāṇapuram upayāti[4] / tasyetthaṃ duṣkarakāriṇo[5]

gantuṃ notsahate netuḥ pṛṣṭhato 'py asato manaḥ // **(k.282cd)**

§30. na kevalam asatām[6] ahaṃkāramamakāravyavasthityānāṃ svayam eva nirvāṇaṃ gantuṃ mano notsahate / api khalu yathopavarṇitasya[7] netuḥ pṛṣṭhato 'py asyāsato[8] nirvāṇaṃ gantuṃ mano notsāhaṃ pravedayate[9] /

§31. kasmāt punar asya[10] netuḥ pṛṣṭhato 'py asataḥ pudgalasya nirvāṇaṃ gantuṃ mano notsahate / śūnyatāyāṃ trāsāt / kasya punar asyāṃ trāso bhavatīti / yasya bhavati taṃ[11] pratipādayann āha /

---

[1] HPS mokṣakāmās tam evaṃ: B mokṣakāmā. B omits tam evaṃ.

[2] B trāsaś cāyaṃ: HPS tatrāyaṃ makes little sense and does not correspond to Tib skrag pa de yaṅ.

[3] HPS °abhiniveśaṃ malavat: B °abhiniveśamalaṃ.

[4] HPS upayāti: B upayātaḥ.

[5] HPS duṣkarakāriṇo: B duṣkarakāriṇo mahākāruṇikasya in keeping with Tib thugs rje chen po mṅa' ba.

[6] HPS asatām . .°vyavasthitānāṃ: B reads singular asato ...°vyavasthitasya.

[7] HPS yathopavarṇitasya: B duṣkarakāriṇo.

[8] HPS asyāsato: B omits asya.

[9] HPS notsāhaṃ pravedayate: B mano notsahate.

[10] B asya: HPS anyasya. Cf. Tib de'i.

[11] Ego taṃ pratipādayann: HPS and B taṃ prati prati°. Tib has no equivalent to this occurrence of prati.

ma mthoṅ skrag par[1] *mi rtsom ste //*
mthoṅ na rnam kun de ldog[2] *'gyur //*
des na ṅes par cuṅ zad cig //
śes la skrag par[3] *bsgrub par bya*[4] *//* **(k.283)**

§32. bstan bcos kyi brda la ma byaṅ ba ni ba laṅ rdzi la sogs pa dag ste de dag ni stoṅ pa ñid lan brgyar **[P.212a]** bstan kyaṅ rnam pa thams cad du rjes su źugs pa med pas stoṅ pa ñid kyi[5] don ma mthoṅ ba'i phyir de la skrag par mi 'byuṅ ste / skad cig mar 'jig pa la der rmoṅs pa lta bu daṅ / dmyal ba'i me la log par lta brgyud bzuṅ ba bźin[6] no //

mthoṅ na rnam kun de ldog 'gyur //

§33. stoṅ pa ñid ces bya ba'i chos mthoṅ na ni de la mkhas pa rnams rnam pa thams cad du skrag pa ldog par 'gyur te / 'jigs pa'i rgyu bdag daṅ bdag gir[7] mṅon par źen pa daṅ bral ba'i phyir ro // thag par mthoṅ na thag pa la[8] sbrul du phyin ci log skyes pa'i sbrul gyi[9] 'jigs pa daṅ bral ba bźin no // gaṅ źig cuṅ zad cig śes[10] śiṅ cuṅ zad cig mi śes pa de la ni ṅes pa ste / gdon mi za bar 'gyur bas skrag par bsrub par bya'o // glaṅ po che **[N.208b]** myos pa'i rkyen bu legs par bslabs pa ni glaṅ po ches spar ba na[11] de la mi 'jigs la / de la bźon[12] par 'dod pa'i[13] groṅ pa śin tu rmoṅs pa

---

[1] PDCNB skrag par: $P_kD_kC_kN_k$VLS skrag pa.

[2] $P_kD_kC_k$NkVLS ldog: PDCNB bzlog. Both are future forms. The commentary in CSV, however, uses ldog.

[3] PDCNB skrag par: $P_kD_kC_kN_k$VLS skrag pa.

[4] DCP_kN_kBVL bsgrub par bya: PND_kC_kS brjod par bya.

[5] DC kyi: PN kyis.

[6] DC bźin: PN yin.

[7] PDC bdag gir: N bdag gi tshe.

[8] PDC la: N omits.

[9] DC gyi: PN gyis.

[10] DCN śes: P ges.

[11] DCN spar ba na: P sbar ba ni.

[12] DCN bźon: P gźon.

trāso nārabhyate 'dṛṣṭe dṛṣṭe 'paiti sa sarvaśaḥ /
niyamenaiva kiṃcijjñe tena trāso vidhīyate // (k.283)

§32. avyutpannaśāstrasaṃketā hi gopālādayaḥ śataśo 'py upadiśyamānāyāṃ śūnyatāyāṃ sarvathā tadanupraveśābhāve saty[1] adṛṣṭatvāc chūnyatārthasya teṣāṃ trāso
° notpadyate tasmin /° kṣaṇabhaṅga iva tadvyāmūḍhasya nārakāgnāv iva mithyādarśanopastabdhasaṃtānasya /
* * dṛṣṭe 'paiti sa[2] sarvaśaḥ /

§33. dṛṣṭe hi śūnyatākhye dharme sa saṃtrāsas[3] tatpaṇḍitānāṃ sarvathāpaiti bhayanimittātmātmīyābhiniveśavigamāt[4] / rajjvām upayātasarpaviparyāsasya[5] rajjudarśane sati sarpabhayāpagamavat[6] / yas tu kiṃcij jānāti tasya niyamenāvaśyaṃbhāvitayā trāso
° vidhīyate /° na hi suśikṣito mattagajāvāhako hastiny utkālyamānas tato bibheti nāpi tadvāhanotsuko 'tyantamūrkho grāmīṇaḥ / sa hi tatpātādidoṣādarśanād vāhanam eva bahu

---

[13] PCN 'dod pa'i: D 'dod pa.

[1] HPS sarvathā tadanupraveśābhāve saty: B sarvathānupraveśābhāvena.

[2] B sa: HPS omits.

[3] Ego sa saṃtrāsas: HPS sa santrāsas; B sa trāsas.

[4] HPS bhayanimittā°: B bhavanimittā°.

[5] HPS upayātasarpaviparyāsasya: B jātasarpasviparyāsasya.

[6] HPS sarpabhayāpagamavat: B sarpabhayavigamavat.

yaṅ ma yin no // de ni de las lhuṅ ba la sogs pa'i skyon ma mthoṅ bas 'źon pa [D.188b] ñid rtog[1] par sems pa na de la mi 'jigs so // cuṅ zad cig śes pa ni bdag ñid de la źon par bya bar rlom pa na ches śin tu 'jigs so // gźan yaṅ bya ba thams cad la 'jug pa na cuṅ zad cig śes pa ṅes par skrag par 'gyur gyi / de kho na ñid rig pa[2] ma yin te ma bsñeṅs pa'i [C.185b] phyir ro // gtan mi śes pa yaṅ ma yin te / gti mug gis btsas pa'i phyir ro // cuṅ zad cig śes pa ni skrag ste / ci 'di nus sam mi nus źig gu sñam du rnam par[3] dpyod pa'i phyir ro //

§34. yaṅ ci'i phyir cuṅ zad śes pa 'di dag gis[4] śes par bya ba yoṅs su rdzogs par ma gyur gyi bar du go 'phaṅ goṅ ma[5] [P.212b] mi tshol źe na / bśad par bya ste / skrag pa'i phyir ro // yaṅ skrag pa'i rgyu ci źig ce na / bśad pa / ma goms pa'o[6] // yaṅ de'i rgyu ci źig ce na / phyin ci log tu goms pa'o // de ñid bstan pa'i phyir bśad pa /

byis rnams ṅes pa kho nar ni //
'jug byed chos la goms pa ste //
de dag goms pa med pa yis[7] //
ldog byed chos la 'jigs par 'gyur // **(k.284)**

§35. 'jug par byed pa'i chos ni 'khor ba'i 'jug pa daṅ rjes su mthun pa ste / sems can so so'i skye bor gtogs pa'i sa la gnas pa rnams ni 'jug par byed pa'i chos la goms so // ldog par byed pa'i chos ni de la goms pa'i gegs dṅos po rnams kyi raṅ bźin stoṅ pa ñid de /[8] 'khor ba ldog pa'i rjes su mthun pa'i phyir ro // so so'i skye bo rnams ni sems kyi rgyud bdag la chags pa daṅ rjes su 'brel pa'i phyir de ldog par byed pa'i

---

[1] PN rtog: DC rtogs.

[2] DC rig pa: PN rigs pa.

[3] PDC rnam par: N rno bar.

[4] DC cuṅ zad śes pa 'di dag gis: PN cuṅ zad cig śes pa 'di dag de dag gis.

[5] DC goṅ ma: PN go ma.

[6] DCN bśad pa ma goms pa'o: P bśad pa la goms pa'o.

[7] C_k yi.

[8] Ego /: PDCN omit.

manyamāno na tato bibheti / kiṃcijjñas tv atitarāṃ bibheti ātmanas tadāsanāparijayaṃ [HPS.496] manyamānaḥ / api khalu sarvakāryeṣv evaṃ pravṛttau kiṃcijjñasya niyataṃ trāso bhavati / na viditatattvasya vaiśāradyāt / nāpy atyantānabhijñasya mohasaṃdhāritatvāt / kiṃcijjñas tu trasyati kim etac chakyaṃ na śakyam iti vimarśotpādāt /

* §34. * kimarthaṃ punar amī kiṃcijjñā uttaraṃ padaṃ na paryeṣante yāvataiṣāṃ jñātavyaparisamāptir bhavatīti / ucyate / trāsāt / kiṃ punas trāsasya kāraṇam / āha / anabhyāsaḥ / tasya punaḥ kiṃ kāraṇam / viparītābhyāsaḥ / tad eva pratipādayann āha /

ekāntenaiva bālānāṃ dharme 'bhyāsaḥ pravartake /
dharmān nivartakāt teṣāṃ anabhyāsatayā bhayam // **(k.284)**

§35. saṃsārapravṛttyanukūlo hi dharmaḥ pravartakaḥ / pṛthagjanaparyāpannāyāṃ ca bhūmau sthitānāṃ pṛthagjanānāṃ[1] pravartaka eva dharme 'bhyāsaḥ / svabhāvaśūnyatā[2] hi nivartako dharmaḥ saṃsāranivṛttyanukūlatvāt / [tadabhyāsa]sya[3] paripanthy ātmasnehaḥ / tadanugatacittasaṃtānatvāt pṛthagjanās tadvyāvartakād dharmāt

[1] HPS pṛthagjanānāṃ: B sattvānāṃ.

[2] HPS svabhāvaśūnyatā: B bhāvānāṃ svabhāvaśūnyatā.

[3] Lacuna of four syllables in HPS. See B who reconstructs from Tib de la goms pa'i. By way of a caution, however, it should be noted that Skt and Tib differ substantially in this particular context.

chos la ches śin tu[1] 'jigs la / dṅos po thams cad raṅ bźin gyis stoṅ pa ñid la g.yaṅ sa'i sul ltar sems pa na ji lta ba bźin rtogs pa mi **[N.209a]** bzod do //

§36. de'i phyir de ltar na gaṅ zag ma rig pa'i mun pa stug pos[2] dṅos po'i de ñid g.yogs śiṅ thog ma daṅ tha ma daṅ mi ldan pa'i 'khor ba'i 'brog dgon par lam bzaṅ po chud zos pa 'ga' źig gal te raṅ bźin stoṅ pa ñid kyi gtam la gus par 'gyur na de daṅ mthun pa'i rkyen ñe bar bsgrub pa'i sgo nas 'ji ltar stoṅ pa ñid la daṅ ba 'phel bar **[D.189a]** 'gyur ba de ltar bya źiṅ sñiṅ rje che[3] ba daṅ / bcom ldan 'das de bźin gśegs pa la byas pa gzo źiṅ bdag ñid kyi dam pa'i chos kyi bar chad kyi rgyu mtshan g.yaṅ sa chen po'i rgyu yoṅs su spaṅ bar 'dod pas yaṅ ba la brten pa daṅ / sbyin par dka' ba yaṅ **[P.213a]** sbyin pa daṅ / bsdu ba'i dṅos po **[C.186a]** bźis kyaṅ bsdu bar bya ste / dam pa'i chos 'di 'bad pa thams cad kyis skye bo dam pa'i chos kyi snod du gyur pa la ñe bar bstan par bya'o //

§37. gaṅ źig ji skad bstan pa la mi gus pa 'ba' źig tu ma zad kyi / gźan yaṅ/

gaṅ źig gti mug 'ga' źig[4] gis //
bsgribs śiṅ de ñid gegs byed pa //
de la dge legs 'gro ba yaṅ[5] //
med na thar pa smos ci dgos[6] // **(k.285)**

§38. gti mug pa 'ga' źig gis śes[7] bya ba ni phrag dog daṅ ser sna daṅ le lo daṅ 'jigs pa daṅ ñan pa po la sdaṅ ba la sogs pas so // gaṅ źig de[8] kho na ñid ñe bar bstan pa'i snod du gyur pa'i skye bo la de kho na ñid lta ba daṅ ñan pa la sogs pa'i

---

[1] Ego ches śin tu: PN chos śin tu; DC omit ches.

[2] DC stug pos: PN 'thug pos. stug po = 'thug po.

[3] PN che: DC omit.

[4] PDCNP$_k$N$_k$BVL 'ga' źig: D$_k$CkS 'ba' źig.

[5] PN 'gro ba'aṅ.

[6] PDCNP$_k$N$_k$BVL smos ci dgos: D$_k$C$_k$S ga la yod.

[7] PN śes: DC źes.

[8] DCN gaṅ źig de: P gaṅ źi bde.

sutarāṃ bibhyati / svabhāvaśūnyatāṃ prapātam iva manyamānā na tāṃ yathāvat pratipattum utsahante /

§36. tad evam avidyāsāndrāndhakārapracchāditapadārthatattve[1] anupalabhyamānāparakoṭike saṃsāramahāṭavīkāntāre pranaṣṭasanmārgasya kasyacin nāma pudgalasya bhavati svabhāvaśūnyatākathāyāṃ ced bhaktiḥ sa tadanukūlapratyayopa[siddhidvāreṇa yathopa-][2] cīyamānaprasādaḥ śūnyatāyāṃ bhavati tathā kāryaṃ karuṇāvatā kṛtajñena ca bhagavati tathāgate[3] saddharmāntarāyanimittaṃ karmātmano mahāprapātahetuṃ parijihīrṣuṇā[4] saṃkaṭam apy avagāhya durdeyam api dattvā saṃgrahavastucatuṣṭayeṇa saṃgṛhya saddharmo 'yaṃ saddharmabhājanebhya upadeṣṭavyaḥ /

§37. yas tu na kevalaṃ yathopadiṣṭaṃ na bahu manyate api tu /

vighnaṃ tattvasya yaḥ kuryād vṛto mohena kenacit /
kalyāṇādhigatis tasya nāsti mokṣe tu kā kathā // **(k.285)**

§38. mohena kenacid itīrṣyāmātsaryakausīdyabhayaśrotṛvidveṣādinā tattvopadeśabhājane jane yas tattvadeśanāśravaṇādivighātakaṃ[5] karoti tasya sugater

---

[1] HPS °tatve-.

[2] Lacuna of seven syllables in HPS. Reconstructed by B on the basis of Tib bsgrub pa'i sgo nas ji ltar ... 'phel bar.

[3] HPS has a daṇḍa here, but such a punctuation is unsupported by the Tib and is also rejected by B.

[4] B parijihīrṣuṇā: HPS parijihīrṣadbhyaḥ. Cf. Tib yoṅs su spaṅ bar 'dod pas.

[5] HPS °vighātakaṃ: B °vighātaṃ.

gegs byed pa de la ni ṅes par ṅan 'gror 'gro bas bde 'gro ste lha daṅ mi'i bdag ñid can yaṅ srid pa med na / de la thar pa'i gtam gyi go skabs su 'gyur ba lta smos kyaṅ ci dgos / 'dis raṅ daṅ gźan gyi rgyud dag la gnod pa ci ma byas / des na śes rab kyi sgron ma phyogs kyi sgo ma lus pa khyab ciṅ snaṅ ba ches[1] gsal ba dus gsum du mthu 'jug pa ñams pa med pa ñin re źiṅ ma rig pa'i mun pa gźom pa'i **[N.209b]** phyir snaṅ ba'i tshogs 'phel bźin par gyur pa / 'gro ba'i bsam pa ma lus par snaṅ bar nus pa rgyud la skye bźin pa la gnod pa rjes su bsgrubs pa yin no //

§39. 'di ñid kyaṅ raṅ daṅ gźan gñis la gnod pa byed pa ñid du gzigs nas / bcom ldan 'das kyis /

tshul khrims las ni ñams bla yi //
lta las cis kyaṅ ma yin no[2] // **(k.286ab)**

źes gsuṅs te / tshul khrims ñams pa ni bla'i lta ba ñams pa ni ma yin no źes ***mdo*** las gsuṅs so // de'i phyir **[P.213b]** de bźin gśegs pa'i gsuṅ 'di 'thad pa daṅ bcas pa ñid du brjod pa'i phyir slob dpon gyis /

tshul khrims **[D.189b]** *kyis ni mtho ris[3] 'gro //*
lta bas go 'phaṅ mchog thob[4] 'gyur // **(k.286cd)**

źes bya ba smos so //

§40. tshul khrims ñams pa na / gal te yaṅ dag pa'i lta ba daṅ ldan pa 'phags pa rnams la bcom par mi 'gyur na / **[C.186b]** chuṅ ṅu daṅ 'briṅ daṅ chen po'i rim pas skyes pa rnams la yi dags daṅ dud 'gro daṅ dmyal bar skye ba'i 'bras bu rnam pa smin pa la 'di tsam źig tu yoṅs su gcad pas 'jug la / tshul khrims rnam par dag pa ni

---

[1] PDC ches: N chos.

[2] PDCNB no: $P_kD_kC_k$VLS te; N_k unclear.

[3] P_kDkC_kN_kVLBS mtho ris: PDCN bde 'gror. However, bde 'gro = sugati. mtho ris = svarga (cf. Skt of k.286) and also figures in CSV.

[4] PDCNB thob: $P_kD_kC_kN_k$LS tu; V du.

api tāvad devamanuṣyātmikāyā[1] nāsti saṃbhavo niyatam apāyagamanāt[2] kim utāsya
° mokṣakathāvakāśaḥ syāt /° kiṃ hy anena svaparasaṃtānayor nāpakṛtam / tena hi
niḥśeṣāśāmukhavyāpinaḥ sphuṭatarālokasyādhvatrayāpratihataprabhāvavṛtteḥ[3] pratidinam avidyāndhakāropaghātāyopacīyamānālokanicayasyāśeṣajagadāśayāvabhāsanasamarthasya prajñāpradīpasya saṃtāne[4] samupajāyamānasya vighāto 'nuṣṭhitaḥ /

* §39. * evam eva[5] parātmanor atyantāpakāritāṃ saṃpaśyatā[6] bhagavatā tathāgatenoktam /

śīlād api varaṃ sraṃso na tu dṛṣṭeḥ kathaṃ cana **(k.286ab)**

iti //

° ***sūtra*** uktam varaṃ śīlavipanno na tu dṛṣṭivipanna iti / ° tad asya tathāgatasya vacasaḥ sopapattikatām udbhāvayann ācārya āha /

śīlena gamyate svargo dṛṣṭyā yāti paraṃ padam **(k.286cd)**

iti //

§40. śīlavipattir hi sūpacīyamānamṛdumadhyādhimātrakramāṇāṃ pretatiryaṅnarakopapattiphalā vipākeyattāparicchedena **[HPS.497]** pravarttate yady ākrāntasamyagdarśaneṣv āryeṣu na vyāpadyate / śīlaviśuddhis tv anākrāntasamyagdarśanānāṃ

---

[1] B tāvad devamanuṣyātmikāyā: HPS tavad eva manuṣyātmikāyā. Cf. Tib *lha* daṅ mi'i bdag ñid can.

[2] Ego apāyagamanāt: HPS apāgamanāt; B durgatigamanāt. Cf. Tib ṅan 'gror 'gro bas; ṅan 'gro is an equivalent for apāya.

[3] Ego prabhāvavṛtteḥ: HPS °prabhāvṛtteḥ. Cf. Tib mthu 'jug pa. mthu = prabhāva; see Lokesh Chandra s.v. mthu.

[4] Ego saṃtāne: HPS santānena. Cf. Tib rgyud *la* skye bźin pa la.

[5] HPS eva: B omits.

[6] HPS saṃpaśyatā: B paśyatā.

yaṅ dag pa'i lta ba ma skyes pa[1] so so'i skye bo rnams la mchog tu gyur par mtho ris kyi 'bras bu can du 'gyur ro // lta ba ñams pa ni gal te ches chuṅ ba źig yin na[2] / de yaṅ rnam par smin pa che ba ñid du tshul khrims ñams pa graṅs med pa brgya stoṅ phrag daṅ mñam par bya bar mi nus na / pham par bya ba lta ci smos / ci ste gaṅ zag de la 'phags pa'i lam skyes pas rkyen las ci źig ltar yaṅ dag pa'i lta ba phun sum tshogs pa skyes na[3] ni de'i tshe 'di gdon mi za bar[4] 'khor ba thog ma daṅ tha ma med par źugs pa'i ma rig pa'i mun pa bsal nas sems can gyi khams ma lus pa mdun du bdar te mya ṅan las 'das par[5] 'gyur ro // de ltar na mkhas pas de kho na ñid la lta ba 'di ni śin tu **[N.210a]** don che ba ñid du rig par byas te / de mi ñams pa'i phyir 'bad par bya'o //

§41. de ñams pa'i 'jigs pa mthoṅ ba 'dis ni thams cad la snod kyi khyad par ṅes par ma bzuṅ bar snod ma yin pa rnams la bdag med par lta ba 'di bstan par bya ba yaṅ ma yin te / de la ñe bar bstan pa ni don ma yin pa'i rgyu kho nar 'gyur ro //**[##]**

blun la ñe bar **[P.214a]** bstan pa ni //
'khrug[6] par 'gyur gyi źi phyir min //
lag 'gro 'o ma 'thuṅ ba ni //
dug 'phel 'gyur ba 'ba' źig go //

źes kyaṅ bśad do //

§42. bcom ldan 'das kyis kyaṅ

'od sruṅs gaṅ zag tu lta ba ri rab tsam[7] ni bla'i / mṅon pa'i ṅa rgyal can stoṅ pa ñid du lta ba ni ma yin no // de ci'i phyir źe na / 'od sruṅs lta bar gyur pa thams cad la ṅes par 'byuṅ ba ni stoṅ pa ñid yin na gaṅ stoṅ pa ñid du lta ba de ni gsor mi ruṅ ṅo

źes gsuṅs so //

---

[1] PN skyes pa: DC skyes pas.

[2] PDC na: N no.

[3] Ego skyes na: PDCN skyes nas. Cf. Skt ājāyet.

[4] PN 'di gdon mi za bar: DC de'i gdon mi za bar.

[5] DC 'das par: PN 'da' bar.

[6] PN 'khrug: DC 'khrugs (past form of 'khrug pa).

[7] PN ri rab tsam: DC rab rib tsam.

pṛthagjanānāṃ prakarṣeṇa svargaphalā / darśanavipattis tu mṛdutarā cet sāpy asaṃkhyeyaśatasahasrair api śīlavipattīnām aśakyā vipākamahattayā samīkartum api prāg eva jetum / atha ced asya pudgalasya katham api pratyayāt samyagdarśanasaṃpattir ājāyed āryamārgotpādāt tadāyam avaśyam avadhūyānādisaṃsārapravṛttam avidyāndha-
* kāram aśeṣasattvadhātupuraskṛto nirvāṇam upayāyād ity * evam atimahārthatām[1] asya tattvadarśanasyāvetyaitadavighātāya viduṣā yatitavyam /

§41. na cānena tadvighātabhayadarśinā satā sarvatraiva anavadhārya pātraviśeṣam etan nairātmyadarśanaṃ upadeṣṭavyam apātreṣu / apātre hi tadupadeśo anarthāyaiva syāt /

<upadeśo hi mūrkhāṇāṃ prakopāya na śāntaye /
payaḥpānaṃ bhujaṃgānāṃ kevalaṃ viṣavardhanam //>[2]

§42.

<varaṃ khalu punaḥ kāśyapa sumerumātrā pudgaladṛṣṭir āśritā na tv evādhimānikasya śūnyatādṛṣṭimālinā / tat kasmād dhetoḥ /... sarvadṛṣṭigatānāṃ śūnyatā niḥsaraṇaṃ yasya khalu punaḥ kāśyapa śūnyatādṛṣṭis tam aham acikitsyam iti vadāmi>[3]

---

[1] B atimahārthatām: HPS atimahārghatāṃ. Cf. Tib śin tu don che ba ñid du.

[2] *Pañcatantra* I, 389.

[3] *Kāśyapaparivarta* §§64 & 65 (ed. A. von Staël-Holstein).

§43. de ñid kyi phyir // **[D.190a]**
dam pa min[1] *la bdag 'dzin mchog //*
bdag med ston pa ma yin te // **(k.287ab)**

§44. bdag med pa'i chos la lhag par mos pa daṅ bral źiṅ bdag tu 'dzin par mṅon par źen pa dam pa'i chos ma yin pa la brten pas lta ba **[C.187a]** thibs po'i rjes su 'braṅ ba'i mi la ni dam pa ma yin pa źes bya ste / dam pa ma yin pa de la ni des ñes par spyod pa ldog pa daṅ mthun pa'i phyir bdag bstan pa mchog yin no // 'di ltar de ni bdag cag la chags pa daṅ rjes su 'brel bas bdag ñid la phan pa daṅ bde ba mṅon par 'dod ciṅ ñes pa spyod pa las log pa la 'tsheṅs par sems la sdig pa las log pa des ni bde 'gror 'gro ba rñed par sla bar yaṅ 'gyur ro // bdag med pa'i chos ston pas ni spoṅ ba daṅ phyin ci log tu rtogs pa dag gis 'di'i lus daṅ ṅag daṅ sems kyi rgyud 'joms par 'gyur ro // de'i phyir de **[N.210b]** ltar na /
gcig ni ṅan 'gro ñid 'gro la[2] *//*
tha mal ma yin źi ñid du'o // **(k.287cd)**

§45. bdag med par lta ba la log par źugs pa'i mi mkhas pa ni ṅan 'gro kho nar 'gro'i źi bar ni ma yin no // gaṅ źig tha mal pa ma yin pa de ni źi ba kho nar 'gro'i ṅan 'gror ni ma yin no // tha mal gyi sgra ni mchog ma yin pa'i tha tshig go // **[P.124b]** mchog ma yin pa la yaṅ gaṅ źig ce na / gaṅ źig stoṅ pa ñid kyi don phyin ci log tu rtogs pa'am spoṅ ba'o // de bkag pas ni tha mal ma yin pa ste / tha mal ma yin pa źes bya ba ni mchog ces bya ba'i don to // stoṅ pa ñid ñe bar bstan pa gaṅ źig kho na las tha mal pa ṅan 'gro'i mthar thug pa'i stoṅ pa ñid bstan pa de ñid las tha mal pa ma yin pa mya ṅan las 'das pa'i mthar thug par 'gyur ro // stoṅ pa ñid mthoṅ ba'i rkyen

---

[1] $DCP_kD_kC_kN_k$VBLS min: PN yin.

[2] $PDCND_kC_k$LS la: P_kN_kBV ba.

§43. ata eva ca /

ahaṃkāro 'sataḥ śreyān na tu nairātmyadarśanam / **(k.287ab)**

§44. nairātmyadharmādhimuktivirahito hy ātmagrāhābhiniviṣṭo 'saddharmasamāśrayād dṛṣṭigahanānucāry[1] asann ity ucyate / tasyāsato varam ātmadeśanā duścaritanivṛttyanukūlatvāt tasyāḥ / tathā hy asāv ātmasnehānugamād[2] dhitam ātmano 'bhivañchan[3] duścaritanivṛttiṃ bahu manyate / nivṛttapāpasya cāsya sugatigamanaṃ bhavati sulabham / nairātmyopadeśas tasya pratikṣepaviparyāsabodhābhyāṃ kāyacittasaṃtānaṃ niyatam upahanti / tad evaṃ

apāyam eva yāty ekaḥ śivam eva tu netaraḥ // **(k.287cd)**

§45. nairātmyadarśanavipratipanno hy avidvān apāyam eva yāti na śivam / yas tu netaraḥ sa śivam eva yāti nāpāyam / itaraśabdo 'yam anutkṛṣṭavācī / kaś cānutkṛṣṭaḥ / yo[4] viparītaṃ śūnyatārtham[5] adhigacchati pratikṣipati vā / tatpratiṣedhena netaraḥ / netara ity utkṛṣṭa ity arthaḥ / yata eva śūnyatopadeśād itaro apāyaniṣṭhas[6] tata eva śūnyatopadeśān netaro nirvāṇaniṣṭho jāyate / śūnyatādarśanapratyayaḥ[7]

---

[1] B adds naro.

[2] HPS °anugamād: B °anugamanād.

[3] B ātmano 'bhivañchan: HPS ātmanābhivāñchan. Cf. Tib bdag ñid la.

[4] B yo: HPS omits. Cf. Tib gaṅ źig.

[5] HPS viparītaṃ śūnyatārtham: B śūnyatārthaṃ viparītam.

[6] B apāyaniṣṭhas: HPS apāyaniviṣṭas. niṣṭha = Tib mthar thug pa.

[7] HPS °pratyayaḥ: B °pratyayena.

gyis thams cad la chags pa spaṅs pa las las daṅ ñon moṅs pa'i tshogs bcom pa ni ṅes par mya ṅan las 'das pa'i go 'phaṅ du ñe bar 'gro'o // **[##]** yaṅ na dam pa ma yin pa[1] gaṅ źig bdag med pa'i chos ñan pa[2] de ni spaṅs pa[3] daṅ phyin ci log tu rtogs pas ṅan 'gro kho nar 'gro la / gaṅ źig mi ñan pa de ni bsod nams kyi las kyi rkyen gyis bde 'gro ñid du'o // **[D.190b]**

§46. **[#]** yaṅ gaṅ źig dam pa ma yin pa dag la bstan par bya ba ma yin źiṅ / dam pa dag la bstan par bya ba bdag med pa źes bya ba **[C.187b]** 'di yaṅ gaṅ źig ce na / de bstan pa'i phyir bśad pa /

źi sgo gñis pa med pa daṅ //
lta ba ṅan rnams 'jigs[4] byed ciṅ //
saṅs rgyas kun gyi yul gyur la[5] //
bdag med ces ni bya bar brjod // **(k.288)**

§47. gaṅ źig źi ba'i sgo gñis pa med pa de[6] ni bdag med pa'o // gaṅ źig lta ba ṅan pa rnams 'jigs[7] par byed pa de ni bdag med pa'o // gaṅ źig saṅs rgyas thams cad kyi yul du gyur pa de ni bdag med pa źes bya'o // de la bdag ces bya ba ni gaṅ źig dṅos po rnams kyi gźan **[N.211a]** la rag ma las pa'i ṅo bo raṅ bźin te / **[##]** de med pa ni bdag med pa'o // **[#]**de ni chos daṅ gaṅ zag gi dbye bas gñis su rtogs te chos kyi bdag med pa daṅ / gaṅ zag gi bdag med pa **[P.215a]** źes bya ba'o[8] // de la gaṅ zag ces

---

[1] DC yin pa: PN yin.

[2] PDN ñan pa: C ñin pa.

[3] PDC spaṅs pa: N spiṅs pa.

[4] P_kBVL: 'jigs: PDCN$D_k$$C_k$$N_k$S 'jig. 'jigs = bhaya, "fear". In the text of CS and especially that of CSV there is a systematic confusion between 'jig ("perish") and 'jigs ("fear").

[5] VB ba.

[6] PN de (= tan): DC omit.

[7] Ego 'jigs: PDCN 'jig. Cf. Skt bhayaṃkaraṃ.

[8] DC źes bya ba'o: PN źes bya'o.

sarvatra saṅgaparityāgān nihatakleśakarmagaṇo niyataṃ nirvṛttim[1] upayāti /

§46. kiṃ punar idaṃ nairātmyaṃ nāma yad asatsu nopadeṣṭavyaṃ satsu copadeṣṭavyam iti tat pratipādayann āha /

advitīyaṃ śivadvāraṃ kudṛṣṭīnāṃ bhayaṃkaram /
viṣayaḥ sarvabuddhānām iti nairātmyam ucyate // **(k.288)**

§47. yad advitīyaṃ śivadvāraṃ tan nairātmyam / yat kudṛṣṭīnāṃ bhayaṃkaraṃ tan nairātmyam / yo viṣayaḥ sarvabuddhānāṃ tan nairātmyam ucyate / tatrātmā[2] nāma bhāvānāṃ[3] yo[4] 'parāyattasvarūpasvabhāvaḥ[5] / tac ca dharmapudgalabhedād dvaitaṃ pratipadyate / dharmanairātmyaṃ pudgalanairātmyaṃ ceti / tatra pudgalo nāma

---

[1] HPS nivṛttim: B nivṛtipadam.

[2] B tatrātmā: HPS tac cātmā. Cf. Tib de la.

[3] HPS bhāvānāṃ: B omits.

[4] B yo: HPS yad.

[5] HPS 'parāyattasvarūpasvabhāvaḥ: B °svarūpaḥ svabhāvaḥ. B adds tadabhāvo nairātmyam ("the lack of that is selflessness") on the basis of Tib de med pa ni bdag med pa'o.

bya ba ni gaṅ phuṅ po lṅa la brten nas btags pa[1] ste / de ni phuṅ po dag la rnam pa lṅas btsal ba ni mi srid do // chos ni phuṅ po daṅ khams daṅ skye mched ces bya ba'i dṅos po rnams so // de'i phyir chos de rnams daṅ gaṅ zag la bdag ñid ji lta ba'i rgyu daṅ rkyen la[2] rag las te skye ba'i phyir daṅ brten[3] nas btags[4] pa'i phyir bdag gi raṅ gi ṅo bo[5] raṅ la rag las śiṅ gźan la rag ma las pa yod pa ma yin pas gaṅ zag daṅ chos rnams raṅ bźin med par rnam par gźag go[6] //

§48. don gaṅ źig la raṅ gi ṅo bos grub pa yod pa[7] ma yin pa de bdag ñid gźan gaṅ źig gis 'grub par 'gyur / de'i phyir dṅos po rnam pa thams cad du raṅ gi mtshan ñid kyis ma grub pa brten[8] nas sam ñe bar blaṅs nas slu[9] ba'i bdag ñid du 'byuṅ ba rnams ni blo blun pa'i chags pa'i gźir 'gyur la / raṅ bźin ji lta ba bźin du yaṅ dag par mthoṅ ba rnams kyis bsgoms pa na chos daṅ gaṅ zag gñis la chags pa yoṅs su zad pa 'dren par 'gyur ro // chags pa yoṅs zad pa ni mya ṅan las 'das pa thob pa'i rgyu yin la / **[##]** raṅ bźin med par lta ba las ma gtogs pa'i chos 'ga' źig de ltar **[D.191a]** chags pa yoṅs su zad pa'i rgyu yod pa yaṅ ma yin no //

§49. de ñid kyi phyir raṅ bźin med pa'i mtshan ñid can gyi **[#]** bdag med pa 'di ni źi ba'i sgo gñis pa med par 'gyur **[C.188a]** te / mya ṅan las 'das pa'i groṅ khyer

---

[1] PN btags pa: DC brtags pa. On the difference between btags pa and brtags pa --a frequent confusion in Tibetan-- see May (1981), n.22.

[2] DC la: PN las.

[3] PN brten: DC brtan.

[4] Ego btags: PDCN brtags.

[5] PDC ṅo bo: N ṅo bor.

[6] DC gźag: PN bźag go. A frequent confusion. rnam par bźag pa is the past form of rnam par 'jog par (i.e. = vyavasthita), whereas rnam par gźag pa is the future translating the passive vyavasthāpyate.

[7] DC yod pa: PN omit.

[8] PN brten: DC bstan nas. Cf. Skt pratītya.

[9] DC slu ba: PN bslu ba.

yaḥ skandhapañcakasyopādānākhyasyopādātā[1] skandhān upādāya prajñapyate / sa ca skandheṣu pañcadhā mṛgyamāṇo na saṃbhavati / dharmās tu skandhāyatanadhātu-saṃśabditāḥ[2] padārthāḥ / tad eṣāṃ dharmāṇāṃ pudgalasya ca yathāsvaṃ hetupratya-yādhīnajanmatvād upādāya prajñapyamānatvāc ca svāyattam aparāyattaṃ nijam akṛtaka-rūpaṃ nāstīti pudgalasya dharmāṇāṃ ca naiḥsvābhāvyaṃ vyavasthāpyate /

§48. yasya cārthasya svarūpasiddhir nāsti tasya kenānyenātmanāstu siddhir iti / sarvathāsiddhasvalakṣaṇā[3] eva padārthā mūrkhajanasya visaṃvādakenātmanā pratītya vopādāya[4] vā vartamānā mūḍhadhiyāṃ saṅgāspadaṃ saṃbhavanti[5] / yathāsvabhāvaṃ tu samyagdarśanaiḥ pratibhāvyamānā dharmapudgalayoḥ [saṅgaparikṣayavāhakā bhavanti
° /][6] saṅgaparikṣayaś ca nirvāṇāvāptikāraṇam / °

§49.... nairātmyam advitīyaṃ śivadvāraṃ bhavati / nirvāṇapurapraveśāya ekam

---

[1] HPS skandhapañcakasyopādānākhyasyopādātā: B omits.

[2] B skandhāyatanadhātusaṃśabditāḥ: HPS skandhā ghanadhātu° Cf. Tib skye mched.

[3] B adds tasmāt sarvathā°.

[4] B vopādāya: HPS copādāya.

[5] HPS saṃbhavanti: B bhavanti.

[6] Missing in HPS, rendering the passage hardly comprehensible. Reconstructed by B on the basis of Tib chags pa yoṅs su zad pa 'dren par 'gyur ro.

du 'jug par bya ba la 'di gcig pu kho na zla med pa'i sgo yin no // gal te yaṅ stoṅ pa ñid daṅ mtshan ma med pa daṅ smon pa med pa źes bya ba rnam par thar pa'i **[N.211b]** sgo gsum yod mod kyi / de lta na yaṅ bdag med par[1] lta ba kho na gtso bo yin te / chos **[P.215b]** ma lus pa bdag med par rig ciṅ dṅos po thams cad la chags pa ma lus pa zad pa la 'gar yaṅ 'ga' źig don du gñer ba'am mtshan mar dmigs pa ga la yod / de'i phyir bdag med pa 'di ni źi ba'i sgo gñis pa med pa kho na źig go //**[##]**

§50. de ñid kyi phyir ***Byaṅ chub kyi tshogs*** las /
raṅ bźin med pas stoṅ la stoṅ pa ni //
yin daṅ mtshan mas ci źig byed par 'gyur //
mtshan ma thams cad log par 'gyur ba'i phyir //
mkhas pas ci ste smon lam 'debs par 'gyur //
źes bśad do[2] //

§51.[#] 'di ni lta ba ṅan pa rnams 'jigs[3] par byed pa ste / lta ba ṅan pa ni ṅan par brtsis[4] pa'i lta ba dag go // bdag med pa yin na ni dṅos po rnams rnam pa thams cad du ma dmigs pas dṅos po'i raṅ gi ṅo bo yoṅs su brtags pa'i rten can lta ba ṅan pa rnams gtan nas 'jig par[5] mthoṅ ba'i phyir bdag med pa 'di ni 'jigs[6] par byed pa'o // bdag med pa ni saṅs rgyas kun gyi yul te saṅs rgyaś kun gyi źes bya ba ni ñan thos daṅ raṅ saṅs rgyas daṅ bla na med pa yaṅ dag par rdzogs pa'i saṅs rgyas rnams kyi'o // ye śes kyi khyad par gyi yul ñid du gnas pa'i phyir na saṅs rgyas kun gyi yul źes bya'o //

---

[1] DC par: PN pa.

[2] From the **Bodhisaṃbhāra* ascribed to Nāgārjuna. See en. 195 for Chinese.

[3] Ego 'jigs: PDCN 'jig.

[4] P brtsis: DC brtses; N brtsas. Cf. *Zidian* p. 632 s.v. brtsi: yin par bsam pa'i don.

[5] PDCN 'jig par is correct (= Skt vināśa).

[6] Ego 'jigs: PDCN 'jig. Cf. Skt bhayaṃkara = 'jigs par byed pa.

evāsahāyam etat dvāram / yady api śūnyatānimittāpraṇihitākhyāni trīṇi vimokṣamukhāni
* / [HPS.498] tathāpi nairātmyadarśanam eva pradhānam / * viditanairātmyasya hi[1]
bhāveṣu parikṣīṇasaṅgasya na kvacit kācit prārthanā kuto vā nimittopalambha ity advitīyam eva śivadvāram etan nairātmyam /

o* §51. tac caitat kudṛṣṭīnāṃ bhayaṃkaram /° kutsitā dṛṣṭayaḥ kudṛṣṭayaḥ[2] /*
nairātmye hi vastunaḥ sarvathānupalambhāt kudṛṣṭīnāṃ vastusvarūpaparikalpasamāśrayaṇād atyantavināśadarśanād bhayaṃkaram etan nairātmyam / viṣayaḥ sarvabuddhānāṃ nairātmyam / sarvabuddhānām iti śrāvakapratyekabuddhānuttarasamyaksaṃbuddhānām / jñānaviśeṣaviṣayatvenāvasthānād viṣayaḥ sarvabuddhānām ity ucyate /

---

[1] B adds sarveṣu.

[2] Ego kutsitā dṛṣṭayaḥ kudṛṣṭayaḥ: HPS kṛtsitā dṛṣṭayaḥ. Cf. Tib: lta ba ṅan pa ni ṅan par brtses pa'i lta ba dag go. The passage is omitted by B.

yaṅ na yaṅ dag par rdzogs pa'i saṅs rgyas kyi[1] chos kyi sku las tha mi dad par bźugs pa thams cad kyi yin par bstan pa'i phyir saṅs rgyas kun gyi źes bśad do // khyad par gyi phreṅ gis ni slob dpon gyis chos thams cad bdag med par gsuṅs so //

§52. bdag med pa 'di ni dam pas skye bo blo źan pa la bstan par bya ba ma yin te / gaṅ **[D.191b]** gi phyir /

chos 'di yi ni miṅ las kyaṅ //
dam pa min pa 'jigs pa skye // **(k.289ab)**

dam pa ma yin pa ni chos 'di gtiṅ **[P.216a]** thug[2] par dka' źiṅ zab pa'i phyir bdag med pa'i **[C.188b]** sgra thos pa las kyaṅ 'jigs pa skye'o // 'di ltar /

gźan[3] la 'jigs pa mi skyed pa'i[4] **[N.212a]** //
stobs[5] ldan źes bya gaṅ źig mthoṅ // **(k.289cd)**

§53. bdag med par lta ba ni stobs daṅ ldan pa yin te / dam pa ma yin pa'i lta ba thams cad druṅ 'byin par nus pa'i phyir ro // dam pa ma yin pa'i lta ba ~~ni~~ stobs chuṅ ba ste druṅs dbyuṅ bar bya ba yin pa'i phyir ro // gaṅ stobs daṅ ldan pa la[6] stobs chuṅ ba 'jigs so źes bya ba 'di ni ṅes pa yaṅ yin no // de'i phyir stobs chuṅ źiṅ lta ba ṅan pas sems kyi rgyud bdag gir byas pa la chos 'di bstan par mi bya ste / 'jigs pa'i rgyu yin pa'i phyir ro //

§54. gal te lta ba ṅan pa ril 'joms pa'i phyir chos 'di bstan par bya ba ma yin nam / 'di ltar phas kyi rgol ba rnams ni gdon mi za bar chos daṅ mthun par tshar gcad par bya ba źig ste / de'i phyir rtsod pa don du gñer źiṅ gźan gyi lugs pham par bya bar 'dod par gyur bas chos 'di snod dag la ñe bar bstan par bya'o źe na / bśad par bya ste 'di ni de lta ma yin te / 'di ltar /

---

[1] DC kyi: PN omit.

[2] DCN thug: P thugs (="heart").

[3] PDCNP_kBVL gźan: $D_k C_k N_k$S źan.

[4] PDN$D_k C_k$S skyed pa'i: C skyed pa'o; $P_k N_k$VBL bskyed pa'i (which is past or future).

[5] B stoabs.

[6] C ldan pas la.

dharmaśarīrāvyatirekavartitāṃ vā sarveṣāṃ samyaksaṃbuddhānām āvedayann āha viṣayaḥ sarvabuddhānām iti / viśeṣaṇamālayā[1] nairātmyam[2] uktam ācāryeṇa /

§52. etac ca nairātmyaṃ satā mandadhiyo[3] nopadeṣṭavyam / yasmāt /

asya dharmasya nāmno 'pi bhayam utpadyate 'sataḥ / **(k.289ab)**

° ° asato hy asya dharmasyātidurgādhagambhīratvān nairātmyaśabdaśravaṇād api bhayam

* utpadyate / tathā hi /*

balavān nāma ko dṛṣṭaḥ parasya na bhayaṃkaraḥ // **(k.289cd)**

§53. balavan nairātmyadarśanaṃ sarvāsaddarśanonmūlanasamarthatvāt / durbalam asaddarśanam unmūlanīyatvāt / niyataṃ caitad yad abalavān[4] sabalād bibhetīti / tasmān na durbalasya kudarśanenātmīkṛtacittasaṃtānasyāyaṃ dharma upadeṣṭavyo bhayahetur iti kṛtvā /

§54. nanu ca upadeṣṭavya evāyaṃ dharmaḥ sakalakudarśanapramāthitvāt / tathā hy avaśyaṃ parapravādinaḥ saha dharmeṇa nigrahītavyāḥ / tataś ca vādārthinā satā paramatavijigīṣuṇāyaṃ dharmo 'pātreṣv apy upadeṣṭavya iti / ucyate naitad evam / yasmāt /

---

[1] B °mālayā: HPS °mālayanairātmyam. Cf. Tib phreṅ gis.

[2] HPS nairātmyam: B sarvadharmanairātmyam.

[3] B adds janasya.

[4] HPS abalavān: B durbalaḥ.

chos 'di de bźin gśegs rnams kyis[1] //
rtsod pa'i ched du ma gsuṅs te[2] // **(k.290ab)**

§55. gal te chos 'di rtsod pa'i ched du bstan par 'gyur na ni 'di de ltar 'gyur ba źig daṅ / 'di ni rtsod pa'i don du bstan pa ma yin te / rnam par thar pa'i sgo ñid du bstan pa'i phyir ro // gal te yaṅ de lta yin mod kyi /**[##]**

de lta'aṅ 'dis[3] *ni gźan smra rnams* //
bsreg ste[4] *me yis*[5] *bud śiṅ bźin* // **(k.290cd)**

§56. rtsod pa'i don du ma bstan yaṅ chos 'di ni pha rol po'i smra ba sel bar byed pa kho na'o // me ñe bar len pa ni btso ba la sogs pa'i bya ba'i don du yin la bud **[P.216b]** śiṅ bsreg[6] pa'i don du ma yin mod kyi / de lta na yaṅ sreg par byed pa'i raṅ bźin yin pas 'dod pa'i bya ba rjes su sgrub ciṅ bud śiṅ yaṅ sreg par byed do // me ji lta ba bźin du chos thams cad raṅ bźin gyis bdag med par śes pa yaṅ dad pa **[D.192a]** can gyi rgyud la ñe bar skye ba na de ltar śes par bya ste / ñon **[N.212b]** moṅs pa'i 'chiṅ ba thams cad sreg par byed pa'i bdag ñid can yin pa'i phyir ro //

* **§57.** * yaṅ ji ltar chos 'di dad pa can **[C.189a]** gyi rgyud la ñe bar skye ba na pha rol po'i smra ba dag sreg par 'gyur źe na / bśad pa /

chos 'di gaṅ gis śes gyur pa[7] //
de ni gźan la mi dga[8] *ste* // **(k.291ab)**

---

[1] N_k kyi.

[2] PNB gsuṅs so.

[3] P_kN_kV 'di.

[4] PDCN bsreg ste: P_kN_kBL bsregs te (=past tense); D_kC_kS sreg ste; V gsregs te.

[5] P_kN_kV yi.

[6] DC bsreg: PN bsregs.

[7] V ba.

[8] V dka'.

vādasya kṛtaśo[1] *dharmo nāyam uktas tathāgataiḥ* / **(k.290ab)**

§55. yadi cāyaṃ dharmo vādasya kṛte [upadiṣṭaḥ][2] syāt syād etad evam / na tv ayaṃ vādārtham[3] upadiṣṭo vimokṣamukhenopadeśāt / yady apy evaṃ

---

[1] HPS vādasya kṛtaśo: B amends to vādasya hi kṛte saying that kṛtaśaḥ "does not give any sense"; V reads vivādasya kṛte. BHSD however has an entry for kṛtaśas, as does Mvyut 5461.

[2] HPS + + + +. B reconstructs on the basis of Tib bstan par 'gyur.

[3] B vādārtham: HPS vādārtha. Cf. Tib ched du.

§58. dam pa'i chos kyi de kho na ñid mthoṅ ba'i bdud rtsi myaṅs pa ni de las gźan pa'i lta ba'i ro la mnog med par byed pa'i phyir de las gźan pa'i lta ba thams cad la de mi dga'o // slob dpon dam pa'i chos kyi bdud rtsi'i ro myaṅs pa lta bur gyur pa[1] skye bo blo daṅ ldan pa'i yid tshim par byed pa'i tshig gsuṅ ba /

des na bdag la chos 'di ni //

'jig[2] pa'i sgo daṅ 'dra bar snaṅ // **(k.291cd)**

§59. slar mi skye bas 'jig pa mthoṅ ba'i phyir chos 'di ni bdag med pa'i chos rtogs pa'i rgyud la dam pa ma yin pa'i lta ba thams cad 'jig pa'i rgyu yin no sñam du slob dpon la snaṅ ṅo // 'di ni mi dmigs pa'i bdag ñid can yin pa'i phyir 'ga' źig yaṅ 'jig pa'i rgyu ma yin pas 'jig pa'i sgo daṅ 'dra bar źes bśad do // yaṅ na bstan pa'i chos la dgoṅs nas 'jig pa'i sgo daṅ 'dra bar źes bśad do // mya ṅan las 'das pa ni gtan du ba'i 'jig pa yin la / der rjes su 'jug pa'i sgo ni rnam par thar pa'i sgo stoṅ pa ñid rtogs pa'i bdag ñid can yin la / bstan pa'i chos kyaṅ slob dpon la de daṅ 'dra bar snaṅ ste **[P.217a]** / ji ltar 'phags pa'i chos kyi raṅ bźin thugs su chud par śes nas dad pa daṅ ldan pa lta ba gźan mṅon par mi 'dod pa de bźin du luṅ gi chos rtogs pa yaṅ gźan la mi dga'o sñam du dgoṅs so //

§60. ci ste 'phags pa rnams la yaṅ ci'i phyir 'di skrag pa'i rgyur mi 'gyur źe na / bdag la chags pa log pa'i phyir ro // gaṅ la bdag la chags pa yod pa de ni[3] de daṅ rjes su mthun pa'i dṅos po'i lta ba 'dod kyi de[4] daṅ mi mthun pas[5] bdag med par lta ba ni ma yin no //

de ñid du bdag med sñam du //

de ltar gaṅ la dgoṅs **[D.192b]** *gnas pa //* **(k.292ab)**

---

[1] NB gyur pa: PDC gyur te.

[2] PDCN$P_k N_k$BVL 'jig: $D_k C_k$S 'jigs.

[3] PNB de ni: DC omit.

[4] PDN de: C di.

[5] DCN mi mthun pas: P (unclear) mi mthun +s; B mi mthun pa'i.

'phags pa /**[N.213a]**

de ni yod pas ga[1] *la dga'*[2] *//*
med pas 'jigs[3] *par ga la 'gyur* // **(k.292cd)**

§61. gaṅ źig la phyi daṅ naṅ gi dṅos po'i raṅ gi ṅo bo yoṅs su mi rtog[4] pa'i phyir źes bya ba'i dṅos po 'ga' yaṅ raṅ bźin gyis yod pa ma yin no sñam pa'i[5] dgoṅs pa rnam par gnas **[C.189b]** pa de ni gaṅ med par mthoṅ ba las de bdag med pa las[6] 'jigs par 'gyur pa yod par lta ba yod pas yoṅs su tshim par ga la 'gyur / de ñid kyi phyir de dag gi rjes su chags pa daṅ khoṅ khro ba daṅ bral ba'o źes bya ste / yod par lta ba la rjes su chags pa med pa'i phyir la / bdag med par lta ba la yaṅ khoṅ khro ba med pa'i phyir ro // de'i phyir gñis la mi spyod ciṅ rtsod[7] pa med pa 'di ni mya ṅan las 'das pa'i groṅ khyer du bde blag tu 'gro ste / de'i phyir mya ṅan las 'das pa dam pa'i gnas yin pa'i phyir na bdag med pa de de'i 'jigs pa'i rgyu ma yin no //

§62. dṅos por lta ba la mṅon par źen pa'i mu stegs can mya ṅan las 'das pa la g.yaṅ sar 'du śes pa rnams ni mya ṅan las 'das pa las 'jig rten gcod par byed ciṅ skye bo sdug bsṅal mtha' yas pa'i rgyu dṅos por lta ba **[P.217b]** la sbyor ba na 'gro ba rnams kyi sdug bsṅal mu mtha' med pa'i sa bon du gyur ba yin no // de'i phyir /

don min sa bon gyur ba yi //
mu stegs ćan maṅ mthoṅ nas ni //
chos 'dod pa yi skye bo la //
su źig sñiṅ mi brtse bar 'gyur[8] // **(k.293)**

---

[1] P_kN_kV gaṅ.

[2] V dka'.

[3] $PNP_kD_kC_kN_kBLS$ 'jigs: DCV 'jig.

[4] PNB rtog: DC rtogs.

[5] PDCN ma yin no sñam pa'i: B ma yin no / smra bar.

[6] PNB las: DC la.

[7] PDCN rtsod: B rtshod.

[8] PDCN sñiṅ mi brtse bar 'gyur: $P_kD_kC_kN_kVBLS$ sñiṅ brtse skye mi 'gyur.

° §63. ° 'jig rten 'di ni mu stegs byed kyi sprul dṅos po daṅ dṅos po med par lta ba dam pa ma yin pa'i tsher ma śin tu 'thibs po'i tshaṅ tshiṅ[1] daṅ ldan pa rnams kyis lam bzaṅ po nas bkug ste / lta ba'i tsher ma'i tshaṅ tshiṅ du bcug nas thar pa'i cha daṅ mthun pa'i dge ba'i srog gi dbaṅ po bcad pa'i sgo nas ñin re źiṅ[2] gsod par byed do // gaṅ źig ci źig ltar skyes bu'i byed pas bdag ñid de las yoṅs su grol bar byas nas lam bzaṅ po la brten pa de ni [N.213b] mdza' bśes tshegs che źiṅ yaṅ bar phyin pa de las grol ba źig sṅar gyi rgyud pa'i gtam thos pas sñiṅ źu ba'i gñen rnams kyis brtse bar bya ba yin pa de [D.193a] lta bu ste de daṅ 'dra bar rnam pa de lta bu'i skye bo rnams la byaṅ chub sems dpa'i rigs can gaṅ źig sñiṅ brtse bar mi 'gyur / sñiṅ brtse ba las kyaṅ gus par byas te de la gaṅ gis na 'dir slar yaṅ mu stegs can gyi sprul ṅag gis[3] phrogs par mi 'gyur ba raṅ bźin med pa'i lam ñe bar bstan par bya'o //

* §64. * yaṅ ci'i phyir sems [C.190a] can rnams dge ba'i bsam pa can[4] yin yaṅ phal cher mu stegs can rnams kyi lugs daṅ rjes su 'brel gyi bde bar gśegs pa pa'i[5] daṅ
° ma yin źe na / de ni phra ba'i phyir ro // ° 'di ltar rags[6] pa mthoṅ źiṅ bde bar gśegs pa pa[7] rnams kyi[8] gtsug lag khaṅ daṅ kha zas daṅ chos gos la sogs pa mchog tu gyur pa dmigs nas lta ba phyin ci log pa rnams de bźin gśegs pa'i gsuṅ rab kyi [P.218a] don zab mo mkhas śiṅ mdzaṅs[9] pas rig par bya ba'i gtiṅ mi dpogs śiṅ mthoṅ ba daṅ thos pa tsam gyis bslus pa na mu stegs can rnams kyi gźuṅ lugs dag la gus par byed do //

---

[1] DC tshiṅ: PN omit.

[2] DC ñin re źiṅ: PN ñin re ñin re źiṅ.

[3] PDC gis: N gi.

[4] PDC dge ba'i bsam pa can: NB dge ba'i bar bsam pa can.

[5] PN gśegs pa pa'i: DC gśegs pa'i; B gśegs pa po'i.

[6] DC rags: PN rag.

[7] PN gśegs pa pa: DC gśegs pa.

[8] DC kyi: PN kyis.

[9] DC mdzaṅs: PN 'dzaṅs, which seems to be equally correct. Cf. Mvyut 2893 'dzaṅs pa = paṇḍita.

* §65. * ji ltar bde bar gśegs pa pa[1] rnams kyi chos 'di phra ba ñid daṅ / de las gźan pa rnams kyi rags pa ñid yin pa[2] de ltar bstan pa'i phyir bśad pa /

śā kya gos med bram ze ste //
gsum po rnams kyi'aṅ[3] chos yid daṅ //
mig daṅ rna ba yis 'dzin pa //
de'i[4] phyir thub pa'i gźuṅ lugs phra[5] // **(k.294)**

§66. bram ze rnams ni 'don pa sñiṅ[6] por byed pa ste / de rnams kyi de ni rna ba'i yul lo // gcer bu pa dag ni gtsaṅ sprar spyod pa[7] daṅ bral ba'i phyir lus dri ṅa ba'i 'dam 'phel bźin pas gos śiṅ lus[8] khrus ras daṅ bral ba graṅ ba daṅ rluṅ daṅ ñi ma daṅ skra 'bal[9] ba la sogs pa'i sdug bsṅal gyi gźir gyur pa rnams te / de rnams kyi lugs de ni mthoṅ bas go bar bya ba yin **[N.214a]** te / de'i phyir de rnams kyi chos ni mig gi rnam par śes pas śes par bya ba yin no[10] // śā kya dṅos po thams cad raṅ bźin med par lta ba'i ñi mas sems kyi rgyud snaṅ bar byas śiṅ dam pa ma yin pa'i lta ba ma lus pas 'thibs[11] śiṅ tshaṅ tshiṅ du gyur pa'i ma rig pa'i mun pa **[D.193b]** bcom pa / 'dus byas

---

[1] PN gśegs pa pa: DC gśegs pa; B gśegs pa po.

[2] PDCN rags pa ñid yin pa: B rigs pa ñid [ma] yin pa.

[3] PDCN gsum po rnams kyi'aṅ: P_kN_kBVL gsum rnams kyi yaṅ; D_kC_kS gsum po rnams kyis. (L's note is erroneous.)

[4] PDCNB de'i: $P_kD_kC_kN_k$VLS de.

[5] PDCNBL phra: $P_kD_kC_kN_k$VS smra.

[6] B sñin.

[7] DCB gtsaṅ sprar spyod pa; PN gtsaṅ sbyar spyod pa. gtsaṅ spra (sbra) spyod pa = caukṣasamudācāra = gtsaṅ sprar spyod pa; cf. Lokesh Chandra s.v. gtsaṅ spra spyod pa and Myvut 6369 s.v. gtsaṅ sbra spyod pa.

[8] D lus: PNB omit; C pus khrus ras.

[9] DCB 'bal: P 'bral; N unclear.

[10] DC mig gi rnam par śes pas śes par bya ba yin no: PN mig gi rnam par śes par bya ba yin no; B mig gis rnam par śes par bya ba yin no.

[11] PDCN 'thibs: B 'jigs.

rmi lam daṅ mig 'phrul daṅ sgyu ma'i na chuṅ[1] daṅ gzugs brñan daṅ sprul pa daṅ mtshuṅs par mthoṅ ba / ñon moṅs pa'i dri ma ma lus pa bsal bas sems kyi rgyud dri ma med par gyur pa rnams ni de ltar mñam par gźag pa[2] dag kho nas ṅes par bya ba yin te / de'i phyir de dag gi dge ba'i **[C.190b]** bsam pa ni yid kyi rnam par śes pas go bar bya ba yin pas thub pa'i gźuṅ lugs phra ba yin no // de'i phyir ma ṅes pas **[P.218b]** bsod nams 'dod kyaṅ skye bo bde bar gśegs pa pa'i[3] chos la mi 'jug go //

§67. 'dir smras pa / gal te blo rags pa'i phyir 'jig rten phyi rol pa[4] la brten[5] nas 'jug na 'o na 'dir yaṅ de ltar rjes su sgrub par gyis śig / phyi rol pa'i bya ba rjes su mi 'grub ste / 'di ltar /

ji ltar bram ze rnams la chos //
phal cher phyi 'chos brjod pa ltar //
de bźin gcer bu rnams la chos[6] //
phal cher blun pa brjod pa yin // **(k.295)**

§68. bram ze rnams ni bzlas brjod daṅ sbyin sreg[7] daṅ / bkra śis daṅ / 'gyod tshaṅs la sogs pa'i bya ba dag gis gźan dag las rñed pa daṅ bkur sti la sogs pa 'dod pas phyi 'chos par 'dod do / de dag gi chos ni phal cher phyi[8] 'chos pa źig ste / phyi[9] 'chos gtso bo yin no źes bya ba'i don to // chos 'di ni thar pa 'dod pa rnams la 'gal ba[10] yin
° te // 'khor ba'i rjes su mthun pa'i phyir la /° kha gsag gis rjes su rig pa'i

---

[1] PDCN na chuṅ: B na chuṅ [ma].

[2] PDCN gźag pa: B bźag pa.

[3] PN gśegs pa pa'i: DC gśegs pa'i; B gśegs pa po'i.

[4] PDNB pa: C la.

[5] DC brten nas: PN bsten nas (= brten nas); B bsten na.

[6] P ches.

[7] DC sreg: PBN bsreg.

[8] DC phyi: PNB phyir.

[9] PNB phyir.

[10] PDCN 'gal ba: B 'gag pa.

bdag ñid can gyi ñe[1] ba'i ñon moṅs pa mṅon par 'phel ba'i rgyu yin pa'i phyir **[N.214b]**
* śā kya pa[2] rnams la ma bstan to //* ji ltar thar pa'i bar du gcod par byed pa'i phyir bram ze rnams kyi chos phyi 'chos phal che ba thar pa 'dod pa rnams kyis spyad[3] par bya ba ma yin pa de bźin du gcer bu rnams kyi chos sems blun pa ñid du byed pa'i rgyu yaṅ blun pa phal che ba'i phyir spyad[4] par bya ba ma yin pas de ltar ñe bar bstan pa rjes su mi sgrub bo //

§69. gaṅ gi phyir bram ze 'di rnams kyi chos phyi 'chos phal che ba de ñid kyi phyir 'jig rten phal cher /

ji ltar rig[5] pa blaṅs pa las //
bram ze[6] gus pa skye ba ltar //
de bźin **[D.194a]** *ñon moṅs blaṅs pa las //*
gcer bu pa la brtse bar 'gyur // **(k.296)**

§70. ji ltar 'don par byed pa tsam gyis sems **[P.219a]** raṅs par gyur pa'i 'jig rten ni rig[7] pa blaṅs pa las bram ze rnams la gus pa skye ba de bźin du ñon moṅs pa blaṅs pa las te mgo 'bal pa la sogs pa lus yoṅs su dub pa rnams las gos med pa rnams la brtse ba skye'o //

§71. 'di **[C.191a]** rnams kyi lus yoṅs su ñon moṅs pa'i sdug bsṅal ñams su myoṅ ba ni chos kyi ched du 'gyur ba 'di ni mi srid de ñes pa spyad pa'i 'bras bu yin pa'i phyir ro źes bstan pa'i phyir[8] /

sdug bsṅal las kyi rnam smin phyir //
ji ltar chos su mi 'gyur ba // **(k.297ab)**

---

[1] PDN ñe: C ña.

[2] DC śā kya pa: PN śā kya.

[3] PDCN spyad: B spyod.

[4] PDCN spyad: B spyod.

[5] DCP_kN_kBLV rig pa: D_kC_kPNS rigs pa.

[6] D_kC_kS bram zer.

[7] DCB rig: PN rigs.

[8] DC phyir: PNB phyir ro.

źes bya ba smos so // ji ltar sgren mos rgyu ba rnams kyi 'di pa'i sdug bsṅal gyi[1] ñams su myoṅ ba yaṅ dmyal ba'i sdug bsṅal gyi ñams su myoṅ ba bźin chos kyi ched du mi 'gyur ba[2] ltar bram ze rnams kyi yaṅ /

de bźin skye ba las kyi ni //
rnam smin phyir na[3] chos ma yin // **(k.297cd)**

§72. gal te las kyi rnam par smin pa yin pa'i phyir mig la sogs pa ltar sdug bsṅal daṅ skye ba[4] chos su mi 'gyur na 'o na chos gaṅ źig yin źe na / bśad par bya ste /

chos ni mdor na mi 'tshe[5] bar //
de bźin gśegs pa rnams kyis gsuṅs // **(k.298ab)**

§73. 'tshe ba ni gźan la gnod par źugs pa'i phyir sems can la gnod pa'i **[N.215a]** bsam pa daṅ / des kun nas bslaṅ pa'i lus daṅ ṅag gi las yin la / mi 'tshe ba ni de las bzlog pa'i sgo nas dge ba bcu'i las kyi lam mo // gaṅ yaṅ cuṅ zad gźan la phan 'dogs pa de thams cad kyaṅ mi 'tshe ba'i khoṅs su 'du ba yin no // de bźin gśegs pa rnams kyis[6] chos ni mdor bsdu na mi 'tshe ba de ñid yin no źes bstan to //

stoṅ ñid mya ṅan 'das par te[7] //
'dir ni[8] de gñis 'ba' źig go // **(k.298cd)**

---

[1] PN gyi: DC omit.

[2] P illegible ('tshol?).

[3] DC: rnam smin phyir na: $P_kD_kC_kN_k$VBLS rnam smin yin phyir; PN rnams smin phyir na.

[4] PN skye ba: DC skye bo.

[5] V 'tshi.

[6] PNB kyis: DC kyi.

[7] PDCNB 'das par te: P_kN_kV 'das par ste; D_kC_kLS 'das pa ste.

[8] V na.

<*dharmaṃ samāsato 'hiṃsāṃ varṇayanti tathāgatāḥ* /> **(k.298ab)**

<*śūnyatām eva nirvāṇaṃ kevalaṃ tad ihobhayam* //> **(k.298cd)**[1]

---

[1] Skt. in Pr. 351.13-14.

§74. raṅ bźin stoṅ pa ñid du gaṅ bśad pa de ñid **[P.219b]** saṅs rgyas bcom ldan 'das rnams kyis[1] mya ṅan las 'das par gsuṅs so /° sdug bsṅal phuṅ po lṅa'i raṅ bźin can gtan ñe bar źi ba gaṅ yin pa de ni mya ṅan las 'das pa yin la / raṅ bźin gyis ma skyes par mthoṅ **[D.194b]** ba'i dus su yaṅ sdug bsṅal raṅ bźin gyis ma skyes par khoṅ du chud pas phyin ci log zad pa yin daṅ de slar yaṅ rnam pa gźan du 'gyur bas yoṅs su brtag[2] pa mi srid pa'i phyir sdug bsṅal 'gags pa kho na'o sñam du dṅos po rnams raṅ bźin gyis stoṅ pa ñid du mthoṅ ba ñid mya **[C.191b]** ṅan las 'das pa'o / źes de bźin gśegs pas gsuṅs kyi dṅos po'i raṅ bźin gyi ṅo bor slar mi skye bas[3] mya ṅan las 'das pa yin no / źes bya bar ni ma yin te raṅ bźin la ldog pa med pa'i phyir ro // de'i phyir raṅ bźin gyis ma skyes pa mthoṅ ba kho na mya ṅan las 'das pa yin no //

* **§75.** * mi 'tshe ba daṅ stoṅ pa ñid ces bya ba'i[4] chos de gñis ni mtho ris daṅ byaṅ grol thob par byed pa ste / de'i phyir

'dir ni de gñis 'ba' źig go //

'ba' źig ces bya ba ni yoṅs su dag pa ste / de bźin gśegs pa'i bstan pa 'di kho nar 'di gñis ches[5] yoṅs su dag par dmigs kyi gźan du ni ma yin no / źes raṅ daṅ gźan gyi bdag ñid la mtho ris daṅ byaṅ grol gyi bde **[N.215b]** ba yaṅ dag par bskyed[6] par 'dod pas rtogs[7] par bya'o //

§76. yaṅ ci'i phyir phyi rol pa 'di dag bde bar gśegs pa'i bstan pa 'di mthoṅ bźin du yaṅ chos gñis po 'di la mi gus śe na / raṅ phyogs la chags pa'i phyir ro // 'di ltar /

---

[1] DCB kyis: PN kyi.

[2] DC brtag: PN brtags.

[3] PDC skye bas: N skye ba.

[4] DC ces bya ba'i: PNB ces pa'i.

[5] PDCN ches: B chos.

[6] PNB bskyed: DC skyed.

[7] DC rtogs: PNB rtog.

raṅ phyogs 'jig rten thams cad la //
skyes sa[1] *bźin du sdug 'gyur na //*
de yi ldog par byed pa'i rgyu //
khyod la gaṅ gis sdug par 'gyur[2] *//* **(k.299)**

§77. raṅ gi **[P.220a]** phyogs la chags pa ni 'khor ba thog ma med pa nas goms pa źig ste / raṅ gi skye ba'i gnas ltar 'jig rten gyis[3] de yoṅs su gtaṅ[4] bar mi nus te / de'i phyir raṅ gi lta ba la mṅon par źen pas byis pa rnams de bźin gśegs pa'i chos 'di la mi 'jug go // mkhas pas raṅ skye ba'i sa yin yaṅ rgud pa'i[5] rgyur gyur ba la re ba spaṅs nas 'byor pa byed pa'i[6] yul la brten par rigs la / 'di ji ltar yin pa de ltar[7] raṅ gi phyogs la chags pa spaṅs nas gźan gyi phyogs yin yaṅ yon tan daṅ ldan pa la yid gźug[8] par bya'o // **[D.195a]** de'i phyir de ltar phyogs su ltuṅ[9] ba med par gyur pas /

rigs pa'i don ni gźan las kyaṅ //
blo ldan legs pa[10] *'dod pas blaṅ*[11] *//*
ñi ma sa steṅ[12] *mig ldan la //*
kun gyi spyi thun[13] *ma yin nam //* **(k.300)**

---

[1] $P_kD_kC_kN_k$BVLS: PN skyes pa; DC skye sa.

[2] PDCND_kC_kBLS sdug par 'gyur: P_kN_kV sdug bsṅal 'gyur.

[3] DC gyis: PNB gyi.

[4] DC gtaṅ: PNB btaṅ.

[5] PNB rgud pa'i: DC brgyud pa'i.

[6] PDC byed pa'i: NB byaṅ ba'i.

[7] B latr.

[8] DCNB gźug: P gźugs.

[9] DC ltuṅ: PNB lhuṅ.

[10] V legs pas.

[11] PN blaṅs.

[12] P_kN_kLS ñi ma sa steṅ: PN ñi mas sa steṅs; BV ñi mas steṅ mig ldan pa la; DCD_kC_k ñi ma sa steṅs.

[13] PN$P_kD_kC_kN_k$BVLS spyi thun: DC spyi mthun.

§78. blo gros daṅ ldan pa bdag ñid kyi yin pa lta bur sems pas gaṅ la lar legs **[C.192a]** par bśad pa dmigs pa de de las blaṅ bar bya'o // chos 'di 'ga' źig tu[1] phrag dog gis[2] gnas pa ni ma yin te / thams cad du ṅo bo mtshuṅs pa'i phyir ro // dper na thams cad la rjes su chags pa daṅ khoṅ khro ba daṅ bral ba'i phyir[3] ñi ma snaṅ ba'i bya ba la mig daṅ ldan pa thams cad la thun moṅ ba[4] yin pa de bźin du chos 'di yaṅ gal te bsgrubs pas rdzogs par 'gyur na / raṅ gi sde pa daṅ gźan gyi sde pa thams cad la phan 'dogs pa yin no // de'i phyir de ltar rig par byas nas gus pa daṅ ldan pas chos 'di bdag tu bya bar rigs so //°

§79. **[N.216a]** slob dpon 'phags pa lha'i źal sṅa nas kyi[5] byaṅ chub sems dpa'i rnal 'byor spyod pa bźi brgya pa las lta bar byas pa dgag pa bsgom[6] pa bstan pa źes bya ba ste rab tu byed pa bcu gñis pa'i **[P.220b]** 'grel pa'o //

---

[1] B du.

[2] B giś.

[3] PBN phyir: DC phyir ro //.

[4] DCB moṅ ba: PN moṅs pa.

[5] PN kyi: DC kyis.

[6] Ego bsgom: PDCN sgom. Cf. the colophons of the other chapters in CS.

SANSKRIT AND TIBETAN TEXTS OF THE CATUḤŚATAKAVṚTTI, CHAPTER XIII: REFUTATION OF THE SENSE ORGANS AND THEIR OBJECTS

CATUḤŚATAKAVṚTTI XIII: TIBETAN TEXT

* **§1.[P.220b1; D.195a5; C.192a3; N.216a2]*** 'dir

rigs pa'i don ni gźan las kyaṅ //

blo ldan legs pa[1] 'dod pas blaṅ //[2]

źes gaṅ smras na / gaṅ źig blo daṅ ldan pas blaṅ bar bya ba rigs pa'i don de yaṅ gaṅ źig yin źes 'dzer to // bśad par bya ste / phyi daṅ naṅ gi dṅos po thams cad raṅ bźin gyis bdag med par mthoṅ ba'o //

§2. gal te dṅos po thams cad raṅ bźin med pa źes bya ba 'di ñid rtogs par mi nus te / yod pa ma yin pa'i boṅ bu'i rwa la sogs pa la ni mṅon sum ñid yod pa ma yin no // bum pa la sogs pa rnams daṅ sṅon po la sogs pa rnams ni mṅon sum yod pa ñid yin no // de'i phyir bum pa la sogs pa'i dṅos po thams cad raṅ bźin daṅ bcas par yod pa kho na'o źe na / 'di ni mi rigs te 'di ltar /

gzugs mthoṅ tshe na bum pa ni //

thams cad kho na mthoṅ mi[3] *'gyur //*

bum pa mṅon sum źes bya **[D.195b]** *ba'aṅ //*

de ñid rig pa su źig smra // **(k.301)**

§3. 'aṅ gi sgras ni de'i ñe bar len pa sṅon po la sogs pa dag kyaṅ mṅon sum yin no źes de kho na ñid śes pa su źig smra bar 'gyur //° de la kha cig dag[4] gis ni bum pa yon tan gsum[5] yoṅs su 'gyur ba'i ṅo **[C.192b]** bor rtogs la / yaṅ gźan dag gis ni bum pa źes bya ba yan lag can gyi rdzas yan lag las tha dad pa mthoṅ ba daṅ / reg pa'i dbaṅ pos gzuṅ bar bya ba[6] yin par rtogs te / de dag gi yaṅ /

---

[1] Ego legs pa (cf. k. 300): PDCNB legs par.

[2] = k. 300ab.

[3] N_k ma.

[4] DC dag: PN omit.

[5] PN bum pa yon tan gsum: DC bum pa la sogs pa'i yon tan gsum.

[6] DC gzuṅ bar bya ba: PN bzuṅ bar bya ba.

CATUḤŚATAKAVṚTTI XIII: SANSKRIT TEXT

<sarva eva ghaṭo 'dṛṣṭo rūpe dṛṣṭe hi jāyate /
brūyāt kas tattvavin nāma ghaṭaḥ pratyakṣa ity api //>[1] **(k.301)**

---

[1] Sanskrit in Pr. 71.6-7.

dṅos po rtag pa las skyes pa //
ji lta bur na mi rtag 'gyur //
nam yaṅ rgyu daṅ 'bras bu gñis //
mtshan ñid mi mthun mthoṅ ma yin //[1]

źes bkag pa'i phyir bum pa ñid yod pa ma yin pas de'i mṅon sum ñid ga la yod /**[N.216b]**

§4. gal te de ltar mi srid na 'o na ji ltar bum pa 'di rnam par gźag[2] **[P.221a]** par rig par bya źe na / de bśad par bya ste / 'byuṅ ba chen po bźi daṅ rgyur byas pa'i gzugs bźi ste / rdzas brgyad po de dag la brten nas bum pa 'dogs te / ji ltar bud śiṅ la brten nas me daṅ / rtswa daṅ śiṅ la sogs pa la brten nas khyim daṅ phuṅ po dag la brten nas bdag tu 'dogs la / de yaṅ raṅ gi rgyu las rnam pa lṅas btsal na ma dmigs pa de bźin du raṅ gi rgyu la brten nas sbraṅ rtsi daṅ chu daṅ 'o ma 'chu źiṅ 'dzin par nus pa mthoṅ ba'i dbaṅ pos go bar bya ba yin pas 'jig rten gyi mṅon sum du gyur pa'i bum pa ñe bar len pa po ñid du rnam par gźag gi[3] / ji skad bśad pa'i brten nas btags pa[4] 'di khas ma blaṅs par rtog pa[5] gźan gyis bum par rnam par gźag[6] par nus pa ni ma yin no //

§5. gaṅ źig gzugs la sogs pa las ma gtogs par bum pa gźan du ma dmigs pa'i phyir gnas skabs de lta bu'i gzugs la sogs pa dag kho na la bum pa'i blor 'gyur gyi bum pa źes bya ba dṅos po 'ga' źig yod pa ni ma yin no sñam du sems pa[7] de ltar rgol ba de'i ltar na rtag tu 'bar ba ñid la sogs pa ñes par thal bar 'gyur ba'i phyir bud śiṅ

---

[1] = k. 211 (CS IX, k. 11). PDCN mtshan ñid mi ldan; but cf. L's ed. of k. 211d: mtshan ñid mi mthun mthoṅ ma yin. See also May (1981) ed. of k. 211 and *Vṛtti*. mtshan ñid mi ldan is incompatible with CSV ad k. 211.

[2] DC gźag: PN bźag.

[3] DC gźag gi: PN bźag gis.

[4] PN btags pa: DC brtags pa. See May (1981) n. 22 on btags pa vs. brtags pa.

[5] PN rtog pa: DC rtag pa.

[6] PN bźag.

[7] DC sems pa: PN sems dpa'.

las ma gtogs par las **[D.196a]** med par gyur pa'i me'i yod pa ñid med pas de yaṅ blos yoṅs su brtags[1] pa tsam du 'gyur la / de bźin du 'byuṅ ba rnams daṅ sems daṅ sems las byuṅ ba rnams phan tshun med par 'byuṅ bar ma grub pa'i phyir bum pa bźin du blos brtags pa[2] tsam ñid du 'gyur źiṅ raṅ gi ṅo bos 'grub par mi 'gyur na / 'di ni de ltar 'dis **[C.193a]** khas blaṅs pa yaṅ ma yin no // de'i phyir bum pa la sogs pa rnams sems daṅ sems las byuṅ ba lta bu daṅ / **[P.221b]** 'byuṅ ba chen po bźin du rten ciṅ 'brel par 'byuṅ ba 'am brten nas btags[3] par ci[4] ste khas mi len te / de'i phyir bum pa rdzas brgyad kyi ñe bar len **[N.217a]** pa can raṅ gi ñe bar blaṅs pa'i ñe bar len pa por gyur ciṅ ñe bar len pa'i bya ba byed pa po 'jig rten gyi mṅon sum du gyur pa'i yan lag can de ltar rnam par gnas pa yin daṅ 'di rnam par dpyad de /

gzugs mthoṅ tshe na bum pa ni //
thams cad 'kho na mthoṅ mi 'gyur te //
* *bum pa rdzas brgyad kyi bdag ñid can yin pa'i phyir ro //

§6. mig gis ni gzugs gcig pu mthoṅ gi dri la sogs pa dag[5] ni ma yin te yul tha
° dad pa'i phyir ro // de'i phyir bum pa thams cad mig gis mi mthoṅ ba'i phyir° na dṅos po'i raṅ gi ṅo bo rnam par ma phye bas 'jig rten ci ruṅ ruṅ ltar raṅ gi rtog pa tshad mar byas nas bum pa bdag[6] gi mṅon sum yin no źes smra la rag mod / gaṅ źig rnam par 'byed par byed ciṅ dṅos po'i raṅ gi ṅo bo la mkhas pa gaṅ phyogs gcig mthoṅ bas ril mthoṅ bar srid par mi byed pa de ni bum pa mṅon sum mo źes bya ba rnam pa de lta bur smra bar mi 'os so //

§7. 'di la rtog ge ba[7] rnams na re bum pa la mṅon sum ñid yod pa ma yin pa kho na ste / gzugs la sogs pa rnams kyi raṅ gi mtshan ñid ni bstan du med pa yin la / mṅon sum gyis bsñad par bya ba'i mig la sogs pa'i rnam par śes pa'i yul yin pa'i phyir

---

[1] DC brtags: PN btags. yoṅs su brtags pa = parikalpita.

[2] DC brtags pa: PN btags pa.

[3] Ego btags: PDCN brtags.

[4] DC ci: PN cis.

[5] PDC dag: NB daṅ.

[6] PN bdag: DC dag.

[7] DCN ba: P omits.

mṅon sum źes bya bar 'dogs so // bum pa ni blos yoṅs su brtags pa tsam yin pa'i phyir raṅ gi **[D.196b]** mtshan ñid du yod pa ma yin la / gaṅ la raṅ gi mtshan ñid yod pa ma yin pa de la ni dṅos kyi gnas pas mṅon sum ñid mi srid pa 'ba' źig tu ma zad kyi de la btags pa'i **[P.222a]** mṅon sum ñid kyaṅ mi ruṅ ṅo // de'i phyir mṅon sum ñid 'gog pa dgos pa med pa'i phyir sgra la mig gis gzuṅ bar bya ba 'gog pa ltar bum pa 'di la **[C.193b]** yaṅ 'gog par[1] rigs pa ma yin no źes zer ro //

§8. rtog ge ba 'di ni 'jig rten pa'i don dag la gtan ma byaṅ **[N.217b]** ba'i phyir byis pa gźon nu ltar je daṅ po kho na nas sbyaṅ bar bya bar[2] gyur pa yin pas de bstan par bya ba'i phyir khyod kyi mṅon sum gaṅ źig yin źes brgal źiṅ brtag par bya'o //

§9. smras pa śes pa mṅon sum yin no // śes pa ci 'dra ba źig / gaṅ rtog pa daṅ bral ba'o // rtog pa yaṅ ci źig / gaṅ don la miṅ daṅ rigs su lhag par sgro 'dogs par źugs pa'i 'du śes g.yer po ste de daṅ bral ba'i phyir dbaṅ po'i rnam par śes pa lṅa ni yul gyi raṅ gi mtshan ñid brjod du med pa tsam źig la 'jug pa'i phyir mṅon sum gyi sgras[3] brjod par bya ba ste / dbaṅ po daṅ dbaṅ po la gnas pa'i phyir ro //

§10. 'o na dbaṅ po'i rnam par śes pa skad cig ma gcig ji ltar mṅon sum ñid yin / de ni dbaṅ po daṅ dbaṅ po la brten nas 'jug pa ma yin te / thun moṅ[4] ma yin pa'i phyir daṅ / dbaṅ po daṅ rnam par śes pa'i skad cig dag skyes ma thag tu 'jig pa ñid kyi phyir ro //

§11. gal te rnam par śes pa'i tshogs lṅa ni bsags pa'i rten daṅ dmigs pa can yin pas dbaṅ po'i rdul phra rab daṅ yul gyi rdul phra rab re re źiṅ rten ñid dam dmigs pa ñid du rtogs pa ma yin te / rab rib can gyis[5] skra śad re re logs su ma mthoṅ ba'i phyir ro / tshogs pa'i naṅ na gnas pa re re yaṅ rgyu'i dṅos po yin pa ltar mig la sogs pa'i rdul phra rab tshogs pa rnams ni re re źiṅ rgyu **[P.222b]** ñid yin no źe na /

---

[1] PN 'gog par: DC 'gog pa'i.

[2] PN bya bar: DC omit.

[3] DC sgras: PN sgra.

[4] DC moṅ: PN moṅs.

[5] DC gyis: PN gyi. Kaḥ thog reads gyis.

§12. dpe mi mthun pa źig ste / rab rib med pas skra re re nas mthoṅ ba'i phyir mig la gnod pa yod na mi mthoṅ bar 'gyur na / dbaṅ po'i rdul phra rab rnams la **[D.197a]** ni tshogs pa'i gnas skabs las phyi rol tu[1] rdul phra rab re re raṅ gi[2] rnam par śes pa'i rten ñid du ma mthoṅ bas tshogs pa la gnas pa rnams la re re rten ñid du brtags pa 'di mi rigs so /

§13. bye ba[3] la nus pa cuṅ zad tsam źig ma dmigs nas tshogs pa la gnas pa la yaṅ de daṅ mthun par brtag par ni[4] rigs par 'gyur ro // 'di ltar rtsa gcig la śa sbraṅ **[N.218a]** daṅ sbraṅ **[C.194a]** bu mchu riṅs la sogs pa'i rkaṅ pa 'chiṅ ba'i nus pa dmigs nas de dag gi tshogs pa la glaṅ po che 'chiṅ ba'i nus pa'i bar srid la / de bźin du til rnams la re re la 'bru mar ñuṅ zad tsam 'byin pa'i nus pa yod daṅ tshogs pa[5] rnams la 'bru mar bum pa gaṅ 'byin pa yaṅ srid na tshogs pa la ma[6] ltos pa'i dbaṅ po'i rdul phra rab rnams la ni de ltar re re rnam par śes pa'i rten ñid du yod pa ma yin pas rdul phra rab la ltos nas kyaṅ nus pa[7] mi srid do // de'i phyir dbaṅ po'i rdul phra rab la brten nas mig gi dbaṅ po źes bya ba rdul phra rab dag daṅ de ñid daṅ gźan ñid rtog[8] pas stoṅ pa raṅ gi rnam par śes pa'i rten du gyur pa brten nas btags pas[9] 'jig rten par

[1] DC tu: PN du.

[2] DC gi: PN gis.

[3] DC bye ba: PN bye ma.

[4] DC ni: PN omit.

[5] PND tshogs pa: C tshogs sa.

[6] DC ma: PN omits.

[7] Ego nus pa ("power"): PDCN gnod pa ("harm"). The context is a discussion of *nus pa*.

[8] PN rtog: DC rtogs.

[9] PN btags pas: DC brtags par.

gyur pa yul la lta ba'i bya ba can źig yod pa ma[1] yin la (/) de yaṅ skad cig ma ñid kyi phyir raṅ gi rnam par śes pa daṅ lhan[2] cig 'gags pas nus pa[3] ga la srid / de'i phyir śes pa gaṅ źig dbaṅ po daṅ dbaṅ po la gnas pa de ni mṅon sum mo źes bya ba mi rigs so //

§14. ci ste rnam par śes pa'i tshogs pa bdag ñid ji lta bu'i dbaṅ po **[P.223a]** dag la gnas pa'i phyir de skad du bye brag tu bśad par 'gyur ro sñam na 'di yaṅ yod pa ma yin no // gaṅ las śe na / mig gi rnam par śes pa'i skad cig ma gcig la de ltar bye brag tu bśad pa mi srid pa'i phyir la / tshogs pa rdzas su med pa la yaṅ dbaṅ po la brten pa ñid med pa'i phyir ro // brten nas btags pas[4] rnam par śes pa'i rten[5] du gyur pa mig gi dbaṅ po'i[6] rnam par gźag[7] pa ji ltar yin pa[8] de bźin du gzugs la sogs pa rnams kyi rnam par gźag[9] pa yaṅ rig par bya ste / de dag kyaṅ brten nas btags[10] **[D.197b]** pa na rnam par śes pa'i rten yin pa'i phyir ro // de ltar na rnam par śes pa la mṅon sum du rtogs pa mi rigs so //

§15. yul la ni rigs te / de la ni zla ba tshes pa la sogs pa la cig car rgyud du ma **[N.218b]** las skyes pa'i dbaṅ po'i yul ñid mthoṅ ṅo // 'jig rten pa'i don la 'jig rten pa'i mthoṅ ba spaṅs nas don gźan la **[C.194b]** brten par rigs pa ma yin no[11] // de'i

---

[1] PN ma: DC omit.

[2] DC lhan: PN ldan.

[3] Ego nus pa: PDCN gnod pa.

[4] PN btags pas: DC brtags pas.

[5] DC rten: PN brten.

[6] PN dbaṅ po'i: DC dbaṅ po.

[7] PN bźag.

[8] PN yin pa: DC omit.

[9] PN bźag.

[10] PN btags: DC brtags.

[11] DC rigs pa ma yin no: PN rig pa yaṅ ma yin no.

phyir 'jig rten na yul kho na dṅos kyi 'jug pas mṅon sum yin la śes pa ni btags pa las so // gźan gyi ltar na ni mṅon sum gyi sgra śes pa la[1] dṅos su yin la yul la ni[2] btags pa yin no // de ni 'jig rten pa ma yin te / 'jig rten la de ltar kun tu tha sñad med pa'i phyir ro // de'i phyir de ltar 'jig rten pa'i tha sñad gnas pa yin daṅ 'jig rten kho na las bum pa mṅon sum mo źes bya bar brjod par rigs kyi / raṅ bźin tshol ba'i dus su de ñid rig pas[3] de skad du smra bar 'os pa ma yin te / bum pa'i raṅ gi ṅo bo rnam pa thams cad du ma dmigs pa'i phyir ro // 'jig rten pa'i rnam par śes pa la[4] ni bum pa la yaṅ mṅon sum yin źiṅ gzugs la sogs **[P.223b]** pa dag kyaṅ mṅon sum yin la de'i ñe bar len pa[5] rnams kyaṅ mṅon sum yin pas ñes pa med do //

§16. gaṅ yaṅ 'dis dbaṅ po'i rnam par śes pa 'di mṅon sum ñid du sgro btags nas gźan tshad ma ñid du rtog par byed de yaṅ ches śin tu ma 'brel ba źig go // mi slu ba'i śes pa ni 'jig rten na tshad ma ñid du mthoṅ na rnam par śes pa yaṅ bcom ldan 'das kyis 'dus byas yin pa'i phyir brdzun pa bslu ba'i chos can daṅ sgyu ma lta bur gsuṅs so // gaṅ źig brdzun pa bslu ba'i chos can daṅ sgyu ma lta bu yin pa de ni mi bslu ba ma yin te / rnam pa gźan du gnas pa'i[6] dṅos po la rnam pa gźan du snaṅ ba'i phyir ro // de lta bur gyur pa ni tshad ma ñid du brtag par rigs pa ma yin te / rnam par śes pa thams cad kyaṅ tshad ma ñid du thal bar 'gyur ba'i phyir ro //

§17. de'i phyir rtog ge ba 'di gal te rtog ge'i chaṅ 'thuṅs pas myos pas smyos par gyur na ni[7] rten ciṅ **[D.198a]** 'brel par 'byuṅ ba daṅ brten nas btags[8] pa źes bya ba lam bzaṅ po spaṅs nas mu stegs can **[N.219a]** gyi gźuṅ las bstan pa'i dṅos po rnams

---

[1] PN la: DC omit.

[2] DC ni: PN omit.

[3] DCN rig pas: P rigs pas.

[4] PN la: DC las.

[5] PN ñe bar len pa: DC ñe bar len pa can.

[6] DC gnas pa'i: PN gźan pa'i.

[7] Ego smyos par gyur na ni: PDCN smyos par ma gyur na ni. I read smyos par gyur na ni instead of smyos par ma gyur na ni ("when he is *not* mad"), as the latter would convey the opposite of what Candrakīrti is driving at.

[8] Ego btags: PDCN brtags.

gsal bar byed pa dam pa ma yin pa'i tshig 'khyal[1] gyi tshogs ches brtol bar mi 'gyur ba źig go // 'jig rten 'di[2] yaṅ phal cher ma'i bźin ltar dpyod ciṅ 'jig rten daṅ 'jig **[C.195a]** rten las 'das pa'i dṅos po gnas pa la rnam par rmoṅs pa 'dis raṅ gi rtog pa tsam gyis sbyar źiṅ mtho ris daṅ thar pa'i lam la bar du gcod par byed pa śin tu don med par rtog ge ba'i lam la bkod pa yin no // de'i phyir 'dir smyo chu 'thuṅs pa ltar don med pa'i ṅag 'khyal las bzlog par mi nus so // spros pas chog go // bum pa mṅon sum yin pa bsal ba **[P.224a]** 'dis ni mthoṅ ba'i dbaṅ po'i[3] yul gyi dṅos po thams cad mṅon sum ñid yin pa bsal bar rig par bya'o //

* **§18.** *ji ltar ji skad bśad pa'i tshul gyis[4] bum pa la sogs pa rnams mṅon sum ñid yin par mi rigs pa de ltar de las gźan pa'i dbaṅ pos yoṅs su gcad[5] par bya ba brten nas gdags pa bsnam[6] par bya ba daṅ myaṅ bar bya ba daṅ reg par bya ba rnams mṅon sum ñid yin pa bsal ba'i phyir bśad pa /

rnam par dpyad pa[7] 'di ñid kyis //
blo mchog ldan pas dri źim daṅ //
mṅar[8] daṅ 'jam pa thams cad dag //
so sor dgag par bya ba yin // **(k.302)**

---

[1] DC 'khyal: PN khyal.

[2] DC 'di: PN omit.

[3] DC dbaṅ po'i: PN omit.

[4] DCB gyis: PN gyi.

[5] DC gcad: PNB bcad.

[6] PDC bsnam: NB bsnams.

[7] V dbyad pa.

[8] B maṅar.

<etenaiva vicāreṇa sugandhi madhuraṃ mṛdu /
pratiṣedhayitavyāni sarvāṇy uttamabuddhinā //>[1] **(k.302)**

[1] Sanskrit in Pr. 71.8-9.

§19. dri źim źes bya ba 'dis ni snas yoṅs su gcad par bya ba sna ma'i me tog daṅ pad ma daṅ ut pa la daṅ tsan dan la sogs pa sna'i dbaṅ po'i yul mtha' dag ñe bar mtshon par byed de[1] / gzugs la sogs pa mthoṅ ba med par mun khuṅ du yaṅ dri tsam 'dzin pa'i phyir ro // de bźin du mṅar daṅ źes bya ba 'dis kyaṅ bu ram daṅ lan tshwa[2] daṅ nim pa la sogs pa lce'i dbaṅ po'i yul thams cad ñe bar mtshon par byed do // 'jam pa źes bya ba 'dis ni śiṅ bal daṅ bye ma daṅ rdo ba la sogs pa lus kyi dbaṅ po'i yul thams cad ñe bar mtshon par byed do // de dag **[N.219b]** kyaṅ rdzas brgyad kyi ñe bar len pa can yin pas bdag ñid ji lta ba'i dbaṅ po dag gis[3] yul re re **[D.198b]** 'dzin pa yin daṅ rnam pa thams cad mi 'dzin pa'i phyir sna ma'i me tog daṅ bu ram daṅ śiṅ bal la sogs pa dag bdag gi mṅon sum yin no źes de kho na ñid śes pa su źig smra / sgra dgag pa ni phyis rgyas par 'chad do //

§20. ci ste bum pa gzugs las tha dad pa med mod kyi gzugs kyis de khyab par byas nas ni gnas **[P.224b]** pas **[C.195b]** gzugs mthoṅ bas bum pa thams cad mthoṅ bar 'gyur ro źe na / 'di yaṅ sñiṅ po med do źes bstan pa'i phyir bśad pa /

gal te gzugs mthoṅ ba yis de //
thams cad mthoṅ bar 'gyur na ni //
ma mthoṅ ba yis[4] gzugs mthoṅ ba //
mthoṅ ba min par cis mi 'gyur // **(k.303)**

§21. gal te gzugs tsam źig mthoṅ bas ma mthoṅ yaṅ bum pa thams cad kho na mthoṅ bar 'gyur na ni bum pa ma mthoṅ bas mthoṅ ba gzugs mthoṅ ba ma yin par ci'i phyir mi 'gyur / yaṅ na 'di ni don gźan yin te bum pa rdzas brgyad kyi ñe bar len pa can yin yaṅ gal te rdzas gcig gzugs[5] mthoṅ bas ril mthoṅ bar rtog[6] na ni

---

[1] DC de: PNB do.

[2] B tshw.

[3] PNB gis: DC gi.

[4] DCD_kLS yis: PN$P_kC_kN_k$VB yi.

[5] PNB rdzas gcig gzugs: DC rdzas gcig gi gzugs.

[6] B rtog: PDCN rtogs.

re źig de dag daṅ so sor mi gnas pa'i gzugs de ñid de de[1] las gźan rdzas bdun ma
° mthoṅ bas na ma mthoṅ ba yin no źes ci'i phyir mi rtog /° 'jig rten na yaṅ phal che
bas brjod pa mthoṅ ba ste mon sran sde'u la sogs pa yod kyaṅ mon sran gre'u'i phuṅ
pos bsñad pa bźin no //

§22. de'i phyir de ltar na ma mthoṅ ba yis te dri la sogs pa yoṅs su ma bcad
* pas mthoṅ ba'i gzugs kyaṅ mthoṅ ba ma yin pa ñid du 'gyur ro // *de'i phyir gzugs ñid
mṅon sum ma yin pa'i phyir bum pa yaṅ mṅon sum ñid du mi rigs so //

§23. ci ste ji skad bśad pa'i rnam par dpyad pas bum pa la mṅon sum ñid mi srid mod / bum pa'i gzugs ni re źig mṅon sum yin te / de'i phyir rgyud nas bum pa yaṅ mṅon sum ñid du 'gyur ro sñam du sems na 'di ni yod pa ma **[N.220a]** yin no // gzugs la mṅon sum ñid yod na ni 'di de skad du brjod par 'gyur ba źig na / gzugs la mṅon sum ñid srid pa ni ma yin no źes bstan pa'i phyir bśad pa /

gzugs ni 'ba'[2] *źig kho na* **[D.199a]** *la //*
mṅon sum ñid **[P.225a]** *ni yod*[3] *ma yin //*
gaṅ phyir de la'aṅ[4] *pha rol gyi //*
cha daṅ tshu rol dbus yod phyir // **(k.304)**

§24. dri la sogs pa daṅ 'brel pa brjod par mi 'dod pa'i gzugs 'ba' źig la yaṅ rnam pa thams cad du[5] tshu rol daṅ dkyil daṅ pha rol gyi cha rnams mthoṅ ba'i phyir mṅon sum ñid mi rigs so // tshu rol daṅ pha rol daṅ dbus kyi cha de dag la yaṅ slar tshu rol daṅ pha rol daṅ dbus kyi cha gźan dag yin la / de dag la yaṅ gźan yin źiṅ[6] de dag **[C.196a]** la yaṅ gźan yin no źes de ltar rnam par phye ba na gzugs de[7] rdul phra

---

[1] PDCN de de: B omits one de.

[2] V 'ga'.

[3] B srid..

[4] PDCN de la'aṅ: $P_kD_kC_kN_k$VBLS de la.

[5] PDC rnam pa thams cad du: N unclear; B rna bar du.

[6] PNB de dag la yaṅ gźan yin źiṅ: DC omit.

[7] Ego rnam par phye ba na gzugs de: PDC rnam par phye ba na gzugs te; N rna bar phye ba na gsugs te; B rna bar phyi gzugs te. But cf. rGyal p. 4: de ltar cha daṅ char phye ba na gzugs *de* rdul phra rab kyi mthar thug par gnas la...

rab kyi mthar thug nas gnas so // brtags[1] bźin pa'i rdul de la yaṅ mdun daṅ rgyab kyi phyogs kyi cha'i dbye ba daṅ / tshu rol daṅ dbus daṅ pha rol gyi cha'i dbye ba las /

rdul la[2] *cha śas yod med ces //*
dpyad[3] *pa der yaṅ 'jug par 'gyur //* **(k.305ab)**

§25. gal te de la mdun daṅ rgyab kyi cha'i dbye ba dag yod na ni de'i tshe bum pa ltar de'i rdul phra rab ñid ñams par 'gyur ro // ci ste med na ni de ltar na yaṅ gsal byed med ciṅ ma bzuṅ ba'i ṅo bo can de la yod pa ñid med do // de'i phyir de la mṅon sum ñid srid par ga la 'gyur /

de'i phyir[4] *bsgrub*[5] *par bya ba yis //*
bsgrub bya 'grub par[6] *mi 'thad do //* **(k.305cd)**

§26. de'i phyir de ltar na mṅon sum ñid ma grub par mi 'thad do // de'i phyir de ltar na mṅon sum ñid ma grub ciṅ bsgrub par bya bar gyur pas[7] bsgrub par bya ba ste (/) dṅos po rnams raṅ bźin daṅ bcas pa ñid du gźan gyis[8] khas blaṅs pa grub pa mi 'thad do //

§27. gźan yaṅ dbaṅ po gzugs can gyis gzuṅ[9] bar bya ba'i don yoṅs su brtags pa na /

---

[1] PDC brtags: N brtogs.

[2] DC rdul la: PNB omit.

[3] V dbyad.

[4] PDCNB de'i phyir: $P_kD_kC_kN_k$VLS de phyir.

[5] V bsgrug.

[6] N_k pa.

[7] PNB de'i phyir de ltar na mṅon sum ñid ma grub ciṅ bsgrub par bya bar gyur pas: DC de'i phyir de ltar mṅon sum ma grub ciṅ bsgrub par gyur pas.

[8] DC gyis: PNB gyi.

[9] DC gzuṅ: PNB bzuṅ.

kun kyaṅ yan lag tu gyur na[1] *//*
slar yaṅ yan lag can du 'gyur // **(k.306ab)**

§28. bum pa ni yan lag gyo mo la ltos[2] nas yan lag can yin la / **[P.225b]** gyo mo de[3] **[N.220b]** dag kyaṅ raṅ gi yan lag la ltos nas yan lag can du 'gyur ro // de bźin du rdul phra rab kyi bar du sbyar bar bya'o // de yaṅ rdzas brgyad la ltos nas sam mdun daṅ rgyab daṅ dbus kyi cha la ltos nas slar yaṅ yan lag can yin pas 'ga' la yaṅ raṅ gi ṅo bos yan lag **[D.199b]** ñid daṅ yan lag can ñid yod pa ma yin te / de'i phyir bum pa la sogs pa rnams la mṅon sum ñid med do //

§29. ji ltar rdul phra rab la rnam par dpyad pa de bźin du miṅ gi[4] mthar gnas pa'i yi ge la yaṅ ste / rdul phra rab ltar ma grub pa'i phyir ro //

de'i phyir[5] *yi ge brjod pa yaṅ //*
'di na[6] *yod pa ma yin no //* **(k.306cd)**

§30. yi ge brjod pa yaṅ mi srid do sñam du dgoṅs so // rnam pa gcig tu na bum pa la sogs pa med na de'i rjod par byed pa'i[7] yi ge **[C.196b]** brjod pa[8] yaṅ mi srid de / don med na śes pa daṅ brjod pa dag 'jug pa mi srid pa'i phyir

yi ge brjod pa yaṅ (/)
'di na yod pa ma yin no //

---

[1] PDCN na: $P_kD_kC_kN_k$VBLS nas.

[2] DC ltos: PNB bltos. Ibidem for subsequent occurrences of ltos nas.

[3] PDCN de: B omits.

[4] PDCN gi: B mi.

[5] PDCNB de'i phyir: $P_kD_kC_kN_k$VLS de phyir.

[6] DCNP_kN_kBL na: D_kC_kS la; PV ni. Cf. CSV which comments on 'di na.

[7] DC rjod par byed pa'i: PNB brjod par byed pa.

[8] DC brjod pa: PNB omit.

§31. gaṅ dag gzugs kyi skye mched kha dog daṅ dbyibs kyi bdag ñid rnam par gñis su rnam par gźag[1] ste de'i sgo nas bum pa[2] mṅon sum ñid du rtog par byed pa de dag la rjod[3] par byed pa ste / 'dir dbyibs 'di rtog pa na[4] kha dog las gźan ñid dam[5] / gźan ma yin pa ñid du rtog graṅ na // de la re źig /

gal te mdog las dbyibs gźan na //
ji lta bur na dbyibs 'dzin 'gyur // **(k.307ab)**

§32. sṅon po la sogs pa'i kha dog ni mig gi dbaṅ po'i yul yin na / gal te de las dbyibs tha dad par[6] 'gyur na ni[7] kha dog las tha dad pa'i phyir sgra la sogs pa ltar mig gi gzuṅ byar mi 'gyur ba źig na / kha dog ltar mig gis 'dzin pa yaṅ yin pas de las gźan[8] ma yin no // ji ltar sṅon po daṅ ser po la sogs pa tha dad pa rnams las **[P.226a]** gaṅ yaṅ ruṅ ba cig[9] bzuṅ nas cig śos kyaṅ 'dzin pa de ltar kha dog las gźan pa'i gzugs ni mi 'dzin to[10] //

'on te gźan min na lus kyis //
mdog kyaṅ ci ste[11] 'dzin mi 'gyur[12] // **(k.307cd)**

---

[1] PNB bźag.

[2] PNB bum pa: DC bum pa ñid.

[3] DC rjod: PNB brjod.

[4] B ni.

[5] PDCN dam: B daṅ.

[6] DC dbyibs tha dad par: PN dbyibs par; B dbyibs [gźan] par.

[7] DC ni: PNB omit.

[8] B gaźan.

[9] DC cig: PNB gcig.

[10] PN to: DC no; B te.

[11] C_k ji ste; PN cis te.

[12] $DCP_kD_kC_kLS$ 'dzin mi 'gyur: PNVB mi 'dzin 'gyur.

§33. gal **[N.221a]** te ji skad bśad pa'i skyon spaṅ bar 'dod pas dbyibs kha dog las gźan ma yin par rtog na ni[1] ji ltar mun khuṅ du lus kyis[2] riṅ po la sogs pa 'dzin pa de bźin du de las tha mi dad pa'i phyir dbyibs ltar kha dog kyaṅ ci ste mi 'dzin te gzuṅ[3] dgos na 'dzin pa yaṅ ma yin no // de'i phyir dbyibs 'dzin yaṅ ma bzuṅ ba'i phyir kha dog las dbyibs gźan ma yin pa ma yin no // de ñid daṅ gźan ñid du rtog **[D.200a]** pa las ma gtogs par rtog pa gźan[4] gźag[5] par nus pa ma yin no // de'i phyir kha dog ltar dbyibs kyaṅ mi rigs la / de med pas kyaṅ 'ga' la yaṅ mṅon sum ñid yod pa ma yin no źes bya bar grub[6] bo //

§34. 'dir smras pa / gzugs kyi skye mched ni yod pa kho na ste[7] (/) de'i rgyu yod pa'i phyir ro // 'dir gzugs kyi rgyu ni 'byuṅ ba chen po bźi yin la / de dag ni re źig yod pa yin no // de dag yod pas de dag gi 'bras bu[8] gzugs kyi **[C.197a]** skye mched kyaṅ yod par 'gyur ro źes smra'o // 'di yaṅ yaṅ dag pa ma yin no źes bstan pa'i phyir bśad pa /

gzugs ni lta[9] źig ma gtogs[10] par //
gzugs kyi rgyu ni mi[11] snaṅ ṅo // **(k.308ab)**

---

[1] PDCN rtog na ni: B brtags ni.

[2] PNB kyis: DC kyi.

[3] DC gzuṅ: PNB bzuṅ.

[4] Ego ma gtogs par rtog pa gźan: PNB ma rtogs par rtog pa gźan; DC ma gtogs pa gźan.

[5] PNB bźag.

[6] PDC grub: NB 'grub.

[7] DC ste: PNB te.

[8] PDC 'bras bu: NB 'bras bus.

[9] PDCN$D_k C_k$BLS lta: $P_k N_k$V blta.

[10] DC$P_k D_k C_k N_k$BVLS gtogs: PN rtogs.

[11] P omits mi.

§35. rdzas brgyad lhan cig 'byuṅ bar[1] ṅes pa 'byuṅ ba chen po bźi ma gtogs par gzugs mi dmigs la / gzugs kyi skye mched ma gtogs par yaṅ gzugs kyi rgyu mi dmigs so // gzugs kyi skye mched ni mig gi dbaṅ pos gzuṅ[2] bar bya ba yin la / gzugs kyi rgyu ni lus kyi dbaṅ pos gzuṅ bar bya ba yin no // de'i phyir gal te **[P.226b]** gzugs kyi rgyu źes bya ba cuṅ zad cig raṅ gi ṅo bos 'grub par 'gyur na ni de'i tshe gzugs kyaṅ raṅ gi ṅo bos grub par 'gyur ba źig na / gzugs kyi rgyu gzugs las tha dad par grub pa gaṅ yin pa 'di ni srid pa yaṅ ma yin no // de'i phyir gzugs kyi rgyu med na rgyu med pa'i gzugs kyaṅ yod pa ma yin no źes bya bar grub bo //

§36. ci ste 'o na ni tha dad pa ma yin par gnas pa'i gzugs kyi rgyu las **[N.221b]** gzugs yin par rag[3] go sñam du sems na / de yaṅ srid pa ma yin no //

gal te de ltar 'gyur na ni //
gñi ga yaṅ ni mig ñid kyis //
'dzin par ci yi phyir mi 'gyur // **(k.308cde)**[4]

§37. gzugs kyi rgyu yaṅ gzugs las tha mi dad pa'i phyir mig gi dbaṅ pos rgyu daṅ 'bras bu gñis ka yaṅ 'dzin par 'gyur na 'di ni[5] srid pa yaṅ[6] ma yin te / dbaṅ po tha dad pa'i yul yin pa'i phyir daṅ / mtshan ñid tha dad pa'i phyir ro // de ñid bstan pa'i phyir bśad pa /

sa ni brtan[7] źes bya bar mthoṅ //
de yaṅ lus kyis 'dzin par 'gyur // **(k.309ab)**

---

[1] DC bar: PNB ba.

[2] DC gzuṅ: PNB bzuṅ. Ibidem for other occurrences of gzuṅ (bar) bya.

[3] PDCN rag: B dag.

[4] Note that this verse has five lines.

[5] B mi.

[6] DC yaṅ: PNB omit.

[7] DCD$_k$C$_k$BLS brtan: PNP$_k$N$_k$V bstan.

§38. 'dzin pa'i las **[D.200b]** kyis[1] rten gyi dṅos por gnas pa'i phyir rten ñid yin pas brtan pa ñid kyis na

sa ni brtan pa źes bya bar mthoṅ la /
de yaṅ lus kyis 'dzin te /

de'i sra ba lus kyi dbaṅ po'i gzuṅ bya yin pa'i phyir ro // gaṅ gi phyir 'di de ltar yin pa /

des na reg[2] pa 'ba' źig[3] 'di[4] //
sa'o źes ni bya bar brjod[5] // **(k.309cd)**

§39. gzugs kyi skye mched ni mig gi **[C.197b]** dbaṅ po'i gzuṅ bar bya ba'o // de'i phyir de ltar na rgyu daṅ 'bras bu gñis tha mi dad pa med de / mtshan ñid tha dad pa'i phyir daṅ / 'dzin par byed pa tha dad pa'i phyir ro //

§40. tha dad pa yod na yaṅ rgyu med pa'i[6] smra bar 'gyur ro // de ñid daṅ gźan ñid daṅ bral ba'i dṅos po 'di 'ga' źig la raṅ gi **[P.227a]** ṅo bos yod pa ñid du rtog[7] par rigs pa yaṅ ma yin te / de'i phyir gzugs kyi rgyu yod pa ma yin no // gzugs kyi rgyu med na yaṅ gzugs raṅ gi ṅo bos yod pa ma yin no źes bya bar grub bo // de ñid kyi phyir bcom ldan 'das kyis /

---

[1] PDCN kyis: B kyi.

[2] D_kS rag.

[3] $PNP_kD_kC_kN_k$BVLS 'ba' źig: DC 'ga' źig.

[4] PDCNB 'di: $P_kD_kC_kN_k$VLS ni.

[5] D brjed.

[6] PNB rgyu med pa'i: DC rgyu med pa par.

[7] B rtog: PDCN rtag.

bya ba ñid 'di yoṅs su brtags nas don blta bar bya ba'i raṅ gi ṅo bo'am / blta bar bya ba ma yin pa'i raṅ gi ṅo bo źig **[D.201a]** la rtog / re źig gal te blta bar bya ba'i raṅ gi ṅo bo la yin na de'i tshe de brtags pas ci źig bya / gaṅ gi don yoṅs su rtog pa de ni med par yaṅ yod pa ñid pas brtag[1] par mi rigs so //

§43. ci ste blta bar bya ba ma yin par gyur pa la blta bar bya ba ñid rtog na de[2] yaṅ **[C.198a]** mi rigs te **[P.227b]** lus can ma yin pa rnams kyaṅ blta bar bya ba ñid du thal ba'i phyir daṅ / blta bar bya ba ñid skyes pa med pa la 'gal ba'i phyir ro[3] //

§44. blta bar bya ba ñid skyes[4] pa med pa

des na blta bya ñid skye ba ltar

te / ji ltar blta bar bya ba ma yin pa'i[5] bum pa la rnam pa thams cad du blta bar bya ba ñid mi rigs pas skye ba mi srid pa de bźin du blta bar bya bar ma gyur pa'i bum pa yod pa'i ṅo bor yaṅ yod pa ma yin[6] la / yod pa yaṅ[7] ma yin pa'i bum pa la ni blta bar bya ba ñid brtag[8] par rigs pa yaṅ ma yin pas 'di ni mi rigs so //

§45. 'dir smras pa / yul gzugs la sogs pa mṅon sum dag ni yod pa kho na ste (/) de'i 'dzin par byed pa mig la sogs pa'i dbaṅ po yod pa'i phyir ro // yod par gyur pa'i[9] dbaṅ po 'di rnams ni gdon mi za bar raṅ gi yul la[10] 'jug par 'gyur dgos la / gaṅ du de rnams 'jug pa srid pa gzugs la sogs **[N.222b]** pa don de dag ni mṅon sum yin no //

---

[1] PDCN brtag: B brtags.

[2] PNB de: DC omit.

[3] B blta bar bya ba ñid skyes pa [blta bar bya ba ñid] med pa la 'gal ba'i phyir ro /. The addition seems unnecessary.

[4] DC skyes: PNB skye.

[5] DC blta bar bya ba ma yin pa'i: PNB blta bar bya ba daṅ blta bar bya ba ma yin pa'i.

[6] =k. 310d with some minor changes. B yod pa'i ṅo bo'aṅ yod pa ma yin.

[7] DC yaṅ: PNB omit.

[8] PDC brtag par: N la rtag par; B rtog par.

[9] PDC gyur pa'i: N gyur; B gyur pa.

[10] DC la: PNB omit.

§46. bśad par bya ste / gal te dbaṅ po rnams kyi[1] yoṅs su gcod par nus par 'gyur na ni gzugs la sogs pa'i don dag tu 'gyur ba źig na / 'gyur ba ñid kyaṅ ma yin no // ji ltar źe na / 'di na mig la sogs pa lṅa po ni spyir 'byuṅ ba las gyur pa ñid du ñe bar ston la / de rnams kyi bya ba ni yul tha dad pas tha dad pa źig go // 'di ltar mig gis gzugs kho na mthoṅ gi sgra mi thos la / rna bas kyaṅ sgra thos kyi[2] gzugs mi mthoṅ ṅo //

§47. gaṅ gi tshe de ltar /
mig ni 'byun 'gyur[3] rna[4] de bźin //
mig gis mthoṅ gi[5] gźan gyis min **(k.311ab)**

pa[6] de'i tshe 'thad pa daṅ 'gal ba'i bya ba mi[7] srid pa'i phyir mig la sogs pa rnams kyi raṅ gi ṅo bo rtog pa ga la yod / 'byuṅ ba las gyur pa ñid du mtshuṅs bźin du yul **[P.228a]** 'dzin pa tha dad pa brtag par ni mi rigs so // **[D.201b]** mig la sogs pa rnams kyi[8] yod pa ñid ni yul 'dzin pa las rjes su dpag[9] pa yin na de yaṅ 'gal bas mi[10] srid de (/) de'i phyir dbaṅ po yod pas yul rnams mṅon sum ñid du mi rigs so //

§48. gal te de ltar mig la **[C.198b]** sogs pa rnams mi srid na / de'i phyir ji ltar mig la sogs pa'i dbaṅ po 'di rnams las kyi rnam par smin pa'i ṅo bor rnam par gźag[11] ce na / ci kho bo cag gis 'di rnams kyi rnam par smin pa'i ṅo bo ñid bkag gam /

---

[1] PNB kyi: DC kyis.

[2] DCB kyi: PN kyis.

[3] D_kC_kBS gyur.

[4] PDCNVBL rna: $D_kC_kP_kN_k$S sna. Candrakīrti comments on rna.

[5] DCD_kC_kBLS gi: PNP_kN_kV gis.

[6] DC pa: PNB omit.

[7] DC mi: PNB omit.

[8] DCB kyi: PN kyis.

[9] PNB dpag: DC dpog.

[10] PNB mi: D ri; C ma.

[11] PNB bźag.

gal te mig la sogs pa rnams 'gog par sgrub pas de ji ltar ma bkag ce na / kho bo cag gi[1] rnam par dpyod pa don raṅ bźin tshol ba lhur byed pa ñid kyi phyir ro // kho bo cag ni 'dir dṅos po rnams raṅ gi ṅo bos grub pa 'gog gi[2] mig la sogs pa byas śiṅ rten ciṅ 'brel bar 'byuṅ ba'i las kyi rnam par smin pa ñid ni mi 'gog pa'o //° de'i phyir de yod pas gaṅ źig rnam par smin pa ñid du bsñad pas[3] mig la sogs pa yod pa ñid do //

§49. gal te de ltar na yaṅ /
mig ni 'byuṅ 'gyur rna de bźin //
mig gis mthoṅ gi[4] gźan gyis min //

źes bya ba'i ñes pa de ñid du 'gyur ba ma yin nam źe na /**[N.223a]**

§50. ñes pa 'di ni med de / las rnams[5] kyi rnam par smin pa bsam gyis mi khyab pa'i phyir ro // las rnams kyi rnam par smin pa ni rigs pa bcug nas bsam par bya bar mi nus te / re źig[6] las de ñid raṅ gi ṅo bos ma[7] grub pa'i phyir ro //[8] gal te de raṅ gi ṅo bos grub par gyur na ni de'i tshe dus thams cad du rnam par mi 'chad par 'gyur źiṅ rnam par smin pa byuṅ[9] zin pa las kyaṅ slar rnam par smin par 'gyur ba'am yaṅ na rnam par smin par mi 'gyur ba ñid de / raṅ bźin gźan ñid du bsgyur bar **[P.228b]** mi nus pa'i phyir ro //

§51. las kyi 'bras bu[10] mthoṅ ba med pa yaṅ ma yin no // de'i phyir mkhas pas 'jig rten pa'i don la ji skad bśad pa'i rnam par dpyad pa de kho na ñid[11] mthoṅ ba daṅ rjes su mthun pa ma bcug par las rnams kyi rnam par smin pa bsam gyis mi khyab

---

[1] B ni.

[2] PDCN gi: B gis.

[3] PDC bsñad pas: N bsñed pas.

[4] DC gi: PN gis.

[5] DC rnams: PN omit.

[6] DC re źig: PN re śig.

[7] DC ma: PN omit.

[8] DC phyir ro //: PN phyir.

[9] DC byuṅ: PN phyuṅ.

[10] PDC 'bras bu: N 'bras bus.

[11] PDC de kho na ñid: N de po na ñid.

pa ñid du khas blaṅs te sprul pa las sprul pa 'byuṅ ba'i tshul du 'jig rten pa thams cad khas blaṅ bar bya'o //

* **§52.** mthoṅ ba la ni bsñon[1] **[D.202a]** par mi nus la / *gaṅ mig 'byuṅ ba las gyur pa yin yaṅ gzugs kho na mthoṅ gi sgra mi thos so[2] źes bya ba la sogs 'di ni mthoṅ ba yaṅ yin no // gaṅ gi phyir 'di de ltar yin pa /

des na ṅes par las rnam smin //
thub **[C.199a]** *pas*[3] *bsam mi khyab*[4] *par gsuṅs //* **(k.311cd)**

§53. dṅos po raṅ bźin med pa rnams kyaṅ bya ba'i 'bras bu ṅes pa'i phyir

° bcom ldan 'das kyis /°

sems can las kyi rnam smin bsam yas pas //
rluṅ las 'jig rten 'di kun 'byuṅ 'gyur te //
mtsho daṅ ri daṅ lha yi gźal med khaṅ //
rin po ches phye sa bon bkram rnams so //

rluṅ las byuṅ ba'i sprin gyis[5] char 'bebs śiṅ //
slar yaṅ rluṅ gis[6] sprin ni rab tu 'jil //
rluṅ las 'jig ten lo tog rgyas 'gyur te //
rluṅ gis 'gro ba kun la bde ba 'dren //[7]

źes bya ba daṅ / de bźin du /

---

[1] PDC bsñon: N bsñom.

[2] B omits so.

[3] $P_kD_kC_kN_k$VLS thub pas: PDCNB thub pa.

[4] B kyab.

[5] DC gyis: PN gyi.

[6] DC gis: PN gi.

[7] Both verses unidentified.

gaṅ dag srid par gyur[1] yaṅ srid pa'i skyon las grol ba rnams //
stoṅ par smra źiṅ las kyi 'bras bu'aṅ 'dor mi 'gyur //
gaṅ dag **[N.223b]** śes pas dri ma bsregs kyaṅ brtse brlan pa //
spyod pa bdag[2] med dbaṅ bsgyur de dag kyaṅ dkris 'gyur //[3]

* źes *las rnams kyi 'bras bu rnam par smin pa bsam gyis mi khyab par gsuṅs so //

§54. 'dir smras pa / mig la sogs pa ni raṅ bźin gyis yod pa ñid de / de'i 'bras bu rnam par śes pa mthoṅ ba'i phyir ro // **[P.229a]** bśad par bya ste / gal te de'i 'bras bu rnam par śes pa ñid yod na ni mig la sogs pa yod par 'gyur na srid pa ni ma yin no // ji lta źe na / de la re źig /

rkyen ma tshaṅ[4] *phyir śes pa ni //*
lta[5] *ba'i sṅa rol yod ma yin //*
'on te phyis na[6] *śes don med //*
gsum par[7] *byed pa don med 'gyur //* **(k.312)**

§55. re źig lta ba'i sṅa rol du ni mig gi rnam par śes pa yod pa ma yin no // mig gi lta ba bdag po'i rkyen ma tshaṅ ba'i phyir ro // ci ste lta ba'i 'og rol du rtog na ni de'i tshe śes pa don med de[8] / gal te rnam par śes pa med pa'i mig gis gzugs mthoṅ na ni 'o na rnam par śes pa yoṅs su rtog pa don med do //

---

[1] DC gyur: PN rgyu.

[2] DC bdag: PN rtag.

[3] Unidentified.

[4] V rgyen ma tshad.

[5] P_kN_kV blta.

[6] C ni.

[7] PDCN gsum par: $P_kD_kC_kN_k$VBLS gsum pa. CSV seems to support gsum par.

[8] DC de: PNB te.

§56. gsum par[1] byed pa don med 'gyur

te (/) rtog pa gsum pa ni lta ba daṅ śes pa gñis cig car 'byuṅ ba ste / de la rgyu **[D.202b]** don[2] med do // 'di lta bas na lta ba ste byed pa de don med par 'gyur ro // lta ba daṅ śes pa gñis cig car yod na ni rnam par śes pa **[C.199b]** gaṅ źig lta ba daṅ dus mtshuṅs pa la[3] de lta ba la rag las te 'byuṅ bar mi rigs so // ba laṅ gi rwa g.yas g.yon lhan cig 'byuṅ ba dag la ni cig śos[4] cig śos la rag las te skye ba ñid mi srid de / de bźin du lta ba daṅ lhan cig 'byuṅ ba'i rnam par śes pa lta ba la[5] rag las te skye
° ba ñid du mi 'gyur bas lta ba don med pa kho nar 'gyur ro //°

§57. ci ste sgron ma daṅ 'od bźin du dus mñam pa dag yin yaṅ lta ba la rag las te gnas pa ñid du 'gyur ro sñam du sems na / de yaṅ yod pa ma yin te / der yaṅ brgal źiṅ brtag pa mtshuṅs pa'i phyir ro // 'jig rten pa'i mthoṅ bas de kho na ñid mthoṅ ba gsal bar rigs pa yaṅ ma yin te / de ni 'jig **[N.224a]** rten pa kho na las tshad ma ñid yin pa'i phyir daṅ / des dmigs pa'i don yaṅ brdzun pa bslu ba'i **[P.229b]** chos
* can ñid du sgrub pa'i phyir ro // *gaṅ gi tshe de ltar rnam par śes pa mi srid pa de'i tshe de yod pas mig la sogs pa rnams yod pa ñid du[6] brtag pa gaṅ yin pa de ni[7] mi rigs so //[8]

§58. 'dir smras pa / mig ni byed pa'i ṅo bo[9] ma yin pa kho na ste / 'o na ci źe na / byed pa po ñid do // de byed pa po'i dṅos por[10] khas blaṅs pa'i phyir /

---

[1] DC gsum par: PNB gsum pa. Note that when k.312d is cited again below in **§58**, PN have gsum par.

[2] PDC de la rgyu don med do: N de la rgyu daṅ med do; B's manuscript was illegible. He leaves out the words ste, rgyu and don.

[3] PNB la: DC omit.

[4] PNB cig śos: DC omit.

[5] DC la: PNB las.

[6] PN yod pa ñid du: DC yod par; B yod.

[7] PNB omit ni.

[8] For the subsequent passages of B's text see his n. 5.

[9] PNB ṅo bo: DC ṅo bor.

[10] Ego byed pa po ñid do // de byed pa po'i dṅos por: PNB byed pa po ñid de de byed pa po'i dṇos por: DC byed pa po ñid do // byed pa po dṅos por.

gsum par byed pa don med 'gyur //
źes gaṅ smras pa de ni mi rigs so //

§59. de ltar brtags na yaṅ mig lta ba'i bya ba daṅ bral ba ñid du 'gyur ro // ji ltar[1] źe na / **[#]** gal te mig gis° gzugs de[2] lta ba na yul gyi yul du soṅ nas sam ma soṅ bar lta graṅ na / gñi ga ltar yaṅ[3] skyon du 'gyur ro źes bstan pa'i phyir bśad pa /

mig de 'gros daṅ ldan 'gyur[4] *na //*
thag riṅ[5] *yun riṅ gis mthoṅ 'gyur //*
ha çaṅ ñe daṅ ches riṅ du //
gzugs de gsal ba[6] *ci ste min //* **(k.313)**

§60. gal te mig phrad nas[7] 'dzin pa'i phyir yul gyi yul du 'gro na ni de'i tshe phye ba tsam gyis zla ba daṅ skar ma la sogs pa'i don dag 'dzin par mi 'gyur ro // 'gro ba'i dus tha dad pa'i phyir na **[##]** 'gro ba daṅ ldan pa'i don gyis[8] yul ñe bar 'dzin pa **[#]** daṅ / dus mñam par yul thag riṅ bar 'dzin **[D.203a]** pa ni mi rigs na / phye ba tsam gyis mig gis thag riṅ ba na gnas pa yaṅ ñe ba na gnas pa[9] ltar mthoṅ ba yaṅ yin pas 'di ni mi rigs so // **[C.200a]**

---

[1] PNB ltar: DC lta.

[2] DC gzugs de: PN omit.

[3] PDC yaṅ: N omits.

[4] D_kC_kS gyur.

[5] PN riṅs.

[6] PDCNB gsal ba: $P_kD_kC_kN_k$VLS gsal bar.

[7] PN nas: DC na.

[8] PDCN gyis: B (n.5) gyi.

[9] DC yaṅ ñe ba na gnas pa: PN omit.

§59. ...[HPS.499][yadi cakṣus][1] tad[2] rūpaṃ paśyed viṣayadeśaṃ vā gatvā paśyed agatvā vā ubhayathā ca doṣa iti pratipādayann āha /

paśyec cakṣuś cirād dūre gatimad yadi tad bhavet /
atyabhyāse[3] ca dūre ca rūpam vyaktaṃ na tac ca kim // **(k.313)**

§60. yadi cakṣuṣaḥ[4] prāptakāritvād viṣayadeśaṃ gacchet tadonmiṣitamātreṇa na candratārakādīn arthān gṛhṇīyāt / [na...][5] tulyakālaṃ ca[6] viprakṛṣṭaviṣayagrahaṇaṃ yuktaṃ[7] gatikālasya bhinnatvāt / paśyati ca cakṣur unmiṣitamātreṇa samīpasthavat vidūradeśastham apīty ayuktam etat /

---

[1] Restitution in B. HPS: °sthaḥ paśyet makes no sense; I omit it. Cf. Tib gal te mig gis.

[2] HPS tad: B omits. Cf. Tib gzugs de.

[3] L atyabhāśe.

[4] HPS cakṣuṣaḥ: B cakṣuḥ.

[5] Nine syllable lacuna in HPS, but the manuscript suggests a longer lacuna. B reconstructs: gatimato 'rthadeśopagrahaṇaṃ. But this seems unlikely in virtue of Tib: 'gro ba daṅ ldan pa'i don gyis yul ñe bar 'dzin pa daṅ / dus mñam par yul thag riṅ bar 'dzin pa ni mi rigs na /. Note that B in his n. 5 changed *don gyis* to *don gyi*, which changes the sense. We should perhaps read something like: na gatimato 'rthasya saṃnihitaviṣayagrahaṇaṃ...

[6] HPS omits ca; B places it after °viṣayagrahaṇaṃ. Cf. Tib daṅ.

[7] Ego °grahaṇaṃ yuktaṃ: HPS °grahaṇayuktaṃ; B °grahaṇaṃ cāyuktaṃ. Cf. Tib in n. 5 above.

gal te yaṅ mig phrad nas 'dzin par 'gyur na ni de'i tshe ha caṅ ñe bar yaṅ mig la gnas pa'i mig sman nam thur ma mthoṅ bar 'gyur la / thag riṅ por yaṅ gsal bar mthoṅ bar 'gyur na / 'di ni srid pa yaṅ ma yin pas 'di ni[1] mi rigs so //

§61. gźan yaṅ gal te mig gis phyin nas gzugs mthoṅ na / de[2] ci ste mthoṅ nas de'i yul du 'gro 'am 'on te ma mthoṅ ba yin / de las cir 'gyur / gñi ga ltar yaṅ skyon du 'gyur ro **[P.230a]** źes **[N.224b]** bśad pa /

gal te gzugs mthoṅ[3] mig 'gro na //
soṅ·bas yon tan 'ga' yaṅ med //
yaṅ na blta byar 'dod pa[4] ni //
ṅes śes bya ba[5] brdzun[6] par 'gyur // **(k.314)**

§62. gal te gzugs mthoṅ nas gzugs kyi yul du mig 'gro'o[7] sñam du rtog[8] na ni 'gro ba ste doṅ bas mig la dgos pa ci yaṅ med do // mig 'gro ba ni yul blta bar bya ba'i phyir yin na / de yul de yaṅ[9] sṅa ñid du 'di na gnas pa mthoṅ bas 'gro ba la dgos pa ci yaṅ med do // ci ste ma mthoṅ bar 'gro na ni de'i tshe blta[10] bar 'dod pa'i yul ṅes par mthoṅ bar mi 'gyur ro // ma mthoṅ bar mṅon par ma rtogs pa'i yul du 'gro ba'i phyir loṅ ba ltar blta bar bya ba'i yul ṅes par mthoṅ bar[11] mi 'gyur ro //

---

[1] PN ni: DC omit.

[2] DC de: PN omit.

[3] P_kN_k maṅ.

[4] PN par.

[5] $P_kD_kC_kN_k$VS ṅes źes bya ba: LB ṅes śes bya ba; PN 'dod ces bya ba; DC ṅes par bya ba.

[6] PDCND_kC_kBLS brdzun: P_kN_kV brjod.

[7] PN 'gro'o: DC 'gro.

[8] PN rtog: DC rtogs.

[9] DC yaṅ: PN omit.

[10] DC blta: PN lta.

[11] DC bar: PN ba.

yadi ca prāptakāri cakṣuḥ syāt tadātyabhyāse 'pi paśyed akṣistham añjanaṃ śalākāṃ va dūre ca vyaktadarśanaṃ syāt na caitat sambhavatīty ayuktam etat /

§61. api ca yadi cakṣur gatvā viṣayaṃ[2] paśyati tat kiṃ viṣayaṃ dṛṣṭvā viṣaya-deśaṃ gacchaty[3] utādṛṣṭvā / ubhayathāpi doṣa iti pratipādayann āha /

gatena na guṇaḥ kaścid rūpaṃ dṛṣṭvākṣi yāti cet /
draṣṭavyaṃ niyameneṣṭam iti vā jāyate vṛthā // **(k.314)**

§62. yadi rūpaṃ dṛṣṭvā rūpadeśaṃ cakṣur yātīti kalpyate gatena tena gamanena cakṣuṣo na kiṃcit prayojanam / viṣayadarśanārthaṃ hi[4] cakṣuṣo gamanaṃ (/) sa ca viṣayaḥ pūrvam evehasthena dṛṣṭa iti na kiṃcid gamanasya prayojanam / athādṛṣṭvā gacchati tadā didṛkṣitaviṣayadarśanaṃ niyamena na prāpnoti / adṛṣṭvā hy andhasyevānabhilakṣitadeśagamanād draṣṭavyasya niyamena darśanaṃ na prāpnoti /

---

[1] HPS akṣisthām añjanaśalākāṃ vā; B omits vā. (HPS adds the long *a* in akṣisthām in square brackets.) But see Tib which justifies the *vā*: mig la gnas pa'i mig sman *nam* thur ma.

[2] HPS viṣayaṃ: B rūpaṃ.

[3] B tat kiṃ dṛṣṭvā taddeśaṃ gacchaty on the basis of Tib.

[4] HPS hi: B omits.

§63. ci ste skyon 'di spaṅ bar 'dod nas gal te /
mig ma soṅ bar 'dzin na ni //
'gro ba 'di kun mthoṅ 'gyur te //
gaṅ la 'gro ba yod min pa //
de la riṅ[1] *med bsgribs*[2] *pa'aṅ med //* **(k.315)**

§64. gaṅ źig mig daṅ yid daṅ rna ba ni yul daṅ ma phrad pa yin no źes bya ba'i luṅ las ni mig gi yul daṅ ma phrad pa kho na'o sñam du sems pa de la brjod par bya ste / re źig luṅ daṅ 'gal ba ni med de phrad nas 'dzin pa ñid tsam źig 'gog pa lhur byed pa'i phyir ro // 'ga' źig tu ni[3] sgrub pa gtso bo ñid yin te gaṅ du de mi 'gal ba'o // la lar ni dgag pa gtso bo ñid yin te gaṅ du de mi 'gal ba'o // de'i phyir 'di la rnam par **[D.203b]** dpyad pa srid pas[4] phrad nas 'dzin pa ñid bkag pa tsam gyis yul daṅ mi phrad pa ñid du rnam par gźag[5] ste /

§65. sgrub pa'i sgo nas yul daṅ ma phrad pa ñid du rtog na ni 'di na gnas pa'i mig kho nas 'gro **[C.200b]** ba thams cad mthoṅ bar 'gyur ro // 'di ltar gaṅ la 'gro ba yod pa ma yin pa de la thag riṅ ba ga la yod de 'dis ni ñe ba na gnas pa'i don **[P.230b]** yaṅ ma soṅ bar blta bar bya ba yin la / thag riṅ ba na gnas pa yaṅ yin pas / thag riṅ bar byas pa'i khyad par du mi 'gyur ro // gaṅ gi tshe ma soṅ **[N.225a]** bar mthoṅ ba de'i tshe 'di na gnas pa bźin thag riṅ po na gnas pa yaṅ mthoṅ bar 'gyur la / **[##]**
de bźin du bsgribs pa[6] yaṅ mthoṅ bar 'gyur ro // **[#]**

---

[1] V 'di.

[2] $D_k C_k$BS bsgribs: PDCN sgrib; $P_k N_k$VL bsgrib. CSV comments on bsgribs.

[3] PN omit ni.

[4] Note that Tib differs considerably from Skt; PDCN rnam par dpyad pa srid pas (= vicārasya saṃbhavāt). Cf. Skt vidher asaṃbhavāt.

[5] DC gźag: PN bźag.

[6] DC pa: PN omit.

§63. athaitaddoṣaparijihīrṣayā[1] yadi

gṛhṇīyād agataṃ cakṣuḥ paśyet sarvam idaṃ jagat /

yasya nāsti gatis tasya nāsti dūraṃ na cāvṛtam // **(k.315)**

§64. yo hi manyate cakṣuḥśrotramano 'prāptaviṣayam ity[2] āgamād aprāptaviṣayam eva cakṣur iti taṃ praty ucyate / prāptakāritāmātrapratiṣedhaparatvād āgamasya tāvad avirodhaḥ / kvacid vidheḥ prādhānyaṃ yatra tasyāvirodhaḥ / kvacit pratiṣedhasya prādhānyaṃ yatra tadavirodhaḥ[3] / tad atra vidher asaṃbhavāt prāptakāritāpratiṣedhamātreṇāprāptaviṣayatvaṃ vyavasthāpyate /

§65. vidhimukhena tv aprāptaviṣayatve kalpyamāna ihastham eva cakṣuḥ sarvaṃ jagat paśyet / yasya hi gatir nāsti tasya kuto dūram / samīpastho 'pi hy anenārtho 'gatvā draṣṭavyo vidūrastho[4] 'pīti dūrakṛto 'pi viśeṣo na syāt / yadā cāgatvā paśyati tadehastham[5] iva vidūram[6] api paśyet / ...

---

[1] B °parijihīrṣayā: HPS °parirjihīrṣayā.

[2] Ego cakṣuḥśrotramano 'prāptaviṣayam: HPS cakṣuḥ śrotramano; B cakṣuḥ śrotraṃ mano. Cf. the text of AK i k. 43cd (ed. Pradhan), the first part of which is being quoted here: cakṣuḥśrotramano 'prāptaviṣayaṃ trayam anyathā. Note that Bhattacharya and Lang both reproduce LVP's inaccurate restitution of AK i 43cd.

[3] B tadavirodhaḥ; HPS tadvirodhaḥ. Cf. Tib de *mi* 'gal ba'o.

[4] B vidūrastho: HPS vidūrasthe.

[5] B tadehastham: HPS tad ihastham. Cf. Tib de'i tshe.

[6] HPS vidūram: B vidūrastham.

'gro ba yod na ni bsgribs pas de[1] bcom pa'i phyir bsgribs pa mi mthoṅ ṅo źes bya bar rigs na / gaṅ gi tshe ma soṅ bar blta bar bya ba yin pa de'i tshe ni bsgribs pa la yaṅ 'gro ba'i gegs med pas ma bsgribs pa bźin mthoṅ bar 'gyur ro //

§66. yaṅ gal te mig lta ba'i raṅ bźin du 'gyur na ni de'i tshe thams cad du raṅ bźin mi ñams pa'i phyir raṅ gi ṅo bo la yaṅ blta bar 'gyur ro // 'di ltar 'jig rten na /

dṅos po kun gyi raṅ bźin ni[2] //
daṅ por bdag la snaṅ 'gyur na //
mig ni mig ñid kyis 'dzin par[3] //
gaṅ źig gis ni[4] *'gyur ma yin* // **(k.316)**

§67. gal te ji ltar me tog tsam pa ka daṅ ut pa la la sogs pa dag gi dri bsuṅ[5] daṅ por raṅ gi rten ñid la dmigs te / phyis de dag phrad pa las til la sogs pa dag la yaṅ yin pa daṅ / yaṅ ji ltar raṅ la gnas pa'i me'i tsha ba de daṅ 'brel pa las gźan gyi bdag ñid la dmigs pa de bźin du[6] mig lta ba'i raṅ bźin du gyur na ni de'i tshe de[7] raṅ gi bdag ñid kho na la lta bar 'gyur te / ci'i phyir mig mig ñid kyis 'dzin par mi 'gyur / dṅos po rnams kyi raṅ bźin yaṅ ches daṅ por raṅ gi[8] bdag ñid la yod pa'i phyir mig kho nas mig 'dzin par rigs na mig ni raṅ gi bdag ñid la blta ba yaṅ ma yin pas boṅ ba[9] la sogs pa ltar gźan la lta ba yaṅ ma yin pas de la mi srid do //

---

[1] DC de: PN omit.

[2] P omits ni.

[3] DC 'dzin pa.

[4] PDCN gaṅ źig gis ni: $P_kD_kC_kN_k$BVLS ci yi phyir na.

[5] DCN bsuṅ: P bsruṅ.

[6] DC du: PN omit.

[7] DC de: PN omit.

[8] DC raṅ gi: PN raṅ ñid kyi.

[9] PDCN boṅ ba = sa rdog gi miṅ (*Zidian* p. 526), i.e. Skt. loṣṭa. B's note 6 on p. 189 about boṅ bu la sogs = kharādi is due to confusion.

gatau hi satyāṃ āvṛte gativighātād āvṛtaṃ nekṣata iti yuktam / yadā tv agatvā draṣṭavyaṃ tadāvṛte gatipratibandhābhāvād anāvṛta iva darśanaṃ syāt /

§66. yadi ca darśanasvabhāvaṃ cakṣuḥ syāt tadā svabhāvasya sarvatraivāvyāghātāt svarūpam api paśyet / tathā hi loke

svabhāvaḥ sarvabhāvānāṃ pūrvam ātmani dṛśyate /
grahaṇaṃ cakṣuṣaḥ kena cakṣuṣaiva na jāyate // **(k.316)**

§67. yathā campakamallikādiṣu saugandhyaṃ pūrvaṃ svāśraya evopalabhyate paścāt tatsamparkāt tailādiṣv api / yathā cāgner auṣṇyaṃ svato vyavasthitaṃ[1] tadyogāt parato 'py upalabhyate / evaṃ yadi cakṣuṣor darśanasvābhāvyaṃ[2] syāt tadā **[HPS.500]** svātmany eva tāvad darśanaṃ syāt / kasmāt punaś cakṣuṣo grahaṇaṃ cakṣuṣaiva na bhavati / bhāvānāṃ svabhāvasya ca svātmany eva prathamataraṃ vidyamānatvāc cakṣuṣaiva cakṣuṣo grahaṇaṃ nyāyyam / na cakṣuḥ svātmānaṃ paśyatīti loṣṭādivat paradarśanam apy asya na saṃbhāvyate /

---

[1] HPS vyavasthitaṃ: B 'avasthitaṃ.

[2] Ego cakṣuṣor darśanasvābhāvyaṃ: HPS cakṣuṣor ddaśanasvābhāvyaṃ; B cakṣur darśanasvabhāvaṃ.

§68. gaṅ źig mig **[D.204a]** 'ba' źig la gzugs lta ba'i nus pa med kyi / 'on **[P.231a]** kyaṅ mig daṅ[1] gzugs daṅ mig gi rnam par śes pa gsum tshogs pa yod daṅ gzugs mthoṅ bar 'gyur ro sñam du sems pa de yaṅ sñiṅ po **[C.201a]** med de / gaṅ gi phyir /

mig la rnam śes[2] *yod min źiṅ //*
rnam par śes pa[3] *lta*[4] *med la //*
gñi ga gzugs la yod min na[5] *//*
de dag gis gzugs[6] *ji*[7] *ltar mthoṅ //* **(k.317)**

§69. de la re źig mig la rnam par śes pa med do / mig gis ni yul rnam par śes pa ma yin te / rnam par śes pa ma yin pa'i raṅ bźin yin pa'i phyir ro // mig ni 'byuṅ ba las gyur pa yin te / bems po yin pas de la yul rtog[8] pa mi srid do // de ltar na

mig la rnam par śes pa med do //

§70. rnam par śes pa la yaṅ mig med do // de ni gzugs can ma yin pa źig ste / de la lta ba ga la yod de med pas na loṅ ba ltar mi mthoṅ ṅo[9] // gzugs la ni gñi ga yaṅ yod pa ma yin no // rnam par śes pa ni ma yin te / rtog pa'i raṅ bźin ma yin pa'i phyir ro // lta ba yaṅ ma yin te lta ba ma yin pa'i bdag ñid can yin pa'i phyir ro // gaṅ gi tshe de ltar dbaṅ po daṅ yul daṅ rnam par śes pa rnams don phan tshun ma tshaṅ ba de'i tshe[10] de dag tshogs par yod kyaṅ de dag gis gzugs mthoṅ ba ma yin pa ñid de/ gzugs lta ba'i yan lag ma tshaṅ ba'i phyir loṅ ba'i tshogs bźin no sñam du dgoṅs so//

---

[1] PDC mig daṅ: N me gis.

[2] P rnam par śes.

[3] PDCNB rnam par śes pa: $P_kD_kC_kN_k$VLS rnam śes la yaṅ.

[4] P_kN_k blta.

[5] N_k no.

[6] P omits gzugs.

[7] P_kN_kV ci.

[8] PDCN rtog pa: B (n. 1) proposes rtogs pa.

[9] Cf. Skt, which differs. B (p. 189, n. 8) erroneously has soṅ ba instead of loṅ ba.

[10] DC de'i tshe (= Skt tadā): PN omit.

§68. yas tu manyate na kevalasya cakṣuṣo rūpadarśanasāmarthyam asti / api tu trayāṇāṃ cakṣūrūpacakṣurvijñānānāṃ sāmagryāṃ satyāṃ rūpadarśanaṃ bhavatīti / tad apy asāraṃ / yasmāt

cakṣuṣo 'sti na vijñānaṃ vijñānasya na darśanam /
ubhayaṃ nāsti rūpasya tai rūpaṃ dṛśyate katham // (k.317)

§69. cakṣuṣas tāvad vijñānaṃ nāsti / na hi cakṣur viṣayaṃ vijānāty[1] avijñānasvarūpatvāt / bhautikaṃ hi cakṣus tasya jaḍatvād viṣayabodho na saṃbhāvyata iti[2] evaṃ

cakṣuṣo 'sti na vijñānam /

§70. nāpi vijñānasya darśanam asti / vijñānaṃ hi vijānāti na tu paśyati / yadi tu vijñānaṃ paśyet tadā tasyāpi rūpadarśanaṃ syād vijñānasadbhāvāt /[3] rūpasya tūbhayam api nāsti / na vijñānam anavabodhasvarūpatvāt[4] / nāpi darśanaṃ rūpālocanābhāvāt / yadā caivam anyonyārthavikalānīndriyaviṣayavijñānāni[5] tadā tatsāmagryām ap satyām naiva tai rūpaṃ dṛśyata iti saṃbhāvayituṃ śakyam / rūpadarśanāṅgavikalatvā(andhasamudāyavad ity abhiprāyaḥ /

---

[1] HPS vijānāti: B jānāty. Cf. Tib rnam par śes pa.

[2] HPS iti: B omits.

[3] For vijñānaṃ hi...vijñānasadbhāvāt, Tib differs significantly. B p. 189 n. 8 restitutes Tib into Skt: na tad rūpavat / kutas tasya darśanam / tan nāstīti gatavan na paśyati /. Cf. Tib: de ni gzugs can ma yin pa źig ste / de la lta ba ga la yod de med pas na loṅ ba ltar mi mthoṅ ṅo.

[4] HPS avabodha°: B anavabodhasvarūpatvāt. Cf. Tib rtogs pa'i raṅ bźin *ma* yin pa'i phyir.

[5] HPS anyonyāthavakalānī°: B anyonyārthavikalānī°.

§71. gaṅ gi tshe de ltar gzugs la lta ba med pa de'i tshe de ñid rig pa[1] su źig gis gzugs mthoṅ ṅo źes bya bar brjod pa'am lta[2] bar 'os / ji ltar de kho na ñid rig[3] pas gzugs lta bar mi 'os pa de bźin du sgra yaṅ mñan par mi 'os te / gzugs lta ba bźin sgra ñan pa yaṅ med pa'i phyir ro //

§72. 'di ni gal te sgra thos na de ñan pa'i yul du phyin pa'am ma phyin pa źig thos graṅ na / gal te re źig phyin te thos na de ñan **[P.231b]** pa'i yul du 'gro ba na sgra 'byin źiṅ 'gro ba'am sgra med pa yin / de la[4] gal te rtog pa daṅ po yin na ni de'i tshe

gal te smra źiṅ sgra 'gro na //
gaṅ gis smra ba por mi **[D.204b]** *'gyur //*
'on te mi smra bar 'gro na'aṅ //
gaṅ gis de la śes pa skye[5] *//* **(k.318)**

§73. de'i phyir smra ba po yin pa'i phyir lhas byin[6] ltar sgrar mi 'gyur ro // ci ste mi smra bar **[C.201b]** 'gro na ni de'i tshe sgra med par 'gro ba'i sgra de la 'di ni sgra'o sñam du ṅes par su źig la 'gyur / ma bzuṅ ba de ni yod pa ñid kyaṅ ma yin pas 'di ni mi rigs so // **[N.226a]**

§74. gźan yaṅ /

---

[1] PN rig pa: DC rigs pa.

[2] PN blta.

[3] DC rig: PN rigs. Cf. Skt tattvavid.

[4] PN de la (= Skt tatra): DC de yaṅ.

[5] PDCNBL skye: P_kN_kV bskyed; D_kC_kS skyed.

[6] PN lhas byin: DC lha sbyin.

§71. yadā caivaṃ rūpasya darśanāsaṃbhavas[1] tadā ko nāmārhati tattvavid rūpaṃ dṛśyata iti vaktuṃ draṣṭuṃ vā / yathā ca tattvavin nārhati rūpaṃ draṣṭuṃ evaṃ śabdam api śrotuṃ nārhati rūpadarśanavac chabdaśravaṇasyāsaṃbhavāt /

§72. iha yadi śabdaḥ śrūyate sa śravaṇadeśaṃ saṃprāpto vā śrūyetāsaṃprāpto vā / yadi tāvat saṃprāptaḥ śrūyate sa śravaṇadeśaṃ vrajañ chabdaṃ vā[2] kurvāṇo vrajen[3] niḥśabdo vā / tatra yadi pūrvaḥ kalpas tadā

na vaktā jāyate kena śabdo yāti bruvan yadi /
atha yāty abruvaṃs tasmin pratyayaḥ kena jāyate[4] // **(k.318)**

§73. tataś ca vaktṛtvād devadattavac chabdo 'sau na bhavati/ athābruvan yāti tadā tasmiñ chabde niḥśabde vrajati śabdo 'yam iti kasyāvasāyo bhavet / na cāgṛhītasyāstitvam iti na yuktam etat /

§74. kiṃ cānyat /

---

[1] Ego rūpasya darśanāsaṃbhavas: HPS rūpasyādarśanāsambhavaḥ; B rūpasya darśanābhāvas.

[2] HPS vā: B omits.

[3] Ego vrajen (=optative): HPS vrajan; B vrajati.

[4] V pratyayo jāyate katham.

gal te phrad de[1] *sgra 'dzin na //*
sgra yi[2] *dan po gan gis 'dzin //*
sgra ni rkyan par[3] *mi 'on na //*
ren[4] *bu ji ltar 'dzin par 'gyur //* **(k.319)**

gal te rna ba'i dbaṅ po'i gnas su phyin pa'i sgra 'dzin na[5] 'o na ni

de'i daṅ po[6] gaṅ gis 'dzin /

phrad nas 'dzin pa'i phyir rna ba la ni sgra'i daṅ por 'dzin pa med la / de'i 'dzin par byed pa'i dbaṅ po gźan yaṅ yod pa ma yin pas 'di dbaṅ po[7] gaṅ gis kyaṅ mi 'dzin no // de'i phyir ma bzuṅ ba'i don de ni sgra ñid du mi 'gyur ro sñam du dgoṅs so //

§75. sgra'i rdul phra rab ni rdzas dgu'i bdag ñid yin pa'i phyir

sgra ni rkyaṅ par mi 'oṅ na /

khyod kyis ni sgra tsam źig kho na rna bas 'dzin gyi / dri la sogs pa dag ni ma yin no źes te mi rigs so // rnam pa gcig tu na sgra yaṅ mi 'dzin par 'gyur ba'am / yaṅ na dri la sogs pa dag kyaṅ zuṅ źig[8] / 'di ni de ltar na[9] yaṅ ma yin pas sgra phrad pa'i yul ñid ma yin no //

---

[1] PN te.

[2] C_k yis.

[3] $P_k D_k C_k N_k$LS rkyaṅ par: DCN rkyaṅ pa'aṅ; PB rkyaṅ ba'aṅ; V rgyad par. Note that below CSV again cites the verse, but with rkyaṅ par.

[4] B riṅ.

[5] PN 'dzin na ni.

[6] PN and B (p. 191, n. 1) daṅ po: DC dbaṅ po.

[7] PDCN all have 'di dbaṅ po, which is meaningful, but Skt (asyādiḥ) would correspond to 'di'i daṅ po.

[8] PN źig: DC śig.

[9] PN na: DC omit.

prāptaś ced gṛhyate śabdas tasyādiḥ kena gṛhyate /
na caiti kevalaḥ śabdo gṛhyate kevalaḥ katham // **(k.319)**

yadi śrotrendriyasthānaṃ prāptaḥ śabdo gṛhyate
[tasyādiḥ kena gṛhyate][1] /
prāptagrāhitvāc chrotrasya śabdasyāder grahaṇaṃ nāsti / na cānyad indriyaṃ tasya grāhakaṃ saṃbhavatīti naiva kena cid asyādir gṛhyate / tataś cāgṛhyamāṇatvāc chabda evāsau na bhavatīty abhiprāyaḥ /

§75. navadravyakatvāc ca śabdaparamāṇor
na caiti kevalaḥ śabdaḥ /
bhavatā ca śabdamātram eva śrotreṇa gṛhyate na gandhādaya iti na yujyate / yad vā śabdasyāgrahaṇam astu yad vā gandhādayo 'pi gṛhyantām / na caitad evam iti na prāptaviṣayatvaṃ śabdasya /

---

[1] Missing in HPS, but restituted by B. Cf. Tib de'i daṅ po gaṅ gis 'dzin.

§76. ci ste /

gal te phrad de sgra 'dzin na //

sgra yi daṅ po gaṅ gis 'dzin //

źes gaṅ smras na / gal te de'i daṅ po[1] ma bzuṅ na de'i tshe ñes pa ci źig yod ce na / gaṅ źig de'i sgra ñid ñams par 'gyur ba 'di ni ñes pa yin no // 'di ltar /

ji srid sgra thos ma gyur pa[2] //

de yi bar du sgrar mi 'gyur //

sgra med pa yaṅ mthar sgra ñid /**[P.232a]**/

'gyur na de ni mi rigs so // **(k.320)**

§77. gaṅ źig mi thos pa de ni thos bźin pa ma yin pa'i phyir dri la sogs pa ltar sgra ñid du mi 'gyur ro // ci ste gaṅ źig gi tshe thos pa de'i tshe sgrar 'gyur ro sñam du sems na // 'di yaṅ srid pa ma yin no[3] // dri la sogs pa phyis sgra ñid du mthoṅ ba ni ma yin te de bźin du sgra med pa 'di yaṅ phyis sgra ñid du mi rigs so //

§78.[##] bcom ldan 'das kyis /

yid du **[D.205a]** 'oṅ ba'i sgra gaṅ thos gyur pa //

de ni nam yaṅ naṅ du źugs pa med //

de yi 'pho ba rñed par mi 'gyur mod //

rtog[4] pa'i **[N.226b]** dbaṅ gis sgra ni 'byuṅ bar 'gyur /[5] **[C.202a]** /

źes bya ba daṅ / de bźin du /

---

[1] DC de'i daṅ po: PN de'i dbaṅ po.

[2] N_k gyur po; V gyur ba.

[3] DCN ma yin no: P ma ma yin no.

[4] DC rtog: PN rtogs.

[5] Cf. the Tib of the verse from the *Upālipariprcchā* in Python (1973) p. 57 and in Pr. May (1959) p. 330 :

yid du 'oṅ ba'i sgra grag gaṅ yin pa //
de yaṅ nam yaṅ naṅ du źugs pa med //
der* 'gro dmigs su yod pa ma yin te //
rtog pa'i dbaṅ gis sgra rnams byuṅ** ba yin //

*Pr. de; **Pr. 'byuṅ.

§76. atha yad etad uktaṃ

prāptaś ced gṛhyate śabdas tasyādiḥ kena gṛhyate /

iti yadi tasyādir na gṛhītas tadā ko doṣa iti / ayaṃ doṣo yad asya śabdatvam eva viśīryate / tathā hi /

yāvan na śrūyate śabdas tāvac chabdo na jāyate /
aśabdasyāpi śabdatvam ante tac ca na yujyate // **(k.320)**

§77. [HPS.501] yo na śrūyate so 'śrūyamāṇatvād gandhādivac chabda eva na bhavati / atha manyase yadā śrūyate tadā śabdo bhaviṣyatīti / etad apy asaṃbhāvyam / na hi gandhādeḥ paścāc chabdatvaṃ dṛṣṭaṃ tadvad evāsyāpy aśabdasya[1] paścāc chabdatvam ayuktam iti /

§78.

<yo 'pi ca śrūyati śabdu manojñaḥ
so 'pi ca nāntari jātu paviṣṭaḥ /
saṃkramaṇaṃ na ca labhyati tasya
kalpavaśāt tu samucchritu śabdaḥ //>[2]

---

[1] B tadvad evāsyāpy aśabdasya: HPS tadvadevāsyāpi śabdasya. Cf. Tib de bźin du sgra *med pa* 'di yaṅ.

[2] *Upāliparipṛcchā* quoted in Pr. 122.1-2. Python (1973) p. 58, §58.

dper na śiṅ daṅ rgyud la brten byas la[1] //
lag pas rtsol ba byas pa gsum tshogs na //
sgrogs byed pi waṅ gliṅ bu la sogs pa //
de dag las ni sgra yaṅ 'byuṅ bar 'gyur //

de nas mkhas pa la las brtag bya ste //
de ni gaṅ nas 'ons la gar soṅ źes //
phyogs daṅ phyogs mtshams kun tu brtag byas na //
sgra yi 'gro ba'am 'oṅ[2] ba mi dmigs so //

źes ji skad du gsuṅs pa lta bu'o //

§79.[#] de ltar re źig dbaṅ po rnams la yul 'dzin pa'i nus pa med par brjod nas yid la yaṅ yul de 'dzin pa'i nus pa med par brjod pa'i phyir bśad pa /

dbaṅ po rnams daṅ[3] bral sems kyis[4] //
soṅ ste'aṅ ci źig byed par 'gyur // **(k.321ab)**

§80. gal te sems yul gyi yul du soṅ nas yul yoṅs su gcod par byed do sñam du rtog na de ni mi rigs so // 'di ni[5] sems 'di dbaṅ po daṅ lhan cig pa źig yul gyi yul du 'gro ba'am / reṅ bu źig yin graṅ na / de la re źig dbaṅ po daṅ bcas pa ni mi 'gro ste / dbaṅ po rnams ni rtag tu lus kho na la ñe bar gnas pa'i phyir la 'gro ba yin na lus dbaṅ po med pa ñid du thal ba'i phyir ro //

§81. ci ste / reṅ bu 'gro na de'i tshe yaṅ /

dbaṅ po **[P.232b]** rnams daṅ bral sems kyis //
soṅ ste'aṅ ci źig byed par 'gyur //

mig la sogs pa dbaṅ po'i sgo spaṅs pa de la ni gzugs la sogs pa lta ba la sogs pa'i nus pa yod pa ma yin te / loṅ ba la sogs pa rnams la yaṅ lta ba la sogs pa yod par thal bar 'gyur ba'i phyir ro //

---

[1] PDN la: C na.

[2] DC 'oṇ: PN 'oṅs.

[3] PDCN$D_k C_k$BLS daṅ: $P_k N_k$V kyaṅ.

[4] PDCN$D_k C_k$BLS kyis: $P_k N_k$V kyi.

[5] DC ni: PN nas.

<yathā tantri pratītya dāru ca
hastavyāyāma trayebhi saṃgati /
tuṇavīṇasughoṣakādibhiḥ
śabdo niścarate tadudbhavaḥ //

atha paṇḍitu kaści mārgate
kutayaṃ āgatu kutra yāti vā /
vidiśo diśi sarvi mārgataḥ
śabdagamanāgamanaṃ na labhyate //>[1]

§79. evaṃ tāvad indriyāṇāṃ viṣayagrahaṇāsāmarthyam udbhāvya manaso 'pi viṣayagrahaṇāsāmarthyam udbhāvayann āha /

viyuktam indriyaiś cittaṃ kiṃ gatvāpi kariṣyati / **(k.321ab)**

§80. yadi cittaṃ viṣayadeśaṃ gatvā viṣayaṃ paricchinattīti kalpyate tad ayuktam / ihedaṃ cittam indriyasahitaṃ vā viṣayadeśaṃ gacchet kevalaṃ vā / na tāvad indriyasahitaṃ yāti / indriyāṇāṃ deha eva sadā saṃnidhānāt / gamane ca sati dehasya nirindriyatvaprasaṅgāt /

§81. atha kevalaṃ gacchati tadāpi

viyuktam indriyaiś cittaṃ kiṃ gatvāpi kariṣyati /

na hi cakṣurādīndriyadvāratiraskṛtasyāsya rūpādidarśanasāmarthyam asti / andhādīnām api darśanādisadbhāvaprasaṅgāt /

---

[1] *Lalitavistara* XIII, verses 114, 115. Ed. Vaidya pp. 127-128. A more reliable Tibetan transl. is quoted in M. av. bhāṣya to M. av. VI, 35: dper na śiṅ daṅ rgyud la brten byas la // lag pa rtsol ba byas pa gsum tshogs na // sgrog byed pi waṅ gliṅ bu la sogs las // de dag las skyes sgra yaṅ 'byuṅ bar 'gyur // de nas mkhas pa la las brtags byas te // de ni gaṅ nas 'oṅs la gar soṅ źes // phyogs daṅ phyogs mtshams kun tu brtags byas na // sgra yi 'oṅ ba'am 'gro ba rñed mi rgyur //.

§82. ci ste yaṅ ci źig ltar 'di la yaṅ yul gyi yul du 'gro bas don dmigs par rtog na de'i tshe na yaṅ[1] don rtogs pa mthar thug pa med pa'i phyir mi ldog par 'gyur ro[2] //

de ltar[3] yin daṅ srog 'di ni //
rtag tu yid med ci ste min // **(k.321cd)**

§83. dus thams cad du bdag sems[4] med pa kho nar 'gyur na / sems med pa ni bdag ñid du srid par rigs pa yaṅ ma yin te / ka ba daṅ bum pa **[D.205b]** la sogs pa **[N.227a]** rnams kyaṅ bdag ñid du thal bar 'gyur ba'i phyir ro // de'i phyir de ltar **[C.202b]** rigs pas rnam par dpyad pa na dbaṅ po daṅ yul daṅ rnam par śes pa rnams la yod pa'i ṅo bo med pas raṅ gi ṅo bos grub pa med do // gal te 'di rnams raṅ gi ṅos bos grub par 'gyur na ni de'i tshe 'thad pas rnam par dpyad pa rnams ches gsal bar[5] ji ltar gnas pa'i ṅo bos yod pa ñid du dmigs par 'gyur na dmigs pa yaṅ ma yin te de'i phyir raṅ bźin gyis stoṅ ṅo źes bya bar grub bo //

§84. gal te de rnams la raṅ bźin med na 'o na gaṅ źig bye brag rnam par gźag pa'i rgyu ñid du ston pa de rnams kyi khyad par yoṅs su gcod par byed pa'i bdag ñid can gyi 'du śes ko ji ltar źe na / brjod par bya ste / dṅos po rnams yod na ni / de rnams kyi bye brag yoṅs su gcod pa'i bdag ñid can gyi 'du śes rigs na / gaṅ gi tshe dṅos po de rnams yod pa ma yin pa ñid du bstan pa de'i tshe / de rnams kyi sgo nas 'du śes de raṅ gi ṅo bos grub par ga la 'gyur //

---

[1] DC yaṅ: PN omit. Cf. Skt tadāpy.

[2] Skt for don rtog pa...mi ldog par 'gyur rc differs from Tib.

[3] PDCNB ltar: $P_kD_kC_kN_k$VLS lta.

[4] DCN sems: P omits.

[5] DC gsal bar: PN gsal ba.

§82. athāpi kathaṃ cid viṣayadeśagamanenārthopalabdhir asya parikalpyate tadāpy aparyavasānatvād arthabodhasyānivṛttau satyāṃ[1]
evaṃ satīha jīvo 'yam amanaskaḥ sadā na kim // **(k.321cd)**

§83. acintaka evātmā sarvakālaṃ prāpnoti / na cācintakasyātmakatvaṃ[2] saṃbhāvayituṃ yuktam stambhādivad acintakatvāt[3] / tad evaṃ yuktyā vicāryamāṇānām indriya[viṣayavijñānānāṃ sadrūpā]saṃbhavāt[4] svarūpasiddhir asatī / yadi hy eṣāṃ svarūpasiddhiḥ syāt tadopapattyā vicāryamāṇā yathāsthitena svarūpeṇa sphuṭataram upalabhyeran / na copalabhyante / tasmāt svabhāvaśūnyā iti siddham /

§84. yadi tarhy eṣāṃ svabhāvo nāma nāsti tat katham eṣāṃ viśeṣaparicchedātmikā saṃjñā padārthaviśeṣavyavasthāhetutvenopadiśyate[5] / ucyate / satsu padārtheṣu tadviśeṣaparicchedātmikā saṃjñā syāt / yadā teṣāṃ ca[6] padārthānām asattvaṃ pra[tipādyate tadā taddvārā kutaḥ][7] svarūpasiddhiḥ syāt /

---

[1] HPS tadāpy aparyavasānatvād arthabodhasyānivṛttau satyām: B tadāpy arthabodhāparyavasānatvād anivṛttiḥ.

[2] HPS °ātmakatvaṃ: B °ātmatvaṃ.

[3] HPS stambhādivad acintakatvāt: B (based on Tib) stambhādīnām apy ātmatvaprasaṅgāt.

[4] Lacuna in HPS restored by B on the basis of Tib yul daṅ rnam pa śes pa rnams la yod pa'i ṅo bo.

[5] HPS padārtha°: B omits padārtha.

[6] Ego yadā teṣaṃ ca: HPS teṣāṃ ca; B yadā teṣāṃ. Cf. Tib gaṅ gi tshe.

[7] Lacuna of ten syllables in HPS restored by B on the basis of the Tib. which B (n.7) gives as bstan pa de'i tshe de rnams kyi sgo nas 'dug° ga la 'gyur. However, the restitution is quite doubtful, as the Tibetan reads bstan pa de'i tshe de rnams kyi sgo nas *'du śes* de raṅ gi ṅo bos grub par ga la 'gyur. We might therefore expect something like... pratipādyate tadā kutas taddvāreṇa tasyāḥ saṃjñāyāḥ svarūpasiddhiḥ syāt.

§85. gal te yul yoṅs su gcod pa 'di rnam pa thams cad du med dam źe **[P.233a]** na / med pa ma yin te / raṅ bźin med pa'i dṅos po[1] yod pa'i phyir ro // 'di ltar /

sṅar mthoṅ ba yi don gaṅ źig //
yid kyis smig rgyu ltar 'dzin pa //
de ni chos kun rnam gźag[2] la //
'du śes phuṅ po źes bya'o // **(k.322)**

§86. 'di ni mig daṅ gzugs la brten nas mig gi rnam par śes pa skyes nas 'gag pa na dbaṅ po daṅ yul rnams daṅ lhan cig 'gag par 'gyur ro // de 'gags na sṅar mthoṅ ba'i don gaṅ yin pa de ñid phyis yid kyis 'dzin to //

§87. yaṅ ji ltar ñe ba ma yin pa la 'dzin pa srid ce na / smig rgyu ltar źes bya ba smros te / smig rgyu la chu bag tsam kyaṅ med mod kyi / 'on kyaṅ rgyu daṅ rkyen gyi dbaṅ gis chu'i rnam pa can gyi 'du śes 'byuṅ ba ñid yin pa de bźin du smig rgyu la bya ba ltar yod pa ma yin pa'i raṅ bźin can gyi dṅos po bzuṅ[3] zin pa **[N.227b]** la yaṅ[4] gaṅ rnam par rtog pa can gyi rnam par śes pa[5] skye ba de ni chos thams cad rnam par 'jog pa'i rgyu yin no // chos thams **[D.206a]** cad rnam par 'jog pa'i rgyu ñid yin pa'i phyir na de ñid la 'du śes phuṅ po śes bsñad de / rnam pa de lta bu'i 'du śes kyi khyad par daṅ mtshuṅs par ldan pa'i **[C.203a]** phyir ro // chos thams cad kyi[6] rnam par gźag[7] pa yaṅ 'du śes kyi dbaṅ gis śes par bya ba'i dṅos po raṅ gi ṅo bo'i rgyu can ni ma yin te raṅ bźin rnam pa thams cad du mi ruṅ ba'i phyir ro //

---

[1] PN dṅos po: DC dṅos pos.

[2] PN rnams bźag; B rnam bźag.

[3] PN bzuṅ (= past): DC gzuṅ (= future).

[4] DC yaṅ: PN omit.

[5] DC gaṅ rnam par rtog pa can gyi rnam par śes pa: PN gaṅ rnam par śes pa.

[6] DC kyi: PN omit.

[7] PN bźag.

§85. kiṃ khalv eṣa viṣayaparicchedaḥ sarvathā nāsti / na nāstīti niḥsvabhāvasya bhāvasya vidyamānatvāt[1] / tathā hi

manasā gṛhyate yo 'rthaḥ pūrvadṛṣṭo marīcivat /
sarvadharmavyavasthāsu sa saṃjñāskandhasaṃjñakaḥ // (k.322)

§86. iha cakṣuḥ pratītya rūpaṃ ca cakṣurvijñānam utpadya nirudhyamānaṃ sahendriyaviṣayair nirudhyate / tasmin niruddhe pūrvadṛṣṭo[2] yo 'rthaḥ sa eva paścān manasā gṛhyate /

§87. kathaṃ punar asaṃnihitasya grahaṇaṃ saṃbhāvyata ity āha / [marīcivad iti / yady api nālpamātram api marī]cikāyāṃ[3] jalam asti api ca hetupratyayavaśāt pravartata eva jalākārasaṃjñā evam avidyamānasvarūpe 'pi pūrvagṛhīte 'rthe marīcyām iva yad vikalpakaṃ vijñānam[4] utpadyate tat sarvadharmavyavasthākāraṇam / sarvadharmavyavasthākāraṇatvāc ca sa eva saṃjñāskandha ity uktas tathāvidhasaṃjñāviśeṣasaṃprayogāt / saṃjñāvaśena[5] ca sarvadharmavyavasthā vijñātavyā na punaḥ padārthasvarūpanibandhanā svabhāvasya sarvathāyujyamānatvāt /

---

[1] B niḥsvabhāvasya bhāvasya vidyamānatvāt: HPS svabhāvasya vidhyamānatvāt. Cf. Tib raṅ bźin *med pa'i* dṅos po yod pa'i phyir.

[2] B pūrvadṛṣṭo: HPS pūrvavaddṛṣṭo. Cf. Tib sṅar mthoṅ ba'i.

[3] Lacuna in HPS restored by B following Tib: smig rgyu ltar źes bya ba smros te / smig rgyu la chu bag tsam kyaṅ med mod kyi /. B's n. 10 contains errors in the Tib.

[4] HPS yad vikalpakaṃ vijñānam: B yad vijñānam. Cf. Tib rnam par rtog pa can gyi rnam par śes pa.

[5] B vaśena: HPS vaśana.

§88. gal te de lta na ni 'on na 'du śes kyi phuṅ po raṅ bźin gyis yod pa yin te de med na ni chos thams cad rnam par gźag[1] par mi nus so źe na / brjod par bya ste / 'du śes de yaṅ rnam par śes pa daṅ mtshuṅs par ldan pa'i phyir rnam par śes pa de ma gtogs[2] par med la / rnam par śes pa de yaṅ 'du śes de ma gtogs[3] par ma grub pa'i phyir raṅ gi ṅo bos med do // 'di las kyaṅ yin te / gaṅ gi phyir /

mig daṅ gzugs la brten nas yid //

sgyu ma **[P.233b]** *bźin du skye bar 'gyur //* **(k.323ab)**

§89. gan źig skye ba'i[4] bya ba'i rten ñid du 'byuṅ bar 'gyur ba rnam par śes pa de skye ba'i sṅa rol na ni yod pa ma yin te / mig la sogs pa'i rkyen rnams yod[5] kyaṅ rnam par śes pa'i raṅ gi ṅo bo med par skye ba'i bya ba mi 'jug pa'i phyir skye ba mi rigs na / rnam par śes pa 'di ni skye ba yin no[6] // de'i phyir sgyu ma'i chos ñid las ma gtogs par ci źig ṅes par bya bar nus /

§90. bcom ldan 'das kyis /

dge sloṅ dag dper na sgyu ma mkhan nam[7] sgyu ma'i mchan bu źig gis lam po che'i bźi mdor sgyu ma'i las rnam pa sna tshogs ston pa 'di lta ste glaṅ po che'i tshogs daṅ rta'i tshogs daṅ / śiṅ rta'i tshogs daṅ / dpuṅ bu chuṅ gi tshogs daṅ źes rgya cher 'byuṅ źiṅ / de skye bu mig daṅ ldan pa źig lta bar byed sems par byed tshul bźin du yoṅs su rtog par byed pa na lta źiṅ sems la tshul bźin du yoṅs su rtog pa de la yod pa ma yin par yaṅ snaṅ / gsog daṅ gsob daṅ sñiṅ po **[N.228a]** med par

---

[1] PN bźag.

[2] DC gtogs: PN rtogs.

[3] DC gtogs: PN rtogs.

[4] PN skye ba'i: DC skye bar.

[5] DC yod: PN omit.

[6] PN skye ba yin no: DC skye ba ma yin no. Cf. Skt utpadyate caitad vijñānam.

[7] DC nam: PN omit.

§88. yady evam asti tarhi svabhāvataḥ saṃjñāskandhaḥ / na hi tasminn asati sarvadharmavyavasthā śakyā kartum iti / ucyate / sāpi hi [HPS.502] saṃjñā vijñāna-saṃprayuktatvād vijñānavyatirekeṇāsatī / tad api ca vijñānaṃ saṃjñāvyatirekeṇāsiddha-tvāt svarūpato nāsti / ito 'pi nāsti[1] / yasmāt

cakṣuḥ pratītya rūpaṃ ca māyāvaj jāyate manaḥ / **(k.323ab)**

§89. na hi tad vijñānam utpādāt prāg asti yad utpattikriyāśrayatvena pravarteta / satsv api cakṣurādiṣu pratyayeṣu vijñānasya svarūpāsaṃbhavāt utpattikriyāyā apravṛtter utpādo na yujyate / utpadyate caitad vijñānam ity ataḥ kiṃ niścetuṃ pāryate 'nyatra māyādharmatāyāḥ /

§90. uktaṃ hi bhagavatā /

tadyathā bhikṣavaḥ māyākāro vā māyākārāntevāsī caturmahāpathe vividhaṃ māyākarma vidarśayet / tadyathā hastikāyaṃ[2] rathakāyaṃ pattikāyaṃ taṃ cakṣuṣmān puruṣaḥ paśyen nidhyāyed yoniśaś copa-parīkṣeta / tasya taṃ paśyato nidhyāyato yoniśaś copaparīkṣa-māṇasyāsato[3] 'py asya khyāyād riktato 'pi tucchato 'py asārato 'pi /

---

[1] B ito 'pi nāsti: HPS omits. Cf. Tib 'di las kyaṅ yin te.

[2] B adds aśvakāyaṃ in accordance with Tib rta'i tshogs.

[3] HPS asato: B °asatto. Cf. Pr. 593.5-7: asatas tucchata...etc.

yaṅ snaṅ ṅo // de ci'i slad du źe na / ci sgyu ma byas pa de la sñiṅ po lta yod dam / dge sloṅ dag de bźin du rnam par śes pa **[D.206b]** gaṅ ci yaṅ ruṅ ba 'das pa daṅ ma 'oṅs pa daṅ da ltar byuṅ ba'am naṅ gi'am phyi'i'am / rags pa'am phra ba**[C.203b]**'am / ṅan pa'am gya nom pa'am thag riṅ po na yod pa gaṅ yin pa'am / ñe ba na yod pa gaṅ yin pa de dge sloṅ źig lta bar byed / sems par byed tshul bźin du yoṅs su rtog par byed pa na lta źiṅ sems la tshul bźin du yoṅs su rtog par byed pa de la yod pa ma yin par yaṅ snaṅ / gsog daṅ gsob daṅ sñiṅ po med pa daṅ nad[1] daṅ 'bras daṅ / zug rṅu daṅ sdig pa daṅ mi rtag pa daṅ / sdug bsṅal ba daṅ stoṅ pa[2] daṅ bdag med par yaṅ snaṅ ṅo // de ci'i slad du źe na / ci rnam par śes pa'i phuṅ po 'di la sñiṅ po[3] **[P.234a]** lta yod dam źes rgya cher gsuṅs te /

§91. ji ltar dmigs pa de ltar rnam par dpyad pa la raṅ gi ṅo bos[4] med pa'i phyir rnam par śes pa sgyu ma'i na chuṅ daṅ 'dra'o źes bya bar ṅes par nus so // de'i phyir /

mig daṅ gzugs la brten nas yid //
sgyu ma bźin du skye bar 'gyur //

źes bya ba 'di[5] legs par gsuṅs pa yin no // yaṅ gal te 'di'i raṅ gi ṅo bo źig tu[6] 'gyur na ni de'i tshe raṅ gi ṅo bos /

gaṅ la yod pa ñid yod de //
sgyu ma źes byar mi rigs so // **(k.323cd)**

---

[1] DC nad: PN nas. nad = roga.

[2] PDN stoṅ pa: C stobs.

[3] DCN sñiṅ po: P sñiṅ po sñiṅ po.

[4] PN ṅo bo: DC ṅo bos.

[5] PN źes bya ba 'di: DC zes bya ba'i.

[6] PN tu: DC du.

tat kasya hetoḥ / kim asmin māyākṛte sāram astīti / evam eva[1] yat kiṃcid vijñānam atītānāgatapratyutpannam ādhyātmikaṃ vā bāhyaṃ vaudārikaṃ[2] vā sūkṣmaṃ vā hīnaṃ vā praṇītaṃ vā yad vā dūre yad vātyantike tad bhikṣuḥ paśyen nidhyāyed yoniśaś copaparīkṣeta / tasya[3] tat paśyato nidhyāyato yoniśaś copaparīkṣamāṇasyāsato[4] 'py asya khyāyād riktato 'pi tucchato 'py asārato 'pi rogato 'pi gaṇḍato 'pi śalyato 'py aghato 'py anityato 'pi duḥkhato 'pi śūnyato 'py anātmato 'py asya khyāyāt / tat kasya hetoḥ / kim asmin vijñānaskandhe sāram astīti /[5]

§91. yathopalabhyate vicāryamāṇasya tathā svarūpāsaṃbhavān māyāyuvatiprakhyaṃ vijñānam iti śakyam avasātum / tataś ca sūktam eva tat

cakṣuḥ pratītya rūpaṃ ca māyāvaj jāyate manaḥ / iti /

yadi punar asya svarūpaṃ syāt tadā svarūpato

vidyate yasya sadbhāvaḥ sā[6] *māyeti na yujyate* // **(k.323cd)**

---

[1] B adds bhikṣavo in accordance with Tib dge sloṅ dag.

[2] Ego vaudārikaṃ: HPS vā audārikaṃ; B vīdārikaṃ.

[3] HPS tasya: B omits.

[4] HPS asato: B asatto.

[5] Cf. *Saṃyutta* iii, 142.

[6] BL sā: HPS V sa.

§92. raṅ bźin gyis[1] mi stoṅ źiṅ yod par 'gyur ba'i bud med ni 'jig rten na sgyu ma źes bya bar mi rigs te / de bźin du rnam par śes pa yaṅ raṅ gi ṅo bos yod pas sgyu ma lta bur mi 'gyur na / rnam par śes pa sgyu ma lta bur bstan pa yaṅ yin no[2] // de'i phyir rnam par śes pa raṅ bźin med do // gaṅ gi tshe[3] rnam par śes pa raṅ bźin med pa de'i tshe raṅ bźin med pa'i rnam par śes pa daṅ mtshuṅs par ldan pa'i 'du śes kyaṅ raṅ bźin med do **[N.228b]** źes bya bar gnas so //**[##]**

§93. bcom ldan 'das kyis /
rab 'dzogs śes pa don can gyi //
'dzin la 'du śes ṅes par bstan //
'du śes de yaṅ 'dzin med de //
rnam par dben pa'i don gyis bstan //

rnam dben gaṅ de'aṅ 'du śes te //
rnam dben gaṅ de bstan pa yin //
de ltar don de bsam byas na[4] //
des na[5] 'du śes 'byuṅ mi **[D.207a]** 'gyur //

'du śes 'di yaṅ spaṅ sñam du //
gaṅ la 'du śes 'byuṅ ba ni //**[C.204a]**
'du śes spros la spyod 'gyur gyi //
'du śes las ni grol mi 'gyur //

'du śes 'di ko ga la 'byuṅ //
gaṅ źig gis ni 'du śes bkag //[6]

---

[1] DC raṅ bźin gyis: PN sṅar bźin gyis.

[2] PN bstan pa yaṅ yin no: DC bstan pa yaṅ ma yin no. Cf. Skt upadiśyate ca māyopamaṃ vijñānam.

[3] PN tshe: DC chos.

[4] DC na: PN nas.

[5] PDC na: N nas.

[6] Two pāda seem to be untranslated in Tib.

§92. na hi loke svabhāvād aśūnyā saṃbhūtā[1] strī māyeti yujyate / evaṃ vijñānam api svarūpato vidyamānatvān māyopamaṃ na syāt / upadiśyate ca māyopamaṃ vijñānam / ato niḥsvabhāvaṃ vijñānam / yadā ca niḥsvabhāvaṃ vijñānaṃ tadā niḥsvabhāvavijñānasaṃprayuktā saṃjñā niḥsvabhāveti sthitam /

§93.

<saṃjñā saṃjānanārthena udgraheṇa nidarśitā /
anudgrahaś ca sā saṃjñā viviktārthena deśitā //

yac co viviktaṃ sā saṃjñā yā viviktā sa deśanā /
saṃjñāsvabhāvo jñātaś ca evaṃ saṃjñā na bheṣyati //

prahāsyāma imāṃ saṃjñāṃ yasya saṃjñā pravartate /
saṃjñāprapañce[2] carati na sa saṃjñātu mucyate //

kasyeyaṃ saṃjñā utpannā kena saṃjñā utpāditā /
kena sā sparśitā saṃjñā kena saṃjñā nirodhitā //>[3]

---

[1] Ego svabhāvād aśūnyā ṣaṃbhūtā: HPS svabhāvāt śūnyā saṃbhūtā; B svabhāvād aśūnyā sadbhūtā. Cf. Tib raṅ bźin gyis *mi* stoṅ źiṅ yod par 'gyur ba'i bud med.

[2] Vaidya reads saṃjñā prapañce, which would make saṃjña the subject of carati. This makes less sense and is not supported by Tib.

[3] *Samādhirājasūtra* 32, verses 92-95.

gaṅ la 'du śes 'byuṅ 'gyur ba'i //
chos ni saṅs rgyas kyis ma brñes //
de ltar don de bsam byas na //
de nas 'du śes 'byuṅ mi 'gyur //

źes **[P.234b]** gsuṅs so //

§94. **[#]** 'dir smras pa / ci nas kyaṅ dbaṅ po rnams yul 'dzin pa mi srid la[1] / mig daṅ gzugs la brten nas mig gi rnam par śes pa yaṅ skye'o źes bya ba 'di ni ṅo mtshar ba źig go //

§95. brjod par bya ste / ci 'di kho na ṅo mtshar gyi gaṅ 'gags pa daṅ 'gag bźin pa'i sa bon las myu gu 'byuṅ bar mi rigs la / sa bon la brten nas myu gu skye ba[2] yaṅ yin pa daṅ / de bźin du byas śiṅ bsags pa'i las 'gags nas yun śin tu riṅ por lon pa la 'gar yaṅ gnas pa med mod kyi / 'on kyaṅ 'gags nas bskal pa du mas chod[3] pa'i las las kyaṅ 'bras bu dṅos su 'byuṅ ba daṅ bum pa la sogs pa rnams raṅ gi rgyu las de ñid daṅ gźan du rnam pa lṅar dpyad pa na yod pa ma yin mod kyi[4] / de lta na yaṅ brten nas btags[5] pas sbraṅ rtsi daṅ chu daṅ 'o ma 'dzin pa daṅ 'chu ba la sogs pa'i bya ba la ruṅ bar 'gyur ba 'di ci ṅo mi[6] mtshar ba źig gam / de'i phyir de ltar na /

gaṅ tshe mkhas la[7] sa steṅ[8] na //
ṅo mtshar can min caṅ[9] med pa //
de tshe dbaṅ rtogs de 'dra la //
ya mtshan źes[10] bya ci źig yod // **(k.324)**

---

[1] PN la: DC pa.

[2] DCN skye ba: P omits.

[3] PDC chod: N chad.

[4] DC kyi: PN omit.

[5] Ego btags: PDCN brtags.

[6] PN mi: DC omit.

[7] D_kC_k pa.

[8] PNP_kN_kBVL steṅ: DCD_kC_kS steṅs.

[9] $PDCNP_kN_kV$ ṅo mtshar can min caṅ: D_kC_kLS ṅo mtshar min pa 'ga'; B ṅo mtshar can min can.

[10] L śes.

<dharmo na labdho buddhena yasya saṃjñā utpadyate /
iha cintetha tam arthaṃ tataḥ saṃjñā na bheṣyati //>[1]

§94. atrāha / āścaryam etat / na cendriyāṇāṃ katham api viṣayagrahaṇaṃ saṃbhāvyate utpadyate ca[2] cakṣuḥ pratītya rūpāṇi ca vijñānam iti /

§95. ucyate / kim etad evāścaryaṃ tvayā dṛṣṭam / idaṃ kiṃ nāścaryaṃ yan na niruddhān nāniruddhād bījād aṅkurodayo yujyate / utpadyate ca bījaṃ pratītyāṅkuraḥ / tathā kṛtasyopacitasya karmaṇo niruddhasya na kvacid avasthānaṃ saṃbhavati / kalpaśatasahasrāntaritanirodhād api karmaṇaḥ sākṣād utpadyata eva phalam / ghaṭādayaś ca svakāraṇāt tattvānyatvena[3] vicāryamāṇā na saṃbhavanti / tathā 'py upādāya prajñaptyā madhūdakādīnāṃ sandhāraṇāharaṇādikriyāniṣpādanayogyā bhavanti / tad evam

yadā na kiṃcid āścaryaṃ viduṣāṃ vidyate bhuvi /
indriyāṇāṃ gatāv evaṃ tadā ko nāma vismayaḥ // **(k.324)**

---

[1] *Samādhirājasūtra* 32, verse 96.

[2] B ca: HPS omits.

[3] Tib adds rnam pa lṅar = pañcadhā.

§96. 'bras bu ni raṅ gi **[N.229a]** rgyu'i rjes su byed par mthoṅ ste / dper[1] na ba laṅ las ba laṅ daṅ / rta las rta daṅ / sā lu las sā lu źes bya ba la sogs pa lta bu yin na / 'byuṅ ba rnams daṅ gzugs daṅ sgra la sogs pa rnams la ni tshul 'di mi rigs so / 'di ltar 'byuṅ ba chen po dag ni lus kyi dbaṅ pos gzuṅ bar bya ba[2] yin źiṅ mñan par bya ba ma yin la / de dag las gzugs mig gis gzuṅ bar bya ba daṅ / mñan par bya ba sgra[3] 'byuṅ ba źes bya ba 'di ni mchog tu ṅo[4] mtshar ba źig go // de bźin du sna la **[D.207b]** sogs pa'i yul daṅ mig la sogs pa dag la yaṅ sbyar bar bya'o //

§97. yaṅ na dbaṅ po rnams kyi **[C.204b]** don rtogs pa **[P.235a]** 'di ni[5] ya mtshan gyi rgyu ma yin no // gal te ṅo mtshar ba[6] 'di dbaṅ po rnams kyi don rtogs pa[7] 'ba' źig kho na la 'gyur na ni / de'i tshe 'di ya mtshan pa'i gnas su 'gyur na / gaṅ gi tshe ji skad bśad pa'i tshul gyis mkhas pa rnams la 'gro ba[8] thams cad mig 'phrul ltar ya mtshan gyi rgyu yin pa de'i tshe 'di ṅo mtshar ba ma yin no // srid par mi 'os pa cuṅ zad cig phyogs 'gar[9] gnas par dmigs pa ni ya mtshan du byed par 'gyur gyi / thams cad du mtshuṅs pa'i ṅo bo ni ma yin te / me'i tsha ba ya mtshan can gyi rgyu ma yin pa'i phyir ro //

§98. gaṅ gi phyir de ltar raṅ gi ṅo bo ma ṅes pas rkyen ji lta ba de lta de ltar rnam par 'gyur ba'i phyir mkhas pa rnams la /

---

[1] PDN dper: C dpen.

[2] DC gzuṅ bar bya ba: PN bzuṅ bar bya ba.

[3] D skra.

[4] DCN ṅo: P ṅe.

[5] DC rtogs pa 'di ni: PN rtogs pa ni 'di ni.

[6] DC ba: PN omit.

[7] DC don rtogs pa: PN don dam pa. Cf. Skt arthagatau.

[8] D 'gro ba: C 'kro ba; PN grol ba. 'gro ba = jagad.

[9] PDN 'gar: C mgar.

§96. kāryaṃ hi svakāraṇam anuvidadhad dṛśyate / yathā gor gaur aśvād aśvaḥ śāleḥ śālir ityādīnāṃ / bhūtānāṃ[1] rūpaśabdādīnāṃ ca vidhir eṣa na dṛśyate / tathā hi kāyendriyagrāhyatvān mahābhūtāny acākṣuṣāny[2] aśrāvaṇāni / tebhyaś cākṣuṣaṃ rūpaṃ śrāvaṇaḥ śabda utpadyata iti / param etad āścaryam / evaṃ ghrāṇādiviṣaye cakṣurādiṣu ca yojyam /

§97. atha vā naiveyam indriyāṇām arthagatir vismayakāraṇam / yadi hīndriyāṇām eva kevalam arthagatāv etad vaicitryaṃ [HPS.503] syāt tadaitad vismayasthānam / yadā tu sarvam eva yathoditena nyāyena jagad viduṣāṃ vismayakaram indrajālam iva tadā nedam āścaryam / pradeśavṛtti hi kiṃcid asaṃbhāvanīyam upalabhyamānaṃ vismayakaraṃ jāyate na sarvatraiva tulyarūpam / na hy agner auṣṇyaṃ vismayāyeti /

§98. ata evāniyatasvarūpatvād yathāpratyayaṃ tathā tathā viparivartamānatvād viduṣām

---

[1] HPS ityādīnāṃ bhūtānāṃ: B ityādi / bhūtānāṃ.

[2] HPS acākṣuṣāny: B omits.

mgal me'i 'khor lo sprul pa daṅ //
rmi lam sgyu ma chu[1] *zla daṅ //*
khug rna[2] *naṅ gi brag*[3] *ca*[4] *daṅ //*
smig rgyu sprin daṅ srid pa mtshuṅs[5] *//* **(k.325)**

§99. ji ltar me daṅ bcas pa'i yog pa myur du bskor ba'i 'gros de mthoṅ ba phyin ci log gi rgyu yin pa'i phyir 'khor lo'i rnam par dmigs par 'gyur mod kyi / de la 'khor lo raṅ gi ṅo bo bag tsam yaṅ yod pa ma yin pa daṅ /

§100. ji ltar sprul pa'i tiṅ ṅe 'dzin gyi rkyen las byuṅ ba'i **[N.229b]** bud med dag yod par 'gyur ba'i bud med rnams ltar 'dod chags can rnams la[6] kun nas ñon moṅs pa'i rgyur 'gyur źiṅ / thub pa rnams kyi(s)[7] sprul pa'i tiṅ ṅe 'dzin gyi stobs kyis sprul pa'i thub pa'i raṅ gi ṅo bo med ciṅ yod par gyur pa'i thub pa'i raṅ bźin daṅ bral ba rnams bden par gyur pa'i thub pa dag[8] ltar skye bo ma lus pa'i yid kyi mun pa 'joms pa na sems can rnams kyi mtho ris daṅ byaṅ grol gyi lam gyi rgyur 'gyur la / de rnams sems daṅ sems las byuṅ ba daṅ bral bas bden par gyur pa ma yin pa daṅ /

§101. ji **[P.235b]** ltar sad pa'i bdag gi dṅos po ltar gñid daṅ mtshuṅs par ldan pa'i rnam par śes pa daṅ ldan pa'i bdag gi dṅos po'i rkyen can rmi lam gyi bdag gi[9] dṅos po **[D.208a]** bdag la chags pa phyin ci log gi rgyu yin la / sad pas de ltar mthoṅ ba med pas de bden par gyur pa yaṅ ma yin pa daṅ /

---

[1] P_k chuṅ.

[2] $PDCND_kC_kS$ khug rna: P_kN_kVLB khug sna.

[3] V grug.

[4] PNB cha.

[5] B mtshuṅs srid pa.

[6] PN la: DC omit.

[7] PDCNB read kyis. For kyi / kyis, see en. 438 and Skt text n. 4.

[8] PDN thub pa dag: C thub de dag.

[9] DC gi: PN gis.

alātacakranirmāṇasvapnamāyāmbucandrakaiḥ /
dhūmikāntaḥpratiśrutkāmarīcyabhraiḥ samo bhavaḥ[1] // **(k.325)**

§99. yathā sajvalasyendhanasyāśubhrāmyamāṇasya[2] tadgatadarśanaviparyāsanibandhanatvāc cakrākāropalabdhir bhavati / na ca tatrāsti cakrasvarūpaleśo 'pi /

§100. yathā ca nirmāṇāni samādhiviśeṣapratyayasaṃbhūtāni vicitrakriyāviśeṣaniṣpādanāt sadbhūtayogisaṃjñāṃ darśanamanoviparyāsād[3] utpādayanti /[4] te tu cittacaittendriyarahitatvān na sadbhūtā yoginām[5] /

§101. yathā ca middhasaṃprayuktavijñānasamāyuktātmabhāvapratyayaḥ[6] svapnātmabhāvo jāgradātmabhāva ivātmani snehaviparyāsanibandhanaḥ / sa cāsadbhūtaḥ prabuddhasya tathādarśanābhāvāt /

---

[1] Quoted in Pr. 173, 552.

[2] B sajvalasye°: HPS sajalasy°. Cf. Tib me daṅ bcas pa'i.

[3] Ego °saṃjñāṃ darśanamano°: HPS °saṃjñādarśanamano°. HPS's Skt text seems confused and Tib differs completely. Note that in HPS's version utpādayanti has no object.

[4] For yathā ca ...utpādayanti I follow HPS. B on the basis of Tib reads: yathā ca nirmitāḥ samādhipratyayasaṃbhūtāḥ striyaḥ sadbhūtāḥ striya iva kāmināṃ saṃkleśahetur bhavanti / munibhir* nirmāṇasamādhibalenānirmitamunisvarūpāḥ sadbhūtamunisvabhāvarahitā api sadbhūtā munaya iva sattvānām aśeṣajanmamano'ndhakāronmūlanena svargāpavargamārgahetur bhavanti /. *The instrumental (thub pa rnams kyis = munibhir) makes little sense. Should the Tibetan be thub pa rnams kyi? B's restitution is very doubtful.

[5] HPS sadbhūtā yoginām: B omits yoginām.

[6] Ego middhasaṃprayukta°: HPS siddhasaṃprayukta°; B nidrāsaṃprayukta°. See Mvyut. 1982, middha = Tib gñid.

§102. ji ltar sgyu ma mkhan gyi **[C.205a]** 'khrul 'khor gyi rgyu can sgyu mar byas pa'i na chuṅ rnams bden par gyur pa'i na chuṅ gis stoṅ bźin du de'i raṅ bźin rnam par mi śes pa rnams kyis sems rmoṅs pa lhur byed par 'gyur ba daṅ /

§103. ji ltar bden par gyur pa'i zla bas stoṅ ba'i chu'i zla ba rten ciṅ 'brel bar 'byuṅ ba'i stobs kyis de ltar 'byuṅ ba na byis pa rnams la zla bar phyin ci log pa'i rgyur 'gyur ba daṅ /

§104. ji ltar yul daṅ dus daṅ rgyu mtshan rnam pa de lta bu dag la brten nas rten ciṅ 'brel bar[1] 'byuṅ ba'i stobs ñid las khug rna byuṅ ba na rgyaṅ riṅ po na gnas pa rnams la bden par 'gyur ba'i du bar phyin ci log pa'i rgyur 'gyur ba daṅ /

§105. ji ltar ri'i tshaṅ tshiṅ daṅ / ri khrod kyi sul daṅ / rluṅ gi zabs[2] rnams kyi naṅ gi brag cas[3] skye bo rnams la yod par gyur pa'i sgrar mṅon par rlom pa skyed par byed pa daṅ /

§106. ji ltar yul daṅ dus kyi khyad par du ñe bar lhags **[N.230a]** pa'i ñi ma'i 'od zer gyi rkyen can[4] gyi smig rgyu chu'i raṅ gi ṅo bos dben bźin du thag riṅ ba rnams la chur phyin ci log skyed par byed pa daṅ /

§107. yaṅ ji ltar sprin rnams thag riṅ po nas ri la sogs pa'i rnam par phyin ci log ñe bar skyed par byed pa

§108. de bźin du mkhas pa ji lta ba bźin rten[5] ciṅ 'brel bar 'byuṅ ba'i raṅ bźin la bzo ba rnams la ma rig[6] pa'i phyin ci log gis 'phaṅs pa las kyi rkyen can gyi 'khor ba rnam par śes pa la sogs pa'i skye ba phyi rol gyi snod **[P.236a]** daṅ bcas par skye bźin pa mgal me'i 'khor lo la sogs pa ltar / brdzun pa slu[7] ba'i chos can yin daṅ

---

[1] DC dag la brten nas rten ciṅ 'brel bar: P dag la brten nas brten ciṅ 'brel bar; N dag la brten ciṅ 'brel bar.

[2] DC zabs: PN zab.

[3] DC cas: PN chas.

[4] C rkyen can: PDN rten can. Cf. Skt ādityaraśmipratyayā.

[5] DC rten: PN brten.

[6] DCN rig: P rigs.

[7] DC slu: PN bslu.

§102. yathā ca māyākārayantranibandhanā māyākṛtayuvatayas tatsvarūpānabhijñānāṃ cittamohanaparā eva sadbhūtastrīśūnyā jāyante /

§103. yathā ca jalacandraḥ sadbhūtacandraśūnyaḥ pratītyasamutpādabalāt tathotpadyamānaś candraviparyāsanibandhano bhavati bālānām /

§104. yathā ca pratītyasamutpādabalād eva tathāvidhakāladeśanimittāni pratītya dhūmikā jātā vidūrasthānāṃ sadbhūtadhūmaviparyāsanibandhanā bhavati /

§105. yathā ca girigahvarodarādīnām[1] antaḥpratiśrutkā[2] pratītya jāyamānā sadbhūtaśabdābhimānaṃ janayaty aviduṣām[3] /

§106. yathā ca marīcikā deśakālaviśeṣasaṃnihitādityaraśmipratyayā jalasvarūpaviviktā vidūrasthānāṃ jalaviparyāsaṃ janayati /

§107. yathā cābhrāṇi vidūrataḥ parvatādyākāraṃ viparyāsam upajanayanti /

§108. evaṃ viduṣāṃ[4] yathāvat pratītyasamutpādasvabhāvakuśalānām[5] avidyāviparyāsākṣiptakarmapratyayo vijñānādijanmasāgaraḥ[6] sa[7] bāhyena bhājanena [jāyamāno 'lātacakrādivan][8] mṛṣā moṣadharmakaḥ

---

[1] HPS °gahvarodarādīnām: B °gahvarakandarādīnām.

[2] Ego antaḥpratiśrutkā: HPS B antaḥ pratiśrutkā. Cf. Tib of k. 325 and CSV: naṅ gi brag ca.

[3] HPS aviduṣām: B janānām.

[4] Ego vidūṣāṃ: HPS B aviduṣāṃ. Cf. PDCN read mkhas pa, rather than mi mkhas pa.

[5] Ego °svabhāvakuśalānām: HPS B °svabhāvākuśalānām. Cf. Tib (PDCN) raṅ bźin la bzo ba, rather than mi bzo ba.

[6] HPS °janmasāgaraḥ: B °janmasaṃsāraḥ.

[7] HPS sa: B saha. sa + instrumental is possible. See Renou (1975) p. 171, §132, (a).

[8] Lacuna in HPS restored by B on the basis of Tib: skye bźin pa mgal me'i 'khor lo la sogs pa ltar.

raṅ bźin gyis stoṅ par gyur du zin kyaṅ byis pa'i skye bo 'drid par snaṅ bar 'gyur te dṅos po'i raṅ bźin śes pa rnams thams cad du[1] chags pa zad pas rnam par grol ba la brten[2] par 'gyur bas[3] 'khor ba mgal me'i 'khor lo la sogs pa ltar raṅ bźin med do źes bya ba 'di mi g.yo bar gnas so // **[##]**

§109. ji skad du /
ji ltar **[D.208b]** mig ni 'khrul ba yis //
mgal me'i 'khor lo 'dzin byed pa //
de bźin dbaṅ po rnams kyis ni //
da lta'i yul dag 'dzin par byed //

ces bya ba daṅ / **[C.205b]**

§110. bden pa'i dge sloṅ dṅos bral dge sloṅ gñis śig gis //
dkon mchog brtsegs[4] las thub pa yoṅs su mya ṅan ma 'das par //
thub dbaṅ zla ba'i dam pa'i chos kyi ñi ma'i 'od zer gyis //
dge sloṅ brgya phrag lṅa de dag gi gti mug mun pa bsal //[5]

§111. de bźin du /
ji tar bu mo gźon nu'i rmi lam na //
bu pho 'byuṅ źiṅ śi ba des mthoṅ nas //
byuṅ nas dga' źiṅ śi nas mi dga' ltar //
chos rnams thams cad de bźin śes par gyis //

---

[1] PN śes pa rnams thams cad du: DC śes pas rnam pa thams cad du. Cf. Skt viditadharmasvabhāvāś ca sarvatraiva.

[2] DCN brten: P rten.

[3] PN 'gyur bas: DC 'gyur bar.

[4] PDC brtsegs: N brtsegs pa.

[5] Unidentified.

svabhāvaśūnya eva san bālajanavisaṃvādakaḥ pratibhāti / viditadharmasvabhāvāś ca sarvatraiva saṅgapari[kṣayād vimuktim āśritā][1] bhavantīti sthitam etad alātacakrādivan niḥsvabhāvaḥ saṃsāra iti /

§109.

<alātacakraṃ gṛhṇāti yathā cakṣur viparyayāt /
tathendriyāṇi gṛhṇanti viṣayān sāṃpratān iva //>[2]

§111.

<yathā kumārī supinān tarasmin
sā putra jātaṃ ca mṛtam ca paśyati /
jāte 'tituṣṭā mṛte daurmanaḥsthitā
tathopamān jānatha sarvadharmān //>[3]

---

[1] Lacuna in HPS restored by B following Tib: zad pas rnam par grol ba la brten par.

[2] *Ratnāvalī* 4, 57 (ed. Hahn p. 114).

[3] *Samādhirājasūtra* 9, 17. Quoted in Pr. 178.5-8 and 550.5-8. The latter quotation, as well as a variant noted in Vaidya's ed., reads svaputra instead of sā putra.

sgyu ma byed pa dag gis gzugs sprul te //
rta daṅ glaṅ po śiṅ rta sna tshogs byas //
de la ji ltar snaṅ ba gaṅ yaṅ med //
chos rnams thams cad de bźin śes par gyis //

ji ltar nam mkha' daṅs par[1] zla śar ba //
de yi gzugs brñan **[N.230b]** daṅ ba'i mtshor[2] snaṅ ste//
zla ba chu yi[3] naṅ du 'phos pa med //
chos kun mtshan ñid de 'drar śes par gyis //

brag phug ri rdzoṅ chu kluṅ ṅogs dag tu //
de dag la brten brag ca[4] 'byuṅ ji ltar //
de bźin 'dus byas 'di kun śes par gyis //
'gro ba thams cad sgyu ma smig rgyu mtshuṅs //

ji ltar **[P.236b]** sos ka'i ñi ma phyed[5] dus na //
skyes bu skom pas[6] gduṅs śiṅ 'gro ba yis //
smig rgyu dag la chu yi phuṅ por mthoṅ //
chos rnams thams cad de bźin śes par gyis //

smig rgyu la yaṅ chu ni yod med na //
sems can rmoṅs pa de la 'thuṅ 'dod de //
mi bden chu ni btuṅ bar yod mi nus //
chos rnams thams cad de bźin śes par gyis //

---

1 DC daṅs par (= dwaṅs par): PN daṅ bar.

2 P mtshor: DC tshor; N unclear.

3 DCN chu yi: P yi yi.

4 DC ca: PN cha.

5 PDN phyed: C byed.

6 DCN skom pas: P sgom pas.

<rūpān yathā nirmiṇi māyakāro
hastīrathān aśvarathān vicitrān /
na cātra kaścid ratha tatra dṛśyate
tathopamān jānatha sarvadharmān //>[1]

<yathaiva candrasya nabhe viśuddhe
hrade prasanne pratibimba dṛśyate /
śaśisya saṃkrānti jale na vidyate
tallakṣaṇān jānatha sarvadharmān //>[2]

<śailaguhāgiridurganadīṣu
yadva pratiśrutka jāyi pratītya /
evimu saṃskṛtu sarvi vijāne
māyamarīcisamaṃ jagu sarvam //>[3]

<yathaiva grīṣmāṇa madhyāhnakāle
tṛṣābhitaptaḥ puruṣo vrajet /
marīcikāṃ paśyati toyarāśiṃ
tathopamān jānatha sarvadharmān //>[4]

<marīcikāyām udakaṃ na vidyate
sa mūḍa sattvaḥ pibituṃ tad icchati /
abhūtavāriṃ pibituṃ na śakyate
tathopamān jānatha sarvadharmān //>[5]

---

[1] *Samādhirājasūtra* Chapter 9, verse 16.

[2] Ibid. 9, 12.

[3] Ibid. 37, 30.

[4] Ibid. 9, 20.

[5] *Samādhirājasūtra* 9, 21.

ji ltar bar snaṅ chuṅ zad sprin med par[1] //
skad cig tu ni sprin gyi dkyil 'khor snaṅ //
thog mar gaṅ nas byuṅ bar śes par bya //
de bźin chos rnams thams cad śes par gyis //

ji ltar smig rgyu dri za'i groṅ khyer daṅ //
sgyu ma ji bźin rmi lam ji lta bur //
mtshan ma sgom pa ṅo bo ñid kyis stoṅ[2] //
chos rnams thams cad de bźin śes par gyis //

źes[3] bya ba la sogs pa gsuṅs **[D.209a]** so //

§112. [#] slob dpon 'phags pa lha'i źal sṅa nas kyi[4] byaṅ chub sems dpa'i rnal 'byor spyod pa bźi brgya pa las / dbaṅ po daṅ don dgag pa bsgom[5] **[C.206a]** pa bstan pa źes bya ba ste[6] / rab tu byed pa bcu gsum pa'i 'grel ba'o //

---

1 DCN par: P pa.

2 PN ṅo bo ñid kyis stoṅ: DC ṅo bo ñid kyis snaṅ. Cf. Skt svabhāvaśūnyā.

3 DC źes: PN śes.

4 PN kyi: DC kyis.

5 PDC bsgom: N sgom.

6 PDC ste: N omits.

<yathāntarīkṣasmi na kiṃcid abhraṃ
kṣaṇena co dṛśyati abhramaṇḍalam /
pūrvāntu jānīya kutaḥ prasūtaṃ
tathopamān jānatha sarvadharmān //>[1]

<yathaiva gandharvapuraṃ marīcikā
yathaiva māyā supinaṃ yathaiva /
svabhāvaśūnyā tu nimittabhāvanā
tathopamān jānatha sarvadharmān //>[2]

§112. bodhisattvayogācāre catuḥśataka indriyārthapratiṣedho nāma trayodaśaṃ prakaraṇaṃ samāptam /

---

[1] *Samādhirājasūtra* 9, 3.

[2] Ibid. 9, 21. Quoted in Pr. 178.9-12.

CHINESE OF DHARMAPĀLA'S COMMENTARY

無邊。是故去來非現有體。但依現在假名建立。謂現在心緣曾當法。似彼相現假說去來。實非過未。由此去來共所許法。非離現在別有實體。自宗所許世所攝故。猶如現在諸立過去。未來有體如現在者。皆同數論外道所計自性體常用有起謝。彼既有過。此亦應然。是故自稱佛弟子者。應捨此執。現在諸法雖世俗有而非勝義。所以者何 若勝義有。應不藉緣。既待緣生猶如幻事。如何可說是眞實有。又現在法有生有滅。猶如幻化。云何實有。若現在法是實有者。應如所執虛空等性。無生無滅。豈名現在。又現在法已生未滅。二分合成。已生待未來。未滅待過去。相待立故。非實有體。如麁細等。攬非實法和合而成。如樹林等。云何實有。又於現在一一法上有多種性。如何實有。謂一一法皆有蘊性處性界性有漏無漏世出世間色心等性有無量種。於諸性中誰實誰假。不可說言。如是等性是義差別同依一體。除此諸性更有何體。亦不可言。一性是體餘性是義。同名爲性無有差別云何一體。餘皆是義。亦不可言。如是等性是名差別。其義是一。若爾不應生別行解。亦不可言。差別行解但緣共名。苦無常等種種行解。皆緣義故。是故一一有爲法體皆用無量性相合成。如舍林等非眞實有。但依世俗說有實體。若言諸性皆是共相。以可說故。如軍林等。是假非實。比量所得。自相是實。現量所得。既言是實。其相如何。現量所得云何可說。若不可說。如何言實。若可言實。卽應可說。云何自相是不可說。若言自相假說爲實 非是眞實。是則一切若假若實。皆依世俗假❶想施設。❷云何汝等定執諸法皆有實體。若一切法皆非實有。如何現前分明可見。鏡像水月健達縛城。夢境幻事第二月等。分明可見。豈實有耶。世間所見皆無有實。云何以見證法是❸眞。覺時所見一切非眞。是識所緣如夢所見。夢心所見決定非眞。亂識所緣如第二月。如是雖無眞實法體。而能爲境。生現見心。因斯展轉發生憶念。前後俱緣非眞有境。是故不可以生憶念證法是眞。法既非眞。時如何實。若緣妄境生於倒見。境可是虛。見應是實。境既是虛。見云何實。如在夢中。謂眼等識緣色等境。覺時知彼二事俱無。妄境倒心亦復如是。愚夫謂有。聖者知無。有倒心境二種皆虛。無倒❹境心俱應是實。世俗可爾。勝義不然。以勝義中心言絕故。若於勝義心言絕者。云何數說。心境是虛。爲破實執。故且言虛。實執若除。虛亦不有。若實若虛。皆爲遣執。依世俗說。非就勝義。勝義諦言亦是假立。爲翻世俗非有定詮。現見心境可言是無。憶念境心云何非有 現見尚無。憶念豈有。若一切法都非實有 如何世間現造善惡。若無善惡苦樂亦無。是則撥無一切因果 若撥因果則爲邪見。豈不怖此邪見罪耶。奇哉世間愚癡難悟。唯知怖罪不識罪因。一切善惡苦樂因果。並世俗有。勝義中無。我依勝義言不可得。不撥世俗何成邪見 於世俗中執勝義有。不稱正理 是爲邪見 今於此中爲破時執 略說諸法俗有眞無。其義虛實研究是非 於後品中當廣分別。已略成立遠離二邊中道實義 諸有聽慧樂勝義人當勤修學 謂常無常二邊邪執。如其次第。略破應知

*大乘廣百論釋論卷第五

---

*大乘廣百論釋論卷第六

聖天菩薩本　護法菩薩釋

*三藏法師玄奘奉　*詔譯

破見品第四

復次若如所言諸法性相世俗事有勝義理空。如來於中智見無礙。言音辯了巧悟他心。如何世間猶爲種種妄見所魅諍論紛紜。由能聞者有過失故。何者名爲聞者過失。謂貪己見。不求勝解。於善惡說不能了知。若無如是三種過失。是則名爲聞正法器。爲顯此義故說頌曰

276 稟和希勝慧　是法器應知
異此有師資　無因獲勝利

論曰。要具三德名爲法器。一者稟性柔和無有偏黨 恒自審察不貪己見 二者常希勝解求法無厭 不守己分而生喜足 三者爲性聰慧於善惡言能正了知。❺德失差別。若無如是所說三德。雖有師資終無勝利。言勝利者。所謂師資開悟證得如其次第。 如彼六師諸外道等。雖聞正法而無所證 非佛於彼無慇濟

❶想＝相【三】【宮】　❷云＝去【明】　❸眞＝實【三】【宮】　❹境心＝心境【明】　❺德＝得【三】

心。亦非聖教不中正理。以於世間所應度者。聞佛聖教皆已度訖。為顯此義故次頌曰

277 說有及有因　淨與淨方便
世間自不了　過豈在牟尼

論曰。諸佛如來無礙智見。觀利他事不過四種。謂所捨證及此二因。體義皆真名言非謬。即是四諦聖教所攝。佛雖廣說而彼不知。過在世間非牟尼失。以諸外道覺慧庸微。及闕正修故不能解。如彼烈日放千光明。盲者不見於日無咎

復次彼諸外道。定為無明放逸睡眠纏覆心識。於自所許不能信依。所以者何。故次頌曰

278 捨諸有涅槃　邪宗所共許
真空破一切　如何彼不欣

論曰。諸外道宗皆言棄捨我所有事。唯我獨存遠離羈纏。蕭然解脫無為❶惔怕。名曰涅槃。離相真空絕諸妄境。亦無分別執有等心。觀此能除一切心境。正歸無上大般涅槃。不違汝等所求解脫。如何憎背而不生欣。我等涅槃唯除我所。空亦破我知何所欣。汝涅槃中若有我者。必不離所何成涅槃。我如前破。不應重執故當欣此離我真空。有則可除空無能遣。執有起過觀空即除。空有二❷途❸德失懸隔。云何汝等黨有誹空。可愍邪徒癡狂無智。不能信受有益真空。常好邪求無益妄有。而於正教反生嫌嫉。如彼惡子婬亂迷心。耽㜰色聲猖蹶無禮。於母慈訓不知敬從。自❹任凶頑反生怨害

復次若離真空畢竟無別捨證方便。故次頌曰

279 不知捨證因　無由能捨證
是故牟尼說　清涼餘定無

論曰。彼諸外道雖復發心。求證涅槃及捨生死。由不善知捨證方便。於所捨證終不能成。除憎背真空耽著妄有。故於方便名不善知。除真空觀無捨生死。及證涅槃別方便故。諸有貪求外道見者。終不能得出世清涼。言清涼者則是一切苦及苦因究竟寂靜。唯有空觀是證得因。除此更無別方便故。如是空觀佛法中有。一切外道邪論所無。故牟尼說四沙門果。我法中有。餘法定無。以諸外道執著己見。誹空觀故不證涅槃。云何應知我等所執定非捨證正方便耶。前已具說。執常句義立實有時。皆有過失後當廣破。執根境等故知汝執非正方便。又諸外道於涅槃處。實不能離我所見等。而謂彼處有自內我。解脫我所名為涅槃。所以者何。我與我所畢竟無有相離義故。汝不可言苦樂等法。於涅槃處遠離於我。汝自立為我所有故。如汝所執我之自體。亦不可言我之自體。非我所有同喻無因。勿汝所執我無自體。便似空華有違宗過。是故汝等外道所執。不能究竟捨離生死。亦不能證究竟涅槃。由此應知非正方便

復次諸外道等。製造書論雖彼所詮少分有實。謂說施等是牽引因。能招善趣及餘勝樂。又說殺等是牽引因。能招惡趣及餘劇苦。然彼書論前後相違。亦復許為殺生等業　又能引發諸惡見趣。亦從如是見趣所生。如有盲人迴遊正道。或時迷失復履邪途。外道書論亦復如是。有實有虛不可依信。若爾如來三藏聖教。或有所說難可信解。是則一切內外經書。無可信者成❺太過失。所以者何。佛經中說種種神變不可思議。又說甚深真實義理。諸有情類不能測量。復說如來三業作用。聲聞乘等所不能知。謂無功用普於十方無量無邊極遠世界。隨諸有情一一根性。無量無數品類差別。如其所樂能於一時現妙色身饒益無盡。雖斷一切尋伺分別。而能為彼無量有情宣說無邊甚深廣大真實美妙無盡法音。於一念頃能除有情無量無邊心行機垢。其心雖無實生實滅。亦無一切能緣所緣。而一念頃普於一切所知境界現見周盡。於現見時遠離一切能見所見分別思惟。雖斷一切隨眠纏縛。而於三有現受死生。雖久離欲而生欲界。現處居家迫迮牢獄。貯畜種種財穀珍奇。養育妻兒親眷僮僕。如是等事皆難信知。故我於此深懷猶豫。事若唯有誠可生疑。然事亦空故。次頌曰

280 若於佛所說　深事以生疑
可依無相空　而生決定信

論曰。此頌意言。如來為怖外道群鹿。大師子吼示現真空。如是真空其義決定。分明理教所共成立。諸有智者用❻為定量。銳難精思皆不能❼越。隨順空理無倒勤修。眾善莊嚴成無上果。於此應生決定信解。唯空是實餘竝非真。但是如來隨物機欲善權方便顯示宣揚。

❶惔＝憺(明)　❷途＝徒(三)(宮)　❸德＝得(明)　❹任＝住(元)　❺太＝大(三)(宮)　❻為＝是(明)　❼越＝起(三)(宮)

又佛所言雖有無量 略唯二種。謂空不空。若於不空有所疑者。可依空理比度應知。諸法皆空云何可見。由識言境有義不成。諸法體相略有二種 謂識所識及言所言。一境同❶時有多識起。隨見差別境相不同。此識不應隨外境起。由一境體多相不成。故知所識決定非有。言是假立唯詮共相。一切共相皆非實有。多法成故如軍林等。又諸共相皆依別法。所依別法其數無邊。諸近見者不能普見。既不見別。不應見總。如二性等依二等物不見所依必不能見。如是共相既非所見。如何依彼建立能❷詮。是故共相但假施設。非爲實有可爲言詮。又諸共相若實有者。一一法上全有分有俱不得成。一一法上若全有者。應如別法共相不成。一一法上若分有者。應成多分非一共相 又實等上無別有一。實等總性慧所緣故。如非實等。總性卽是諸法共相。是故共相非有實體 但諸世間假共施設。如是諸法 或識所識 或言所言 二種推徵俱非實有。除此二境更無別法 故應信解諸法皆空。由此契經有如是說。諸法實性無示無對。皆同一相。所謂無相。諸法性相非言所行。言不能詮故名無示。非心心法所行境故。非緣有對之所能對故名無對。非❸超二種所行相外別有餘相故名無相。空相無二故名一相。不可了故名爲相。又眞空理離有無等一切法爲妄執貪等毒箭損害。眞見所證眞空分明相故名無相 無相無二故說爲一。卽以如是無相爲相 故名爲相非別有相

復次彼諸外道作如是言。諸佛所說略有二種謂空不空 空言若實餘說應虛。若佛所言一分是實 則類餘分亦非虛者。我等所言亦應如是 云何總撥言不可信。汝等外道於現事中有謬失故不可依信。所以者何。故次頌曰

281ab 觀現尙有妄　知後定爲虛

論曰 彼諸外道邪覺亂心。淺近事中尙有顚倒。況於後世深遠難知 因果理中而無謬失。是故所言不可依信。於何淺近我有倒❹耶 謂勝論者計同異等是現量境。諸數論者計苦樂等是現量境。如是等事其數無邊。皆有顚倒。所以者何。如勝論執同異性等是現量境。其理不成。牛馬等性 分別意識。於色等法假施設有。越諸根境非現量得 遍諸所依無差別故 如和合體。彼計第六和合句義。其體是一遍諸所依。越諸根境非現量得。同異等性共義亦爾。云何執爲現量境界。又彼論說有實句義。是現量境。理亦不然 所以者何。瓶衣等物分別意識。於色等法假施設有。云何執爲現量境界。 然彼論說瓶衣等物因德業實同異合故。爲眼所見及身所觸。故是根境現量所知。此必不然。先明因德所引實智非現量攝。謂因青等煖等諸德所引實智。定非見觸現量所攝。 非業同異實所引生依隨餘相合所生故。如因香味所引實智。因業引生實智亦爾。如其所應比量遮破。謂因諸業所引實智 亦非見觸現量所攝。非同異性實所引生依隨餘相合所生故 如因香味所引實智。因實引生所有實智。如見叢等知是牛等。既破叢等諸實句義。非所見觸。卽已破彼所引實智。以叢等智必因德業方乃得生。此前已破。是故亦非現量所攝。因同異性所引實智。亦非見觸現量所攝。依隨餘相合所生故。如非實等所有諸智。 謂非實智於德業等言此非實依隨餘相合所生故。 定非見觸現量所攝。餘智亦爾。由是應知。一切句義假合生智。皆非眞實緣彼現量。謂緣實智非是眞實。緣實現量假合生故。 如德等智。如是乃至緣和合智亦非眞實。緣彼現量假合生故。如實等智故不應執六句義中有現量境。 是故勝論於其現世淺近事中亦有顚倒

復次彼數論者執色等法三德合成。 是實非假現量所得。理亦不然。多法成故。如軍林等。色等應假。云何言實。又樂等三共性別故。如未變位不應成一。又色等法若是實有。應如樂等非三合成。又樂等三其相各異。云何和合共成一相。不可合時轉爲一相。與未合時體無別故。又樂等三性既各異。相不應同。汝執性相定是一故。性應如相同。相應如性異。又樂等別。色等是總。汝執總別既定是一。總應如別。是三非一。別應如總。是一非三。云何別三成於總一。 又轉變時樂等三德若不和合共成一相。如未轉時其相差別。不應現見是一色等。 若三和合共成一相應失樂等三種別相不可說言樂等三德各有二相。 一總二別。所以者何。總相若一不應卽三。總相若三不應見一。若言樂等一一皆有。樂等三相

❶時＝隨【三】　❷詮＝證【宋】【元】【宮】　❸超＝起【三】【宮】　❹耶＝邪【三】【宮】

共相和雜難可了知。故見一者。此亦不然。各有三相還應見三。如何見一。云何可知樂等有異。又若一一皆有三相。何須和合共成色等。即應一一能成色等。根境差別爲我受用。又此三德各有三相。互有差別。如何色等共相是一。又若樂等一一皆能成色等法。一一法體皆三合成。是則諸法若性若相。應無差別。同以三德三相成故。若爾所有大等因果。唯量諸大諸根差別。一切不成世間現見情與非情淨穢等物 現比等量亦無差別。違諸世間現所見故。成大過失。如是等類。外道邪師所執雖多。皆不應理。誰能撓攪糞穢聚爲。我佛法中多諸法將。已摧彼敵。故不煩詞。如是外道於淺近處。白日夷途尙致顚蹶。況於深遠嶮絕稠林亙夜重昏而無謬失。誰有識者信彼邪言爲❶止歸邪。故復頌曰

281cd ❷諸依彼法行　被誑終無已

論曰。若諸有情隨彼外道昧見倒執所說法行。彼隨惡友邪教化力。妄見熏習所任持故。誹毀如來證所起法。獲大罪業其量無邊。由是因緣墮諸惡趣。受大憂苦無有出期。故有智者。勿類愚夫隨惡友行而自欺誑。應隨諸佛眞實無罪。速證出離聖教修行

復次如上所言。佛經中說種種神變不可思議。又說甚深眞實義理。諸有情類不能測量。乃至廣說 如是等事。難信知者誠如所言。諸佛功德所說義理。皆甚深故難可信知 汝等愚夫薄福少智。唯求自利不顧濟他。未飲大悲甘露法味。豈能信解如是法門。若有慧光破無明闇。深心悲愍一切有情。求佛菩提具廣大福。乃能信解如是法門。謂諸如來昔無量劫。悲慧種❸姓熏發其心。爲拔有情生死大苦。爲求無上正等❹菩提。於諸佛所恭敬供養。聽聞正法繫念思惟。修集無邊法隨法行。謂施戒忍勤定慧等。種種難行微妙勝行。殷重無間修習圓滿。證得無上正等菩提。獲不思議自在神力。本願❺所引妙用無窮。於此何緣而不信解。現見世間機關等事。先勢所引任運動搖。如是如來殊勝神變。本願所引任運施爲。又如世間習幻術者。若極成滿處多人衆妙用難思。何況如來。久修勝定增上滿足。神通作用而可測量。是故汝等於諸如來不思議事。應生信解。於佛圓德自在神通當至心求。勿懷放逸。有聲聞等於佛無邊不思議力。自知絕分悲號傷歎。聲振三千。汝等云何誹謗不信

復次諸有智者。自往涅槃昧識逢師不能隨學。爲顯此義。故說頌曰

282 智者自涅槃　是能作難作
愚夫逢善導　而無隨趣心

論曰。煩惱纏縛無始時來。數習堅強牢固難斷。涅槃虛寂無相無名。勝德無邊高深難證。諸有智者。不因他教。自然能度生死大海。證得究竟大般涅槃。是大丈夫能作難作。愚夫久沒諸欲淤泥。耽味歡娛不求出離。如狗貪齩染血枯骨。雖杖逼之猶不棄捨。愚夫亦爾。味著諸欲聖言訶責。亦不厭離。如是智者。自然開覺證大涅槃。是作難作。愚夫放逸無所覺知。雖遇聖言不希寂滅

復次生死甚苦涅槃極樂。過失功德麁著易了。如何有情安然不欲。厭背生死欣趣涅槃。以彼愚癡有怖畏故。謂懷我愛聞涅槃空。恐證無餘我便斷滅。由此怖畏。是故不欲厭背生死欣趣涅槃。如是怖畏由少智生。所以者何。故次頌曰

283 不知無怖畏　遍知亦復然
定由少分知　而生於怖畏

論曰。若諸有情都無覺慧。於一切法無所了知。彼於涅槃不生怖畏。若有遍知諸法正理。彼達生死及與涅槃。生死生時唯假苦生。生死滅時唯假苦滅。本來無我諸法皆空。故於涅槃全無怖畏。若有但解般涅槃時。諸行皆滅都無所有。不知行苦任運自滅。無實體用離我我所 彼由身見我愛所持。聞涅槃中空無所有。懼我斷滅便生怖畏。如是怖畏因少智生。故有智者應正除斷。又非串習故生怖畏。所以者何。故次頌曰

284 生死順流法　愚夫常習行
未曾修逆流　是故生怖畏

論曰。諸異生者說名愚夫。煩惱隨眠無不成就。欣生❻厭死不樂涅槃。從無始來數曾受領。增上生道可愛異熟。未曾修習決定勝道。增上生道諸果異熟。貪等隨眠所依止處。雖爲苦火常所焚燒。而不覺知歡娛遊戲。於生死苦常習行故。不知過患無厭離心。於其解脫無罪樂味。由不曾知不樂修證。如世溷猪耽樂糞穢。淸閑美膳非所欣求。如是愚夫樂

❶止＝正【元】【明】【宮】　❷諸＝說【宮】【聖】　❸姓＝性【明】　❹菩＝苦【明】　❺所＝行【宮】　❻厭死＝死樂【明】

生死苦。於解脫樂無希慕意。由未串習。聞說其名不能信受。反生怖畏。諸有智者由思擇力。於解脫樂應正勤求。勿類愚夫倒生厭怖

復次諸有信求無倒解脫。或性賢善。或由慧力。將修眞實見方便時。若於其中爲作障礙。所獲罪業其量無邊。爲顯此義。故說頌曰

285 諸有愚癡人　障他眞實見
無由生善趣　如何證涅槃

論曰。眞實空見是證圓滿無上智因。又是永滅一切無義涅槃方便　此方便道是不思議功德生處。由是展轉疾證菩提。不住涅槃利樂無盡。隨其所化無量有情根性不同。安立種子及成熟等。利樂無窮諸有愚人。由無明闇覆自慧眼。不見眞空。復以邪說及餘方便。障他所修。如前功德。彼獲罪業無量無邊。唯有如來能知其際。由重惡業染壞其心。後生善趣法之甚遠。隨眠纏縛相續堅牢。種種業因能爲重障。方便順忍尙不得生。正見涅槃如何可證。知障正法罪業既深。智者應當自防勿犯

復次諸有障他修正法者。彼後自引邪見令生。此邪見罪過於毀戒。爲顯此義。故復頌曰

286ab 寧毀犯尸羅　不損壞正見

論曰。如契經言。寧毀淨戒不壞正見。此意云何。毀淨戒者唯能自壞。若壞正見兼壞自他。令無量生受大苦果。及失無量無邊利樂。又毀戒者由犯戒故常懷慚愧訶厭自身。壞正見者無慚無愧。讃成邪見恒自貢高。又毀戒者不增邪見。若壞正見令破戒惡未生而生。生已增廣堅固難壞。又毀淨戒但障生天。壞正見者障涅槃樂。所以者何。故次頌曰

286cd 尸羅生善趣　正見得涅槃

論曰。毀戒壞見。雖復俱能損壞善因障礙樂果。然毀戒輕。壞見極重。所以者何。持戒生天增長結縛受生死苦。正見能證三乘菩提得涅槃樂。是故智者勿壞正見

復次諸法眞理何者是❶邪。謂一切法空無我理。若爾此理亦有過失。所以者何。如有一類聞空無我謂法皆無。誹撥一切因果正理。乃至斷滅一切善根。此自見有過。非空無我咎。由惡取空妄起邪見。行諸惡行空無我理。心言不測非彼所證。愚夫聞說諸法皆空。不知聖意。便撥世俗因果亦無滅諸善法。此豈是空無我過失。聖說空教有何意耶。爲遣一切虛妄有執。若爾亦應說諸法有。爲遣妄執諸法空故。實爾若有執諸法空。如來亦說諸法是有。既爲遣執說有說空。諸法眞理爲空爲有。諸法眞理非有非空。分別戲論皆不能及。何緣聖說非虛妄耶。爲除邪執故非虛妄。空有二教俱能除執。何故如來多說空教。以諸有情多分執有。生死多分從有執生。是故如來爲除有執滅生死苦。多說空教。若空若有皆是教門。何故前說空爲眞理。方便假說亦不相違。　又此空言是遮非表。非唯空有亦復空空。遍遣執心令契諸法。非有非空究竟眞理。諸法眞理實非空性。空爲門故假說爲空。眞理非空。空爲門者。眞理非有。應有爲門。隨機說門•有亦無過。然其門義順在於空有。有有等皆順執心。空空空等皆違妄執。故有智者。聞說空言應離一切有無等執。悟法眞理非有非無。勿起有無分別戲論

復次劣慧者。前不應輒說空無我理增其惡見。所以者何。故次頌曰

287 寧彼起我執　非空無我見
後兼向惡趣　初唯背涅槃

論曰。彼謂世間諸劣慧者。我執卽是薩迦耶見。其我所見亦帶我執。故我執言亦攝彼見。我執雖復不稱正理。而寧彼起過失輕故。空無我見雖稱正理。然彼不能如實了達。因斯誹撥諸法皆無。過失重故。寧彼不起。云何此二過失輕重。謂初我執唯背涅槃。後惡取空兼向惡趣。彼劣慧者惡取空時。尙厭善根。況諸含識。彼由厭背善及世間。斷滅善根損害含識。非唯棄背清涼涅槃。亦持自身足地獄火。起我見者。無如是事。所以者何。彼貪我樂欲我離苦。不造衆罪廣修諸福。脫諸惡趣不失人天。但怖涅槃不證解脫。故契經說。寧起我見如妙高山。非惡取空增上慢者。若爾諸法空無我理。隣近險趣。聖不應說。劣慧者前實不應說。而勝慧者隨此修行獲大義利。故須爲說。所以者何。故次頌曰

288 空無我妙理　諸佛眞境界
能怖衆惡見　涅槃不二門

論曰。求解脫者除妙空觀。無別方便能證涅槃。智者欲除諸惡見垢。離此無有餘勝方便。

❶邪＝耶【三】【宮】

有見執有所緣境故。如餘有見不證涅槃。亦不能除諸惡見垢。修此空行至究竟者。能證極果無上菩提。普爲有情方便開示。復令圓證所求妙果。諸有能成自他利樂。空無我觀最爲勝因。故應善知有情根性。方便開示令其悟入

復次如來爲除惡見鬼魅。說空無我阿揭陀藥。所以者何。諸惡見者。聞說空名皆生怖畏。漸次調伏自然息除。爲顯此義。故說頌曰

289 愚聞空法名　皆生大怖畏
如見大力者　怯劣悉奔逃

論曰。愚謂惡見。損覆慧眼。彼聞空名。諸惡見命自然損害。空雖無心欲害惡見。而力大故。聞名自滅。如聞虎名怯者自喪。又如世間調善龍象。於其兩❶頰威汗交流。雖復無心損害物命。而彼龍象威力大故。其見聞者驚怖奔逃。空理亦然。威力大故。令惡見者聞名驚怖。自然損滅。空理無心。非爲損物。證空理者應爲害他。若證眞空其心寂靜。平等無二。豈欲害他。然爲利樂諸有情故。方便開示空無我理。懷惡見者。聞之自滅。爲顯此義。故次頌曰

290 諸佛雖無心　說摧他論法
而他論自壞　如野火焚薪

論曰。諸佛無心欲❷摧他論。然爲利樂所化有情。開示昔來諸佛廣路。謂一切法性相皆空。前後如來無不遊履。從因至果引導群迷。外道邪徒諸惡見論。聞斯空教自然壞滅。如在山林野火騰焰。濕薪積木烈日所乾。雖無有人持火來就。然薪逼火如自引燒。惡見邪徒諸論亦爾。空教勢力而自崩摧

復次諸外道宗皆說妄有。欲令棄捨故說眞空。所以者何。故次頌曰

291 諸有悟正法　定不樂邪宗
爲餘出僞門　故顯眞空義

論曰。有智自能簡別眞僞。遇此正法不樂邪宗。如識寶人得無價寶。終不復樂餘水精珠。諸外道宗皆立妄有。去正法遠如假僞門。誑惑有情令失大利。故我顯示佛教眞空。令彼邪徒趣眞背僞

復次何緣外道欣樂邪宗。厭背聖教。由身見力。若知無我必無欣厭。所以者何。故次頌曰

292 若知佛所說　眞空無我理
隨順不生欣　乖違無厭怖

論曰。若知佛教空無我理。斷除身見所起隨眠。觀察世間如空舍宅。虛妄諸行生死輪迴。興盛無欣。衰損無厭。無憂無喜無畏泰然。若有身見謂我損益。衰盛起時便生憂喜。因斯便有怖畏無窮。故有智人應除我執

復次諸外道衆。由著我執。能爲自縛亦縛有情。所損既多。深可悲愍。爲顯此義。故說頌曰

293 見諸外道衆　爲多無義因
樂正法有情　唯不深悲愍

論曰。諸外道衆貪愛我執。能令自他起無量罪。薩迦耶見是一切惡生根本故。如說所有惡不善法。一切皆以薩迦耶見爲本而生。諸有中懷樂善法者。自無定執隨順他緣。爲彼外道邪言誑惑。亦貪我見起無量罪。如是外道能令自他俱起種種堅固纏縛。唯有智人而不悲愍。故樂正法淨意有情。起利樂心應深悲愍。慇懃爲說無我眞空。令修正見離諸繫縛

復次諸佛菩薩常住於世。實有眞淨利樂他心。何故世間猶有無量信邪倒見謗法有情。由佛所說境智甚深微細難悟。外道不爾。所以者何。故次頌曰

294 婆羅門離繫　如來二所宗
眼耳意能知　故佛法深細

論曰。諸婆羅門唯常習誦虛言爲道。耳識能知。非是深細離繫外道。唯以露形身體臭穢種種猛利自苦爲道。眼識能知。亦非深細如來聖教。以證眞空無漏慧劍。永斷所有內煩惱賊。獲得無上正等菩提。利益安樂一切含識。理教意趣甚深微細。諸有通達如實理者。於佛聖教或知不知。由佛理教最深細故。外道愚夫不能悟入。外信外道麁淺邪言。少信如來深細聖教。世間多信婆羅門者。以婆羅門多行誑詐。誦呪祠火自苦除愆。矯設吉祥妄說禍福。爲活命故種種方便。誑諸女人成達羅等。令於彼所生希有心。供給所須推爲尊貴。古昔黠慧諸婆羅門。隱造明書言自然有。唯得自誦不許他觀。讚婆羅門最爲尊貴。剎帝利等皆是卑賤。給施所須獲無量福。愚夫無智不能測量。謂眞福田信敬供養。然彼明書非自然有。有所❸詮故如世俗言。又彼明書非審稱理。非聖說故如虛誑言。婆羅門種

❶頰＝類【三】【宮】　❷摧他＝推地【明】　❸詮＝說【三】【宮】

非實尊貴。非眞福田。常行乞匃養妻兒故如貧癩者故。有智人不應歸信。婆羅門法既多誑詐。離繫外道所學如何。彼所學法多順愚癡。所以者何。故次頌曰

295 婆羅門所宗　多令行誑詐
離繫外道法　多分順愚癡

論曰。離繫外道都不知眞。唯貪後樂現受劇苦。諸有所言多不合理。愚癡種類聚結成群。爲世愚癡之所歸信。云何決定知彼愚癡。以露身形無羞恥故。如狂如畜。如似嬰兒。若婆羅門實非尊貴。何緣貴勝亦敬事之。以彼習誦諸明論故。諸婆羅門。實無所識爲活命故於一切時誦諸明論。詐現異相。以動人心。世間貴勝不審觀察謂其有德故敬事之。又明論中雖無勝義。而有世俗少分禮儀。世間貴勝爲習學故。彼雖無德亦申敬事。餘有不誦諸明論者。以同類故世俗相承不審觀察亦衆敬事。離繫外道與彼不同。云何世間亦多敬事。以其薄知星歷道度觀鳥解夢❶占相吉凶。故凡愚人多申敬事。又婆羅門誦諸明論以難成故世共敬之。離繫外道以苦行故世共愍念。此皆不能解脫生死。諸有智者當正了知。勿隨彼見。故次頌曰

296 恭敬婆羅門　爲誦諸明故
愍念離繫者　由自苦其身

論曰。婆羅門法勤誦諸明。世以爲難故共恭敬。然諸明論非解脫因。但有虛言無實義故。離繫外道極自苦身。亦以爲難。世共愍念。云何自苦非解脫因。是異熟果非善法故。彼拔髮等所生身苦。由過去世惡行所招。是業異熟非善法故。如樂異熟非解脫因。若言此苦現功力生。非異熟果因不成者。此亦不然。彼所受苦是異熟果。以無所益與色根識俱生苦故。如地獄中所受身苦。自部亦有不許此苦。是異熟者。應以此量而決了之。諸有身苦非異熟者。亦非能證解脫親因。有漏身受現緣生故。如婬欲樂。又彼自苦非解脫因。違聖教故。如自害苦。彼師所說。非是聖教。非如來等所共說故。如婬書等。故彼自苦。但是前世惡行所招。及以現在愚癡所起。定非能證眞解脫因

復次有作是言。依尊勝身能得解脫。世間尊勝謂婆羅門。故婆羅門能證解脫。非餘雜類可得涅槃。此說不然。故次頌曰

297 如苦業所感　非眞解脫因
勝身業所生　亦非證解脫

論曰。如離繫宗所受身苦。業異熟故非解脫因。婆羅門身設許尊勝。亦業所感非解脫因。身雖不能親證解脫。而身中善是解脫因。若爾餘身善亦如是。云何但說婆羅門耶。又婆羅門根境等法。與餘種類一切皆同。云何自言彼勝餘劣。是故彼說。唯誑愚夫。諸有智人不應信受。然婆羅門非勝餘類。此洲人故。如成達羅。成達羅等非劣彼姓。此洲人故。如婆羅門既言外道所說皆虛。未知如來法有何實。爲❷遣此疑。故說頌曰

298 略言佛所說　具二別餘宗
不害生人天　觀❸空證解脫

論曰。佛說無量深妙法門。利樂有情要唯二種。一者不害能感人天。二者觀空能證解脫。身語二業總名爲害。若能斷彼所說害法。修諸善因名爲不害。謂十善業。布施愛語利行同事。及諸靜慮無色定等。由此得生人天善趣。受諸勝妙無染果報。依此能除一切煩惱。及能修習無量善因。眞如實際離相名空。正觀此空。證涅槃樂空無我理。於諸法中無相無名。咸同一味寂靜安樂。即是涅槃。此必觀空。方可證故。如是善趣解脫二因。唯佛法中具足可得。外道雖說施等少分。生人天因而不圓滿。所以者何。彼諸外道無有顯析因果智故。不言意思生勝福故。無別解脫律儀法故。善趣麁業尚不委知。涅槃妙因故其絕分。如來所說理教周圓。外道邪徒如何不樂。由佛正教違彼邪宗。乖本所貪。故不欣樂。爲顯此義。而說頌曰

299 世人耽自宗　如愛本生地
正法能摧滅　邪黨不生欣

論曰。如本生地雖不膏腴。久處其中而不願捨。❹自宗亦爾。雖與理違。以本師承故不能離。尚不欲樂餘外道宗。況慕如來甘露聖教。甚深實相眞空智火。能焚外道邪執積薪。違彼本心。故不欣樂。諸有智者應善思惟。勿染邪宗致違正法

復次佛法普照如盛日輪。求勝智人應當信仰。爲顯此義。故說頌曰

300 有智求勝德　應信受眞宗
正法如日輪　有目因能見

❶占＝瞻(宋)　❷遣＝違(元)　❸空＝宗(明)　❹自＝其(明)

論曰。此中顯示要具二德能信大乘。一者有❶知。二者希求殊勝功德。大乘能滅一切邪宗。隨順大乘多所饒益。謂自能證無上涅槃。普令他有情亦出生死。大乘正法如彼日輪。普爲世間破無明闇。有慧目者因此法光。分明照知眞僞色像。背邪從正避嶮求安。利樂自他無不成辦。諸有智者應信大乘。勿顧邪宗誹毀正法。自受沈溺生死淤泥。誑惑有情令失大利。智與愚異。謂識是非智勿似愚不辨眞僞。若有眞實利樂他心。應以大乘摧邪立正。勤修空觀速證菩提利樂有情窮未來際

*大乘廣百論釋論卷第六

*大乘廣百論釋論卷第七

聖天菩薩本　護法菩薩釋
*三藏法師玄奘奉　*詔譯

破根境品第五

復次如上所言。後當廣破根境等者。我今當說。根是了別境界所依。將欲破根先除其境。境既除已根亦隨亡。迦比羅云。瓶衣等物唯色等成。諸根所行體是實有。爲破此計。故說頌曰

301 於瓶諸分中　可見唯是色
言瓶全可見　如何能悟眞

論曰。汝宗自說眼等諸根各取自境不相雜亂。眼唯見色。瓶通四塵。豈見色時全見瓶體。此顯瓶體非眼所見。非唯色故。猶如聲等。豈不瓶體亦是色耶。我不言瓶體唯非色。但言瓶體非唯色成。故所立因無不成失。汝於現事既有乖違。而言悟眞。此何可信。如眼所見唯色非瓶。香等亦然。故次頌曰

302 諸有勝慧人　隨前所說義
於香味及觸　一切類應遮

論曰。鼻舌身根。其境各異。全取瓶體。義亦不成。瓶非三根所取境界。一一比量如前應知。聲既非恒。故此不說類其色等。聲亦應然。如是一切瓶衣車等。皆非色根所取境界。非定意識取於外境。必隨色根。瓶等既非色根境界。意亦應爾。若不爾者。盲聾等人。亦應了別色等外境。如是瓶等非根所行。皆是自心分別所起。若言瓶等與色等法體無異故。眼等諸根。如取自境。亦取瓶等。是故諸根。亦能漸次取瓶等境。若爾瓶等應是一切色根所行。即違諸根各取自境。或一瓶等體應成多。或許諸根不取瓶等。唯色等體是根境故。色等各別既非是瓶。如何合時成實瓶體。若言瓶等衆分合成。見一分時言見瓶等。如見城分亦名見城。此亦不然。城非實故。城體是假衆分合成。見一分時不名全見。瓶等若爾。是假非眞。汝等云何執實可見。又見一分言可見者。其理不然。故次頌曰

303 若唯見瓶色　即言見瓶者
既不見香等　應名不見瓶

論曰。若和合中有衆多分。由一分故全得其❷名。謂於一瓶有色等分。由見色故言見瓶者。所餘香等既不可見。應從多分言不見瓶。亦不應言色體是勝。瓶一分故。猶如香等。色等於瓶既無勝劣。應從香等名不可見。世間立名。或從多分。或就最勝。色上全無。香等有一。是故瓶等應從香等名不可見。是則外色亦應非實。是可見性。是瓶衣等不可見法一分攝故。猶如香等。世間共知。瓶色可見。云何得立不可見耶。世間所知隨自心變。假說可見非外實色。今遮心外實有可見。故不相違。不可見法。無所有故。應不可說。所以者何。可見無故名不可見。無法都無如何可說。可見之法以有體故。可爲他說。此亦不然。無體之法亦是說因。若不爾者。不可見言現應無有。又見於色都無所爲。何故說色以爲可見。非不可見。所以者何。非由能見及不能見。令色有異。云何由見說色可見。非由不見說不可見。如瓶上色是可見故。說瓶可見。瓶上香等不可見故。亦應說瓶爲不可見。其理等故。又眼見時。說色可見。眼不見時。亦應說色爲不可見。其理等故。瓶之與色。既有可見不可見義。何故今者。偏破可見立不可見。可見起執。遮可見故言不可見。非立瓶色爲不可見。又色亦非全體可見。如何由色而說見瓶。所以者何。故次頌曰

304 有障礙諸色　體非全可見
彼分及中間　由此分所隔

論曰。有障礙色非全可見。彼分中間此分所隔。如隔壁等所❸有諸色。雖見一分而不見餘。故應如瓶名不可見。於諸分中此分非勝。

❶知＝智【宋】【宮】　❷名＝有【明】　❸有＝見【明】

餘分爲多。此應從多名不可見。麁色漸❶析未至極微。常有多分。若至極微非色❷根境。是故諸色皆不可見。豈不極微外面傍布無所障隔。相隣而住全可見耶。衆微總相是假非實。一一別相非色根境。有礙極微面有彼此。如何得立色法實有全體可見。雖諸極微總相是假。一一別住實不可見。然諸極微和合相助。不可分析。而有彼此。故一一微其體實有。全分可見。此亦不然。故次頌曰

305 極微分有無　應審諦思察
引不成爲證　義終不可成

論曰。極微亦與餘物合故。應如麁物有分是假。破常品中已❸辨極微有分非實。極微一一既不可見。云何和合相助可見。若相助時。不捨本相。不應相助。若捨本相應非極微。以相助時。若如本細應無助力。應不可見。若轉成麁應非極微。應假非實審思極微。由有礙故。有分非實不可全見。是故不可引證諸色實而可見。如色中前所說道理。有分無實非色根境。如是一切有質礙法。皆衆分成非色根境。爲顯此義。故復頌曰

306ab 一切有礙法　皆衆分所成

論曰。諸有礙法以慧析之。皆有衆分相依而立。析若未盡。恒如麁事。衆分合成是假非實。析之若盡便歸於空。如畢竟無越色根境。諸可見者皆衆分成。世所共知。並假非實。細分障隔不可全見。極微相助。理復不成。諸有礙物皆可析之。盡未盡時歸空是假。是故都無眞實色法可見可聞可嗅嘗等。所詮色法既非根境。能詮亦然。故次頌曰

306cd 言說字亦然　故非根所取

論曰。一切所聞音聲言說。漸次分析至一字名。此亦如前。猶有細分。復漸分析乃至極微。此非所聞。猶有細分。復漸分析乃至都無。析未盡來。是有礙故。常有細分。是假非實。又聲細分前後安立。互不相續。體無合義。非實詮表。非實可聞。其理分明。故復別說。若聲細分同時而生。非前後立如色細分。薩羅羅薩。如是等字。同時可聞。義應無別。如是已破色等五塵。體是實有色根所得

復次有說。形色是眼所見。今應徵問。如是形色。爲離顯色。爲卽顯耶。若離顯者。應非眼見。離青等故。如樂音等。若卽顯者。應如顯色。亦非眼見。前已廣論。又說頌曰

307ab 離顯色有形　云何取形色

論曰。若離顯色別有形者。云何依顯而取形耶。如離顯色有樂音等。自根取時不依於顯。然依顯色而取於形。如遠見火。知燧總相。是故形色決定應非色根所取。或非眼見。若復有言。不依青等而取形者。應如是破。不動顯處形色了別。必色根境。了別爲先。緣形相故。諸緣形相必色根境。了別爲先。如旋火輪形相了別。或如闇中形相了別。有作是言。形顯二色共體各別。能了異故。如香味等。現見世間長等青等。能了各異。若爾世間諸大造色。與金銀等能了異故。應有別體。因既不定。宗義豈成。或復云何取形色者。若形實有是眼所見。云何依觸而取形耶。不見青等依觸而取。形既依觸而可了知。應如澁等非眼所見。此因若言定依於觸而了形者。依於顯色。應不了形。若言依觸定了形者。觸風水等應亦了形。此難非理。我意但言。形可依觸而了知故非眼所見。不言形了依觸決然。若爾顯色亦依觸了。應不可見。如依觸故。知火色等。此必長等差別所隔。方可了知。故所立因無不定失。所以者何。若依於觸了別青等。定是比知非眼所見。青等共相此必長等差別所隔。非親依觸。不可難言。形亦應爾。以形於觸無決定故。顯有決定。故不相類。如是已破離顯有形。卽顯亦非。故次頌曰

307cd 卽顯取顯色　何故不由身

論曰。形若卽是青等顯色。顯色如形應由身取。是則顯色身觸應知。卽是形故。猶如形色。身觸知形不知其顯。故知顯色非卽是形。此意❹說形非卽顯色。不同知故。猶如樂音。形若與顯非卽非離。應如車等其體非眞。形體若實。如青色等。應與顯色或卽或離。又諸形類無別極微。一一極微無長等故。離顯極微別有長等。極微自性難可了知。形顯極微。豈既無別。云何離顯別有實形。亦不可說。一一極微有長等相。長等如麁體可分析。何謂極微。又諸極微量無差別。彼此共許。今說極微有長等相。便違自宗。汝所學宗許極微量。無差別故。亦應信受。離顯無形。若言極微雖無長等而由積集成長等形。卽顯極微集成長等。何須別執有形極微。又長等形非如青等。極細分析本相猶存。故長等形非色根境。無

❶析＝拆㊂下同　❷根＝沮㊄㊅　❸辨＝辯㊂㊅*　❹說＝談㊂

實體故。猶若空花。若諸極微非實長等。如何積集成長等耶。汝許極微體非麁大。云何積集成麁大耶。是故長等非實有性。但是青等積集所成

復次勝論宗中。離色等外別立實有同異性等。彼由能依色等勢力爲色根境。此亦不然前說色等非色根取。故彼亦非色根境界。彼宗有說。實等要因麁德色德合故方見。若無二德。應如極微及空中風。雖有不見。此亦不然。麁如長等。析卽歸無。色非可見。並如前說。如何因斯能見實等。彼復有說。所依實等要由能依色故可見。如熱水中。水覆火色。雖有火實而不可見。卽彼論中有破此說。青等染色染白衣時。不見白色應不見衣。不可說言。由見染色見染所依。❶染所依實與衣合故。亦得見衣。所以者何。水火二實既共和合。由見水色卽見於水。亦應由此見於火實。彼宗二師俱不合理。且借彼一以破彼宗。爲破彼執。復說頌曰

308 離色有色因　應非眼所見
二法體既異　如何不別觀

論曰。色所依實名爲色因。如是色因若離青等。應如味等非眼所見。色與色因性相若異。如青黃等應可別觀。實既離色。不可別觀。應如色體無別實性。實之與色亦可別觀。如見青❷黃二解別故。如是二解非色根識。假合生故如非實心

復次或勝論者作如是言。諸色實有。而❸言聚色非實有故不可見者。若執一處。有衆多色可有此過。我說同類處必不同。故於一處唯有一色。無此過者。此亦不然。若色實有應不可見。無細分故。如虛空等。此因不定。以色性等亦無細分而可見故。汝云何知離色體外別有色性。復云何知色性可見。爲破彼執。故說離色有色因等。此中色性說爲色因。色智色言藉此生故。若此色性異色體一。周遍一切離青等處。亦應可見離青等處。既不可見。色性定應非眼所見。有作是言。若執色性其體周遍。容有此失。我說色性隨自所依。各各不同。無斯過者。此亦不然。若色性等隨自所依體不同者。無青等處。青等數生。有青等處。青等數滅。爾時色性與所依色。其處不同。應各別立。而汝不許云何無過。若言色性有遷動能。轉至餘處或復新起。是卽此性非一非常。既許一常體應周遍。還同前失。離青等處亦應可見。既不可見應非眼境。豈不中間或餘法上無了因故不可見耶。何名爲了因。謂形量差別。若爾色性應不可見。所依諸色無形量故。又此色性應非眼見。體周遍故。如聲性等。色與色性體相若異。應可別觀如青黃等。然此二種不可別觀。是色是性故無有異。不可說言。見而不了。是色是性二相差別。色性相異應如青黃。爲緣發生似己見故。能見既同。所見應一。故離色外無別色性。既無色性離色可見。如何比量因不定耶。餘聲性等隨其所應。一一研尋例如前破

復次勝論宗中說。地水火有色觸故。皆爲眼身二根所得。世間共許。地等三大是眼所見身所覺故。風唯身得。以無色故。此亦不然。已破眼見。當破身覺。若隨世間共所許者。身唯能覺觸德非餘。所以者何。故次頌曰

309 身覺於堅等　共立地等名
故唯於觸中　說地等差別

論曰。世間身覺堅濕煖動。便共施設地水火風。是故唯觸名爲地等。非離觸外有別所依。地等四實此義意言。地等四實不離於觸。身所覺故。如堅等觸。若執地等非觸所攝。應如味等非身所覺。若於堅等立地等名。則無所諍。體無別故。若立地等是觸所依。非卽堅等違此比量。頌中初半明地等大。自相身覺卽觸所攝。後半明彼地等共相。非觸所攝。身不能覺。唯是分別意識所知。前色性等自相共相。隨其所應類亦應爾

復次地等諸大。於燒等時無異相生。故非根境。如燒瓶等。於熟位中有異相生。謂赤色等。此諸異相德句所攝。離此無別實句❹相生。如何可言。離德別有地等實句身根所覺。爲顯此義。故復頌曰

310 瓶所見生時　不見有異德
體生如所見　故實性都無

論曰。瓶等燒時有赤色等。諸德相起現見異前。除此更無實句瓶體。與未燒位差別而生。瓶等實句若別有體。應如德句有異相起。能燒所燒和合等位。既無有別實句相生。應如空等非實有性。亦非色根所取境界。但是分別意識所知。世俗諦收假而非實

復次外道餘乘。各別所執麁顯境相。我已略

❶（所）十染㊂㊉　❷黃二花㊂㊉　❸言二此㊂㊉　❹相二根㊂

進。今當總破外道餘乘遍計所執一切境相。謂彼境相略有二種。一有質礙。二無質礙。有質礙境皆可分析。有質礙故。如舍如林。析卽歸空。或無窮過。是故不可執爲實有。無質礙境亦非實有。無質礙故。猶若空花。又所執境略有二種。一者有爲。二者無爲。諸有無法從緣生故。猶如幻事非實有體。諸無爲法亦非實有。以無生故。譬❶似龜毛。又所執境一一法上。隨諸義門有衆多性。若是實有。應互相違。復析歸空或無窮過。又所執色應非實色。是所知故。猶如聲等。廣說乃至。所執諸法應非實法。是所知故。猶如色等。由此道理。一切所執若有若無皆非眞實。諸有智者應正了知。有無等境皆依世俗。假立名相。非眞勝義。復次已破其境。復爲破根。先破餘乘。故說頌曰

311ab 眼等皆大造　何眼見非餘

論曰。眼等五根皆四大種。所造淨色爲其自性。故契經言。謂四大種所造淨色。名眼等根。此世俗言非勝義說。若執爲實其義不成。所以者何。同是造色。何緣見用。唯眼非餘。未見世間二法相似所❷起作用更互不同。豈不諸根其相有異。謂各能作自識所依。此果有異非相差別。相既無別。果如何異。用有異故。其果不同。現見世間用殊相一。如諸藥草。損益用別。堅等相同。相既是同。用應非異。又應諸根卽是大種。生識用別名眼等根。如卽堅等作用不同。得藥草名種種差別。此不應然。相用體一。名有異故。由見等用有差別故。卽顯眼等相有差別。非有別用。依無別相。用既不同相必有異。故離大種別有義成。若爾藥草用既不同。亦應離大別有共體。許有別體於義何違。若如見等全離大種。義可無違。然非全離。何得無違。若言眼等性類雖同而相有異。便違自宗。汝宗性類卽法體相。性類既同。相❸由何異。不可一體有同不同。二相差別俱非假有。如一色上無有青黃二相差別。若一法性可分二相。於中一一復應可分。如是展轉應析至空。或至無窮。常非實有。又眼等根體由何異。由見等因有差別故。豈非見等同用大種。以爲其因。云何有別。若由大種有差別故。所生見等有差別者。卽應依此差別大種。眼識等生何用眼等。非唯大種是見等因。如何可言彼無異故見等無別。復有何因。謂善惡業。此業復由貪樂見等衆緣展轉差別而生。由此業故見等有異。若多滿業別感見等。其義可然。若唯一業總感一身。如何有異。又色界身業無差別唯厭味等一業所招。彼界諸根應無差別。若言一業有多功能。故所感身諸根別者。業與功能俱是作用。如何一用而有多用。不言一用復有多用。但說一體有多功能。由此功能發生多果。如同分眼。體雖是一而能生識及生自類。假說可然。實云何爾。一卽是多理相違故。若許一業有多功能。感多根者何不許業。唯感一根能生多識。如是抑難於理何益。又一根處有損益時。餘根亦應同有損益。又若一根身應鄙陋。我不抑汝。❹令唯一根。但欲挫汝❺一業多用。又業力故。無有諸根同時損益。如地獄中。雖有猛火焚燒其身。而彼有情諸根不滅。又由根處身相端嚴。如靑盲人形非鄙陋。又若一業能生多果。以生別識證有別根。如是比量應不成立。此有彼有。此無彼無。但可成立差別功能。不應證有差別體相。又卽此業差別功能。何不能生差別諸識。諸識生時業已滅故。無能生用。若爾眼等應不從彼業用而生。若業所引習氣猶存能生眼等。何不從彼業引習氣諸識生耶。此不應然。生無色界眼等五識。應亦現行業習所依。識體有故。立有色根。無如是失。生無色界大種無故。造色亦無。何緣生彼無大種耶。離❻色貪故。卽由此因損害識種。故眼等識於彼不生。此不應然。非於境界離貪欲故。能緣識種亦被損害。勿於欲界得離欲者。或於三界得離欲者。能緣彼識畢竟不生。若言所依由❼自地業所引發故能生諸識。身生色界於欲界境應不能緣。若爾應言。生無色界無境界故。彼識不生。何故不緣下地境起。若言於彼已離貪故不能緣者。此先已說。先何所說。謂生上地應不能緣下地境界。若卽業種能生五識。不應根處有損益故。識隨損益。所以者何。非業習氣用彼爲依。彼變異故。識隨變異。由現彼識有損益故。令業習氣亦有損益。所以者何。世間現有緣卽心境妄分別識。能令餘法損益事成。如在夢心妄謂心等。若不覺知根處損益。能依之識損益應無。此中必有微細覺受。如是等類問答無窮。恐厭繁詞。故應且止。諸法性相微細

❶似＝如【明】 ❷起＝造【明】 ❸由何＝何由【三】【宮】 ❹令＝今【明】 ❺一＝果【聖】 ❻色貪＝貪色【三】【宮】 ❼自＝是【明】

甚深。淺識之儔極難開悟。且應隨俗說有諸根。非卒研窮能契實義。故次頌曰

311cd 故業果難思　牟尼眞實說

論曰。此頌義言。諸業眼等異熟因果。不可思議。唯有如來能深了達。非餘淺識智力所行。應隨世間且說爲有。非暫思擇能會其眞。諸法實性內證所知。非世尋思所行境界。若執實有。理必不然。所以者何。違比量故。謂眼非見。如耳等根。耳亦非聞。如眼根等。鼻不能嗅。如舌等根。舌不能嘗。如鼻根等。身不能覺。如上諸根。一切皆由造色性故。或大種故。❶或業果故。又眼等根皆有質礙。故可分析令悉歸空。或無窮過。是故不應執爲實有。但是自心隨因緣力。虛假變現如幻事等。俗有眞無

復次數論外道作如是言。色等境界皆二根取。謂眼等見及內智知。今應審察見智於境爲同一時。爲有先後。設許先後。誰後誰先。先後同時。皆不應理。所以者何。故次頌曰

312 智緣未有故　智非在見先　居後智唐捐　同時見無用

論曰。見是智緣隨見起。若未有見智必不生。如生盲人無了色智。是故智起定非見❷先。若居見後智卽唐捐。見已了色智復何用。汝宗法起必爲我須。非但隨因任運起故。若見已了復須起智。應一境上了了無窮。若二同時見應無用。兩法俱有因果不成。如牛二角。如苦樂等。汝應不許見爲智因。若智❸知境不由見生。盲聾等人應明了境。又不應有盲聾等人。以皆分明了色等故。又不應立五有情根。意獨能了色等境故

復次有立眼耳境合方知。其理不然。故次頌曰

313 眼若行至境　色遠見應❹遲　何不亦分明　照極遠近色

論曰。眼謂眼光是眼用故。不離眼故。❺亦得眼名。若此眼光行至色處。何故遠色見不淹遲。如何月輪與諸近色。擧目齊見無遲速耶。未見世間有行動物一時俱至遠近二方。由是因緣應立比量。照遠色見不至遠色。照近色見時無異故。如近色見。照近色見不❻至近色。照遠色見時無異故。如遠色見。又若眼光至色方見。極遠近色應見分明。與非近遠見應無異。旣有差別。故非至境。非鼻等❼根。於香味觸有此遠近明昧不同。由是比知眼不至境。於近遠境用差別故。猶如❽磁石。又眼趣色先見不見。二俱不然。故次頌曰

314 若見已方行　行則爲無用　若不見而❾往　定欲見應無

論曰。本爲見色行趣於境。其色已見。行復何爲。見已方行。又違先立眼之與耳境合方知。亦不可言不見而往。眇無指的行趣何方。如瞽目人所欲趣向不定能至。此亦應然。不見而往應無住期。或於中間遇色便止。期心往者或果所求。或由力竭中塗而住。如是二種理❿旣不成。更無第三。故非境合

復次有說。眼根不合故見。此亦不然。故次頌曰

315 若不往而觀　應見一切色　眼旣無行動　無遠亦無障

論曰。不合體無相無別故。應見一切。或全不觀。所以者何。緣無差別。從緣有法差別不成。豈不諸色由遠由障而不見耶。眼旣不行何遠何障而令不見。若眼與色不合而見。應無遠近障無障殊。不合之因無差別故。有見不見。理不得成。又極遠名無實有體。云何能礙令見不生。非二中間諸法名遠。彼於見用不能礙故。若執中間諸法名遠。礙見用者。遠障應同。言眼趣色。亦有此過。謂極遠名無實體等。執眼爲常行趣於色。實有此過。所以者何。執眼無常行趣於色。可言力竭不至遠方。若執眼常用無變壞行趣於色。過與前同。行與不行二俱有過。故眼見色非行不行。豈不光明助眼令見光明被障故不見耶。夜分遠望⓫珠燈中色。旣隔闇障應不能觀。若言眼根雖不至色然同*磁石遠近用殊。此亦不然。疑難等故。世間共見。何疑難耶。此亦不然。眞俗異故。世間見俗汝執爲眞。世亦不知不合而見。如何可說與*磁石同

前諸頌中雖正破眼。亦兼破耳。以義同故。謂若耳根境合知者。不應遠近一時俱聞。聲從質來。旣有遠近。不應一⓬念同至耳根。耳無光明。不應趣境。設許趣境。過同眼根。又聲離質來入耳聞。亦不應理。鍾鼓等聲現不離質遠可聞故。若耳與聲無聞而取。應如香等不*辨方維。若耳與聲不合而取。應無遠近一切皆聞。不合體無⓭相無別故。或應一切皆不能

❶或＝成（宮）　❷先＝無（宮）　❸知＝智（三）（宮）　❹遲＝逆（宮）　❺亦＝不（明）　❻至＝生（宮）　❼根＝相（元）（明）　❽磁＝慈（宋）（元）（宮）*　❾往＝住（宮）　❿旣＝俱（三）（宮）　⓫珠＝殊（明）　⓬念＝合（宮）　⓭相＝根（三）（宮）

聞。是故耳根聲合不合。實取自境二俱不成

復次若執眼根能見於色。應見自性。所以者何。故次頌曰

316　諸法體相用　前後定應同
　　如何此眼根　不見於眼性

論曰。法體相用前後應同。展轉相望無別性故。眼若能見應如我思。於一切時以見為體。是則眼根不對境位。應常能見如對境時。彼位色無而有見用。應以眼體為其所觀。若無色時眼不能見。應有色位亦不能觀。又若眼根以見為體。應能自見如彼光❶明。即違自宗。根非根境。若不自見。應不見他。如生盲人都無所見。又汝宗言。眼等色等諸法相用樂等所成。相用雖殊其體無別。眼見色體即是自觀。亦違自宗。根非根境。又眼見色稱實而觀。色與眼根體異是一。如能見色應見眼根。既不見根。應不見色。不可眼色體實有殊。勿違自宗。同樂等性不應說眼不稱實觀。勿違自宗。現量所攝。若言自見世事相違。此亦不然。體用別故。若言見用即是樂等。青等亦然。應不可見。若言根境共體有殊。便違自宗。俱樂等性不可一性。有樂多體轉變亦然。不離性故。若言共體即別即同。除汝巧言誰能說此。根境體一見境非根。如是宗言。極難信解。如破眼見。耳等例然。根境皆同樂等性故、又應一境一切根行。亦應一根行一切境。是則根境安立不成。故不應言諸根實有

復次鵂鶹子言。我宗根境共性有異。不同彼失。所以者何。眼等五根隨其次第。即是火空地水風實。眼見三實。謂火地水及見於色。身覺四實。謂除其空。兼覺於觸。耳唯聞聲。鼻唯嗅香。舌唯嘗味。故我師宗不同彼失。若爾根境有異有同。異且可然。同如彼失。眼等火等其相不同。如何五根五實為性。地水火實異青等故。非眼所觀。地水火風若體異觸。應非身覺。是故汝宗亦有多過。又彼宗執眼色意我四法合故能見於色。此亦不然。故次頌曰

317　眼中無色識　識中無色眼
　　色內二俱無　何能合見色

論曰。眼色識❷二各別無二。非和合故。無見用生。三法合時與別無異。如何可執有見用生。有小乘說。此難不然。誰言合時與別無異、諸法一一雖各無能。而和合時相依有用。若和合位有異相生。與前不同。應非眼等。若和合位無異相生。與前既同。應無見用。若言同類有異相生。此亦不然。理相違故。類之與相其體不殊。如何可言類同相異。同異二義互相乖違。而言體一。必不應理。若眼等三能生見用。爾時見用應亦生三。不可同時有因有果。而三起見。非見起三。一剎那中彼此俱有。如何相望有因非因。又應同時無因果義。果體已有。豈復須因。若不同時應許先後。同時不立先後豈成。果時無因。果是誰果。因時無果。因是誰因。若爾應無一切因果。尚不許有。況立共無。而說種種因果不同。此世俗言。非為勝義。正破外道。兼破小乘。故此頌中唯破眼等。我❸或已破。故不重論。如破眼等合故見色。耳等亦應隨義而破

復次耳所聞聲能成名句詮表法義勝色等塵。故於此中重審觀察。令知詮表俗有真無。為所聞聲能詮表義。為不爾耶。若爾何失。初且不然。故次頌曰

318ab　所聞若能表　何不成非音

論曰。所聞與音聲之異目。俱能顯義。表即是詮。此中顯示聲不能詮。設許能詮。便失聲性。以聲自相定不能詮。無分別識所了知故。如餘自相。又聲自相定不能表。所欲說義。同喻無故。如不共因。聲之共相非耳所聞。一一皆依多法成故。有細分故。如非實等。此若能詮便失聲性非所聞故。猶如樂等。非離聲性別有所聞。猶如色等。非聲性故。後亦不然。故次頌曰

318cd　聲若非能詮　何故緣生解

論曰。若所聞聲不能詮表。不應由此名句智生。唯句與名能詮表義。故於此處不說文身。又若語聲不能詮表。應同餘響非義智因。若爾不應聞聲了義。聞既了義應是能詮。豈不意識耳識後生。依所聞聲假立共相。此能詮表引義智生。意識生時聲與耳識二俱已滅。共相何依。聲體既無。誰之共相。若謂念力追憶前聲。心等依之假立共相。應心心法各別所緣。不隨心緣應非心法。若謂共相不要依聲。唯分別心假想建立。如何此相唯屬於聲。若言因聲而得起者。耳根識等豈非此因。又耳識生不緣共相。如何定作立共相因。若言

❶明＝眼〔宮〕　❷二＝三〔宋〕〔元〕〔明〕　❸或＝惑〔宋〕〔元〕〔明〕

如色見已便增。此亦同疑。不可爲證。若言諸法功力難思。既爾云何强立共相。若言二相同依一聲自相先聞後意俱了。聲相既異。體云何同。心相既殊。體亦應別。不可意識二相合緣。念唯記前所❶取相故。若聲共相念不由聞。自相亦應不聞而憶二先別了後可合緣。別了既無。合緣豈有。是故共相非實能詮。亦非音聲。定不能表。雖廣諍論而理難窮。應

❷止傍言推尋本義

復次執聲與耳合不合聞。多同色破。又聲與耳合故能聞。理必不然。故次頌曰

319ab 聲若至耳聞　如何了聲本

論曰。本謂說者。聲起源故。若聲離本來至耳聞。如何得知能發聲者。既了發處聲必不來。亦不應言耳往聲處。用無光質。何以知行。又詮表聲不可全了。所以者何。故次頌曰

319cd 聲無頓說理　如何全可知

論曰。名句細分漸次而生。耳不頓聞。如何全了。亦不應說追念故知。念必似前❸具如先*辨。不可離念率爾能知。應不藉聞意別能了。若爾聾者應自了聲。或能說人言音無用。若言聞聲次第緣力引故全了。此亦不然。次全了心不必生故。若言全了必次聞生。此亦不然。天耳通後必隔定心。方全了故。又餘意識從聞聲後。亦經多時方全了故。不可執有實詮表聲。先耳能聞後意能了。但是虛妄分別識心。變現言音謂爲詮表

復次應審推徵聲名何法。其體實有。是耳所聞。若爾不然。故次頌曰

320 乃至非所聞　應非是聲性
先無而後有　理定不相應

論曰。未來聲體非耳所聞。眼等五根取現境故。則未來聲應非聲性。非所聞故。如色等塵。若未來聲與現同類。現可聞故。彼亦名聲。應現在聲與彼同類。彼非聲故。現亦非聲。又從未來流入現在。現可從彼說爲非聲。未來不從現在流入。如何由現說彼爲聲。若現可聞是聲性者。應此聲性本無而生。則違汝宗。先有聲性。聲性先有。應非始生。既非始生。後應無滅。無生無滅聲性應常。又過去聲應非聲性。非所聞故。如未來聲。若未非聲。流入現在。現是聲故。說彼爲聲。應現在聲流入過去。過非聲故。現亦非聲。若爾則應三世聲性相待而立。皆非實聲。又現在聲從未來至得名生者。應過去聲從現在至亦說名生。則過去聲應名現在。後應更滅。若過去聲從現在至得名滅者。應現在聲從未來至亦說名滅。則現在聲應名過去。後應不滅。未來無二應說爲常。有滅有生應名過現。如是推徵聲性散壞。色等亦爾。如理應思

復次有數論者作是執言。心往境處方能了別。此亦同前根往境破。又不應說心離於根獨能了境。故次頌曰

321ab 心若離諸根　去亦應無用

論曰。心若離根定不能了。色等諸法去亦唐捐。若不待根心獨了境。盲聾等類應了諸塵。或復應無盲聾等類。此前已*辨。無假重論。又養諸根心則明利。是故決定心不離根。有執內心其體周遍。用依各別往所了塵。用卽是心現境行相。起卽了境。去復何爲。不可執言別現別了。勿現色等了聲等塵。又心不應離用趣境。汝執體遍行趣何方。又不應然。故次頌曰

321cd 設如是命者　應常無有心

論曰。心若趣塵。體則不遍。心常往境。我應無心。然微細心身中恒有。睡眠❹悶等諸位常行。有息等故。夢可得故。勞倦增故。引覺心故。❺任持身故。觸身覺故。又若內身恒無心者。如死屍等。害應無愆。供應無福。則與空見外道應同。有執心體不遍不行。但用有行亦同此過。心用心體不相離故　又若心體往趣前塵。有觸內身應無覺受。應勤思慮不損內心。若執其心非自境合。應如餘境。亦不能知。應一一心知一切境或一一境一切心知。如是諸宗執實根境。皆不應理。應信非真。豈不大乘亦同此過。設許少實。此過應同若爾應無世間諸事。想顚倒故。謂彼非無想者是何。而由顚倒令❻謂世事是有非無。想謂想蘊。故次頌曰

322 令心妄取塵　依先見如焰
妄立諸法義　是想蘊當知

論曰。初心生時取青等相。如立❼標幟爲後憶持。取越色根所行境相。故名爲想。❽由此想故。後時能憶境相分明。雖一切心皆有共想。而果位勝故說依先。以後分明顯先是有。如此❾想妄立一切世間有情無情諸法義相。如依陽焰有水想生。誑惑自心亦爲他說。由此

❶取＝共(明)　❷止＝正(宋)(元)(宮)　❸具＝共(宋)(元)(宮)　❹悶＝鬧(宮)　❺任＝住(宮)　❻謂＝諸(宋)(宮)　❼標＝摽(元)(明)　❽由＝比(明)　❾想＝應(宮)

妄想建立根塵及餘世間諸事差別。爲顯此想依多法成是假非眞。故說想蘊。又顯世間法義差別。皆由想立。故說當知。豈不五識緣實有塵。隨五識行。意識亦爾。想與諸識境界必同。何得定言想爲顚倒。誰言諸識緣實有塵。而妄爲難。故次頌曰

323ab 眼色等爲緣　如幻生諸識

論曰。如諸幻事體實雖無而能發生種種妄識。眼等亦爾。體相皆虛。①如嬌誑人。生他妄識想隨此發。境豈爲眞。根境皆虛。如先具述。此所生識亦復非眞。所現皆虛猶如幻事。非諸識體卽所現塵。勿同彼塵。識無緣慮。亦不離塵別有識體。離所現境識相更無。如何可言識體實有。如有頌②曰

彼能緣諸識　非卽所現塵
亦不離彼塵　故無相可取

有說幻事皆實非虛。呪術功能加木石等。令其現似車馬等相。此相或用聲等爲體。或體卽是識之一分。爲破彼救。故次頌曰

323cd 若執爲實有　幻喩不應成

論曰。若幻是實聲等爲體。如餘聲等應不名幻。若言幻事迅速不停。如化所爲。故說名幻。此亦不然。體既實有。如餘聲等。何不名眞。迅速不停亦非幻相。勿電光等亦得幻名。若言誑惑世間名幻。幻相非虛。何名誑惑。若言能生常等倒故。卽應餘法亦得幻名。又不應言幻是識分。非解了性。豈卽是心。③或應異名。說唯識義。應信諸法皆不離心。如何一心實有多分。或應信受識體非眞。若識是眞而許多分。應一切法其體皆同。若識體一而現二分。如陽焰中現似有水。則不應言幻是識分。其體實有識無二故。非所執水是陽焰分。如何喩識體一分多。若爾大乘說何爲幻。我所說幻。如世共知。覺慧推尋諸幻事性。實不可得。言豈能詮。故一切法皆如幻事。其中都無少實可得。如有頌言

以覺慧推尋　諸法性非有
故說爲無性　非戲論能詮

是故諸法因緣所生。其性皆空猶如幻事。若法性空而現似有。何異羂索籠繫太虛。法性理然汝何驚異。世事難測。其類④寔繁。爲證斯言。故次頌曰

324 世間諸所有　無不⑤皆難測
根境理同然　智者何驚異

論曰。如一⑥思業能感當來。內外無邊果相差別。極善工匠所不能爲。是名世間第一難測。又如外種生長芽莖。無量枝條花葉根果。形色間雜嚴麗宛然。是名世間第二難測。文如婬女身似糞坑九孔常流種種不淨。而貪欲者見發婬情。是名世間第三難測。又如花樹。名曰無憂。婬女觸之。衆花競發枝條垂拂如有愛心。是名世間第四難測。又如花樹名好樂音。聞作樂聲擧身搖動。枝條⑦裊娜如舞躍人。是名世間第五難測。又如花樹名好鳥吟。聞鳥吟聲卽便搖動。枝條*裊娜如喜抃人。是名世間第六難測。又如生上經無量生。退下生時便求母乳。騰躍嬉戲寢食貪婬。是名世間第七難測。又如欣樂無上菩提。應正勤修微妙善法。而行放逸撥法皆無。是名世間第八難測。又如厭捨迫迮居家。至道場中而營俗務。貪著財色無悔愧心。是名世間第九難測。又如淨定所發神通。妙用無邊不相障礙。隨心所欲一切皆成。是名世間第十難測。如是難測世事無邊。根境有無方之甚易。世俗故有。勝義故空。諸有智人不應驚異。爲顯諸法俗有眞空。故於品終。復說頌曰

325 諸法如火輪　變化夢幻事
水月彗星響　陽焰及浮雲

論曰。如旋火輪變化夢等。雖現似有而實皆空。諸法亦然。愚夫妄執分別謂有。其體實無。離妄執時都無所見。如淨眼者不覩空花。無爲聖智所見乃眞。能緣所緣行相滅故。如是善順契經所言。有爲識心所行非實。是故根境皆俗非眞。由識所行如火輪等。諸外道輩所見非眞。由執有無如眩瞖等。欲求聖智除⑧妄契眞。應順如來圓淨法敎

*大乘廣百論釋論卷第七

*大乘廣百論釋論卷第八

聖天菩薩本　護法菩薩釋
*三藏法師玄奘奉　*詔譯

破邊執品第六

如是已⑨辨根境皆虛。復爲遣除非眞句義邊執垢穢。故說頌曰

①如＝知【三】【宮】　②曰＝言【三】【宮】　③或＝感【三】【宮】　④寔＝實【三】【宮】　⑤皆＝能【宮】　⑥思＝異【宮】　⑦裊＝嫋【宮】*　⑧妄契＝契妄【元】【明】　⑨辨＝辯【宋】【元】，辯【宮】

INDEXES

Errata

(with regard to Chinese texts pp. 131-145)

The arabic numeral equivalents to the Chinese page numbers in the following texts got omitted at the printing stage. Read serial 'no. 215' for the first page, serial 'no. 216' for the second page and so on; the last serial no. will be 229. For their correct placements, see serial no. 227, 228 and 229.

INDEX OF SANSKRIT TERMS

ā-KṢIP "project" 152
ā-MNĀ "read"; recite" en. 127
abhijñā "super-knowledge" en. 5
abhiniṣpatti "complete" 113
abhiniveśa "erroneous grasping" 93, 104
abhiprāya "thought"; "intention" 108, fn. 48
abhivyakti "manifestation" 184
abhrānta "not mistaken" fn. 88, en. 367
abhūtaparikalpa "false conceptualization"; "unreal notion" 166, fn. 127
abhyāsa "training"; "habit" 100
abhyudaya "good position" 117
acintya "inconceivable" en. 392
adhikagrahaṇa "apprehension of [objects] bigger [than the sense organ]" en. 290
adhikaraṇa "locus" 145, en. 252
adhimukti "zealous application" 87, en. 3, 45
adhipatipratyaya "dominant condition" 187, en. 287, 397, 428
adhyāśaya "disposition" 115
ādhyātmikāyatana "internal domain" en. 187, 236, 264
ādi "beginning" 191
adṛṣṭa "non-empirical" 121
adveṣa "absence of aversion" en. 97
advitīyaṃ śivadvāram "the unrivalled door to peace" en. 108
agada "antidote" 105, en. 109
āgama "scripture" 27, fn. 58,
āgamāśrita "[inference] based on scripture 24
āgantuka "adventitious" en. 198
agha "an impurity" 194
ahaṃkāra "conception of an I"; "ego" (Sāṃkhya) 104, 107, 122, 125, en. 286
ākāra "image", "aspect" 9, 41, 42, 44, 45, 49, 51-53, 61, 67, 167, 173, 194, fn. 91, fn. 92, en. 193, 344, 432
ākāśa "space" en. 262, 356
ākāśaguṇatva "being a quality of space" 33
akliṣṭa "undefiled" 112, 115
akṣam akṣaṃ prati vartate "occurs in connection with the various individual sense organs" 177
akṣara "syllable" 140, 181
ākṣepahetu "propelling cause" 90, en. 26
ākṣepakakarman "propelling karma" en. 269
alam atiprasaṅgena s.v. ity alaṃ prasaṅgena en. 334
ālambana "object [of mind]" 164, en. 332
ālambanapratyaya "objective condition" en. 227, 397
alātacakra "circle traced by a whirling firebrand" 141
alobha "absence of desire" en. 97
amoha "absence of bewilderment" en. 97
anāgāmin "non-returner" en. 19
anaikāntika "inconclusive" 142, 145
anāsrava "undefiled" 108
anātman "selfless" 195
anidarśana "indescribable" 93
animitta "without characters" 112, en. 135

ānimitta "lack of characters" 127, en. 193
ānimittasamādhi "[meditative] trance directed towards the lack of characters" en. 193
anitya "impermanent" 194
anivṛtāvyākṛta "not defiled and not defined" en. 128
antadvaya "binary doctrinal extremes" 72
antaḥkaraṇa "internal organs" en. 286, 288
antara "between" 158
antyaviśeṣa "ultimate particular" en. 53
anudharma "secondary dharma" en. 80
ānulomikī kṣānti "patience of amenability" 101, en. 92
anumāna "inference" 136, 142, fn. 37, 49, en. 232, 314
anupalabdhi "non-perception" 129, fn. 75.
anupaśyanā "contemplation" en. 432
anupūrvavihāra "states following one another in regular succession" en. 134
anuśaya "[latent] propensities [for passions]" 91, 100, en. 32, six anuśaya en. 87
anutpāda "non-arisal" 54
anuttarasamyaksaṃbodhi "unexcelled perfect enlightenment" 98
anuttarasamyaksaṃbuddha "unexcelled perfectly enlightened ones" 128
anyathātva "other than before" 148
anyayogavyavaccheda "exclusion of connections with something else" en. 240
apara "near" 180
aparasāmānya "lower universal" en. 252a
apauruṣeya / apauruṣeyatva "not man-made" en. 124
apavāda "denigrate" 172
apavarga "emancipation" 133
apoha "exclusion" 22, 71, en. 329
apraṇihita "no focusing [on objects] 127, en. 193
apraṇihitasamādhi "[meditative] trance which does not focus on anything" en. 193
aprāptaviṣayatva "contact the object" 189
aprāpyakāritva "[the sense organ] does not operate by contacting [the object]" en. 294
aprāpyakāritvavāda, see Index of Proper Names.
apratigha "without resistance" 93, en. 48
āpta "an authority" fn. 49, 54.
āptavacana "authoritative words"; "trustworthy words" fn. 49, 54, en. 314
āptavāda "authoritative words" 24
āptopadeśa "the teaching of an authority" 33, fn. 84
artha "object"; "entity"; "state of affairs" 135, 162, en. 18, 89, 347
arthacaryā "beneficial conduct" 112, en. 134
arthākāra "aspect of the object" 9
arthakriyā "practical efficacity" 45, 47, 68, fn. 101, en. 366
ārūpyadhātu "formless realm" 153
ārūpyasamāpatti "formless meditative absorption" 112, en. 134
ārya "Noble One" 125, 129
āryamārga "noble path" 125
asādhāraṇa "specific"; "exclusive" 177
asādhāraṇahetu / asādhāraṇakāraṇa "specific cause" en. 367
asādhāraṇānaikāntikahetu "a reason which is uncertain because it is [too] exclusive" 163, en. 329a
asādhāraṇatva "having nothing in common"; "being specific"; "exclusive" 163
aśaikṣamārga "path of no more learning" en. 80
asaṃskṛta "unconditioned" 149, 173, three sorts en. 262, 356
asāra "insubstantial" 194
asat "inexistent" 194
āśaya "resting-place"; "basis" 157
aśeṣa "without remainder" 100
asiddha "unestablished" 135
āsravakṣayajñānasākṣātkārābhijñā "the super-knowledge which realizes an understanding [capable] of destroying defilements" en. 2, 5
āśraya "basis"; "locus" 94, 145, en. 252, 430
āśrayāsiddha "the [fallacy that] the locus is unestablished" fn. 48
astidṛṣṭi; bhavadṛṣṭi "the view of existence" 105
asty eva "really exists" 92
atiprasaṅga

— "absurdity" 31, 91
— "digressions" 164
ativyāpti "over-pervasion" 65
ātmabhāva "the body" 168, en. 439
ātmadṛṣṭi "the view of the self" en. 86
ātman "self" 159, 161
ātmasneha "self-cherishing" 100, 123
ātmīya "possession of the self" 88, 118, en. 86
ātmīyadṛṣṭi "view of the possessions of the self" 104
atyantaparokṣa "completely imperceptible" 24-28, 31-34, 77, 91, fn. 59, fn. 73
atyantāyogavyavaccheda "exclusion of absolute non-connection" en. 240
audārika "coarse" en. 249
avadhāraṇa "restriction"; "necessity" en. 240, 242
avasthāviśeṣa "different states" en. 40
avayavin "whole" 175, en. 40
avidyā "ignorance" 88, en. 10, 26, 128
avijñapti "unmanifest" en. 236
avinābhāva "necessarily connected" en. 22
avinābhāvaniyama "necessary connection" en. 276
aviparīta "non-erroneous" 101
avisaṃvādi jñānam "non-belying consciousness" en. 376
avisaṃvādin "non-belying" 179, fn. 54, 86, en. 375
avyakta "unmanifest" en. 68
avyapadeśya "inexpressible" en. 366
āyatana "domain" 127, en. 187, 188, 193, 273, 397
ayogavyavaccheda "exclusion of non-connection" en. 240
ayukta "incoherent" 152
bādhaka "invalidator" fn. 75
bāhyārtha "external object" 58, fn. 131
bāhyāyatana "external domain" en. 187, 236, 264
bhāga "part [of consciousness]" 8, fn. 25
bhāvalakṣaṇa "character of existence"; "existential character" 93, en. 47 §a, §c
bhāvanā "meditation" en. 80
bhāvāntara "distinct entity" 93, en. 51
bhautika "derivatives [from the elements]" 142, 150, 185, 190, 196, en. 236, 237, 264, 362, 383, 385, 417
bhoga "enjoyment" 97
bhoktṛ "enjoyer" en. 75
bhūta "element" 196, en. 236, 237, 264
bhūtakoṭi "the true endpoint" 112, en. 135
bhūtalakṣaṇa "the true character [of things]" 113
bhūtatathatā "true thusness"; "real nature" 155, en. 356
bīja "seed" 101, 153, en. 26, 90, 125, 278
bodhi "enlightenment" en. 94
bodhimaṇḍa "seat of enlightenment" 172
brāhmaṇa "Brahmin" 108
buddhi "intelligence" 88, en. 68, 286
caitanya "conscious principle" en. 309
caitta "mental factor" 164, en. 131, 332, 427, 439
campaka "yellow magnolia" en. 405
catuṣkoṭi "tetralemma" 61, 72-77, fn. 16
catvāraḥ pratyayāḥ "the four conditions" en. 339, 397
caura "thief" en. 122a
citta "mind" 164, 192, en. 131, 332, 427, 439
cittacaitta "minds and mental factors" 93, 164, 176
cittotpāda "generating the mind of enlightenment" en. 18
cyutyupapādajñānasākṣātkārābhijñā "the super-knowledge which realizes an understanding of birth and death" (= divyacakṣus) en. 5
dāna "giving" 98, 112, en. 134
dānādi "giving and the other [perfections]" 90
darśana "sight"; "view" en. 2, 180, 190, 287, 397
daśakuśalakarmapatha "ten virtuous actions" 112, en. 134
daurmanasya "despondency" en. 352
deha "body" en. 132
dharmadhātu "sphere of the Dharma" en. 198
dharmakāya "Dharma-body" 184, en. 198
dharmanairātmya "selflessness of dharmas" 127, fn. 117
dharmānudharma s.v. dharmānudharmapratipatti en. 80
dharmānudharmapratipanna s.v. dharmānudharmapratipatti en. 80
dharmānudharmapratipatti "practices in keeping with the Dharma" 98, en. 80

dharmaparyāya "approach to the Dharma" 98
dharmaśarīra s.v. dharmakāya en. 198
dharmatā "nature of things" 184
dharmin "subject" fn. 95, 107, en. 24, 329a
dhātu
— "elements" 127, en. 188
— "phenomenal constituents" en. 188
— "realm" en. 188
dhyāna "meditative trance" 98, 112, en. 79, 134, 340
dhyānacitta "mind in meditative trance" 165
divyacakṣus "the divine eye" en. 5, 340
divyaśrotrābhijñā "the super-knowledge known as 'the divine ear' 165, en. 340
doṣa "fault" en. 121
draṣṭavyatva "perceptibility" 184, en. 259, 399
dravya "substance" 96, 135, 175, en. 42, 219, 308
— dravyaparamāṇu "atom" en. 417
— eight substances in Abhidharma en. 362, 417
— nine substances of the Vaiśeṣika en. 61
dravyato 'sti; dravyasat "substantially existent" 92, en. 40
dravyatva "substanceness" 145
dṛṣṭa "empirical" 121, en. 314
dṛṣṭānta "example" 29, en. 129
dṛṣṭāntābhāsa "fallacy of the example" en. 24
dṛṣṭi "heretical view"; "view"; "vision" vi, 87, 115, en. 86, 282
dṛṣṭigata "heresy" 90, en. 121
dṛṣṭipāpta "possessed of [philosophical] vision" en. 44
duḥkha "suffering"; "painful" 194, en. 54, 85
duḥkhaduḥkhatā "suffering *qua* suffering" en. 85
dvadāṣāyatana "twelve domains" en. 187
dvīpa "continent" 111
dvitvādi "two, etc." 92, en. 39
ekalakṣaṇanirvāṇa "the nirvāṇa of one [unique] character" en. 49
ekānekaviyogahetu "the 'neither one nor many' reasoning" 63, fn. 93, 133, 134, en. 37, 244
eva "only"; "alone" 153, en. 240
gambhīra "profound" 31, en. 28
gaṇḍa "abscess" 194
gati "path"; "way" 105
gocara "object" 93
gotra "lineage" 98, en. 78
grāhaka "what apprehends" 55, 91, 173, fn. 25
grāhakākāra "subjective aspect" 9, fn. 92
grāhya "what is to be apprehended" 55, 91, 173, fn. 25, fn. 135
grāhyākāra "objective aspect" 9, fn. 92
guṇa
— "excellent quality" 87
— "quality" (Sāṃkhya and Vaiśeṣika) 32, 95, 96, 148, 160, 175, en. 23, 39, 42, 54, 68, 72, 74, 219, 248, 308, 361
guṇasaṃdrāva "collection of the qualities"; "synthesis of the qualities" en. 72, 219
guṇasamudāya s.v. guṇasaṃdrāva en. 72, 219
hetu "reason" 90, en. 24, 129, 258, 329a
hetuphalabhāva "causality" 162
hetupratyaya "[general] causal condition" en. 397
heya "what is to be abandoned" 116
homa "fire offering" 131
indrajāla "Indra's net" 196, en. 210
indriya "organ"; "sense organ" 97, en. 236, 283 286
indriyārtha "sense organs and their objects" vii, ix, 135, 175
indriyavṛtti "operation of the senses" en. 286
indriyāyatana "sense domain" 152
iṣṭavipāka "desirable [karmic] retributions" 100
itara "ordinary" 126
ity alaṃ prasaṅgena "Enough of these digressions!" 179
jaḍa "inert matter" 190
janman "birth"; "origin" en. 132
jāti "kind" 162, en. 252a, 391
jātikusuma "nutmeg blossoms" 179
jātimant "having arisal"; "coming into being" 167
jīvitendriya "vital faculty" en. 206
jñānadarśana "insightful vision" 87, en. 2
jñānadharmakāya "wisdom-dharmakāya" en. 198
jñeya "object of cognition" 149
kalpa "conceptualization" 192

kalpanā "conceptualization"; "concept" fn. 88, en. 364, 367
kalpanāpoḍha "free of conceptualization" 37, 49, 177, fn. 88, en. 367, 428
kāmadhātu "the realm of desire" 91, 141, en. 385
karaṇa "instrument" 187, 188, en. 395
kāraṇahetu "effective cause" en. 397
kārāpakāra "aided or impaired" en. 274
kāritra "operation" 91
karkaśatva "hardness"; "roughness" en. 239
karman
— "action"; "act" 95, 152, 196, en. 42
— "object" 176
kartṛ "agent" 188, en. 395
kārya "effect" fn. 75,
kāryahetu "reason consisting in an effect" en. 397
kāryakāraṇabhāva "causality" 162
kāya
— "body" en. 132, 198
— "collection" en. 327
ke cit "some people" 102
keśa "hair" en. 227, 370
keśoṇḍuka "tangled hair"; "a mesh of hair" en. 155, 370
kevala
— "alone" 191, en. 415
— "pure" 132, 133, en. 214
kleśa "passions" 99, 100, en. 17, 32, 87, 99, 121, 122a
kliṣṭa "defiled" en. 131
kṛtajña "grateful" 124
kṛtakatva "being a product" 25
kṣānti "patience" 98, en. 92
kuśalajīvitendriya "virtuous vital faculty" 130
kuśalamūla "root of virtue" 103, en. 97
kuṇapa "corpse" 168
lakṣaṇa
— "character" 58, 59, 74, 88, 183
— "rule" 118
lakṣaṇaniḥsvabhāvatā "absence of nature concerning characters" fn. 124, en. 50
lapanā "vaunting oneself" 131
lokottara "supramundane" 89
luk "suppression"; "dropping out" 118, en. 154
mahābhūta "gross elements"; "elements" 97, 142, 150, 195, en. 383, 385
mahat "great one" (Sāṃkhya) en. 68
mahattva "largeness" en. 249
mala "defilement" en. 198
mamakāra "the conception of [what is] mine" 122
māṃsapiṇḍa "ball of flesh" en. 264
manas "the mind"; "mental organ" 112, 161, 164, 192, fn. 26, en. 60, 187, 286, 321, 326, 397, 425
manasādhiṣṭhitā "controlled by the mind" en. 344
mānasāpratyakṣa "mental perception" en. 425, 428
maṅgala "auspiciousness" 131
manovijñāna "mental consciousness" 94, 136, 163, 169, fn. 26, en. 428
manovṛtti "operation of the mental organ" en. 286
mantra "spells" 32, 108, 170
marīci "mirage" 169
māṣa en. 378
māyā "illusion" 149, 169, 179, 194
middha "sleep"; "sloth" 88, en. 10, 439
middhasaṃprayukta "associated with sleep" en. 439
mithyāsaṃvṛti "false convention" 41, 46, 50, 68, fn. 106
moha "bewilderment" 99, 101, 109, 124, en. 54, 131
mokṣa "liberation" 101, 115, en. 128
moṣadharmaka "deceptive" en. 375
moṣadharman s.v. moṣadharmaka en. 375
mṛṣā "false"; "deceptive" 112, 169
mṛṣā moṣadharmaka "false and deceptive" 188, 198
mudga en. 378
mūrchā "unconsciousness" 168
na yuktaḥ "incoherent"; "irrational"; "incorrect" 94
na siddhaḥ "unestablished" 94
nairātmya "selflessness" 26, 102, 105
nairātmyadarśana "the view of selflessness" 125
nāman "name" 162
naraka "hell"; "hells" 104
nāsti kiṃcit "do not exist at all" 138
netara "out of the ordinary" 126, en. 181

neyārtha "interpretative meaning" 54
nidhyāna "discrimination" 101
niḥsaraṇa "deliverance" 98
niḥśreyasa "what is supremely excellent" 100, 117
niḥsvabhāva "no-nature" "absence of nature" 54, 58, fn. 124
niḥsvabhāvatā "absence of nature" fn. 124, en. 50
nimitta
— "character" 127, en. 193
— "ground" en. 44
nirabhilāpyasvabhāvatā "inexpressible nature" fn. 119
nirāmiṣa "free from worldliness" 116
nirmāṇa "magically created being", "magical being" 170, en. 441
nirodha "cessation" 99, en. 262, 356
nirupadhiśeṣaṃ nirvāṇam / nirupadhiśeṣanirvāṇa "nirvāṇa without remainder" en. 17, 215
nirveda "revulsion" 101
nirvikalpaka "non-conceptual" en. 60
nirvikalpakaṃ pratyakṣam "non-conceptual perception" en. 60
nirvṛtti "cessation" 126, en. 182
niścaya "certainty" fn. 48.
niścita "ascertained" fn. 48
niścitagrahaṇa "the word 'ascertained' [in the *trairūpya*]" fn. 48
nītārtha "definitive meaning" 55
nivartaka "quietening" 123
niyama "restriction"; "necessity" en. 240, 242
nyāya "reason"; "rationality" 87
pada "phrase" 162
padārtha
— "category" (Vaiśeṣika) 32, 94, en. 42, 44, 61, 53, 54
— "entity" 89
pāka "heating"; "cooking" en. 257
pakṣa "thesis" 32, 75, en. 25, 129
pañcadhā "five ways" 127, en. 363
pāpa "evil action" 105
para "distant" 180
paramāṇu "atoms" 139
paramārtha
— "really true" 110
— "ultimate reality" 87, 158
paramārthaniḥsvabhāvatā "absence of nature concerning the ultimate" en. 50
paramārthasatya "ultimate truth" en. 198, 366
paramārthika "really true" 110
pāramitā "perfection" 98
pāraṃparyeṇa "step by step" 101
parapravāda "rival assertions" en. 112, 200
parapravādin "rival teacher" 128, en. 200
parārthānumāna "inference-for-others" fn. 37
paratantra / paratantrasvabhāva "dependent nature" 41, 44, 45, 51, 52, 54-61, 66, 68, 74, fn. 2, 92, 108, 127, 141, en. 50
paravāda "rival assertions" en. 112
pari-CHID "cognize" 135
pariccheda "discrimination"; "individuation" 185, 193
parihāra "reply" 170
parikalpita / parikalpitasvabhāva "thoroughly imagined nature" 42, 51, 55, 56, 58-61, 66, 68, 74, 149, fn. 2, 26, 92, en. 50
parimāṇa "size" 143, (five sorts) en. 249
pariṇāma
— "development" 55, 154, en. 68, 281, 283
— "transformation" (Sāṃkhya) en. 68
pariṇāmaduḥkhatā "suffering of change" en. 85
pariniṣpanna / pariniṣpannasvabhāva "thoroughly established nature" 54, 56-60, 74, fn. 2, en. 50
paripāka "maturation" 101, en. 90
paripūrakakarman "accomplishing karma" 152
pariśuddha "pure" 133
parokṣa "imperceptible" 25-28, 31, 91, 120, en. 28
paryanuyoga "issue" 188
paryavasthāna "ensnarements" 91, en. 9, (ten sorts) en. 32
paryāya "approach" 103
paryāyaśabda "synonym" 170
pāṣaṇḍin "heretic" 117
PAṬH "read" en. 127
paṭu "keen"; "intelligent" 167
pradhāna (Sāṃkhya) "the Principle" 21, 22, 69, 71
prāgvāyu "primordial wind" en. 394

prajñā "wisdom" 98, en. 2, 97
prajñācakṣus "eye of wisdom" 101, 105, en. 91
prajñapti "designation" 64, 92, 137, en. 40, 100, 363
prajñaptisat "existent as [simply] a designation" 64, en. 40
prajñaptito 'sti s.v. prajñaptisat 94
prakṛti "Primordial Nature" (Sāṃkhya) 21, 32, 159, 160, fn. 51, en. 54, 75, 219, 289, 308, 312, 361
prakṛtisthagotra "naturally abiding buddha-nature" en. 198
pramāda "carelessness" 88, 99, 172, en. 10
pramāṇa "means of valid cognition" 28, 30, 33, 35 97, 160, 179, 188, fn. 25, 37, 51, 64, 75, 78, 79, 86, 107, 109, 117, en. 124, 292, 314, 375, 376, 428
pramāṇabhūta "became a *pramāṇa*" fn. 59
pramāṇaphala "the result of the means of valid cognition 9, fn. 25,
prameya "what is validly cognized" fn. 25, 75
praṇidhāna "vow" 98
prāṇin "sentient being" en. 106
prāpaka(tva) "making one arrive at" fn. 86
prapañca "proliferations" 59, 103, 171, fn. 119, en. 100
prāptakāritā s.v. prāpyakāritva 189
prāptakāritva s.v. prāpyakāritva 188, en. 294
prāpyakāritva "[the sense organ] operates by contacting [its object] en. 294
prāpyakāritvavāda, see Index of Proper Names.
prasajyapratiṣedha "non-implicative negation" en. 102, 223
prasiddha "commonly acknowledged [linguistic conventions]" fn. 49
pratijñā "thesis" 75
pratiṣedha "negation" 103, 189, en. 102, 401
pratītya "depending on"; "dependent" 127, en. 18[illegible]
pratītyasamutpāda "dependent origination" en. 185
pratyāhāra "condensed form" en. 158
pratyakṣa 40, 44, 176, 177, 178, fn. 71, en. 358
— "perceptible" 26-28, 44, 175, 179, 180, fn. 71, en. 373, 374
— "perception" 37, 44, 91, 94, 177, fn. 37, 49, 97, en. 53, 60, 314, 365, 367, 428
pratyaya
— "[causal] condition" 154, 187, en. 397
— "conviction" 125, en. 45, 178
— "knowledge" 191, en. 413
pratyāyaka "refer" 140, en. 328
pratyekabuddha "solitary enlightened one" 128, en 94, 197
pravartaka "activate"; "set in motion" 123, en. 144
pravṛtti "functioning" 167, en. 345
prayāsa "effort" 110
prayoga "reasoning" 29, fn. 75, en. 129
preta "hungry ghost" 125
priyavacana "pleasant speech" 112, en. 134
pṛthagjana "the profane [people] 100, 123
puṇya "merit" 98
puṇyakṣetra "field of merit" 109, en. 125
pudgalanairātmya "selflessness of the person" 127
puruṣa "Spirit" (Sāṃkhya) 159, en. 75, 289, 309
pūrvaka "be preceded" 141
pūrvanivāsānusmṛtijñānasākṣātkārābhijñā "the super-knowledge which realizes an understanding [capable] of remembering past lives" en. 5
rajas "agitation" 94, 156, en. 54
rasa "taste" 140, 141, en. 292
raśmi "light-ray" en. 291
ṛddhi "miraculous powers" 31, 91, en. 27, 81
rikta "empty" 194
roga "sickness" 194
rūpa 161, 162, en. 321
— "character [of a logical reason]" fn. 94
— "colour" 94, 144, 161, en. 56, 241, 248
— "form" i.e. synonym of "matter" 26, en. 229
— "[visual] form" = colour and shape 135, 180, en. 362, 383
rūpadhātu "realm of form" 152
rūpādi "colour, etc." s.v. rūpa 94
rūpaprasāda "subtle matter" 150, en. 236, 264
rūpatva "colourness" 145

rūpavat "physical"; "having form" 190
rūpāyatana "domain of [visual] form" 141, 182, en. 229
rūpin "physical"; "having form" 190
rūpīndriya "physical senses" 111, 136
śabda "sound" 163, en. 327
śābda/śabda "testimony" 28, 33, fn. 37, fn. 51, 84
śabdatva "soundness" 146, 166, 167
śabdārtha "meaning of a word" en. 37
sabhāga "has its own activity" 152, en. 272
ṣaḍāyatana "six domains" en. 187
sādhana "means of proof" 27, 81, fn. 75
sādharmyadṛṣṭānta "homologous example" 90, fn. 79, en. 329a
sādhya "the [proposition] to be proved"; "something to be proved" 135, 181
sādhyadharma "property to be proved" fn. 107, en. 24, 258, 329a
sādhyasama "[the reason] is similar to what is to be proven" 81, 139, 181, en. 227, 379
sahopalambhaniyama "necessity for being apprehended together" fn. 131
sakṛdāgāmin "once returner" en. 19
sākṣādvṛtti "applying directly" 71
sākṣāt "directly"; "manifestly" 105, 111, 142
sākṣātkaraṇa "realization" 87
sākṣātkriyā s.v. sākṣātkaraṇa 87
śakti "power" 152, en. 283
śalya "splinter" 194
samādhi
— "[meditative] trance" 197, en. 193
— = samāpatti en. 134
sāmagrī "collection" 137
samānajāti "same [natural] kind" 145, en. 252a
samanantarapratyaya "immediately preceding condition" 165, en. 339, 397
samānārthatā "sameness of goal" 112, en. 134
sāmānya "universal" en. 38, 42, 53, 57, 60, 72, 390
sāmānyalakṣaṇa "universal character" 8, 92, 139, 141, 142, 148, 163, fn. 89, en. 40, 66, 221, 232, 330, 333, 366
sāmānyaviśeṣa "limited universal" 94, 144, en. 53
samāpatti "meditative absorption" en. 134
samāpatticitta "mind in meditative absorption" 165
samāpattiviśeṣa; samādhiviśeṣa "various meditative absorptions" 99
samārambha "apply oneself"; "undertake" en. 18
sāmarthya "power" 152
samāsatas "in brief" 112, en. 133
samatā
— "equanimity" 106
— "similarity" en. 332, (fivefold) en. 427
samavāya "inherence" 94, en. 42, 390
saṃ-CAR "pass over" 166
saṃghāta "collection" 137
saṃghātaparamāṇu " molecule"; "atoms which are aggregates" en. 417
saṃgraha "summary" 88
saṃgrahavastu "way of gathering [disciples]" 124, en. 134, 175
saṃjñā "notion" 164, 168, 193, en. 348, 427, 432
saṃjñāskandha "the aggregate of notions" 84, 168, 193
saṃkhyā "number" en. 39
saṃkleśa "defilements" 118
saṃprajānāḥ pratismṛtāḥ "fully conscious and mindful" 98
saṃprāpta "reached" 191
saṃprayoga "association" 194
saṃprayuktakahetu "associated cause" en. 427
saṃskāra "conditioned things"; "conditionings" 48, 100, 116, fn. 108
saṃskāraduḥkhatā "suffering due to conditioning" 100, en. 85
saṃskṛta "conditioned" 149, 179
saṃsthāna "shape" 141, 182, en. 235
saṃtāna "continuum"; "stream" en. 40, 206
samudāya "synthesis"; "aggregate" 96, en. 38, 43, 72
saṃvedana "cognition" 38, fn. 131, fn. 135
saṃvṛti "convention" 158, fn. 108
saṃvṛtimātra "simply conventional" 40, 48, fn. 108
saṃvṛtisatya "conventional truth" 44, 46, 48, 148, en. 198, 366
saṃvyavahāra "convention" 178

sāntara "having an interval"; "set apart" 158, en. 301
sāntaragrahaṇa "apprehension from a distance" en. 290, 301
sapratigha "having resistance" 93, en. 48
saras "lake" 140, 141, en. 292
śarīra s.v. deha en. 132
sārūpya "same sort" 110
sāsrava "defiled" 111, en. 128, 129
śāstra "treatise" fn. 58
sat "existent" 59
satkāryavāda — see Index of Proper Names
satkāya en. 86
satkāyadṛṣṭi "the [erroneous] view concerning the personality 100, 104, 107, en. 86, 121
sattā "existence" 58, 59, en. 53
sattva
— "ontological excellence" (Sāṃkhya) 94, 96, 97, 156, 160, en. 54
— "sentient being" en. 106
sattva, etc. (Sāṃkhya) = three guṇas en. 219
sāvaraṇa "having resistance" 138
savikalpaka "conceptual" en. 60
savikalpakapratyakṣa "conceptual perception" en. 60
siddhānta "doxographical literature"; "philosophical system" 7, en. 94
śīla "moral discipline" 98, 102
śiva "tranquillity" 89
skandha "aggregate" 127, en. 86, 188, 427
skandhān upādāya prajñapyate "designated in dependence upon the [five] aggregates" 127, en. 185
SMṚ "recall" 163
smṛtaḥ saṃprajānaḥ s.v. saṃprajānāḥ pratismṛtāḥ en. 79
smṛti "memory" 163
sopadhiśeṣaṃ nirvāṇam "nirvāṇa with remainder" en. 215
sparśa "touch sensations" 147
sparśana "bodily feelings" 147
SPHAR "spread out"; "distribute" en. 226
sphaṭika "crystal"; "quartz" 107
sphoṭa en. 230
śraddhādhimukti "faithful application" en. 45
śrāmaṇyaphala "fruit of religious practice" 89, en. 19
śrāvaka "hearer" 128, en. 94, 197
srotaāpanna "stream enterer" en. 19
sthiti "duration" en. 206
su "nominative singular *s*" 118, en. 154
śuddhakadhyāna "pure meditative trance" 172
sugati "fortunate state of existence" 90
sukha "pleasure" en. 54
śūnya "void" 58, 59, 195, en. 98
śūnyatā "voidness" 58, 59, 88, 103, 120, 127, fn. 82, en. 11, 98
śūnyatāsamādhi "[meditative] trance directed towards voidness" en. 193
sup "case-ending" 118, en. 154
svabhāva en. 184
— "essential property" fn. 75, en. 184
— "nature" 37, 40, 41, 44, 47, 50, 53, 55, 56, 58, 60, 67, 78, 90, 190, 194, fn. 92, 114, 123, 131, 147, 148, fn. 109, en. 40, 50, 184, 304, 363, 380
svabhāvahetu "reason which is an essential property" fn. 135, en. 184
svabhāvapratibandha "essential connection" 25, fn. 70, en. 184
svabhāvena "by nature" 175
svābhāvikakāya / svabhāvakāya "essential-body" en. 198
svalakṣaṇa "particular"; "particular character" 8, 22, 37, 38, 39, 44, 50, 52, 69, 70, 127, 147, 163, 176, fn. 88-89, 95, fn. 112, 131, en. 37, 40, 184, 333, 364, 367
svarga "heaven" 26, 133
svārthānumāna "inference-for-oneself" fn. 107
svarūpa "essence" 126, 181, en. 37, 184
svasaṃvedana "self-awareness" = svasaṃvitti 8, 40, 45, 51, 52, fn. 25, fn. 92, fn. 131
svasaṃvitti "self-awareness" 8, 9, 40, fn. 25, fn. 131
svasaṃvittibhāga "the part [of consciousness] consisting in self-awareness" fn. 25
svasaṃvittisvasaṃvitti "self-awareness of self-awareness" fn. 25

svasaṃvittisvasaṃvittibhāga "the part [of consciousness] consisting in self-awareness of self-awareness" fn. 25

svātmani kriyāvirodha "the contradiction of there being an action [directed] to itself" en. 310

tādātmya "essential identity" fn. 131

taimirika "one who has the eye disease known as *timira*" 118, 177, en. 370

tamas "dullness" en. 54

tanmātra "subtle element" 97, en. 68, 219

tārkika "logician" 176, en. 364

tathatā "thusness" 58, 112, 117, en. 103, 135

tathatālakṣaṇa "defined as thusness" en. 356

tathyasaṃvṛti "correct convention" 41, 46, 50, 52, 68, fn. 106

tatsabhāga "that which is analogous to a *sabhāga*" en. 272

tattva "truth"; "true nature" 31, 91, 101, 102, 117, 186

tāvat "to that degree" 155

timira "opacity / obscurity of one's vision" 64, 118, 119, 173, 177, fn. 107, en. 156, 157, 227, 370

tiṅ "verbal ending" 118, en. 158

tīrthakara "Outsider" 118

trairūpya "the triple-characterization [of a reason]" fn. 48

trayaduḥkhatā "three sorts of suffering" en. 85

trikāla "three times" 167

trisvabhāva "three natures" 55, fn. 2, 116

tṛṣṇā "craving" en. 128

tryadhvan "three times" 167

tuccha "insignificant" 194

tuṇa — a type of musical instrument 192, en. 419

ubhayaprasiddhi "acknowledgment by both parties" fn. 107

ubhayasiddha "established for both parties" fn. 94

udvega "fear" en. 118

upacāra "metaphorical description" 103, en. 228

upādāna en. 185
- "appropriated object" 127, en. 185
- "appropriation" en. 185
- "material cause" 178, 180, en. 185
- "substratum" 175, en. 363, 364

upādātṛ "appropriator" 127, 176, en. 185, en. 363

upādāya "on account of", "dependent upon" 127, en. 185

upādāya prajñapti "dependent designation" 64, 175, 196, en. 40, 363

upādāya prajñapyamānatva "being dependently designated" 127

upādeya
- "what is to be appropriated" (s.v. upādāna) en. 185
- "what is to be realized" 116

upamāna "comparison" fn. 37

upāya "method"; "means" en. 16

upāyakauśalya "skillful means" 92, en. 34

utkṛṣṭa "superior" 126

utpattiniḥsvabhāvatā "absence of nature concerning production" en. 50

vāda "argument"; "assertion" en. 112

vaidharmyadṛṣṭānta "heterologous example" en. 258

vaktṛ "speaker" 191

vākya "sentence" 163

varṇa "colour" 141, 182, en. 235

vāsanā "[latent karmic] tendencies" 98, 153, fn. 117, en. 278

vaśitā "mastery" 98

vastu "real entity" en. 333

vastubalapravṛttānumāna / vastubalapravṛtta "inference which functions by the force of reality" 24-29, 33-35, 67, fn. 79

vāyu "wind"; "air" 187

vidhi "affirmation" 189, en. 102

vidyā "knowledge" en. 53

vi-JÑĀ "cognize" 135

vijñaptimātra(tā) fn. 28, 127, 131

vikalpa "conceptualization"; "concept" 22, 88, 91, 103, en. 2, 31, 54, 428, 364

vikalpakaṃ vijñānam "conceptual consciousness" 194, en. 427, 428

vikurvaṇa "miraculous transformations" 31, 91, en. 27

vimokṣamukha "access to liberation" 127, 128, en. 193

vimukti "emancipation" 133
vīṇā "lute" 192, en. 419
vineya "[person] to be trained" 101
vinivṛtti "cessation" 89
vi-PAC "[yield a] retribution" 111
vipāka en. 131
vipāka "retribution" 125, 132, 186, en. 131
vipākahetu "retributive cause" en. 128, 131
vipākaphala "retributive effect" 110, en. 128, 131
viparīta "erroneous" 168
vipatti "misfortune" 130
viruddha "contradictory" 103
vīrya "vigour" 98
viṣaya "object" 135, en. 280
viṣayākāra "aspect of the object" 9
viṣayin "subject" en. 280, 373
viśeṣa "particular" 92, en. 42, 43, 53, 60, 72, 390
vi-ŚṚ "crumble to pieces" 167
vitarkavicāra "ratiocination and investigation" 91, 155, en. 31
vivāda "dispute" 147
vivakṣā "speech-intention" 70
vṛtti "operation" 168
vyañjana "letter" en. 327
vyañjanakāya "collection of letters" 163
vyāpti "implication"; "pervasion" fn. 135, en. 276, 329a
vyartha "pointless" 155
vyasana "misfortune" 130
vyatirekavyāpti "contraposition of the implication" en. 258
vyavahāra "convention" 103, 158
yāna "vehicle" 102
yathākramam "in their due order" 87, en. 5
yathāyogam "duly" 95
yāvat "up to" 96
yāvat ... tāvat 20, 21
yoga "connection" 95
yugapad "all at once" en. 337
yukta "coherent" 109
yukti "reason"; "reasoning" 87

INDEX OF TIBETAN TERMS

'ba' źig "alone"; "pure"
= kevala 132, 133
bag chags "[latent karmic] tendencies"
= vāsanā fn. 117
bdag gi ba "possessions of the self"
= ātmīya 118
bdag po'i rkyen "dominant condition"
= adhipatipratyaya 187
bden grub "true establishment" fn. 109
bden par yod pa "true existence" 73
bkra śis "auspiciousness"
= maṅgala 131
blaṅ bar bya ba "what is to be realized"
= upādeya 116
blo rigs bdun du dbye ba "the sevenfold classification of cognition" fn. 86
bram ze "Brahmin" en. 208
brdzun pa bslu ba'i chos can "false and deceptive"
= mṛṣā moṣadharmaka 188
brgal źiṅ brtag pa "issue"; "at issue"
= paryanuyoga 188
brjod par 'dod pa "speech-intention"
= vivakṣā 70
brten nas 'dogs pa "dependently designated"
= upādāya prajñapti 175
bsags pa "accumulation" 177
bsam gyis mi khyab pa "inconceivable"
= acintya en. 392
bsgrub bya "something to be proved"
= sādhya 181
bsgrub bya daṅ mtshuṅs pa "[the reason] is similar to what is to be proved"
= sādhyasama 81
bslu ba'i chos can "deceptive"
= moṣadharman; moṣadharmaka; moṣadharmiṇaḥ en. 375
btags pa tsam "mere designation" en. 40
btags pa yod pa "existence as a designation"
= prajñaptisat en. 40
byaṅ grol "emancipation"
= apavarga; vimukti 133
byed pa "instrument"
= karaṇa 175, 188, en. 395
byed pa po "agent"
= kartṛ 188, en. 395
'byuṅ ba chen po "elements"; "gross elements"
= mahābhūta 195
'byuṅ 'gyur "derivative from the elements"
= bhautika 185
chos can 'ba' źig pa "the nominal subject" fn. 48
chos can mthun snaṅ ba "commonly appearing subject" fn. 94, 95, 107
chos daṅ rjes su mthun pa'i chos la źugs pa
= dharmānudharmapratipanna en. 80; see chos daṅ rjes su mthun pa'i chos kyi nan tan
chos daṅ rjes su mthun pa'i chos kyi nan tan "practices which are in keeping with the Dharma"
= dharmānudharmapratipatti en. 80
cuṅ zad lkog gyur "imperceptible" fn. 71.

dbaṅ po daṅ dbaṅ po la gnas pa "occurs in connection with the various individual sense organs"
= akṣam akṣaṃ prati vartate 177
dbyibs "shape"
= saṃsthāna 182
de kho na ñid
= tattva "truth" 116, 117, 186
= tathatā "thusness" 117
dgag bya "the object to be refuted" fn. 48
dgag bya ṅos 'dzin "recognizing the object to be refuted" fn. 109
dge ba'i srog gi dbaṅ po "virtuous vital faculty"
= kuśalajīvitendriya 130
dgoṅs pa "thought"; "intention"
= abhiprāya fn. 48
dgoṅs gźi "intentional foundation" fn. 48
dṅos po raṅ mtshan pa "particular entities" en. 379
dṅos po'i lta ba "realist views" 129
dṅos por lta ba s.v. dṅos po'i lta ba en. 205
don dam bden pa "ultimate truth"
= paramārthasatya en. 366
don gyi sdod lugs "objective mode of being" 43, fn. 95
don spyi "object-universal" fn. 48, en. 367
dor bar bya ba "what is to be abandoned"
= heya 116
dpyad pa gsum "the threefold analysis" 24, fn. 75
'du byed "conditioning"
= saṃskāra 116
'du śes g.yer po "clear and distinct notion" 177
'du śes kyi phuṅ po "the aggregate of notions"
= saṃjñāskandha 84
'dus byas "conditioned"
= saṃskṛta 179
'dzud par byed "guide"; "set in motion"
= parvartaka en. 144
gegs byed "impediment" fn. 75
gliṅ bu "flute" en. 419
gnod byed "invalidator" fn. 75
gos med "Jain" en. 208
grub mtha' "philosophical system"; "doxographical literature"
= siddhānta en. 428
gtan tshig kyi gźi ma grub pa "the reason's locus is unestablished" fn. 94
g.yer po "intelligent"; "clear"
= paṭu en. 367
gźan dbaṅ "dependent phenomena"
= paratantra fn. 2
gźan smra ba "rival assertions"
= paravāda en. 201
gźan stoṅ "voidness of what is other" fn. 2, fn. 126
gzigs pa "see" 48
gzugs can "physical"; "having form"
= rūpavat; rūpin 190
gzugs kyi skye mched "the domain of [visual] form"
= rūpāyatana 182
ji lta ba "how things are" en. 198
ji sñed pa "how things appear" en. 198
'jigs tshogs la lta ba "the view concerning the personality"
= satkāyadṛṣṭi en. 86
kha gsag "vaunting oneself"
= lapanā 131
kha dog "colour"
= varṇa 182
'khrugs pa "confusion" en. 141
khyab par byed pa "spread out"; "pervade"
= SPHAR en. 226
kun brtags "thoroughly imagined"
= parikalpita fn. 2
kun nas dkris pa "ensnarement"
= paryavasthāna en. 32
kun nas ñon moṅs pa "defilements"
= saṃkleśa 118
kun nas ñon moṅs pa'i phyogs "orientation towards the completely defiled" 115
kun rdzob bden pa "conventional truth"
= saṃvṛtisatya en. 366
kun rdzob tsam "simply conventional" fn. 48
= saṃvṛtimātra fn. 108.

kun tu tha sñad "convention"
= saṃvyavahāra 178
las
= karman "object" 176
= karman "action"; "act" 186
lhag pa'i bsam pa "disposition"
= adhyāśaya 115
lkog gyur "imperceptible"
= parokṣa 31
log śes "erroneous cognition" fn. 86
lta ba "sight"; "vision"
= darśana en. 297
lta bar bya ba ñid "perceptibility"
= draṣṭavyatva 184
luṅ "scripture" en. 204
= āgama 27
luṅ gegs byed / luṅ gegs byed du 'dod pa'i lugs "the position which holds that scriptures [can at most] be an "impediment" [to the truth of an opposing proposition] fn. 75
luṅ gnod byed / luṅ gnod byed du 'dod pa'i lugs "the position which holds that scriptures [can] invalidate [an opposing proposition] fn. 75
mchiṅ bu "rhinestones" en. 164
mi bslu ba / mi slu ba "non-belying"
= avisaṃvādin 179, fn. 86, en. 375
mi dmigs pa "non-perception"
= anupalabdhi 129
mig "eye" en. 409
mig 'phrul "illusion"; "Indra's net"
= indrajāla en. 210
mṅon par gsal ba "manifestation"
= abhivyakti 184
mṅon par tho ba "a good position [in the world]"
= abhyudaya 117
mṅon sum
= pratyakṣa "perception" fn. 97
= pratyakṣa "perceptible" 175, 185, en. 373
mṅon sum pa "perceptible" en. 428
mtho ris "heaven"
= svarga 133
mthun snaṅ ba / mthun par snaṅ ba "similarly appearing" 42, fn. 94; cf. chos can mthun snaṅ ba
mtshan gźi "illustrative example" en. 128
mtshan ñid "character"; "rule"
= lakṣaṇa 118, 183
mtshuṅs ldan gyi rgyu "associated cause"
= saṃprayuktakahetu en. 427
mu stegs byed pa "Outsiders"
= tīrthakara 118
ṅag "speech" fn. 78
ñe bar len pa
= upādāna "substratum" 175
= upādāna "material cause" 178, 180
ñe bar len pa po "appropriator"
= upādātṛ 176
ñe bar len pa'i bya ba "action of appropriation" 176
ṅes par legs pa "what is supremely excellent"
= niḥśreyasa 118
ñon ma moṅs pa
= akliṣṭa "undefiled"
pha rol "distant"
= para 180
pha rol po'i smra ba "rival assertions"
= parapravāda en. 201
'phags pa "Noble Ones"
= ārya 129
phan pa daṅ gnod pa "aided or impaired"
= kārāpakāra en. 274
phas kyi rgol ba "rival teachers"; "rival assertors"
= parapravādin; paravādin en. 201
phra rgyas "propensities [for passions]"
= anuśaya en. 87
phyi 'chos "outward show" 131, en. 212
phyi rol gyi don "external object"
= bāhyārtha fn. 131
rab rib can "one who suffers from timira"
= taimirika 118, 177
rab tu 'jug pa "functioning"
= pravṛtti en. 345
raṅ bźin "nature"
= svabhāva 78

raṅ bźin gyis "by nature"
= svabhāvena 175
raṅ bźin gyis yod pa "existence by [the entity's own] nature" 73
raṅ gi mtshan ñid "particular"; "particular character"
= svalakṣaṇa 176
raṅ gi ṅo bo "essence"
= svarūpa 181
raṅ rig "self-awareness"
= svasaṃvedana fn. 2
raṅ rten chos can "the real subject" fn. 48
raṅ stoṅ "voidness of [the entity] itself" fn. 126
rdzas "substance"
= dravya 175
rgyu mtshan med pa'i yid dpyod "true presumption where there is no reason" fn. 86
rgyud pa "misfortune"
= vipatti; vyasana 130
ri mo'i skyes bu'i rnam pa ltar "like a [mere] simulacrum"; lit. "like the aspect of a painted person" 115
rkyen "[causal] condition"
= pratyaya 187
rluṅ "wind"; "air"
= vāyu 187
rnam bden pa "real images/aspects"
= satyākāra fn. 91
rnam bden pa daṅ mthun pa "inclined towards Satyākāravāda" fn. 113
rnam pa daṅ bcas pa "having images/aspects"
= sākāra[vādin] fn. 91
rnam pa med pa "without images/aspects"
= nirākāra[vādin] fn. 91
rnam par rtog pa "conceptualization"
= vikalpa 22
rnam par rtog pa med pa "without conceptualization" fn. 97
rnam par smin pa "retribution"
= vipāka 186
rnam rdzun pa "deceptive images/aspects"
= alīkākāra fn. 91
rnam rdzun daṅ mthun pa "inclined towards Alīkākāravāda" fn. 113
rnam smin "retribution"
= vipāka 132
rnam smin gyi rgyu "retributive cause"
= vipākahetu en. 128
rta'i tshogs "cavalry corps"
= aśvakāya en. 431
rtog bral "free from conceptualization"
= kalpanāpoḍha 177
rtog ge ba "logician"
= tārkika 176, en. 364
rtogs pa "realization" en. 204
rtogs pa'i blo / rtogs pa "knowledge" fn. 86,
rtsa myon drug "six principal passions" en. 87
śa sbraṅ "gadfly" 177, en. 370a
śākya (pa) "Buddhist" en. 208
sbraṅ bu mchu riṅs "mosquito" 177, en. 370a
sbyin sreg "fire offering"
= homa 131
sbyor ba "reasoning"
= prayoga fn. 75.
sdaṅ ba "dislike" 116
sems can "sentient being"
= sattva en. 177
sems daṅ sems las byuṅ ba "mind and mental factors"
= cittacaitta 176
śes pa "consciousness" fn. 78
śes pa la snaṅ ba'i cha "something appearing to consciousness" 46, fn. 94
śes pa la snaṅ ba daṅ mthun par dṅos po gnas pa "the entity conforms to the appearance to consciousness" 46
sgra spyi "word-universal" en. 367
sgyu ma "illusion"
= māyā 179
śin tu lkog gyur "completely imperceptible"
= atyantaparokṣa 24, 77, fn. 73
skra śad "hair" 118, en. 155
skra śad 'dziṅs "tangled hair"; "a mesh of hair"
= keśoṇḍuka en. 155
skyes bu "person" fn. 78,

sna ma'i me tog "nutmeg blossoms"
= jātikusuma 179
snaṅ ba "appearances" 51
snaṅ ba'i cha "appearances" 51, fn. 94
sñan dṅags mkhan "poet" 12, fn. 2
snaṅ la ma ṅes pa'i blo "inattentive cognition" fn. 86
sñom par 'jug pa "meditative absorption"
= samāpatti en. 134
spros pas chog "Enough of these digressions!"
= ity alaṃ prasaṅgena 179
spyi "universal"
= sāmānya en. 38, 390
spyi mtshan "universal character"
= sāmānyalakṣaṇa en. 40
tha sñad du raṅ bźin gyis grub pa "conventionally established by its nature" 43, fn. 95
tha sñad du raṅ ṅos nas grub pa "conventionally established from its own side" 43, fn. 95
*thal phyir "sequence and reason" fn. 47
thar pa "liberation"
= mokṣa 115
the tshom "doubt" fn. 86
thun moṅ ma yin pa "specific"
= asādhāraṇa 177
tshad ma "means of valid cognition"
= pramāṇa 179, fn. 78
tshad ma'i skyes bu "person of authority" 29, 30, fn. 48, fn. 78
tshul mtshuṅs pa "same way" fn. 76
yid ches kyi rtags "reason based on authority/trust" fn. 75.
tshaṅ tshiṅ "tangle"; "thicket" en. 206
tshig 'grel "word-commentaries" 15
tshu rol "near"
= apara 180
ya mtshan can "heretic"
= pāṣaṇḍin 117
yan lag can "whole"
= avayavin 175
ye śes gzigs pa "insightful vision"
= jñānadarśana en. 2
ye śes mthoṅ ba s.v. ye śes gzigs pa
yi ge "syllable"
= akṣara 181
yid ches kyi rtags "reason based on authority" fn. 75
yid ches pa'i rjes dpag "inference based on [scriptural] authority" en. 428
yid ches pa'i tshig "authoritative words"; "trustworthy words"
= āptavacana fn. 54
yid dpyod "true presumption" 34, 35, 67, fn. 54, 86
yoṅs grub "thoroughly established"
= pariniṣpanna fn. 2
yoṅs su dag pa "pure"
= pariśuddha 133, en. 214
yoṅs su gcod pa "discrimination"; "individuation"
= pariccheda 185
yul can "subject"
= viṣayin en. 373
zaṅ ziṅ med pa "free of worldliness"
= nirāmiṣa 116

INDEX OF CHINESE TERMS

ā jiē tuó 阿揭陀 "antidote"
= agada 105

ài yǔ 愛語 "pleasant speech"
= priyavacana 112

bàng yán 傍言 "digressions"
= atiprasaṅga 164

běn 本 "origin" 165

běn yuàn 本願 "vow"
= praṇidhāna 98

bǐ liáng 比量 "inference"
= anumāna 136

bǐ zhī 比知 "inference"
= anumāna 142

biàn jì suǒ zhí 遍計所執
"thoroughly imagined"
= parikalpita 149

biàn jì suǒ zhí xìng 遍計所執性
"thoroughly imagined natures"
= parikalpitasvabhāva 56

biàn 變 "transformation" (Sāṃkhya)
= pariṇāma en. 68

biàn xiàn 變現 "conjurings" 155

biàn yì 變異 "developments"
= pariṇāma 55, 154

biǎo 表
= "positive assertion 103 vidhi? en. 102
"state"; "show" 163

biāo zhì 標幟 "symbol" 169

bié 別 "particular" 96
= viśeṣa 92

bié jiě tuō lü yí 別解脱律儀
"Pratimokṣasaṃvara" 112

bié yǒu 別有 "distinct entity"
= bhāvāntara 93

bō 撥 "denigrate"
= apavāda 172

bù shī 布施 "giving"
= dāna 112

bù chéng 不成 "unestablished"
= asiddha 135

bù dìng 不定 "inconclusive"
= anaikāntika 142, 145

bù gòng yīn 不共因 "reason which is [too] exclusive"
= asādhāraṇahetu, asādhāraṇānaikāntika-hetu 163, en. 329a

bù gòng yuán 不共緣 "specific cause"
= asādhāraṇahetu; asādhāraṇakāraṇa en. 367

bù xiāng lí 不相離 "necessarily connected"
= aviyukta; avinābhāva en. 22

chà dì lì 剎帝利 "Kṣatriya" 109

chán fú 纏縛 "ensnarements"
= paryavasthāna 91

chén 塵 "object"
= artha; viṣaya 135

chēng lǐ 稱理 "coherent"
= yukta 109

chéng 乘 "vehicle"
= yāna 102

chéng bàn 成辦 "complete"
= abhiniṣpatti 113

chéng shú 成熟 "maturations"
= paripāka 101

chū lí 出離 "deliverance"
= niḥsaraṇa 98

chū shì 出世 "supramundane"
= lokottara 89

chù 處 "locus"
= āśraya; adhikaraṇa(?) 145

chù 觸 "touch-sensations"
= sparśa 147

chuàn xí 串習 "training"; "habit"
= abhyāsa 100

cì dì yuán 次第緣
"immediately preceding condition"
= samanantarapratyaya 165

cū 麁
= mahattva "large" en. 249
= audārika "coarse" en. 249

cū dà 麁大 "massive" 144

dà 大 "gross elements"; "elements"
= mahābhūta 97, 142

dà zào 大造 "derived from the elements"
= bhautika 150

dà zhǒng 大種 "elements"
= mahābhūta 150

dào chǎng 道場 "seat of enlightenment"
= bodhimaṇḍa 172

dé 德 "quality"
= guṇa 95, 96, 148

dì yù 地獄 "hell"
= naraka 104

diān dǎo 顛倒 "erroneous"
= viparīta 168

dìng 定
= samādhi; samāpatti "meditative absorption" en. 134
= eva "only" en. 240

dìng xīn 定心 "mind in meditative trance"
= dhyānacitta; samāpatticitta 165

dùn 頓 "all at once" 165
= yugapad en. 337

èr xìng děng 二性等 "two, etc."
= dvitvādi 92

fǎ mén 法門 "Dharma approaches"
= dharmaparyāya 98

fǎ suí fǎ xíng 法隨法行
"practices in keeping with the Dharma"
= dharmānudharmapratipatti 98

fǎ yì 法義 "states of affairs"
= artha 162

fán nǎo 煩惱 "passions"
= kleśa 99, 100

fāng wéi 方維 "direction" en. 307

fàng yì 放逸 "carelessness"
= pramāda 88, 99, 172

fēn 分 "part [of consciousness]"
= bhāga fn. 25.

fēn bié 分別 "conceptualization"
= vikalpa 88, 91, 103

fēn míng 分明 "representation" 169

fēn wèi chā bié 分位差別 "different states"
= avasthāviśeṣa en. 40

fú "merit"
= puṇya 98

fú tián 福田 "field of merit"
= puṇyakṣetra 109

gǎn 感
= vi-PAC "retribution" 111
= ā-KṢIP "project" 152

gēn 根 "organs"; "sense organs"
= indriya 97

gēn chù 根處 "sense domain"
= indriyāyatana 152

gēn jìng 根境 "the sense organs and their objects"
= indriyārtha vii

gōng lì 功力 "effort"
= prayāsa 110

gōng néng 功能 "power"
= śakti; sāmarthya 152, en. 283

gòng xiāng 共相 "universal character"
= sāmānyalakṣaṇa 92, 142, 148, 163

hán shì 含識 "sentient being"; see yǒu qíng, en. 106

hé 合 "connection"
= yoga 95

hé hé 和合
= samavāya "inherence" 94
= saṃghāta; sāmagrī "collection" 137

huà 化 "magical creation"
= nirmāṇa 170

huàn shì 幻事 "illusion"
= māyā 149, 169

huì xīng 彗星 "comet" 172

huì yǎn 慧眼 "eye of wisdom"
= prajñācakṣus 101, 105

jí 即 "alone"; "only"

= eva 153

jí miè 寂滅 "cessation [of suffering]" en. 195
= nirodha; śānti 99

jí wēi 極微 "[subtle] atoms"
= paramāṇu 139

jiǎ 假 "designated" 100;
also "false"; "borrow" en. 40
= prajñapti 137

jiǎ hé 假合 "designated connection" 95

jiǎ hé shēng 假合生 "arise from designated connections" en. 64

jiǎ lì 假立 "designation"
= prajñapti 92, en. 40

jiǎ míng 假名
= upādāya prajñapti "dependent designation" en. 40

jiǎ shè 假設 s.v. jiǎ lì en. 40

jiǎ shī shè 假施設 s.v. jiǎ lì en. 40

jiǎ shī shè yǒu 假施設有
"exists as a designation"
= prajñaptisat; prajñaptito 'sti 94

jiǎ shuō 假說 "metaphorical description" 137
= upacāra 103, en. 228

jiǎ xiǎng 假想 "[false] notion"
= saṃjñā 164

jiàn 見
= dṛṣṭi "heretical views" vi
"view" en. 180
"perception" fn. 25.

jiàn qù 見趣 "heresies"
= dṛṣṭigata 90

jiě tuō 解脫 "liberation"
= mokṣa 101

jiè 戒 "moral discipline"
= śīla 102

jìng 境 "object" en. 36

jìng dìng 淨定 "pure meditative trance"
= śuddhakadhyāna 172

jìng lü 靜慮 "meditative trance"
= dhyāna 112

jìng sè 淨色 "subtle matter"
= rūpaprasāda 150

jiù 救 "reply"
= parihāra 170

jū fēn 俱分 "both"
= sāmānyaviśeṣa "limited universal" cf. tóng yì en. 53

jù 句 "phrase"
= pada 162

jù yì 句義
= padārtha "entity" 89
= padārtha "category" 94

jué 覺 "bodily feelings"
= sparśana 147

jué dìng 決定 "necessity"; "restriction"
= avadhāraṇa; niyama en. 240, 242

jué dìng shèng dào 決定勝道
"what is ultimately excellent"
= niḥśreyasa 100

jué huì 覺慧 "intelligence"
= buddhi 88

kě ài yì shú 可愛異熟 "desirable [karmic] retributions"
= iṣṭavipāka 100

kōng 空 "void"; "voidness"
= śūnya; śūnyatā en. 98

kōng kōng kōng děng 空空空等
"voidness, voidness of voidness, etc." 104

kōng wú wǒ 空無我 "selflessness"
= nairātmya 102, 105, en. 96

kōng xíng 空行 "the sphere of voidness" 105

kōng xìng 空性 "voidness"
= śūnyatā 103

kǔ 苦
= rajas en. 54
= duḥkha "suffering" en. 54

lè 樂
= sattva en. 54
= sukha "pleasure" en. 54

lè děng 樂等 "sattva, etc." 96, en. 54

lèi 類 "kind"
= jāti 162

lí xì 離繫 "Jain"
= nirgrantha 108

lí xiāng 離相 "the lack of characters"
= animitta 112

lǐ bù chéng 理不成 "incoherent"; "irrational"
= na yuktaḥ; na siddhaḥ 94

lǐ xiāng wéi 理相違 "incoherent"
= ayukta 152

lì xíng 利行 "beneficial conduct"
= arthacaryā 112

liáng 量
= pramāṇa "means of valid cognition" 97
= parimāṇa "size" 143

liǎo bié 了別 "cognize"
= vi-JÑĀ; pari-CHID 135

lín jìn 隣近 "manifestly"
= sākṣāt 105

liú rù 流入 "pass over"; "pass into"
= saṃ-CAR 166

lùn 論 "argument"
= vāda en. 112

lüè shuō 略說 s.v. lüè yán en. 133

lüè yán 略言 "in brief"
= samāsatas 112, en. 133

mǎn yè 滿業 "accomplishing karma"
= paripūrakakarman 152

mēn 悶 "unconsciousness"
= mūrchā 168

mén 門 "door"; "approach"
= paryāya 103

méng 虻 "gadfly" en. 370a

míng 名 "name"
= nāman 162

míng lì 明利 "keen"

= paṭu 167

míng lùn 明論 "Vedas" 110, en. 127

míng shū 明書 "Vedas" 109

nǎi zhì 乃至 "up to"
= yāvat 96

nán cè 難測 "hard to fathom" 171

nèi shēn 內身 "the body"
= ātmabhāva 168

nèi zhì 內智 "inner mind" 155, en. 286

néng duì 能對 "resister" en. 48

néng jiàn 能見 "what perceives" 91

néng quán 能詮 "referring expressions" 92

néng yuán 能緣 "what apprehends"
= grāhaka 55, 91, 173

niàn 念 "memory"
= smṛti 164

niè pán bù èr mén 涅槃不二門
"the unrivalled door to nirvāṇa" en. 108

niú méng 牛虻 "cattle-fly"; "horsefly" en. 370a

páng bù 傍布 "spread out"; "distribute"
= SPHAR; spharitvā en. 226

píng děng 平等 "equanimity"
= samatā 106

píng tǐ 瓶體 "the vase's nature" 135

pó luó mén 婆羅門 "Brahmin"
= brāhmaṇa 108

qī xīn 期心 "basis"
= āśaya 157

qǐ 起 "functioning"
= pravṛtti? 167

qiān yǐn yīn 牽引因 "propelling cause"
= ākṣepahetu 90

qiǎn 遣 "cease"
= vinivṛtti 89

qiě 且 "to that degree"
= tāvat 155

qīn 親 "direct"
= sākṣāt 111, 142

qīng liáng 清涼 "tranqillity" en. 17
= śiva 89

qù 趣 "path"; "way"
= gati 105

quán 全 "whole"; "totality" en. 415

quán 詮 "state" 163

quán biǎo 詮表 "refer" 162
= pratyāyaka 140, en. 328

rú qí cì dì 如其次第 "in their due order"
= yathākramam 87

rú qí suǒ yīng 如其所應 "duly"
= yathāyogam 95

rú shí lǐ 如實理 "correctly" 108

sà jiā yé jiàn 薩迦耶見
"the [erroneous] view with regard to the personality"

= satkāyadṛṣṭi 104

sān qiān 三千 "three thousand [worlds]" 99

sān qiān dà qiān shì jiè 三千大千世界
s.v. sān qiān en. 82

sān qiān shì jiè 三千世界
s.v. sān qiān en. 82

sān shì 三世 "three temporal realms"; "three times"
= tryadhvan; trikāla 167

sàn huài 散壞 "crumble to pieces"
= vi-SṜ 167

sè 色 "form"; "colour"
= rūpa 135, 144, en. 241

sè 澁 "roughness", "hardness", "astringency"
= karkaśatva en. 239

sè děng 色等 "colour, etc."
= rūpādi 94

sè gēn 色根 "physical senses"
= rūpīndriya 111, 136

sè jiè 色界 "realm of form"
= rūpadhātu 152

sè xìng 色性 "colourness"
= rūpatva 145

shā mén guò 沙門果 "fruit of religious practice"
= śrāmaṇyaphala 89

shàn gēn 善根 "root of virtue"
= kuśalamūla 103

shàn qù 善趣 "fortunate state of existence"
= sugati 90

shàn quán fāng biàn 善權方便
"skillful means"
= upāyakauśalya 92

shāo 燒 "heat"; "cook" 148

shēn 深 "profound" 31
= parokṣa 31, 91
= gambhīra 31

shēn shì 深事 s.v. shēn
= parokṣa en. 28

shēn 身 "body"; "birth" 111
= deha; kāya; śarīra "body" en. 132
= janman "birth"; "origin" en. 132

shēn jiàn 身見 "[false] view concerning the personality"
= satkāyadṛṣṭi 100, 107

shén biàn 神變 "miraculous transformations"
= vikurvaṇa; ṛddhi 31, 91, en. 27

shén lì 神力 "miraculous powers"
= ṛddhi en. 81

shén tōng 神通 s.v. shén biàn; shén lì
= ṛddhi en. 27, 81

shèn shēn 甚深 "extremely profound" 31
= atyantaparokṣa? 31, 91, en. 28
= gambhīra 31, en. 28

shēng 聲 "sound"
= śabda 163

shēng xìng 聲性 "soundness"
= śabdatva 146, 166

shèng dìng 勝定 "various meditative absorptions"
= samāpattiviśeṣa; samādhiviśeṣa 99

shèng jiě 勝解 "zealous application"
= adhimukti 87, en. 3, 45

shèng lì 勝利 "excellent qualities"
= guṇa 87

shèng yì 勝義
= paramārtha "ultimate reality" 87
= paramārtha; paramārthika "really true" 110

shī děng 施等 "giving, etc."
= dānādi 90

shī huǒ lún 施火輪 "circle traced by a whirling firebrand"
= alātacakra 141

shī zī 師資 "the teacher's assistance" en. 4

shí 實 en. 37
= dravya "substance" 93, 94
"true" "real" 93, en. 40

shí jì 實際 "the true endpoint"
= bhūtakoṭi 112

shí xiāng 實相 "true character [of things]" en. 47
= bhūtalakṣaṇa 113

shí xìng 實性
"true/real nature" 93
= bhūtatathatā "true thusness" 155
= dravyatva "substanceness" 145

shí yǒu 實有 "substantially existent"; "really existent" en. 37
= dravyato 'sti; dravyasat; asty eva 92

shí shàn yè 十善業 "ten virtuous actions"
= daśakuśalakarmapatha 112

shì sú 世俗 "conventional"
= vyavahāra; saṃvṛti 103

shì sú dì 世俗諦 "conventional truth"
= saṃvṛtisatya 148

shòu yóng 受用 "enjoyment"
= bhoga 97

shù dá luó 戍達羅 "Śūdra" 109

shuài ěr 率爾 "randomly" 165

shuǐ jīng 水晶 s.v. shuǐ jīng zhū en. 116

shuǐ jīng zhū 水精珠 "crystal"; "quartz"
= sphaṭika 107, en. 116

shuì mián 睡眠 "sleep"; "sloth"
= middha 88

shùn rěn 順忍 "patience of amenability"
= ānulomikī kṣānti 101

sī zé 思擇 "discrimination"
= nidhyāna; vicāra 101

sǐ shī 死屍 "corpse"
= kuṇapa 168

sòng 誦 "recite"; "read"
= ā-MNĀ; PAṬH en. 127

sú 俗 "conventional"
= vyavahāra; saṃvṛti 158

suí mián 隨眠 "propensities [for passions]"
= anuśaya 91, 100

sǔn yì 損益 "impaired or aided"

= kārāpakāra en. 274

suǒ duì 所對 "resisted" en. 48

suǒ huà 所化 "[sentient beings] to be trained"
= vineya 101

suǒ jiàn 所見 "what is perceived" 91

suǒ lì 所立 "what is to be proved"
= sādhya 135

suǒ shě 所捨 "what is to be abandoned" 88

suǒ shè 所攝 "summary"
= saṃgraha 88

suǒ wén 所聞 "what is heard" 163

suǒ xíng 所行 "object"
= gocara 93

suǒ yī 所依 "basis"
= āśraya 94

suǒ yuán 所緣
= grāhya "what is (to be) apprehended" 55, 91, 173
= ālambana "object [of mind]" 164

suǒ yuán yuán 所緣緣 "objective condition"
= ālambanapratyaya en. 227

suǒ zhèng 所證 "what is to be realized" 88

suǒ zhī 所知 "object of cognition"
= jñeya 149

suǒ zōng 所宗 "doctrine" 108

tā lùn 他論 "rival assertions"
= paravāda; parapravāda en. 112

tài guò shī 太過失 "gross absurdity"
= atiprasaṅga 31, 91

táng juān 唐捐 "pointless"
= vyartha 155

tǐ 體
= dravya? "substance" 96, 135
= svabhāva "nature" 135, 159, 160, en. 219, 308
= artha en. 219
"nature" 135, 138
"thing"; "entity" 152, 157

tǐ xiāng 體相 "nature and characters" 92

tǐ yì 體義 "meaning" 88

tiān ěr tōng 天耳通 "super-knowledge known as 'the divine ear'"
= divyaśrotrābhijñā 165

tóng fēn 同分 "having its own activity"
= sabhāga 152

tóng lèi 同類
= sārūpya "same sort" 110
= samānajāti "same [natural] kind" 145

tóng shì 同事 "sameness of goal"
= samānārthatā 112

tóng yì 同異
= sāmānyaviśeṣa "limited universal" 94, 144, en. 53

tóng yù 同喻 "homologous example"
= sādharmyadṛṣṭānta 90, en. 329a

wài dào 外道 "Outsider" 30

wài jìng 外境 "external object"
= bāhyārtha 58

wàng wèi 妄謂 "[erroneous] view"
= dṛṣṭi en. 282

wàng zhí 妄執 "erroneous grasping"
= abhiniveśa 93, 104

wéi liáng 唯量 "subtle elements"
= tanmātra 97

wéi xiān 爲先 "be preceded"
= pūrvaka 141

wèi biàn wèi 未變位 "untransformed state"
96

wèi lái jì 未来際 "bounds of the future" en. 140

wén shēn 文身 "collection of letters"
= vyañjanakāya 163

wǒ 我
= ātman "self" 159, 161
= puruṣa "Spirit" (Sāṃkhya) 159

wǒ ài 我愛 "self-cherishing"
= ātmasneha 100

wǒ suǒ jiàn 我所見
"[erroneous] view of the possessions of the self"
= ātmīyadṛṣṭi 104

wǒ suǒ yǒu shì 我所有事 "the possessions of the self"
= ātmīya 88

wǒ zhí 我執 "conception of an I"
= ahaṃkāra 104, 107

wú bù yóu lǚ 無不遊履
"actively engaged" 106, en. 115

wú dào 無倒 "non-erroneous"
= aviparīta 101

wú duì 無對 "without resistance"
= apratigha 93

wú lòu "undefiled"
= anāsrava 108

wú míng 無明 "ignorance"
= avidyā 88

wú rǎn 無染 "undefiled"
= akliṣṭa 112

wú sè dìng 無色定
"formless meditative absorption"
= ārūpyasamāpatti 112

wú sè jiè 無色界 "formless realm"
= ārūpyadhātu 153

wú shàng zhèng děng pú tí 無上正等菩提
"unexcelled perfect enlightenment"
= anuttarasamyaksaṃbodhi 98

wú shì 無示 "indescribable"
= anidarśana 93

wú suǒ yǒu 無所有 "do not exist at all"
= nāsti kiṃcit 138

wú wéi 無爲 "unconditioned"
= asaṃskṛta 149, 173

wú xìng 無性 "absence of nature"
= niḥsvabhāvatā en. 50

wú yǒu xiāng lí 無有相離
"mutually inseparable" 90

wú yú 無餘 "no remainder"
= aśeṣa 100

xí qì 習氣 "[latent karmic] tendencies"
= vāsanā 153

xì lùn 戲論 "proliferations"
= prapañca 103, 171

xì niàn sī wéi 繫念思惟
"fully conscious and mindful"
= saṃprajānāḥ pratismṛtāḥ 98

xiǎn sè 顯色 "colour"
= varṇa 141

xiàn 現 "present" 94

xiàn jiàn 現見 "direct perception"; "perception"
= pratyakṣa 91

xiàn liáng 現量 "direct perception"; "perception"
= pratyakṣa 94

xiāng 相 "character" 151, fn. 25, en. 47, 308
= lakṣaṇa 88

xiāng wéi 相違 "contradictory"
= viruddha 103

xiāng xù 相續 "continuum"
= saṃtāna en. 40

xiǎng 想 "notion"
= saṃjñā 168

xiǎng yùn 想蘊 "the aggregate of notions"
= saṃjñāskandha 168

xīn xīn fǎ 心心法 "minds and mental factors"
= cittacaitta 93, 164

Xīn sà pó duō 新薩婆多 "Neo-Sarvāstivādin
en. 227

xìn jiě 信解
= śraddhādhimukti "faithful application"
en. 45
= adhimukti "zealous application" en. 45
= pratyaya; saṃpratyaya "conviction" en. 45

xíng 行 "conditioning"
= saṃskāra 100

xíng kǔ 行苦 "suffering due to conditioning"
= saṃskāraduḥkhatā 100

xíng xiāng 行相 "aspects"
= ākāra 167, 173

xíng sè 形色 "shape"
= saṃsthāna 141

xíng xiāng 形相 "shape"
= saṃsthāna 129

xìng 性
"nature" 96, en. 47
= prakṛti "Primordial nature" (Sāṃkhya) 159, 160, en. 308

xìng lèi 性類 "nature" 151

xìng xiāng 性相
= bhāvalakṣaṇa "existential character" 93, en. 47
"nature and character" 106, en. 47, 69

Xiū liú 鵂鶹 = Ulūka 160, en. 316

Xiū liú zǐ 鵂鶹子 = Aulūkya en. 316

xū 虛 "deceptive"; "false" 94
= mṛṣā 112, 169

xū jiǎ 虛假 "false" 155

xū kuáng yán 虛誑言 "lies" 109

xū wàng 虛妄 "false" 103

xū wàng fēn bié 虛妄分別
"false conceptualization"
= abhūtaparikalpa 166

xūn xí 熏習 "[latent karmic] tendencies"
= vāsanā 98

xún sì 尋伺. "ratiocination and investigation"
= vitarkavicāra 91, 155

xuàn yī 眩醫
= timira 173

yǎn guāng 眼光 "the eye's light-rays" 156, en. 302

yàn 焰 "mirage"
= marīci 169

yàn bù 厭怖 "fear"
= udvega en. 118

yàn lí 厭離 "revulsion"
= nirveda 101

yán quán 言詮 "figures of speech" 92

yáng yàn 陽焰 "mirage"
= marīci 169

yè 業 "action"
= karman 95, 152

yī lèi 一類 "some people"
= ke cit 102

yī tā 依他 "dependent nature"
= paratantra 56

yì lǐ 義理 "object"; "entity"
= artha en. 89

yì 意 "mind"; "mental organ"
= manas 161, 164

yì qù 意趣 "thought"
= abhiprāya 108

yì shí 意識 "mental consciousness"; "mental cognition"
= manovijñāna 94, 136, 163, 169

yì sī 意思 "mind"; "mental organ"
= manas 112

yì shú guǒ 異熟果 "retributive effect"
= vipākaphala 110

yì mén 義門 "accesses to the entity" 149, en. 263

yì míng 異名 "synonym"
= paryāyaśabda 170

yì qián 異前 "other than before"
= anyathātva 148

yì shēng 異生 "the profane [people]"
= pṛthagjana 100

yīn 因 "reason"; "cause" en. 298
= hetu 90

yīn guǒ yì 因果義 "causality"
= hetuphalabhāva; kāryakāraṇabhāva 162

yīn 音 "sound" 163

yǐn yè 引業 "propelling karman"
= ākṣepakakarman en. 269

yōu 憂 "despondency"
= daurmanasya en. 352

yǒu 有 "exist"; "existence" en. 98
= sattā "existence" en. 53

yǒu duì 有對 "having resistance"
= sapratigha 93

yǒu fēn 有分 "whole"
= avayavin en. 40

yǒu jiàn 有間 "having an interval"
= sāntara en. 301

yǒu jiàn 有見 "the view of existence"
= astidṛṣṭi; bhavadṛṣṭi 105

yǒu lòu 有漏 "defiled"
= sāsrava 111

yǒu qíng 有情 "sentient being"
= prāṇin; sattva en. 106

yǒu shēng 有生 "that which has coming into being"
= jātimant 167

yǒu wéi 有爲 "conditioned"
= saṃskṛta 149

yǒu xìng 有性 "existence" en. 53

yǒu yǒu yǒu děng 有有有等
"existence, existence of existence, etc." 104

yǒu zhàng ài 有障礙 "resistant"
= sāvaraṇa 138

yòng 用
"function" 150, en. 308
= vṛtti "operation" 167, 168

yú chī 愚癡 "bewilderment"
= moha 99, 101, 109

yǔ 語 "sentence"
= vākya 163

yù jiè 欲界 "the realm of desire"
= kāmadhātu 91, 153

yuán 源 "source" 165

yuán 緣 "[causal] condition"
= pratyaya 154

yuán lǜ 緣慮 "ideation" 170

yuán chéng 圓成 "thoroughly established nature"
= pariniṣpanna 56

Zá ā hán jīng 雜阿含經 (Saṃyuktāgama) en. 265

zào sè 造色 "derived [matter]"; "derivatives"
= bhautika 142

zhǎn zhuǎn 展轉 "step by step"
= pāramparyeṇa 101

zhē 遮 "negation"
= pratiṣedha 103, en. 102

zhē biǎo 遮表 s.v. zhē, s.v. biǎo en. 102

zhēn 眞
= paramārtha "ultimate" 158
"true" 173

zhēn kōng 眞空 "voidness"
= śūnyatā 88, en. 11

zhēn kōng lǐ 眞空理 "voidness"
= śūnyatā en. 11

zhēn lǐ 眞理 "true nature"

= tattva 102

zhēn rú 眞如 "thusness"
= tathatā 112

zhēn shí 眞實 "truth"
= tattva 31, 91, 101

zhēng 諍 "dispute"
= vivāda 147 (= *zhèng*)

zhèng dé 證得 "realizations"
= sākṣātkaraṇa; sākṣātkriyā 87

zhèng kōng yǒu 諍空有 "debate on voidness and existence" fn. 114

zhèng lǐ 正理 "reason"; "rationality"
= nyāya; yukti 87

zhèng zì zhèng 證自證 "self-awareness of self-awareness"
= svasaṃvittisvasaṃvitti fn. 25.

zhì jiàn 智見 "insightful vision"
= jñānadarśana 87

zhōng jiàn 中間 "between"; "set apart"
= antara; sāntara? 158, en. 301

zhǒng xìng 種姓 "lineage"
= gotra 98
= vaṃśya; gotra en. 78

zhǒng zi 種子 "seeds"
= bīja 101, 153

zhōu 洲 "continent"
= dvīpa 111

Zhòng xián 衆賢 (Saṃghabhadra) en. 227

zhòu 呪 "spell"
= mantra 108

zhòu shù 呪術 "spell"
= mantra 170

zhū fǎ shí xiāng 諸法實相
s.v. shí xiāng en. 47

zhū fǎ xìng xiāng 諸法性相
"nature and character of dharmas" 87, en. 1, 114, 142

zhuī yì 追憶 "recall"
= SMṚ 164

zì 字 "syllable"
= akṣara 140

zì hài 自害 "self-refutation" en. 124

zì rán yǒu 自然有 "exist naturally" 109

zì sàng 自喪 "think oneself to be lost" 106

zì tǐ 自體 "nature"
= svabhāva 90

zì xiāng 自相 "particular character"; "particular"
= svalakṣaṇa 147, 163

zì xìng 自性 "nature"
= svabhāva 143

zì zài 自在 "masteries"
= vaśitā 98

zì zhèng 自證 "self-awareness"
= svasaṃvitti fn. 25.

zōng 宗 "thesis"
= pakṣa en. 25

zǒng 總 en. 38, 72
"universal" 92, 93
= samudāya? "synthesis" 96
= sāmānya "universal" en. 38

zǒng xiāng 總相 "universal character"
= sāmānyalakṣaṇa 139, 141

zǒng xìng 總性 "universal nature" 93

zuì 罪 "evil action"
= pāpa 105

zuò yòng 作用 "operation"
= kāritra 91

INDEX OF PROPER NAMES

A kya yoṅs 'dzin dByaṅs can dga' ba'i blo gros (18th C.) fn. 86, en. 397
A lag śa Ṅag dbaṅ bstan dar (1759-1840) 29, fn. 79
Abhidharma 141, 151, 182, en. 128, 239, 266, 401, 439
Abhidharmakośa fn. 123, en. 2, 5, 10, 19, 27, 31, 32, 45, 48, 85, 86, 87, 97, 122b, 128, 131, 187, 188, 193, 204, 206, 226, 228, 235-238, 245, 256, 262, 264, 265, 269, 272, 290, 307, 327, 339, 340, 342, 353, 356, 362, 370, 381, 385, 386, 388, 394, 397, 401, 417, 427. Vol. II, 91, fn. 2
Abhidharmakośabhāṣya en. 128, 206, 226, 256, 264, 265, 272, 327, 342, 381, 388, 397, 401, 427, 432
Abhisamayālaṃkāra en. 94, 91, 198
Abhisamayālaṃkārāloka fn. 93
Adhyāśayasaṃcodanasūtra 116, en. 146
Ajitamitra en. 428
Akṣaraśataka 7
Akutobhayā fn. 123
Ālambanaparīkṣā 8, 13, 38, 61, fn. 129, 131, 132, en. 227, 283, 369
Ālambanaparīkṣāvṛtti fn. 132, en. 283, 369
Alīkākāravāda 42, 51, fn. 91, 92, 113.
Ālokamālā fn. 113
Annambhaṭṭa en. 57
Aprāpyakāritvavāda 157, 165, 189, en. 290, 299, 304
Atiśa Dīpaṃkaraśrījñāna fn. 26
Arundhatī (the star, Alcor) 121, en. 163
Āryadeva 1, 2, 5-7, 13, 14, 15, 18, 19, 23, 29, 30, 31, 37, 54, 56, 57, 58, 62, 67, 68, fn. 88, en. 8, 13, 68, 77, 157, 290, 299, 321, 326
— life and dates 5, 6
— the Tantric Āryadeva (Āryadeva II) 6, 7
— works of Āryadeva 6, 7
Ārya Vimuktisena fn. 26
Asaṅga 51, 55, 56, 74, fn. 2, 25, 26, 91, 117, 119, 123, 126, 127, 131, en. 80
— as Alīkākāravādin 51, fn. 91
— on the inexpressibility of dharmas' natures fn. 119
— on *parikalpita* 55, 56, fn. 117
— theory of voidness fn. 126, 127
Aṣṭādhyāyī en. 154, 158. Vol. II 9, fn. 3
Aṣṭasāhasrikā Prajñāpāramitā fn. 115
Aśvaghoṣa en. 134
Atharvaveda en. 210
Ātmatattvaviveka en. 360
Aulūkya 119, 160, en. 316
Avalokitavrata fn. 123, en. 363
Avataṃsaka en. 92
Ayer, A.J. 38, 39
Bǎi lùn 6, fn. 14, en. 68, 259, 302, 344, 396, 404
Bǎi zì lùn 7, fn. 15
Berkeley, G. 39

Bhartṛhari 12, fn. 85
Bhāvaviveka 1, 6, 8, 13, 45-47, 54, 55, 57, 64, fn. 19, 114, en. 102, 272
— his debate with Dharmapāla. See entry for Dharmapāla.
— on *tathyasaṃvṛti/mithyāsaṃvṛti* 45-47,
— recent research on Bhāvaviveka fn. 114
Bì ná (= *Prakīrṇaka?*) 12, fn. 32
Blo gsal grub mtha' fn. 91, 106
Blo rigs kyi sdom tshig blaṅ dor gsal ba'i me loṅ fn. 86, en. 397
Bodhibhadra fn. 20, 25, 91, 92.
Bodhicaryāvatārapañjikā fn. 98, 106, 134, en. 166. Vol. II 79, fn. 1
Bodhipathapradīpa 30
**Bodhisaṃbhāra* 127, en. 195
Bodhisattvabhūmi 55, fn. 119, 126, 127, en. 134
Bodhisattvayogācāracatuḥśataka 134, 199
Brahmins 108-111
bsDus grwa en. 40, 128, 236, 256, 339, 342
bsTan bcos bźi brgya pa źes bya ba'i tshig le'ur byas pa'i mchan 'grel fn. 45
bsTan 'gyur fn. 27
Bu ston Rin chen grub (1290-1364) 13
Buddhapālita 13, fn. 123
Byaṅ chub kyi tshogs (= **Bodhisaṃbhāra*) en. 195
Bye brag pa (Vaiśeṣika) en. 159
bŹi brgya pa'i rnam bśad legs bśad sñiṅ po 77-84, fn. 45, 78
Candragomin fn. 27.
Candrakīrti 1-3, 5, 7, 8, 12-15, 19, 29, 40-53, 53, 63-68, 72, 74, fn. 43, 59, 89, 113a, 119, 121, en. 102, 108, 151, 154, 158, 184, 185, 227, 259, 287, 308, 363-365, 370, 374, 390, 391, 396, 397, 401, 403, 412, 414, 415, 424, 425, 427, 428, 439
— author of the **Madhyamakaprajñāvatāra* (Candrakīrti II or III) 13
— discussion of Yogācāra 44, 45, 65, 66, fn. 119
— his anti-reductionism 53, fn. 89
— life and dates 13
— on *mānasapratyakṣa* en. 428
— on *ākāra* 52, 53, fn. 113a
— on perception and the given 37, 40-53, 67, 68, en. 364, 365, 374
— on the *catuṣkoṭi* 72, 74
— recent research on Candrakīrti 1-5
— the Tantric Candrakīrti (Candrakīrti II) 13, fn. 43
— works of Candrakīrti 13, 14
Candramati en. 53, 317
Candrānanda en. 53
Carnap, R. 39, fn. 89
Catuḥśataka 1-4, 6-8, 11, 14, 15, 23, 29, 31, 34, 37, 44, 54, 72, fn. 6, 26, 59, 79, 83, 122, 131, en. 14, 20, 47, 53, 54, 56, 68, 99, 102, 184, 326, 361, 404, 415, 428
Catuḥśatakaṭīkā (= *Catuḥśatakavṛtti*) 1, 14
Catuḥśatakavṛtti 1-4, 14, 15, 16, 37, 40, 46, 52, 53, 72, 77-84, fn. 7, 26, 45, 88, 105, 143, 144, en. 93, 107, 108, 144, 151, 158, 179, 185, 201, 208, 214, 227, 309, 335, 361, 365, 369, 375, 391, 395, 397, 399, 403, 409, 415, 421, 428
Chéng wéi shí bǎo shēng lùn 13
Chéng wéi shí lùn (**Vijñaptimātratāsiddhi*) 8, 13, 54, 58, fn. 22, 25, 124, 127, en. 52, 53, 64, 227, 228, 283
Chéng wéi shí lùn shù jì en. 53, 72, 227
Chéng wéi shí lùn zhǎng zhōng shū yào fn. 29
Chos 'grub fn. 15
Cittaviśuddhiprakaraṇa 6
Cūḷasuññatāsutta fn. 126
Dà chéng bǎi fǎ míng mén lùn fn. 27
Dà chéng zhōng guān shì lùn fn. 123
Dà zhì dù lùn en. 47 §d, 138
Daśabhūmikasūtra en. 375
Daśapadārthaśāstra en. 53, 317
dBu ma bźi brgya pa'i 'grel pa fn. 45
dBu ma bźi brgya pa'i rnam par bśad pa rgya mtsho'i zeg ma fn. 45
dBu ma dgoṅs pa rab gsal fn. 98, 109
dBu ma'i spyi don en. 428
Deva 5, fn. 14
Devadatta 191, en. 292

Devaśarman 57, fn. 123
dGe 'dun chos 'phel (20th C.) fn. 109
dGe 'dun grub pa (1391-1474) fn. 47, 75, en. 428
dGe lugs pa en. 40, 428
Dharmadāsa fn. 26
Dharmakīrti 10, 18, 19, 22-35, 41, 51, 63, 67, 71, fn. 24, 25, 26, 47, 49, 58, 73, 75, 88, 91, 101, 131, en. 22, 25, 44, 124, 230, 240, 366, 367, 425, 428
— arguments against Vaiśeṣika idea of *ātman* en. 22
— his being a disciple of Dharmapāla 10, 30, fn. 26
— his denial of external objects fn. 131
— his "distortions" of Dignāga 18, 19, 22
— his Sākāravāda / Satyākāravāda 41, 51, fn. 91
— his theory of *apoha* 71
— on *atyantaparokṣa* 26, fn. 73
— on *kalpanā* en. 367
— on *mānasapratyakṣa* en. 425, 428
— on *pakṣa* 32, 33, fn. 49, en. 25
— on scripture 23 et seq.
— on the definition of perception fn. 88, en. 367
— on *vastubalapravṛttānumāna* 25-28, 33
— use of *eva* en. 240
Dharmapāla 1, 2, 4-6, 8-12, 18, 19, 22, 29-31, 37, 54-68, 72, 74, fn. 2, 21, 25, 26, 29, 32, 35, 83, 114, 123, 127, 131, en. 1, 3, 13, 16, 18, 24, 26, 31, 35-37, 40, 44, 47, 50-54, 57, 58, 60, 63, 64, 69, 72, 80, 102, 107, 108, 113, 124, 127, 131, 219, 221, 227, 228, 230, 231, 234, 238-240, 243, 259, 268, 281, 283, 286, 287, 290, 291, 299, 308, 315, 317, 318, 321, 326, 329a, 335, 340, 344, 345, 347, 397, 414, 415, 430
— and Asaṅga on *manas* fn. 26
— and Dharmadāsa fn. 26
— approach to *catuṣkoṭi* 61, 72, 74
— as a precursor of *gźan stoṅ* ("other voidness") fn. 2
— debate with Bhāvaviveka 1, 8, 54, fn. 114
— his being a guru of Dharmakīrti 10, 30, fn. 26
— his being a poet 12, fn. 35
— his being a teacher of Devaśarman 57, fn. 123
— his connection with the Epistemologists 8, 9, 18, 19, 22, 30, fn. 25, 26
— his position on the parts of consciousness, *svasaṃvitti* and *pramāṇaphala* 8, 9, fn. 25
— his *vijñaptimātra* according to Kuī jī fn. 127
— his *Vyākaraṇa* treatise 12, fn. 29, 32
— life and dates 8, fn. 21
— on Mīmāṃsā fn. 83, en. 124, 230
— on proving imperceptible states of affairs 31, 32
— on the unreality of *lakṣaṇa* fn. 127
— philosophy of perception and idealism 54 et seq.
— research on Dharmapāla 4
— Tibetan views on Dharmapāla fn. 2
— works of Dharmapāla 11-13
Dharmapāla of Suvarṇadvīpa fn. 26.
Dharmapāla, the Theravādin fn. 26.
Dharmottara 51, fn. 54, 86, 91, en. 428
Dharmottarapradīpa en. 428
Dhruva (the North Star) 121
Dīghanikāya en. 161
Dignāga 7-9, 12, 13, 18, 19, 21-27, 29, 32, 38, 41, 51, 61, 70, 71, fn. 24, 25, 49, 56, 75, 91, 107, 131, en. 25, 36, 40, 53, 54, 60, 227, 232, 283, 290, 291, 299, 301, 366, 367, 369
— his *apoha* 71
— his Aprāpyakāritvavāda en. 290, 291, 299
— his denial of external objects 38, 61, fn. 131
— his Sākāravāda / Satyākāravāda 41, 51, fn. 91
— on *bhāga* ("parts") of consciousness 8, 9, fn. 25
— on *kalpanā* en. 367
— on *pakṣa* fn. 49, en. 25
— on *prakṛti* 21, 22

— on *pratyakṣa* and *kalpanāpoḍha* en. 367
— on Sāṃkhya en. 54, 343
— on scripture 19-22, 23 et seq.
— on *svasaṃvitti* and *pramāṇaphala* 8, 9, fn. 25
— on the sense organs en. 283
— on Vaiśeṣika en. 36, 53, 60
Dī pó pú sà shì léng jiā jīng zhōng wài dào xiǎo chéng niè pán lùn 7, fn. 17
Dī pó pú sà shì léng jiā jīng zhōng wài dào xiǎo chéng sì zōng lùn 7, fn. 16
Dī pó pú sà zhuàn fn. 8
dKar po rnam par 'char ba fn. 123
Dol po pa Śes rab rgyal mtshan (1292-1361) fn. 2
Don bdun cu en. 91, 198
Draṅ ṅes legs bśad sñiṅ po fn. 114, 117, 133
Durveka Miśra fn. 86, en. 428
Frege, G. fn. 48
Gautama 32, en. 53
Gautama Prajñāruci fn. 123
Gaṇḍavyūhasūtra en. 80
Gauḍapāda en. 54, 71, 286, 313
'Gos khug pa lhas btsas 13
Guhyasamājatantra 6, 13
Grub mtha' rin chen phreṅ ba fn. 25, 95, 113
gSer mdog paṇ chen Śākya mchog ldan (1428-1507) fn. 2, 75
Guān suǒ yuán lùn shì 13, fn. 34, 132
Guǎng bǎi lùn 6, 11 fn. 13
Guǎng bǎi lùn shì lùn 2, 13, 31, 56, 57, fn. 114, 119, 121, 131, en. 47 §c, 64, 124
Guṇamati 57, fn. 123
Guṇaśrī fn. 123
gŹan dga' gŹan phan chos kyi snaṅ ba (19th C.) fn. 45
gŹan stoṅ pa fn. 2, 126
gŹan stoṅ seṅ ge'i ṅa ro fn. 126
gZegs zan (Kaṇāda) en. 159
Haribhadra fn. 91, 93, 113.
Hastavālaprakaraṇa 7, fn. 18, en. 157
Hastavālaprakaraṇavṛtti 7, fn. 18, en. 157
Hīnayāna 161, 162, en. 197, 321
Hossō en. 47 §b
Huì lì 11, 12, fn. 29
Jaimini en. 124, 159
Jaiminīya en. 124
Jains 108-111
'Jam dbyaṅs bźad pa'i rdo rje Ṅag dbaṅ btson 'grus (1648-1722) fn. 25, en. 428
'Jam mgon koṅ sprul Blo gros mtha' yas (1813-1899) fn. 2
Jayanta fn. 131
*Jīn qī shí lùn (*Suvarnasaptati)* en. 54
Jinendrabuddhi 27, 31, 69, 71, fn. 73, en. 53, 60, 283
Jitāri fn. 113
Jñānagarbha 45-47, 51, fn. 94, 97, 103, 108
Jñānasārasamuccaya 7, fn. 20
Jñānasārasamuccayanibandhana fn. 20, 91
Jñānaśrīmitra fn. 91
Jo naṅ pa fn. 2
Kaḥ thog mkhan po Ṅag dbaṅ dpal bzaṅ (1879-1941) fn. 45, en. 142, 143, 207, 208, 371, 379, 438
Kamalaśīla fn. 48, 94, 107, 108, 113, 135, 139, en. 292, 296, 357
— on Aprāpyakāritvavāda (reply to Uddyotakara) en. 292
— on the Svātantrika interpretation of *paratantra* fn. 108
Kambala fn. 113
Kaṇāda 119, en. 53, 159, 316
Kapila 119, 135, en. 159, 219
Karṇakagomin 28
Kāśyapaparivarta 105, 125, en. 107, 179, 441. Vol. II 35, fn. 3
Klu sgrub dgoṅs rgyan fn. 109
Kokuyaku Issaikyō 4, en. 12, 33, 35, 41, 47, 73, 89, 95, 109, 120, 122, 123, 126, 129, 133, 139, 231, 261, 297, 322, 338, 341a
Kripke, S. fn. 48
Kuī jī 12, fn. 25, 28, 29, 127, en. 53, 64, 72, 227
Kumārajīva 6, fn. 14
Kumārila fn. 131, en. 299, 428

Lakatos, I. 16, fn. 48

Lalitavistara 192, en. 419. Vol. II 103, fn. 1

lCaṅ skya grub mtha' fn. 25, 95, 107, 113, 117, en. 44, 94, 366, 367

Luṅ gi rjes su 'braṅ pa'i sems tsam pa ("Vijñānavādins who follow scripture") fn. 25

Madhyamaka / Mādhyamika 1, 2, 5, 8, 13, 14, 30, 32, 37, 40-42, 46, 47, 51, 54, 57, 58-61, 63-66, 68, 72-76, 171, 196, fn. 88, 95, 113, en. 37, 40, 94, 184, 223, 290, 403, 425, 428

Madhyamakabhramaghāta 6, fn. 19

Madhyamakahṛdaya 6, 54, fn. 114

Madhyamakālaṃkāra 16, fn. 93, 94, 133, 134, en. 37

Madhyamakālaṃkārapañjikā fn. 94, 133

Madhyamakālaṃkāravṛtti fn. 94, 96

Madhyamakāloka fn. 100, 108, en. 221

Madhyamakaprajñāvatāra 13

Madhyamakaratnapradīpa fn. 114

Madhyamakārthasaṃgraha 45, 46

Madhyamakāvatāra 14, 40, 44-46, fn. 41, 48, 98, 106, 108, 111, 119, 138, en. 85, 86, 121, 201, 284, 310, 323, 363, 370

Madhyamakāvatārabhāṣya 14, 48, 52, fn. 41, 108, 112, en. 86, 201, 419. Vol. II 103, fn. 1

Madhyāntavibhāga 59, fn. 118, 126, 127, en. 26, 45, 100, 135

Madhyāntavibhāgabhāṣya 59, fn. 126, en. 100, 135

Mahābhāṣya 118, fn. 59, en. 158, 219. Vol. II 11, fn. 1

Mahāparinibbānasuttanta en. 161

Mahāparinirvāṇasūtra 119, en. 79, 161

Mahāprajñāpāramitāśāstra (Dà zhì dù lùn) en. 47 §d

Mahāvyutpatti en. 2, 27, 38, 80, 81, 85, 128, 134, 187, 201, 339, 367, 375, 431

Mahāyāna 5, 8, 113, 114

Mahāyānasaṃgraha 55, fn. 26, 116, 117, en. 80

Mahāyānasūtrālaṃkārabhāṣya fn. 2

Majjhimanikāya en. 34, 406

Mallavādin en. 219

Manorathanandin en. 44, 124

Mīmāṃsaka 27, en. 124, 159, 290

Mīmāṃsāsūtra en. 124, 230

Mi pham rgya mtsho (1846-1912) fn. 126

mKhas grub rje = mKhas grub dGe legs dpal bzaṅ po (1385-1438) fn. 75, 107

Mokṣākaragupta fn. 131, en. 428

Mūlamadhyamakakārikās 37, 57, fn. 123, en. 34, 179, 323, 324, 356, 363, 396, 404

Mūlasarvāstivāda Vinaya en. 6

Nāgārjuna 1, 2, 5-7, 13-15, 37, 57, 63, 74, 75, fn. 2, 12, 15, 107, 123, en. 179, 195, 356, 428

Nāgārjunapāda 6

Naiyāyika fn. 88, en. 37, 290, 291

Neo-Sarvāstivādin en. 227

Nirākāravādin fn. 25, 91.

Nirgrantha = Jain 108, 119

Nyāya en. 221, 360

Nyāyabhāṣya 32, fn. 83, 84, en. 291, 344

Nyāyabindu fn. 88, en. 367, 428

Nyāyāgamānusāriṇī Nayacakravṛtti en. 54

Nyāyakandalī en. 60

Nyāyamukha 8, 11, fn. 49, 94, en. 24, 25, 53, 367

Nyāyānusāra en. 227

Nyāyapraveśa en. 24, 53, 240, 367

Nyāyasūtra 32, fn. 84, en. 53, 291, 317, 344, 379

Nyāya-Vaiśeṣika 14, 32, 33, 175, en. 252, 257, 360, 361

Nyāyavārttika en. 290

Pa tshab Ñi ma grags (1055/54-?) 2-4, fn. 3, 36

Pad ma dkar po fn. 48

Padārthadharmasaṃgraha s.v. *Praśastapādabhāṣya*

Pañcakrama 6

Pañcaskandhaprakaraṇa 14, fn. 42, en. 32, 87, 97, 187, 188, 362

Pañcatantra 125. Vol. II 35, fn. 2

Pañcaviṃśatisāhasrikā Prajñāpāramitā en. 46

Pāṇini en. 154, 158

Paramārtha en. 75

Patañjali en. 158

Pei na = Bì ná 12, fn. 32

Phyogs glaṅ yab sras 29

Phya pa Chos kyi seṅ ge (1109-1169) fn. 86
Popper, K. fn. 48
Pradīpoddyotana 13
Prajñākaragupta en. 428
Prajñāpāramitā en. 138, 198
Prajñāpāramitāsūtra 54
Prajñāpradīpa 45, 54, fn. 114, 122, en. 222, 404
Prajñāpradīpaṭīkā fn. 123, en. 363
Prakīrṇaka 12, fn. 32
Pramāṇasamuccaya 19-21, 24, 26, 71, fn. 25, 44, 48, 49, 59, 73, 94, en. 25, 36, 54, 60, 70, 221, 232, 286, 290, 299, 301, 343, 344, 366, 367, 368
Pramāṇasamuccayaṭīkā 21, 24, 69-71, fn. 57, 61, en. 54, 284, 286, 343
Pramāṇasamuccayavṛtti 20, 21, 24, 31, 69-71, fn. 49, 57, 60, 73, 74, en. 25, 36, 40, 232, 291, 366, 367
Pramāṇavārttika 26-29, 32, 33, 71, fn. 25, 44, 47, 49, 58, 59, 64, 70, 72-75, 79, 83, 88, 131, en. 22, 25, 37, 44, 54, 121, 124, 221, 230, 240, 366, 376
Pramāṇavārttikabhāṣya fn. 49, 73, 94, en. 37, 232, 366
Pramāṇavārttikasvavṛtti 32, fn. 52, 67, 70, 73, en. 230
Pramāṇavārttikasvavṛttiṭīkā 28, fn. 62, 63, 67, 73
Pramāṇavārttikavṛtti fn. 63, 64, 65, 68, 73, en. 22, 25, 37, 44, 124
Pramāṇaviniścaya fn. 54, 86, 131, en. 37, 240, 367
Pramāṇaviniścayaṭīkā fn. 54, 86
Prāmāṇyaparīkṣā fn. 86
Prāpyakāritvavāda 156, 165, 188, en. 290, 299, 412
Prasaṅgika 1, 13, 49, 51-53, 65, fn. 36, en. 94, 428
Prasannapadā 1, 14, 37, 47, fn. 38, 89, 107, en. 17, 19, 34, 121, 151, 159, 179, 185, 188, 193, 204, 272, 324, 356, 363, 365, 370, 374, 379, 387, 396, 397, 406, 432. Vol. II: 7, fn. 2; 55, fn. 1; 61, fn. 1; 69, fn. 1; 79, fn. 1; 119, fn. 1
Praśastapāda en. 23, 53, 57, 60, 61, 317, 320, 321
Praśastapādabhāṣya en. 23, 39, 53, 60, 61, 252a, 317, 390, 412
Prātimokṣasaṃvara en. 137
Price, H.H. 39
Pú tí zī liáng lùn (= **Bodhisaṃbhāra*) en. 195
Qīng mù (= *Piṅgala) fn. 17
Qŭ yīn jiă shè lùn (= **Upādāyaprajñapti-prakaraṇa*) en. 40
Raṅ rgyud pa (= Svātantrika) fn. 36, 95
Ratnākaraśānti fn. 91
Ratnakūṭasūtra 105, 198, en. 146, 179, 441
Ratnāvalī 119, 198, en. 105, 160, 168, 428, 437, 440. Vol. II 13, fn. 1; 123, fn. 2
Red mda' ba gŹon nu blo gros (1392-1481) fn. 45, en. 141, 142, 144, 207, 209, 215, 216, 218, 421
rGya gar chos 'byuṅ fn. 26
rGyal tshab rje = rGyal tshab Dar ma rin chen (1364-1432) i, 29, 77, 81, fn. 2, 45, 75, 78, 143, 144, en. 142, 207, 208, 211, 212, 373, 379, 390, 397, 416
Rigs pa'i rjes su 'braṅs pa'i sems tsam pa ("Vijñānavādins who follow reasoning") fn. 25
rJe btsun pa'i grub mtha' fn. 117
rNam 'grel spyi don fn. 48
rNam 'grel thar lam gsal byed fn. 75, 78
rÑiṅ ma pa fn. 45
Rorty, R. 38, 52, 53
rTsa ba'i śes rab kyi dka' gnas brgyad 65, fn. 140, en. 94
rTsa śe ṭīk chen 72, fn. 98
Russell, B. 39
Sa skya pa en. 428
Sākāravāda / Sākāravādin 52, fn. 25, 91
Śālistambasūtra en. 432
Samādhirājasūtra 117, 118, 120, 121, 195, 198, en. 154, 158, 193. Vol. II 8, fn. 2; 19, fn. 2; 21, fn. 1; 113, fn. 3; 115, fn. 1; 125, fn. 1-5; 127, fn. 1, 2

Saṃdhinirmocanasūtra 54, 55, fn. 6, 116, 117, en. 50, 370

Saṃghabhadra en. 227, 369, 370

Saṃghatissa 5

Śaṃkara Miśra en. 60, 249

Śaṃkarānanda en. 428

Sāṃkhya 21, 27, 32, 96, 117, 119, 135, 155, 156, 159-161, 167, 168, 175, en. 52, 54, 56, 65, 68, 70, 72, 74, 75, 159, 219, 221, 286, 287, 289, 290, 308, 314, 315, 343, 344, 360, 361, 397

— on *guṇasaṃdrāvo dravyam* en. 65, 72, 219

— on perception en. 54, 286, 344

— their system en. 54, 68, 219

Sāṃkhyakārikās en. 54, 68, 74, 75, 286-289

Saṃyuktāgama en. 265

Saṃyuttanikāya 194, en. 406, 432. Vol. II 111, fn. 5

Śaṅkarasvāmin en. 53, 296

Śāntarakṣita 13, 16, 46, 51, 63, fn. 91, 93, 94, 96, 113, 131, 134, 139, en. 37, 296, 299, 360, 367

— his use of the *ekānekaviyogahetu* 63, fn. 134

— on "similar appearances" (*mthun snaṅ ba*) and *āśrayāsiddha* fn. 94, 96

Sarvadharmaniḥsvabhāvasiddhi fn. 107

Sarvāstivādin fn. 90, en. 134, 227, 256, 278

Śātavāhana 5, fn. 12

Śatasāhasrikā Prajñāpāramitā en. 46

Śataśāstra en. 53

Satyadvayavibhaṅga 45, fn. 94, 100, 101

Satyadvayavibhaṅgavṛtti fn. 94, 96, 97, 101, 104

Satkāryavāda en. 68, 323

Satyākāravāda / Satyākāravādin 41, 42, 45, 51, fn. 91, 113

Sautrāntika 52, 64, 119, en. 86, en. 159, 227, 206, 342

sDe bdun la 'jug pa'i sgo don gñer yid kyi mun sel en. 366

sGom sde Nam mkha' rgyal mtshan (19th C.) fn. 107

Se ra rje btsun Chos kyi rgyal mtshan (1469-1546) 72, fn. 48, 95, 100, 117, en. 86, 91, 198, 428

Sellars, W. 53

Sēng zhào fn. 14

Śes bya kun khyab fn. 2

Shēng míng zá lùn 11

Shōzōgaku "the study of the nature and the characters" en. 47 §b

Śīlabhadra 8, fn. 21

Siṃhala 5

Siṃhaladvīpa 5

Siṃhasūri en. 54, 219

Six Heretics (viz. Pūraṇa Kaśyapa *et al.*) en. 6

sKabs daṅ po'i spyi don 72, fn. 95, 100, en. 204

Skhalitapramathanayuktihetusiddhi 7, fn. 19

Ślokavārttika en. 299, 305

sṄags rim chen mo 29, fn. 76

Sphuṭārthā Abhidharmakośavyākhyā en. 370

Śrāvakayāna 150

Śrīdhara en. 53, 60

Sthiramati 57, fn. 25, 123, en. 227

sTon pa tshad ma'i skyes bur sgrub pa'i gtam 29, fn. 79

Sūkṣmajana 2

Sum pa mkhan po Ye śes dpal 'byor (1704-1788) 13, fn. 26

Śūnyatāsaptati en. 437

Śūnyatāsaptativṛtti 14, fn. 40, 99

Śūraṃgamasamādhisūtra en. 125

**Suvarṇasaptati* en. 54

Svātantrika 39, 40, 42-48, 50, 51, 53, 67, 68, fn. 36, 95, 97, 107, 109, 113, en. 94

Tāranātha 10, 12, 13, 30, 57, fn. 2, 26, 123

Tarkajvāla 6, fn. 19

Tarkasaṃgraha en. 57

Tarkabhāṣā fn. 131

Tathāgataguhyasūtra en. 121

Tattvasaṃgraha en. 277, 290, 292, 294, 296, 299, 305, 323, 324, 357, 360, 367

Tattvasaṃgrahapañjikā fn. 135, en. 290, 292, 294, 296, 357, 360, 367

Thal 'gyur pa (= Prāsaṅgika) fn. 36

Theg pa chen po'i chos brgya gsal ba'i sgo bstan bcos fn. 27
Triṃśikā 13, fn. 22, 116
Triṃśikāvijñaptibhāṣya en. 227
Triśaraṇasaptati 14, fn. 43
Trisvabhāvanirdeśa fn. 116
Tshad ma rigs pa'i rgyan fn. 75, en. 428
Tshad ma'i brjed byaṅ chen mo 29, fn. 76
Tshig gsal stoṅ thun gyi tshad ma'i rnam bśad en. 428
Tsoṅ kha pa Blo bzaṅ grags pa (1357-1419) 16, 23, 29, 65, 72, fn. 36, 48, 76, 87, 98, 107, 109, 114, 117, 133, en. 94, 198, 366
Udayana en. 360
Uddyotakara fn. 131, en. 290, 292
Ulūka 160, en. 316
**Upādāyaprajñaptiprakaraṇa* en. 40
Upāliparipṛcchā 192. Vol. II 101, fn. 2
Vāgbhaṭa en. 227
Vaibhāṣika 119, en. 32, 86, 134, 159, 206, 342, 362, 427
Vaiśeṣika 14, 31-33, 37, 94-96, 117, 119, 144, 145, 147, 160-162, en. 22, 36, 39, 42, 44, 52, 53, 56, 57, 59, 60, 61, 64, 72, 159, 248, 249, 251, 254, 257, 258, 290, 316, 317, 321, 326, 360, 361, 390, 412
— on perception en. 53, 60
— their *padārtha* en. 42, 53, 61
Vaiśeṣikasūtra en. 39, 53, 60, 61, 249, 316, 320, 321, 412
Vaiyākaraṇa 32
Vajracchedikasūtra 184. Vol. II 79, fn. 1
Vākyapadīya 12, fn. 85, en. 230
Vākyapadīyavṛtti en. 53
Vārṣagaṇya s.v. Vṛṣagaṇa
Vasu 6, fn. 14.
Vasubandhu 8, 13, 61, 63, fn. 2, 25, 26, 27, 116, 126, 131, 134, en. 227, 369, 370
Vātsyāyana 32, fn. 84, en. 291, 344
Vedāntin en. 290
Vedas 12, 109, 110, en. 124, 127, 154
Vetullavāda 5, fn. 11
Vibhūticandra fn. 65
Vigrahavyāvartanī 75, fn. 107
Vijñānavāda / Vijñānavādin 2, 8, 38, 41, 44, 54, 57, 119, fn. 2, 21, 22, 25, 26, 91, 92, 108, 113, 117, 136, en. 47 §b, 90, 94, 159, 228, 262, 278, 281, 283, 349, 356
Vijñaptimātratāsiddhi 11, fn. 28
Viṃśatikā 13, 61, fn. 25, 130
Vinaya en. 17, 137
Vinītadeva en. 227
Viśuddhimaggaṭīkā fn. 26
Vivṛtagūḍhārthapiṇḍāvyākhyā en. 80
Vohārikatissa 5
Vṛṣagaṇa en. 54, 343
Vyākaraṇa 12
Wéi shí èr shí lùn shù jì fn. 25, 127, en. 227
Wéi shí lùn 11, fn. 28
Wittgenstein fn. 48, 109
Wŏn ch'uk (= Yuán cè) 54, fn. 6, 114
Xī yóu jì 8, fn. 12
Xuán zàng 2, 4, 8, 11, 13, 54, fn. 12, 21, 22, 26, en. 2, 11, 45, 47, 53, 54, 135, 239, 240, 286
Yaśomitra en. 227, 370
Yi ge'i mdo'i 'grel pa (*Varṇasūtravṛtti*) fn. 27
Yì jìng 12, 13, fn. 26, 29, 32
Yogācāra / Yogācārin (= Vijñānavāda) 44, 45, 48, 51, 54, 55, 58-60, 64-68, 75, fn. 48, 91, 92, 99, 108, 109, 114, 117, 119, 124, 126, 127, 131, 136, 139, 141, en. 215, 218
— denial of the external world 55, 58, fn. 131
— on *parikalpitasvabhāva* 55, 56, fn. 117
— on the *trisvabhāva* 55
— their idealism 64-66
— their notion of *dharmanairātmya* fn. 117
— theory of voidness 58-60, fn. 126, 127
Yogācārabhūmiśāstra fn. 25, 131, en. 2, 26, 193, 215
Yoṅs 'dzin blo rigs fn. 86
Yoṅs 'dzin rtags rigs fn. 75
Yuán cè 54, fn. 6
Yuktidīpikā en. 54, 74, 344
Yuktiṣaṣṭikā en. 215, 437
Yuktiṣaṣṭikāvṛtti 14, 52, fn. 39, 113a, en. 94

Zá bǎo shēng míng lùn 12, fn. 29
Zokuzōkyō fn. 6